PUBLIUS AGAIN
A New Defense of the Constitution

LANTZ McCLAIN

Cover Art: Howard Chandler Christy - The Indian Reporter, Public Domain, https://commons.wikimedia.org/w/index.php?curid=662340

Published in the USA

INDIE
PUB
PRESS

Indie Pub Press

ISBN -13: 978-1-956806-01-4

For Leslie

TABLE OF CONTENTS

"My conclusions will not be starting – originality in this sphere is almost always a sign of error … I console myself with Justice Holmes' observation that sometimes the vindication of the obvious is more important the elucidation of the obscure – especially when the obvious is challenged." – *Sidney Hook*

1.00 – OPENING STATEMENT

1.01 - Publius Again

There's a lot to be said for the U.S. Constitution, but from where I sit, looking out my law office window toward the Creek County Courthouse, nobody seems to be saying it. That made me think we needed another Publius again. We needed a new defense of the Constitution like in the old *Federalist Papers*. That made me think, Why not me? In these articles for the "Daily Herald," I've been trying to keep you current on what's goes on with the law and in the courts. What's going on with the Constitution no more than the same topic write large. But what gave me pause was the deserved reverence for the great originals. Anyone who sets out to rival their eloquence is riding for a hard fall. But if we value the Constitution, someone has to appear for the defense. Someone has to try and do their best. The long and the short of it being, I decided to have a go. I figured I had at least this much going for me. I could stand on their shoulders and had the over two hundred years experience since.

Back in 1787 and 1788, three of the Founding Fathers (Alexander Hamilton, James Madison, and John Jay) collaborated on writing the *Federalist Papers*, 85 essays that appeared in the New York newspapers. They were advocating for ratification of the Constitution. Following the custom in their day, they didn't write under their own names, but under a joint pseudonym – *Publius*. That referred to the Roman *Publius*, also called *Publicola*, the friend of the people, who played a lead role in overthrowing the last of the Roman kings and founding the Roman Republic, traditionally in 509 BC. Hamilton, Madison, and Jay saw themselves as taking up a similar role again, as trying to found a new American republic.

1

Hamilton receives the credit for *Federalist No. 1*, and he began with these words, "After an unequivocal experience of the inefficiency of the subsisting federal government, you are called upon to deliberate on a new Constitution for the United States of America." In other words, he was saying that "the subsisting federal government" (since 1781 under the Articles of Confederation) was "inefficient" and we needed "a new Constitution." But if we could imagine that brilliant gentleman to come back to life, sit down at his desk, dip his quill pen in the inkwell, and begin to write again, he would have to reverse that start. He would have to begin with something like, "After over two hundred years unequivocal experience of the efficacy of the existing Constitution, we are now constantly told that the Constitution is dysfunctional."

At least, that's the sort of thing one reads all the time. Take a 2012 article in "New York Times," bearing this title, "Our Imbelic Constitution." The contributor, a distinguished constitutional law professor at a leading law school, went on to inform us that, "Critics across the spectrum call the American political system dysfunctional, even pathological. What they don't mention, though, is the role of the Constitution itself in generating the pathology." During the budget crisis the same year, the "Times" followed with another article titled, "Let's Give Up on the Constitution." This time the contributor, another distinguished professor of constitutional law from a prestigious university, told us that, "As the nation teeters at the edge of fiscal chaos, observers are reaching the conclusion that the American system of government is broken. But almost no one blames the culprit: our insistence on obedience to the Constitution, with all its archaic, idiosyncratic and downright evil provisions."

But I want to say, Hasn't America had over two hundred years unequivocal experience of the efficacy of the existing Constitution? These critics must not think so. A dysfunctional constitution can't have functioned well. A pathological constitution can't have produced a healthy body politic. Then what do they say the malfunctions and maladies? They don't hesitate to tell us. In addition to filling the editorial pages, their books fill the mainstream and scholarly press with titles such as *The Frozen Republic: How the Constitution is Paralyzing Democracy* (1996) or *Our Undemocratic Constitution* (2006). Who has the time to read all this stuff? But who doesn't catch the drift?

Hamilton wrote in *Federalist No. 1*, "I will not amuse you with an appearance of deliberation when I have decided. I frankly acknowledge to you my convictions, and I will freely lay before you the reasons on which they are founded." Let me follow his example. "I frankly acknowledge to you my conviction" to answer these critics. After what I hope you will agree more than "an appearance of deliberation," I am decidedly a friend to the Constitution. It only remains for me to lay before you the reasons on which my friendship is founded that you may decide for yourselves whether to be or remain a friend.

1.02 – Half Empty or Half Full

If you're willing to sit on this jury, there's an open invitation. It's the case of the critics (the plaintiffs) versus the Constitution of the United States of American (the defendant). I've not so modestly appointed myself as the lawyer for the Constitution (to appear for the defense). If you've ever watched a trial, you know that after the jury seated and sworn to fairly try the case, the lawyers make their opening statements. That's their chance to tell the jurors what the case about and what the evidence will show. Then here goes my opening statement.

Ladies and gentlemen of the jury, used to seem to me that when my generation in grade school, as long ago as the 50s, Americans were optimists about the Constitution. They regarded their constitutional cup as full to overflowing. Used to seem to me around our college years, the famous 60s, they began to turn pessimists. They often regarded the same cup as half empty (at most), the vintage that suited past tastes as now more than a little distasteful. But I've come to learn the pessimism goes way back, although lately the cup does seem draining faster.

Probably the past optimism was fullest around the time of our nation's youthful maturity, say around 1900. Back then, most Americans seemed to regard the Constitution like the sacred text of a civic religion. By following this faith, America was seen as having become "one nation under God, indivisible, with liberty

3

and justice for all." This same faith was seen as holding out the promise of a better life to other peoples of the world. Dedicated in this era in 1886, the imagery of the Statue of Liberty well conveyed the reigning orthodoxy. A gift from the French people, her name properly translates as "Liberty Enlightening the World." Her right arm holds aloft the torch of progress. Her left arm embraces a tablet with the date of the Declaration of Independence (July 4, 1776). A broken chain lies at her feet. At the base the plaque with the poem by Emma Lazarus reads, "Give me your poor, your tired, your huddled masses yearning to breathe free, … I lift my lamp beside the golden door!"

This old time civic religion preached "the American dream," the hope of a better life for you and your children. The preachers' sermons urged, Leave behind the Old World. Sail away from those shores ruled over by privilege and class. Come to this New World, the "land of opportunity." On these shores good values and hard work were the rulers. Horatio Alger's rags to riches novels have gone out of fashion, but once made such optimism a staple of popular fiction. But never mind the fiction, didn't the nation teem with real life success stories? Read a biography of Andrew Carnegie. Born poor in Scotland (1835), emigrated with his parents at the age of thirteen (1848), and by 1900 (age 65), owned Carnegie Steel Company and one of the richest men in the world. Weren't there thousands of such real-life success stories across America, even if not quite so spectacular? Then how not see earthly salvation on a vast scale?

But already, some skeptics saw this civic religion as riddled with hypocrisy and fraud. They called for a cleansing of the temple, sometimes rejected the faith altogether. One of the earliest and longest running denunciations cried out against the pollution of slavery within the precincts. As long ago as 1833, the abolitionist David Lloyd Garrison called the Constitution, as a "compact" which bound the non-slave states to the slave states, "a covenant with death and an agreement with hell." While during industrialization, the progressives of that era began to denounce the civic religion as nothing more than worshipping at the Temple to Mammon. In 1907, a progressive historian wrote, "It may be said without exaggeration that the American scheme of government was planned and set up to perpetuate the ascendency of the property holding class." They called for casting out the buyers and sellers and overturning the tables of the moneylenders. In our present time, we hear increasing complaints about "structural flaws," such as the Electoral College that can elect a president who wins only a minority of the popular vote or the separation of powers that can lead to gridlock. Over the years, the skepticism has reached a bottom where a Jeremiah was recently heard preaching from his pulpit, "No, no, no. Not God Bless America; God Damn America!"

Well, our constitutional cup may be half full, filling, or full to overflowing. It may be the fullest cup around the table. It may be like the jars at the wedding feast in Cana, which constantly refilled with new good wine. But when people start to regard the cup as drained, leaving a sour taste behind, it can turn into a self-fulfilling prophecy. "The sea of faith was once, too, at the full, but now I only hear its melancholy, long, withdrawing roar." If enough people withdraw their belief in our fathers' constitutional faith, it will become a dead religion. But there's no atheism or agnosticism. You have to practice a constitutional faith. If you don't choose a constitution for yourself, someone else will impose one on you. Nor is one constitutional faith as good as another. Don't we know of false constitutional faiths like fascism or communism that led their believers into a wasteland? We better figure it out. What's the true constitutional faith, leading to the Promised Land?

1.03 – Come into My Parlor

Ladies and gentlemen of the jury, on first hanging out my shingle in this town, an older lawyer told me practicing law was a lot like loafing. That can be true, if you just want to follow some easy, well-worn path of the law and make a comfortable living like he did. But followed far enough, all the paths of the law lead into a legal labyrinth. A more committed lawyer can't but follow those paths. The harder you try, the more the law becomes a toil, time-intensive, labor-intensive. It's an all-consuming choice. "Then come into my parlor said the spider to the fly." By inviting you into my new defense of the Constitution, I'm not promising you a rose garden. Constitutional law is the most central law, right in the center of the tangle. When King Ptolemy asked for an easier way to learn geometry, Euclid replied, "There's no royal road to geometry, your majesty." There's no easier way to follow all the twists and turns in this labyrinth than by the sweat of our brows.

Ladies and gentlemen, in the *Federalist Papers No. 1,* Alexander Hamilton wrote, "I propose, in a series of papers, to discuss the following interesting particulars," and he set forth a lengthy agenda, concluding, "In the progress of this discussion, I shall endeavor to give a satisfactory answer to all the objections [to the Constitution] which have made their appearance that may seem to have any claim to your attention." In my new defense of the Constitution, I don't think I can do better than to try to follow his example. I propose to discuss the Constitution and try to answer "all the objections" along the way.

But we won't be discussing quite the same Constitution that he discussed. It's changed a lot since his day. We'll have to discuss those changes, the Constitution as it has become. Moreover, our agenda has to reach beyond the Constitution itself. The law, including the constitutional law, is never more than an instrument and an instrument never without some purpose. Then unless we understand the purposes, how can we ever hope to understand how well or poorly the instrument designed to serve the purposes? And the Constitution is a complicated instrument with a great many moving parts, such as Congress, the presidency, and the courts, all designed to interlock and interact to serve a great many purposes, such as the Preamble says, "to form a more perfect Union, establish justice, insure domestic tranquility, provide for the common defense, promote the general welfare, and secure the blessings of liberty."

You'll agree that to understand all these "interesting particulars" must set forth a lengthy agenda. Our situation is really worse than a lawyer just researching the law. It reminds more of a good friend of mine (not a lawyer) who got sued. One day I came across him up in the law library that the county maintains on the top floor of the courthouse, trying to look up the law on his case. An extremely intelligent guy, he was perfectly capable of understanding what he read. But there he sat, surrounded by a couple thousand law books, and not being trained in the law, he didn't have the context. He was just finding some bits and pieces.

He might as well have tried to put together a jigsaw puzzle without the picture on the box and without knowing whether some of the pieces were missing. Then don't we find ourselves in an even bigger library? All around from ceiling to floor stretch books on history, political science, sociology, and psychology. To understand the purposes of the Constitution and how well it serves those purposes, we're going to have to find all the relevant pieces and fit them together into the right picture.

Then you've been warned. Gird your loins. As the self-appointed lawyer for the defense, I've made the commitment to present the case to you. You've got to make the commitment to sit as the attentive jurors on the case, paying careful attention to the evidence throughout, letting nothing escape your notice. If my task not an easy one, neither is yours. My client (the Constitution) is a very serious and complicated gentleman. He can't be understood on a superficial acquaintance. He's not a solitary, but a sociable sort. To understand him, we have to understand his social nature and his place in society. He's an institution. To understand him, we have to understand his institutional nature. The Founding Fathers brought him to life with a single act of creation with the Constitutional Convention in 1787, yet he's the product of a long history. To understand him, we have to understand his history. He's grown and changed a lot over the years, too. To understand him, we have to understand him as he has become. Only by coming to thoroughly understand him can we put ourselves in a position to fairly and intelligently judge him.

If all this sounds a daunting task, why would we want to make the effort? Well, first of all, that reminds of still another legal war story. When I had the honor to serve as a judge, I had a good ole boy in front of me one day, an affable sort, who according to his own testimony, had managed to spend his life mainly coon hunting and drinking a little whiskey. He didn't have much formal education, but mentioned he liked to read. When somebody says they like to read, I'm always curious to know what. His response was, "I like to read encyclopedias, anything. I just like to know." Wow! He was a true child of nature. Aristotle says, "All men by nature desire to know." Then we'll want to make the effort simply because we desire to know. What could be more in our nature?

But who doesn't know the Constitution is foundational? When

some self-appointed engineers start digging around our foundations, we better have them up for an inquiry. Maybe they're undermining or weakening the foundations. But no doubt they'll protest the very best motives. They'll claim that like the architects who built those old Gothic cathedrals, they only aspire to raise towers that soar ever higher to Heaven. We might be interested in building higher ourselves. But some of those old churches collapsed during their construction. Their builders aspired beyond their science. Then good intentions aren't enough. We need some convincing science. We don't want our constitutional structure to fall down around our heads and have to live in the ruins.

But whether we want to make the effort or not, the case against the Constitution is a class action, and we're all joined as parties. We're all living in the same constitutional structure, and if the structure is condemned, we're all going to have to find someplace else to live. We better not let the judgment go against us by default. We better choose to make the effort required to defend our interests in the case.

The Constitution not only a very serious and complicated gentleman, he's a very important one. John Jay wrote in *Federalist No. 2*, "When the people of America reflect that they are now called upon to decide a question, which, in its consequences, must prove one of the most important, that ever engaged their attention, the propriety of their taking a very comprehensive, as well as a very serious view of it, will be evident." In the next article, let me try to convince you that neither the importance of the question, the consequences of deciding it, or the propriety of our taking a very comprehensive and serious view of the Constitution has declined in the intervening years.

1.04 – Covered with Flies

Ladies and gentlemen of the jury, let me tell you about an adventure my father went on right after World War II. Before the war, he worked for the Gulf in the oil fields around Kiefer, Oklahoma. During the war, he served as a Chief Petty Officer in the SeaBees. After the war, one morning he stepped out his front door to look for a job. "It's a dangerous business going out your door. You step into the road, and there is no knowing where you might be swept off to." He was looking for a job in the green hills of eastern Oklahoma, but he found a job with Aramco (the Arabian American Oil Company) and was swept off to the arid deserts of Saudi Arabia. "Home is behind, the world ahead." My mother and myself followed shortly after in his wake.

It was an adventure all right, and who would miss an adventure? And that adventure taught me that failure in government is not an option, although I didn't grasp the lesson for a number of years. We crossed more than time zones traveling to the Middle East. We crossed into the zone of failed governments. We arrived where "the splendor of their early history has been dimmed ... by economic distress, and by the debasing tradition of centuries of misrule."

Our lives in Arabia were a blue-collar version of the British in India. We were the colonialists and lived the good life. Aramco recreated for us a version of small-town America in the wastes of the Arabian desert. The company shipped in all the necessities and most of the comforts from home. They had to. In those days, only a Lawrence of Arabia sort could have survived on the local economy. Down at the local souk, raw meat hung on hooks covered with flies. That image pretty much sums up their standard of living.

They say a picture is worth a thousand words. When I taught political science as an adjunct over at Tulsa Community College, I would show my class old black and white photos from those days in Arabia. To stick with the ever-present flies, one was picture of an infant in a mother's arms, the mucous on its face covered with flies she didn't even bother to shoo away. I was trying to make the point that failure in government is not an option.

I would go on to say that failure in government is the Four Horsemen of the Apocalypse (Famine, Pestilence, War, and Death). If that sounded like pitching it too strong, I asked them only to consider. What has happened throughout history can surely happen again. What has happened elsewhere can surely happen here. Then consider what has happened throughout history and what has happened elsewhere.

How many has Famine (on the red horse) carried away? During the Irish Potato Famine from 1845 to 1852, about a million died, about an eighth of the population. Yet in those days, Ireland was still a part of Great Britain, and the country as a whole grew enough food to have bridged the Irish over. But no such bridge got thrown across the Irish Sea. Some early Irish accounts accused the British government of genocide (deliberately starving them), but later and more dispassionate accounts failed to prove so much. The British authorities had no malice aforethought to starve the Irish. Rather than first-degree murder, they were merely guilty of negligent manslaughter caused by mistaken policy and bureaucratic bungling. First, they failed to grasp the scale of the catastrophe, and second, they failed to grasp the scale needed for relief, which arrived too little or too late.

But governments can starve people without Mother Nature's help, as shown between 1948 and 1952 by the Chinese Communists under Chairman Mao. His Great Leap Forward planned to transform China from an agrarian economy into an industrial juggernaut overnight. But so bad was the planning that the juggernaut went in reverse. China went from barely feeding her hungry masses to mass starvation. Much later with the Great Leader safely embalmed and on display in his Mausoleum, the Chinese government officially admitted to an astounding 14 million deaths, but unofficial estimates go as high as between 20 and 43 million.

But governments have starved their people not just by mistake, but in cold blood. Between 1932 and 1933, the Soviet Communists under Stalin deliberately starved to death millions of Ukrainians (the Terror Famine). The peasants had resisted collectivization, and that man of steel resolved to introduce them to the twentieth century one-way or the other. If they didn't believe in the promise of his communist utopia, let them believe in the guarantee of communist terror. After forcibly exporting their grain, the communist authorities as forcible interdicted all aid. Known as the Holodomor (or Ukrainian Holocaust), some 7 million died.

Pestilence (on the white horse) usually hunts with Famine, starvation weakening the victims for disease to kill. But Pestilence can ride alone, striking down with such deadly weapons as the Spanish influenza, which between 1918 and 1920 killed some 50 to 100 million, some three to five percent of the world population. Nor do we ever drive Pestilence farther than just over the horizon.

But out of sight should not be out of mind. Witness the recent (2014) ebola outbreak in Africa. Only government has the resources to avert or fight such plagues.

While as for War, who rides the red horse if not government? During World War II, the warring governments between them killed some 63 million, about 3 percent of the world population. While as for Death (pale rider, pale horse), has government not already glutted on death? Not to repletion, since governments have turned to genocide. The Nazis murdered about 6 million Jews and others in the Holocaust. The Soviet Communists murdered even more, 20 million being an often mentioned figure. But the Khmer Rouge of Cambodia achieved the all-time highest kill ratio. From 1976 to 1979, they murdered approximately 25 percent (2 million) of Cambodia's population.

Do we say it can't happen here? Why not? What do we require except failed government? We don't even require malice aforethought like the Nazis or the Communists. All we require is the failure of good intentions like the British during the Irish Potato Famine. Those murdered by the worst tyrants in history are no more dead than those killed by bureaucratic bungling.

Writing and rewriting constitutions is a dangerous business. That's because government is a dangerous business. You never know where you might get swept off to. Failure is raw meat covered with flies. Failure is the Four Horsemen of the Apocalypse. We don't want to go off on such an adventure. Failure in government is not an option.

1.05 – Trust the Process

Ladies and gentlemen of the jury, one morning when still a young lawyer, on the first day of a jury docket, I walked into the main courtroom of the Creek County Courthouse. Potential jurors crowded the courtroom and spilled out into the halls. All the lawyers on hand were crowded together on the other side of the rail, tightly jammed into a narrow corner between the bench and the door to the judge's chambers. It was like a herd instinct. It was like they were afraid of the jurors and trying to get as far away from them as possible. Jury trials are judgment day all right, and not a few have a cause to fear the Day of Judgment.

But ladies and gentlemen, in those days this county still boasted some of the finest trial lawyers who ever trod the boards. None of those guys must have had a case on the docket that day. They didn't fear a jury trial any more than a matador fears a bullfight. To them a jury trial was no more than another chance to don their suit of lights and enter the ring to kill the bull (in the process killing the fatted calf). But despite their self-confidence, winning a jury trial is far from as guaranteed as a bullfight. Over the years, I've seen many a renowned trial lawyer tossed and gored in the courtroom, prostrate and covered with the blood of his dying case, wanting only somehow to rise and stagger to another venue, there to rinse away the bitter taste of defeat with some cool beverage, there to begin to restore the bruised tissues of the ego. But they're a tough lot, the trial lawyers. Usually, they recuperate as soon as the next jury docket, rising to even greater heights on the steppingstones of their dead cases. But the process takes a toll. A lot of trial lawyers look on the verge of a coronary, and they're not a long-lived breed.

Nope, winning a jury trial is seldom a guarantee. But as one of the best of those old Creek County trial lawyers (none better) used to say, "Trust the process." He meant that a jury trial is a good process. He meant that a lawyer who knows his business and takes care of business should win the jury trials he should win and lose the ones he should lose. Not every time, since juries make mistakes and can go rogue. But the run of verdicts will square with justice. Having attended not a few of these spectacles both as an observer and a participant, my experience says he was right. A jury trial is a good process.

Ladies and gentlemen, why am I telling you this legal war story at the start of my defense of the Constitution? I'm trying to make a fundamental point that will carry all the way through. The Constitution or any constitution is more like a jury trial than a verdict. A jury trial is a process to render a just verdict, but doesn't guarantee either party (the plaintiff or the defendant) a favorable verdict. In the same way, a constitution sets up a process to decide on laws and policies, but doesn't guarantee the outcomes. A jury trial is a good process and the run of verdicts will square with justice. In the same way, a good constitutional process will lead to a run of good laws and good policies even though not every outcome as good.

Ladies and gentlemen, let me try to hammer home this point, which critical to my defense of the Constitution. In *Alice in Wonderland* the King of Hearts says, "Verdict first, and trial afterwards." But in the real world, the verdicts don't cause the jury trials, the jury trials cause the verdicts. In the very same way, the outcomes (the laws and policies) don't cause the constitutional process, the constitutional process causes the outcomes.

What came first, the chicken or the egg? You aren't faced with that dilemma. You know what came first. The constitutional process has to come before the outcomes, since the first causes the second. Before you can have a law, you have to pass the law. Then ask yourself a question. Unless you have a good constitutional process, how can you have good laws? Don't we begin to see a good constitution is a necessary cause for good government and a bad constitution will cause bad government. "Be assured that the laws … grow out of the constitution, and they must fall or flourish with it."

Ladies and gentlemen, if you will but grasp this point and keep it constantly in mind, you will immediately begin to see what's wrong with most of the case the critics try to make against the Constitution. Their criticisms mainly amount to quarrelling with the verdicts. They didn't get the verdicts they wanted or not as soon or as big as they wanted. But if the trial was fair, how can they complain about the verdict? If the constitutional process was fair, how can they complain about the laws and policies (the outcomes)?

Ladies and gentlemen of the jury, what's this case about? Remember, it's the case of the critics versus the Constitution. "It's a constitution we're talking about." Then first and foremost, this case has to be about the constitutional process. It's about whether the Constitution sets up a good process. But lest the critics accuse me of unfairly limiting the question, I don't mean to do that. They're perfectly within their rights to ask for not just a good process, but for the best process. We shouldn't have to settle for a good constitution, if a better one available. But the evidence in this case will show that if the Constitution not the best process, it will puzzle our ingenuity to set up a better one. But I've run out of space and need to continue my opening remarks in the next article.

1.06 - The Lawyerly View

Ladies and gentlemen of the jury, to remember where we are in these articles, I'm signed on as the lawyer for the Constitution to defend it against the critics, and I'm right in the middle of my opening statement to you, the jury of public opinion. Let me proceed by asking a question. Do you think the Constitution more about your rights or your responsibilities? Let me tell you how most any lawyer representing you will answer that question. Ladies and gentlemen, I've watched them in and out of court for a long time. They view the Constitution as all about your rights, or to have it both ways, all about the responsibilities the government and others owe you. Lawyers make their fees by asserting their clients' rights and the responsibilities others owe to their clients, not by asserting the responsibilities their clients owe to others (the rights of other people). As a result, the legal mind has come to view the Constitution as all about your "rights." There they are guaranteed in the Constitution. All that remains for you, the public, to do is hire them, the lawyers, to claim your guarantees. The Constitution is the law. All you need do is "go to law."

But ladies and gentlemen, as the lawyer for the Constitution, I take another view. And just as the other lawyers take their view based on their clients' interests, I take my view based on my client's interests. Peculiar, isn't it, how a lawyer's views tend to change depending on his client's interests and so his own? However, before coming to my own view, let me say the lawyers seem to have persuaded you, the public, to share their lawyerly view. After all, who doesn't want their "rights?" Viewing the Constitution from that angle makes sense to you, the public, for the same reason it makes sense to them, the lawyers. You want to claim your rights against others, and they want to make a fee by claiming your rights for you. As a result, both the lawyers and you, the public, have come to view the Constitution as all about your rights and the responsibilities owed to you.

To confirm how widespread this lawyerly view, only open your morning newspaper and you routinely come across headlines something like, "Muslim woman files a federal lawsuit alleging County Sheriff's Officers forced her to remove her hajib in public in violation of her rights." Or, "Lawsuit claims a question on the census form about their citizenship violates minority rights." Or, "Lawsuit claims law forcing a baker to make a cake for gay wedding violates his rights." Such headlines and such lawsuits appear never-ending. Is there anything the lawyers haven't managed to make into a right that they can sue over and so make a fee from?

Or only listen to the way our public discourse constantly phrases our political controversies. "My client has a right to own a handgun," or "My client has a right against prayer or Bible reading in the public schools," or "My client has a right against racial discrimination," or "My client has a right to possess pornography," or "My client has a right against questioning by the police without an attorney present," or "My client has a right to an abortion," or "My client has a right against sexual harassment," or "My client has a right against the death penalty," or "My client has a right to marry a person of the same sex," or "My client has a right to health care." Rather than trying to make a complete list, we might as well ask, what political controversy hasn't been phrased as a constitution right and then demanded as a constitutional right?

Ladies and gentlemen, it's really amazing, isn't it, how many rights the lawyers have discovered in the Constitution not originally found there? Back in 1789, no one would have imagined a right to abortion or same sex marriage just to give two outstanding examples. Perhaps even more amazing, some rights have turned into opposite rights. For example, originally, the people had a right to pass laws against pornography, but later in the 1960s, that turned into a right against their passing any such laws. You almost can't name a constitutional right that hasn't gone through significant change with a lot of totally new rights added. Then don't all these alterations and additions force you to ask, how say our "rights" are guaranteed by the Constitution, when our rights have so constantly changed?

As much as that, and however all these new rights regarded as a good thing (or maybe not), where does all this "rights talk" leave us, not to mention leave my client, the Constitution? As for us, the public, we're left with nothing more than an ongoing and endless arguments between competing "rights." For instance, over that still controversial right to an abortion, one side says there's "a right to a

15

choice" and the other says there's "a right to life" and never the twain shall meet. Virtually all the arguments about our rights reach a similar deadlock. But whatever their view about their rights and however new, novel or unexpected their views, all seem to see their rights as non-negotiable. After all, if you have a "right," why compromise? A gay rights advocate recently well summed up the prevailing attitude, saying, "We lose when our rights are considered debatable." Such appears the attitude taken by all. Their rights aren't debatable. While as for my client, the Constitution, everyone demands that he conform to their view of their "rights." Otherwise, they condemn him. So my client, the Constitution, has no way to win an argument phrased in terms of "rights." Whichever side my client takes, he's fated to face constant and repeated condemnation from some side or other.

Ladies and gentlemen, if these were fair terms, my client would have to take them however disadvantageous. But as the lawyer for the Constitution, I say to you, these aren't fair terms, but a false view. Not that the Constitution isn't about rights. But this lawyerly view thinks about and has gotten you, the public, to think about the Constitution the wrong way around. If you will only recall the last article, I tried to make the fundamental point that the constitutional process produces the laws, including the laws about our rights. Then before the Constitution can be about our rights, it has to be about the process to determine our rights. I tried to drive home that point by comparing a constitution to a jury trial rather than a verdict. A jury trial is a process for arriving at a verdict, and a constitution is a process for arriving at our laws, including the laws about our rights. In either case, the process comes first. Then the Constitution can't be first of all about our rights. Rather, it has to be first of all about the process for determining our rights and the other laws. Doesn't the fact our rights have so often been changed prove the point? The constitutional process has repeatedly changed our rights. Then the process had to come first.

Ladies and gentlemen, since the constitutional process produces our laws, including our rights, how can we have good laws without a good constitutional process? Since the constitutional process determines our rights, how can we fairly determine our rights except with a fair constitutional process? Then before we argue about our rights, shouldn't we ask about the best and fairest process to settle our arguments about our rights?

While here's another thing about it. Although we might argue endlessly over our rights, yet might we manage to agree on a fair process to settle the arguments? You've seen a couple of kids agree to settle a dispute with a quick game of scissors, paper, rock. An adult group might agree to go with a show of hands. Although we constantly disagree, yet might we agree on some fair way to settle our disagreements and so reach an underlying agreement? While as for my client, the Constitution, if he can show his processes fair, neither side could condemn him anymore.

Ladies and gentlemen, you see what I'm trying to do. I'm wanting you to leave behind a "rights centered" (lawyerly) view of the Constitution, which has become the widely accepted view. I'm wanting you to take a fresh view of the Constitution. I don't ask you to check your "rights" at the door. You can bring along your views to the performance. But I ask you to start viewing the Constitution as being first of all about a fair process to determine all our rights and a fair process comes even before your rights.

Now ladies and gentlemen, if my client, the Constitution, innocent of the charges against him, surely his defense can rest on no better grounds than truth ("actual innocence"). If I say to you in truth he's innocent, it can't be in his interest to be misunderstood. Rather, to be truthfully understood should clear him of the charges. Since the lawyerly ("rights centered") view of him gets it wrong, what would be a more truthful view? Ladies and gentlemen, on to the next article.

1.07 – Human Architecture

Ladies and gentlemen of the jury, you may never have had the occasion to go in the main courtroom on the third floor of the Creek County Courthouse. Several generations of lawyers have cycled through there since that structure completed in 1914. No one seems to know who adorned the back walls with the large portraits of Franklin D. Roosevelt and Robert E. Lee, a pairing unique so far as known to our courthouse. However, in the recent renovation, these two gentlemen as mysteriously disappeared, replaced by the official portraits of the sitting president and vice-president. But with the exception of such minor trappings as the pictures on the walls, you don't have to go in. You're familiar with the standard design for an American courtroom.

But pause a moment to consider how the architecture structures the human interaction there. Go in and watch a jury trial. At the top (head) of the room, the raised bench gives the judge a commanding presence, putting him firmly over the proceedings (in charge). The jury box (somewhat lower than the bench, but higher than the floor) carefully locates the jurors off to one side. That leaves them somewhat under the wing of the judge, yet somewhat independent of him, too. He runs the trial and hands down to them his instructions on the law, yet they're able to render an independent verdict. At the same time, they're higher than the parties and their lawyers (in a position to judge them). The two identical counsel tables (on the floor) place the parties (the plaintiff and defendant) and their lawyers on the same level (on an equal footing), pleading up to the judge and jury. The witness stand between the bench and the jury box forces the witnesses to confront the parties while testifying before the jury, not sponsored by the judge, yet somewhat under his supervision and even protection on one flank. In front of the bench (inconspicuously) sit the court reporter and a court clerk to record the proceedings. A bailiff and sometimes an armed guard hovers around the edge to maintain order in the court. Behind the rail, some rows of seating make the trial open to the public. Recall the Constitution guarantees "a public trial." Could we think of a better design for a courtroom (a stage setting that better put all the actors in their proper role)?

Ladies and gentlemen, let me try to make a point with a comparison. Just as a courtroom structures human interaction such as the process of a jury trial, a constitution structures human interaction such as the processes for passing the laws or carrying out government policies. But while a courtroom uses a physical architecture, a constitution uses an institutional architecture.

Ladies and gentlemen, if you look in the dictionary, you'll find "institution" defined as an "organization." Although economists, sociologists, and political scientists all the time insist on the significance of institutions in our lives, apparently any more precise definition not that easy. One example from a topnotch political scientist was, "Institution. The word does not have a meaning sufficiently precise to enable one to state with confidence that one group is an institution while another is not. Accepted examples, however, include the courts, legislatures, executives, and other political institutions, families, organized churches, manufacturing establishments, transportation systems, and organized markets." That's a lot of good examples, but if "the word does not have a meaning sufficiently precise," I have a hard time working with that definition.

The general agreement seems an "institution" a way people organize to attain mutual goals by following rules, and significant institutions have leaders (management) and are set up in a durable way (a lasting, self-perpetuating way)." Hopefully, that's good enough to go down the road with, but does leave the thing a matter of degree.

To flesh it out, say you take a walk in Kelly Lane Park on a Saturday afternoon and see some kids playing a pickup baseball game at one of the diamonds. They're organized to attain a mutual goal (their mutual entertainment) and following rules (the rules of the game), but that's too informal (lacking clear leadership) and ephemeral (just for the afternoon) to qualify as an institution. Next go down to the Salvation Army baseball fields and watch the Youth Baseball League, a citywide organization that has gone on from year to year. Next watch the Little League World Series, which put on by Little League International, draws teams from around the world, and has lasted for some seventy years. By the time you attend an MLB game, you've definitely watching an institution in action and a fairly significant one. They're attaining a mutual goal (making lots of money) by following a lot of highly formal rules regulating the interaction between the owners, the players and the commissioner, not to mention the rules of the game, and have a very formal and hierarchical leadership (the management, that is, the owners and the commissioner). They're also set up in a durable (long-lasting, self-perpetuating) way. Team ownership passes from one owner to another. The current commissioner's office dates back to the long tenure of Kennesaw Mountain Landis, who served from 1920 to 1944, and the present commissioner (Rob Manfred) the tenth in the line. The players come and go as do the managers. But the league itself (the institution) has been around well over a century.

Whether or not we see an institution or a significant one may remain a matter of degree, but no doubt we see them all around and all the time. No doubt either about their significance to our lives. They give an architecture (a structure) to our human interaction (to our very lives). As we heard the political scientist quoted above say, "Accepted examples … include the courts, legislatures, executives, and other political institutions, families, organized churches, manufacturing establishments, transportation systems, and organized markets." That's a lot of highly significant institutions that structure a lot of our lives, but doesn't even begin to give a complete list.

Ladies and gentlemen, I've said that just like the architecture of a courtroom structures our human interaction such as the process of a jury trial, the architecture of institutions structures our human interaction such as the processes for passing laws or carrying out government policies. But we've run out of space again. To show how, we need to go on to the next article.

1.08 – The Reserve Clause

Ladies and gentlemen of the jury, in the last article, I said that the architecture of institutions structures our human interaction. But more than that, the architecture structures the interaction in certain ways, and very often, the only way to change the interaction is to change the architecture. To illustrate, let's stick with MLB a moment.

Until 1974, all the players had to sign a form contract with a "reserve clause," a rule which prevented them from jumping to another team, although the teams could trade the players. A player either had to take the owner's salary offer or hold out (not playing and receiving no salary at all). This institutional architecture decisively structured the human interaction between the owners and the players. It gave the owners a big leverage, letting them keep down the players' salaries, keeping more money in the owners' pockets.

But in 1974, that rule changed, changing the institutional architecture, changing the human interaction. Baseball entered the era of "free agency," which gave the players more freedom to move from to team to team. The owners were forced to bid against each other for the best players, whose salaries quickly exploded into the multimillion-dollar range. How this happened makes a fascinating story in and of itself, but outside our purposes. What we want to take away is that the institutional architecture structured the human interaction, that changing the architecture changed the interaction, and that the interaction wouldn't have changed unless the architecture had changed. The reserve clause structured the institution, giving the owners a big advantage over the players. That wasn't going to change until the architecture changed.

Ladies and gentlemen, coming to government, what do we come to except another institution? What is a constitution except the fundamental laws (the architecture) that structure the institution? The government organizes people to attain their mutual goals. It decisively structures their interaction (their lives). It structures their interaction in a certain way. And often, the only way to change their interaction is by changing the structure of their government (by changing their constitution).

Ladies and gentlemen, it's something of a hobby of mine to read constitutions, and none better illustrates this point than the present Constitution of Iran. Promulgated in 1979 after the Iranian (or Islamic) Revolution, the guys who wrote it, obviously some highly educated Islamic clerics, knew just what they were about. Obviously, they had read a lot of constitutions themselves. They took one clause from one and another from another. To give credit where credit due, they creatively came up with a combination of clauses to structure exactly the sort of government they wanted.

They called their work-product the "Constitution of the Islamic Republic of Iran." That is, they claimed to be setting up a "republic." Nor did they fail to write in clauses that gave lip service to democratic values. Article 19 proclaims, "All people of Iran … enjoy equal rights." Article 20, "All citizens … equally enjoy the protection of the law." Article 58, "The functions of the legislature are to be exercised through the Islamic Consultative Assembly, consisting of the elected representatives of the people." Article 114, "The President is elected for a four-year term by the direct vote of the people." So far so good.

But then they starting writing in reserve clauses, starting with

21

the office of the Supreme (or Religious) Leader, described as "a holy person possessing the necessary qualifications." A number of clauses reserved to him what amounted to supreme powers. He can declare war or peace, serves as the commander-in-chief, appoints the top military commanders, appoints the highest judges, and appoints the head of the state-run media. Another clause designated the Ayatollah Khomeini as the original Supreme Leader, and after his demise, a Council of Experts appoints his successors. To which we need only add, since the Supreme Leader controls the appointments to this Council, he can handpick his own successor.

Ladies and gentlemen, it should be obvious these reserve clauses make the Supreme Leader like the owner of a baseball team in the days of the reserve clause and other Iranians the players. He's got the leverage. The way the Iranian constitution structures their government, they're going to play by his rules. The only way to change that would be to change the institutional architecture by changing the constitution.

Ladies and gentlemen, I don't think we need any more examples. We've reached a true view of my client, the Constitution. He's the clauses that structure our government's institutional architecture. He structures our human interaction and in a certain way. To understand the Constitution, we have to understand how he structures the government and our interaction.

Ladies and gentlemen, it's taken me quite a while to get to this point in my defense of the Constitution, but I didn't see any shorter route. First, we needed to dispel a misapprehension. The lawyers have got you to thinking it's all about your rights. And it is about your rights, but that starts at the wrong end. The Constitution is more like a jury trial than a verdict. The constitutional processes are the trial; your rights are the verdict. The processes produce and determine your rights, not the other way around. So the processes come before the rights. Second, we needed to see that the Constitution structures the institution. It's this institution that runs the processes. The architecture of this institution (the government) crucially structures the processes.

If we've come so far, we've made a crucial start on our journey. But before concluding my opening statement and going on to hear the evidence (the next step in a trial), we need to cover a few more preliminaries in the next articles.

1.09 – Passing Judgment

Ladies and gentlemen of the jury, there used to be a free show in the Creek County Courthouse any time a jury docket going. We had some great trial lawyers (masters of the art). They could work on a narrow ledge and scale what seemed a sheer rock face to improbable verdicts. One had to admire their skill, if not always applaud their triumphs. Sometimes, they reached the ambitious heights of the ancient sophists, making the worst case seem the better (outsmarting justice). But however ingenious, they still had to win by some rules. To walk a client on a murder charge, they had to convince the jury that the case not proved beyond a reasonable doubt. No matter the type of case, there were some rules.

Well, if there are rules in court, when the critics try the Constitution in the court of public opinion, shouldn't there be some rules? While if some friend self-appoints himself to defend the Constitution (like myself), shouldn't he have to abide by the same rules? How pass judgment on the Constitution or any constitution without some rules?

Then in the first place, we can't hope for absolute, ideal perfection in a constitution. If we demand the Peaceable Kingdom from government, we can only suffer continual disappointment. Nirvana doesn't step off the night train. Let the perfect not become the enemy of the good. Things might be better, but things could be worse. When it comes to government, those who try to make it better have often only made it worse and sometimes a great deal worse. Politics being the art of the possible, let's judge by the possible.

In the second place, when someone sets up as a critic in the political theater, he should have to do more than criticize. Finding fault with the current political actors seldom hard, but putting on a better performance as seldom easy. Before the French Revolution in 1789, critics like Voltaire and Rousseau mercilessly ridiculed the *Ancien Regime*, so inciting the audience as to drag the reigning stars off the stage and murder them as the final act in that old drama. But the revolution then staged a lousy performance and the public paid a high price for admission. In the new first act, Madame Guillotine stole the show (the Terror and maybe 40,000 executions). The second act featured a merciless civil war in the Vendee (maybe 170,000 casualties). After an interlude filled with several farcical governments, the curtain raised on the grand climax, the endless wars of the Napoleonic Empire (maybe a million French casualties). A great many critics in the twentieth century, prominently communists and fascists, when given the chance to strut across the stage of history, have performed to still less applause and at still higher costs.

"Just because I don't have a solution doesn't mean there's not a problem." But booing the current political actors off leaves an empty stage, and this show must go on. We, the public, have to stay in our seats. Many a political farce has been followed by a worse political tragedy. One might name some political melodramas where any change of cast seems an improvement, say the dictatorship of the late and unlamented Muammar Gaddafi in Libya. But short such a bad actor, we need more than a revolutionary catharsis. We need some realistic solutions for the complications of the plot.

In the third place, the Constitution itself guarantees, "No … ex post facto Law shall be passed." In other words, the government can't make something a crime after the fact. The Constitution itself should benefit from a similar rule. It shouldn't suffer condemnation for not being farther ahead of its time than it was. Nor should it suffer continued condemnation for wrongs no longer committed, especially when the Constitution itself remedied the wrongs. For the most prominent example, the Constitution itself abolished slavery with the 13th Amendment in 1865. For another example, the Constitution itself guaranteed women the vote with the 19th Amendment in 1920. Why condemn or continue to condemn the Constitution in either case?

But finally, it would be great to have some objective rules by which to pass judgment on the Constitution or any constitution for that matter. It would be great to have something like a yardstick. And actually, some good objective yardsticks do exist. One is "the index of freedom," which measures such things as free elections and civil liberties. As a well-known example, Freedom House (an

NGO, a non-governmental organization) puts out an annual report (Freedom in the World). Another good way to measure is by per capita GDP (gross national product divided by the population). If counting the money sounds too materialistic, leaving out what really counts, yet a higher per capita income counts for a higher standard of living with better housing, infrastructure, education, jobs, healthcare, and a longer life.

Both these measurements fit well with our intuition. When we think we see a good government, we see a higher index of freedom and a higher per capita GDP. If the voice of the people counts for anything, they've voted with their feet. The tide of immigration sets strongly toward countries higher by these measurements.

We would leave behind a great deal of confusion and unfairness if we agreed up front on some rules for passing judgment on the Constitution or any constitution. First, don't demand absolute (ideal) perfection, but settle for the possible. Second, don't accept mere criticism, but require constructive criticism. Third, don't condemn the past on standards not yet invented or the present for errors no longer committed. Fourth, measure success by the index of freedom and the per capita GDP.

Ladies and gentlemen of the jury, hopefully we can agree on so much. But there's still another measure we need to apply when judging the Constitution. That's how well it measures up to its own principles. Let me take up that topic in the next article to my opening statement.

1.10 – The Declaration

Ladies and gentlemen of the jury, if we're going to talk about the Constitution, which ratified in 1789, we should start by talking about the Declaration of Independence, which proclaimed in 1776. Not only does the Declaration come first in time, but in pride of place. There's the law, there's the spirit of the law. The one is dead without the other. There's the Constitution, there's the Declaration. The Constitution creates the government, but the Declaration proclaims the spirit for the creation. The one is dead without the other.

We can't re-read the words too often, "We hold these truths to be self-evident: that all men are created equal, that they are endowed by their Creator with certain unalienable rights, that among these are life, liberty, and the pursuit of happiness. That, to secure these rights, governments are instituted among men, deriving their just powers from the consent of the governed." Not least for writing these words, Thomas Jefferson has come down to history with a great name.

Yet what exactly do the words mean? How say "all men are created equal," when they're obviously not? "Equal born? O yes, if yonder hill be level with the flat." Rather, they seem born on a bell curve. The genetic lottery picks winners and losers unequally. You can't coach speed. If you're not born fleet of foot, forget about ever winning the 100-meter dash at the Olympics. While as for competing in the mental events, the speed of guys like Newton and Einstein leaves us ordinary mortals panting behind in their intellectual dust. But if not nature, it's nurture. "Duke's son, cook's son, son of a hundred kings." In the race for the good things of life, some are born with a head start, have a hand up, and a hand to catch them if they fall. While life relentlessly grades on a curve. No matter how talented or how hard you try, only a very few can ever make an NFL roster, whose size limited. Daniel Webster said of the legal profession, "There's always room at the top," and he shouldered his way in. But by definition the top rests on the bottom, leaving some at the bottom, and generally, a narrow top rests on a much wider bottom, excluding most from the top.

Legal or economic "equality" glimmers like a will-o'-the-wisp, forever leading on, never quite in reach. Nothing better illustrates than that pursuit of racial equality in our time. First, racial equality meant repeal segregation (laws that mandated racial separation); next, it meant integration (laws to break down racial separation); next, it meant affirmative action (laws to make up for past discrimination). Yet blacks are still behind by many socio-economic indicators. As long as such statistics persist, does the gap equate to failure in racial equality? Another illustration comes from all the recent talk about "income inequality." In 1915, the richest 1 percent of Americans had 18 percent of the income, but by 2006, their share was all the way up to 24 percent. A Noble Prize winning economist commented, "The most important problem that we are facing now today, I think, is rising inequality."

Unless we somehow more equally redistribute the income, do these figures equate to inequality?

What exactly are our "unalienable rights?" We might agree on some godlike generalities, but the devil is in the details. We might agree "thou shalt not kill." So many say "an eye for an eye" and put the murderer to death. But many say the death penalty violates the commandment. We might agree about the "free exercise of religion," but what amounts in detail to "free exercise?" Can the Mormons practice polygamy? (No.) Can the Church of Lukumi Babalu Aye sacrifice animals and scatter the body parts around the city? (Yes.) The list of such questions about our rights and the sometime surprising and sometimes dubious answers goes on and on.

Yet Americans believe "all men are created equal" and "endowed with certain unalienable rights." They believe in these ideals. If someone wants to disagree, they can. It's a free country. But it's a country that agrees with Jefferson. And it's a country that has worked out "equality" and "rights" in some considerable detail. But we shouldn't be surprised that considerable details remain to be worked out. That's the way with ideals. They remain a work in progress.

Which brings us to the final words, "That, to secure these rights, governments are instituted among men, deriving their just powers from the consent of the governed." We might almost call those the forgotten words, since often left off the quote for some unaccountable reason. But at least we know their meaning. The "consent of the governed" means democracy. Then why would we ever leave those words off the quote? What's more fundamental to our equality or our rights than democracy? And isn't democracy fundamental for another reason? If "equality" and "rights" a work in progress, how do we work out the progress? If we can't be equal or have our rights without democracy, how can we work out the progress except through the democratic process?

Ladies and gentlemen of the jury, does that somehow get it wrong? Doesn't the Declaration of Independence proclaim the principles for the U.S. Constitution? Aren't those principles above all democracy? And while in one sense democracy an outcome, as a choice among types of governments, once that choice is made, isn't it a process, a method of government? That's why as earlier said, the Constitution is more like a jury trial than a verdict. Just as a jury trial a process to reach a verdict, democracy is a process to arrive at the laws. Just as a jury trial doesn't guarantee any particular verdict, democracy doesn't guarantee any particular laws. Rather, what's guaranteed is the process itself (the democratic process itself).

Perhaps Lincoln gets quoted too much, but that's because he so often gets it right. He got it right this time, too. He said, "Now, my countrymen, if you have been taught doctrines conflicting with the great landmarks of the Declaration of Independence; if you have listened to suggestions which would take away from its grandeur, and mutilate the fair symmetry of its proportions; … let me entreat you to come back. Return to the fountain … come back to the truths that are in the Declaration of Independence." As we study the Constitution, let's never forget "the fountain" and to "come back to the truths that are in the Declaration of Independence." Let's never forget that democracy is the spirit of the Constitution.

1.11 – Take a Seat

Ladies and gentlemen of the jury, there's an armchair philosopher in this town. One afternoon over in the Courthouse Grill, holding forth across the coffee table, he said philosophy was a stool with four legs. He ticked them off on his fingers – the nature of reality, how we know it, the problem of conduct (morality), and the problem of governance (political science). Everyone is sitting on their own stool, however unsteady the legs. Ladies and gentlemen, to take "a very comprehensive, as well as a very serious view" of the Constitution will require us getting at least one of our legs solid under us (political science).

How can we take such a solid seat? Someone else has said, "Philosophy is getting it right." How can we "get it right?" Fortunately for us, a lot of great thinkers, not least the Founding Fathers, have already broken the trail, and the classic guys all followed the same trail. They all go from psychology to sociology to political science, all by way of history. Don't see how we can do better than to follow along (follow the "classic tradition" of political science).

As with so much else, Aristotle long ago laid down the point of departure, saying, "As in other departments of science, so in politics, the compound should always be resolved into the simple elements or least parts of the whole." All the classic thinkers follow him. They all start by breaking down "politics" into the "simple elements or least parts of the whole." And since individuals are "the least parts of the political whole," they all start with individual human nature (psychology), As he said, the "other departments of science" do the same. For example, in physics they break down matter to the least particles and the forces operating on them. From that starting point, they try to arrive at an understanding of the physical universe. Why should political science vary? We have to start by breaking it down to the least particles (the individuals) and the forces operating on them (their psychology).

Aristotle also famously said, "that man is more of a social animal than bees or any other gregarious animals is evident," which next brings us to the nature of society (sociology). When you study bees, you may start with the individual bee, but except for a few solitary types, bees live in a hive. The bees' behavior makes up the hive, but the hive has behaviors all its own not described by describing the behavior of any individual bee. The same goes for humans. We may start with individual human nature (psychology), but except for a few hermits, humans live in a society. Men make up society, but society has behaviors all its own. Individuals make up American society, but you can't describe American society by describing any individual. As the English philosopher Thomas Hobbes said to kick off his great work on government, *Leviathan*, "I will consider them [mankind] first singly, and afterwards in train, or dependence upon one another."

Aristotle further famously said, "Man is a political animal." Instincts organize the bees, but government organizes humans. That brings us the study of governments (political science). And that finally brings us to the study of constitutions and our Constitution, since the constitutions organize the governments.

While all these sciences share the same laboratory – history. A psychologist, sociologist, or political scientist may run some experiments on some rats or even some sophomores. They may run their subjects through some mazes or over-crowd them, ask them to respond to some pictures or play some games. But whatever their theories, the real test comes from the history in the real world. How well does it hold up in practice? And with humans, your ability to experiment is pretty limited. Some experiments you shouldn't do, and some they won't do. More than that, the real human phenomena occur in history, either the past or the ongoing. So that's the laboratory.

Ladies and gentlemen, to take "a very comprehensive, as well as a very serious view" of the Constitution, I can't think of a better trail to follow that the one broken and followed by classic political science. My new defense of the Constitution will follow that trail. Admittedly, that lays out a bit of a long itinerary, but no shorter journey will reach our destination.

Remember, it's the case of the critics versus the Constitution. You, the public, are sitting as the jury on the case. I've not so modestly self-appointed myself as lawyer for the Constitution. It's my duty to present you the evidence. It's your duty to bring in a just verdict. Ladies and gentlemen of the jury, take a seat.

2.00 – THE BODY POLITIC

2.01 – Dissect the Body Politic

Like the Jewish lady who kept referring to "my son, the doctor," anyone with a child who graduated from medical school can hardly resist the reference. Then let me get that out of the way. When "my daughter, the doctor," went to medical school, the first thing she did was dissect a body. That's not a bad way to start with the study of constitutions either. Dissect the body politic.

"For by art is created that great LEVIATHAN called a COMMONWEALTH or STATE (in Latin, CIVITAS), which is but an artificial man, though of greater strength and stature than the natural." The body politic resembles a LEVIATHAN all right. It can make way with surpassing strength, as Rome conquered the known world or Britain an empire on which the sun never set. It can swallow lives whole like the whale swallowed Jonah or the gulags swallowed so many. Its vast bulk can blunder about shortsighted and clumsy, wrecking all sorts of havoc and unintended consequences like European nations stumbled into the mass slaughter of World War I. It can beach in the shallows to die and rot like a whale again or the decline and fall of the Roman Empire, leaving behind bleached bones or the ruins of Rome.

The body politic seems like "an artificial man" as well (like a living organism). It comes to birth like our Constitution brought into being the United States. Like an organism made from cells, this body made from individuals (over 300 million now in America). Like the cells form organs, these individuals organize to form institutions. It can maintain a homeostasis (an inner stability, as the U.S. has maintained its existence for over two hundred years). It has a metabolism (can extract energy from the environment, as what else are your taxes)? It can reproduce as

31

Britain gave birth to our thirteen colonies and grow like we spread across the continent. It can adapt, as say America to the industrial revolution. It can respond to external stimuli, as say America to the Japanese attack on Pearl Harbor. Finally, it can die, as Rome again, not yet us.

This body politic seems to share all the ills that flesh is heir to. It can suffer from cancers and cognitive disorders, go about covered in festering sores or openly psychotic. But just as medicine aspires to health, political science (the science of government) aspires to a healthy body politic. Can a government not move with the athleticism and intelligence that Michelangelo imagined for Florence with the David? Can a government not promote the civic calm and justice that Pericles imagined for Athens when crowning the Acropolis with the Parthenon? If such asks too much, can government not at least walk upright and normal (a healthy mind in a healthy body)?

But if we think we know health or an athletic or beautiful body when we see it, when the doctors began dissecting cadavers, it was far from clear what they were seeing. Cutting into the chest, they saw the dead heart, but couldn't see how the living heart pumped the blood throughout the body. It took considerable ingenuity for William Harvey in 1628 to figure out how the living heart works and the circulation of the blood. While the doctors still don't understand a lot of things about the human body like the brain or how to prevent cancer. When we dissect the body politic, do we know what we're seeing? Only if we can we figure out how it works.

But fortunately, that's not as hard as medicine for the same reason law school not as hard as medical school. To learn medicine takes a lot of complicated math and chemistry, subjects sometimes beyond our average minds. To learn the law just takes some average common sense, since the subject adapted to the purpose. If the average person couldn't figure out the law, how could they be governed by it? Since the body politic no more than individuals living together in an organized way (in society), figuring that out takes no more than common sense either. We're all pretty well adapted to figure out each other and society. We just require some common sense psychology and sociology. But although this book not that hard to read, it has a lot of pages, and if we don't read all the pages, the story won't make sense. In other words, I'm saying you have to stick with me. We have quite a bit to cover and we have to cover it all.

One thing seems clear from the start. The body politic resembles a human body in a crucial way. "To understand Italy nationally, you have to understand Italy locally, and to understand Italy locally, you have to understand Italy nationally." In the human body, the higher functions depend on the lower functions and the lower on the higher. The brain depends on the stomach to digest the food, and the stomach depends on the brain to find the food. A sore on the toe can turn into gangrene and kill the whole body, including the brain. If the brain can figure out how to treat or prevent the sore, it can save not only the toe, but the whole body and itself. In exactly the same way, the higher functions in the body politic depend on lower functions and the lower on higher. A paralysis in the lower functions, say in the economic system, can cripple the whole body, say with a depression, and a paralysis in the higher functions, say the government's mismanagement of the monetary supply, can cripple the lower functions, say causing a recession. A healthy body politic requires higher and lower functions to work together as the economy and the government must work together.

Taking a page from the medical profession, let's start by dissecting the body politic. Just like the human body is made from individual cells, the body political is made from individual people. First, let's look at these individuals (the local level). Next, just as the cells form the organs, the people organize at what we might call the regional level (into institutions). Let's look at these regions (the institutions). Finally, let's go onto the national level (look at the organism as a whole). Along the way, we'll want to pay special attention to the highest organ or level (the government, corresponding at least in part with the brain). Let's try to figure out how it all goes together and works. Let's try to figure out what amounts to a healthy body politic (one with a healthy constitution).

2.02 – Only as Good as the Client

Lawyers have a saying that "a case is only as good as the

client." Back in the days before the public defender system, we younger lawyers learned that lesson the hard way. The judges would court appoint you in rotation to represent indigent defendants. Before you knew it, you found yourself seated at counsel table next a client charged with armed robbery, a couple prior convictions, and a teardrop tattoo in the corner of one eye. You might as well have taken a seat in a plane with a pilot determined to fly into the side of a mountain. Didn't matter how good you were. You were going to crash and burn right along with him.

But good or bad, clients share a dominant trait. They want to win their cases. Good or bad, lawyers share the same dominant trait. They want to win their cases. It's a blood sport for the same reason so much of the law descends from vengeance and the feud. The cases are about deeply held passions and fiercely held interests like murder, divorce, and money. In the old days of trial by combat, the legal warriors actually fought to the death, making them highly motivated, since their lives depended on it. Today's lawyers don't actually shed each other's blood, but they're about as highly motived, since their professional lives depend on it.

This psychology serves as the foundation for the Anglo-American (adversarial) legal system. We pit highly motivated adversaries in the legal coliseum, the judge and the jury the audience in the stands. Under the theory, the legal gladiators (the lawyers) will attack each other with every available fact and argument, revealing between them all sides of the case. The impartial judge and jury turn thumbs up or thumbs down. Thus, justice should prevail. The theory makes good sense except lawyers fight at different weights. When you get a mismatch, a heavyweight against a lightweight, the higher-class lawyer is more likely to win, not necessarily the better case.

But if this psychology dominates in the legal forum, why would we expect some other psychology to dominate over in the political arena? Winning is the dominant trait in either venue. When the lawyers win, they win their cases. When the politicians win, they win power. Winning cases is the lawyers' lifeblood, winning power is the politicians' lifeblood. That led the English philosopher Thomas Hobbes, who lived 1588 to 1679, to lay down as the first principal of political psychology, "So that in the first place, I put for a general inclination of all mankind, a perpetuall and restless desire of Power after power."

How right he was. In the political universe, the will-to-power works like the force of gravity in the physical universe. You can no more defy the one than the other. You can no more erect a political structure (a government institution) that violates his "first principle" than erect a physical structure, say a bridge, that violates the law of gravity. To design either, you have to start by calculating what your material will carry. A designer of bridges has to calculate how much weight the timber, stone, or steel will bear aloft. A designer of governments (writer of constitutions) has to make the same calculation, except his structure rests on the backs of living humanity. In either case, faulty structures collapse with disastrous results, and making a mistake in your calculations just ends up another manmade disaster.

The former Soviet Union gave an absolutely classic demonstration of such a miscalculation. They based their constitution on Marx's theory that, "The abolition of private property" would lead to a state of equality ("from each according to his ability, to each according to his needs"). However, under the theory, the "transformation" first required "a political transition period in which the state can be nothing but *the revolutionary dictatorship of the proletariat.*" Following this logic, the Soviet constitution demolished private property and raised a dictatorship on the ruins. Unfortunately, the predicted "transformation" failed to occur.

In making his calculations, Marx had left out Hobbes' first principle of political psychology. He rightly saw the capitalists' power rested on their property and taking away their property would cause their power to collapse. But the power of the state is the ultimate power. A dictatorship has a monopoly on that commodity, and the Soviet dictator's will-to-power worked no different the capitalists' will-to-power. A capitalist with a monopoly charges the highest price the market will bear. Since the Soviet dictator could deal in terror as a commodity, he could extract the ultimate human price (utter servitude). The apparatchiks (the party bureaucrats) distributed this commodity with blind obedience in abject terror themselves and received as their reward the lesser spoils of office. Before the capitalists had the good things of life, but now the dictator and his minions had it all. The people were as firmly excluded as ever. The tiger didn't change, but merely re-arranged his stripes.

To avoid such disasters in government (in writing constitutions), let's never forget that a lawyer's case in only as good as the client, and a constitution is only as good as the human material. A bridge can't defy the laws of gravity. A political structure (a government institution) can't defy the "first law of political psychology" (the will-to-power). In the next articles, let's consider some other aspects of the human material (of human psychology) we need to take into account in designing any constitutional structure.

2.03 – What Makes Sammy Run

Successful trial lawyers can't let themselves get out of touch with the jurors (their constituency), just like successful politicians can't let themselves get out of touch with the electorate (their constituency). Since they share the same constituency (the public), neither lawyers nor politicians can let themselves get out of touch with Hollywood and the media, which reflect and form the public taste. It doesn't hurt if their personal tastes run that way, but I knew a lawyer who imposed the task on himself of going to movies and watching TV. He took the view that if you didn't dine on the public fare, you might miss a change in the public appetite. He told a jury once, "I'm going to give you the raw meat," and he kept his promise. He knew what they wanted and how to give it to them.

But if the lawyers want to win (their cases) and the politicians want to win (their elections), what do Hollywood and the media types want? What else, if not the same thing? They want to win (fame, money, an Oscar, a Grammy, a star on the Hollywood Walk of Fame). They're all running on that same first principle of political psychology, "a perpetual and restless desire of power after power" or the equivalents like fame, money, or prestige. Like the bumper sticker says, "I'll give up my gun when you pry my cold, dead fingers off the barrel." Only death can pry their fingers off grasping for more celebrity.

But remember *What Makes Sammy Run?* In that best-selling novel and Broadway musical about the Hollywood rat race, Sammy betrayed everyone on his way to a hallow success. He was running on that same first principle of political psychology. He was running after the power of success. He clawed his way to the top. But the pursuit left him empty, not fulfilled. What went wrong for Sammy?

An American psychologist, Abraham Maslow, who lived 1908 to 1970, pioneered a model for human psychology that makes good sense. He said people are motivated by "a pyramid of needs." If George Mallory had to climb Mt. Everest "because it's there," we have to climb this pyramid for the same reason. That's how we're set up. But to climb the pyramid at Giza, you have to go up stone by stone, just like to reach the summit of Everest you have to go in stages from base camp to the peak. In the same way, Maslow said we have to get our lower needs before we can get our higher. First, we have to get our bodily needs (such as food or sex). Next, we need safety (from fear) and shelter. Next, we need relationships (friends, families, lovers). At about the same level, we need respect (from others and self-respect). At the highest level, we need self-actualization (a sense of meaning, purpose, and fulfillment in our lives). Throughout runs a need for knowledge (not least about how to get our other needs). There also seems an aesthetic need (for beauty and order). We're motivated to get all our needs (even to the highest). But generally, we can't leap to the final level (to self-actualization). When food, safety, and shelter are hard to come by, it's hard to give much thought to friendship or love. Without friendship or love, it's hard to feel much self-respect. Without all the others, it's hard to feel a sense of fulfillment in our lives. To become a fully developed and healthy individual we have to get all our needs.

Maslow's model seems to fit well with what we see whether we look inside ourselves or outside at others. What normal behavior not explained? Through all vicissitudes, we pursue our needs. While it has another feature of a good scientific theory. It has predictive power. It lets us predict how (normal) individuals will behave. But maybe there's a flaw. It's not hard to call to mind historic figures who clearly felt on top of the world, but deluded if not delusional. Recall the old black and white photos of Hitler at

Berchtesgaden, gazing out over the Bavarian Alps, every inch the great leader in his own mind. The newsreels of Stalin's smiling face from the top of Lenin's Tomb in Red Square, reviewing the annual May Day parades, have the same self-satisfied glow.

But to return to Sammy, let's apply the psychology. Now we know what made him run. He was running after his needs. Now we know what made him fail. His constant betrayals kept others from trusting him, and without their trust he couldn't get his needs for friendship, love, and the respect of others. He was like a runner in a relay race who throws away the baton. No matter how fast he ran, he couldn't know the thrill of victory, only the agony of defeat. He had disqualified himself. He had made a basic mistake about human psychology. He had forgotten that life is a team sport.

When it comes to government and constitutions, let's not lose touch with our constituency. We can't leave the psychology of winning (the will-to-power) out of account, but neither can we leave the rest of human psychology (our other needs) out of account. Either would be a fatal miscalculation. Lawyers, politicians, the Hollywood and media types, all the rest of us, we're all running to win. We're all running on Hobbes' first principle of political psychology, "a perpetual and restless desire of power after power" (or fame, money, prestige, or the equivalents). But let's not make Sammy's mistake. The late, great Vince Lombardi said in a line lifted from a John Wayne movie, "Winning isn't everything, it's the only thing." Better what Grantland Rice said, "It's not whether you win or lose, but how you play the game." Unless we play the game the right way, we can never win.

2.04 – Ask Not

They've started calling our parents "the greatest generation," but they're still calling us (the baby boomers) "the me generation." In our youth, we watched Kennedy's inauguration live and still remember (don't we), "Ask not what your country can do for you, but what you can do for your country." But over the years (if our name fits), our generation has asked not so much what we could do for our society (our country), as what our society could do for us. But any generation should learn from experience, and so sooner or later we should learn such "me first" thinking threatens to turn into a self-defeating strategy. Unless we give some thought to society, we're neglecting the preconditions for our own success.

To put that thought on a sound scientific basis, start with "the beetle in a box" thought-experiment. We hand out a box to the students in the class. We ask them to say what in their boxes. They all say, "A beetle." Everyone knows what everyone else means. But only because we all know what the word "beetle" means. We all learned that word as a child from someone else, who learned it from someone else, who learned it from someone else. But what if no one was around to teach a child a language? What would happen?

Forget Romulus and Remus being suckled by a wolf or Mowgli in the *Jungle Book*. Wild animals eat human young. The actual cases come from horrendous neglect, being locked in a closet or some such thing. So we know what happens. Past a certain age, children cannot acquire language. Worse than that, something else won't happen. The human brain won't develop normally in such extreme social isolation, causing severe cognitive and emotional disorders. If rescued, such children prove tragically beyond rehabilitation, leading short lives bereft of their full humanity.

Without a doubt, the science proves our very thoughts and minds require a society. Left to our own devices, we cannot acquire so much as the mental apparatus to think. In the face of such overwhelming isolation, where is the man who can proclaim, "I am the master of my fate, I am the captain of my soul?" Nowhere. He can't even learn to think the thoughts, let alone to speak the words.

Every day and all around us, how ignore the clear evidence of our social dependence? An adult hunter-gatherer might live off the land, but bereft of his band, his other needs would go abegging, not least for friendship and love. Mere loneliness would soon reduce him to a dull despair. But abandoned in the sands of the Kalahari, the average American would serve as no more than quick and easy protein for the scavengers. However, no need to conduct such unethical experiments, since in every American city the homeless wander the streets. No doubt about money being a socially generated device, and they lack the necessary. If not for the Salvation Army or the John 3:16 Mission, they would starve to death in the alleys in the midst of plenty. Being broke has forced a harsh lesson upon not a few of us, teaching our social dependence.

When was the last time a natural disaster like a hurricane or an ice storm struck your region? Remember Katrina? Maybe your disaster was less bad, just an ice storm that blocked roads and knocked out the power. But if your grid stayed down for more than a couple days, something ominous began to happen. The shelves in the grocery stores began to empty out. For a brief moment, didn't your social dependence cross your mind? Do you grow your own food? If not, you're totally dependent on others.

Americans take pride in being rugged individualists. We like to see ourselves as self-made men. But we much prefer to play the cowboy rather than the farmer, much prefer to mount a horse and boss the herd rather than walk sweating (and swearing) behind the plow (lashed to the mule). We much prefer to get astride society (if we can) rather than harness ourselves to work in tandem with society. As a stepstool to mount this noble steed, we display real ingenuity and bottomless self-justification. Like Thoreau, we want to decide for ourselves which social rules to obey. Like him, we strike heroic poses, make up legends, depict ourselves as in an epic struggle against the ignorance and prejudices of our society. But however much we manage to delude ourselves or succeed in shifting the burden onto others, we never escape our social dependence.

"No man is an island, entire of itself. … ask not for whom the bell tolls. It tolls for thee." We can't escape our dependence on society. A generation may well ask what society has done for them, since everyone requires society to do so much for them. But they better not forget to ask what they've done for society either. Otherwise, they risk neglecting the preconditions for their own success. The sooner a generation learns that lesson, the better the generation. Maybe our generation better hope it's never too late.

2.05 – You Didn't Build That

As a presidential candidate, Barack Obama never carried a single county here in Oklahoma. His popularity in these parts only seems to have declined since. Apparently, a lot of Oklahomans would regard quoting him as somewhat the opposite of the devil quoting scripture. But I'm defending the Constitution in these articles. If some president or anyone else says something useful to my defense, I mean use it. Mr. Obama said something too good to pass up.

Remember the 2012 campaign, when he said, "If you've got a business – you didn't build that." His critics here in Oklahoma and elsewhere pounced like tigers on crippled prey. They accused him of denying the cherished American creed of the self-made man. But come on, folks, our Oklahoma sense of fair play should compel us not to take his quote out of context. He said, "Somebody helped to create this unbelievable American system that we have that allowed you to thrive. Somebody invested in roads and bridges. If you've got a business – you didn't build that. Somebody else made that happen." So to play fair, he wasn't saying, "If you've got a business – you didn't build that." Rather, he was saying that "somebody helped" to build "this unbelievable American system that allowed you to thrive." That becomes still clearer by quoting the still fuller context, "The point is that when we succeed, we succeed because of our individual initiative, but also because we do things together." These passages may not well display Mr. Obama's famed eloquence, if clarity a part of eloquence. But he was spot on when he said, "When we succeed, we succeed because of our individual initiative, but also because we do things together."

If we don't want to take it from Mr. Obama, let's take it from the Marine Corps, who say *gung ho* (work together). We better work together, because we can't achieve a lot of our goals working alone. We have to come together in society to achieve these "social goals."

Right up front come our economic goals. Like the man who said, "Give me the luxuries of life and the necessities will take care of themselves," most of us would settle for a society that poured out the proverbial horn of plenty (the cornucopia) in our laps. But for most of history, the human race has lived a hardscrabble existence for the bare necessities. Even today, it's still the economy, stupid. Presidential elections still turn on the latest economic indicators because the economy still so basic. Napoleon said an army marches on its stomach, and a society marches on its economic stomach. Without a well-fed economy, it won't march very far or arrive on the field in very good order.

About as soon comes the social goal for self-defense. As *Federalist No. 41* said, "Security against foreign danger is one of the primitive objects of civil society." Excavations from the earliest times reveal towns with defensive walls. By 1,200 BC, monumental stone battlements guarded Troy, yet Euripides tells the fate of the Trojan women. Patrick Henry said give me liberty or give me death, but they got neither. They got slavery. Their society failed at the social goal of self-defense. While still today, if you travel long enough and far enough, one morning you'll wake up to the sound of gunfire, hopefully in the distance. "We're at war, we just don't know it." A society that wants liberty rather than death or slavery better attain the social goal of self-defense.

About as soon comes law and order. How soon did Cain murder Able? As soon comes this goal. Bonnie and Clyde stick a gun in your face or Don Corleone makes you a deal you can't refuse. They say the death penalty doesn't deter crime, but if they say law enforcement doesn't deter crime, let them visit some town run by the outlaws. When Pablo Escobar ran Medellin, he murdered who he wanted and took what he wanted. After the Columbian police finally shot him through the head, he stopped doing those bad things anymore. If termination with such extreme prejudice offends your sensibilities, yet we'll have to handle the Pablos of this world somehow or other.

Not too distantly related comes the goal of socialization, instilling some habits of cooperation. We're naturally competitive. Like a bunch of kids who never grow up, we play king of the mountain all our lives, pulling the other guy down to pull ourselves up. That may serve useful purposes, say in playing the free-market game. But if we're not careful, we can end up playing a real-life version of family feud, dueling in the streets like the Montagues and the Capulets or bushwhacking each other like the Hatfields and the McCoys. We can end up playing at ethnic cleansing and civil war like in the Balkans. Too much dissension is counterproductive. Society requires some consensus, some sufficient general agreement to go on with. We need to play some games that teach cooperation (socialize us).

Neither last nor least come the social goal of knowledge and not least about how to attain all the other social goals. Knowledge is power. In a war for national survival, you better not bring a knife to a gunfight. Your society better know how to make a gun. If you want the luxuries of life, let alone the bare necessities, you better know how to make a good economy. Closely related comes the goal of efficiency, getting the most from always more or less scarce resources. Closely related comes social adaptability, a society's ability to adapt to changing circumstances. As the old Greek said, we never step in the same river twice. Change is constant. The fossils of the dinosaurs and the ruins of Rome are both colossal, and both show what can happen. Unless you can adapt, your species can go extinct and your society can collapse.

If we have to do things together for success, that leaves the question how to organize for success. As Moustache said, "That's another story." In the next articles, let's turn to how we organize, hopefully for success, through two connected ways – laws and institutions.

2.06 – The Law Library

Over at the Tulsa Law School, hardly anybody ever goes in the law library except faculty and students. In fact, no one else can get in without paying for a not so cheap library card. Down at the Oklahoma Law School in Norman, they're less exclusive. Being a public university, they let in the public, but just during the daytime hours. Law schools regard their libraries as precious institutional resources. Their promotional literature brags about the size of their collections, and it ain't just brag. If they do let you in, rows upon rows, thousands upon thousands of law books greet your eye. Walking down the aisles, you notice most are thwacking great tomes with mysterious numbers on the spines rather than titles, a code known only to the legally initiate. In the great law libraries, the collection goes back hundreds of years and the older volumes bound in leather. Alas, such elegant binding a thing of the past, but any law school worth its salt still makes an effort for some elegance in the furnishings, maybe some dark, expensive looking wood shelves, maybe some comfortable leather chairs, maybe some old-fashioned reading lamps with green shades on long tables. You're entering a temple of the profession. They want you properly impressed with the decorum, the quiet opulence, even with the unspoken power to command such impressions.

There you have the law library as a physical embodiment of the dignity and majesty of the law and of the profession. But might one wonder? Why do we need so many laws as in all these thousands upon thousands of books? Such a proliferation of law must signal a top-down social organization, since the top hands down laws to govern the bottom. Why do we at the bottom need so much governance from the top? Why can't we have more of a bottom-up social organization, where we at the bottom are less ruled over by the top or even give rules to the top?

Why can't social organization be more like walking down a crowded city street? Sociologists have studied that phenomenon in some detail, and they can tell you what you already noticed on your own. On a crowded city street, say New York City at rush hour, people spontaneously organize themselves. With no real conscious effort, people slightly alter their pace and path in response to each other. It's not perfect, but they give elbowroom, avoid bumping into each other, and move along in an orderly fashion. All on their own, they organize themselves to attain a social goal, the smooth flow of the traffic. Everyone gets to their destinations with a minimum of inconvenience to or from others. Sociologists call that bottom-up as opposed to top-down organization. With pure bottom-up you don't have any top-down. The top doesn't need to hand down a bunch of laws (rules) telling the bottom what to do. The cooperative "emerges" from the bottom spontaneously. Why can't living together in a society be more like that?

Yet look again. Notice the sidewalks, streets, traffic lights, and crosswalks. That framework sets the preconditions for the cooperation to emerge. There was a lot of pre-planning, and that required a lot of top-down (a lot of management). The city government had to design this framework. That was top-down. While if the top-down hadn't gotten it right, the bottom-up wouldn't have emerged right. If the sidewalks were designed too narrow or too winding, if the traffic lights were wrongly timed, the pedestrian traffic would snarl, as has been known to happen. We're not really seeing pure bottom-up organization, but a combination, top-down combined with bottom-up.

Economists talk about the free-market as the classic model for bottom-up organization. Rather than the laws being handed down from the top, the free-market runs on choices made at the bottom. The laws don't force people to produce goods or services, don't force them to buy and sell, don't set their prices. Instead, the invisible hand runs the market. Productivity, innovation, and wealth emerge spontaneously from the bottom.

Yet look again and notice some preconditions again. Without property rights (laws to secure property and enforce contracts), without a monetary system, the free-market can't emerge. That's top-down. The government has to create the property rights and the monetary system. So once again, it's a combination, top-down combined with bottom-up. Notice something else once again. Unless the top-down gets it right again, the bottom-up can't emerge right. If the top-down gets the monetary supply wrong, it can cause runaway inflation or the opposite (deflation), crippling the market. On the other hand, too much top-down will convert the free-market into a command-and-control economy, a fully socialized economy, stifling the market and the productivity, innovation, and wealth will no longer emerge from the bottom.

There seems no way out of it. It won't do any good to rise like the French peasants in 1789, kill all the aristocrats, and burn their title deeds. It won't do any good to kill all the lawyers and burn their libraries. They'll just be back. Cooperation (organization) can emerge bottom-up, but seldom without some top-down planning (some laws and rules). What we have to figure out, if we can, is the right combination of both.

2.07 – Laws Not Men

In early 2017, at his confirmation hearings as U.S. Attorney General, then Senator Jeff Sessions (R-AL) said, "You know I … am committed to the rule of law." Later he said, "I have always loved the law. It is the very foundation of our great country." Lawyers, judges, and legal scholars say such things all the time. But what exactly is "the rule of law" or "the law" that they're "committed to" and "always loved?"

A very famous definition of "law" comes from the English legal philosopher, John Austin, who lived 1790 to 1859. "Every law … is a command. … The evil which will probably be incurred in case a command be disobeyed … is frequently called a sanction." That seems to back into it cautiously enough. More directly we might say that a law is a command backed with the threat of a punishment. "Don't do the crime, if you can't do the time." But later commentators noted not all laws have a sanction (a punishment). Sometimes, the laws only provide a procedure to make legal determinations about facts or rights. The law for a jury trial provides for a procedure to determine guilt or innocence; the law to probate an estate provides a procedure for determining the heirs to the property.

If "the law" a command backed by a punishment or a procedure to determine facts or rights, what's "the rule of law?" The idea goes way back. Aristotle said, "law should govern." But still another English legal philosopher, A.V. Dicey, who lived 1835 to 1922, gets credit for popularizing the phrase "the rule of law." He wrote, "We mean, … that no man is punished or … made to suffer in body or goods except for a distinct breach of law established in the ordinary legal manner before the ordinary Courts of the land."

Reading him carefully, "the rule of law" requires two connected things. First, if "no man is punished … except for a *distinct breach* of the law," the law must be *distinctly* stated, that is, with the sufficient clarity that a breach can be clearly "established" (clearly seen). Second, if "no man is to be punished except for a distinct breach of the law *established* in the ordinary legal manner," the "ordinary legal manner" of proceeding against him must also be clearly "established," that is, the legal procedure must also be clearly stated (so it can be clearly followed).

Dicey adds that, "the rule of law is contrasted with every system of government based on the exercise by persons in authority of wide, arbitrary, or discretionary powers." In other words, by clearly stating the laws and procedures and following them, we leave behind "arbitrary." Further, Dicey goes on to say, "We mean … when we speak of the 'rule of law' … not only that … no man is above the law, but … every man, whatever be his rank or condition, is subject to the ordinary law of the realm," in other words, "equal protection of the laws."

All that sounds wonderful, doesn't it? It's even more wonderful when we remember Aristotle said that law is "reason without passion." It's still more wonderful when we remember St. Thomas Aquinas said that law is "an ordinance of reason, promulgated by one who is responsible for the good of the community." How could it get any more wonderful? The famous phrase "a government of laws not men" about sums it up. The law will govern by "reason without passion" and "for the good of the community." Under the rule of law, we'll have rational and equal, rather than arbitrary justice. No wonder Jeff Sessions said he had "always loved the law" and was "committed to the rule of law."

And it is wonderful. Let's strive for that. But before we get too carried away, let's notice two things about it. First, a law is a command backed by a punishment. The laws are promulgated by the government and backed with force. The laws are a way for the government to force people to do things, whether they want to or not. Second, the law can't make, interpret, or apply itself. Men have to do that. And men have been known to make, interpret, and apply the laws with neither "reason without passion" nor "for the good of the community," but to satisfy their own passions (ambitions and appetites) or for their own good (in their own interests). Even when well-intended, men have made mistakes. Recall the well-intended 18th Amendment ratified in 1919, prohibition. How well did that turn out?

For our purpose to understand the body politic, let's take away a couple lessons about the law. For all this talk about "an ordinance of reason" and "the good of the community," the laws are a way society organizes itself (enforces cooperation). They're "commands" backed by "sanctions" (punishments). The "rule of law" requires clearly stated ("established") laws and legal procedures to avoid arbitrariness as well as "equality before the law" (equal treatment for everyone). But since men must make, interpret, and apply the laws, we're never going to completely attain "the rule of law not men." Men are always going to rule, not the law.

2.08 – Institutions Matter

Institutions matter. But since they're not made out of matter, we tend to look right through without seeing them. That's a fault in our vision. We need to start seeing institutions. They matter.

Institutions are like the molds that turn out the products we need or want. Go to Italy and you're likely to see some Bernini bronzes, their ornate grandeur being hard to miss. You may like that sort of thing. But you won't see the mold, which long since discarded, and out of sight is out of mind. Yet unless Bernini had made the mold, you would never have seen the statue. Unless he'd done a great job on the mold, the statue wouldn't have turned out a great job either. The mold imprinted its nature on the statute. Then didn't the mold matter? Institutions work the same way and imprint their nature on their products.

Economic and political institutions mold whole societies. Rather than Italy, go to England and tour the Tower of London. That's a medieval castle; that's a product turned out by medieval institutions; that's a pretty impressive sight. But you don't see feudal institutions, which long since gone. Yet feudal institutions produced the Tower of London as well as all the other medieval castles, not the other way around. Without the institutions, the castles would never have been there to see. Much more than that, those institutions formed the whole of medieval society. Like a narrow neck on a wide mouthed funnel, they compressed that society into a form with a wide bottom and a tight top. The mass of the people (the peasants) poured in their labor at the wide bottom. A few people (the nobles) collected their lion's share at the tight top. To form some other sort of society, you would have had to break the mold. All the mold of feudal institutions was ever going to pour out was the product of feudal society. Don't we begin to see that institutions matter?

While not made out of matter, institutions can be as solid as matter, as solid as say a medieval castle. A castle's solid walls and towers let you dominate the lands round about and dominate whoever lives there. But remember the Spartans, who deliberately never built a wall around their city? Their institutions (their state and army) were so solid they didn't need walls. They dominated the lands around and whoever lived there with just their institutions. The Romans were the same way. Sure, they built walled cities and fortified camps, but their real strength came from their institutions, again the state and the army, with which they dominated the known world. Institutions can be as solid as walls (as solid as matter). Don't we begin to see that institutions matter?

In the dictionary, you'll find two definitions for "institution." In one sense, an institution is a widespread custom or practice, such as "the institution of marriage," "the institution of slavery," or "the institution of private property." In another sense, an institution is an organization, such as a corporation, a church, or a government. Let's not get confused between these two definitions. While institutions as customs or practices matter, institutions as organizations matter much more.

When we come to study institutions (as organizations) we see they serve as an essential way people come together to attain their social goals, such as economic goals or self-defense. They govern their members by rules of conduct, nowadays usually written down. They have leaders with authority to make decisions and enforce the rules. And they're durable. set up in such a way as to be self-sustaining.

To flesh it out, look at a modern, publicly held business corporation. You see people coming together to attain a social goal, this time to run a business, make money, manufacture a product, or provide a service. They're united by rules, the corporate bylaws and corporate policies. The shareholders own and hopefully profit from the corporation. They elect the board of directors, who hire the officers to run the company, providing leadership (management). The institution is set up in a lasting, self-perpetuating way. The stock passes from hand-to-hand, directors and officers come and go, but the successful corporation endures, sometimes for generations.

If we become convinced institutions matter and start looking for them, we start to see them everywhere. We see educational institutions, economic, political, cultural, religious, scientific, political, and on and on. And we can't but notice how institutions built into and onto each other. Our larger government institution includes legislative, executive, judicial, bureaucratic, and military institutions. And we can't but notice that all these institutions serve like a matrix connecting society or a scaffolding beneath and holding up society. While of course, government is the dominant institution. Government claims legitimacy in the use of force to carry out its rules (its laws).

So finally, don't we see that institutions are a way people come together to attain social goals (to organize to do things they can't do on their own, everything from the economy to national defense). They mold people together to turn out the products (goods and services we may need or want). But the first product any institution has to turn out is itself. Before it can mold anything else, it has to mold itself. And creating the mold changes the material going to make the mold just as surely as the mold will later change any material going through the mold. We don't just produce (change things) with institutions, the institutions change us as well. Let's turn to that important and neglected topic in the next article.

2.09 – A Life of their Own

Have you heard about "Lawyers For Less Litigation?" Nope, such a group doesn't exist. Lawyers are for more litigation, not less. More litigation means more money and power and influence for them. If you go to a meeting of say a trial lawyer association, you'll find a simple, underlying formula sums up their agenda. The more money the trial lawyers make, the better America will be. They're faithful advocates for any laws or legal reforms fitting their formula. They've convinced themselves and only need to convince the world.

But the lawyers aren't different. They're typical. They're just thinking in the institutional box. Who doesn't think in their institutional box? "What's good for General Motors is good for the country." When we get inside an institution, the institution gets inside our head and starts doing our thinking for us. It's easy to understand why. When we're inside an institution, what's good for the institution becomes what's good for us, since when the institution profits, we profit. Just like there's no "Lawyers For Less Litigation," there's no "bureaucrats for smaller budgets." Nope, just give them more money and staff, and their institution will save the world or more of it. Just give them enough paint and canvas, and they will paint a masterpiece. The fact they'll do nothing of the kind never enters their minds. They come to believe it. In exactly the same way and despite "Democrats for Nixon," there's no "Democrats for Republicans" or vice versa. Nope, those who belong to a political party think resolutely in their party's box. The more offices held by their party, the better the world will be. However nonsensical the party propaganda, they come to believe it. Over and over, our institutions do our thinking for us.

Even more disturbing, institutions have a mind of their own. They often do what not even those inside want them to do. Congress passes many a law not a single member of Congress wanted, the law being a compromise making no one happy. The institution had a mind of its own and did what no one wanted it to do. Economic institutions constantly show such an independence of mind. No one wanted the Great Depression in 1929. No one wanted the more recent Great Recession in 2008. The economic institutions had a mind of their own.

That brings up a still more troubling side to institutions. They often take over our lives. Political institutions are the worst. If you were drafted into the Prussian army under Frederick the Great, who reigned 1740 to 1786, that institution made you into a uniformed automaton, flogging and shooting you into mindless obedience. Prussian soldiers marched in lockstep to battle, maneuvered with precision in the face of the enemy, stood in rigid rank as the shot and shell poured in, fired their volleys and charged with the bayonet, all exactly on command. But if such Prussian discipline admirable, Prussian casualties were ghastly. In 1756, when Prussia entered the Seven Years War, their army numbered about 140,000. By the end, they had taken about 180,000 casualties. That's right, more than 100 percent. Frederick bore the attrition with manly fortitude, resolutely called up fresh conscripts, and eventually not only won the war, but won the title of "Frederick the Great." No doubt the man was a military genius, nor did he lack physical courage, having seven horses killed under him in battle. But serving in his institution doesn't sound so great to me.

Another troubling thing, institutions can outlive their useful lives. After the fall of the Roman Empire, feudalism had a good reason to come to life. You had to fight for every foot of ground against guys like the Vikings. Feudalism covered every foot of that ground with castles and armored knights. The peasants' labor went to grow the food, build the castles, and support the knights, letting the knights devote their labor completely to defending the institution. Who wouldn't rather hoe the nobles' row on that deal? Yet at least they paid for the privilege, hoeing a pretty rough row themselves. But by say 1600, feudalism had lost its reason for living. Gunpowder had made castles and armored knights obsolete. Yet the dead hand of feudal institutions clung to the living. The nobles still owned the land, and the peasants still had to work for them. What began as a symbiotic relationship, where the nobles gave something back, now lived on as a parasitic one, the nobles sucking the people's blood. It took shedding quite a bit of the nobles' own blood like during the French Revolution to finally kill off feudal institutions.

Institutions, again especially political ones, even have a will-to-power all their own. The staff they come and go, the times they come and go, but the institution keeps right on acquiring more power. In the early days, Congress lacked even the power to fund internal improvements like canals and wilderness roads. By the time of the Civil War, they had acquired the power to finance the intercontinental railroads. By the Second World War, they had acquired the power to build the interstate highways system. Congress has acquired so much power on so many fronts, what can't Congress do nowadays? The presidency has as relentlessly acquired more power. The Constitution says only Congress can declare war. But although Congress hasn't declared a war since 1941, we've fought a number such as the Korea War, the Viet Nam War, the Gulf War. The president has, in fact, acquired the power to declare war. Wherever you look, you see the same tendency. The institutional will-to-power never rests.

What is this, the tale of Dr. Frankenstein? We bring institutions to life. But they have a way of getting into our heads (changing the way we think). They can do what no one wants them to do (have a mind of their own). They can lead lives of their own. They can take over our lives (and use us like cannon fodder). They can outlive their useful lives. They have a will-to-power.

When we come to bring such a creature to life, we better give some careful thought to the act of creation. As the Emperor Charles V remarked, "If I had been around at the Creation, I could have offered some helpful suggestions." A helpful suggestion might be not to create institutions quite so much in our own image, but leave out so much free will and willfulness. We might want to insert carefully at birth some parental controls into our institutional offspring.

2.10 – A Fair Translation

A thing not widely known about me is my brief stint working for Vinson & Elkins, a mega law firm with hundreds of lawyers, headquartered in Houston and branch offices around the world. Let me hasten to add for the sake of their reputation and my own, they didn't and would never hire me as a lawyer. I'm not their kind of guy, and they're not mine. But after law school, no one was beating down my door, and meditating the heresy of a move to Texas' greener pastures, I went down there to take the bar exam. To make ends meet while waiting on the results, I found this job in the mailroom of Vinson & Elkins. Even from that vantage point, my few months in their employ confirmed my prior views about the big law firms without confirming their views about me, since they didn't notice me any more than a fly on the wall. But I noticed them and especially the salary readouts that routinely came through the mailroom. Apparently, there was no secret about it, since an open copy went in every lawyer's box right there for any fly to read. A few top partners, not more than a dozen, were making big bucks, but the rest of the lawyers, the vast bulk, were making not much more than wages.

If you know about the big law firms, you know that's how they operate. Their narrow institutional top rests on a wide institutional bottom. The top partners are rainmakers, legal aces (sometimes both), or possess some less obvious talents. They can make it rain (fees, by bringing in big clients), have a record of legal kills, or have clawed their way to the top some less obvious way. The partnership's articles that set up the institution vest them with control, including control over distribution of the fees. Beneath them toil for mere wages the much larger number of associates or junior partners. And toil they do, putting in sixty and more hours a week, billed at an hourly rate far exceeding the mere wages, the extra going to swell the partners' share. Promotion to a senior partnership being far from a guarantee, many a young lawyer has toiled early and late, toiled into middle age, only to suffer a discard when flagging at the pace or worn out. As a footnote, twenty years later a lawyer friend visited a law school classmate who had worked in the same big firm ever since graduation. He reported our friend still dwelt in a small office behind a small desk without even his own secretary. Such is life in the big law firms.

Thus, the big law firms teach a lesson about what sociologists call the iron law of oligarchy. Society translates our individual needs (like making a living) into our social goals (like a good economy). Maybe something has to be lost in translation, but the best translation stays faithful to the original, and a version of society that leaves out our individual needs isn't a fair translation. And nothing causes more trouble with this translation than this iron law of oligarchy. By coming together in society, we gain the advantage of working with many hands and many heads and gain the further advantages of a division of labor and specialization. But to gain these advantages, we have to organize ourselves to work together into institutions. Institutions require management (leaders with authority to direct the work). That's the iron law of oligarchy. Institutions require management (leaders with authority). But frequently, these leaders manage to take over the institutions, directing the work for their benefit, leaving out the needs of others.

Thus, the partners in the big law firms work the associates to death. Thus, corporate CEOs draw their huge salaries while paying their workers minimum wage. Thus, throughout history, petty and not so petty tyrants, always claiming to act in the name of society, have replaced the real social goals with their selfish goals, replaced working for the common good with working for their good. Over and over, this mistranslation has recurred like a good song played over bad speakers. We could hear the initial good intentions, but "look what they've done to my song, Ma. It's turning out all wrong."

Well, as a lawyer, you don't have to go to work for a big law firm. To hell with their translation. You don't have to step on their treadmill. Write your own translation. Hang out your shingle in your hometown and work for yourself. You may not get rich, but at least you won't not get rich by making them rich. But if you do work in a top-down (oligarchic) institution like a big law firm, you're going to be working for them rather than them for you. You're going to be trapped in their translation.

Make no mistake about it either. When it comes to the institution of government, you can't tell them to "take this job and shove it, I ain't working here no more." They're the only firm in town. There's just one translation (one constitution) at any one time. Then you better make sure your government a fair translation. Otherwise, they've got you trapped.

But how make a fair translation? Social contract theory (so dear to the hearts of the Founding Fathers) offered a hopeful version. The theory viewed a constitution as like a legal contract. To gain the benefits of government, the people bargained away some rights on entering the contract, but carefully retained others. And the really clever part was writing in a self-enforcing clause. Under the contract the people retained the right to consent to the government, a consent manifested by electing or un-electing the leaders. Thus, the theory came up with a practical way to counter the iron law of oligarchy. To win and keep office the leaders were forced to take into account the people's needs, keeping the institution nearer to the real social goals, keeping the leaders from totally usurping the institution to serve their own goals.

If someone wants to work for a big law firm, it's a free country. But if you let them write a constitution like the partnership articles for the big law firms, it won't stay a free country long. You better not let them do it. You better write another sort of constitution.

2.11 – Bad Money

"Bad money drives out good." That's Gresham's Law, named after Sir Thomas Gresham, a Tudor financier, who lived as long ago as 1519 to 1579. Although this law has been around a long time and proved right again and again, a lot of people still don't get it or why it's true. We can't afford to make that mistake.

Let's offer the proof with a story from Lord Macaulay's *History of England,* published in 1848 and one of the great history books.

At the time, "money" meant coin (specie), and a coin was supposed to contain a specific weight in gold or silver. It was before the days of paper (fiat) money. Macaulay being so eloquent, let's hear the story mainly from his mouth.

"Till the reign of Charles the Second [1660 to 1686] our coin had been struck by a process as old as the thirteenth century. ... The metal was divided with shears, and afterward shaped and stamped by the hammer. In these operations much was left to the hand and eye of the workman. It necessary happened that some pieces contained a little more and some a little less than the just quantity of silver; few pieces were exactly round, and the rims were not marked. It was, therefore, in the course of years discovered that to clip the coin was one of the easiest and most profitable kinds of fraud. ... about the time of the Restoration [in 1660], people began to observe that a large proportion of the crowns, half-crowns, and shillings which were passing from hand to hand had undergone some slight mutilation."

People had shaved or clipped a tiny fleck from the edge of these coins (say from a silver shilling). When they bought something in a shop, their clipped coin would still pass for the full value of a shilling. Gradually, they collected enough silver shavings to make the value of another shilling. Just as gradually, more and more of the coin became "bad money," debased in value, not weighing the proper amount.

However, in the 1660s, "A great improvement in the mode of shaping and striking the coin was suggested. A mill, which to a great extent superseded the human hand, was set up in the Tower of London. ... The pieces which it produced ... were among the best in Europe. It was not easy to counterfeit them; and, as their shape was exactly circular, and their edges were inscribed with a legend, clipping was not to be apprehended." These coins were "good money," not debased in value, weighing the proper weight.

Macaulay goes on, "The hammered coins and the milled coins were current together. They were received without distinction in public, and consequently in private, payments. The financiers of that age seem to have expected that the new money, which was excellent, would soon displace the old money, which was much impaired. Yet any man of plain understanding might have known that, when the State treats perfect coin and light coin as of equal value, the perfect coin will not drive the light coin out of circulation, but will itself be driven out. A clipped coin, on English ground went as far in the payment of a tax or a debt as a milled crown. But the milled crown, as soon as it has been flung in the crucible or carried across the Channel, became much more valuable than the clipped crown. It might therefore have been predicted, as confidently as anything can be predicted which depends on the human will, that the inferior pieces would remain in the only market in which they could fetch the same price as the superior pieces, and that the superior pieces would take some form or fly to some place in which some advantage could be derived from their superiority.

"The politicians of that age, however, generally over-looked these obvious considerations. They marveled exceedingly that everybody should be so perverse as to use light money in preference to good money. In other words, they marveled that nobody chose to pay twelve ounces of silver when ten would serve the turn. ... Fresh wagon loads of choice money still came forth from the mill; and they still vanished as fast as they appeared. Great masses were melted down; great masses exported; great masses hoarded; but scarcely one new piece was to be found in the till of a shop, or in the leathern bag which the farmer carried home after the cattle-fair."

The bad money was driving out the good as predicted by Gresham's Law. Never mind that under the law the penalty for clipping was death. "At every session that was held at the Old Bailey terrible examples were made. Hurdles, with four, five, or six wretches convicted of counterfeiting or mutilating money, were dragged, month after month, up Holborn Hill. One morning seven men were hanged and one woman burned, for clipping. But all was vain."

This bad money eventually caused some bad consequences. "At length it became an insupportable curse to the country. ... in the autumn of 1695, it could hardly be said the country possessed for practical purposes, any measure of the value of commodities. It was a mere chance whether what was called a shilling was really tenpence, sixpence, or a groat. ... when the great instrument of exchange became thoroughly deranged, all trade, all industry were smitten as with a palsy. The evil was felt daily and hourly in almost every place and by almost every class, … . Nothing could be purchased without a dispute. Over every counter there was wrangling from morning to night. … The laborer found that the bit of metal, which, when he received it, was called a shilling, would hardly, when he wanted to purchase a pot of beer or a loaf of rye-bread, go as far as sixpence."

Every monetary transaction had turned into a dispute, from buying a pot of beer or rye-bread to the largest financial transactions. Everyone who could from the day laborer to the rich merchant refused to take a coin at face value, but insisted on weighing it out. These disputes not only cheated many who often not in a position to insist, like usually the day laborer, but the total effect clogged up commerce so bad as threatened to bring the national economic life to a virtual standstill.

Macauley goes on to tell how Britain managed to reform its currency. Beginning in this same year of 1695, they succeeded in driving the bad money out of circulation. On this success, all their later enormous commercial, industrial, and indeed, military success ("money is the sinews of war") depended. He says, "the deep and solid foundation had been laid on which was to rise the most gigantic fabric of commercial prosperity that the world as ever seen." But the cure caused a huge amount of financial pain at the time, almost enough to kill the patient. Just about everybody got stuck holding some bad money, which no longer worth more than the melted value. However, that's the rest of the story and falls outside our purposes.

What we want to take away is why the law holds true. We earlier heard Hobbes lay down the first law of political psychology as "a perpetuall and restless desire of Power after power." Gresham's Law rests on a similar first law of economic psychology. People perpetually and restlessly seek to make a profit. You can't repeal either of these psychological laws with a statutory law passed by the legislature. Whatever laws the legislature passes, the laws of human psychology remain the same. However many malefactors went to the gallows for clipping, it didn't change the psychology.

Just like we better never forget the first law of political psychology in constructing our government, we better never forget this first law of economic psychology in constructing our economy. To consider further, on to the next article.

2.12 – A Law of Nature

A lady friend of mine won't go into Wal-Mart except to use the toilet. On a road trip, there's a Wal-Mart right off the interstate at convenient intervals, and she can trust their restrooms. But she won't shop there. Being something of a socialist, she regards Wal-Mart as amoral, if not immoral.

She's got one thing right. Wal-Mart operates on the law of supply and demand. All the law of gravity cares about is how much you weigh, and if you weigh a little more, you land a little harder. The law of supply and demand doesn't even care that much about you. It doesn't care how hard you land. It's amoral, if not immoral. But it's also why Wal-Mart cares about you enough to furnish clean restrooms.

Unlike the laws that govern the physical universe as laid down by hard sciences such as physics or chemistry, the social sciences such as economics, psychology, or political science can't lay down many hard laws. But economists claim "the law of supply and demand" makes the grade. Their statistics seem to prove them right. Supply goes up as the price rises, down as the price falls; demand goes down as the price rises, up as the price falls. It seems a law of nature.

Rather than operating on physical forces like physics or chemistry, this law operates on a force of human psychology. Just like people seek power in political life, they relentlessly seek a profit in economic life by buying low and selling high. If people weren't around, presumably the laws of physics and chemistry would go right on operating and the universe would keep on doing whatever it's doing, but the law of supply and demand would no longer operate.

There's still another precondition – a free-market. Unless people can buy and sell freely what they want, when they want, the psychology (the profit motive) would still exist, but couldn't operate. But only set up this precondition and stand back. $E=MC2$. Nature locks away tremendous energy in the atom. The free-market releases the tremendous energy locked away in people.

Turned lose by the free-market, their productivity and creativity explodes.

Nothing better illustrates than Wal-Mart. If my lady friend went in for more than to use the toilet, she would walk down aisles stocked with thousands of products and good products at a good price. Not so long ago, nature poured out no such bounty, and only science fiction imagined many of the items on their shelves such as televisions or computers. Not so long ago, you earned your daily bread in the sweat of your brow, and nature often failed to cooperate, rather than raining down plenty, sending floods, droughts, and plagues. But Wal-Mart isn't a force of nature. The law of supply and demand is the force. All those millions of people out there competing to make a profit generate the ocean. Wal-Mart is just surfing on the wave. And incidentally, the same force cleans Wal-Mart's restrooms to attract customers to make a profit.

Yet my lady friend has a point. The law of supply and demand is a "social Darwinian" mechanism and lacks a "social conscience." It's "survival of the fittest." It just cares whether you're better equipped to survive in the economic ocean. It don't care if you're a whale, a shark, a tuna, or an octopus. It don't care if you get eaten or drown beneath the waves. It just cares whether you make a profit. If you're ill-adapted for the environment for whatever reason, you're liable to find yourself at the bottom of the food chain, a bottom feeder scrounging for scraps. And so, since Wal-Mart operates on the law of supply and demand, my lady friend sees Wal-Mart as not really caring about anything except their profits. And so, she sees them as amoral, if not immoral. And so, she won't shop there.

Somewhat this same train of logic explains "socialism" or "the welfare state." Both want to replace the free-market wave with a rising tide that lifts all boats. Both want an economic ocean with a social conscience. "Am I my brother's keeper?" Yes, you are. If you can man an oar, man an oar and pull the boat. And "no child left behind." No one gets thrown out of the lifeboat. If you're not an able-bodied seaman, the more able will row you to shore. In Marx's famous formulation, "From each according to his means to each according to his needs."

But there's a distinction between socialism and the welfare state. A standard dictionary definition for "socialism" is "any of various economic and political theories advocating collective or governmental ownership and administration of the means of production and distribution of goods." Such "governmental ownership" closes down the free-market and re-opens for business under state ownership. Since people no longer own "the means of production and distribution," they can no longer buy and sell freely and make a profit. Rather than the law of supply and demand sorting out the winners and losers, now the state does the sorting, presumably with a social conscience so everyone comes out a winner. By contrast, the welfare state leaves the free-market open, but redistributes the profits. Like Robin Hood, the state takes from the rich by taxing their profits and gives to the poor to achieve "equality of results." But since their profits drive the market, if the state taxes away enough of the driving force, it can end up stifling, strangling, or even closing down the market from the other end.

What's wrong with socialism? We should know by now. It's been tried. The evidence is in. It wants to repeal the law of supply and demand with the operation of human laws with a social conscience. But "you can't fool Mother Nature." You can't repeal a law of nature with a human law.

When you pass a law taking all the property away from the capitalists like Wal-Mart, now who owns it? The state, which to say, the politicians. All you've done is to transfer the title deeds. You haven't repealed the underlying law of nature that people will seek to make a profit. Depending on your form of government, you'll have one of two results. In an autocracy, the new owners (the autocrats) will behave just like the old owners (the capitalists). Nothing restrains them. Before the plutocrats lived at the top of the trees, now the autocrats dine there, leaving most folks trying to survive on the crumbs that fall to the forest floor. With a democracy, you can hope for better. Since the politicians are accountable to the people, they will at least try to administer the property "as a trust, for the general benefit."

But in any event, when you kill off the free-market, you've killed off the precondition for the law of supply and demand to operate. Now what force is going to fill your shelves? And the free-market doesn't just give people incentives (the profit motive), but manages them with the "invisible hand." Go in a department store and count the fashions in ladies' shoes on sale. Who decides which fashions and how many to produce? Nobody. The market decides. Turn to the stock market page in a newspaper. Who decides what stocks to offer, how many, and at what price? The market again. How many such questions could we ask? Literally millions. The free-market answers them all (bottom-up). Responding to the demand in the market, people adjust their production toward the "equilibrium point," where the market produces sufficient goods and services at an affordable price.

If you close the free-market, who answers all those millions of questions? You have to substitute a "command and control economy," where the state tells everybody what or produce and at what price to sell. You have to substitute top-down management for the market's bottom-up mechanism. But the government just can't hope to succeed in answering so many questions. Not only have you taken away the incentives for hard, productive, and creative work, you've taken away the mechanism to manage the production. "Allowing people to make their own decisions via markets is the best way for society to efficiently use its resources. When the state ... controls all the resources instead, neither the right incentives will be created nor will there be efficient allocation of the skills and talents of the people."

By contrast, what's wrong with the welfare state? Maybe nothing, depending on how far it goes. But if it goes too far, it has the same result. As said, sufficient taxation will strangle, stifle, or even close the free-market by taking the profit motive out. You can end up with socialism by another name.

If my lady friend had lived in the old Soviet Union under a thoroughgoing socialist regime, likely enough she would have found herself standing in a bread line, hoping some left when she made it in the store. If they had a toilet on premises and she needed to use it, she couldn't for fear of losing her place in line, not to mention, one rather doubts the cleanliness of their public toilets. Tell her that, and she just smiles knowingly. Like so many others, she's convinced that sooner or later socialism is going to work.

Maybe. But the law of supply and demand seems a law of nature. So far, nobody has figured out how to repeal the laws of nature with human laws. Until they do, we better not let our hopes triumph over our experience. Let's try to work with Mother Nature rather than against her. Let's not close down the free-market. Wal-Mart may not have a social conscience, but it does have clean restrooms.

2.13 – The Maxim Gun

A lawyer who doesn't know the law is fighting blind. Another lawyer who knows the law will strike him down in the courtroom and he won't even see the blow coming. The same goes for whole societies. Some societies have a lot more knowledge than others. And in the Darwinian scheme of things as in the courtroom, better knowledge gives you a big competitive advantage. When it comes to survival of the fittest, your society better be able to say, "Whatever happens, we have got the Maxim gun, and they have not." A society should want all the knowledge it can get.

"Knowledge is power." That's easy to see with technology. A Maxim machine gun can shoot down any number of Zulu spearmen no matter how brave. An atom bomb can give a still more convincing demonstration, convincing to any rational decision maker. The power of institutions is easy to see as well. When the Spartan phalanx or a Roman legion came marching over the hill, you immediately perceived a powerful institution, coming right at you. But renounce warlike intent. Resolve, say, to feed the hungry or bring about world peace. You still have to figure out how to do it. Knowledge may be of good and evil, but knowledge is power.

How can a society come by better knowledge? Those who have turned their minds to the question say, "innovate and diffuse." Create new and useful knowledge (innovation) and spread it around (diffusion). And rather than waiting on the accidents of inspiration (some genius leaping naked out of the bath shouting, "Eureka, I've found it"), institutionalize the process.

The familiar story of technological evolution shows the basic process. Starting with fire, stone tools, and the wheel, now we have nuclear energy, computers, and the internet. It all started with the ideas in our heads. Someone came up with a better idea (an innovation). But a better idea isn't much use until spread around to other people (diffusion). They say the Chinese learned how to vaccinate for smallpox centuries ahead of Dr. Edward Jenner in 1798. But the Chinese innovation never diffused to Europe. Jenner had to make his discovery independently. Meanwhile, the disease continued to kill and disfigure.

We're familiar, too, with the way technology speeds up the process. Take the invention of writing. The written word transmits faster than the spoken. You can read a book in less time than you can listen to the same book on tape. Until the radio, the written word also broadcast much farther than the spoken. More people could read Aristotle than hear his lectures at the Lyceum. Writing also gives an assist to the mind, letting you go back to refresh your memory, restart your thoughts, recheck your logic. It sets up a lending library, saving ideas in a collective memory bank to loan out to others. It creates a community of problem solvers. Two heads are better than one and a thousand better yet. A problem might stump the bright guys in Athens, but maybe the bright guys in Alexandria could come up with a solution. The printing press (another technology) joined millions in this community. The computer (still another technology) took writing to the next level. We gained an accessory to our brains that could run calculations faster than our brains, run models too complex for our brains. The internet (yet another technology) connects an online community of problem solvers, worldwide and close to instantaneous. We might say that technology has constantly raised the "velocity" of knowledge, speeding up the creation (innovation) and speeding up the spread (diffusion).

Not only technology can raise the velocity. Institutions can too. You can locate such institutions by no more than marking up a map. Make a check for the inventions that marked the progress of the industrial revolution; make another check for the inventions of the more recent digital revolution. The checks will mostly cluster on the map in the UK and the US. Why? We know why. Those countries have long run "open societies." They have long had two closely connected institutional sets – representative democracy and free-markets. Those institutions are open to innovation and diffusion and so speed the velocity of knowledge.

By contrast, closed societies with authoritarian institutions slow or shut down the current of knowledge, insulating against innovation and diffusion. They spend their creative energy running in place, since the authorities mainly concerned to stay in place. Take the Soviet Union under Stalin, that rigid man of steel. When it came to staying in place, his creative juices flowed, qualifying him as a creative genius of sorts. Who else other than an evil genius could have thought up such innovations in terror and diffused them so widely? He killed with a fine and arbitrary hand, sending a jolt of fear throughout the society. The overwhelming force of that current kept Stalin in place, but slowed and shut down the current of knowledge.

For example, in the 1930s, the census didn't grow to Stalin's satisfaction, not giving off the image he wished to convey. In a happy proletarian paradise, the proletariat should procreate as happily. Since he was murdering in the millions and shipping other millions to the gulag, the census data no more than reflected the reality. But Stalin found an innovative way to fix his image. He simply shot some census bureau staff and sent some others to the gulag. The next census had the kind of statistics Stalin wanted to read.

Something similar happened over in academia. A geneticist named Lyshenko had a theory that made him a favorite with Stalin. Under this theory, parents could hand down acquired characteristics to their offspring. Stalin liked the theory because he wanted to create a new human type, who would acquire a communist ethos and pass on the characteristic. But the theory was nonsense. Only genetic characteristics pass on, not acquired ones. Serious Soviet scientists knew it was nonsense. But any scientist who dared openly to contradict Lyshenko was likely to disappear from the faculty, never heard from again or next heard about performing manual labor in Siberia.

How can knowledge flow with any velocity, when even the statistics and science are made to lie? "There is no mystery about the thing itself. Every effect is just such as any intelligent man knowing the causes, would anticipate." Creativity stagnated in the Soviet Union.

A society should want maximum knowledge. It should want innovation and diffusion. It should try to institutionalize the process. Otherwise, it's like a lawyer who doesn't know the law. It's fighting blind. It will fall all over itself. It will not do well in attaining its social goals. Facing an adversary with better knowledge, it will be struck down.

3.00 – THE GOVERNMENT

3.01 – Ends of Government

In *Federalist No. 51*, Madison wrote, "Justice is the end of government. It is the end of civil society." Well, yes, let's write justice at the top of our shopping list. But when we go shopping for a government, let's not forget to bring home some other items as well. There are quite a few other "ends of government" besides "justice." We don't want to leave any necessary item off our list.

To start at the bottom of the list, what's more at the bottom than our individual needs, yet what more often left at the bottom? We all need food, shelter, and safety. We all need an education, a job, friends, and family. The list goes on, and at the top of each individual's list comes a need to flourish, a chance to realize his full potential, a chance for a meaningful life. But no one can get all their needs all on their own. At bottom, then, our individual needs are what cause us to come together in society in the first place and why we organize governments. Then getting our individual needs must be at the bottom of government as an end of government. Yet what more often gets left at the bottom by the government?

The historian Thomas Carlyle famously wrote, "The history of the world is but the biography of great men." That accurately sums up the way the "great men" have routinely written the history. They've contrived the plots as their own biographies, leaving the rest of us to play no more than the supporting roles. We're no more than the off-camera grips who build the stage for the star to strut across or the uncredited extras for the hero to cut down in the battle scenes. Napoleon bragged to the great Austrian diplomate Prince Metternich he could afford to lose 30,000 men a month, and since no one else could afford such a casualty list, he didn't need to negotiate, but would simply win the wars and dictate the treaties.

In such scripts as written by the "great men," they get their needs, but the rest of us are cannon fodder. We have to find a way to live on the scraps from their table or starve. That leaves most of us living history as a sort of contradiction in terms. To get our needs, we come together in society and organize governments. But only the "great men" get their needs, leaving our needs to go begging. There must be a better way to write history.

The rest of us need to contrive our own plot, one where our needs aren't left out of the story. The needs of the rest of us need to come at the end of the story as an end of government. Better than Carlyle's view is what Colonel Thomas Rainsborough said back in 1647, and the only famous thing he ever said, "The poorest he that is in England hath a right to live as the greatest he." Better is what James Madison said in *Federalist No. 45*, "It is too early for politicians to presume on our forgetting that the public good, the real welfare of the great body of the people is the supreme object to be pursued; and that no form of Government whatever, has any other value, that as it may be fitted for the attainment of this object."

Once we do come together in society, our individual needs translate into our social goals. We organize society to attain those goals. We want a good standard of living with a good economy. We want national defense against foreign enslavement and law and order against internal disorder and lawlessness. We require some socialization, some ways to learn to cooperate with each other. We require some ways to reach some consensus, some sufficient general agreement to go on with. We should want all the knowledge we can get, not least about how to attain our social goals. We should try to institutionalize the process of the innovation and diffusion of new and useful knowledge. Since change constant, we better have some social adaptability, some facility to adapt to the changing circumstances. Since resources always more or less limited, we better practice some efficiency at getting the most out of the resources. Since government a crucial way we organize, these social goals must also come as ends of government.

While if we're to judge success in government by the index of freedom, those freedoms must be an end of government. Such items as open and fair elections, freedom of speech, the rule of law, and property rights (it's a long list) are an end of government. While if we're to judge success in government by the standard of living, a high per capita GDP must be an end of government. While if we're to judge success by progress in both areas, such progress is an end of government.

All of which begins to sound a tall order, but the tallest yet to come. What about "equality," "inalienable rights," and "the consent of the governed" as proclaimed in the Declaration of Independence? If those principles are fundamental, they must come before any other ends of government. Nor let us forget about "justice," which Madison said "the end of government?" Perhaps if government achieves all the other ends on this list, it will attain "justice" too.

If this long list sets forth the ends of government, the best government must be the one that best achieves all these ends. What government would that be? If someone says democracy, will we believe it? Probably, since we're been taught to believe in democracy. But can we prove that to ourselves?

3.02 – Pick a Door

Choosing a government is a lot like the old story of the young man in an arena facing two doors. He has to choose which door to open or suffer a cruel and lingering death on the scaffold. Behind one door paces a ferocious tiger, ready to leap out and devour him. Behind the other door awaits a beautiful princess, eager to step forth and become his bride, bringing an ample dowry. He knows which choice he wants to make, but he doesn't know which door to choose.

Choosing a government is a lot like that since the choice compelled, the wrong choice a bad result, and the right choice a good result. The choice is compelled since no government (ANARCHY) the very worst result (like a cruel and lingering death on the scaffold). But when choosing a government there are three clearly marked doors –MONARCHY, ARISTOCRACY, DEMOCRACY. Why would someone not open the door to democracy? But for a long time, few got to make a free choice. For a long time, too, many failed to understand the choices. No excuse exists for making such a mistake in the present. Then why does so much confusion still persist?

Let's get it straight once and for all. The distinction between the types of government depends on the power (the ability to impose one's will). In monarchy, ONE has the power. In aristocracy, a FEW have the power. In democracy, the MANY have the power. The political process (or political structure) keeps control in the chosen hands. Let's get another thing straight once and for all. There are only three types of government, the logic as compelled as the choice. One rules, a few rule, or the many rule. One cannot rule if the few rule, the few cannot rule if the many rule, and so forth.

However, constitutions (ancient and modern) have shown considerable ingenuity at mixing and matching the types. The British Parliament has two chambers, the House of Lords and the House of Commons. For centuries, some aristocrats inherited a seat in the Lords with their title, making them an aristocratic institution. You won a seat in the Commons with an election, making them a democratic institution. Under the U.S. Constitution, we elect Congress and the president, but appoint Supreme Court justices for life, making for two democratic institutions and one aristocratic type. Then more precisely, there aren't just three types of government, but rather just three types of political institutions, which can be combined in the same government.

But what's so significant about the type of the government anyway? Why not an enlightened despotism? Why not a benevolent dictator? Why not a good king? But you might as well say, Why not a contradiction in terms? Only democracy rules in the people's interests. That conclusion follows inexorably from the first principle of political psychology, "So that in the first place, I put for a general inclination of mankind a perpetuall and restless desire of Power after power." As others have said, the aphrodisiac of powers allures irresistibly.

In the political sphere the force of interests (the will-to-power) works like the force of gravity in the physical universe. In a planetary system, gravity exerts a force on any object passing through the system, altering the course. In a political sphere, self-interest exerts a force on any question passing through, warping the answer. Whoever controls the political process bends the answers to serve their interests. Plug the exact same question into one type of political institution, and a very different answer will come out than from another type of institution. The answer will favor whoever has the power. Monarchy will perform in the monarch's interest, aristocracy in the aristocrats' interest, and only democracy will perform in the people's interest (the public interest).

As the Scottish philosopher David Hume well, if cynically, summed it up, "In contriving any system of government, and fixing the several checks and controuls of the constitution, every man ought to be supposed to be a knave; and to have no other end, in all his actions, than private interest. By this interest, we must govern him, and, by means of it, make him, notwithstanding his insatiable avarice and ambition, co-operate to public good." As Hamilton wrote in *Federalist No. 72*, "The best security for the fidelity of mankind is to make their interest coincide with their duty."

In monarchy or aristocracy nothing effectively "checks and controuls" their "insatiable avarice and ambition," nothing "makes them co-operate to the public good." But democracy rather cleverly reverses this image like a mirror. In democracy, the officials have to win elections to gain and retain power. This mechanism reverses their "insatiable avarice and ambition," making them "co-operate to the public good." They are forced to serve the people's interests to serve their "private interest." The mechanism works "to make their interest coincide with their duty." Nothing else, not all the good intentions in the world, will hold them to it.

Let's get and keep it straight once and for all. First, every political institution is controlled by one, a few, or the many (the people). Second, every political institution will perform in the interests of whoever controls it. Third, since only democracy controlled by the people, only democracy performs in the public interest.

If we want to live happy ever after with our government, we better go through the door marked DEMOCRACY. There awaits a comely bride with all the virtues of a wife and mother in her lap. Behind the other two doors (MONARCHY or ARISTOCRACY) awaits a dominatrix with a whip. However much the allure of turning these ladies loose against our foes, we cannot do so without submitting to them ourselves. Such a mistake would prove fatal to our happiness.

3.03 – The Golden Word

Some of my readers may still remember I once managed to win a fairly hard-fought election for district attorney around here. That brings to mind the saying, "Be careful what you wish for, you may get it." Not that I regret winning. Far from it. But frankly, I didn't realize the job was quite so labor intensive. It all turned out for the best though. I was all the better for the hard work and learned up close and personal why "accountability" is the golden word in government.

A couple years later, a big-time criminal lawyer was in my office. We had the goods on his defendant, and he knew it. He told me, "Those ass kickings are hell." He didn't want to take an ass kicking at a jury trial, but wanted to work out a plea bargain. If the lawyers feel that way over losing a jury trial, the same goes at least as much for losing an election. Remember the local banker on the school board, not even a paid position, who entirely unexpectedly drew an opponent in the next election? He started out acting like it was no big deal, like it didn't really matter to him whether he won or lost. But by the time it was over, it must have been a big deal. He and his whole family had knocked on every door in town and called in favors across a couple generations. The acrimony got so bad as to break a couple close friendships. Nobody wants to take a public ass kicking. While as for winning elections, as Texas football coach Mack Brown once said, "In this business, if you're not careful, you end up just feeling a sense of relief when you win, and you're devastated when you lose." In electoral politics, the thrill of victory is only a momentary relief, while the agony of defeat continually threatens with the next election.

That's how accountability works in a democracy. His law partner (William Herndon) said Abraham Lincoln's ambition was "a little engine that never slept." Accountability is that same little engine. It motivates with a sleepless ambition not to lose an election.

You've heard said, "The arc of the moral universe is long, but bends toward justice." That image conveys a moral universe where the moral force operates like the force of gravity in the physical universe. Just like gravity bends the planets' course around the sun, the moral force bends toward justice. For myself, I believe in the moral force. But for long ages of human history, the arc more resembled a flatline. The patient looked nearly dead on the operating table.

That's because the moral force not the only one just like the physicists tell us other forces besides gravity operate in the physical universe. As someone who has spent a lifetime in the universe of the courts, I can tell you the moral force operates strongly there, bending the cases toward justice. Yet other forces operate on the cases as well, such as interests and ambitions, which operate as strong forces, often bending the cases away from justice. Other similar and powerful forces operate in the political universe as well, often bending away from justice.

But the strongest force in the political universe is this same "accountability." If you can hold a man accountable, you can make him do what you want. That's the very definition of political power (being able to impose your will). For those long ages that justice flatlined, the autocrats could hold the government accountable, and this strongest force operated in line with their interests and ambitions. They could and did bend justice to serve themselves. But with the fairly recent arrival of democratic accountability, suddenly the forces realigned. The force of the people's ambitions and interests began to bend the government. The moral force came to life and began to bend toward "justice" for the people.

Democratic accountability revolutionizes the political universe. No longer do the people have to cool their heels waiting interminably in the antechambers of the great for an audience with an unsympathetic ear. Rather, the powers-that-be have to pay some court to the people to get and hold their power. They can no longer say, "Throw this rascal out on his ear," rather, they have to lend an ear. Now they say, "How may I be of assistance to you, sir?" The former masters become the servants. Like the old ballad says, "you see the world turned upside down."

The body politic re-organizes in a much more healthful way. The top (the government) starts to listen to and take account of the bottom (the people). Is an end of government the people's needs such as for jobs, housing, education, or healthcare? Is an end of government the "social goals" such as a good economy? Now it is. If you don't believe it, just compare the per capita GDP in democracies with the same statistic in autocracies. The higher GDP in the democracies reliably reflects more people getting their needs and the attaining of more social goals.

Is an end of government and the most important one "equality, inalienable rights, and the consent of the governed" as the Declaration of Independence proclaims? You can't have equality except in a democracy. You can't have your rights unless you can decide on your rights, which your most important right. By definition, you can't have the consent of the government except in a democracy. If you don't believe it, compare the index of freedom in the democracies against the autocracies.

While as for "justice," which Madison proclaimed the end of government, the arc of justice won't bend toward justice for the people without democratic accountability. It's the strongest force in the political universe.

Take it from the horse's mouth. When I had the honor to serve as your district attorney, I like to think I tried to do the right thing because it was the right thing. I like to think I would have done the right thing even when unpopular. But I never forgot how it would look in the eyes of the electorate. I never forgot the next election. I never forgot I was accountable. Every elected official feels the same force acting on him. Can you think of a better force? All the people want is for you to do the right thing. All you have to do is figure it out and do it. If you think the people may sometimes misunderstand the right thing, then it's part of your job description to show some leadership and explain it to them. The force of accountability operates in line with the moral force, bending the arc toward justice for the people.

Someone may say with all sincerity, "If I were King of the Forest, … Though my tail would lash, I would show compash, for every underling! If I, if I were king." Sure they would, somewhere over the rainbow. But meanwhile, let's not be underlings and rely on their compassion. Let's rely on a more reliable force. Accountability is the golden word in government.

3.04 – The Horse and Carriage

Majority rule and democracy used to go together like the old song said, "love and marriage go together like a horse and carriage." Majority rule was thought as natural to democracy as love to marriage, as pulling along democracy as naturally as the horse pulls the carriage. But just as love without marriage has gradually become more popular, so has democracy without majority rule. Just as marriage has been gradually re-defined, so has democracy. While the voice of the people was once called "the voice of God," now we never cease to hear about "the tyranny of the majority" and how the majority discriminates against and oppresses the minority. Gradually, democracy has become conceived much less as majority rule and much more as "minority rights." We constantly hear said such things as, "Indeed, as democracy is conceived today, the minority's rights must be protected no matter how singular or alienated that minority is from the majority society; otherwise, the minority's rights lose their meaning."

Whoa, big fella, slow down. Doesn't that put the cart before the horse? First, consider the logic. The horse is the political process, the laws are the cart, and the cart can't move without the horse. The laws, including the laws protecting minority rights, can't even exist until promulgated through some political process. Then the first question must be what horse (what political process) we want pulling our cart (making our laws). And there are just three available political processes (three available horses to hitch to this cart). Either someone (a monarch) makes our laws, some group (an aristocracy), or the people (a democracy). Either some minority rules through a monarchy or aristocracy, or the majority rules through a democracy. Since that exhausts our choices, do we want minority rule or majority rule? If we believe all men created equal and that the most fundamental right, don't we have to choose democracy and majority rule, since that's the only political process that counts all men equal?

Don't take it from me. Take it from Thomas Reed, Speaker of the U.S. House from 1889 to 1891 and again from 1895 to 1899, "Our government is founded on the doctrine that if 100 citizens think one way and 101 think the other, the 101 are right. It is the old doctrine that the majority must govern. Indeed, you have no choice. If the majority do not govern, the minority will; and if the tyranny of the majority is hard, the tyranny of the minority is simply unendurable. The rules, then, ought to be arranged as to facilitate the action of the majority."

But these aren't just horses of a different color, they're horses with very different temperaments. Since when did either monarchy or aristocracy show the temperament to protect any minority rights except their rights as the ruling minority? Nope, only democracy has ever exhibited a temperament friendly to the people's rights, including minority rights. A friendship for minorities is bred into democracy for the reason that Hamilton mentions in *Federalist No. 85*, "Many of those who form the majority on one question may become the minority on a second, and an association dissimilar to either may constitute the majority on the third." The majority has a care not to trample on the rights of the minority, since they'd be trampling on parts of their own anatomy.

Madison memorably developed this point in *Federalist No. 10*, "The smaller the society, the fewer will probably be the distinct parties and interests composing it; the fewer the distinct parties and interests, the more frequently will a majority be found of the same party; and the smaller the number of individuals composing a majority, and the smaller the compass within which they are placed, the more easily will they concert and execute their plans of oppression. Extend the sphere, and you take in a greater variety of parties and interests; you make it less probable that a majority of the whole will have a common motive to invade the rights of other citizens."

You see his point. In a small society, a narrow majority easily forms, but not in a large society where the majority made from minorities. As an example of a small society, recall the Puritans who early immigrated to New England. A highly religious majority dominated their small society and enforced a rigorous religious conformity. As an example of a larger society, recall American colonial society as a whole. In the south, the Church of England had a majority, in the middle colonies the Presbyterians, in Pennsylvania the Quakers, while Maryland was a Catholic redoubt, and elsewhere were enclaves devoted to almost every Protestant sect. Across the whole society, every religion was a minority. That goes far to explain why the national majority later ratified the 1st Amendment in 1791, assuring religious toleration. The national majority was for religious rights for the minority, since the majority was made up of minorities.

There's just no way around it. Majority rule still goes with democracy, if not like love still goes with marriage, at least like a horse still goes with a carriage. If the majority doesn't rule, some minority rules. That has to violate the fundamental principle that "all men are created equal." Nor will the majority oppress the minority provided that the sphere of your society large enough that the majority made up of minorities. So let's never forget as said *Federalist No. 22*, "that fundamental maxim of republican government, which requires that the sense of the majority should prevail." As a distinguished political scientist more recently put it, "The political equality embedded in majority rule is the most fundamental component of a democratic form of government."

3.05 – Five Minutes

Winston Churchill once quipped, "The best argument against democracy is a five-minute conversation with the average voter." But given more than five-minutes (given enough time), the average voter will refute the great man. But democracy doesn't work by giving the average voter enough time. Rather, democracy works because the politicians like Churchill have the time. So the best argument for democracy is a five-minute conversation with the average politician, not the average voter.

To say something complimentary about our political class may sound a rank heresy, causing many to throw this book at the preacher and leave his church. If we must praise democracy, the orthodoxy seems to praise the people, not the politicians. But have a little patience. Retrieve the book and resume your seats. Listen to the sermon. Give a hearing to some tried and true democratic doctrine, backed with ample evidence and sound common sense.

To start with, let's not fail to praise the people, not giving them credit they don't deserve, but some credit they seldom receive. True, a five-minute conversation with the average voter will show him ill-informed, if not misinformed on political topics. But switch the topic. Let the average politician take a seat at the average coffee table in the average small town. He'll find the regulars well informed on many a topic that may puzzle him like farming, plumbing, or working on cars. Those topics are just as complex as political topics. The locals are just as intellectually capable as the politician. They just haven't had the inclination and taken the time to figure out the politician's topic.

Look what happens, for example, when racing season opens, over in Oaklawn in these parts. Guys who don't look literate or capable of basic math go around with racing forms under their arms. Not only can they read and do the math, they're pretty good at figuring out the odds. In fact, without the odds, most of them could pick the winners. That's why the big Vegas' sport books have to give odds. Your average sports fan can pick the winners in football, basketball, and so forth. If they could bet straight up, a big majority would pick the winners, and the books would lose their shirts. The bookmakers have to give odds to make it harder to figure out the winners.

If your average voter as smart as your average politician, they can figure out political topics, and if your average politician as smart as your average bookie, he knows the average voter can figure them out. Just like the bookie has to figure out the odds, the politician better figure out the odds. And what are his better odds? His better odds are to place winning bets for the voters and keep placing them. If the voters backing him win and keep winning, odds are they'll keep placing their bets on him. When they start losing, they'll switch their bets to another horse, and he'll lose his next race (his next election). A politician who fails to figure out these odds likely loses his political shirt (loses office).

Oddly enough, then, the average voter doesn't need to be that well informed on political topics. He doesn't even have to be interested enough to turn out and vote in high numbers. That's because the racing season never ends for the politicians. The voters don't have to take the time to constantly figure out the odds because the politicians are constantly doing it for them. And you never know when the stakes may suddenly go up like with a recession or a foreign crisis. When such a season comes around, the average voter will suddenly start to take the time to figure out the odds. When that happens, unless a politician has been saddling winners, his odds won't be too good.

Here's another thing about it. In any profession, some are better at it that others. The better ones tend to stay in the business and gain the experience to get even better. Successful bookies are better than average at setting the odds. The same goes for politicians. Successful politicians are better than average at the business. They tend to stay in the business by getting re-elected, gaining the experience to get even better. Successful politicians aren't just average at picking winners, they're better than average.

Here's still another thing. To paraphrase slightly a famous philosopher, "It is not sufficiently considered how little there is in most men's ordinary life to give any largeness either to their conceptions or to their sentiments. But giving him something to do for the public, supplies, in a measure, this deficiency. It makes him an educated man. He is called upon to weigh interests not his own; to be guided by another rule than his private partialities; to apply, at every turn, maxims which have for their reason of existence the common good." In other words, we do "not sufficiently consider" how "giving a man something to do for the public" educates an elected politician. In private business, a man constantly consults his own interests. But an elected politician is "called upon, to weigh interests not his own" and "to apply, at every turn, maxims which have for their reason of existence the common good." He becomes educated about the public interest.

As Madison wrote in the *Federalist No. 10*, "It may well happen that the public voice pronounced by the representatives of the people, will be more consonant to the public good, than if pronounced by the people themselves convened for the purpose." We begin to see some reasons why. Our politicians have the time and the interest to figure out the odds for us. They're better than average at picking winners. By placing the right bets for us, they're placing the right bets for themselves. That adds up to a pretty good argument for democracy.

3.06 – The Sin Qua Non

Hypocrisy being the tribute vice pays to virtue, what dictator

79

hasn't confessed to vice by paying tribute to democracy? What dictator hasn't tried to hide under the name of democracy, the people, a republic, or sometimes all at once? Stalin and his successors assumed the name of the Union of Soviet Socialists Republics from 1922 until 1991, but their regime was as far from a "republic" as you could get, being a totalitarian state. After World War II, some combination of the words "Democratic People's Republic" became a code for the puppet communist dictatorships across Eastern Europe, such as the Democratic Republic of Germany (East Germany from 1949 until 1990), the People's Republic of Poland from 1945 to 1989, and so forth. The Far East joined this name game with the People's Republic of China from 1949 to the present and the Democratic People's Republic of Korea (North Korea, from 1945 to the present). More recently, the Middle East has gotten into the same name game with some local color added, such as the Syrian Arab Republic, since 1963, and the Islamic Republic of Iran, since 1979.

If you can't go by the name, what can you go by? We need a reliable way to recognize a real democracy when we see one, a reliable test to see through the hypocrisy. But that's not really hard. We just have to look for the *sin qua non* (the without which nothing). When we look for a democracy, what's the least we can see without which seeing nothing that qualifies as a democracy?

And we need to see at least these three things: 1) frequent and fair elections, 2) universal enfranchisement, including the right to stand for office, and 3) freedom of speech, including freedom of association. If we don't see those three things, we're not seeing a democracy no matter what the name.

How frequent the elections? Machiavelli's advice to princes serves as sound advice for the people as well. Better gratitude, but gratitude has a short memory, asking what have you done for me lately. Better still love, but you can't necessarily persuade this lady to love you or keep her love alive, however much you may yearn for, earn, or deserve her love. Instead, Machiavelli advised princes not to rely upon either the people's gratitude or their love, although to try and win both. Rather, he recommended the respect paid to a healthy fear, an emotion a ruler can both reliably instill and maintain. In their turn, the people, if they aspire to rule, should heed the advice. Elections should come around soon enough to instill and maintain a healthy fear in the hearts and minds of the elected officials. Let them live in fear of the people's wrath at the next election. The familiar cycle of two, four, or six years seems to excite the necessary state of mind.

What about fair elections? There's a vexed question, so vexed as sometimes lacks a perfect answer. Yet the answer must have two parts. First, fair elections must mean free elections, free from intimidation, fraud, or corruption. Second, fair must mean all votes count the same. But while we can hope to come close to the first (free elections) with laws to prevent say bribery or stuffing the ballot box, the second (counting all votes the same) evades a perfect solution.

You can apportion electoral districts the same size so that the same number of votes elect the same number of representatives. That does away with mal-apportionment, would do away, for example, with California and Wyoming each having two senators, although the one state has 37 million people as compared to only 600 thousand in the other. But you can never entirely do away with the gerrymander effect caused by the way the electoral districts are apportioned. A state may have as many Democrats as Republicans, but when the Democrats win a few districts with a large majority, while the Republicans win more districts with a narrow majority, the same number of Democrats may end up electing fewer representatives than the same number of Republicans. Even when not intended, you can't entirely avoid these effects.

But elections amount to nothing unless you can vote in them. Democracy requires universal enfranchisement. And you have to be able to stand for office, too. Take Iran, where you can vote, but can't necessarily stand. The Guardian Council (twelve clerics and jurists) may refuse to let you enter the race. Candidates who don't line up with the Guardians' political line never reach the starting line, eliminating their chance to cross the finish line. By picking the horses who can run in the race, they can pick the horses who can win. That's a hobbled democracy at best.

Finally, democracy requires freedom of speech. Without free speech, including a free press, people can't know what's going on. They can't know whether to throw the rascals out, keep a good man, or chose a better one. They can't know whether to stay the course or change course. Nor can isolated individual hope to make

81

a difference. People need to be able to join with others (freedom of association).

Often other things are included in the definition of democracy. Traditionally, free-markets and property rights have gone along with democracy. Sometimes, a long list of other rights are included such as the separation of church and state and so forth. But generally, these three basic things imply or lead to the others. Freedom of speech implies freedom of religion, since religion an aspect of speech. And democracy will preserve the people's other rights, too, since the people will insist on it.

The next time some great leader of the latest "people's revolution" starts laying his rhetoric on you, filled with moving eloquence, brimming with compassion and a call for social justice, lay a question back on him. All that sounds wonderful, great leader, but will the new government have frequent and fair elections, universal enfranchisement, the right to stand for office, and freedom of speech and association? If not, he's nothing except the latest in a long time of hypocrites paying lip service to democracy while pursuing the vices of dictatorship.

3.07 – Not a Shield but a Spear

Go into any courtroom in the land and watch the lawyers at work. You'll notice them all the time trying to turn their client's rights from a shield into a spear. Rather than merely defending their clients' rights, they're trying to use their clients' rights to attack the rights of others. Listen to the wider political discourse (or cacophony), and you'll notice the same tactic. People are all the time trying to use their legal rights not just as shields (as defensive armor), but as spears (as offensive weapons).

Take a basic right – the "right to property." The Founding Fathers were real big on that right. In *Federalist No. 54* Madison wrote, "Government is instituted no less for protection of the property, than of the persons of individuals." That sounds like a shield (a "protection"). But not much later in a book published in 1840, the celebrated French anarchist Proudhon proclaimed, "Property is theft." He regarded the right as a spear (an offensive weapon to commit "theft"). Shortly later, Karl Marx reached for his own spear (the rights of the proletariat) to advocate a violent revolution to attack and destroy the right to property. He wrote in *The Communist Manifesto* (1848), "the theory of Communists may be summed up in the single sentence: Abolition of private property." Which is it (a shield or a spear)?

Way back in 1689, John Locke in his *Second Essay Concerning Civil Government* had provided the classic rationale for the right to property. He wrote, "every man has a 'property' in his own 'person.' This nobody has any right to but himself. The 'labour' of his body and the 'work' of his hands, we may say, are properly his. Whatsoever, then, he removes out of the state that Nature hath provided and left it in, he hath mixed his labour with it, and joined to it something that is his own, and thereby makes it his property." A man has a right to the property from his own labor. Makes sense and sounds no more than a defensive right.

Yet Locke was too careful a thinker not to perceive how this right might easily turn into a weapon. He went on, "It will, perhaps, be objected to this, that if gathering the acorns or other fruits of the earth, etc., makes a right to them, then any one may engross [monopolize] as much as he will. To which I answer, Not so. The same law of Nature that does by this means give us property, does also bound that property, too. … As much as any one can make use of to any advantage of life before it spoils, so much he may by his labour fix a property in. Whatever is beyond this is more than his share, and belongs to others." Further, "As much land as a man tills, plants, improves, cultivates, and can use the product of, so much is his property." Locke was trying to set the proper limit on the right as a defensive right rather than as a way to attack the rights of others.

But Locke's agricultural imagery wasn't entirely clear or complete. Did "the labor of his body and the work of his hands" mean only his personal labor? Could he hire other men and acquire a right to the product of their labors as well? Was the reference only to physical labor? Men work as much or more with their minds than their hands. Didn't a man have a right to the products of his mind as well, say his invention of a medicine or a machine? Nor did this agricultural imagery cover commerce. Men were buying and selling commodities, importing and exporting, making fortunes. What defined or properly limited their rights to that sort of property?

To stick for the moment with landed property, in Locke's day, a few men owned virtually all the land, leaving most men with nowhere to "gather acorns or the other fruits of the earth," leaving them no way to earn their daily bread except by selling their labor. Notoriously, the landlord class, a tiny minority, grew rich, but the huge laboring class were poor. Locke had said a man's right to property was only "so much he may by his labour fix a property in [and] beyond this is more than his share, and belongs to others." Then wasn't the landowner getting "more than his share," getting what by right "belongs to others?" Weren't his excessive property rights dispossessing others, turning his rights from a shield into a spear?

By the time of the Industrial Revolution in the mid and late 1800s, any image drawn from an imagined "state of nature" could no longer hope to describe the reality. A few "capitalists" owned the new factories, which churned out a mass production, far more the owners could personally "use the product of." Once again, the vast majority, the workers, had nowhere "to gather their acorns" except by selling their labor. However much the muckraking journalists of the progressive era heightened the negative for effect, such works as Sinclair Lewis' still read *The Jungle*, published 1906, drew upon ample evidence, attesting to real ills associated with industrialization. The list included such items as starvation wages, long hours, child labor, dangerous factories, and defective, unsanitary, or unsafe products. Weren't the capitalists using their property rights not as a shield, but as a spear?

Some such thought led Proudhon to say, "Property is theft." Some such thought led Marx to formulate his remedy, "abolish private property." Such thoughts led to socialism, to the thought of abolishing the right to private property in the name of right to equality. But socialists didn't stop there. They went on to formulate another right in the name of equality, "from each according to his ability to each according to his needs." Under this formula, a man doesn't just have a right to the labor of his own hands, as Locke had said, rather those who produce less or nothing have a right to the produce of the labor of others. If the capitalists had weaponized the right to property, weren't the socialists guilty, in their turn, of the same tactic? They had weaponized the right to equality. Before, one man's right to property forced other men to labor for him. Now, one man's right to equality forced other men to labor for him.

What's the proper definition and limit for the right to property, leaving every man his due rights? For that matter, what's the proper definition and limit for the right to equality, leaving every man his due rights? You've got me. Both are complicated questions incapable of perfect answers.

About the best one can do is quote what Chief Justice Charles Evans Hughes said in a 1937 case about another right, the right to contact, "The Constitution does not speak of freedom of contract. It speaks of liberty and prohibits the deprivation of liberty ... In prohibiting that deprivation the Constitution does not recognize an absolute and uncontrollable liberty. ... But the liberty safe-guarded is a liberty in a social organization which requires the protection of law against the evils which menace the health, safety, morals, and welfare of the people. ... This essential limitation of liberty in general governs freedom of contract in particular." In other words, yes, there's a "right to contract," but not an "absolute and uncontrollable liberty" (right). It's subject to other rights, such as the rights "against the evils which menace the health, safety, morals, and welfare of the people." We may be able to discern the shape, but the precise contours have to be worked out so that the one right does not unduly impinge on another right.

The same goes for all our rights to property, to equality, to contract, etc. These will always remain a matter of degree and continual adjustments. The abstractions may sound like absolutes, but the absolutes never quite work in practice. As much as that, people are always going to try to turn their rights from a shield into a spear. They're always going to try to use their rights to put other people to work for them.

That has to throw the questions about our rights back on the process. What political process is best going to give the best answers? Let's take that up in the next article.

3.08 – The Rights of Man

Remember the movie "Gettysburg" with Martin Sheen of all

people as Robert E. Lee? Remember the scene where some Union soldiers, passing a young Confederate prisoner by the roadside, ask him, "What you fighting for, reb?" He answers what sounds to them like, "My rats." After a bit of confusion, they figure out he's saying, "My rights." Not only were their accents near incomprehensible to each other, what they meant by their "rights" would have turned out as near incomprehensible. But that should come as no surprise. No words have stood for more different meanings than "rights," except maybe "freedom," "liberty," or "equality." More than that, no words have been made more often to stand for their exact opposites than these related words. As a great English historian remarked, "There is no end to the paradoxes for which liberty has been the excuse or the justification. The crimes perpetuated in its name have been as multifarious as the sins committed on behalf of religion or the battles fought for the sake of peace."

The problem is you're never going to be ruled by your rights, rather, you're always going to be ruled by your government. Then unless your constitution writes down the right sort of government, writing down your rights in your constitution won't do you much good. Unless the constitution gives you an effective way to control the men who control your government, those men will use their control to interpret away your rights. To believe otherwise is a fallacy summed up by the notion of "a government of laws not men." The phrase sounds good, but since men interpret the laws, you can't have a government of laws rather than men. Unless restrained, men with the power to interpret the laws will re-interpret them, changing their meaning to favor themselves. They will turn the words upside-down and inside-out (into a paradox).

The French Revolution of 1789 offers a classic example of this paradox. To kill off their old constitution, they guillotined poor King Louis XVI and Queen Marie Antoinette. To bring to life a new constitution, they began by writing their famous Declaration of the Rights of Man and the Citizen. The Marques de Lafayette, assisted by our own Thomas Jefferson, in France at the time as a diplomat, receives much of the credit for the drafting. The preamble begins, "The ... National Assembly ... have determined to set forth in a solemn declaration the natural, unalienable, and sacred rights of man." The document goes on through some seventeen articles, such as, "1. Men are born and remain free and equal in rights. 2. The aim of all political association is the preservation of the natural … rights of man. These rights are liberty, property, security, and resistance to oppression. … 4. Liberty consists in the freedom to do everything which injures no one else." It's like they were afraid to leave out some "right" and wrote down all they could think of.

Now writing down this long list of noble rights was no harder than putting a quill pen to parchment. But the French failed miserably at writing a constitution that forced the men who controlled the government to respect these rights. First, the Committee of Public Safety murdered thousands by judicial decree (the Terror). Eventually, the Emperor Napoleon turned himself into a military dictator. All the time, every French ruler kept pledging allegiance to the "rights of man," but all the time, they kept interpreting the rights into a paradox, first as a justification for their reign of terror, finally as a justification for a military dictatorship.

In the same way, the several constitutions of the Soviet Union, starting with one in 1918, proclaimed a list of rights as long as your arm. The 1918 version guaranteed freedom of the press with these words, "For the purpose of securing freedom of expression to the toiling masses, the Russian Socialist Federated Soviet Republic … turns over to the working people and the poorest peasantry all technical and material means for the publication of newspapers, pamphlets, books, etc., and guarantees their free circulation throughout the country." But the Soviet Union never had freedom of the press or any other rights. The men who controlled the government never ceased to proclaim the freedom of the press and all other rights, but never ceased to simply interpret them away into the opposite.

By contrast, the Glorious Revolution of 1688 in England shows how to run a revolution and write a constitution. Not only did their revolution avoid bloodshed, almost too much to ask, but they wrote into their constitution controls over the men who controlled the government. They didn't fail to write a bill of rights, but the most important right was, "That election of members of Parliament ought to be free." Rather than interpreting the people's rights away, Parliament respected their rights, since the people demanded it, they could hold Parliament accountable at the ballot box, and so Parliament saw to it.

These two opposite story lines have repeated with monotonous regularity. In the more usual story line, the revolution proclaims the rights of man, but the revolutionaries take the path more traveled. They write a constitution giving themselves control over the government and use that control to interpret away the people's rights. More rarely, the revolutionaries take the path less traveled like the English and later the Americans. They write a constitution that gives the people control over the government. Only down that path do the rights of man stand a chance.

If you want to be right when you say you're fighting for "your rights," you better be fighting for your right to democracy.

3.09 – The Economy, Stupid

Remember the mantra from Bill Clinton's first presidential campaign back in 1992, "It's the economy, stupid." How right that was. A poor economy was a key factor in his win over the incumbent, the first George Bush. The incumbent president takes the blame or sometimes the credit for the economy. Never mind the tools for economic management not entirely in his hands and the economy too complex to manage entirely anyway. As the most visible symbol of the government, the people hold him responsible. At least they've got the underlying premise right. The government is more responsible for the economy than anyone else.

A lot of economists talk like the economy more important than the government. That's the wrong way around. Political power (force) trumps economic power (money), and the sort of economy you have depends on the sort of government you have, not the other way around. Just as you can only have three sorts of government (monarchy, aristocracy, or democracy), you can only have three sorts of economy (socialism, a free-market, or something in between). Any sort of autocratic government (monarchy or aristocracy) will strongly prefer socialism, but democracy will show more preference for a free-market. As a practical matter, you'll end up with a mixed economy, something in between, tilted more or less one way or the other.

With socialism, the government owns the economy. No wonder the autocrats prefer it. Who wouldn't prefer to own it all? They already own all the political power. Socialism lets them own all the economic power, too. Since they already have all the political power, sooner or later, they take all the economic power, too. It's no more than another exemplification of that first law of political psychology (the "perpetual and restless desire of power after power"). But the people would prefer to own it, too. A free-market leaves the economy in their hands. Since they have the political power in a democracy, they've shown more preference for a free-market. It's still another exemplification of the same first law.

But while your sort of economy reflects your power politics, your economic success or failure reflects your sort of economy. It took some failures of biblical proportions, but the collapse of the Soviet Union in the 1990s finally convinced all except the stupids such as Fidel Castro in Cuba or Hugo Chavez in Venezuela. The socialists' dream turned out to predict the "lean and ill-favored kine" (the scarcity and famine in Pharaoh's dream). The free-market was the "fat and well-favored kine" (the years of plenty). All the smart guys gave up on the dream of socialism and preferred the free-market.

But if some took the lesson to heart, many found it an inconvenient truth. Weren't they the smartest guys in the room? They started trying to figure out how to milk this truth without the inconvenience of buying the cow, in other words, how to steal the milk. But as has been said, contented cows give more milk. The more of their milk you steal, the less contented the free-market cows, and the less milk they give.

The Communist Chinese offer a very prominent example. Chairman Mao was a committed socialist as well as a committed dictator. Following his teachings, they butchered China's free-market cows. By the time of his own death in 1974, their "lean and ill-favored" economy forced the lesson on his successors. So urgent the truth, the world witnessed a rare sight indeed – an autocracy actually surrendering some power. They signed away much of their economic power by moving from socialism toward a free-market. They resurrected a huge herd of free-market cows, who promptly began to give huge amounts of milk. Their economy was now the "fat and well-favored kine." If anything proved the truth, China proved it. Their new free-market economy vastly out performed their old socialist one. China turned into a very profitable business.

But regarding themselves as the smartest guys in the room, they structured the deal much to their advantage. Remember what Lenin said? "The capitalists would sell you the rope to hang themselves by." No doubt the Chicoms regard themselves as having pulled off some such trick. Their free-market cows are giving them lots of milk (selling them the rope). The trick is the Chicoms can steal all they want by butchering and hanging any cows they want. Since political power trumps economic power, and they didn't give away any political power, they're still the real owners of the economy. And so far, they look like the smartest guys in the room. China came out with a much more powerful economy and so much more powerful in every way, including militarily. Since they still own China, they came out with not less, but more power. But how well this trick works in the long run remains to be seen. So far, the Chinese free-market cows seem content. It doesn't hurt the Chicoms let their cows steal milk from other cows, steal technological and other innovations from other nations. But are the Chicoms smart enough in the long run? Historically, no autocracy has been that smart. Sooner or later, they start stealing too much and mistreating their cows. The economy grows discontented and starts to stall and stagnate. Only time will tell.

But the autocrats like the Chicoms aren't the only ones who regard themselves as the smartest guys in the room. Democratic politicians have just as high a regard for themselves. If they can't own it all, they want to own as much as they can, and what they can't own outright, own through regulation and taxation. But the people want to own it, too, and each of them wants to own as much as they can. Since the people have the political power in a democracy, the politicians stumble against the people. Helping the politicians over this hurdle, the free-market divides the people against themselves into the "haves" and the "have-nots." What Plato said so long ago still holds true, "Any city however small is in fact divided into two, one the city of the poor, the other of the rich. These are at war with one another." By forming an alliance with the poor, who always greatly outnumber the rich, democratic politicians can muster enough votes to take over much, if not all of the economy. Such explains why today every developed democracy has become more or less a welfare state, where the politicians take and always want to take more from the haves for redistribution to the have-nots. All of which is fine. Except contented cows give more milk. The more milk the politicians take, the less contented the cows, and the less milk they give. Somewhere along the line, you reach the point of diminishing returns, where the economy starts to do less well and can start to stall and stagnate as bad as with socialism.

As a practical result, everyone ends up with a mixed economy tilted one way or the other, but not only as an outcome of power politics. Given the free-market out performs, the government still has to create the preconditions for the performance. At the least, it has to secure property rights, enforce contracts, and provide a monetary supply. This last requirement forces the government to own a crucial piece of the economy, the monetary supply, about which more in later articles. Moreover, the free-market suffers from "market failures," turns out self-defeating or inadequate in some ways. Monopolies can set price, defeating the mechanism on which the market operates, and forcing the government to prevent monopoly. On the other hand, you have the "natural monopolies," where a monopoly actually turns out more price efficient. The classic examples are utilities such as water, gas, electricity, where competition drives the cost up not down. Building two or more sets of utility lines to serve a city costs more than only one. But if you're only going to have one, the government either needs to own or regulate it to prevent price gouging. The free-market also fails to produce "social goods" such as highways, schools, or national defense. That forces the government to produce them. Then there are the "negative externalities" produced by the market such as the pollution from a business, which forces the government to regulate the problem.

Let's not get fooled about the economy, stupid. We, the people, should much prefer a free-market. We should much prefer to own as much as we can.

3.10 – Happy Ever After

In fairy tales, we never hear what happens to the happy couple after their marriage. But when a people marry a government, we know what happens. If they live happy ever after, they married Lady Democracy and stayed faithful to her.

Compare the marriages made by the English and the French. Both carried off their brides with revolutionary violence. The English divorced their monarch with the English Civil War (1642 to 1651), and imitating Henry VIII, finalized the decree by cutting off the head of unfortunate King Charles I, making him a martyr to the divine right of kings. But reverting to form, they remarried another monarch with the Restoration, his son, Charles II, who reigned 1660 until 1686. But that rogue's infidelities and those of his brother, James II, who succeeded him on the throne in 1686, finally convinced them. With the Glorious Revolution of 1688, they finally contracted a lasting union with democracy.

The French were more laggard and less fortunate ·in their wooing. Not until a century later with the French Revolution of 1789 did they finally divorce their monarch, imitating the English by guillotining the unfortunate Louis XVI. But they left democracy standing at the altar and went philandering after monarchs for another century. Initially, they espoused that dashing Corsican adventurer, Napoleon from 1798 to 1815. Later, they let his flashy and unreliable nephew seduce them, Napoleon III from 1852 to 1870. The happiness and prosperity of England in her democratic marriage, as compared to the misery of France with her monarchs, serves as a cautionary tale. However urgent the search for an eligible government, a nation, young or old, rich or poor, had better accept no proposals except from democracy.

Democracy brings to marriage the virtues that a people should want from a government, while monarchy has settled vices. Democracy is a good provider, growing a nation's wealth, growing the per capita GDP, while monarchs waste the people's dowry and despoil their estate. Rather than a domestic tyrant, democracy respects the people's rights. Monarchy is an abusive relationship, a police state with censorship. Democracy is handy around the house, an inventive sort, who comes up with all sorts of useful inventions, making life easier. Monarchy cares only for its own comforts. Democracy prefers the calm of civil life. Napoleon contemptuously called England a nation of shopkeepers, and how right he was. Democracies recoil from bloodshed not from any moral superiority, but because they don't like the sight of their own blood. True, when business (shopkeeping) stands to profit by shedding a little blood, if mainly the blood of other peoples, they can show willing, which helps explain the British Empire. But routinely, democracy prefers the safe profits from business as usual and winning glory in the cannon's mouth a highly risky business. But since monarchs don't lead such charges, but order others to make them, war to them like Napoleon is business as usual, having all the attractions of a commercial speculation carried on at the risk of other people's blood and treasure.

Yet when backed against the wall, democracy has proved a mighty man of war. Since the modern era, democracy has soundly drubbed autocracy in all the big wars. In the War of the Spanish Succession (1701 to 1714), England fought the ambitions of Louis XIV, that epitome of hereditary and absolute monarchy, to a standstill. In the first truly world war, the Seven Years War from 1756 to 1763, England chased his weaker successor, Louis XV, from most of France's world empire, putting their own British Empire well on its way. In the Napoleonic Wars (1803 to 1815), England brought down the Emperor Napoleon, a figure of titanic ambition, resource, and military genius. In World War I (1914 to 1918), the allied democracies (Britain, France, and finally the U.S.) brought down the German and Austrian autocracies. In World War II (1939 to 1945), the allied democracies (Britain and the U.S.) crushed the German (Nazi) dictatorship and the Japanese militarists, although it's true, with more than a little help from the autocratic Soviet Union. However, in the Cold War (1947 to 1991) the U.S. democracy settled the Soviet autocracy in its turn.

They say you can fall in love with someone rich as easy as someone poor. Then why not fall in love with a government so rich in so many ways? "How do I love thee? Let me count the ways." Whether we count freedom (as shown by the index of freedom), the standard of living (as shown by the per capital GDP), the wealth of technology, or the national strength, the attractions of democracy leave other suitors behind. A people had better pledge to love, honor, and obey. They better pledge till death do us part. Otherwise, their tale won't have a happy ending. They won't live happy ever after.

4.00 – THE HISTORICAL EXPERIENCE

4.01 – Illumination from the Past

A great thing about the law, it's right there in the law books going back for literally hundreds of years. Not only can you read the first English statute, the Statute of Merton from 1235, during the reign of Henry III, you can read English cases, decisions handed down by their judges going back even farther. You can research the law right down to the bedrock. Generally, your labor will reveal not just how the later laws built on the earlier, but the reasons beneath the laws. That's why a lawyer who wants to find the reasons that support his case hits the law books and looks up the precedents (the history). Generally, understanding the history is a great way to understand the reasons beneath the laws.

The same goes for the constitutional law. If we want to understand the Constitution, a great way is to research the history of constitutions going all the way back. Excavate right down to the bedrock, uncover all the layers of government, and reveal how each built on the other. This archeology takes some time and effort, but besides just the intrinsic interest of digging up the past, will reward the labor (as that distinguished archeologist, Professor Henry Jones said) with "illumination."

Reaching for our pick and shovel and starting to dig, we strike the earliest solid constitutional rock at the level of ancient kingships. In J.R.R. Tolkien's the *Return of the King* (a classic in epic fantasy), Aragon returns as king and restores Middle Earth to a golden age. To imagine the age of real-life kings as golden would require an even more epic sort of fantasy. Yet once upon a time, the real-life kings were as good as it got (the best available government).

When Americans knew their Bible, they knew the story of Saul,

Israel's first king, and that story preserves a memory about the reason for the rise of kingships across the ancient world. When the twelve tribes finally crossed the Jordan River into the land of Canaan, they followed judges (not judicial officers, but warrior chieftains). They had no king (no centralized government). Before too long, other nations with kings, especially the Philistines, began to press hard against them.

The Biblical narrative picks up from there, "Then all the elders of Israel gathered themselves together and came unto [the prophet] Samuel … And said to him, Behold, thou art old … make us a king to judge us like all the nations. And [Samuel] said, This will be the manner of the king who shall reign over you: He will take your sons, and appoint them for himself, for his chariots, and to be his horsemen; ... . And he will take your fields, and your vineyards, even the best of them, and give them to his servants. And he will take the tenth of your seed, and of your vineyards, and give to his officers, and his servants. Nevertheless, the people refused to obey the voice of Samuel; and they said, Nay, but we will have a king over us; That we also may be like all the nations; and that our king may judge us, and fight our battles."

Despite Samuel's warnings, the people wanted a king to "fight our battles" just "like all the nations." They had come to realize that without a king (a more centralized government), they were going to keep losing the battles to their better organized foes. Samuel gave in and anointed Saul the first king. But Saul didn't fare too well, being killed in battle with the Philistines, who "fastened his body to the wall of Beth Shan." His successors, David and Solomon, fared better, ushering in a brief era of national glory.

Yet already, the people had cause to recall Samuel's dire predictions. When Solomon's son (Rehoboam) succeeded him on the throne, "All the congregation of Israel came, and spake unto [him] saying, Thy father made our yoke grievous: now therefore make thou the grievous service of thy father, and his heavy yoke which he put upon us, lighter, and we will serve thee." But the young king returned a haughty reply, "Whereas my father laid upon you a heavy yoke, so shall I add tenfold thereto." A more mature diplomacy might have better served him. The ten northern tribes promptly rebelled, splitting the kingdom into halves (Israel and Judah).

To leave that story, early kingship had a competitive advantage over tribalism. A kingship is fairly easy to set up and fairly stable. Tribalism disperses power, leaving a vacuum at the center. An ambitious chieftain has only to conceive the scheme to fill this empty space. He can recruit a revolutionary cadre with a straightforward and highly persuasive sales pitch. Make me a king, and I'll make you a nobleman. Together they can carry out the revolution and seize power over the tribes. Their mutual interests serve as the glue for the new government. They adhere against all comers foreign and domestic. By uniting the power at the center, the king can govern a larger population over a larger area. He can mobilize more available national resources. By so doing, kingship triumphed over tribalism as a form of government.

Nor does kingship lack some virtues any government should want. First, unanimity. Kings can unite the nation. Second, dispatch. Kings can act when their minds made up, acting with speed to carry out their policies or respond to crises. Third, secrecy. Kings can keep their plans as close as their own minds, keeping their foes foreign or domestic off balance and taken by surprise (get there firstest with the mostest). Such qualities serve extremely useful purposes, especially in the conduct of foreign diplomacy or in waging war.

With kings, not only does the center hold, the center attracts. The nation gathers and grows around them. Kings found capital cities and raise monumental palaces, temples, and fortifications. They create professional bureaucracies and standing armies. Essential to all the rest, they set up a regular system of taxation. They reach out to bring all a nation's resources to flow toward themselves. In this process, kings encourage some useful arts like literacy, engineering, and architecture. In this same process, a central elite appears, who contribute much to the early progress of the arts and sciences. Yet as Samuel warned and as Rehoboam showed, kingship has besetting flaws. Let's turn to those in the next article.

4.02 – Black Robe Fever

Lawyers call it "black robe fever." Some lawyer gets appointed a judge, and before you know it, turns into a petty tyrant, making life miserable for the lawyers who practice in his court. While if a man can catch a fever from no more than a black robe, imagine the galloping consumption he can catch from the royal purple. Not surprising, kings tend to go power mad. Not just them, the institution of the kingship tends to go power mad. In the grievous nature of the disease, the longer the king lives or the institution lasts, the madder they go.

Just the ceremonials show this tendency. When Augustus seized kingly power over the Romans (27 BC), he styled himself no more than First Citizen (*Princeps Civitatis*) and managed affairs from behind the scenes, never openly stepping on the stage with a crown and scepter. Even a century later, an old woman could still approach Trajan (emperor 96 to 117 AD), pluck the sleeve of his toga, and demand a hearing for her petition. But by the time of Diocletian (284 to 305), the emperor "had become an absolute monarch and was elevated above all his subjects" and "hardly ever appeared in public, but if he did he wore a diadem of pearls and beautiful clothes embroidered with jewels. In his presence people had to prostrate themselves (*adoratio*) and only a few senior officials were allowed to kiss the hem of his robe. Anything that was linked to the emperor ... was regarded as sacred."

As part of their power madness, kings seldom fail to exhibit symptoms of paranoia. "This is a sickness rooted and inherent in tyranny: that he that holds it does not trust his friends." They're insanely suspicious of every imaginable threat to their throne or their lives. Crushing all imagined fears by crushing all imaginable resistance, they crush all freedom. As another part of the disease, they seldom fail to exhibit symptoms of kleptomania. "Now king David was old and stricken in years; ... So they sought for a fair damsel throughout all the coasts of Israel, and found Abishag a Shunammite, and brought her to the king." If they can take the most precious and delicate commodity of all, what can't they take? Nothing. "A king is like a robber permanently on the prowl, always probing, always searching for the weak spot where there is something for him to steal." More or less gradually, but inexorably, kings, their families, and their courtiers take until they own it all. Their governments degenerate into a kleptocracy, crushing the free-market. The nation presents the spectacle of overwhelming oppression combined with abject poverty.

Kingship suffers from another besetting ill, the disorders that fester around the succession. When Madame de Stael praised benevolent despotism to Czar Alexander, that perceptive despot replied, "Yes, madam, but it is only a happy accident." The genealogy of royal houses amply proves his point. Kings strongly prefer the hereditary principle, preferably inheritance by the eldest son. Passing down the crown with their blood appeals not just to their exalted vanity, but eases their settled fears. A rule for inheritance by the eldest male cuts off the otherwise constant quarrels within the royal house over the succession. And who will wait for the legacy as patiently as a son guaranteed the bequest, while his patient waiting ousts the impatient ambition of others for the same legacy. But unfortunately for the hereditary principle, the royal line has rather frequently been known to fail and run out of male heirs. At least as frequently, kings have failed to pass down their capacity as reliably as a thoroughbred horse passes down a physique. Many a noble king, who beat all comers, sires only sons who never won a race. "It has been said, not truly, but with a possible approximation to truth, that in 1802 every hereditary monarch was insane."

Nor do the sons always wait with the hoped for patience. "Absalom! Absalom!" King David cried out in grief over the death of that rebellious son. Many a king has so cried out in grief, but not the sons have always died. Royal offspring have been known to eat (or poison) the parent. While this ill extends well beyond the royal family. "Is this a dagger which I see before me, the handle toward my hand?" Many an ambitious usurper like Macbeth has grasped the handle and plunged the blade into the breast of a King Duncan. In the late Roman Empire, it got so bad you needed a scorecard to keep track of the murdered emperors. The civil wars over the succession ousted orderly government and ruined whole provinces. But if the king can last, he can sometimes live on into his dotage, leaving the government in a state of cognitive disorder.

But what galls most about kings is the subservience. Who would not enjoy being paid kingly honors, but who enjoys paying the honors? Which of us longs to bend the knee, doff the hat, or kiss the ring? Who likes to say, "Your majesty" or "sire?"

However long taught, who reconciles with such habits and would not rather learn better habits? The pride of kings never went down easy with their subjects. The surviving sources testify to an abiding resentment.

Yet viable alternatives were slow to emerge. Let's turn to those efforts next.

4.03 – Fire From Heaven

Back in 1787, James Madison carefully researched past constitutions before packing his bags to attend the Constitutional Convention. You can still go to the library and read his research notes in the edition of his works. He went all the way back to the ancient Greeks, who invented democracy. And what didn't they invent? Fire from heaven rained down on classical Greece. In their mythology, they mated with gods and goddesses. Maybe aliens came down. Whatever the cause, their intelligence and creativity went through the roof. Yet as Madison noted, their form of democracy suffered from a fatal flaw, leading to a demise.

Around 335 BC, Aristotle founded the Lyceum, his great school for philosophy. As an aid to their studies in political science, we know his students collected some 170 constitutions from the Greek city-states. Some were probably merely different constitutions for the same cities from different times. Yet such a high number shows the height of Greek disunity. A small peninsula divided between so many city-states must be fatally divided against itself. So it would prove. But Aristotle's collected constitutions were all lost except for one. In the late 1800s, some papyri were found in Egypt with a copy of his Athenian Constitution. As fate would have it, that's the one we would most want to have.

Athens was the most illustrious and influential Greek city-state. Students of constitutions like Madison already knew a lot about her democracy from other sources such as Thucydides, but now we had the specifics. Athens had a highly "direct" form of democracy where all citizens could "directly" participate. Every citizen could attend and vote in the Assembly, where final authority resided. Ten-member boards carried out the day-to-day executive functions such as managing the naval arsenal or maintaining the public buildings on the Acropolis. Any citizen could put forward his name as a candidate to sit on a board, and the winners were drawn by lot. Their term of office lasted only a single year, a man could serve only one term on any board, and only two terms total on all the boards. This rapid turnover and the luck of the draw gave everyone a chance to share in the glory of office with one exception. The Assembly elected the Ten Generals each year, who commanded the army and navy, and a man could serve any number of terms. For all their egalitarianism, the Athenians didn't want to pick their generals by chance, and when they picked a winner, wanted to keep on picking him.

This constitution looks democratic enough for the tastes of the most ardent populist. But if such total participation a virtue, that was the fatal flaw. That placed a narrow limit on the practical size of the state. If every citizen was to participate in the Assembly, every citizen had to live close enough to attend on a regular basis. As Madison would note in the *Federalist No. 14*, "the natural limit … is that distance from the central point, which will just permit the most remote citizen to assemble as often as their public functions demand." The Athenian city-state covered some 700 square miles, but that's smaller than Rhode Island and many a U.S. county. That geographic limitation left direct democracy a fairly small phenomenon.

That left Athens swimming a smaller fish in a much bigger sea. And we know what happens to smaller fish. Bigger fish eat them. That's exactly what happened to Athens and the other Greek city-states as well. First, the Macedonians devoured them, later the Romans digested them. In the Darwinian world of international diplomacy and warfare, the species "direct democracy" went virtually extinct, being too small to survive.

The ancient Greeks gave the Founding Fathers no useful institutional forms to copy. Yet the Greeks influenced them in significant ways. Their literary remains, especially Plato's *Dialogues*, preserved an appealing image of free men living free lives in a democracy. The Founders aspired to live with the same freedom in a democracy. But the Greeks' failure to unite into a single nation did serve as a cautionary tale. The Founders didn't want to stay disunited like the Greeks and like them fall a prey to larger nations. In the words of a song popular in the days of the

American Revolution (the "Liberty Song"), "in Freedom we'll live. … By uniting we stand, by dividing we fall." So much they learned from ancient Greece.

4.04 – Republican Empire

People seem fascinated by the Roman Empire and the Roman Emperors. Movies and books continue to display this fascination, such as the old PBS series "I, Claudius" or the more recent "Gladiator." What seems to get overlooked is that Rome conquered the known world as the Roman Republic, declined and fell as the Roman Empire. As a republic (a type of representative democracy), her system ran the table. When her system altered into an empire (into an ever more onerous military dictatorship), she slowly lost all her winnings and went broke (declined and fell). When she won with one system (one constitution), but went bankrupt when she changed systems, doesn't that make you think the change in her systems (in her constitutions) had something to do with the change in her fortunes?

The Greek historian Polybius, who was around to witness her rise, living from about 200 to 118 BC, wrote, "Can anyone be so indifferent or idle as not to care to know by what means, and under what kind of polity, almost the whole inhabited world was conquered and brought under the dominion of the single city of Rome, and that too within a period of not quite fifty-three years?" He went on, "Now in every practical undertaking by a state we must regard as the most powerful agent for success or failure the form of its constitution; for from this as from a fountain-head all conceptions and plans of action not only proceed, but attain their consummation."

What was the constitution under which Rome conquered? What the constitution under which she declined and fell? Rome's founding fathers, whose names largely lost, had devised a republican constitution (a form of representative democracy). And they achieved a combination of virtues never before achieved in government.

Every Roman citizen could attend the assemblies of which there were several. But rather than govern directly, the assemblies elected the magistrates (the executive officers), who actually carried on the government. The assemblies also passed the laws, which the magistrates had to propose. Concerned to prevent the magistrates from seizing too much power, the constitution weakened them with a "collegial system" and only short (one year) terms of office. That is, several officials shared each office, and a whole new set came in each year. For example, ten quaestors handled the state's finances, and two consuls were the highest magistrates and commanded the armies. These magistrates' natural rivalry was expected to serve as a check on their ambitions and keep them honest, each official checking the excessive ambitions of the others and watching over their honesty.

This constitution retained the virtues of a democracy. The government stayed responsible (accountable) to the Roman people. But it acquired the virtue of sufficient executive vitality (provided by the magistrates). Moreover, since the assemblies only met occasionally, the Roman city-state could grow to a much larger size than a direct democracy. Since the citizens didn't have to attend very often, they could come a much farther distance, letting there be a lot more of them.

How well did Rome's founding fathers do their job? For centuries, Romans enjoyed freedoms seldom matched in the ancient world. For centuries, her assemblies elected capable magistrates, who stayed restrained within their authority and honest, who yet had sufficient authority to govern with firmness and energy. For centuries, this freedom and this leadership made for a dynamic combination. The Roman city-state was big enough to compete, and she out-competed. The Roman Republic conquered the known world, leading to the *Pax Romana*. As Hamilton observed in *Federalist No. 34*, "The Roman Republic attained to the utmost height of human greatness."

But the size of her success eventually overwhelmed her constitution. To rule her vast provinces, she sent out proconsuls. While in theory these magistrates remained accountable to the republic, no effective mechanism actually held them accountable. They were able to rule their provinces like mini-military dictators, and a thought soon occurred to some of them. Why not turn their armies back against Rome, making themselves the masters rather than the servants of the republic? Such thoughts were fathers to such deeds, causing a series of civil wars. In 49 BC, Julius Caesar not only crossed his Rubicon, but took the Republic with him. Marching his legions back from Gaul, he overthrew the Roman Republic once and for all, changing the Roman constitution into a kingship under any other name, since the Romans hated the name of a king. Having crossed this line, the Roman constitution took on the form of an ever more onerous military dictatorship.

The philosopher David Hume well summed up the process, "The despotism of its monarchs, extinguished all emulation, debased the generous spirits of men, and depressed that noble flame by which all the refined arts must be cherished and enlivened. The military government, which soon succeeded, rendered even the lives and properties of men insecure and precarious, and proved destructive to those vulgar and more necessary arts of agriculture, manufacture, and commerce." In other words, the Roman Emperors gradually went more and more power mad, gradually killing off Roman freedom, gradually killing off the dynamic vitality of the system. Not that Rome died in a day. The Empire lived on for centuries, feeding off the huge carcass of the Republic. Aspects of the republican system survived in the imperial administration and at the local level in the towns and cities and continued to provide some nourishment. But the emperors' appetites inexorably devoured more and more, until finally nothing was left but the eaten out ruins.

Our own Founding Fathers knew their Roman history. But the Roman Republic offered them no useful institutional forms to copy, suitable to the Founders' own times and circumstances. Our republic bears no resemblance to theirs any more than our Senate resembles the Roman Senate. Yet Roman history did influence the Founders. The Roman Republic showed that a carefully crafted constitution could combine personal liberty with national strength. On the other hand, the fall of the Republic excited their fear of too much democracy. In the standard telling, the most famous Roman of them all (Julius Caesar) had played on the ignorance of the mob to overthrow the Republic and make himself a dictator. They feared unbridled democracy might suffer from an inherent flaw, a vulnerability to the arts of a demagogue. This fear helps explain why they hedged the franchise with property qualifications, entrusted state legislators with the election of senators rather than the people, and created the Electoral College for an indirect rather than popular election of the president. But something else survived from Rome as well, preserved perhaps nowhere better than in the literary works of Cicero (106 to 43 BC). This was a very appealing image of the sort of freedoms offered by a republic, which contrasted very strongly with the sort of subservient lives of people under monarchs.

However, as John Jay would write in *Federalist No. 5*, "The history of Great Britain is the one with which we are in general the best acquainted, and it gives us many useful lessons. We may profit from their experience, without paying the price which it cost them" Let us turn to that history and those lessons in the next articles.

4.05 – Mother of Parliaments

The better our lawyer forefathers knew their Blackstone (Sir William Blackstone's *Commentaries on the Laws of England*, published 1765 to 1769), the better they knew American law. That's because American law descends directly from the "laws of England." The same goes for our constitutional law. The U.S. Constitution descends directly from the English Constitution, bearing as close a resemblance as a mother and daughter, who look, think, and act very much alike. To understand the daughter, a good place to start is with the mother. To understand the U.S. Constitution, a good place to start is with the Mother of Parliaments.

The lady wasn't born to sovereignty, but had to fight her way from the cradle for her very life. Some great minds like John Locke later wrote some great books about her theory of government. But on her way up, she never used a theory except as a weapon to strike down a foe. In her rise, she displayed an eminently practical, not to say ruthless, turn of mind. She meant to climb. With some luck and by the skin of her teeth, she reached the top of the greasy pole. By the time of the American Revolution in 1774, she (Parliament and especially the House of Commons) had long reigned as the real power in the British Constitution. Her reign had already proved the value of her only real theory of government (that she rule). Britannia ruled the waves, dined on the roast beef of Old England, and enjoyed the rights of freeborn Englishmen. The Mother of Parliaments had scored the hat trick in government (national strength, prosperity, and liberty). Her career had finally given the world a working model for a republic (a representative democracy).

Although she long remained the exception rather than the rule, she didn't start out so unique. In feudal times, other European peoples had rudimentary national assemblies much resembling her such as the French *Estates General* or the Spanish *Cortes*. Every so often, the medieval monarchs would summon these gatherings, which somewhat haphazardly included members of the three estates, the nobility, the clergy, and the commons. Neither really representative nor with real power, yet these loose institutions served some useful purposes. Medieval kings weren't securely enough mounted to ride roughshod. A country filled with castles and armed men requires some coaxing. These assemblages gave the kings a chance to hear the latest news from the reaches of the realm, sense which way the wind blew, test the waters, and rally waverers with persuasion, promises, and the royal largesse, or if such blandishments failed, threats, confiscations, and executions. As to the others in attendance, they got a chance perhaps at least to offer some advice, maybe even vent some grievances. But during the late Middle Ages, the older feudal decentralization gradually gave way before a newer royal centralization at about the same rate as castle walls gave way before the new technology of gunpowder. These old national assembles began to be overgrown by royal authority, languish in the shade, and wither on the vine. On the eve of the French Revolution in 1789, the *Estates General* hadn't met for over a century, since 1614. The Spanish *Cortes* had continued to meet, but only to hear the royal command.

But something unique happened over in England. Rather than shriveling, the Mother of Parliaments grew in strength through the accident of events. Initially, she came under the protection of the armed nobility as a useful device with which they could resist the king. Later and oddly enough, the situation reversed, and she came under the royal protection as a useful device with which the king could reduce the power of the barons. Still later, the situation changed again, and she served as a refuge for opponents to a further extension of royal authority as the center for resistance to the establishment of a royal despotism. In this last role, she finally managed to step forward and claim sovereignty (ultimate power) for herself.

By the long reign of Edward I (from 1272 to 1307) custom had firmly established the calling of Parliaments. In 1295, he summoned what later called the Model Parliament. The king sent out writs (an order to attend) to the great nobles, the bishops, and also to the shires and towns, who themselves selected who to send. Lacking authority to pass laws, yet Parliament could petition the king for a law. Already a legal principle had appeared that later proved highly consequential. The king could tax only through Parliament, not just by his personal fiat. Initially, the armed barons successfully defended this principle for obvious reasons. Later the House of Commons would defend it with even more success for the same obvious reasons. It was the rock on which the monarchy would eventually break.

But at this early stage, that wasn't evident. And not only was Parliament not a democratic institution, democracy wasn't even in the wind. Rather, the initial struggle for power was between the king and the feudal barons. And initially, the barons enjoyed some success in resisting the king both inside and outside Parliament. But as the late Middle Ages wore on, the greater power at the center in the hands of the kings began to wear down the barons, and the kings found Parliament a useful weapon to hand. Many the holder of an illustrious noble title suffered attainder before Parliament, a procedure whereby Parliament found the accused guilty of treason, skipping over the inconveniences of a trial by a court. The convicted went to the headmen's block and their lands escheated (forfeited) to the crown.

By the time of the Tudor monarchs, Henry VIII, who ruled from 1509 to 1547, and his peerless daughter, Elizabeth I, who ruled 1558 to 1603, the monarchy had broken the nobility. By that time, too, Parliament had divided into the familiar two chambers, the House of Lords (the nobility, who inherited their seats with their title, and clergy, who took their seats with their appointment to a bishopric) and the House of Commons (selected by the shires and towns). And the Tudors monarchs reigned comfortably over their Parliaments, dictating the outcomes. But a subtle shift was occurring, a gradual move from feudalism toward a landed and commercial society. Beneath the king, the power no longer resided in the strong arm of the feudal barons, but in the wealth that came from land or trade. Those with this new wealth (this new power) naturally found their way into the House of Commons, while at the same time, the monarchy naturally wanted to tap into (tax or expropriate) their growing wealth. But this desire stumbled against the principle that the king could tax only through Parliament, where the new wealth found not only a ready place to rally against him, but this ready principle around which to rally.

In the next era after the death of Elizabeth I in 1603, a classic power struggle developed between the competing political institutions (the monarchy and Parliament). The first two Stuart kings, James I (reigned 1603 to 1625) and Charles I (1625 to 1649) longed to become absolutist monarchs like Louis XIV over in France, while Parliament sought to further limit the powers of the monarchy. The outcome was decided by nothing except the bloody English Civil War (1642 to 1651). The Parliamentary forces, led by Oliver Cromwell, won the war, finally decapitating King Charles I, the only English monarch to die on the scaffold.

The Mother of Parliaments had led a precarious life. Born in early feudal times in a time of decentralized government, she had fortuitously avoided the fate meted out to her sisters by later feudal monarchs as part of making themselves absolute. In early modern times, she had gathered under the slender protection of her skirts the growing landed and commercial wealth, recruiting gradually more power to herself. Finally, she had leveled the power of the monarchy by cutting off a king's head. But her sovereignty was still tenuous. Only with the Glorious Revolution of 1688 did she finally consolidate her power once and for all, about which more in the next articles.

4.06 – The Tyranny of King George III

If you're not careful, you can start believing your own propaganda. Thomas Jefferson, rightly classed a great man and president, seems to have done that over King George III. During the American Revolution, Jefferson got so worked up calling King

George a tyrant, he seems not only to have convinced himself, but never ceased believing it. He should have known better. King George was no tyrant, but a constitutional monarch. Americans didn't revolt against tyranny, but for independence.

When we think of the Declaration of Independence, we think of Jefferson's stirring language, "We hold these truths to be self-evident." Great stuff we can't re-read too often. But when we keep reading, coming to the parts no longer much read, we come to stuff maybe not as great. Jefferson starts to sound like a prosecuting attorney drawing a bill of indictment, accusing King George of all sorts of heinous crimes. And the effort starts to suffer from a very lawyerly failing, starting somewhat to stretch the facts to make the case. He arraigns King George thus, "The history of the present King of Great Britain is a history of repeated injuries and usurpations." He convicts him thus, "A Prince whose character is thus marked by every act which may define a Tyrant, is unfit to be the ruler of a free people." But the ringing tone can't quite hide the overreach. How condemn King George as "unfit to be the ruler of a free people" when he ruled as a constitutional monarch in tandem with Parliament over the freest people in the world, the British?

As much as that, except for some leading strings, Americans were about as free. Under their colonial charters, every colony had a mini-constitution after the English model. The royal governor served as the chief executive and took his marching orders from the British colonial authorities, one of the main leading strings. But each colony had an elected assembly like the House of Commons and an appointed council like the House of Lords, which served as their local legislatures, passing the local laws and levying the local taxes. These assemblies had often copied Parliament's past tactics against the monarchy and often successfully. In a series of conflicts with the royal governors, they had resisted unpopular taxation or gained concessions in return. However, Parliament not King George did have the final authority to pass colonial laws and levy taxes, another main leading string. But except for some annoying economic regulations, benefiting British merchants at colonial expense, for a longtime Parliament did little leading, leaving the colonies largely to follow their own lead. The colonials also had British style courts in which they enjoyed the usual "rights of Freeborn Englishmen." Americans didn't live under a tyranny, but had a lot of self-government and liberty, more than about anybody else in the world at the time.

Long after the American Revolution, writing in 1826, Chief Justice John Marshall, whose credentials as a patriot impeccable, having fought in a Virginia regiment and survived Valley Forge, confessed as much, writing, "Our resistance was not made to actual oppression. Americans were not pressed down to earth by the weight of the chains nor goaded to resistance by actual suffering. … The war was a war of principle against a system hostile to political liberty, from which oppression was to be dreaded, not against actual oppression." Where "oppression was to be dreaded," but there was no "actual oppression," any tyranny appears more potential than real.

While for another fact, as long as Americans still needed the British Empire, they showed themselves willing enough as subjects. And they had still needed the Empire as long as the French had still held Canada. Remember James Fenimore Cooper's *The Last of the Mohicans*? That fictionalized the bloody fighting along the frontier during the French and Indian War (1754 to 1763), but the savagery was no fiction. In the winter, the French and Indians put on their snowshoes and traveled overland hundreds of miles, coming down with a war whoop and the dawn on isolated settlements. In the summer, they paddled their canoes down the rivers on still bigger raids. That was until 1759, when Wolfe beat Montcalm at the Battle on the Plains of Abraham just outside Quebec. In the peace treaty (the Treaty of Paris, 1763), the French lost Canada, the Indians lost the French, and the Americans lost their need for the British Empire.

Americans already needed the mother country less, having grown to youthful maturity and now better able to look out for themselves. And they had grown up independent minded. After all, what were they except the heirs to English history, English traditions, and English institutions? What did that legacy teach, if not a stubborn adherence to their liberty as well as how to govern themselves? Only adding to this independent frame of mind, they had been conveyed to a distance shore and there largely left to fend for themselves, since the mother country far away and more concerned with the children who stayed at home.

As soon as the French threat disappeared, it didn't take long for

Americans to start asking what the mother country had done for them lately. In the same timeframe, the mother country began to ask, perhaps not unreasonably, why the colonials shouldn't show some gratitude by helping pay down the huge British national debt run up winning the French and Indian War. Weren't the Americans among the prime beneficiaries of the victory? With that thought in mind, Parliament finally did begin to impose some taxes on the colonies, the infamous Stamp Act and the Townsend Duties, including the one on tea that led to the Boston Tea Party. These taxes weren't really that onerous. But here the theory ("oppression to be dreaded") threatened to turn into the practice ("actual oppression"). Americans, perhaps not unreasonably in their turn, raised the cry of "no taxation without representation." Political passions being what they are, a lot of Americans, even reasonable men like George Washington or John Marshall, soon worked themselves into a lather and started calling King George a tyrant.

With the calmer hindsight of history, the American Revolution wasn't a revolt against the tyranny of King George. It was more like a family quarrel, where the grownup children (the colonials) were eager to escape parental (British) control and take on the responsibilities and pleasures of adulthood. Americans were already used to having their head, used to having their liberty and governing themselves. At the very time they ceased to need so much parental protection, the parent was tightening, rather than loosening the leading strings. Well, they knew what to do about that. Just as their English ancestors had rebelled, they would rebel. Just as they would later imitate the English model in writing the U.S. Constitution, they would imitate the English models for revolution, the English Civil Wars (1642 to 1651) and the Glorious Revolution of 1688.

4.07 – The Model Revolution

Why do so many intellectuals still gush over the French Revolution of 1789? That was no model revolution. The model revolution was the English Glorious Revolution of 1688. Our American Revolution of 1776 falls in between, not only in time, but in method.

To take the events in the order of their occurrence, with the Glorious Revolution of 1688, the English kicked out King James II after just three years on the throne. For once, a people seem to have learned from their history rather than merely repeating the errors of the past. In a still earlier revolution (the English Civil War, 1642 to 1651), the parliamentary forces under Oliver Cromwell had thoroughly whipped the royalists and signalized their victory by cutting off the head of the unfortunate King Charles I. But the overall body count ran to roughly 190,000 of lesser known folk out of a population of just five million, not to count the economic cost and social disruption. Nor did this revolutionary violence reap a permanent reward. Unable to settle on a constitution lacking a monarch as the head, the English eventually invited back as king Charles II (the eldest son of the beheaded Charles I), who ruled from 1660 to 1685 (the Restoration). So far, they were merely repeating the errors of their history. Both Charles I and II were absolutists to the core, who never reconciled themselves to sharing power with Parliament. Both constantly schemed to seize absolute powers and rule like Louis XIV over in France. When Charles II died, his younger brother succeeded him as James II, and if anything, he was the most rigid absolutist in the family.

But the sequel showed that people can learn from their history. Enough was enough, and with the Glorious Revolution of 1688, the nation expelled James II from the throne. This time around the revolution was gloriously bloodless. Although James fell into their hands, they refrained from shedding even his blood. Rather than making him into a martyr, they let him escape to an ignominious exile in France. The revolution was further glorious in finally establishing once and for all the sovereignty of Parliament. Never again would a British monarch openly harbor absolutist ambitions, however much they may have longed for such power in the privacy of their hearts and minds. We still call Britain a constitutional monarchy, but from that day to this, their government has been effectively a representative democracy.

These events were recent and familiar history and their own history to our Founding Fathers. As we heard John Jay say in the *Federalist No. 5*, "The history of Great Britain is the one with which we are in general the best acquainted, and it gives us many useful lessons. We may profit from their experience, without paying the price which it cost them." But we didn't entirely manage to "profit from their experience, without paying the price it cost them." Our American Revolution in 1776 was far from bloodless, about 50,000 dead in a population of just four million and caused significant social and economic dislocation. But we did "profit from their experience" by establishing a representative democracy, although not an effective national one until the ratification of the Constitution in 1788.

If our attempt to imitate the model fell somewhat short, the French Revolution in 1789 created another model altogether. The Terror and Madam Guillotine still stand as the model for revolutionary terror. A great many modern revolutionaries such a Stalin or Mao have preferred to copy this French model. Nor did the French Revolution establish a democracy, rather, falling back to become a military dictatorship under Napoleon. A great many modern revolutionaries, again like Stalin or Mao have also preferred to copy this part of the French model as well. Not that the French Revolution accomplished nothing. It swept away the remnants of feudalism, made their society more egalitarian, their government more efficient. But at what cost? The Terror claimed thousands of lives, Napoleon's wars claimed tens of thousands. Nor did they end up with a democracy. Is that any way to run a revolution, however it may appeal to such as Stalin and Mao?

Let's get it right. What we want from any revolution is maximum progress at minimum cost. We want to end up with a democracy. We want to get there with as little bloodshed and social and economic dislocation as we can. The model revolution is the Glorious Revolution of 1688, not the French Revolution of 1789. Our American Revolution of 1776 falls somewhere in between.

4.08 – The Swing of the Pendulum

Historically, a lot of revolutions have swung back and ended close to their start. The French Revolution of 1789 started out dethroning the autocratic Bourbon kings, only to swing back and crown Napoleon as emperor. The Russian Revolution of 1917 started out toppling the despotic Romanoff czars, only to swing back and elevate Stalin as a more than oriental despot. Apparently, it's easy enough to kill off a ruler or a dynasty the way Lenin had Czar Nicholas II and his family slaughtered in the cellar at Yekaterinburg in 1918, but government institutions die harder and tend to resurrect themselves in their former shape. Nor does our American Revolution of 1776 differ much from this pattern. We swung back as close as we could get to where we started.

When a revolution overthrows an existing regime, often an interregnum follows, when the government institutions are in flux. Napoleon didn't manage to seize monarchical power until 1799; Stalin wasn't entirely a dictator until about 1929. During this interval, it's often like a pendulum. The government institutions swing away from their starting point only later to swing back. The same goes for the American Revolution. We started out under a strong British national government with an elected legislature (the House of Commons), a strong chief executive (not the king, but the prime minister and his cabinet), and an independent judiciary. With the Revolution, the pendulum began to swing away from this institutional shape.

In late 1774, the First Continental Congress convened from September 5 to October 26 at Carpenter's Hall in Philadelphia. Reps from twelve colonies attended, but didn't even pretend to form a national government. The main outcomes were a petition of grievances to the king and a call for a boycott of British goods to pressure Parliament into some sort of compromise with colonial demands. By the next year (1775) when the Second Continental Congress met, the revolutionary war had already broken out spontaneously, and they became, in effect, our revolutionary government in being, lasting from May 10, 1776 until March 1, 1781.

This Congress was an incomplete government at best, being no more than a gathering of delegates from the colonies, which soon began to call themselves independent states. However, on July 4, 1776, they did publish the Declaration of Independence. And they did manage to carry out some of the functions of a national government. They created the Continental Army and appointed George Washington the commanding general. They raised money to finance the war by requests to the states and loans, and they printed a currency (the Continental). They sent Benjamin Franklin as ambassador to France, where his negotiation of an alliance proved critical to victory in the Revolution. One of their committees also wrote the Articles of Confederation to set up a permanent national government. After ratification by the last state (Maryland in 1781), these Articles became our national constitution until superseded by the U.S. Constitution in 1789.

The very first sentence of *Federalist No. 1* reads, "After an unequivocal experience of the inefficiency of the subsisting federal government, you are called upon to deliberate on a new Constitution for the United States of America." The "subsisting government" was these Articles of Confederation, our constitution from 1781 to 1789, technically "the first American constitution." What exactly was "the unequivocal experience of the inefficiency?"

The Articles of Confederation swung away from the shape of British government institutions. The Articles failed to create a strong national government, but only a weak confederacy where the states greatly predominated in power over the national government. The Articles said, "Each state retains … every power, jurisdiction, and right, which is not by this Confederation expressly delegated to the United States, in Congress assembled." And the Articles "expressly delegated" to the national government not much more than the conduct of foreign affairs, the raising of an army and navy, and the declaring of war. No provision gave this government sufficient strength to carry out even these limited roles.

Under the Articles, the national government consisted only of a legislative branch, a single chamber Congress, having neither an executive nor a judicial branch. The state legislatures annually appointed from two to seven delegates to the Congress, but each state had only one vote in the chamber, and no law could pass without a vote of nine out the thirteen states. Since such a high level of agreement was seldom attainable, the Congress could as seldom take much action. Without a chief executive to give a steady impetus, action drifted. Crucially, the national finances were also adrift. To raise taxes, the national government could do no more than requisition the states to pay their share. Since no effective mechanism existed to make them pay up, we should see where that's headed. Many states neglected or refused to write the check, the nation's bills went unpaid, and the national treasury was empty.

Federalist No. 15 gives a litany of the resulting woes. "Do we owe debts to foreigners and to our own citizens contracted in a time of imminent peril for the preservation of our political existence? These remain without any proper or satisfactory provision for their discharge." Since we couldn't collect the necessary taxes, we had defaulted on the loans made to finance the Revolution. "Have we valuable territories and important posts in the possession of a foreign power which, by express stipulations, ought long since to have been surrendered? These are still retained." In the Treaty of Paris (1783) ending the Revolution, Great Britain had agreed to turn over certain western posts and forts, but was refusing to do so. "Are we in a condition to resent or to repel the aggression? We have neither troops, nor treasury." Which words expressed the exact truth. "Are we even in a condition to remonstrate with dignity? The just imputations on our own faith, in respect to the same treaty, ought first to be removed." We had failed to live up to our own obligations under the same treaty. We had agreed to pay British citizens some reparations, but having no money in the treasury, had defaulted on that obligation as well. Furthermore, Spain had closed the Mississippi River against us. Commerce was languishing and real property going down in value. The credit and the monetary systems were in disarray. "We may indeed with propriety be said to have reached almost the last stage of national humiliation. There is scarcely anything that can wound the pride or degrade the character of an independent nation which we do not experience."

There was only too much truth in this long list. But then, the pendulum started to swing back. In 1786, a call went out for a Meeting of Commissioners to Remedy Defects of the Federal Government. Called the Annapolis Convention because they met in Annapolis, Maryland, only twelve delegates from five states attended, but among them were both James Madison and Alexander Hamilton. Supposed to discuss issues of commerce and trade, they concluded those issues required a larger political reform. In a unanimous report, they recommended that a convention "meet at Philadelphia on the second Monday in May next, to take into consideration the situation of the United States, to devise such further provisions as shall appear to them necessary to render the constitution of the Federal Government adequate to the exigencies of the Union."

Prodded by this report, the Congress under the Articles passed a resolution for a convention, but only to revise the Articles. This call led to what became the Constitutional Convention, which would meet in Philadelphia from May 25 to September 17, 1787. They wouldn't just revise the Articles, but write an entirely new U.S. Constitution. In so doing, they would swing back to the institutions of the British Constitution, leaving out the monarchy and aristocracy, taking account of America's own peculiar circumstances, and particularly the existence of thirteen independent states, who were reluctant to surrender all their sovereignty.

The American Revolution started out under a strong national government with an elected legislature, a strong chief executive, and an independent judiciary. During the Revolution, the pendulum swung away from these institutions. With the Constitutional Convention it would swing back. With the U.S. Constitution, we would end up as close to our start as we could get.

5.00 – THE CONSTITUTION

5.01 – A Gathering of Bourgeoisie

The historian Charles A. Beard, who taught at Columbia before World War I, got famous with a revisionist book. Beard looked back at the Constitutional Convention through a Marxist lens. Where earlier historians saw the Founding Fathers as heroes (patriots and lovers of liberty), he claimed to reveal their feet as the common clay of capitalism. He claimed they were out to make a profit with their new Constitution. Far from a gathering of eagles, he regarded the Convention as a gathering of bourgeoisie.

Beard's book (*The Economic Interpretation of the Constitution of the United States*, published in 1913) began with these questions, "Did the men who formulated the fundamental law of the land possess the kinds of property which was immediately and directly increased in value or made more secure by the result of the labors at Philadelphia? Did they have money at interest? Did they own public securities? Did they hold western lands for appreciation? Were they interested in shipping and manufacturing?" Of course, he answered all these questions with a ringing, "Of course!"

All these "kinds of property" looked to gain ("immediately and directly increase in value") with the new Constitution. A strong new national government would make property secure and money sound. Thus, someone with "money at interest" (owed money like bankers and bondholders) would not only collect the money owed them, but collect in sound money (not devalued by runaway inflation). The prior government (under the Articles of Confederation) had been unable effectively to raise money through taxation and had defaulted on the national debt. But the new one could effectively tax. Thus, someone holding "public securities" (government bonds) would now get paid. The new government could also raise the money to pay for an army, and it could admit new states to the union. America's vast western frontiers were under attack by hostile Indian tribes and threatened by the meddling of European nations (Britain, France, and Spain). Now this territory could be defended and organized. Thus, someone who "held western lands for appreciation" (had speculated in them) could now expect that speculation to pay off. Last but not least, the new government could set up a national marketplace (free of internal custom barriers) and could regulate foreign commerce. Thus, someone in "shipping and manufacturing" could now expect to do well, too.

Thus, Beard claimed the Founding Fathers had self-interested motives. They were no more than capitalists out to make a profit. Some later historians took up his gauntlet and flung it back in his face. They claimed he was self-interested himself and had fudged his research to support his thesis. Their claimed their counter-research showed the Founders had little, in most cases no, such property. But so what? Where can you find men above interests? While as for interests, what's so wrong with property rights, sound money, paying your debts, opening the west, and commercial prosperity? We should hope such interests motivated the Founding Fathers. But we should expect the love of liberty and democracy motivated them as well, since what was more in their interests?

Both Beard and his detractors go right past the real point. No, the Founding Fathers didn't rise above interests. Rather, their interests marched comfortably with their society. They were revolutionaries all right, but not the familiar modern type, generally Marxists, who leave behind civil society and wage a violent, lifelong struggle to overthrow the existing order. The pleasures of Che Guevara's lifestyle had not yet been invented. Nor of course, did those pleasures turn out disinterested, since the main pleasure turned out having total power over everybody else and all their property.

The resumes of the fifty-five delegates to the Constitutional Convention reveal a conspicuous absence of decreed academics, professional philosophers, or public intellectuals. Yet they were not failed or insignificant men, but men of family, men of property, well educated, many professionals, successful in life, and comfortable with their society and the society of others. More than half were college graduates and thirty-three lawyers. One and all, they had long and wide experience in democratic institutions. Eight had signed the Declaration of Independence, seven had served as state governors, and thirty-nine as members of the Congress under the Articles. In their debates at the Convention, they exhibited neither unrealistic idealism nor contempt for established society, rather an acceptance of men as they were, a tolerance for the imperfectability of human nature, a willingness to compromise, and a desire to make progress where possible.

Contrast George Washington, who presided at the Convention, or James Madison, one of the most influential members, with those great, modern Marxist revolutionaries, Lenin, Stalin, and Mao. The Americans were already successful men before leading their revolution. They were comfortable with their society and its values. Lenin, Stalin, and Mao were all utter failures before seizing dictatorial powers and regarded the existing social order with contempt. Washington and Madison helped father a constitution that strengthened their society. As presidents, they were patient with others, tolerant of dissent, and made do with compromise. Lenin, Stalin, and Mao imposed constitutions that strengthened nothing but their own power. They never compromised on their power and silenced dissent by murdering the dissidents.

A gathering of bourgeoisie, you say? If bourgeoisie means sociable, normal, and successful in life, bring them on. If bourgeoisie means pragmatic and democratic, bring them on. In 1787, the Constitutional Convention brought them on. They brought on the sort of constitution you would expect such men to bring on.

5.02 – The Moving Finger

The U.S. Constitution is short, elegant, economical, and beautifully written. The original without later amendments runs to just around 4,500 words. It doesn't take that long to re-read, and it might not be a bad idea to set aside a national day each year to do just that, maybe as part of the annual Fourth of July celebrations. It wouldn't hurt to become more familiar with what the Constitution actually says, rather than with what we've heard it says. Except it wouldn't be enough to become more familiar with the words without becoming more familiar with their meanings. Except many of the words no longer mean what they originally meant or seemed to mean. Truth to tell, often they didn't say enough, and often what they said or seemed to say turned out inconvenient or even unworkable over time. So not only have more words been added with the constitutional amendments, but much of the original meaning of the words has been changed over time. So to understand the Constitution, we have to understand it as it has become. Re-reading the words just makes a good start.

"The moving fingers writes, and having writ, moves on, nor all your tears wash out a word of it." Some such thought goes a long way to explain mankind's enthusiasm for writing down their laws. People long for permanence in their lives, and written laws seem to offer permanence. "Now, O king, establish the decree, and sign the writing, that it be not changed, according to the law of the Medes and Persians, which altereth not." Hammurabi went to the length of carving his law code into a stone stele, which he erected in the marketplace for all to see, although probably few could read it. God handed the Ten Commandments to Moses on Mt. Sinai engraved in stone. "And the Lord delivered unto me two tables of stone written with the finger of God." The underlying idea seems that since the writing stays the same, writing down the laws makes them unchanging as well. In much this same way, Americans have always longed to regard their written Constitution as fixed and established once and for all (almost like sacred writ). "Other creeds have waxed and waned, but 'worship of the Constitution' has proceeded unabated."

But while you can't change what written by the dead hand of the past, although historians keep re-writing and revising history, what's written in the laws or a constitution can never be entirely clear or complete. For example, the 4th Amendment says, "The right of the people to be secure … against unreasonable searches and seizures, shall not be violated." But what exactly amounts to an "unreasonable search?" While at the same time, the moving finger keeps on writing ("the times they are a changing"), and so what originally written in the laws or the constitution can never hope to account for all the changes over time. When the 4th

Amendment was ratified back in 1791, no one anticipated the telegraph, the radio, the telephone, the cellphone, or the internet. How exactly did the right against unreasonable searches apply to these new technologies? Not only do the laws and the constitution require constant interpretation to clarify their meaning, but constant re-interpretation and even revision to adapt to the changing times. The Supreme Court has handed down dozens of cases on the 4th Amendment, clarifying and even changing the meaning.

With a written constitution, the Founding Fathers claimed a virtue for necessity. Their necessity was to bring forth a government with a single act of constitutional creation. The still unwritten English Constitution had evolved over time, but the Founding Fathers had to give birth. No practical way existed other than to promulgate a written constitution. But under "social contract theory," then a recent theory, they claimed a written constitution as a virtue. In many of life's most significant transactions, unless you can do business on a handshake, you can't do business. But when it comes to doing business, people reasonably want something more solid. They want a clear and binding written contract that guarantees their rights (their interests) under the contract. Social contract theory applied the same logic to government. Under the theory, writing down the people's rights in a constitution (in the social contract) would guarantee their rights (their interests under the contract). The moving finger having writ, there it would be, unchanging and permanent.

But what made the words in the Constitution near indelible was a corollary the Founders tacked onto the theory and an untried corollary at that. Back in Britain they had a social contract, too, embodied in their Constitution. But the British Constitution remained and remains unwritten, and Parliament could and can change it just by passing a law. But this untried corollary sought to make the words more permanent still. The Founders wanted a written contract that could only be changed by the people themselves, not just by their representatives in Congress. As *Federalist No. 53* said, "The important distinction so well understood in America between a constitution established by the people, and unalterable by the government; and a law established by the government, and alterable by the government, seems to have been little understood and less observed in any other country." The Founders wrote this "important distinction" into the Constitution. Article V provides that only the people can amend the Constitution, saying, "The Congress, whenever two thirds of both Houses shall deem it necessary, shall propose Amendments ... or, on the Application of the Legislatures of two thirds of the several states, shall call a Convention for purposing amendments, which, in either Case, shall be valid to all Intents and Purposes, when ratified by the Legislatures of three-fourths of the states, or by Conventions in three-fours thereof."

As so often with untried political theories, neither did this one work in practice as the theorists planned. It turned out near impossible to amend the Constitution by the formal process in Article V. But as already said, much of the original meaning of the words was far from clear, and over time, those same words had to stretch to try and cover a lot of unforeseen and changing circumstances. So through force of necessity, informal methods have largely replaced the formal method. The words in the Constitution have remained the same. But their original meaning has been constantly re-interpreted and changed by Congress, the president, and the Supreme Court. In this way, the Constitution has been constantly amended without admitting to the deed.

The moving finger may have writ. You may be able to read the words written in the Constitution. But over time, the original meaning of the words has been greatly changed. As Woodrow Wilson, our only president with a Ph.D. and that in political science, would later write, "The Constitution in operation is very different thing from the Constitution of the books." In these articles we next need to turn and try to understand "the Constitution in operation," as it has become.

5.03 – More Perfect

With the Constitution, the Founding Fathers reached as said in the Preamble for "a more perfect union." But your reach should exceed your grasp. They may not have grasped enough "perfect," but they did grasp a "union." No one should seriously want to relax that grip even today.

We can read the aspirations they reached for in the Preamble. "We the People of the United States, in Order to form a more perfect Union, establish Justice, insure domestic Tranquility, provide for the common defence, promote the general Welfare, and secure the Blessings of Liberty to ourselves and our Posterity, do ordain and establish this Constitution for the United States of America."

What more concretely were they trying to grasp? By a "more perfect Union" they meant a strong federal government, one with sufficient strength to attain all the other stated aspirations. To "establish justice" (the rule of law and protection for property), to "provide for the common defense" (against foreign enemies), to "insure domestic tranquility" (against insurrection and civil war), to "promote the general Welfare" (especially by creating a national marketplace), and to "secure the blessings of Liberty" (democracy and the rights of the people).

To see how crucial this "more perfect Union," imagine some alternative history. Imagine America had failed to ratify the Constitution, instead remaining a weak confederacy under the Articles of Confederation, the existing constitution from 1781 until superseded by the U.S. Constitution in 1789. This failure would have radically altered the national course and doubtful for a better destination. In real history, such national weakness invariably invites, really guarantees national calamities.

In the *Federalist No. 18*, Madison reviewed the actual historical record compiled by weak confederacies. "Among the confederacies of antiquity, the most considerable was that of the Grecian republics, associated under the Amphictyonic council. ... it bore a very instructive analogy to the present Confederation of the American States." That is, this ancient Greek confederacy had no more than a weak national government much like ours under the Articles of Confederation. He tells the result, "The more powerful members, instead of being kept in awe and subordination, tyrannized successively over all the rest." To resist the stronger members, the weaker members then called in foreign allies, Macedon and later Rome. Again, Madison tells the result, "they soon experienced, as often happens, that a victorious and powerful ally, is but another name for a master." The ancient Greeks soon lost their independence, first to the Macedonians and with finality to the Romans. Madison draws the obvious conclusion, "Had Greece ... been united by a stricter confederation, and persevered in her union, she would never have worn the chains of Macedon; and might have proved a barrier to the vast projects of Rome." Let Americans learn the object lesson and turn over the reverse side of that old adage "divide and conquer." Let them "unite and resist conquest."

But for the ratification of the Constitution, why would Americans not have suffered the same fate as the ancient Greeks? In the first federal census (1790), Virginia had a population of 747,610, while neighboring Delaware only 59,094. Massachusetts had 373,787, her neighbor Rhode Island only 68,825. What would have kept these two powerful states from tyrannizing over their weaker neighbors? Next, what would have kept Virginia and Massachusetts from turning on each other? As Madison notes, "Athens and Sparta ... became first rivals and then enemies." What would have kept the national regions from entering into hostile alliances against each other, which actually happened with the Civil War? What would have kept them from calling in foreign allies, as the Confederate States actually tried to call in Britain and France? Finally, what would have kept Britain or France from dominating over America like Macedon and Rome dominated over Greece? But for the Constitution, what would have kept Americans from re-losing their independence and ending up a subject people like the ancient Greeks?

The failure to grasp "a more perfect union" would have left a lot of other good things beyond our reach as well. Instead of a great national economy, we would have stayed thirteen small and rival economies. Already, some states had erected tariffs barriers against each other. Instead of speaking with one national voice in commercial negotiations, we would have continued to speak with thirteen discordant voices, letting foreign nations play off one against the other. Already, the states had begun to cut private deals for foreign trade, one state bidding against the other. As an added grief, some states suffered from internal discords and their own weak state governments, a combination friendly to civil strife and insurrection. Already, Shay's Rebellion in 1786 and 1787, an uprising of debtor farmers against their city creditors, had shaken Massachusetts.

Without "a more perfect union," America's alternative history would not have turned out the saga of a political giant, but diminished into a sorry tale about a race of quarrelsome, weak, and impoverished pygmies. Not able to get along among ourselves, not able to defend ourselves, not able to prosper ourselves, we would have lived out a stunted national existence. No doubt such a national history would have proved less offensive to others. America wouldn't have had the same weight to throw around. But it would have proved more offensive to ourselves. Rather than other nations having to put up with our bad manners, we would have had to put up with theirs. Justice Holmes said, "at bottom … however tempered by sympathy and all the social feelings, is a justifiable self-preference." In our alternative history, our justifiable self-preference would have been considerably tempered by the lack of sympathy and social feeling shown us by other nations.

Back in the days when they still gave eloquent speeches in the Senate and those speeches were widely reported and swayed public opinion, Daniel Webster gave the most famous speech of all. His "Second Reply to Hayne" (delivered on January 26, 1830) came at the height of an early crisis in the sectional conflict that would finally lead to the Civil War. Webster said, "I profess, Sir, in my career hitherto, to have kept steadily in view … the preservation of our Federal Union. It is to that Union we owe our safety at home, and our consideration and dignity abroad. It is to that Union that we are chiefly indebted for whatever makes us most proud of our country. That Union we reached only by the discipline of our virtues in the severe school of adversity. It had its origin in the necessities of disordered finance, prostrate commerce, and ruined credit. Under its benign influences, these great interests immediately awoke, as from the dead, and sprang forth with newness of life. Every year of its duration has teemed with fresh proofs of its utility and its blessings; … It has been to us all a copious fountain of national, social, and personal happiness."

How right silver-tongued Daniel was and still is. The Founders reached for "a more perfect Union." They may not have grasped enough "perfect," but they did grasp "a Union." We better not relax that grip (ever).

125

5.04 – Nothing If Not

The Constitution meant nothing if not a republic. As Alexander Hamilton wrote in *Federalist No. 39*, "The first question that offers itself is, whether the general form and aspect of the government be strictly republican? It is evident that no other form would be reconcilable with the genius of the people of America; with the fundamental principles of the revolution; or with that honorable determination, which animates every votary of freedom, to rest all political experiments on the capacity of mankind for self-government." That last word says it all – "self-government."

A republic is nothing more, but nothing less than what today more often called a representative democracy or simply democracy, where the people govern themselves through their elected representatives. As Hamilton wrote in *Federalist No. 70*, "The circumstances which constitute safety in the republican sense are, first a due dependence on the people, secondly a due responsibility." Above all else, a republican constitution must hold the government accountable to the people. The underlying axiom, proved by long and painful experience, is that unless the people can hold the officials of the government to "a due dependence" and "a due responsibility" (accountable), the people won't govern themselves. Rather, whoever can hold the government accountable will govern the people.

This axiom works the same as the distinction between being an owner and employee. An owner can run the business hopefully to his profit. An employee works in the business for the owner's profit. With accountable government, the people stand in the position of the owners and hopefully can run the government to their profit. The government officials stand in the position of their employees and work in the government for the people's profit. Otherwise, someone else stands in the position of owner and the people their employees. Who doubts which the better stand?

In a republic, the right to elect their representatives must stand as the people's most important right. Other than elections, no one has ever devised an effective mechanism to hold the government accountable (to "a due dependence on the people" or "a due responsibility"). Without elections, "safety in the republican sense" disappears and some other form of government appears. Above all other rights, a republican constitution must guarantee the right to vote.

It would be nice for a republic to guarantee all sorts of other nice rights, too, say such as the right to a jury trial, which the Constitution does in fact guarantee, in the 6th Amendment. But you can have a republic without jury trials and without all sorts of other nice rights, too. But you can't have a republic without the right to vote, since electing your representatives the only effective way to hold them accountable. Hopefully, with an accountable government, the people will guarantee themselves all sorts of other nice rights, too. Yet let's not get confused. Any so-called rights inconsistent with the fundamental right to "self-government" are inconsistent with a true republic.

Why did the Founders believe in a republic? First of all, they believed "self-government" simply a fundamental right. The Declaration of Independence proclaimed "self-evident [that] governments are instituted among men, deriving their just powers from the consent of the governed." For a second reason, they had faith as Hamilton just heard to say in "the capacity of mankind for self-government." But they didn't worship in blind faith. They believed all human history provided the proofs.

Speaking much later, a well-known political scientist would sum up these historical proofs in a list worth taking the time to quote, "1) Democracy helps prevent government by cruel and vicious autocrats. 2) Democracy guarantees … fundamental rights that nondemocratic systems do not, and cannot grant. 3) Democracy insures … a broader range of personal freedom than any feasible alternative … 4) Democracy helps people protect their fundamental interests. 5) Only a democratic government can provide a maximum opportunity for persons to exercise the freedom of self-determination – that is, to live under laws of their own choosing. 6) Only a democratic government can provide maximum opportunity for exercising moral responsibility. 7) Democracy fosters human development more fully than any feasible alternative. 8) Only a democratic government assures a relatively high-degree of political equality. 9) Modern representative democracies do not fight wars with one another. 10) Countries with democratic government tend to be more prosperous."

The Founding Father didn't express themselves in this same way (in the language of modern social and political science). But they expressed the same truths in the language of their day. But why were and are all these good things true? It was obvious then and should be obvious now. All these good things result directly from "self-government" (from accountability, from the "due dependence on the people" and the "due responsibility"). Elected officials can't get away with being "cruel and vicious autocrats." Under an elected government, the people will demand in their own interests "guarantees for fundamental rights, a broad range of personal freedom, protection for their fundamental interests, and the freedom of self-determination." At the same time, the people will live "under laws of their own choosing" and remain "morally responsible" for themselves and their government. All of which will "foster human development more fully and assure political equality." The people will be "more prosperous" because they will insist on their own prosperity and not let the officials turn the government into a kleptocracy. Finally, since wars cost the people's blood and money, the people won't like wars, at least not bloody and expensive ones.

As Chief Justice Marshall would later write in a famous case, "The Government of the Union then … is, emphatically and truly, a Government of the people. In form and in substance, it emanates from them. Its powers are granted by them, and are to be exercised directly on them, and for their benefit." The Constitution meant nothing if not a republic.

5.05 – All About the Power

The U.S. Constitution was all about the power. Above all, it was about "power to the people." The Preamble begins, "We the People … do ordain and establish this government." Since as the Declaration of Independence proclaims, governments must derive "their just powers from the consent of the governed," the people must possess the sovereign power (the ultimate power). They and no one else must "ordain and establish" the government. Nor with the Constitution did the people mean to surrender their sovereignty. By creating a republic (a representative democracy), they meant to retain the ultimate power (through "self-government"). Through keeping the government to "a due dependence on the people" and "a due responsibility," they meant to govern themselves rather than let someone else govern them.

This overriding concern for "power to the people" (for "self-government," for a "due dependence" and "due responsibility") dominates the constitutional structure. The institutions then conceived the most powerful (Congress and the presidency) were made dependent and responsible through elections. While originally the Senate wasn't elected directly, but through the state legislatures, and the president elected through the Electoral College, yet the same design applied, although incorporated in a two-tier structure. At the same time, the separation of powers divided the government into three connected institutions (the legislature, the executive, and judiciary), and the institution then conceived the most powerful of all (Congress, the legislature) was further subdivided against itself into two chambers, the House and the Senate. Under the theory, the institutions would check and balance each other, further contributing to a "due dependence" and "due responsibility" by preventing any branch from acquiring enough power to usurp the sovereignty of the people.

But however much the Constitution meant "power to the people," however much the people meant to retain their sovereignty (their ultimate power), finally they had to surrender quite a lot of power to the new federal government to have an effective government at all. And first of all, they surrendered a direct power over themselves. The prior national government under the Articles of Confederation couldn't act directly on the people, but only through the medium of the states. Alexander Hamilton observed in the *Federalist No. 15*, "The great and radical vice in the construction of the existing Confederation is in the principle of legislation for states or governments, in their corporate or collective capacities, and as contradistinguished from the individuals of whom they consist."

Why was that "the great and radical vice?" Because as a practical matter, the national government lacked any effective way to carry out the national laws. If a state didn't want to obey, no mechanism existed to force them short of civil war. But the new

Constitution remedied this vice. As Justice Sandra Day O'Conner would observe much later in a 1992 case, "In the end, the Convention opted for a Constitution in which Congress would exercise its legislative authority directly over individuals rather than over States; … In providing for a stronger central government, therefore, the Framers explicitly chose a Constitution that confers upon Congress the power to regulate individuals, not States."

Now the national laws applied directly to individuals, and if someone didn't want to do it, the federal government could force them. To give a crucial example, under the Articles of Confederation, the national government would direct the states to pay their share of the taxes, but a number of states neglected to send in the money, causing the national government to actually default on the national debt. But under the Constitution, the federal government could levy taxes directly on the people, and if someone didn't pay up, fine or imprison them.

This transfer of power took a huge chunk out of state sovereignty, as well as giving the new federal government a great deal of power over the people themselves. But the transformation wasn't over. The Constitution also gave the specifically "enumerated" (or "delegated") powers to the federal government. The main ones came under the following heads, First, the taxing power. ("Congress shall have the Power To lay and collect taxes.") Second, the spending power. ("Congress shall have the Power to pay the Debts and provide for the common Defense and general Welfare.") Third, the commerce power. ("To regulate Commerce with Foreign Nations, and among the several States.") Fourth, power over foreign relations. ("appoint Ambassadors … to make Treaties). Fifth, the war-making power. ("To declare War. To raise and support Armies. To provide and maintain a navy.") But less specifically, the Constitution went on and gave all the powers "necessary and proper" to carry out the specifically enumerated powers. ("To make all Laws which shall be necessary and proper for carrying into Execution the foregoing Powers, and all others Powers vested by this Constitution in the Government.")

What did all these powers amount to specifically? Would you believe that back then no one knew (specifically)? Because that would be the truth. For an instance, back in 1789 someone could have told you the taxing power meant the national government could pass a tariff on imports, but nobody could have told you for sure whether it had a power to impose an income tax, which not in contemplation. When in 1894, Congress did pass an income tax, a lot of people claimed the law unconstitutional as beyond the powers delegated to the national government. In a ruling too absurd to waste time discussing, the Supreme Court sided with them and held the income tax law unconstitutional. That was so out of whack with reality we actually managed to pass a constitutional amendment, the 16th Amendment, ratified in 1913, which says, "The Congress shall have the power to lay and collect taxes on incomes." Yet the incident serves to illustrate a truth we need to grasp. The Constitution had few specifics, and it left a lot for the future to sort out.

As an inevitable result and as Chief Justice John Marshall would write in a famous 1819 case, "But the question respecting the extent of the powers actually granted is perpetually arising, and will probably continue to arise so long as our system shall exist." And as that "question respecting the extent of the powers actually granted has perpetually arisen," the government has repeatedly answered the question in its own favor. The people are still sovereign, but "the extent of the government's powers" has greatly changed. Until today, the national government possesses a plentitude of powers never originally conceived.

But let's hasten to add that's not necessarily a bad thing and often has clearly been a good thing. The people have repeatedly asked the national government to take more power to do things the people wanted done. But whether good or bad, it's simply a fact that the national government has gradually acquired a great deal more power. To understand the Constitution as it has become, we need to turn to examine those national government powers as those have become.

5.06 – Montesquieu's Theorem

Back in high school civics class they taught us about the wonders of the "separation of powers" and the "system of checks and balances." They taught us about the separation between the

131

three branches, the legislature (Congress), the executive (the president), and the judiciary (the Supreme Court). They taught us how each checks the other, keeping any branch from gaining too much power, keeping any branch from growing despotic, thus keeping our liberty safe in the balance. But why didn't they teach us that such a separation of powers often keeps the government from acting at all or delays and obstructs action? Why didn't they teach us that liberty doesn't necessarily result from inaction, but often demands government action? As *Federalist No. 1* says, "the vigor of government is essential to the security of liberty."

Montesquieu, who lived 1699 to 1755, gets more credit than anyone else for this theorem about the separation of powers. In the *Federalist No. 47*, Madison both adopts his basic premise and gives him the credit, saying, "The accumulation of all powers legislative, executive, and judiciary in the same hands, … may justly be pronounced the very definition of tyranny. … The oracle who is always consulted and cited on this subject is the celebrated Montesquieu." But Madison wasn't the only one who bought into Montesquieu's theory. One political scientist counted up and discovered the Founding Fathers quoted him more than any book except the Bible.

Montesquieu lived in France under an absolutist monarchy. Casting his gaze no farther than across the English Channel, he saw the neighbors living under a constitutional monarchy, which looked highly preferable as a domestic arrangement to him. But being outside looking in, he somewhat mis-perceived the British household. He thought he saw a thoroughgoing separation of powers, and he thought this separation the central virtue to their constitution. In his great book, *The Spirit of the Laws* (published 1748), he turned these thoughts into his very influential theorem. But eventually, a great English journalist, Walter Bagehot, would publish a long overdue correction in his *The English Constitution*, 1867. Bagehot wrote, "It is laid down as a principle of the English polity [by such as Montesquieu], that in it the legislative, the executive and the judicial powers are quite divided … that no one of these can interfere with the work of the others." But Bagehot points out the exact opposite more nearly true, saying, "The efficient secret of the English Constitution may be described as the close union, the nearly complete fusion, of the executive and legislative powers."

We have only to look at the facts to prove that as usual the indigenous native (Bagehot) grasped the local customs better than the anthropologist (Montesquieu). Under the British Constitution, their monarch must appoint as prime minster the leader of the dominant party in the House of Commons. The prime minister then appoints the cabinet from among other members of the House Commons. So not only is there no separation between the executive branch (the prime minister and the cabinet) and the legislative branch (the House of Commons), but rather a "close union, the nearly complete fusion." Moreover, that's the "efficient secret of the English Constitution." A member of the House of Commons who wants to serve in the cabinet (their keenest ambition) has to stay in favor with the prime minister. While if the other members of his party (the backbenchers) vote against him on a key vote (a vote of confidence), his government falls, leading to an immediate new election. In other words, by voting against him, they vote themselves out of office. Needless to say, such an event rarely occurs. The system is "efficient" because the prime minister has the reins in his hands, if not the whip hand. He can drive both horses in tandem (the executive and legislative branches).

But our Founding Fathers bought into Montesquieu's theorem. They wrote the separation of powers into our Constitution. Nothing is more prominent in their words and deeds. As for their words, Madison said, "If there is a principle in our Constitution … more sacred than another, it is that which separates the Legislative, Executive and Judicial powers." As for their deeds, Article I creates the Congress, Article II the presidency, and Article III the courts. Each can check the others.

But does that create a balance in favor of liberty or merely amount to a formula for inaction? Since we know from hard and continual experience that action often frustrated, the theory can only work by presuming that liberty naturally emerges as a result of inaction. But "it ain't necessarily so." Without government, people often violate each other's liberty, and to protect their liberty often requires government action, not inaction. For a basic example, doesn't government have to act to protect our lives by passing and enforcing laws against murder and other violence? For another basic example, doesn't government have to act to protect our property against robbery, theft, and fraud? In fact, what liberty can exist without government action except the liberty of anarchy?

Back in the Founders' day, this basic truth looked less self-evident. For centuries, the chains of monarchy had bound down the people. They were bound by government action (bound down by the laws). It looked like if you just struck off their chains, the people would rise on their own to claim their liberty. And in those agrarian times, that image was more real. People being largely self-sufficient, they didn't need the government to lead, just to get the hell out of the way. But in today's highly complex, industrialized, digitalized, and interconnected society, that's not nearly as true. Today, we often need government action, not inaction. Being much more interdependent, we interfere with each other much more. We need much more government action to manage our interaction.

If the "close union, the nearly complete fusion" of the executive and legislature "describes" the "efficient secret" of the British Constitution, Montesquieu's theorem describes the not so secret cause for much of the inefficiency charged against the U.S. Constitution. The separation of powers often makes it very difficult for our government to work efficiently. That seems to be becoming more and more of a problem.

5.07 – A Legal Urban Legend

In law school the professors still talk about the "doctrine of enumerated powers" (or "delegated powers"). In their decisions, the Supreme Court still talks about the doctrine. But the talk isn't confined to the legal profession. The doctrine has passed into American folklore, becoming a legal urban legend. You often hear said that the federal government has only "limited powers" (only the powers "enumerated" or "delegated" by the Constitution). As long ago as the celebrated case of McColloch v Maryland in 1819, Chief Justice John Marshall wrote, "This Government is acknowledged by all to be one of enumerated powers. The principle that it can exercise only the powers granted to it … is now universally admitted." As late as another celebrated case in 2012, one of the Obamacare cases, Chief Justice John Roberts wrote, "In our federal system, the National Government possesses only limited powers." But like so many other urban legends, what started out based on some truth has become less and less true with each re-telling.

An early re-telling comes from that just mentioned and celebrated case from back in 1819 (McColloch v Maryland). At issue was the constitutionality of the Second Bank of the United States. In 1816, Congress had passed a law to incorporate this second national bank to replace the earlier First Bank of the United States, incorporated for twenty years by a congressional law in 1791, and which lapsed out of existence in 1811. But the Constitution fails to specifically enumerate (or delegate) a power to charter a national bank. Then was such a bank unconstitutional? Nope, ruled Chief Justice Marshall. Rather, he re-told the doctrine of enumerated powers. In his re-telling, the Constitution "implied" a great many other powers not specifically enumerated, including the power to create a national bank.

Here's his re-telling. He writes, "The first question made in the cause is – has Congress power to incorporate a bank?" Next, he states the doctrine of enumerated powers as already heard, "This Government is acknowledged by all to be one of enumerated powers. The principle that it can exercise only the powers granted to it … is now universally admitted." Next, he has to admit that the Constitution contains no specific enumeration of such a power, "Among the enumerated powers, we do not find that of establishing a bank or creating a corporation." Then it's beginning to look bad for the bank and incidentally for Congress. Just a literal re-telling of the doctrine of enumerated powers would leave Congress without such a power. Not only would the bank have gone out of existence as unconstitutional, but such a literal interpretation would have highly limited Congress, since not many powers are specifically enumerated in the Constitution.

But wait. Chief Justice Marshall hasn't finished re-telling the doctrine. Next, he writes, "Although, among the enumerated powers of Government, we do not find the word 'bank' or 'incorporation,' we find the great powers, to lay and collect taxes; to borrow money; to regulate commerce; to declare and conduct a war; and to raise and support armies and navies." Then he quotes "the necessary and proper clause" found in Article I, Sec. 8, which grants to Congress a further power, "To make all Laws which shall be necessary and proper for carrying into execution the foregoing powers and all other powers vested by this Constitution in the Government of the United States." So finally, in his retelling, Marshall can join the specifically enumerated powers with the power of "the necessary and proper clause." This lets him tell a different tale. His version finds "implied" in the Constitution all the powers "necessary and proper" to carry out the specifically "enumerated powers." In his own famous words, "Let the end be legitimate, let it be within the scope of the Constitution, and all means which are appropriate, which are plainly adapted to that end, which are not prohibited, but consistent with the letter and spirit of the Constitution, are Constitutional."

Thus, the Second Bank of the United States survived as constitutional, implied as an appropriate means to carry out the specifically enumerated powers. Thus, already back in 1819, the doctrine of enumerated powers had started to turn into a legal urban legend. It's not quite true. Literally, the doctrine said, "This Government is … one of enumerated powers. … the National Government possesses only limited powers." But what precisely defines (limits) "necessary and proper?" Nothing precisely (only "all means which are appropriate"). Then if nothing precisely limits "necessary and proper," what precisely limits the enumerated power? Nothing precisely. Nevertheless, the doctrine persists as a legal fiction. Yet it has been so continually re-told, and in these re-tellings has become so continually less and less true, that today it's harder and harder to find any truth at all in it.

Rather than re-telling this legal urban legend about the doctrine of enumerated powers and limited government, let's tell the truth. Today, the doctrine of enumerated powers limits almost nothing Congress wants to do. And let's tell another truth. That's not necessary a bad thing. After all, there are lots of things we need and want the government to do for us, and not all of these things are specifically enumerated in the Constitution. For example, do we think it would have been better for Congress to lack the power to create a national bank? Coming forward to today, how would we manage the monetary supply without the FED, the Federal Reserve Bank, our present national or central bank? The list of such examples goes on and on, where we needed and wanted the government to do something good for us, but no power was specifically enumerated in the Constitution. It's hard to say what bad things a literal telling might have prevented, but it's easy to point out many good things the constant re-tellings have permitted.

What limits a government from doing bad is seldom some doctrine (some theory) anyway. What limits them to doing good is nothing except effective accountability to the people. We don't want that ever to turn into a legal urban legend. As long our government stays accountable, it stays true to the Constitution in the most important and only really effective way.

5.08 – Senator Sherman's Bill

You've heard of General William Tecumseh Sherman, the Civil War general who said, "War is hell," and pretty much proved his point "marching through Georgia" to the sea in 1863. But General Sherman had a brother as distinguished, if not as well remembered. That would be Senator Charles Sherman (R-OH). After entering Congress in 1855, this other Sherman stayed in office for the next forty-three straight years until 1898. And in 1889, he filed a piece of legislation that would carry his own name to posterity as the Sherman Anti-Trust Act. In his speech from the floor of the Senate, he said, "If we will not endure a king as a political power, we should not endure a king over the production, transportation, and sale of any of the necessities of life. ... We should not submit to an autocrat of trade, with power to prevent competition and to fix the price of any commodity." What was his bill all about?

First, it was about monopoly, but second, it was about the federal government's power or lack thereof to "regulate commerce" under the Constitution. As for monopoly, that's where somebody or some entity manages to seize a vital slice of the economic pie. As Senator Sherman put it, where they can control "the production, transportation, and sale of any of the necessities of life," say for example, a commodity such as sugar. When they can manage that, they can become as Senator Sherman put it, "an autocrat of trade" and can "fix the price" (charge the public whatever the market will bear). While as for the federal government's power or lack thereof, the "commerce clause," in Article I, Sec. 8, says, "The Congress shall have Power ... to regulate Commerce … among the several States." Who won't agree that monopoly an evil, but does the "commerce clause" give the federal government the power to prevent it as part of "regulating commerce?"

Monopolies are nothing new. By the late Middle Ages, John D. Rockefeller's spiritual ancestors had already figured out the formula. Corner a market and name your price. While the public had already eaten enough monopoly price bread to figure out the profit margin stuck in their throats. By 1516, Sir Thomas More, that renowned "man for all seasons" and Chancellor of England, who so unfortunately lost his head in the matrimonial and religious squabbles of Henry VIII's reign, had advised in his *Utopia*, "Suffer not thies ryche men to bye vp all, to ingrosse and forstalle, and with theyr monoplye to kepe the market alone as please them."

Yet in writing the Constitution, the Founding Fathers gave absolutely no thought to monopoly and for very a good reason. In their day, economic activity was highly localized, leaving any monopoly no more than a local matter for state rather than federal regulation. But as industrialization gathered steam after the Civil War, monopolies suddenly started to emerge on a national scale and in more virulent form. At the same time as the new factories churned out a mass production, the new railroads linked them together into national networks. These altered conditions fostered the rise of "the trusts," gargantuan, nationwide monopolies, such as Rockefeller's Standard Oil, Carnegie's U.S. Steel, the Southern Pacific Octopus in railroads, the Sugar Trust, the Whiskey Ring, the Big Four in meatpacking, the list goes on.

The world had never seen anything quite like it. The shrewdness, tenacity, and wealth, not to mention ruthlessness of the titans of business who forged these mega-firms makes up not a small part of the legend of all-out American capitalism. Their dynamic personalities propelled them toward monopoly, a dominant trait being the passion to stand triumphant upon a stricken economic field, all rivals bankrupt at their feet. On one hand, here was creative destruction hurled on a gigantic canvas, driving technology and business methods to dizzying heights, generating amazing production and stupendous wealth. On the other hand, it was Scrooge before his memorable Christmas conversion, "a tight-fisted hand at the grindstone ... squeezing, wrenching, grasping, scraping, clutching, covetous." Their defenders argued they brought efficiency and economies of scale to the marketplace. Their detractors countered that their main efficiency was gouging profits at the expense of consumers.

Increasingly, the latter description better fit the spectacle. If this was the survival of the fittest, perhaps it was time to think about revising the laws of the economic jungle, which brings us back to Senator Sherman's bill. When finally passed in 1890, it would carry his name to posterity as the Sherman Anti-Trust Act and outlawed monopolies. It declared that, "Every contract, combination in the form of trust or otherwise, or conspiracy, in restraint of trade or commerce among the several States, or with foreign nations, is hereby declared illegal ... Every person who shall monopolize, or attempt to monopolize any part of the trade or commerce among the several States, or with foreign countries, shall be guilty of a misdemeanor."

But what about the Constitution? Did Senator Sherman's new law exceed the powers delegated to Congress? He didn't neglect to address this concern in his speech, saying, "I believe this bill is clearly within the power conferred expressly upon Congress to regulate commerce with foreign nations and among the several States. ... Can it be with this vast power (over commerce) Congress cannot protect the people from combinations in restraint of trade ... ? It may 'regulate commerce;' can it not protect commerce, nullify contracts that restrain commerce, turn it from its natural course, increase the price of articles, and therefore diminish the amount of commerce?"

He was referring to the already mentioned "commerce clause" in Article I, Sec. 8, which as already quoted reads, "The Congress shall have Power ... to regulate Commerce ... among the several States." Although the Constitution nowhere specifically mentions any power for Congress to regulate or outlaw monopolies, was Senator Sherman right? Did the "commerce clause" imply such a power?

Perhaps rather surprisingly, in a few short years the Supreme Court would rule Senator Sherman had been wrong, and Congress lacked the power to outlaw monopolies. This ruling would come in 1895 in the E.C. Knight Case, which involved the "sugar trust" (a/k/a, the American Sugar Company). In 1890 at the time of the passage of the Sherman Act, American Sugar produced and sold about 65 percent of the nation's sugar. By 1892, their directors had arranged to buy four other sugar companies (E.C. Knight, Franklin, Spreckels, and Delaware), which produced and sold another 33 percent of the total sugar, leaving nobody out of the ring except little ole Revere up in Boston with a minuscule 2 percent share. With 98 percent control, American Sugar would have affected a corner on refined sugar in the United States. Having destroyed (absorbed) the competition, the monopoly could have set and raised the price. But the administration of President Grover Cleveland filed suit to bust the trust under the provisions of the Sherman Act.

Unfortunately for the fate of Senator Sherman's bill, the Supreme Court very narrowly read "the commerce clause" and so very narrowly construed the federal government's power to regulate commerce under it. Justice Melvin Weston Fuller wrote, "The argument is that the power to control the manufacture of refined sugar is a monopoly over a necessary of life, to the enjoyment of which by a large population of the United States interstate commerce is indispensable, and that, therefore, the general government in the exercise of the power to regulate commerce may repress such monopoly." Indeed, that's the argument we just heard from Senator Sherman, deducing from the "commerce clause" congressional authority to regulate monopolies. However, Justice Fuller has only stated the argument to reject the logic.

To do so, he draws a distinction between "commerce" and "manufacture." He writes, "Doubtless the power to control the manufacture of a given thing involves in a certain sense the control of its disposition, but this is a secondary and not the primary sense; and although the exercise of that power may result in bringing the operation of commerce into play, it does not control it, and affects it only incidentally and indirectly. Commerce succeeds manufacture and is not a part of it." By his logic, since "manufacture" isn't "commerce," Congress lacked the power to regulate or outlaw the monopoly under "the commerce clause."

Of course, this distinction made absolutely no sense in the real world. If a company that produces and sells 98 percent of the refined sugar isn't engaged in commerce, then who is? The answer was almost nobody. As a result, the federal government's power to regulate the economy through "the commerce clause" amounted to almost nothing either. If they couldn't regulate an outfit as big as American Sugar, they couldn't regulate much else either. But the story didn't end there. However, we've run out of space and need to go onto the next article for the next episode in the history of the commerce clause.

5.09 – Farmer Filburn's Wheat

When you read a constitutional law textbook, you notice something when you come to the part about "the commerce clause." First, there's a chapter titled something like "the pre-1937 cases." Next, there's a chapter titled something like "the commerce cases from 1937." Why? In that year, the words in "the commerce clause" didn't change, but their meaning changed abruptly, dramatically, and forever. The federal government's power as abruptly and dramatically expanded forever. The textbook probably won't mention that in this same year (1937), President Franklin D. Roosevelt threatened the Supreme Court with his famous or infamous "court packing plan." To understand how the one relates to the other requires some background.

In the last article, we saw the Sherman Anti-Trust Act of 1890 meant to outlaw monopoly. We heard Senator John Sherman, who sponsored the law, argued that Congress had the power under "the commerce clause" to pass such a law. That clause says, "The Congress shall have Power ... to regulate Commerce with foreign Nations, and among the several States." But in just a few short years (in 1895 in the E.C. Knight Case), we heard the Supreme Court rule Senator Sherman was in error. The judges said that "manufacture" wasn't "commerce." They said that a company (American Sugar) manufacturing and selling 98 percent of the refined sugar in the country was engaged only in "manufacture" and not "commerce." And so, they ruled that the federal government lacked any power under the commerce clause to outlaw the monopoly. Obviously, that was a totally unrealistic definition of "commerce." Just as obviously, that left almost all the economy outside the feds' power to regulate as commerce. If they couldn't regulate a company as big and pervasive as American Sugar, what could they regulate?

But in only a few short decades in 1929, the country fell into the crisis of the Great Depression. To get out and stay out, most of the experts as well as most of the public seemed to agree the government would need to regulate the economy a whole lot more in future. In the presidential election of 1932, Franklin D. Roosevelt was swept into office on a pledge to do just that with his New Deal. In the hundred days after his election, Congress helped him redeem this pledge by passing a record number of laws regulating the economy. These laws fall outside our story. All we need to know is that the Supreme Court between 1933 and 1937 declared virtually all of these New Deal laws unconstitutional. Using their old, narrow, unrealistic definition of the commerce clause, the justices kept ruling Congress lacked the power to pass laws to regulate the economy.

But the justices not only badly miscalculated the demands on government made by a modern economy, they badly misjudged their man. Their rulings trapped both the economy and the president in a hopeless situation. They had left the economy adrift like a ship without a rudder on a stormy sea. They had left the president like the captain on the quarterdeck of his burning ship, but forbidden to touch the wheel or adjust the sails, not able to do anything except hope the ship somehow drifted safe into harbor. Roosevelt wasn't a man so easily discharged from his command.

In 1937, he turned the tables on the justices, attacking them with his famous or infamous "court packing plan." For a long time, nine justices had sat on the Supreme Court, but the Constitution doesn't fix the number, leaving that to Congress. Roosevelt proposed adding a new justice to the Court for every justice over seventy who didn't retire. For all the savage criticism heaped on him before and since, Roosevelt's convinced his severest critics. Suddenly sensing their own powers in peril, the justices abruptly did "the switch in time that saved nine." Somewhat ignominiously, they "switched." They started automatically approving New Deal laws exactly like the ones they had previously declared unconstitutional. By so doing, they raised the white flag and "saved nine" as the number of justices on the Court. Roosevelt accepted their surrender, and the plan to add new judges withered away in

Congress.

Fundamental to their retreat, the Court abruptly abandoned their old, narrow definition of the commerce clause. Instead, they changed the meaning into an almost unlimited power for the feds to regulate. In 1937 in the Jones & Laughlin Case, Chief Justice Charles Evans Hughes wrote, "The fundamental principle is that the power to regulate commerce is the power to enact 'all appropriate legislation' for its 'protection or advancement' .... Although activities may be intrastate in character when separately considered, if they have such a close and substantial relation to interstate commerce that their control is essential or appropriate to protect that commerce from burdens and obstructions, Congress cannot be denied the power to exercise such control."

Thus, the definition of "interstate commerce" changes abruptly and forever. From that day to this, if "activities" have "a close and substantial relation to interstate commerce" and cause "burdens and obstructions," Congress can regulate under the commerce clause. It only need be added as immediately became clear that a "burden," or an "obstruction," required no more than a touch. In future, this horse would run with reins loose on its neck.

This looser definition immediately revived the Sherman Anti-Trust Act, which we earlier saw virtually done to death. Now the federal government could outlaw monopolies. But it went much further. Perhaps in 1942, Wickard v Filburn reached the outer limits. That case held the feds had the power to prevent a farmer (Filburn) from growing wheat for personal consumption by his family. Justice Jackson reasoned, "But even if [a farmer's] activity be local and though it may not be regarded as commerce, it may still, whatever its nature, be reached by Congress if it exerts a substantial economic impact on interstate commerce." If Farmer Filburn's activity fits that description, what more need be said? Before the feds could regulate almost nothing under the commerce clause, but now they could regulate almost anything under it.

Then once again, the Constitution changed, and once again, the federal government acquired a great deal more power. But if there's a downside to giving the government more power over our lives, there's often also an upside. It's hard to imagine how we can run a modern economy without a great deal of government regulation.

5.10 – The Turn of the Screw

No doubt you heard about the recent Supreme Court case over Obamacare. Actually, there've been several, the reference being to the first one handed down. You may recall that case challenged the constitutionality of the Obamacare law. You know that law was all about health care and insurance coverage, and you may also recall the Court upheld the law as constitutional under the congressional power to tax. That may have left you wondering what health care and insurance had to do with taxes. But the case was no more than the latest turn of the screw. Over the course of our history, the federal government has tightened down on us their constitutional power to tax until the power goes way beyond taxation.

Alexander Hamilton says in *Federalist No. 30*, "Money is with propriety considered as the vital principle of the body politic; as that which sustains its life and motion, and enables it to perform its most essential functions. A complete power therefore to procure a regular and adequate supply of it … may be regarded as an indispensable ingredient in every constitution." In other words, as he goes on to say in *No. 31*, "the Federal government must of necessity be vested with an unqualified power of taxation in the ordinary modes."

But where does or should the power to tax end or does it? We begin to see the importance of the question when we recall what Chief Justice Marshall observed so long ago, again in the 1819 case of McColloch v Maryland, "the power to tax involves the power to destroy." For an example in the law books, in 1902 Congress raised the tax on oleomargarine so high as to price the product out of the market. Not really a tax to raise revenue, this law was passed at the behest of the dairy industry, whose butter competed with the artificial product. In other words, Congress meant to destroy the business of manufacturing oleomargarine. Nevertheless, the Supreme Court upheld the tax as constitutional in 1904, in the case of McCray v United States.

What are the limits on taxation written in the Constitution? As usual, that question led to some controversy. The Constitution says only a couple things about taxation. Article I, Sec. 8 says, "The

Congress shall have the Power To lay and collect Taxes ... to ... provide for the common Defence and general Welfare of the United States." Since "general welfare" can mean just about anything, you could construe those words as giving the federal government a virtually unlimited power to tax. But the counter-argument went that the words gave only a much more limited power, that Congress could only tax to carry out the enumerated powers (those specifically granted). In the early days of the Republic, Alexander Hamilton, being a Federalist and so a strong advocate for a strong national government, argued for the wider view of the taxing power. James Madison, having gone over to the Jeffersonian Republicans and so being obsessed with limiting the national government's power as long as the Federalist controlled the national government, which they initially did, argued for the narrower view.

In a much later Supreme Court case (the Butler Case in 1936), Justice Owen Roberts, writing the opinion for the Court, summed up this early controversy and ruled for Hamilton's view (for a broader taxing power). He wrote, "Since the foundation of the Nation, sharp differences of opinion have persisted as to the true interpretation of the phrase. Madison asserted it amounted to no more than a reference to the other powers enumerated in the subsequent clauses of the same section; that, as the United States is a government of limited and enumerated powers, the grant of power to tax and spend for the general national welfare must be confined to the enumerated legislative fields committed to the Congress. ... Hamilton, on the other hand, maintained the clause confers a power separate and distinct from those later enumerated, is not restricted in meaning by the grant of them, and Congress consequently has a substantive power to tax and to appropriate, limited only by the requirement that it shall be exercised to provide for the general welfare of the United States."

As said, Justice Roberts rules for the broader (Hamiltonian) view, although he does go on to say, "But the adoption of the broader construction leaves the power to spend subject to limitations." However, we might wonder where to find such "limitations" since none specifically mentioned. While by the time of the Obamacare case in 2012, any limitations appear largely imaginary.

Obamacare (the Patient Protection and Affordable Care Act) meant to expand health insurance coverage to everyone. As part of that, the Act required everyone to buy insurance or pay a penalty in the form of a tax to the IRS. But where does the Constitution enumerate (or delegate) a power to Congress to pass such a law, forcing people to buy insurance? Perhaps surprisingly, the Court upheld the law under the taxing power. In his opinion, Chief Justice Roberts writes, "The Federal Government does not have the power to order people to buy health insurance. ... The Federal Government does have the power to impose a tax on those without health insurance." In other words, they can't order you to do it, but can punish you for not doing it. We might feel that's a distinction without a difference.

However that may be, we should see the taxing power has become a very great power. The celebrated doctrine of a government limited to enumerated powers has suffered another erosion. Way beyond any enumerated powers, the feds can tax you "for the general welfare," whatever that may be. They can ban your product like oleomargarine. They can force you to buy a product like insurance. What can't they do by merely calling it a tax?

As a footnote, Article I goes on to say, "No Capitation, or other direct tax, shall be laid." There was a controversy over those few words as well. In 1895, in a decision too absurd to take the time to discuss in detail, the Supreme Court managed to construe these words in such a way as to strike down as unconstitutional an income tax law recently passed by Congress. That ruling was so ridiculous the country managed to ratify a constitutional amendment and overrule the Court. The 16th Amendment (1913) says, "The Congress shall have the power to lay and collect taxes on incomes from whatever source derived." So much for that. As we all become very much aware every year come April 15, the feds now have the power to collect income taxes.

Let's recall that old slogan from the American Revolution, "No Taxation Without Representation." Today, that about sums up the only real limitations left on the fed's power to tax. The limits aren't written in the Constitution, but the ballot box can still set some limits. As Chief Justice Marshall wrote in 1819, again in McCulloch v. Maryland, "the only security against the abuse of this power is found in the structure of the government itself. In imposing a tax, the legislature acts upon its constituents. This is, in general, a sufficient security against erroneous and oppressive taxation." We better hope that's "sufficient security," since that's the only real security left.

5.11 – The Best Money

No power belongs more exclusively to a democratic legislature than "the power of the purse." Very early in English history the legal principle appeared that the king could not tax except through Parliament. As the centuries rolled on, the Parliament gradually leveraged this power, gradually forcing more concessions from the king in return for raising more revenue. But giving into parliamentary demands whenever short of funds, a rather frequent occurrence, grew as gradually more irksome to the kings, who were as gradually losing more power to Parliament. Eventually in the middle 1600s, the Stuart monarchs tried to rebel against this legal principle. But the Parliament rebelled in turn, rallied the nation behind the principle, and finally broke the king's power instead once and for all with the Glorious Revolution of 1688. In their turn, later the American colonies would rally around the same principle ("no taxation with representation"), using it to the same good effect.

No wonder, then, the Constitution carefully reserves the power of the purse to Congress. As Madison wrote in *Federalist No. 58*, "They [the House of Representatives] in a word hold the purse; that powerful instrument by which we behold in the history of the British constitution, an infant and humble representation of the people, gradually enlarging the sphere of its activity and importance, and finally reducing, as far as it seems to have wished, all the overgrown prerogatives of the other branches of the government. This power over the purse, may in fact be regarded as the most complete and effectual weapon with which any constitution can arm the immediate representatives of the people, for obtaining a redress of every grievance, and for carrying into effect every just and salutary measure."

But there's a tendency to think about "the power of the purse" only in terms of taxation (as raising revenue). But taxation only fills the purse, and "the best money is spent money" (spent to buy what you want). Then let's not forget "the spending power" (the power to spend the tax revenues to buy what Congress wants). And Congress has often wanted to spend the money to acquire still more power for itself and the federal government.

If the power to tax is a huge power, the same goes for the power to spend. Just as the feds have leveraged the taxing power, they have leveraged the spending power to acquire still more power. By now, people should know only too well how the feds play this game. In that other version of the golden rule, whoever has the gold makes the rules. The feds have the gold through taxation, so they make the rules through spending. Congress dangles a pot of federal gold in front of the greedy eyed states. To reach into the pot, they have to agree to play the game by the feds' rules. Otherwise, the feds take their ball and go home. Since the states can't resist the carrot, they take the stick. Not only has this game become gradually more and more widely played, the feds' rules have gradually given them more and more power over the states and the people.

For a routine example, back in 1939, Congress passed a law that the states had to administer all federally funded programs through a civil service (not a patronage) bureaucracy. The feds, in effect, forced the states to change their prior bureaucratic practices, since most state agencies received some federal funding. Rather than hiring and firing their state employees on a patronage (a partisan) basis, they were forced to convert to a civil service system, where theoretically, the bureaucrats are hired and promoted on merit and fired only for cause. Nothing in the Constitution gave the federal government any such power over the states. The feds leveraged their spending power to acquire more power over the states.

For another more recent example, take Medicaid. As Justice John Roberts wrote in a recent case, "Enacted in 1965, Medicaid offers federal funding to States to assist pregnant women, children, needy families, the blind, the elderly, and the disabled in obtaining medical care. … In order to receive that funding, States must comply with federal criteria governing matters such as who receives care and what services are provided at what cost. By 1982 every State had chosen to participate in Medicaid. Federal funds received through the Medicaid program have become a substantial part of state budgets, now constituting over 10 percent of most States' total revenue." Nothing in the Constitution specifically gave the feds the power to regulate the medical services offered by the states in such minute detail. But by leveraging the spending power, they have acquired the power to regulate the states down to the minutest detail.

Now remember, under the doctrine of enumerated powers as stated by the Supreme Court, "This Government is acknowledged by all to be one of enumerated powers. The principle that it can exercise only the powers granted to it ... is now universally admitted." Further, "In our federal system, the National Government possesses only limited powers." But when it comes to "the spending power," the Supreme Court ruled in a recent case in 2012, "when Congress acts under the Spending Clause, ... Congress can use that power to implement federal policy it could not impose directly under its enumerated powers."

Well, doesn't that seem like the Court talking out of both sides of its mouth at once? The feds have only their enumerated (limited) powers, but when acting under the spending clause, they're not limited by their enumerated powers. Then what exactly limits their spending power? The Supreme Court has also said Congress can't "coerce" the states. But what would specifically amount to "coercion" has never been defined. Rather, as a noted political scientist has said, "the Court has seemingly found no area in which Congress might not spend its way around what would otherwise be the constitutional prerogatives of state power." So once again, the federal government has acquired more power.

The best money is spent money (to buy what you want). The feds have often spent their money to buy more power. That's what they wanted. But also once again, that may not be a bad thing, but a good thing. The feds may have used their greater power in the public good. Maybe forcing a civil service system on the states was a good reform. Most people seem to support Medicaid. But whether good or bad, the Constitution has changed. The feds have a lot more power under the spending clause than back at the start.

5.12 – Down Mexico Way

"South of the border, done Mexico way," the rules change. Behavior not tolerated this side of the border may pass on the other side, which why Americans wanting to go on a party have been known to head for the border. It's the same with the U.S. Constitution. Outside our borders, the rules change, and the U.S. government can get away with behavior not tolerated inside the borders. Why and how do the rules change?

The rules change because the borders mark the limit of U.S. sovereignty (a government's full powers). Across that line, our laws don't run. A nation's laws cover only their part of the map. The only global law is international law, a far from a complete code and notoriously lacking effective law enforcement mechanisms. International "laws are like cobwebs, which may catch small flies, but let wasps and hornets break through." A lone individual being a "small fly," occasionally you see someone caught in the web of international law. The International Tribunal, which sits in the Hague, tried Slobodan Milosovic, the former prime minister of Serbia, for war crimes under international law, a trial lasting some five years from 2001 to 2006 and ending without a verdict when Milosovic died in prison. But such trials are rare, since nation states tend to shield their nationals from international law. And the nation states themselves like the "wasps and hornets break through." Between nations the rule is still *force majeure* (the rule of superior force). As long ago said, "You know as well as we do that right, as the world goes, is only in question between equals in power, while the strong do what they can and the weak suffer what they must."

Across the border, the U.S government confronts a constant if undeclared war of all against all between nation states. Nations constantly strive to gain an advantage over other nations, either by gaining a strategic advantage or some commercial advantage. This striving can easily lead to armed hostilities and occasionally escalates into open warfare. Hiding amidst the confusion, petty and not so petty criminals constantly try to pull off and get away with their crimes such as smuggling drugs, hacking computers, or committing terrorist acts.

With what powers does the U.S. Constitution arm the U.S. government facing outward toward this lawless combat zone? Remember that oft stated constitutional rule, "This Government is acknowledged by all to be one of enumerated powers. The principle that it can exercise only the powers granted to it … is now universally admitted." Forget that. The rule changes at the borders. In a 1936 case the Supreme Court said, "The broad statement that the federal government can exercise no powers except those specifically enumerated in the Constitution, and such implied powers as are necessary and proper to carry into effect the enumerated powers, is categorically true only in respect to our internal affairs. … the federal power over external affairs [is] in origin and essential character different from that over internal affairs." In other words, across the borders, the U.S. government's powers aren't so limited.

What is "the origin and essential character" of "the federal power over external affairs?" The "origin" comes from the overriding necessity for self-preservation (for national survival). We have to defend ourselves by carrying out diplomacy, and if need be, with armed force. The "essential character" of such a power is whatever required for the mission. Then do any limits exist? No, not really. Congress has sometimes passed laws saying the president or the military can't do something outside the borders. The Constitution says that Congress may "make Rules for the Government and Regulation of the land and Naval forces," and the U.S military serves under a code of military justice, prohibiting such things as torturing or killing prisoners of war. But "all's fair in love and war," and this is war, even if usually undeclared. What's more remarkable than the few rules is the general lack of rules when push comes to shove.

For a prominent instance of how the rules change at the borders, back in 2011, a team of U.S. Navy Seals terminated with extreme prejudice Osama bin Laden in Abbottabad, Pakistan. In the years before and since, the U.S. military has taken out quite a few terrorists with drone strikes in various locations. But all this lethal activity happened outside the borders. Inside the borders, a terrorist might have the misfortune to get killed in a shootout, but one who throws down his weapon, holds up his hands, and surrenders suffers a less drastic fate. The officers can't summarily execute him, rather he has a right to all the panoply of due process and a jury trial with lawyers appointed at the public expense no less, if he's indigent. The rules change at the borders.

We could stretch the list of how the rules change to some length. But the exercise wouldn't help us to sketch some bright line, limiting the government's powers outside the borders. Not only that, the U.S. government's powers facing outside can sometimes migrate back inside, giving the government more power inside our borders. During the Korean War in 1952, a labor strike threatened to shut down the nation's steel production. To prevent that, President Harry Truman issued an executive order to the Secretary of Commerce (a guy named Sawyer) to take over and run most of the steel mills. Nothing in the "enumerated powers" gave the president such a power. What was Truman's reasoning? He argued that steel production was essential to the manufacture of weapons and other war materials and a work stoppage would jeopardize the war effort. In other words, he argued his powers outside the country to wage war gave him a power inside the country to seize the steel mills. In this particular case the Supreme rebuffed him (in Youngtown Steel and Tube v Sawyer), ruling he'd gone too far, since Congress hadn't authorized the action. But notice that didn't say the government couldn't seize the steel mills for national security reasons, only that Congress would need to authorize such a step.

As Justice Frankfurter noted in concurring, "Congress has frequently – at least 16 times since 1916 – specifically provided for executive seizure of production, transportation, communication, or storage facilities." He was referring to the numerous instances during World Wars I and II. For example, the Lever Food and Fuel Control in 1917, during World War I, gave the president the power to regulate the import, manufacture, mining, storage, and distribution of necessary commodities; to requisition food, feed, and fuel; to take over and operate factories, packing houses, pipe lines, and mines; to fix a minimum price for wheat; and to fix the price of coal and to regulate the production, sale, and distribution.

As a matter of constitutional fact, the much less limited powers of the government outside our borders can migrate back inside, giving it much more power. While there's still another way the government's power facing outside can result in more power facing inside. The Constitution provides the president "shall have the Power, by and with the Advice and Consent of the Senate, to make Treaties." Further, "all Treaties made ... shall be the Supreme Law of the Land." Then what limits the government's power to make "the supreme law of the land" (American law) by making treaties?

As an example, back in 1916, the U.S. and Great Britain entered into a treaty to protect the migratory birds flying back and force across the U.S. and Canadian borders. To carry out the treaty, Congress passed the Migratory Bird Treaty Act of 1918, protecting the birds. That law led to the well-known case of Missouri v Holland in 1920. In the case, the state of Missouri argued the treaty and the law invaded that state's sovereignty, since the Constitution enumerated no power for Congress to regulate on the topic. But the Supreme Court ruled the government had the power. The opinion by Justice Holmes carefully refrained from drawing any bright lines. The closest he comes is to say, "the question is whether the United States is forbidden to act." Then the government is not limited in making treaties by the enumerated powers. It is only limited were it "is forbidden to act" by some specific prohibition in the Constitution. Then, for example, the government presumably couldn't enter into a treaty that abrogated religious toleration or freedom of speech. But you can't cite many such specific limitations.

To see how far our obligations under a treaty might carry us, let's come back to President Truman and the Korean War. The Constitution says, "Congress shall have the Power ... To declare War." But Korea was an undeclared war. How was it legal under the Constitution? One argument made was based on the treaty making power. After North Korea invaded South Korea in 1950, the U.N. Security Council passed a resolution for U.N. member states to provide military forces to throw back the North Koreans. The U.S. was a member of the U.N. through our treaty obligations. Therefore, this argument went, the treaty authorized the U.S. government to enter the war without any declaration of war by Congress.

"Across the border, down Mexico way," the rules change and for very good reasons. The U.S. government has far more power across than within our borders. Those greater powers on the outside sometimes given them greater powers inside. Where does it all end? Nobody knows for sure.

5.13 – The Foreign Policy Coach

A Russian supposedly pointed out a troika (a three-horse sleigh) to a friend who doubted the doctrine of the Holy Trinity. "See, the Holy Trinity is just like a troika, the Father, the Son, and the Holy Ghost, three horses pulling the same sleigh at the same time." The doubtful friend wasn't convinced. "To show me the Holy Trinity, you'll have to show me the same man sitting in three sleighs at the same time." How the separation of powers pulls the coach of American foreign policy isn't open to such doubt. It's like we have three coachmen all striving to drive the same coach at the same time. The president may have the reins, but Congress has a brake and sometimes tries to grab the reins, while the political parties constantly backseat drive. It's a wonder how it goes down the road as well as it does.

On its face, the Constitution divides the power over foreign policy between the president and Congress, and where the presidents and Congress are involved, you can reliably expect the political parties to get involved, too. It makes the president the commander-in-chief, but leaves most of his commands dependent on Congress's funding. He has the authority to "make treaties," but only with the "advice and consent of the Senate," a two-thirds majority being required to ratify. So on its face, the Constitution sets up an interface between the president and Congress, which further interface along party lines. These three drivers often turn a hostile face toward each other, often making for a rough and rocky ride, sometimes threatening to career off the road altogether.

No better example exists than the lurching course our foreign policy went down between the World Wars. With President Woodrow Wilson driving, we had finally galloped full speed ahead into World War I. But after our late arrival snatched the Allies (Britain and France) back from the brink, Congress suddenly applied the brakes. Completely reversing President Wilson's course, they uncoupled from our allies, unhitched the horses, and put the coach back in the barn. We demobilized and refused to join the League of Nations. Even when World War II started looming down the road, Congress stubbornly kept their foot on the brake and constantly tugged at the reins. President Franklin Roosevelt was trying to steer through a treacherous landscape strewn with boulders and precipices all around. But they kept interfering, and we almost went off the brink ourselves.

Way back in 1796 with his Farewell Address, George Washington had warned against foreign and especially European entanglements. "It is our true policy to steer clear of permanent alliances with any portion of the foreign world. ... Europe has a set of primary interests which to us have none; or a very remote relation. Hence she must be engaged in frequent controversies, the causes of which are essentially foreign to our concerns. Hence, therefore, it must be unwise in us to implicate ourselves ... in the ... combinations and collisions of her friendships or enmities. Our detached and distant situation invites and enables us to pursue a different course. ... Why forego the advantages of so peculiar a situation? Why quit our own to stand upon foreign ground? Why, by interweaving our destiny with that of any part of Europe, entangle our peace and prosperity in the toils of European ambition, rivalship, interest, humor or caprice?"

Per usual, George's advice made eminent common sense, and going forward, the central tenet for American foreign policy became "isolation" from Europe. Behind the "distant situation" of the Atlantic and Pacific Oceans, we pursued our "primary interests" on this continent. In 1803, we acquired the Louisiana Purchase; in 1823 we declared the Monroe Doctrine, warning the Europeans to stay on their side of the ocean; in 1846-48 we fought the Mexican-American War to acquire still more territory. But even in this early era, the other party tended to oppose the president on foreign policy. For an example, in his lone term in Congress (1847-49), Abraham Lincoln (then a Whig) gave his "show me the spot speech," attacking the justification offered by President James K. Polk (a Democrat) for declaring war on Mexico. Nor did we even firmly adhere to our isolation. In 1812, President James Madison (a Democrat-Republican) somewhat stumbled into a war with Great Britain. Despite the Battle of New Orleans, we got pretty soundly thumped for our trouble, the British even burning Washington, D.C. Once again, the party-out-of-power (this time, the Federalist) assailed the president's foreign policy, going so far as to threaten secession in some New England states.

During the latter part of the nineteenth century, "the advantages of so peculiar a situation" began to erode, eaten away by steam technology. About as rapidly as the railroad linked the nation more tightly, the steamship linked the nation more tightly to the wider world. People might lament the passing of the romance of sail, but sailing ships were obsolete. People might cling to isolationism, but such a foreign policy was becoming obsolete. In 1898, we took our first real step into deeper waters with the Spanish-American War. Not only did we fight a war with a European power, albeit a weak sister, the war stretched around the globe, and we came out with some overseas possessions, most prominently the Philippines, Guam, and Puerto Rico.

Washington had said, "the period is not far off when" our growing national strength would permit us to "take such an attitude as will cause [our] neutrality … to be scrupulously respected." But during World War I, despite President Wilson's repeated demands, our "neutrality" wasn't "scrupulously respected." In 1917, Germany declared unrestricted submarine warfare and began sinking our merchant ships without warning. Convinced we could no longer stand aloof from Europe, Wilson finally asked Congress to declare war, which they did on April 6, 1917. Had we left behind Washington's advice "to steer clear of permanent alliances with any portion of the foreign world," or were we still following his advice by merely trusting "to temporary alliances for extraordinary emergencies?"

For President Wilson's part, he took the boat over to France and negotiated the Treaty of Versailles signed in 1919. Having rather grandly proclaimed a "war to end all wars" and "to make the world safe for democracy," he had come up with a rather grand scheme to make good on his lofty promises. At his insistence, the treaty created the League of Nations. In Wilson's vision for the future, this institution for "collective security" would replace the old "balance of power." Rather than nations making treaties to try and achieve a balance of power that discouraged wars, all nations would belong to the League, which would enforce collective security and prevent wars. Still a far cry from the old dream of a world government ("the battle-flags were furled in the Parliament of Man, the Federation of the world. ... the kindly earth shall slumber, lapt in universal law"), yet Wilson wanted to lead the world and America in such a direction, replacing national might with moral right, the rule of law enforced by a world organization.

Obviously, Wilson had become a convinced "internationalist" and was determined to abandon "isolation." By joining the League, America would permanently engage with the world, serving as a strong balance in the weight to maintain the peace. Never mind the League appeared to lack the strength to enforce peace and failed in the event. Given a try, who knows how his grand idea might have worked in the interwar years? But it was never given a fair try, since Congress abruptly applied the brakes and seized the reins. They refused to ratify the treaty and America never joined the League. Instead, Congress returned the country to an isolationist foreign policy. Nor did partisanship fail to exercise an influence, the Republicans in Congress leading the charge against the Democratic president. The fight about killed Wilson, who while campaigning to rally public support for the treaty, suffered a debilitating stroke. His defeat did effectively kill any hope for the League, which probably wouldn't have worked anyway, but without America, lacked a member who might have contributed a critical strength.

What might have been will never be known. But we do know something similar happened in the run up to World War II. President Franklin Roosevelt was another committed internationalist, but isolationist sentiment still ran strong in Congress, not to mention Republican sentiment still ran strong against another Democratic president. Roosevelt wanted to engage internationally again. But Congress jerked on his reins, seriously undermining his room to maneuver and injuring his credibility. Between 1935 and 1937, they passed several Neutrality Laws, forbidding arm sales or loans to belligerent nations during a state of war. Roosevelt was trying to deter Hitler and the Japanese imperialists by warning them our immense industrial productivity and boundless financial resources, if not our military, would show up against them in the event of a war. But Congress was sending the opposite message.

In 1936, a civil war broke out in Spain between the

Republicans, the existing government, a hard left-leaning coalition, and the Nationalists, a hard right-leaning coalition, who were supported by the German and Italian fascists. Roosevelt wanted to aid the Republicans, once again as a way of deterring fascist Germany, but the Neutrality Laws tied his hands. In early 1939, when he tried to get these laws repealed, Congress refused. When Hitler invaded Czechoslovakia in March, 1939, he tried again with the same discouraging result. Only after Hitler finally invaded Poland in September, 1939, did Congress relent somewhat, passing a law to allow arm sales, but still only on a cash and carry basis.

"When a people is divided … about the conduct of its foreign relations, it is unable to agree on the determination of its true interest. It is unable to prepare adequately for war or to safeguard successfully its peace." The surprise attack on Pearl Harbor (December 7, 1941) proved the proposition, as did the disastrous defeats at Bataan and Corregidor which shortly followed. But it's not the "people" who are "divided about the conduct of foreign relations," it's the drivers of our foreign policy coach who are "unable to agree." Since their political interests are divided, they're generally divided. Nor has this changed.

With World War II and the Cold War, America permanently left behind "isolation" for an "internationalist" foreign policy. For a time, we even left behind most of the division between the president and Congress and even the political parties over foreign policy. But that was only as long as the foreign threat was big enough. Surrounded by hostiles, the drivers laid aside their separate interests to pursue the common interest in survival. But by the later part of the Vietnam War from 1961 to 1975, the divisions re-asserted themselves, and it's been an uneven ride ever since.

Is this any way to run a country or least its foreign policy? It's the way we do it. But maybe that's not so bad after all. On the one hand, a lot of other nations are driven by a single-whip hand (a dictator) and can take a single-minded course. That gives them a chance to out-maneuver and take us by surprise like the Japanese Imperialists did. But having a single driver didn't turn out so well for Japan or Germany. Maybe it's not so bad to have a coach with three drivers.

5.14 – Lawyer Henry

Patrick Henry best remembered for saying, "Give me liberty or give me death." He delivered that eloquent and memorable line in 1775 on the eve of the American Revolution in a fire breathing speech before Virginia's House of Burgess, their colonial legislature. But Patrick Henry said a lot of other eloquent things, too. The most renowned trial lawyer of his day in Virginia and probably the nation, no tongue was more golden, no antagonist more feared, either in the courtroom or the political platform. Not only was his famed eloquence heard stoking the revolutionary fires, but later in the debates over ratification of the Constitution. In point of fact, he was opposed, although changing his mind in later years. Being a lawyer, he attacked the Constitution in a very lawyerly like way. No rhetorical device comes more readily to a lawyer's tongue than claiming some violation of his client's rights. Deploying this familiar tactic, Henry claimed the Constitution threatened the people's rights.

Article VIII sets out the method to ratify the Constitution, "The Ratification of the Conventions of nine states, shall be sufficient for the Establishment of this Constitution between the States so ratifying the Same." On September 28, 1787, the existing Congress under the Articles of Confederation voted that the proposed new Constitution "be transmitted to the several legislatures in order to be submitted to a convention of delegates chosen in each state by the people thereof." This call set off a fierce debate across the country. The "federalists" supported the proposed federal union, and the "anti-federalist" were opposed. In the event, the ratification turned out a close-run thing.

Have you ever noticed a Delaware license plate? The motto reads, "First State." They were the first state to ratify in their convention on December 7, 1787 with a unanimous vote of 30 to 0. Elsewhere the victory was harder fought and more narrowly won. The Massachusetts' convention ratified by a close vote of only 187 to 168 on February 6, 1788. Since Massachusetts a large state whose adherence essential to an effective national union, a mere ten men changing their votes could have changed our national fate. New Hampshire became the crucial ninth state on June 21, 1788, technically all the states required. But the new nation could not succeed without the adherence of the two large and influential states of Virginia and New York. Virginia finally came in with another close vote of 89 to 79 on June 25, 1788. New York with a razor thin margin of only 30 to 27 on July 26, 1788. North Carolina failed to ratify until 1789, and Rhode Island held out until May 29, 1790.

To return to Patrick Henry, he led the anti-federalists in the Virginia convention on ratification. Fortunately for the Constitution, in that assembly he crossed verbal swords with a foeman worthy of his steel, James Madison, the father of the Constitution himself. For once, lawyer Henry lost his case, yet did manage to draw blood with some debating points. Henry kept hacking away at the lack of a bill of rights in the Constitution, claiming this lack threatened the people's rights. At one point, Henry said, "For upwards of a century, [England] was involved in every kind of calamity, till the bill of rights put an end to all, by defining the rights of the people, and limiting the king's prerogative." At another, "Mr. Chairman, the necessity of a bill of rights appears to me greater in this government than ever it was in any government before."

A bill of rights is a very appealing idea, and much of the appeal comes from regarding a constitution as like a contact. If you write down your rights in a contract, later you can enforce your rights by going to court. As the next step in the analogy, if you write a bill of rights into your constitution, later you can enforce your rights the same way by going to court. Indeed, that's true up to a point. But a constitution isn't like a contract between private parties. Rather, it's a contract between the people and their government, and being part of the government, the courts and the judges are parties to the contact. At which point the analogy begins to break down. When you go to court to enforce a private contract, you can hope for an impartial judge, but when you go to court against the government, you can only hope for an impartial judge up to a point. As long as you're asserting your rights against the legislative or executive, you can still hope for an impartial judge. But when it reaches the point where you're asserting some right against the power and prerogatives of the judiciary itself, you can no longer hope for an impartial judge. At that point, the judges are sitting as judges in their own case as to the extent of their power over you. They're no longer impartial and will rule for themselves and against you.

As a result, this appealing idea won't quite work as hoped and promised. A bill of rights may serve to guarantee some of the people's rights against legislative or executive infringement. But when it comes to questions about the people's rights versus the judges' rights, that is, the judges' powers, it won't likely serve as much protection. As we'll see in later articles, it will more likely serve as a way for the government and particularly the judges to acquire still more power over you, the people.

Back in Patrick Henry's day, few saw this flaw in a bill of rights and many still refuse to see it. He and other anti-federalists were able to use this appealing idea to beat the federalists over the head. They constantly attacked the lack of a bill of rights in the Constitution as threatening the people's rights. The long and short of it being, that's how we ended up with the Bill of Rights, of course, the first ten amendments to the Constitution. To mollify their critics, Madison and other federalists took the easy way out. They promised that once the Constitution ratified, they would later add a bill of rights. Madison himself, who served in the first House of Representatives, would go on to draft these amendments and see them through the legislative process.

As for the Bill of Rights itself, no need to go over each one. For example, the 1st Amendment says, "Congress shall make no law respecting an establishment of religion, or prohibiting the free exercise thereof; or abridging the freedom of speech, or of the press; or the right of the people peaceably to assemble." The other amendments guarantee such things as the right to jury trial, the right against unreasonable searches and seizures, and so forth. Wonderful things all.

But the Bill of Rights didn't turn out quite the way Lawyer Henry claimed and as most lawyers still claim. Up to the previously mentioned point, the Bill of Rights has protected our rights. But beyond that point it has served as still another way for the federal government and particularly the judiciary to acquire still more power over us. Let's turn to what happened in the next articles.

5.15 – Our Rights

The law professors and the lawyers constantly wax rhapsodic over the Bill of Rights. They never cease dinning in our ears the notion that the Bill of Rights guarantees our freedoms by limiting the government's power over us. A highly respected legal scholar makes their underlying point this way, "To an American interested in constitutional history, the great theme in the country's development is the idea of law as a check upon governmental power." Except with the "constitutional history" so far seen in these articles, the "development ... of law as a check upon governmental power" hardly seems "the great theme." Rather, the great theme seems the growth of the federal government's powers. Nor when we come to the Bill of Rights, does this theme vary much. Rather, our rights have served as still another way for the federal government to gain still more power over us.

In this connection, the doctrine of "state rights" has fallen into disrepute through past association with nullification, secession, and segregation. But "state rights" started out life as thoroughly respectable. Let's not forget this earlier and more respectable career, which as much as the Bill of Rights, reflected a concern to guarantee our freedoms (serve as "a check upon governmental power" by limiting the federal government).

The Founders feared giving the new federal (national) government too much power. The Constitution granted it only specific (enumerated) powers, intending to limit it to no more. When later added, the Bill of Rights guaranteed such freedoms as freedom of speech and freedom of religion, further limiting the federal government. And let's take the time to notice something largely forgotten today, but crucial to our story about the Constitution as it has become. As written, intended, and originally interpreted, the Bill of Rights applied only against the federal government, not against the states, that is, limited only the federal government, not the states.

The early case of Barron v Baltimore (1833) makes this crucial point absolutely clear. The plaintiff (some guy named Barron) owned a profitable wharf in Baltimore harbor. The defendant (the City of Baltimore) ruined the property's value by diverting the flow of water with some street construction and causing the access to silt up. The "taking clause" in the 5th Amendment of the Bill of Rights says, "nor shall private property be taken for public use, without just compensation." Barron sued the city, arguing what they had done amounted to taking private property for public use and claiming a right to just compensation. But the Supreme Court ruled the 5th Amendment only applied against the federal government, that is, didn't apply to a state or a municipality such as the City of Baltimore. Chief Justice Marshall wrote, "These amendments [the Bill of Rights] contain no expression indicating an intention to apply them to the State governments. ... We are of opinion that the provision in the Fifth Amendment to the Constitution declaring that private property shall not be taken for public use without just compensation is intended solely as a limitation on the exercise of power by the Government of the United States, and is not applicable to the legislation of the States." Barron might have a right to compensation, but his right would have to come from somewhere else than the Bill of Rights. Those rights limited only the federal government, not the states.

Let's remember something else. The doctrine of "state rights" started out as part of the same scheme to limit the federal government's power. In this connection, let's remember the now largely forgotten 10th Amendment, the last amendment in the Bill of Rights, which says, "The powers not delegated to the United States by the Constitution, nor prohibited by it to the States, are reserved to the States respectively, or to the people." In other words, except for the powers specifically assigned the feds or specifically withheld from the states, all the other power belonged to the states "or to the people." At least as much as the Bill of Rights guaranteed other rights such as freedom of speech and freedom of religion, it guaranteed "state rights," the right of the people to govern themselves through the states and not be governed by the federal government. Just as much as the other rights, "state rights" limited the powers of the federal government.

There you have the original and highly respectable doctrine of state rights. As a practical matter, that left the people a lot of right to govern themselves through their states, rather than being governed by the federal government. Back at the time, this right was highly regarded, and in fact, a national consensus. In every era, Americans have been touchy about their rights. In that era, they regarded "state rights" (the rights reserved to the states and the people) as among their most fundamental rights.

But also in every era, people have never ceased to try and stretch the "rights tent" to bring their version of rights under the canvas. Before the Civil War, political theorists opposed to particular federal laws, say a tariff, began to argue that states had a right to nullify (invalidate) the laws they didn't like. In the 1832 Nullification Crisis, South Carolina actually tried to nullify the Tariffs of 1828 and 1832. President Andrew Jackson worked out a compromise that plastered over the schism. But in 1861, the Confederate states took the argument to the extreme, claiming their states had a right to secede from the union. Either argument reduced the federal government to nothing or dissolved it altogether. Both were finally rejected as outcomes of the Civil War. Yet still later, some states sought with success for a while to shelter laws that segregated blacks under a state rights argument.

Yet still more lately, not only have such arguments suffered rejection, virtually the whole doctrine of state rights has gradually disappeared in the national rearview mirror. In these articles, we've already seen one way the nation traveled down this highway. We've seen how the powers specifically delegated to the feds were gradually enlarged such as the commerce power or the power to tax and spend. This growing federal power has gradually left behind the powers reserved to the states. Next, we need to look at another way the federal government picked up speed. We need to look at how the Bill of Rights served as a vehicle for the federal government to gain still more power over the states, and indeed, over the people.

While once again, these signposts on the constitutional road may lead down a good or bad turning. But to understand the Constitution as it has become, we have to have to follow this turn in the road. In the next article, let's take that turn by following as our religious rights took an unexpected turn.

5.16 – Our Religious Rights

For some reason, there seems some confusion together with

some misrepresentation over what the Constitution said about our religious rights (originally). But the facts stand uncontroverted on the face of the historical record. To dispel the confusion and refute the misrepresentations, we need only to make the effort to look these facts squarely in the face. Conveniently enough, the same effort will show how the "religious clauses" and the Bill of Rights served as still another way for the federal government to gain more power over the states and the people.

The Bill of Rights was ratified in 1791, and the "religious clauses" are found in the 1st Amendment. "Congress shall make no law respecting an establishment of religion, or prohibiting the free exercise thereof." And right up front, let's take the care to notice a crucial fact. These words limit *only* the federal government, *not* the states. The words say, "*Congress* shall make no law," but says absolutely nothing about the states making no law.

That's because as originally intended the Bill of Rights applied *only* against and *only* limited the federal government and didn't apply against or limit the state governments, and these religious clauses didn't apply against or limit them either. In an 1845 case (the Permoli Case), the Supreme Court would specifically affirm this original intent, saying, "The Constitution makes no provision for protecting the citizens of the respective States in their religious liberties; this is left to the State constitutions and laws; nor is there any inhibition imposed by the Constitution of the United States in this respect on the States."

Then first and crucially, originally these religious clauses only limited the federal government, not the states. But what did the clauses mean to prevent? Over in the mother country, the British had an "established church" (the Anglican Church), officially endorsed and supported by the national government. The "establishment clause" meant the new, federal government couldn't establish such a national church. Over there, too, non-Anglicans faced barriers to the "free exercise" of their religion. The "free-exercise clause" meant the new, federal government couldn't erect such barriers.

Where did this meaning leave our religious rights (originally, in 1791)? Let's also recall the 10th Amendment, the last one in the Bill of Rights, which says, "The powers not delegated to the United States by the Constitution, nor prohibited by it to the States, are reserved by it to the States respectively, or to the people." Since the Constitution "delegated" no power over religion to the federal government and "prohibited" no power over religion to the states, that left our religious rights "reserved" to the people acting through the states. Acting through Congress, the people couldn't establish a national church or interfere with the free exercise of religion. But otherwise and by acting through the states, they could decide on the place of religion in the national life (the "religious settlement"). In fact, that was one of their fundamental rights under the Bill of Rights.

Back at the time in 1791, all the states had some guarantee for religious rights in their constitutions, yet the 1st Amendment didn't even prevent a state from having an "established" church. In fact, seven of the fourteen states did have established state churches, with the last one in Massachusetts not being abolished until 1833. The states and the people had the right to decide for themselves.

Nor did the 1st Amendment even prevent all recognition or support of Christianity by the new federal government. As a later judge would write in a much later case in 1962, "No historical fact is so easy to prove by literally countless illustrations as the fact that belief and trust in a Supreme Being was from the beginning and has been continuously part of the very essence of the American plan of government and society. The references to the Deity in the Declaration of Independence; the words of our National Anthem: 'In God is our trust', the motto on our coins; the daily prayers in Congress; the universal practice in official oaths of calling upon God to witness the truth; the official thanksgiving proclamations beginning with those of the Continental Congress and the First Congress of the United States and continuing till the present; ... the directions by Congress in modern times for a National Day of Prayer and for the insertion of the words 'under God' in the Pledge of Allegiance to the Flag; innumerable solemn utterances by our Presidents and other leaders --- all of these make historically inescapable the flat statement [by the Supreme Court in the 1952 Zorach Case] that: 'We are a religious people whose institutions presuppose a Supreme Being', which paraphrased the Supreme Court's similar assertion in 1892 in the Holy Trinity Church case."

As a further legal authority on this original meaning of the 1st Amendment, let's turn to Justice Joseph Story, who served on the

Supreme Court from 1811 to 1845, simultaneously held down a professorship at Harvard Law School, and in his spare time wrote a comprehensive treatise on the Constitution, his *Commentaries on the Constitution of the United States*, published in 1833. Story says this, "Probably at the time of the adoption of the Constitution, and [of the 1st Amendment], the general if not universal sentiment in America was, that Christianity ought to receive encouragement from the State so far as it was not incompatible with the private rights of conscience and the freedom of religious worship. An attempt to level all religions, and to make it a matter of state policy to hold in utter indifference, would have created universal disapprobation, if not universal indignation. ... The real object ... was not to countenance, much less to advance, Mahometanism, or Judaism, or infidelity, by prostrating Christianity; but to exclude all rivalry between Christian sects and to prevent any national ecclesiastical establishment."

For an authority on the original practice under the 1st Amendment, we can turn to that insightful French visitor, Alexis de Tocqueville, who extensively toured this country in 1831 and 1832 and recorded the prevailing view in his often quoted *Democracy in America*, in two volumes published 1835, 1840, "Religion in America takes no direct part in the government of society, but nevertheless it must be regarded as the foremost of the political institutions of that country; for if it does not impart a taste for freedom, it facilitates the use of free institutions. Indeed, it is in this same point of view that the inhabitants of the United States look upon religious belief. I do not know whether all Americans have a sincere belief in their religion, for who can search the human heart? But I am certain that they hold it to be indispensable to the maintenance of republican institutions. This opinion is not peculiar to a class of citizens or to a party, but it belongs to the whole nation, and to every rank of society."

Finally, we can turn to the Supreme Court and read their decision in the Church of the Holy Trinity Case (1892). Justice David Josiah Brewer wrote for a unanimous Court. After passing in review a number of state constitutions, he says, "There is a universal language pervading them all, having one meaning. They affirm and reaffirm that this is a religious nation. These are not individual sayings, declarations of private persons. They are organic utterances. They speak the voice of the entire people. … this is a Christian nation."

As a matter of historical fact, originally (in 1791) the 1st Amendment didn't change our religious rights at all, but left in place an existing "religious settlement." This arrangement no more than reflected and accepted the traditional Christian pattern brought over from the Old World, but which arrived turned upside down. In America, the official Anglican Church stood on a narrow foundation except in the South, since not many Anglicans had emigrated except to the South. Rather, America had served as a refuge for the dissenters and nonconformists. They had made New England a Puritan stronghold, the Middle Colonies a home to the Presbyterians, and Pennsylvania a Quaker haven. But you could have located an enclave devoted to almost any Protestant sect, as well as Catholic redoubts. The trans-Atlantic migration had reversed the traditional European "religious settlement." Rather than a cathedral like national church, America offered a bazaar-like choice of churches, one for almost any taste. Yet while no church dominated the landscape, Christianity thoroughly dominated as the national religion.

Then let neither the confusion nor the misrepresentations continue. We know what the Constitution (originally) said about our religious rights. But in the last half of the last century, the federal government and specifically the Supreme Court would change what originally said. Interpreting away the original limits in the Bill of Rights on the federal government's power over our religious rights, they took for themselves this power previously reserved to the states and the people. Then they changed the existing "religious settlement," moving away from being a Christian nation toward becoming a thoroughly secular state. In our story about the Constitution as it has become, this chapter offers the most prominent example of how the Bill of Rights served as another way for the federal government to gain still more power. But we've run out of space and need to turn to this next chapter in the next article.

5.17 – Second Chapter

The last article talked about our religious rights, first chapter. This article talks about our religious rights, second chapter. The first chapter started the story with the Founding. This second chapter picks up the story in 1947. And a significant change in the narrator marks this change in the chapters. The people, speaking through the states, started out telling the story. Their version merely carried forward the American religious tradition (the prior "religious settlement"). Starting out as a nation without any "established" church, yet America started out as "a Christian Nation." But now the federal government and specifically the Supreme Court takes over as narrator. Turning the page on the older tradition, they start rewriting and revising the earlier edition. Closing the chapter on America as "a Christian Nation," they open a new chapter on America as a nation with a secular future.

For our larger tale of the Constitution as it has become, these religious chapters aren't just significant in themselves, but serve to illustrate a larger power shift toward the feds. As originally conceived and interpreted, the Bill of Rights limited only the federal government's power, which left a lot of power with the people, acting through the states, to decide on their rights. But in the era after the Second World, the federal government and specifically the Supreme Court, assumed a power to apply the Bill of Rights against the states, thus taking away the power previously reserved to the states. Not only that, the feds, and again specifically the Supreme Court, assumed a power to redefine the rights (to change their meaning). In combined effect, the people lost their previous power to decide their rights by acting through the states. Instead, the Bill of Rights became a source of still more power for the feds, and again specifically for the Supreme Court.

To turn to the second chapter in the story of our religious rights, we need to start by reading the Everson Case from 1947. The New Jersey legislature had passed a law which offered some assistance to private, non-profit schools by picking up some of the transportation costs, a measure especially benefitting the numerous Catholic parochial schools. However, someone named Arch Everson objected and filed a lawsuit, arguing the law violated the "establishment clause" of the 1st Amendment by using tax dollars to support a religion. However, under the long-accepted doctrine, the "establishment clause" applied only against the federal government, not against state governments such as New Jersey. Under this rule, the state of New Jersey and the people acting through the state could legally pay whatever transportation costs they wanted even to religious schools.

But in the opinion, the Supreme Court suddenly re-interpreted the "establishment clause" to now apply against the states. Writing the majority opinion, Justice Hugo Black said, "The First Amendment, as made applicable to the states by the Fourteenth ... commands that a state 'shall make no law respecting an establishment of religion or prohibiting the free exercise thereof.'" These two sentences, which sound so matter of fact, actually reversed the long-accepted doctrine. Because remember as discussed in the last article, the 1st Amendment reads, "*Congress* shall make no law respecting an establishment of religion." This language limited *only* the federal government (*not* the states) and had been so interpreted down to that very day. But suddenly Justice Black has chopped out the key word "*Congress*" and substituted the word "*state*." He has ruled that: "The First Amendment ... commands that a *state* 'shall make no law respecting an establishment of religion.'" He has changed the original meaning of the Bill of Rights, in effect, amending the Constitution. In the process, the power moved away from the states, and indeed, away from the people. They lost the power over their religious rights previously reserved to them.

But Justice Black wasn't through. He shortly proceeds to re-interpret the meaning of the "establishment clause." He writes, "The 'establishment of religion' clause of the First Amendment means at least this: Neither a state nor the Federal Government can set up a church. Neither can pass laws which aid one religion, aid all religions, or prefer one religion over another. ... No tax in any amount, large or small, can be levied to support any religious activities or institutions ... In the words of Jefferson, the clause against establishment of religion by law was intended to erect 'a wall of separation between Church and State.'"

With these words, the "wall of separation," a phrase used by Jefferson in a private letter, entered the public consciousness and the legal lexicon. But let's not let Jefferson's appealing metaphor distract us from what Justice Black has just done. He has just radically altered the meaning of "the establishment clause."

Because remember as shown in the last article, originally the clause only meant to keep Congress from "establishing" a national church, a federally endorsed, supported, and controlled church like the Anglican Church in Great Britain. Now he's utterly changed the meaning. Now the "establishment clause" has been suddenly extended to prohibit any "aid" to religion or to "support any religious activities." And so, as the rest of the second chapter in our religious rights unfolds, the federal government and specifically the Supreme Court will shortly go on to prohibit such things as Bible reading in school, prayer in school or school events, or posting the Ten Commandments on classroom walls. If America's past had been as a "Christian Nation," apparently her future was as a thoroughly secular nation.

While at the same time, this second chapter on our religious rights illustrates a larger trend. First, using a recent doctrine called "incorporation," the federal government and specifically the Supreme Court "incorporates" the Bill of Rights against the states. That is, they rule those rights now apply against (limit) the state governments as well as the federal government. Next, they reinterpret the rights (changing their meaning). In net effect, the people acting through the states have lost much of their power to decide and define their rights. Instead, the feds and specifically the Supreme Court have gained a lot more power.

We just saw how the process worked with our religious rights. And most of the Bill of Rights has been changed through the same process. The 1st Amendment right to "freedom of speech" now protects most obscenity. The same right mandates a civil service system. The 4th Amendment right against "unreasonable searches and seizures" and the 5th Amendment right against self-incrimination have been extended. The 8th Amendment right against "cruel and unusual punishments" has been extended to cover the death penalty. The list goes on.

All of these changes may be good things, depending on our point of view. But whatever our point of view, we can't help but see that the federal government has gained a great deal more power. Under the Bill of Rights as originally conceived and interpreted, the power to decide and define all these rights remained with the people through the states. Now the federal government has that power. While as an afterthought to be developed in later articles, we might mention that all this power was transferred not just from one set of democratic institutions (the state legislatures) to another democratic institution (the Congress). Rather, all this power went to the Supreme Court (an unelected institution). Not only did the people lose the power to govern themselves through their states, they lost the power altogether.

Then how say the Bill of Rights limits the federal government's power over us? In some ways it does, but in other ways it has come to enlarge the fed's power over us. In the name of our rights, the feds gained a great deal of power. That may be a good or a bad thing, but to understand the Constitution as it has become, we have to understand the change.

5.18 – The Second Constitution

We conceive nothing more central to American values than "all men are created equal." In 1776, the Declaration of Independence so proclaimed. Yet nothing in the Constitution as it came off the press spoke directly to "equality." That had to wait for publication of the Reconstruction Amendments, which so much revised the original as sometimes called "the Second Constitution." The 13th Amendment (ratified 1865) abolished slavery. The 15th Amendment (ratified 1870) guaranteed the vote. But it's the one in between, the 14th Amendment (ratified 1868), which says, "No state shall make or enforce any law which shall deny ... to any person ... the equal protection of the laws."

Surely, this "equal protection clause" sounds like a restraint (a limit) on the government's power, saying, "No state ... shall deny ... equal protection." The negatives add up, and negatives amount to a restraint. Yet lately the clause has turned into a source of still more positive power for the feds. Once again, to understand the Constitution as it has become, we have to unravel something of a legal paradox.

To make a start and given nothing more, what would we think "the equal protection of the laws" means? Surely, at least what the words say, that "the laws shall not deny to any person the equal protection." For example, the criminal laws against murder, rape, robbery, etc., should not deny to any person their equal protection, but protect all the same. For a connected example, the laws of criminal procedure such as the right to a jury trial or against unreasonable searches and seizures should also protect all the same against wrongful conviction for crime. Such examples seem easy enough. In sum, we seem able to say that the law should treat people the same, not give a preference, not discriminate.

But take another example. The 26th Amendment (ratified in 1971) says, "The right of citizens … who are eighteen years of age or older, to vote shall not be denied." That protects all "citizens over eighteen years of age," but not under eighteen. Then does the 26th Amendment contradict the 14th Amendment ("deny … the equal protection of the laws")? No, because we regard the distinction as rational (or reasonable). Children and adolescents lack the same maturity, and so the law may reasonably treat them differently from adults.

When we come to think about it, our laws are shot through with similar distinctions, which we regard as reasonable. The criminal laws treat juveniles differently, more leniently. You can't try the mentally incompetent for their crimes, since they're incapable of aiding in their own defense. You can't convict the insane for their crimes, since they can't appreciate the nature and consequences of their acts. Yet the sane and mentally competent can be tried, convicted, and punished. We could keep on giving such examples, where the laws make distinctions regarded as reasonable. People with seizures can't get a driver's license. People without a license can't practice medicine or law. People with a higher income pay a higher percentage of income tax. Many, many legal distinctions treat people differently, yet aren't regarded as denying "the equal protection of the laws," since regarded as making reasonable distinctions.

But where do the rational (reasonable) distinctions leave off? Take the right to vote again. Back in days of the founding of the republic, the laws hedged the franchise with property qualifications, and only people with a certain amount of property could vote. Until 1920 and the ratification of the 19th Amendment, women couldn't vote. Until 1971 and the above mentioned 26th Amendment, eighteen-year olds couldn't vote. At the time, these earlier legal distinctions were regarded as reasonable and not a violation of equal protection of the laws. Now these same distinctions are labeled as "invidious" or "discriminatory," as not making a reasonable distinction. Now such laws are regarded as violating the "equal protection of the laws."

Again, without much effort, we could come up with quite a number of similar examples, where past laws regarded at the time as making a reasonable distinction, but where more recently the same laws have become regarded as "invidious" or "discriminatory." But of course, legal segregation offers the classic example. In the not too distant past, some states had laws that made distinctions along racial lines. The infamous Louisiana Separate Car Law from 1890 read, "All railway companies carrying passengers in their coaches in this State shall provide equal but separate accommodations for the white and colored races, by providing two or more coaches for each passenger train, or by dividing the passenger coaches by a partition so as to secure separate accommodations." How did such laws not violate equal protection of the laws? Yet back at the time, the Supreme Court held this law made a rational distinction in the famous case of Plessy v Ferguson (in 1896). Only much later in the even more famous case of Brown v Board of Education (in 1954) did the Supreme Court change its mind and rule the distinction now invidious or discriminatory.

Then when it comes to "equality" and the Constitution, might we agree on this much? The "equal protection of the laws" means the laws should treat everyone the same. But that doesn't mean the laws can't make "reasonable" (rational) distinctions, Rather, it only means the laws can't make "invidious" or "discriminatory" distinctions. Unfortunately, that still leaves a messy problem. We have to figure out what's reasonable or rational as opposed to invidious or discriminatory. But at least such agreement would bring the discussion so far.

However, more recently, "the equal protection of the laws" has come to mean quite a bit more. It's come to serve not just as negative on government power, but as another way the feds gained still more positive power. Let's see how in the next article.

5.19 – The Power in Equality

In the last article, we saw that "the equal protection clause" in the 14th Amendment reads, "No state shall make or enforce any law which shall deny ... to any person ... the equal protection of the laws." Hopefully, we agreed that means "the laws" should treat people "equal." Yet hopefully, we also agreed that the laws can make rational distinctions, for example, treating juveniles differently than adults, but shouldn't make "invidious" distinctions, for example, by race. Now we need to go on to understand how "the equal protection clause" served as another source of still more power for the federal government beginning in the latter part of the twentieth century.

While not confined to race, these new powers originated in cases over race, and a famous Supreme Court case about race serves as the best place to start. Decided in 1971, the Swann Case was about desegregating the public schools in Charlotte, North Carolina. In writing the opinion, Chief Justice Warren Earl Burger began by summarizing the facts. "The Charlotte-Mecklenburg school system, the 43rd largest in the Nation, encompasses the city of Charlotte and surrounding Mecklenburg County, North Carolina. The area is large --- 550 square miles, spanning roughly 22 miles east-west and 36 miles north-south. During the 1968-1969 school year the system served more than 84,000 pupils in 107 schools. Approximately 71% of the pupils were found to be white and 29% Negro. As of June 1969 there were approximately 24,000 Negro students in the system, of whom 21,000 attended schools within the city of Charlotte. Two-thirds of those 21,000 --- approximately 14,000 Negro students --- attended 21 schools which were either totally Negro or more than 99% Negro."

Notice something about these facts. This huge school district included Charlotte and the surrounding suburbs. The blacks lived mainly in the city ("there were approximately 24,000 Negro students in the system, of whom 21,000 attended schools within the city of Charlotte") and the whites mainly in the suburbs. The laws didn't cause the racial separation between the city and suburban schools, all such laws having been wiped off the books twenty-five years gone by (in 1954, by the decision in Brown v Board of Education). The racial separation wasn't caused by the existing laws, but by the existing demographic patterns. How, then, can these facts violate the "the equal protection of the laws," since "the laws" didn't treat anyone different?

Yet reading on, Chief Justice Berger discovers a violation of "the equal protection of the laws." He writes, "The basis of our decision must be the prohibition of the Fourteenth Amendment that no State shall 'deny to any person within its jurisdiction the equal protection of the laws.'" Based upon this violation, he orders thoroughgoing integration (racial mixing) between the city and the suburban schools. He orders massive busing to transport children to racially mix them and highly gerrymandered school attendance zones, radically re-drawn into a pie shape pattern, the wedges extending from the city center outward to the suburban rim.

Yet maybe good justifications exist. No doubt the prior laws had contributed to the present demographics. Restrictive covenants in deeds had prevented selling houses to blacks, confining them to specific neighborhoods. Schools had been deliberately located to maintain a segregated pattern. Reasonably perhaps, the prior laws justify the present remedies. Perhaps it's not enough to cancel out the prior unequal laws, but the present laws need to rectify the lingering effects. But if such a sufficient justification, the same facts were lacking in other cases. For example, Michigan never had laws that segregated the schools. But in another famous case (Milliken v Bradley from 1974) the local federal judge ordered massive busing to mix up the races in the Detroit metro area schools. Across the country, the federal courts and the federal bureaucracy ordered such massive integration programs whether or not a state's prior laws had mandated segregation.

Then do we see how the feds just gained a great deal more power? Not only does "the equal protection of the laws" prevent invidious laws, but now prevents invidious distinctions whether or not caused by law. The law doesn't just have to treat people equally, rather, now the law requires equal treatment throughout society. The "equal protection clause" is no longer just a restraint on government power, limiting the laws the government can pass, but a new power for the government to pass laws to eliminate all distinctions regarded as invidious.

Other school desegregation cases show the vast extent of this new federal power. As mentioned, in 1974, Milliken v Bradley ordered massive busing in the Detroit schools. The local federal judge ordered some 300,000 students bused back and forth from the white suburbs to the black inner city. The Supreme Court later cut down the size of this plan somewhat, yet tens of thousands of children were still bused in this way in the Detroit metro area and across the country. In 1977, a local federal judge in Kansas City got even more creative. He ordered that "every senior high school, every middle school, and approximately one-half of the elementary schools" become magnet schools. "Finding that construction of new schools would result in more 'attractive' facilities than renovation of existing ones, [he] approved new construction at a cost ranging from $61.80 per square foot to $95.70 per square foot as distinct from renovation at $45.00 per square foot." His capital improvements went on to include "a 2000-square-foot planetarium; greenhouses and vivariums; a 25-acre farm with an air-conditioned meeting room for 104 people; a Model United Nations wired for language translation; broadcast capable radio and television studios with an editing and animation lab; a temperature controlled art gallery; movie editing and screening rooms; a 3,500-square-foot dust-free diesel mechanics room; ... swimming pools; and numerous other facilities." When the costs for all this far exceeded the limits on taxation written into the Missouri Constitution, he simply held those limits unconstitutional and raised the taxes himself. Whatever happened to "no taxation without representation?"

As said, while originating with race, these new powers aren't confined to race. Here's a statement recently put out by a federal agency, "This entire organization is fully committed to ensuring a safe, comfortable and diverse work environment where all individuals, regardless of sex, race, color, religion, gender, or sexual identity or orientation, are treated fairly and equally. We have work to do to achieve this goal, but we are going to meet it." Every federal agency follows this same policy. And that's not just a rule about the "work environment" inside the agencies applying only to the federal civil servants. That's a federal law across the whole country, applying to virtually every workplace and public place.

Well, again, all this may be a good thing, not a bad thing, depending on your point of view. But how fail to see the federal government has gained a great deal more power? The "equal protection of the laws" has come to mean not just that the laws can make no invidious distinctions. It has come to mean the feds have the power to remedy any distinctions perceived as invidious throughout society and however caused. Turns out there's a lot of power in equality.

5.20 – The Great and Chief End

In writing the Declaration of Independence, Thomas Jefferson paraphrased the English philosopher John Locke, who lived 1632 to 1704. In the *Second Treatise on Government*, Locke had written, "all men by nature are equal, … no one ought to harm another in his life, health, liberty, or possessions." Jefferson altered the phrasing to the more powerful, "all men are created equal, … with certain unalienable Rights, that among these are Life, Liberty, and the pursuit of Happiness." Apparently, too, he hesitated to elevate the right to "possessions" (read property) to quite the same level as "life and liberty," instead replacing it with "the pursuit of Happiness." Yet the "right to property" was near and dear to the hearts of the Founding Fathers.

Locke, the Founders' favorite philosopher, himself had gone on to say, "The great and chief end, therefore, of men … putting themselves under government, is the preservation of their property." James Madison would echo that in the *Federalist No. 54*, saying, "Government is instituted no less for protection of the property, than of the persons of individuals." A similar high regard for property fills the Founding Fathers' writings, speeches, and deeds. Yet today, one seldom hears the "preservation of property" proclaimed as "the great and chief end" of government. Other rights are far more popular, especially rights against "discrimination" based on race or gender. Lately, too, we're hearing a great deal about a new "right" to a basic income for all, even if that requires redistributing one man's property to another man. Nevertheless, the Founders laid the right to property at the foundation of their constitutional structure, where it remains a cornerstone.

Why were the Founders so big on the right to property? We have only to recall their immediate history that still spoke to them in moving terms. As we heard Professor Beard say in an earlier article, the Founding Fathers were bourgeoisie. Originally, that term referred to anyone living in a borough (a city or town). Their immediate history was the rise of their class. It had been a revolution, bitter, sometimes bloody, and far from over. The old feudal order hadn't gone softly into that good night, nor was the body quite dead and buried. The victory of the bourgeoisie was still tenuous, and in much of the world, they had yet to win at all. The whole thing had been about nothing so much as their right to property.

During the feudal era, the king and the nobility owned all the property in the form of land. We might almost say the vast majority (the peasants) didn't own property, but were property. They were bound to the land, being forbidden by law to leave. They had to render services to the lord (their feudal dues) for their farms. If the land sold, they went right along with it. But in the later middle ages, more cities and towns (the boroughs) began to grow up and commerce revived. And "town air makes free men." The townspeople (the bourgeoisie) didn't owe feudal obligations. They didn't have to labor for a lord, but could labor for themselves. A peasant who escaped into a town could gain a similar freedom. Inside these towns, the artisans and merchants owned their own houses, shops, tools, merchandise, wharves, ships, and trade goods. Increasingly, they also possessed a lot of that highly desirable and highly mobile form of property – money. On this moveable feast, the kings soon began to cast an envious and covetous eye. They longed to tax and expropriate this rising class's property to their heart's content and put the bourgeoisie under their heel like the peasants.

Except as already mentioned in these articles, that scheme failed in England. There, the rising bourgeoisie found a protector in Parliament, where many of them had a seat or some influence. In the English Civil Wars from 1642 to 1651 and finally with the Glorious Revolution of 1688, Parliament fought not just for political primacy, but against arbitrary taxation and expropriation, which they regarded as almost the same thing. In other words, they were fighting for their right to property. Parliament's victory hedged that right with an effective defense. It established the principle that only the people's representatives in Parliament could tax them. Since they had an effective check on their representatives (through elections), that gave them an effective defense for their right to property.

It was Locke himself who served as their philosopher, coming up with the theory that served as their rationale. He argued that the government "cannot take from any man any part of his property without his own consent." He went on, "Nor can any edict ... by what power soever backed, have the force and obligation of law which has not its sanction from that legislative which the public has chosen and appointed; for without this the law could not have that which is absolutely necessary to its being a law, the consent of the society, over whom nobody can have power to make laws but by their own consent and the authority derived from them." Finally, "If any one shall claim a power to lay and levy taxes on the people by his own authority and without such consent of the people, he thereby invades the fundamental law of property, and subverts the end of government."

We should begin to see why the right to property so fundamental to the Founding Fathers. No wonder they fought under the slogan, "No taxation with representation." And although no "right to property" was specifically mentioned in the Constitution, yet the right is carefully protected.

The 5th Amendment says, "No person ... shall be ... deprived of ... property, without due process of law; nor shall private property be taken for public use without just compensation." Article I, Sec. 10 goes on to say, "No State shall ... pass any ... law impairing the obligation of contracts," since a great deal of property is in the form of contractual rights. And there can be no taxation without representation, since Article I, Sec. 8 says, "Congress shall have power, To lay and collect taxes."

The right to property remains near and dear to the hearts of many an American and especially the ones with ample funds on deposit. Yet through the years the right has taken a lot of abuse. Until today, a lot of people would not agree that, "The great and chief end, therefore, of men ... putting themselves under government, is the preservation of their property." Yet not only did the right to property rest on the Founders own experience and interests. Our experience has since further proved the great value of the right.

The right to property is the foundation for a free-market

economy. The free-market is the source of America's long running economic success. We should, therefore, recognize the continued importance of this right and be very reluctant to see it forgotten, ignored, or disappear.

5.21 – The Second Bill of Rights

Have you heard about the Second Bill of Rights? While not yet quite in the Constitution, this Second Bill of Rights is a work well along, if still a work in progress. But the newer version varies from the original in a significant way. The original Bill of Rights meant to guarantee our rights against the government. This Second Bill of Rights means to guarantee our rights from the government. The first said hands off, but the second says hands on. That's because the original guaranteed us against government action, but the newer version guarantees us government action. Thus, while the original Bill of Rights started as limiting the government's power of action, this Second Bill of Rights starts by increasing the government's power of action.

This proposal for a Second Bill of Rights (also called an "economic bill of rights") was influentially announced by President Franklin D. Roosevelt in his last State of the Union Address, delivered on January 11, 1944. He said, "It is our duty now to begin to lay the plans and determine the strategy for … the establishment of an American standard of living higher than ever before known. We cannot be content, no matter how high that general standard of living may be, if some fraction of our people— whether it be one-third or one-fifth or one-tenth—is ill-fed, ill-clothed, ill-housed, and insecure."

He went on, "This Republic had its beginning, and grew to its present strength, under the protection of certain inalienable political rights—among them the right of free speech, free press, free worship, trial by jury, freedom from unreasonable searches and seizures. They were our rights to life and liberty. As our nation has grown in size and stature, however — as our industrial economy expanded — these political rights proved inadequate to assure us equality in the pursuit of happiness. We have come to a clear realization of the fact that true individual freedom cannot exist without economic security and independence. 'Necessitous men are not free men.'"

He concluded, "In our day these economic truths have become accepted as self-evident. We have accepted, so to speak, a second Bill of Rights under which a new basis of security and prosperity can be established for all — regardless of station, race, or creed. Among these are: ... The right to earn enough to provide adequate food and clothing and recreation; ... The right of every family to a decent home; The right to adequate medical care ... ; The right to adequate protection from the economic fears of old age, sickness, accident, and unemployment; The right to a good education. ... We must be prepared to move forward, in the implementation of these rights, to new goals of human happiness and well-being."

As Roosevelt said, the original Bill of Rights "protected our inalienable political rights" such as "free speech" or "trial by jury." But as he went on to say, this "so to speak, a Second Bill of Rights" will guarantee "economic security" (the "right to earn enough," the right "to a decent home," the right to "medical care," the "right to adequate protection from the economic fears of old age, sickness, accident, and unemployment," the right to "a good education"). In sum, this newer, second version will guarantee all the entitlements of a welfare state from the cradle to the grave.

If we put the two versions side by side, we can't help but notice that the original Bill of Rights expressed negative commands against government action. For example, the 1st Amendment say, "Congress shall make no law ... abridging the freedom of speech." The 4th Amendment say, "The right of the people ... against unreasonable searches and seizures, shall not be violated." But the Second Bill of Rights expresses positive commands that require government action. The government must provide "economic security and independence," "adequate food," "a decent home," "medical care," "a good education," and so forth.

Thus, the Second Bill of Rights isn't hands off, but hands on. If the federal government is going to provide all these entitlements, it's going to have to take a great deal more power unto itself to make things happen. Indeed, that describes what already well along, beginning with Roosevelt's own New Deal programs. "Adequate food." Think of food stamps. "Decent housing." Think of public housing. "A good education." Think of federal grants and guaranteed student loans. "Medical care." Think of Medicare, Medicaid, and Obamacare. "The economic fears of old age, sickness, accident, and unemployment." Think of Social Security retirement and disability or unemployment insurance. The list goes on, and proposals are constantly made to lengthen the list.

Thus, the Second Bill of Rights has already served to add vastly to the federal government's powers. While if these rights aren't yet quite in the Constitution, the effort is well underway to write in such guarantees. As one distinguished legal scholar has hoped, "The day may indeed come when a general doctrine … recognizes for each individual a constitutional right to a decent level of affirmative government protection in meeting the basic human needs of physical survival and security, health and house, work and schooling." In other words, the hope is to make all these entitlements into constitutional rights that the government cannot deny.

This Second Bill of Rights may be a very good thing, although not everyone convinced. But neither the original Constitution nor the original Bill of Rights contemplated anything like the welfare state or granted the federal government the powers required to make it happen. Still once again, the feds have gained still more power.

5.22 – The Second-Best Thing

The "due process clause" of the 14th Amendment (ratified in 1868) says, "No State shall … deprive any person of life, liberty, or property, without due process of law." The 5th Amendment in the Bill of Rights (ratified back in 1791) already said, "No person shall be … deprived of life, liberty, or property, without due process of law." Why put the same clause in twice, and what is "due process of law" anyway?

But if we read carefully, these two amendments don't say quite the same thing. Back in 1791, the 5th Amendment said, "*No person shall be deprived.*" In 1868, the 14th Amendment said, "*No state shall deprive.*" This slight variation mattered a lot. Because remember, originally the Bill of Rights and so the 5th Amendment only applied against (only limited) the federal government, not the state governments. Then in 1791, when the 5th Amendment had said *"no person* shall be deprived," that had only protected someone against the federal government. But when in 1868, the 14th Amendment said *"no state* shall deprive," that extended the protection against the states. In particular, the intent meant to protect the new freedmen (the slaves freed by the Civil War), assuring their rights to "due process" against the former slaveholding states.

But what is "due process of law" anyway? The term goes way back in Anglo-American law, so far back as to start out another term. As long ago as 1215, Magna Charta used the words "law of the land" for roughly the same meaning. By 1354, during the reign of Edward III, a statute used the form "due process" of law. By the time of Lord Coke, a renowned authority, he could state in his *Institutes* (published between 1628 and 1644) that "by the law of the land" was meant "by the due course and process of the law." By 1788 when the U.S. Constitution ratified, the two terms were still interchangeable, and several state constitutions still used the form "law of the land." However, today, we always hear "due process of law."

Crucial to our proper understanding, "due process of law" refers mainly to "procedural law" as opposed to "substantive law." In the technical language of the law, the substantive law is the substance of the laws, while the procedural law is the procedures to enforce the substance. The law that makes murder a crime is a substantive law. The law for a jury trial in a criminal case is a procedural law to enforce the substantive laws against crimes such as murder. The law setting forth the requirements to make a valid last will and testament is a substantive law. The procedure for probating a will after the death of the testator is a procedural law.

However, due process does refer to the substance of the law in one respect. Due process requires clearly stated laws. Otherwise, we couldn't rely on the law. Vaguely worded laws let people get away with way too much, and much more troublesome, let the authorities get away with way too much. People can easily slip through the noose, cheating and defrauding other people. The authorities can swing a wide lasso, convicting people they may not like under loosely worded laws. For example, what's the difference between bribing a congressman to influence legislation or making a campaign contribution in the hope of influencing legislation? What's the difference between tax avoidance (structuring a financial transaction to legally avoid taxes) and tax evasion (illegally evading taxes by say not reporting income)? Unless the laws clearly stated, no one is either confined by or safe in the corral.

With this start in mind, look back at the "due process clause," which says, no one "shall be deprived of life, liberty, or property without due process of law." The first part ("life, liberty, and property") refers to the substantive law. Those laws set forth our rights (to life, liberty, and property). The second part ("due process of law") refers to the procedural law such as the right to a jury trial or the procedure to probate a will. Putting the two parts together, we cannot be deprived of our substantive rights (to "life, liberty, and property") unless certain procedural rights are followed ("without due process of law").

What are these procedural rights (what amounts to due process)? Over many centuries, English law had developed some careful procedures to protect the people's rights. Few other legal systems had such protections and the English and later the Americans rightly treasured this legal heritage. With that in mind, we can approach the best-known early attempt by the Supreme Court to give an overall definition of "due process." Back in 1856 in Murray's Case, they indicated two sources for the concept. First, due process required those procedures required by specific provisions in the Constitution, such as the right to jury trial or the right a lawyer. Second, due process was "those settled usages and modes of proceeding existing in the common and statute law of England, before the emigration of our ancestors, and which are shown not to have been unsuited to their civil and political condition by having been acted on by them after their settlement of this country."

Then in the first place, due process meant those procedures required by specific provisions in the Constitution and the Bill of Rights. Two of the most important are found in the body of the original Constitution. First, "The privilege of the Writ of Habeas Corpus shall not be suspended." (Article I, Sec. 9). That's a procedure requiring the government to show some legal cause for holding someone and prevents arbitrary arrest and detention.

Second, "The Trial of all Crimes … shall be by Jury." (Article III, Sec. 2) Other important procedural ones are the "right … against unreasonable searches and seizures" (in the 4th Amendment), the right against self-incrimination (in the 5th Amendment), "the right to a speedy and public trial, … to be informed of the nature and cause of the accusation; to be confronted with the witnesses against him; to have compulsory process for obtaining witnesses in his favor, and to have the Assistance of Counsel for his defence" (all in the 6th Amendment), and that "Excessive bail shall not be required" (in the 8th Amendment).

All these are "specific provisions in the Constitution." What about those other "due process" rights? What are "those settled usages and modes of proceeding existing in the common and statute law of England, before the emigration of our ancestors, and which are shown not to have been unsuited to [the American] civil and political condition?" More recently, the Supreme Court has set forth the basic requirements. In the 1970 case of Goldberg v Kelly, they said, "The fundamental requisite of due process of law is the opportunity to be heard." This "opportunity to be heard" requires timely and adequate notice of the contemplated government action, an effective opportunity to defend by confronting adverse witnesses, present one's own evidence, and make an oral argument. In a later case, they said, "the Due Process Clause provides that certain substantive rights – life, liberty, and property – cannot be deprived except pursuant to constitutionally adequate procedures. … As essential principle of due process is that a deprivation of life, liberty, and property 'be preceded by notice and an opportunity for hearing appropriate to the nature of the case.' We have described 'the root requirement' of the Due Process Clause as being 'that an individual be given an opportunity for a hearing *before* he is deprived of any significant property interest.'"

The lawyers love due process because they make their living in the process (through running the procedures). For once, the lawyers have it right, although as usual, they've been known to push a good thing too far along. Other than democracy, due process is the best thing in the Constitution. It's the second-best thing. Democracy keeps the government in line through periodic elections. But due process keeps the government in line through the courts and all the time. Under due process, the government can't deprive you of your rights except through "due process."

It's hard to exaggerate the importance of this protection. Elected officials live in constant fear of the electorate at the next election. But all the officials in the government live in constant fear of due process all the time. Virtually every action they take impacts the lives, liberty, and property of someone. All of those someones have a right to due process. If an elected official has to constantly keep the electorate in mind, all officials, including the unelected bureaucrats, have to constantly keep due process in mind. They can't violate someone's rights with impunity. Rather, a process exists for anyone to vindicate their rights. It's the second-best thing in the Constitution.

5.23 – The Political Sun

Through his three months as president of the Constitutional Convention, George Washington presided in an armchair on a raised dais facing the other delegates. You can still see the armchair at Independence Hall in Philadelphia. On the back, you'll notice a carved image of the sun. On the final day of the Convention, as the delegates were signing their signatures to the document, Benjamin Franklin pointed to the chair and remarked, "I have often looked at that behind the president without being able to tell whether it was rising or setting. But now I … know that it is a rising … sun."

Indeed, the new federal government was a rising sun. As the most massive object in our new political solar system, it would exert more gravitational force (more power) than any other object. And gradually, it would attract all the rest of our political universe into orbit around it. This force was exerted especially by the "supremacy clause" in Article VI, "This Constitution, and the Laws of the United States which shall be made in Pursuance thereof; and all Treaties made, or which shall be made, under the Authority of the United States, shall be the supreme Law of the Land." The power in those words made federal law supreme (more powerful).

Back in 1824 in the case of Gibbons v Ogden, Chief Justice John Marshall formulated the legal doctrine that flows from the "supremacy clause," saying, "if a law passed by a State … comes into conflict with a law passed by Congress … they affect the subject and each other like equal opposing powers. But the framers of our Constitution foresaw this state of things, and provided for it by declaring the supremacy [of the federal government and laws]. … In every such case, the act of Congress or the treaty is supreme, and the law of the State, though enacted in the exercise of powers not controverted, must yield to it." As the Court has said in a much more recent case in 1992, "Under the supremacy clause … any state law … which interferes with or is contrary to federal law, must yield."

The "supremacy clause" holds the states into orbit around the center of the federal sun. Without the force of this supremacy, the states would come unstuck and blunder away on courses dictated by their own interests. But the federal sun didn't just rise in 1789, it's been climbing higher in the political sky ever since, gathering more power unto itself and coming to almost totally eclipse the states.

Nothing better shows this gathering of the powers than the marshalling of the host. Originally, the federal government could marshal only a small host (less than a hundred-member Congress representing thirteen states, the president, a three-man cabinet, some 3,000 lesser officials, a six-judge Supreme Court, a few other federal judges, and an insignificant military). Today, the Congress has more than five hundred members representing fifty states, the cabinet and other agencies run into the hundreds, the federal bureaucracy numbers in the millions, the nine-man Supreme Court sits atop a nationwide network of federal courts, and the military number over 1.5 million on active duty.

This formidable array is armed to the teeth with powers. But while we can count their numbers, their powers have grown so vast and complicated that any attempt to give a complete list would numb the reader's mind and still leave something out. Perhaps the best way to convey the size to ask, as one political scientist recently did, "Just try to identify any activity in which you engage; any space you traverse; any building that you enter (including your own private home); any product or service that you produce, buy, or sell (including private health insurance); or, for that matter, any air that you breath on which there is no government policy, program, or regulation." The answer gives some idea of the powers the federal government has gathered unto itself.

Whatever happened to "limited" government? Back in 1819 in the McColloch Case, Chief Justice John Marshall wrote, "This Government is acknowledged by all to be one of enumerated powers. The principle that it can exercise only the powers granted to it ... is now universally admitted." As late as 2012 in the first Obamacare Case, Chief Justice John Roberts wrote, "In our federal system, the National Government possesses only limited powers." If these words not a legal fiction back in 1819, what more did this oft repeated formula amount to by 2012?

Only consider how the "enumerated powers" have spread. Already back in 1819 in that same McColloch Case, we heard Chief Justice Marshall open-handedly interpret the "necessary and proper clause." He ruled, "Let the end be legitimate, let it be within the scope of the Constitution, and all means which are appropriate, which are plainly adapted to that end, which are not prohibited, but consist with the letter and spirit of the Constitution, are Constitutional." In other words, all powers "necessary and proper" to carry out the specifically enumerated powers were "implied." While since nothing specifically limited what was "necessary and proper," now nothing specifically limited the "enumerated powers" either, already by 1819. In the years since, the enumerated powers have been extended to an almost unlimited extent.

Take, for example, the power enumerated in the "commerce clause" ("to regulate commerce among the several states"). Initially, that power was narrowly construed. In 1895 in the E.C. Knight Case, we heard the Supreme Court say that the Congress lacked the power to regulate a monopoly that produced and sold 98 percent of the refined sugar in the country. But by 1937 in the Jones & Laughlin Case, we heard them say, "The fundamental principle is that the power to regulate commerce is the power to enact 'all appropriate legislation' for its 'protection or advancement' ... if [activities] have such a close and substantial relation to interstate commerce that their control is essential or appropriate to protect that commerce from burdens and obstructions, Congress cannot be denied the power to exercise such control." That was a much more open-handed construction. While by 1942 in the Filburn Case, we heard them rule that Congress had the power to prevent a farmer from growing wheat for personal consumption by his family. What can the "commerce power" not now reach? What limits remain?

What have the feds done with "the commerce clause," if not used it to gather more power unto themselves? As we've seen in these articles, the same goes for all the other "enumerated powers" such as the taxing and spending power or the treaty power. The same goes for the Bill of Rights such as the 1st Amendment religious rights and other Amendments such as the "equal protection clause" of the 14th Amendment. The feds have even used what originally looked like restraints on their power to gain still more power to themselves.

Yet this gathering of the powers may not be a bad thing, but a good thing or maybe a mixed blessing. After all, things have changed. Not only are there more things we want the federal government to do for us, there are more things we need the federal government to do for us, given modern circumstances. At any rate, the Constitution has changed. To understand it as it is as it has become, we have to understand those changes. So far, we have only looked at those in general terms. In the future articles, we need to turn and look in more detail. We need to look at the Congress, the presidency, and the Supreme Court to see how these were set up, how they have come to function, and their present powers. Only by so doing can we understand the Constitution as it has become and then hope to answer our larger question. Is the Constitution as it has become a good thing or a bad thing or maybe a mixed blessing?

5.24 –Perpetual and Restless

Let's recall again Thomas Hobbes' first principal of political psychology, "So that in the first place, I put for a general inclination of all mankind, a perpetuall and restless desire of Power after power." One could offer no better proof than the history of our federal government. In these articles, we've seen the feds gain "power after power." But this same "general inclination" and "desire" motivates not only the whole government, but each branch. The Congress, the president, and the Supreme Court have "perpetually and restlessly" vied for more power over and against each other.

What would seem most odd to the Founders about this, the Congress has lost the most through these inter-governmental power struggles. The prior experience in England and America suggested the legislature was the strongest branch. Madison wrote in *Federalist No. 51*, "In republican government the legislative authority, necessarily, predominates." But when we think about federal power today, our thoughts start with the president's powers.

The Constitution may still say, "All legislative Powers herein granted shall be vested in a Congress." Back at the start, Congress jealously guarded this prerogative and resisted any presidential intervention. Madison disapproved of President Washington's draft of his first inaugural speech as "its lengthy legislative proposals would be interpreted as executive meddling with the legislature." But over the years, the presidents have elbowed their way into the process. The Constitution may still say, "All bills for raising Revenue shall originate in the House of Representatives." That's still literally true in the sense all revenue bills are filed in the House first. But today the national budget begins its legislative career in the Office of Management and Budget, an agency under direct presidential supervision. The OMB drafts the bill, which then handed off to some congressman for the formality of filing. Most other significant legislation follows a similar career path, an agency under the president's authority writing the bill, which then filed with the Congress. It's gone so far the country expects every president to come up with an entire legislative agenda, such a Woodrow Wilson's Fair Deal or Franklin Roosevelt's New Deal. To say all legislative power is still vested in Congress no more than to say Congress still has to pass the laws. So much legislative influence has become vested in the president, the political science textbooks have taken to calling him "the chief legislator."

Over foreign policy, the presidents have demonstrated the same perpetual and restless desire. The Constitution says, "[The president] shall have Power, by and with the Advice and Consent of the Senate, to make Treaties, provided two-thirds of the Senators present concur." But the custom has become not only for presidents to neglect asking for the Senate's advice before making a treaty, but even dispense with asking for their consent afterwards. Called technically only "executive agreements," yet these agreements legally commit the nation as much as a formal treaty. To give an idea of how common this practice, in the fifty years from 1889 to 1939, the U.S. entered into 524 formal treaties, but the president signed the country up to another 917 executive agreements. Maybe even more than that, the Constitution also says, "The Congress shall have the Power … To declare War." Yet although the Congress hasn't formally declared war since World War II in 1941, that little detail hasn't kept the presidents from leading the country into a number of undeclared wars. For outstanding examples, think of the Korean War (1950 to 1953), the Vietnam War (1961 to 1975), or the Iraq War (2001 to 2011). By stretching their constitutional powers over foreign policy and as commander-in-chief, the presidents have largely displaced Congress.

It's easy enough to see how the original powers of the president put him in a good position to acquire still more power relative to Congress. Yet the same perpetual and restless desire has sometimes motivated Congress to push back. Take the budget. Congress has the power to appropriate the money, but the president through the executive branch controls the expenditure. Some presidents sought to expand this control by "impounding," refusing to spend money appropriated by Congress. If some president didn't like some congressional program, this tactic let him thwart them. But Congress finally pushed back, passing the Budget and Impoundment Act of 1974. This law required the president to spend monies appropriated for a specific purpose. Or take an example related to foreign policy. When in 1984, President Ronald Reagan sought to extend aid to the contras in Nicaragua, Congress blocked him by cutting off the funding.

Yet overall, the perpetual and restless desire of the presidents has clearly succeeded more than the same emotions in the hearts of Congress. The presidents have aggrandized much more power relative to Congress. But what perhaps more surprising, the Supreme Court has proved the most successful aggressor of all, acquiring much more power over both Congress and the president. Alexander Hamilton wrote in *Federalist No. 78*, "the judiciary, from the nature of its functions, will always be least dangerous to the political rights of the constitution; because it will be least in a capacity to injure or annoy them. ... It may truly be said to have neither Force nor Will, but only judgment." No prediction could have proved more wrong. But we've reached a complicated topic, requiring we put off a full discussion until the later articles devoted specifically to the judiciary.

Yet already, we've seen one outstanding example of judicial aggression. When talking about our religious rights, we saw how the Constitution originally left America's religious settlement to the people acting through the states. But we saw how beginning in 1947 with the Everson Case, the Supreme Court took this power away from the people and the states, changing the prior religious settlement, moving from being a Christian Nation toward becoming a thoroughly secular state. This example only typifies many others. The Court has continually acquired greater powers, taking over more and more items on the national agenda.

When we recall the judiciary a non-democratic institution, the justices holding lifetime offices, we should begin to see how this has seriously altered not just the power relationship between the branches, but the form of the Constitution itself. The Constitution meant nothing if not a republic. But it is much less a republic today, the unelected Court have come to greatly dominate over the elected branches, indeed, over the people themselves.

Nor in this brief summary at the start, let us entirely neglect to mention what has become the largest branch – "the fourth branch," the bureaucracy. Although technically very much under the sway of the other three branches, the bureaucrats have shown considerable ingenuity in asserting their own "restless and perpetual desire of power after power." Their very size has greatly assisted their efforts, since they can often avoid detection by hiding in the maze. The very inertia of such a mass also assists them, as they bear down from so many points and so constantly. They have also shown some skill at playing off the other branches against the other. They sometimes manage to call in Congress to resist the president or the other way around. They have also developed techniques to seek judicial protection against the both the president and the Congress. Specific examples must await the later articles.

In sum, then, under the Constitution as it has become, not only have the federal powers greatly enlarged, but the power relationships between the branches have greatly changed. Congress started out looking the master, but the president has often proved the master of Congress. The Supreme Court has often proved the master of both. In the later articles, we'll explore these changes in more detail.

5.25 – Dead or Alive

There's a big argument among legal scholars about whether the Constitution is "dead or alive." The late, great Justice Antonin Scalia (a conservative) used to say the Constitution was dead. But the late, great Justice William Brennan (a liberal) used to say the Constitution was alive. Both sides make some good points. But as the lawyer for the Constitution, let me say I think they're both abusing my client for their partisan purposes.

First, for the good points made by either side (conservative and liberal). By saying the Constitution dead, Justice Scalia was advocating a doctrine called "originalism" as how to interpret the Constitution. Under this doctrine, the Constitution is supposed to mean what it originally meant. When interpreting it, he claimed to follow the "original intent" of the Founders. Then surely, the "originalists" make a good point. As one distinguished legal scholar said, "almost everyone is an originalist at some level." After all, constitutional interpretation has to start somewhere, and where else except with the Founders' original intent? By contrast, Justice Brennan was advocating a doctrine called "the living constitution." He asked, "What do the words of the text mean in our time?" When interpreting it, Justice Brennan claimed to follow what it should mean in our time. Then surely, the "living constitutionalists" make a good point, too. Since "time changes everything," a constitution has to change with the times. A government seized into a state of constitutional rigor mortis can only go on to decay.

But listening to them argue, you realize both sides are no more than lawyers making up clever arguments for their side of the case. It turns out "originalism" means the conservatives win, and "the living constitution" means the liberals win. Up at the Supreme Court, the justices from either side have done no more than use their respective doctrines to interpret the Constitution so their side wins. For examples, recently conservative justices used "originalism" to find the 2nd Amendment guaranteed a very strong version of the right to bear arms (a conservative cause). Less recently, liberal justices used "the living constitution" to find a constitutional guarantee for a right to abortion (a liberal cause). But surely, we need a better way to interpret the Constitution than just doctrines that mean no more than it's good when conservatives win or it's bad when liberals lose.

Let's put their arguments together, hopefully in a better and hopefully the right way. Yes, the Constitution dead in one way. The Founders meant to settle the argument over the form of our government once and for all. They meant to fix our institutions as democratic. They meant power to the people. But yes, the Constitution alive in another way. They meant to create living institutions (a living democracy). They meant for those living institutions to settle all the other arguments such as between the conservatives and liberals. And notice that puts together the arguments about interpreting the Constitution in a non-partisan way. It doesn't say which side should win (the conservatives or the liberals). It just says how they should agree to settle their differences (through the democratic process).

The Founding Fathers didn't go on such a fool's errand as to try to write down all our laws and rights once and for all. They knew better. They knew you can never write down all your laws and rights completely or clearly enough. Something is always left out; something always remains open to interpretation. They knew, too, that present laws can never hope to cover all future eventualities and circumstances. With the future, the unexpected should be the expected. Rather than trying to lock down all our laws and rights, they left the door open to adaption and change as needed.

A true doctrine of "originalism" and a true doctrine of "the living constitution" would both recognize this original intent of the Founders. If "everyone is an originalist at some level," that should be the level. Both sides should accept the Constitution is both dead and alive. It's dead as to the form of the government, but created a living democratic government. The living democratic institutions are the way to settle all the live controversies.

To close with a quote from another late, great jurist, Oliver

Wendell Holmes, Jr., writing in a 1920 case, said, "when we are dealing with words that also are a constituent act, like the Constitution of the United States, we must realize that they have called into life a being the development of which could not have been foreseen completely by the most gifted of its begetters. It was enough for them to realize or hope that they had created an organism; it has taken a century and has cost their successors much sweat and blood to prove that they created a nation."

Holmes was born in 1841 and served in the Civil War, being wounded three times and near fatally. When referring to the "sweat and blood," he was no doubt thinking especially about that irrepressible conflict. But conflict is always irrepressible. What you have to have is a way to settle your conflicts short of bloodshed. The Constitution meant to call into life such a being and create such a nation.

6.00 – THE CONGRESS

6.01– Last in the Hearts

Congress seems last in the hearts of the American people. Mark Twain said, "Suppose I were a member of Congress. Suppose I were an idiot. But I repeat myself." Oklahoma's own Will Rogers said, "Every time Congress makes a joke, it's a law, and every time they make a law, it's a joke." More recently, a survey by some outfit called Public Policy Polling found Congress less popular than lice, cockroaches, and traffic jams. The firm's director said, "When you're less popular than cockroaches … it might be time to reevaluate." Making jokes and expressing disdain for Congress seems a national pastime.

But when not poking fun at the political class, Twain and Rogers were known at times to hobnob with them. They were just making fun of the foibles of a friend. Surely, there's nothing wrong with having a laugh at the expense of Congress and laughing at the government a luxury of living in a democracy. But seriously, folks, the results of that poll remind of another legal war story. A lawyer friend was trying a divorce case in front of a tough old judge, who when it came to the custody of the children, told both parents, "Neither of you is fit to raise hogs." But if you feed him fat, even a hog has the sense to feel some sort of gratitude. Congress has fed the American people fat. Just look at all the obese people on the sidewalks and in the stores. But according to that poll, a lot of them want to bite the hand that feeds them. People that dumb aren't good for much more than bacon, and without Congress, they'd be on their way to the slaughterhouse. If "it might be time to reevaluate," it's not Congress will come up short on brains. It's all those people who fail to appreciate what Congress has done for them all these years and still doing.

The Founding Fathers had better sense. Congress came first in their hearts, not last. They put Congress first in the Constitution. The very first words of Article I read, "All legislative Powers herein granted shall be vested in a Congress of the United States." In the *Federalist No. 51* (Madison) says, "In republican government the legislative authority necessarily predominates." Congress not only came first, they meant for Congress to "predominate" over the government.

Why? Above all because they were convinced republicans and believed in representative democracy. They meant to follow "the consent of the governed." How else follow that consent except through an elected legislature? While just as much, in their experience, an elected legislature had always led the way they wanted to go. In England, the House of Commons had led the way, away from monarchy to parliamentary democracy. In America, the colonial assemblies had led the way, and later, the Continental Congress and state legislatures had led the way to independence. To go the rest of the way, they meant to follow Congress. Why wouldn't they "dance with the one who brung us," when that partner had brought them so far?

Were they wrong? Can we think of a better way to pass our laws than through an elected legislature? Who else will care more about our freedom and prosperity than our elected representatives? Who else will be as open and responsive? They have every incentive to answer their phone calls, read their mail, and listen. They consult a constituency as broad as the nation. They represent the public interest as broadly. While if a law disappoints, the people can quickly reflect their disapproval, leading to repeal or reform of the law. In sum, they're an open institution, conducting information and knowledge at high velocity. The widest variety of ideas can find an entrance and get a hearing, and better ideas have a chance to convince by simply being better ideas. As for the people's rights, who's going to protect their rights better than their elected representatives? As for the people's prosperity, who's going to promote that better than these same representatives?

Some folks take exception to calling America "exceptional," saying we're no better than anybody else. But to think America not exceptional in some excellent ways is as simple minded as to think that Congress has nothing to do with the excellent exceptions. It's simply a fact America exceptional, the freedom, the prosperity, the opportunity, all exceptional. If someone can't see that much exception, they're exceptional. Our immigrant forefathers saw it, as do all the present-day immigrants. That's why they came and are still coming. While if someone thinks that Congress didn't and doesn't have a lot to do with the exceptions, if the right one don't get you, the left one will. Either Congress passed the laws that caused the exceptionalism, or Congress didn't pass the laws that prevented the exceptionalism. Congress has to deserve a lot of the credit, one way or the other.

If "it might be time to reevaluate," what needs reevaluation is all the loose and negative talk about Congress. A lot of Americans seem so spoiled they not only expect Congress to feed them fat, they expect Congress to do their dieting and exercise for them. But that's not how it works. If you want to stay healthy and get in shape, you have to take the responsibility on yourself. Then we better take on the responsibility to understand what Congress does for us. Otherwise, we're like those spoiled rich kids, who since they've always had it, think they'll always have it. Failing to understand how their parents acquired it, they fritter away their inheritance with their ignorance and incapacity. "God bless the child who has its own." We better come to appreciate Congress. We better stop putting them last in our hearts and give them some love and attention, not to mention respect.

6.02 – Why Two

At the time of writing, the repeal or revision of Obamacare looks stuck in the Senate. The House passed a bill, but the Senate can't cobble together a majority. Whatever if anything finally passes the Senate will likely have undergone some big revisions. Since a bill must pass both chambers in precisely the same form, the House will then have to repass the Senate version. Since the two chambers seem pretty far apart, this back and forth may take a long time or may never reach an end and no bill pass.

Which brings up the question, Why two? Why have two houses to your legislature? Once again, the Founders were copying the British Constitution. Parliament has the House of Lords and the

House of Commons; Congress has the Senate and the House of Representatives. But the Founders weren't just slavish copyists. By the time of the Constitutional Convention in 1787, a two chambered (bicameral) legislature had picked up a theoretical justification. Madison wrote in *Federalist No. 51*, "In republican government the legislative authority, necessarily, predominates. The remedy ... is, to divide the legislature into two different branches." In other words, they thought of Congress as the most powerful branch ("necessarily predominates"), and as a part of the separation of powers, they further separated Congress against itself into two sub-branches, the House and the Senate. Not only would the three branches (the legislative, the executive, and the judiciary) check and balance each other, these two sub-branches would further check and balance the legislature.

If the repeal of Obamacare or any other law can't pass Congress, the difficulty just results from the design. The legislature is just acting as a check upon itself. If that makes it sometimes hard to carry out even the vital functions of the government such as passing the budget, that's just the way it is.

But the Founders also put this two-chambered design to another use. At the Constitutional Convention in 1787, one of the main stumbling blocks was a conflict between the smaller and the bigger states. Under the principle of majority rule, the less populous such as Connecticut or Delaware feared the more populous such as Massachusetts or Virginia would consistently outvote them in the new national legislature, and their interests would as consistently lose out. To modify majority rule in their favor, they demanded a Congress where each state regardless of size would have the same number of votes. That put the shoe on the other foot. The bigger states feared that under such a rule the more numerous small fry would dominate. This caused a stubborn impasse that threatened to derail the whole project until Roger Sherman of Connecticut got things back on track. Under the Connecticut (or Great) Compromise engineered by him, the Constitution apportions the House of Representatives by population, giving the bigger states an advantage there, but each state has two senators, giving the smaller states an advantage there.

Thus the apportionment remains to this day, and as a result, the Senate has been called the most malapportioned legislative body in the world. At the extremes, the biggest state (California with a population over 39 million) and the smallest state (Wyoming with only close to 600,000) each have two senators with the other states falling somewhere in between. Perhaps not surprising, then, careful studies show the smaller states have managed to leverage this advantage to extract somewhat more in federal dollars out of the process. While as another not unintended consequence, the Senate continues to stand as a bulwark against any complete dismantling of the states' sovereignty. However much the population may shift around, it's unlikely enough states won't continue to defend the influence their two senators give them and so will block any change.

The Founders also put the two chambers to still another use. Fearing somewhat the ignorance and inexperience of the masses, they feared somewhat a too direct democracy. As a partial remedy, they left electing the House of Representatives directly in the people's hands, but put electing the Senate in the hands of the state legislatures. The Constitution originally read, "The Senate of the United States shall be composed of two Senators from each State, chosen by the Legislature thereof." The underlying idea was the state legislators were more knowledgeable and experienced than the average voter, and so this indirect election of the Senate would serve as something of a check upon the populist enthusiasms of the House. As George Washington would later remark to Thomas Jefferson, "We pour the House into the Senate to cool them." The thought was carried even farther by giving the senators six-years terms and staggering their terms so only a third come up for election every two years. This looked to confer even more stability on the Senate, whereas all the Representatives are up for election every two years. But of course, in 1913, the 17th Amendment made the Senators also popularly elected, saying, "The Senate of the United States shall be composed of two Senators from each State, elected by the people thereof."

Over time, both the Senate and the House have grown in size. The Senate has 100 members and the House size was set at 435 by a law in 1911. But the two chambers remain very different places. The senators with their longer terms and few numbers remain a somewhat more exclusive club. Each senator carries quite a bit of weight, and they've used that weight to resist any tight institutional controls. For a very long time, a small group of senators or even one could stymie all action with the filibuster, although lately that seems largely done away with. Yet the Senate remains a place hard for the leadership to ramrod. Trent Lott, the Senate majority leader from 1996 to 2002, titled his memoir *Herding Cats* for good reason. On the other hand, the House has much stronger institutional controls. In the House, the leader, the Speaker, can usually get his way, although far from always and not without carefully watching his step.

At any rate, there you have to basic institutional pattern of the Congress. It's a two-headed monster. These two heads sometimes don't think alike and even fall into quarrels. In the Senate, the smaller states enjoy a disproportionate representation. Next, let's look at the inner organization of the institution.

6.03 – Size and Terms

We take for granted the size of Congress and their terms of office. But back at the Constitutional Convention in 1787, the Founders Fathers gave a lot of thought to both. Their forethought resulted well for us.

The Constitution says, "The Senate of the United States shall be composed of two Senators from each State." That meant the First Congress had only 26 senators, but as we know, the size has grown with the admission of new states to an even 100, a fourfold increase. The Constitution set the numbers in the House of Representatives in the first Congress at only 65, but provided for a reapportionment based on the census, which "shall be made within three Years," and thereafter every "ten Years." It also provided, "The Number of Representatives shall not exceed one for every thirty Thousand," but left Congress to set the exact number by law. In 1793 after the very first census, the number jumped to 105. Just before the Civil War in 1857, it had reached 237, but with the loss of the seceding states, went down for a few years. However, in the next decades began another long rise tracking the rise in the population. Until finally, with the Apportionment Act of 1911, Congress passed a law limiting the size to 435. That familiar number has stayed the same for over a century, although Congress could always change it again.

What would be the ideal size for a legislature anyway? In *Federalist No. 55*, James Madison took on the question by first admitting the difficulty with any precise answer. "In general it may be remarked on this subject, that no political problem is less susceptible of a precise solution than that which relates to the number most convenient for a representative legislature." As typical with his pragmatic approach, he next turned to try and learn the lessons taught by actual experience, examining the size of state legislatures and the British House of Commons. From this survey, he drew three general conclusions. First, too small a legislature tends to turn into a cabal, since just a few men can easily conspire among themselves or be easily corrupted through bribery. Second, a legislature should contain enough members to represent its total constituency so as to understand and share the totality of the people's interests. Third, it shouldn't be so large as to turn into a mob swayed by passions and with individual responsibility lost in the mass. *No. 55* concludes, "The truth is, that in all cases a certain number at least seems to be necessary to secure the benefits of free consultation and discussion, and to guard against too easy a combination for improper purposes; as, on the other hand, the number ought at most to be kept within a certain limit, in order to avoid the confusion and intemperance of a multitude. In all very numerous assemblies, of whatever character composed, passion never fails to wrest the sceptre from reason."

But there's another aspect to legislative size. "How much wood would a woodchuck chuck if a woodchuck could chuck wood? As much as he could if a woodchuck could chuck wood." How many voters should a representative represent? As many as he could? How many would that be before the size of his constituency made any meaningful representation a nonsense phrase?

As just seen, the Constitution said, "The Number of Representatives shall not exceed one for every thirty Thousand." And 30,000 is not more than the size of a town where everybody knows everybody else's business. A representative can know and so can represent such a constituency pretty well. But the first census in 1790 showed a population of close to 4 million, while the last in 2010 counted well over 300 million. As an inevitable result, our congressmen have come to represent more and more people.

The size for a House district is now over 650,000. While of course, many senators have much larger constituencies. The two senators from California represent over 39 million people. Then can we still say our representatives are still in touch with their constituents? Probably we could still say that about the members of the House and the senators from the smaller states. But those senators from the really big states are probably past the outer limits on the size.

Leaving behind the size of Congress, let's turn to their terms of office. *No. 52* says, "As it is essential to liberty that the government in general should have a common interest with the people, so it is particularly essential that [the Congress] should have an immediate dependence on, and an intimate sympathy with, the people. Frequent elections are unquestionably the only policy by which this dependence and sympathy can be effectually secured." But how frequent? It was a popular saying back at the time of the Constitutional Convention in 1787 that, "where annual elections end, tyranny begins." But obviously, the delegates rejected this advice. The Constitution says, "The House of Representatives shall be composed of Members chosen every second Year," and, "The Senate of the United States shall be composed of two Senators from each State, chosen … for six years," with one-third of them elected every two years. The *Federalist No. 53* vigorously defended these terms by again pointing to experience where legislators elected for even considerably longer periods, up to seven years for the British House of Commons, had not resulted in tyranny. Without going any further into the controversy, our experience since seems to have conclusively settled the argument. Two-year terms for the House and six-year terms for the Senate have "effectually secured" their "dependence on the people."

Let us mention, too, the issue of the quorum. Article I says, "a Majority of each shall constitute a Quorum to do Business." In other words, only 50 percent plus one need be present for either the House or the Senate to conduct business. *No. 58* notes that, "It has been said that more than a majority ought to have been required for a quorum." Even today, some states require more for a quorum in their legislatures, say two-thirds. But this requirement allows a minority to totally frustrate the majority by simply refusing to attend, as has happened in some states. Rather and more wisely, the Constitution follows the reasoning in *No. 58*, "In all cases where justice or the general good might require new laws to be passed, or active measures to be pursued, the fundamental principle of free government would be reversed. It would be no longer the majority that would rule: the power would be transferred to the minority."

Let us not pass by these institutional features of the Congress without pausing to remark their importance. Congress seems about the right size to be able to get through its business. It's not too small or too large. It seems about the right size to represent it constituencies, but it's pushing the upper limit in some respects there. The terms of office seem not too short and not too long. Their terms are not so short the members have to devote all their time and energy to running for office with none left over to do the job they were elected to do and not so long that the members can forget about their responsibility to the electorate. A legislature which meets all these criteria might seem a commonplace. But it hasn't been in history and so should be ranked as quite an accomplishment.

6.04 – Compared to What

People all the time call Congress "dysfunctional." But compared to what? Let them point out some more functional legislature in the real world. Turns out they can't. They imagine smooth sailing on some calm legislative sea somewhere, but storm and stress fill the political seas of the real world. So turns out they can't point out a legislature as well designed to navigate such troubled waters as Congress, except again, the British Parliament. By comparison with others, Congress turns out a well-designed legislative ship-of-state (more functional).

In making such a comparison between legislatures, a recent book deserves a wider audience. Professor Joel M. Ostrow, a political scientist, writes for the scholarly press, and his book (published in 2000) bears the rather ungainly title, *Comparing Post-Soviet Legislatures: A Theory of Institutional Design and Political Conflict*. But the title well describes the project. The book "compares" the "institutional design" of "post-soviet legislatures" in Russia and her former satellites after the fall of the Soviet Union. Making these comparisons leads him to comes up with "a theory of institutional design" for legislatures. This comparison shows why Congress is a legislature well-designed to manage "political conflict," the key to a functional as compared to a dysfunctional legislature.

After the fall of the Soviet Union in 1991, Russia replaced her dictatorship with a democracy and good for her. Their new constitution provided for an elected president, a post won by Boris Yeltsin, and an elected legislature, the Supreme Soviet. But within a few short years, as Professor Ostrow tells us, "Russian President Boris Yeltsin decreed the Supreme Soviet out of existence and, on October 4, 1993, used the firepower of T-72 tanks to enforce the decree. The Supreme Soviet has pursued such an intractable line of conflict that it provoked the Russian president to bomb it out of existence." Their legislative ship went down with all hands. That's dysfunctional.

What had gone wrong? No doubt whoever wrote the new democratic Russian Constitution had good intentions, but they lacked the know-how to design a functional legislature that could navigate through the political conflicts. As Professor Ostrow points out, it's not enough to elect your legislators, although that's fundamental to the design. You also have to design the institution so it can resolve both the conflicts within the legislature itself and with the executive branch. Professor Ostrow says, "Democracy presupposes the existence of conflict. Rather than eliminating conflict, democracy requires institutions to provide for its ... expression and resolution. ... Democratic institutions ... are successful insofar as they are able to manage and channel political conflicts to productive ends."

But while the "expression" of the conflicts just happens, their "resolution" doesn't just happen. Rather, a legislative institution has to be designed to make it happen. Otherwise, the legislators' conflicts with each other and/or with the executive branch become intractable and the institution won't function well.

Then first, let's look how the U.S. Congress functions to "manage and channel political conflicts to production ends." Professor Ostrow calls our congressional design a "linked dual channel system." When we understand what he means by that rather academic description, we see he has laid his finger on some essential elements in the congressional design (and elements often overlooked). He means that Congress functions through two ("dual") channels (the "committees" and the "political parties"), and these two channels are "linked" together.

All congressional business gets assigned to a particular committee, and there are numerous committees. That's one channel. Because this channel has so many tributaries, it can carry a lot of traffic at the same time. Congress can function to carry on a large volume of business all at once. The second channel (the political parties) links these tributaries together and directs the traffic. The majority party elects the congressional leaders, assigns all the committee chairmen, and has a majority on every committee. Generally, then, the leaders of the majority party can manage the Congress. They can resolve the conflicts within the institution. Congress not only can get through a lot of work, it can move as a coherent whole. While at the same time, the party leaders can interface with the chief executive and the bureaucracy, resolving the conflicts with those branches.

Not to say the Congress functions flawlessly (far from it). But compared to the Supreme Soviet, the congressional design is much more functional. The design of the Supreme Soviet carefully excluded parties as an organizing principle. Perhaps they'd listened to all the complaints about "partisanship" in our Congress, and they thought by excluding the parties from any control, their legislature would function more smoothly. Instead, their design was totally committee centered. Ostrow says, "The Supreme Soviet, with its non-partisan, committee centered design, reached extraordinary internal consensus on technical legislative issues, resulting in a highly consensual legislative process." So much of the design looked good. Their legislature was able to solve the conflicts within itself.

But hold it, that's only half the problem. Remember that it also needed to interface with the chief executive. That's where their design failed. Ostrow goes on, "However, by denying an institutional role for partisan interests, the Supreme Soviet lacked mechanisms for managing political conflict with the executive branch. The absence of organized partisan structures enabled individual Supreme Soviet members and, most notably, the

Chairman to pursue and unconstrained line of confrontation with the executive branch. The conflict and extended deadlock that ensued culminated in the President's abolishing that legislature by decree and destroying it in a hail of artillery fire." You see what he's saying. Their design lacked an effective way to resolve the conflicts between the legislature (led by the chairman) and the chief executive (the president), leading to a deadlock between the two finally resolved only by an appeal to armed force.

Good intentions aren't enough. Institutional design is crucial. It's not enough to say we're going to have a democracy. Just electing your legislators isn't enough. The institutional design of the legislature has to allow for the resolution of the continual and endless political conflicts. To understand how Congress manages to achieve this, we have to understand the points made by Professor Ostrow in his "theory of institutional design." We have to understand the "dual, linked channels" (how the committees and parties work in Congress).

When people call Congress dysfunctional, it's generally because Congress hasn't done exactly what they think it should have done as soon as they think it should have done it, which usually the day before yesterday. But the truth is, they don't have in mind a better design for a more functional legislature. The truth is, Congress is well designed to do what we want a legislature to do, that is, reflect the will of the people, resolve the conflicts in public opinion, resolve the conflicts within Congress itself, and resolve the conflicts with the executive and bureaucracy. Truth is, nobody has come up with a way to make it more functional. Truth is, for over two hundred years it has functioned well in the public interest. Truth is, no other legislative institution in the world has such a record of success, except once again, the British Parliament.

6.05 – Committee Government

No other profession has produced as many presidents as the lawyers, a fact they're rather fond of reminding people. But who was the only president with a Ph.D.? That was Woodrow Wilson, president from 1913 to 1921. Perhaps not coincidentally, Wilson took his doctorate in political science, a new discipline back then.

Before going into politics, he taught at the university level and published rather than perished, churning out a long list of books on politics and history. His best and most original was *Congressional Government* (published in 1884), but his main thesis may sound rather odd to present-day readers. It's a bit to get through, but here it is, "There has been a vast alteration in the conditions of our government; ... the checks and balances which once obtained are no longer effective; ... The noble charter of fundamental law given us by the Convention of 1787 is still our Constitution; but it is now our form of government rather in name than in reality, ... the actual form of our present government is simply a scheme of congressional supremacy. ... I know not how better to describe our form of government in a single phrase than by calling it a government by the chairmen of the Standing Committees of Congress."

Now at the present-day, it wouldn't sound odd for someone to say, "there has been a vast alteration in the conditions of our government" or "the checks and balances which once obtained are no longer effective." People say those sorts of things all the time. But it would sound rather odd to say, "our present government is simply a scheme of congressional supremacy." Presently, we don't think about "our government" as "a scheme of congressional supremacy." To the contrary, we think about either "the imperial presidency" or "judicial supremacy." In the present-day scheme, Congress seems the least of the branches, having been thrown into the shade by the growth of presidential and judicial power. But as acute an observer as Wilson didn't get it wrong. Back when he was writing in 1884, Congress had dominated for a period. Earlier and stronger presidents such as Washington, Jefferson, Jackson, and Lincoln had managed their reins so as to lead the Congress, but after the Civil War, Congress managed to take the bit between their teeth and run away with some weaker presidents such as Andrew Johnson or Chester Arthur. But before too long, another "alteration in the conditions" would set in, shifting power back toward the presidents. Wilson himself would take notice of this shift in a later book, *Constitutional Government in the United States*, 1908, and after taking office as president in 1913, no one could have accused him of not doing his part to shove along the shift.

But notice something more from the quote, "I know not how

better to describe our form of government in a single phrase than by calling it a government by the chairmen of the Standing Committees of Congress." Wilson wasn't just saying the government "a scheme of congressional supremacy." He was "calling it a government by the chairmen of the Standing Committees of Congress." But if that were true, who were these "chairmen" and whence came their power? Where does the Constitution mention "the standing committees" or their "chairmen," let alone confer power on them?

No, if you re-read the Constitution, you won't find any words about congressional committees, their chairmen, or their powers. Rather, these institutional features later spontaneously emerged within Congress. Wilson lays his finger on the reason why. "Time would fail it to discuss all the bills brought in, for they every session number thousands, … . Accordingly, no futile attempt it made to do anything of the kind. The work is parceled out to the forty-seven Standing Committees." In other words, the whole Congress couldn't possibly "discuss all the bills" filed, so Congress quite soon and quite sensibly developed a system of committees to "parcel out the work." After being filed, the bills are referred to the proper committee, "who," Wilson goes on to say, "sift the chaff from the wheat in the bushels of bills every week piled upon the clerk's desk." Through this winnowing process, the committees and their chairman acquire their power. They can decide what bills to take up (hold hearings on) or ignore (bury), and they can amend the bills. Only the ones they "refer out" (send back to the floor for final passage) have a chance to become law.

Let us pause to applaud this marvelously practical invention of American political genius. Apparently, in Wilson's day, the Congress had "forty-seven standing committees" and the number has varied. But whatever the precise number, all these committees can carry on their business at the same time. That serves as a multiplier. Rather than being able to work on just one bill at a time, Congress can work on any number of bills simultaneously. Otherwise, they couldn't possibly get through all the work. Another advantage comes with this division of labor, which brings the advantage of specialization. Every committee has an assigned area of specialization, the Agriculture Committee, the Armed Services Committee, and so on. The members on these committees, who often serve for years, can acquire real expertise in the specific areas under their jurisdiction. Congress cannot only get through more business, they can become experts at the business.

But if look back at his book, remember published in 1884, we find Wilson wasn't lauding the committee system, but finding fault. He argued the committees and especially their chairmen, who can usually dominate their committees, had way too much power. He argued the chairman had managed to form an inner oligarchy inside Congress. Rather than operating democratically, he argued these few men had effectively seized control over the Congress. At the time, that may have been a good argument. Since then, Congress has somewhat reformed itself to answer this argument. Yet a perfect balance has proved hard to strike. Complaints still sometimes sound against the excessive power of the committee chairmen.

But the fact remains that the institution of the committees provided a vital component to the institution of the Congress. Without committees, Congress couldn't hope to get through all the business or get through it as efficiently. Then can we take away at least this much? Once again, the Constitution has not stayed static, but continually evolved. As Wilson said, there has been a continual "alteration in the conditions of our government." Not only did committees emerge within Congress, but just as the power of Congress has waxed and waned, the power of the committees and their chairman has waxed and waned within Congress. Moreover, the institution of the committees is essential to the efficiency of the institution of Congress.

6.06 – Partisan Government

In 1962, at a White House dinner honoring Noble Prize winners, President John F. Kennedy remarked, "I think this is the most extraordinary collection of talent, of human knowledge, that has ever been gathered together at the White House, with the possible exception of when Thomas Jefferson dined alone." Jefferson would have been gratified. But if the man possessed one talent more than another, it was for politics (for winning power). That talent caused him to come up with a stroke of genius. As a way to win power, he invented the American political party.

As the new government under the Constitution got up and running back in 1789, the new Congress would shortly attract Jefferson's talent for politics (and for winning power). Not that Jefferson sat in Congress, and he never did. Rather, Washington had tapped him for a more prominent seat, the one reserved in the cabinet for the very first Secretary of State. There he found himself rubbing uncongenial shoulders with Alexander Hamilton, the very first Secretary of the Treasury. These two men's soaring ambitions made them bitter rivals, since each stood in the way of other. It was Jefferson's early frustrations in their conflict that attracted his talent for politics (and for winning power) toward Congress.

The Constitution says not much about the leaders or the internal organization of Congress. Article I says no more than, "The Vice President ... shall be the President of the Senate, ... the Senate shall chuse their other Officers, ... [and] the House of Representatives shall chuse their Speaker and other Officers." It goes on, "Each House may determine the Rules of its Proceedings."

Nor when the First Congress met in 1789 were there many members either, just 26 senators and 65 representatives. Not a lot, but enough to mill around on the floor, start to fall out among themselves, and start to form loose factions against each other largely along sectional lines and interests. For a conspicuous example, New Englanders wanted tariffs to protect their infant manufactures against mature foreign competitors. Southerners opposed such tariffs, which raised the cost of manufactured goods to their agricultural region. Herein lay the seeds for that fierce sectional discord over tariffs which later served as a prelude to the Civil War.

Meanwhile over in the cabinet, Jefferson was suffering nothing except vexation. As president and with his overwhelming prestige, Washington called the shots in the cabinet and kept siding with Hamilton. Never happy to play second fiddle even under Washington's baton, Jefferson's eye had always been on the prize anyway, the presidency for himself eventually. So his talent conceived his original and brilliant political invention (to win power for himself). He would resign from the cabinet and switch his base of operations to Congress. First, he would organize a political party to win control inside Congress. Then he would use that party to spread the control outside Congress. By inventing this device, he planned to win control over Congress, the states, and the nation and elect himself to the presidency. As we know from the events, his invention proved a stroke of political genius, propelling Jefferson to all his goals.

It was a classic move into a power vacuum. The loose factions in Congress left no faction dominant there. But if he could organize a tighter faction (what we've come to call a political party), and if the party could recruit a majority of the members of Congress, they could dominate the body. From this start, they could spread their dominance across the nation. Although nothing quite like what Jefferson imagined had ever been done before, his many friends both inside and outside Congress quickly grasped the potential. The top spot might be reserved for Jefferson, but such a party offered rich rewards to whoever signed on as his lieutenants and followers. Through organizing themselves more tightly, together they could enjoy the pleasures and profits of power.

With Jefferson's master-hand working the levers, his new political invention quickly proved it value in practice. His party (the Democrat-Republicans or the Jeffersonian Republicans) elected him president for two terms (1801 to 1809), elected his top protégé (James Madison) for the next two terms (1809 to 1817), and elected a second protégé (James Monroe) for the next two terms (1817 to 1825). It doesn't get much better than that in politics, winning six presidential campaigns in a row for twenty-four straight years. They were so successful they ran the competition out of business. The Federalist Party disappeared after around 1820, and with no one else to fight with, the Jeffersonian Republicans began quarreling among themselves over the power.

But regard what Jefferson's talent had wrought in the halls of Congress. From then until now, the political parties have organized the Congress. The majority party elects the Speaker of the House and the Majority Leader in the Senate, as well as the other assistant leaders. The majority party appoints all the committee chairmen and a majority of their members to all the committees. The majority party controls Congress.

Thus, Congress is organized along partisan lines. This partisanship is often decried, but along what other lines would you have Congress align? If partisanship often leads to partisan strife, yet the partisanship is how things get done. Without that organizing principle, you'd have nothing more than what Congress started out, that is, a bunch of members milling around and forming loose factions. How would they ever get through the business?

Jefferson wasn't involved in constitution building, but in constituency building (to win power for himself). But in the process, his genius created what in effect has become an integral part of the Constitution, the political party as an organizing principle both inside and outside Congress.

6.07 – Democracy in Congress

In this day of reality TV, surely Congress must be next. But they'll have to find a way to spice up the script. You can already watch Congress live on C-SPAN, and generally, the proceedings are as dull as dishwater. Yet there have been the occasional episodes of high legislative drama. Back on January 29, 1890, one such played out on the House floor, following a script written by then Speaker of the House, Thomas B. Reed (R-ME).

Not much remembered today, Reed offers an interesting case study for the American type of the professional politician. Representing Maine in the House for twenty-two years from 1876 to 1899, Reed was an imposing figure at six-three and over 250 pounds. He was possessed of a biting wit. Asked whether he planned to attend the funeral of a political foe, he replied, "No, but I approve of it." When a fellow congressman concluded a speech by saying he would rather be right than president, Reed growled, "The Honorable Member need not worry because he will never be either." He's also credited with the saying "a statesman is a dead politician." In 1896, Reed would lose a bid for the Republican presidential nomination in a close contest with fellow congressman William McKinley. But the day we meet him, as said January 29, 1890, he was riding high on the wave of a political triumph, having just been elected Speaker of the House when the Fifty-First Congress assembled on December 1, 1889.

The loyal opposition in the House, the minority party (on this day the Democrats), seldom pause in their efforts to thwart the majority (on this day the Republicans led by Reed). In those bygone days, one familiar and highly effective tactic was "the disappearing quorum." The Constitution says, "a majority of each house shall constitute a quorum to do business." In other words, "to do business" the House needs at least half the members plus one present. But during the long and tedious sessions, members often absented themselves from the floor, being busy or not so busy elsewhere. Looking around and seeing some majority members off on such errands, the minority would often move for a quorum call (move the clerk to call the roll to show whether a quorum present). As the clerk called the roll, the minority members wouldn't answer when their names called, and so wouldn't be counted for the purpose of making up a quorum. Especially when the chamber closely divided, their silence would cause a quorum to fail when only a few majority members were absent. The eye of the beholder could count a quorum, but the refusal of the minority members to answer created a fiction in the ear of the listener. Business would grind to a halt until the majority could summon enough of their vagrant members back to the floor. Thus was the precious resource of limited legislative time frittered away in a trivial pursuit, but playing a game the minority much enjoyed.

But on this particular day (January 29, 1890), Reed, as the new Speaker, meant to re-write this familiar script. The pages of the Congressional Record have preserved the drama. In 1890, the House had only 330 members (a quorum being 166). After calling for a vote on a motion unimportant in itself, Reed announced the count as "the ayes are 161, the nays 2" (which of course, was three short of a quorum). At which point, the Democratic leader, Charles F. Crisp (D-GE) made the expected objection, calling out, "No quorum." But then Reed did the unexpected.

"Directing the Clerk to record the following names of members present and refusing to vote," Reed started naming Democrats actually present in the chamber, easily more than enough to make a quorum. In other words, he suddenly and dramatically signaled his intention to break with the tradition of "the disappearing quorum." From now on, he (as Speaker) meant to count any member actually present, whether or not they answered to their name on the rollcall.

As the Democrats caught on to what he was doing, they

promptly flew into a passion. When Reed came to name of Mr. Breckenridge of Kentucky, that gentlemen responded, "I deny the power of the Speaker and denounce it as revolutionary" (to loud applause from the Democratic side of the House, which was renewed several times). Reed responded, "The Chair is making a statement of fact that the gentleman from Kentucky is present. Does he deny it?" (to laughter and applause from the Republican side).

After three tumultuous days of such back and forth bickering, "the disappearing quorum" itself disappeared into history. The Constitution says, "Each House may determine the Rules of its Proceedings." Since the majority in the House (at the time the Republicans) could outvote the minority (at the time the Democrats), they could change the rules and did. Fiction was replaced with fact. The minority lost a tool with which to obstruct the majority.

That wasn't the only rule the majority changed. Under Reed's leadership, they promulgated a whole new set of rules for governing the House (the "Reed Rules"). If before the minority had too much power to obstruct and stall the majority, the complaint soon sounded that the "Reed Rules" let the majority, and especially the Speaker, run roughshod over the minority. Under these new rules, the Speaker appointed all the committee members and chairman, a power it was asserted that made him a "virtual dictator" over the House.

Not to go into all that for our present purposes, let's take away the larger point. To preserve the democratic process inside Congress or any legislative body, for that matter, you need some carefully crafted rules. On one hand, if the minority can totally frustrate the will of the majority, they can as totally frustrate the principle of majority rule. On the other hand, if the leaders in the body can entirely dominate its proceedings, you turn the legislature into an oligarchy. Either extreme destroys the democratic nature of the institution. It's not enough to have an elected legislature. You have to have internal rules that pass the will of the majority throughout the process.

In the history of Congress, the fights over the internal rules have seesawed back and forth. The minority wants rules that let them frustrate the majority. The members want rules that keep the leadership from dominating the body. The leadership wants to dominate. The balance has tipped back and forth and sometimes gotten out of balance. It's a struggle that will and must go on. But in general, we don't have the impression that either the majority has been totally frustrated or that the leadership has been able to totally dominate the chamber. If a perfect balance seems elusive, yet we're left with the impression the will of the majority has been passed through by the internal rules.

6.08 – Gridlock in Congress

We constantly hear about "gridlock" in Congress. Such complaints are nothing new. Back in 1963, Walter Lippman, one of the most famous and influential columnists ever, described the Eighty-Eighth Congress in 1963 as "accomplishing practically nothing, … feebly led, wedded to its own lethargy and impervious to criticism, … a scandal of drift and inefficiency." His conclusion, "This Congress has gone further than any other within memory to replace debate and decision by delay and stultification. This is one of those moments when there is reason to wonder whether the congressional system as it now operates is not a grave danger to the Republic." In a book the same year, *The Deadlock of Democracy*, James MacGregor Burns, a distinguished historian, said, "we are at a critical stage of a somber and inexorable cycle that seems to have gripped the public affairs of the nation, … mired in governmental deadlock, as Congress blocks and kills not only" President Kennedy's programs, but Republican programs as well. His conclusion, "We … underestimate the extent to which our system was designed for deadlock and inaction" and maybe the system would have to be changed. The popular "Life" magazine piled on with their conclusion, "This scandal has put our whole system of Parliamentary democracy in question."

That was in 1963. But suddenly the very next year (1964), Congress passed a major tax cut bill and the Civil Rights Act of 1964, the law that finally broke the back of segregation, a breakthrough if ever there was one. In the same year, Lyndon Johnson swept to re-election in a landslide that carried the Democrats to a supermajority in the next Congress, the Eighty-

Ninth from 1965 to 1967. About this Congress it has been said, "The first session of the Eighty-Ninth Congress passed more landmark legislation than any legislature since 1933." These laws included the Voting Rights Act of 1965 (to further guarantee black voting rights) and Johnson's vast Great Society programs, such as Medicare and Medicaid, the Elementary and Secondary School Act (greatly expanding federal funding for education), the Immigration and Naturalization Act of 1965 (doing away with the preferences for northern and western Europeans), the Housing and Urban Development Act (greatly expanding federal funds for housing and subsidies for the elderly and disabled), the Freedom of Information Act, and let us not forget, Lady Bird's Highway Beautification Act.

The reference back to 1933 as another landmark year for congressional legislation is significant. That refers back to the Seventy-Third Congress from 1933 to 1935, which came into office on another landslide. In response to the crisis of the Great Depression, the voters in 1932 swept both Democrat Franklin Roosevelt into the White House and a Democratic supermajority into the Congress. Their landmark legislation included an Emergency Banking Act (requiring all banks to undergo federal inspection to assure their stability), the Agricultural Adjustment Act (intended to protect farmers with subsidies and production controls), the National Industrial Recovery Act (an effort to stabilize industrial production, prices, and wages), the Glass-Steagall Act (establishing the Federal Deposit Insurance Corporation), the Securities Act (establishing the Securities and Exchange Commission), and the list goes on.

Why did the gridlock break in 1933 and 1964? It's simple, isn't it? Congress exhibits a high degree of gridlock when the American people are fairly evenly divided and so Congress is fairly evenly divided between the two parties. But the gridlock relaxes when a clear popular majority elects one party with a clear majority to Congress. That's what happened in 1933 and 1964. That's why those Congresses could pass a lot of landmark legislation. But that's doesn't happen very often. More usually, Congress is fairly evenly divided and so has a hard time passing any big-ticket items. Yet year in and year out, they still manage to carry out the routine business, such a keeping the government funded and running.

Then is such a situation really a bad thing? John C. Calhoun wouldn't have thought so. Thoroughly out of fashion today, as the leading defender of slavery in his day, yet the South Carolinian was definitely a man to reckon with in his day, and some of his other ideas are still very much in fashion even today. He served as Vice-President, Secretary of State, Secretary of War, and senator from South Carolina, dying in office in 1850. As well as being a formidable political actor, he was a formidable political theorist. One of his theories now goes under the name "consensual democracy." Rather than a mere legislative majority being enough to pass a law, Calhoun argued that to treat the minority fair passing a law should require a consensus (virtual unanimity). In the form he advocated it, all the states should have to agree on any federal law. Of course, he came up with this argument as a way to try and prevent Congress from ever passing any laws to abolish slavery. Today, that cause discredits the theory coming from his mouth, but it remains very much alive and well when coming from other mouths. Today, all sorts of folks advocate all sorts of limits on majority rule in favor of all sorts of minorities and causes. We're told that Switzerland and the Netherlands actually have "consensual democracies," where doing anything of real importance requires not merely a legislative majority, but a consensus.

Maybe that goes too far. Maybe every minority shouldn't possess a veto over all legislation. But maybe there's something to be said for more than a bare majority, at least when passing landmark legislation. Maybe there's something to be said for not taking a radical turn with every shift of the electoral tide, but waiting until the tide runs strong enough. Then if Congress often gridlocks until one party wins a clear majority, maybe that's not such a bad thing. The gridlock is frustrating, sometimes even threatens to go over the edge, as when Congress can't pass the budget or raise the debt limit on time. But so far, they've never gone over the edge. Then maybe we shouldn't talk so much about gridlock, but talk more about a certain delay and caution designed into the system, which not necessarily a bad thing.

The truth seems to be that year in and year out, Congress manages to get through the routine business such as passing the budget. In fits and starts, Congress manages to get done the big-ticket items. If anyone can suggest a better or smoother system, let them come forward with their suggestion. Meanwhile, we'll have to get along with what we have, which may not be so bad.

6.09 – The Stagnant Congress

People express a low opinion for Congress, but what seems contradictory, seem to have good opinions about their own congressmen. At least, they keep re-electing the same ones. In the 2014 elections, over 90 percent of incumbents won re-election, and such a high "retention rate" goes fairly far back. Political scientists began noticing this trend in the 1970s, and they began referring to the phenomenon as "congressional stagnation." What causes such a seeming contradiction? Why would Congress suffer a low approval rating, but congressmen enjoy a high approval when and where it counts, at election time? And does that amount to "stagnation" or maybe just stability, and what's so wrong with stability?

As far as the high retention rate, maybe we should however reluctantly give some credit to the congressmen themselves. A guy who wins election to Congress has proved he can play in the bigs, and once in Congress, has a chance to perfect his game and rack up some statistics. He may not hit spectacular home runs, but has the chance to score some runs and win some applause from the crowd. At the least, he gets his name in the papers, winning the advantage of "name recognition." But if he's on his game, he will deliver for his constituents, running errands for them on Capitol Hill and with the bureaucracy (case work) and bringing home some pork. With such favors to trade, he can make new friends and expand his base. And he gains another major advantage. In the major leagues a guy makes the big bucks, and playing in Congress, a guy can raise the big bucks. Donors give steadily to incumbents, who already have the influence that comes with office. By comparison, most challengers enter the race from a standing start. They're unknown quantities and have to finance their campaign in a hurry and on a hope of some future influence. The only thing they have reliably going for them is the hostility of the out-party for the in-party's congressman.

But if this story has a villain, his name is "gerrymander." As most know by now, this term traces back to Elbridge Gerry, who lived from 1744 to 1814. A Founding Father of some prominence, Gerry signed the Declaration of Independence, but although a delegate to the Constitution Convention, refused to put his name to the finished document, thereby missing a second sure entry into the national hall of fame. Nevertheless, later he sat in the U.S. Congress from 1789 to 1793 and climbed as high as the vice-president's seat under James Madison from 1813 to 1814, dying in office. In between, Gerry found time to serve as the Governor of Massachusetts from 1810 to 1812. A convert to Jefferson's Republican Party, in 1812 while governor, he signed into law a bill passed by a Republican dominated legislature. This law drew some very odd shaped electoral districts, which sprawled across the political landscape on a partisan mission. Their boundaries gave the Republicans an electoral advantage over the Federalists, the other major party in those days. One of these strange shapes looked, as someone quipped, like a salamander, and it was only a short step to call the drawing of such partisan districts a "Gerry-mander," which has come down to us as "gerrymander."

The basic legal rule about legislative districts is "one-man, one-vote." The Supreme Court has ruled the Constitution requires districts roughly equal in population to assure a vote in one district counts as much as another vote in another district. Since the population moves around and grows, that rule forces a redrawing of the electoral districts with each census every ten years. Traditionally, that was a task for the state legislatures, and even before Gerry's memorable efforts, the majority party in the legislature already knew how to use the occasion as a way to gain a partisan advantage for themselves.

A gerrymander relies on "packing and cracking." Packing is "concentrating one party's backers in a few districts that they win by overwhelming margins." Cracking is "dividing a party's supporters in multiple districts so that they fall short of a majority in each one." By cleverly using these techniques, an electoral mapmaker can virtually assure one party wins more seats in the legislature than the other, at least if the electorate fairly evenly divided between the two parties. The disfavored party will "waste" a lot of votes, winning by big margins in a few districts. The favored party will win more districts by a narrower margin, making its votes more "efficient." One pundit says that due to gerrymandering "in 1981 … the Democrats [won] 62 percent of California's districts while receiving only 51 percent of the votes cast—an 11 percent gerrymandering bonus. … The same was true in Texas where Democrat candidates regularly won considerably more than 57% of the congressional seats with as little as 39% of the vote."

How exactly do we know a gerrymander when we see it? After all, one party will win in any given district. Any win may largely reflect a local candidate's superior stump presence or turn on some immediate local controversy or pressing issue. But the traditional hallmark of a gerrymander was, as the name suggests, those oddly shaped electoral districts needed to achieve the desired result. If instead, one saw compact and contiguous districts, conforming to county and municipal boundaries, it was generally regarded as refuting a gerrymander. However, with the advent of computer modeling, cleverly designed electoral districts can achieve a gerrymander more subtly without odd shaped districts. The political scientists who deal in such metrics have come up with several complex formulas purporting to detect such schemes. Unfortunately, none of the formulas work to perfection and their results sometimes disagree. That seems to leave a gerrymander largely, but not entirely, in the eye of the beholder. If one party wins say 50 percent of the votes, but 55 percent of the seats, we might not suspect anything. But if one party consistently over several elections wins only say 40 percent of the votes, but 60 percent of the seats, we might strongly suspect we're seeing a gerrymander.

But what's wrong with the gerrymander anyway? That's politics. If the people vote one party in, drawing the electoral districts is one of the prerogatives and pleasures the people conferred on the party. But surely, that goes too far. The people may vote one party in, but it goes too far to say they meant to vote them in permanently, meant for the winner of one election to entrench themselves behind a gerrymander to win the future elections. As much as that, it just doesn't seem fair for one party to win more votes, but come away with fewer seats. Such outcomes seem to violate the fundamental democratic principle of majority rule. "The workable democracy that the Constitution foresees" must include "a method for transforming the will of the majority into effective government." And, "Each political group in a State should have the same chance to elect representatives of its choice as any other political group."

As another consequence, the gerrymander creates "safe districts" for both parties. Each party's candidates can except to win in those districts without much of a fight. Such safety will likely cause them to lose interest in broadening their base or working across the aisle. Instead, they're likely to play to their party's more extreme wing. "A [legislator] who has won with only 51% of the vote will very likely govern differently than one who has a safe seat, ... It is exceptionally likely that legislators in swing districts will adopt more moderate, centrist positions than some of their colleagues, and they will of necessity be more responsive to the 49% of the electorate that did not vote for them. It would not be surprising if legislators from [safe] Democratic districts or [safe] Republican districts, for example, represented viewpoints further from the center of their respective parties' ideologies, being more concerned about a primary challenge from *within* their own party than any threat from a candidate from the other party."

What's the solution to the gerrymander? No one seems to have found one. A few states have set up independent commissions to draw their electoral districts. That likely just substitutes the hidden partisanship of a supposedly bipartisan commission for the open partisanship of the legislature. Increasingly, too, the state and federal courts have intervened and drawn supposedly fair electoral districts. That likely just substitutes the often avid partisanship of the supposedly nonpartisan judges. In short, there appears no perfect solution.

Left with an imperfect system, perhaps we can comfort ourselves with the thought it hasn't performed that badly over the years. Despite the gerrymander, the fortunes of the political parties have gone up and down. Overall, the majority will appears to have prevailed in Congress.

6.10 – Duverger's Law

Did you ever wonder why we have just two political parties in Congress, the Democrats and the Republicans? Why not three or four, or for that matter, a dozen like in the German Bundestag or the French National Assembly? A French political scientist named Maurice Duverger got famous by answering that question. Not that he made a discovery not long ago made by the keen-eyed pols who operate on the American political scene. But he put the discovery on the academic map by putting the formula in academic language. Called Duverger's Law, he put it this way, "the simple-majority single-ballot system favors the two-party system." When we unpack that, we're going to find something of real significance for our study of the Constitution and how Congress works.

If we look at continental European democracies, we don't see just two political parties. Take this rather mind-numbing list of the parties with seats in the German legislature (the Bundestag) – the Christian Democratic Party (CDU) with 200 seats, the Social Democratic Party (SDP) with 153 seats, the Alternative Party (AfD) with 92 seats, the Free Democratic Party (FDP) with 80 seats, the Left Party (LINKE) with 69 seats, the Green Party (Grune) with 67 seats, the Christian Social Union of Bavaria (CSU) with 46 seats, as well as several other parties with just one seat such as the Blue Party (B).

Obviously, no party has a majority. Just as obviously, their chancellor (their chief executive) has to govern through putting and holding together a coalition. Recently, their present chancellor, Angela Merkel, has had a hard time cobbling together a stable coalition and so has had a hard time governing. No wonder. When we recall how well the Democrats and the Republicans get along in our Congress, it gives us a pretty good idea about how well these parties get along in the German Bundestag.

If rather than looking all the way to continental Europe, our gaze had paused at Great Britain, we would have seen another political landscape. The British have just two major political parties, presently the Conservatives and Labor. Why does their political scenery resemble the American rather than the European? But actually, it's the other way around. The American two-party system resembles the British two-party system since we inherited our electoral system from them. It's not that fewer varieties of political opinion flourish in Great Britain and America than on the continent and so we have fewer political parties. It's the outcome of a shared electoral system and initially an unintended consequence.

When the English kings began to summon the commons to attend the Parliament, they summoned them from the counties and towns. Where else than from where they lived? The members of the House of Commons started out representing and still represent "geographic districts." Each district elects their member by a plurality. The winning candidate doesn't have to win by a majority (50 percent plus one), but just by the most votes. Here's a quote from a biography of Ramsay MacDonald, who later became the first Labor Prime Minister in 1924, "MacDonald was returned at the head of the poll, with 14,318 votes to Byass's 11,111 and Edwards's 5,328." He didn't win by a majority, but just by a plurality (about 46 percent).

This electoral system seemed natural enough to the Founding Fathers, and they followed it. We elect our Congress and our state legislatures from geographic districts. That's what Duverger meant when he said "the simple-majority, single-ballot system." As he went on to say, this "system favors the two-party system." It makes it very difficult for new parties or fringe parties to gain any traction. They may take some votes from one of the major parties, but that just helps the other major party win. A new or fringe party wins no or very few seats, and so languishes in the political wilderness and perishes from lack of access to the wells of political power. Eventually, their supporters desert them rather than continue throwing away their votes on a hopeless cause.

By contrast, much of continental Europe has "proportional representation." Under this electoral system, a party wins seats in the legislature in "proportion" to the total votes it wins across the country with some minimum required to win any seats. Say the legislature had a hundred seats. If the White Party wins 40 percent of the votes, the Reds 40 percent, and the Greens 20 percent, the Whites win 40 seats, the Reds 40, and the Greens 20. This system leads to a multiplication of parties, since a new or even a fringe party can hope to win some seats. And since the largest parties seldom have a majority in the legislature, even small parties can hope to gain some access to power by offering their support to a larger party to form a coalition.

Duverger's law is why we have just two political parties in our Congress and has important consequences for how Congress works. Since there are only two parties, one party has a majority. However much we may deride "partisanship" in Congress, that partisanship is exactly how things get done. The majority can get things done. By contrast, under "proportional representation," one party seldom has a majority. A coalition of parties has to run things. Not only is it difficult to put and hold together such a coalition, but their competing aims make any coherent course difficult. Since one of the major parties often has to align with a minor party to attain a majority, that minority party often ends up calling the shots on issues crucial to it. We are told, for example, that the extreme religious party in Israel has often managed to call the shots on that nation's religious laws. Although they're a minority, their support has often been crucial to the governing coalition, and their price has been religious policies that don't to reflect the opinion of the majority, but of their minority.

Our system seems much more functional. But the Founders didn't plan it that way. It was an unforeseen and unintended consequence of the electoral system inherited from Great Britain. It's great to be good, but it's even better when you're lucky as well.

6.11 –My Congressman

In Oklahoma, we know all about the McClellan-Kerr River Navigation System, but folks in most of the country probably never heard of it. To let them in on the story, when finished in 1971, this navigation system was the most expensive civil works project ever built by the Corps of Engineers to that time, costing $1.3 billion. In these parts, the power and influence of two men in Congress, whose power and influence extended to naming it after themselves, gets the credit for winning the approval and funding. That would be Senator John L. McClellan (D-AR) and Senator Robert S. Kerr (D-OK). That brings up the issue of the "pork barrel," or as we now call it, "earmarks."

There's no question about the economic benefits of this project for our region. By massive dredging and digging canals, the Corps opened a 445 mile long navigation channel from the White and Mississippi Rivers in Arkansas to the Arkansas and Verdigris Rivers in Oklahoma. Freight moves by barge at about a third the cost of rail and a fifth the cost for trucking. Driving down those transportation costs stimulated commerce across a wide swath of middle America. A 2015 study claimed an annual contribution to the economy of $8.5 billion in sales, $289 million in taxes, and the creation of over 55,000 jobs.

Yet if those figures sound a sweet outcome, the smell of the "pork barrel" has often been regarded as giving off a bad odor. The general idea seems our congressman should do something more elevated than "bring home the bacon" (bring home to their districts the funding for projects such as this navigation system). Political scientists have even gone so far as to label this "the two-Congress problem." Under this theory, there are really "two Congresses." The one Congress is a national body supposed to represent our national interests, but since the congressmen represent their districts, the other Congress represents state and local interests. This is seen as a problem since the congressmen are then seen as neglecting the national interest in pursuit of their constituents' interests. The critics have also often singled out powerful congressmen's pet projects as wasteful or not needed. In 2005, Alaska's congressional delegation managed to "earmark" some $398 million to build a bridge to Gravina Island, which although it had an airport that handled about 250,000 passengers a year, had only about fifty residents. Although supporters argued the new bridge would better serve the airport than the existing ferry and open the island to development, opponents labeled the project as "the bridge to nowhere" and eventually succeeded in killing it.

Well, all I can say is, the pork barrel may sometimes give off a bad whiff, but hallelujah somebody in Washington has a real motive to care about us, their lowly constituents. Thank heavens somebody wants to bring us home the bacon and build us things like the McClellan-Kerr Navigation System. Otherwise, we would languish in neglect. No doubt some more powerful congressman carves off more pork for his constituents than some less powerful one. No doubt more powerful interests dine higher on the hog than less powerful interests. No doubt some pie-in-the-sky projects should never have been built. But if Congress isn't going to decide what, when, and where to build, who's going to do it? Some imaginary panel of bureaucratic experts who will scientifically and objectively do the right thing? Good luck to such a hopeful thought.

No, give me "my congressman." Give me a congressman elected by me in my district. Give me a congressman who wants to do everything he can for me. And while we take such a tie-that-binds between the representatives and ourselves for granted, we shouldn't. A lot of electoral systems around the world don't create such an intimate relationship. We only do so because our congressmen are elected in geographic districts. But as said in an earlier article, you can do it another way. You can have proportional representation like in continental Europe.

Look how a pure system of proportional representation works. A party wins representatives in the legislature in proportion to the popular votes they win in the election. Say you have a hundred-member legislature. Each party puts up a slate of candidates. The party selects the candidates, and the candidates don't run in geographic districts. They run as a slate across the whole country. Say a party wins 40 percent of the votes. The top 40 names on its slate get seats in the legislature. But now who represents you? You no longer have your representative tied to your interests. Instead, you have representatives with loyalty tied to their party's interests, and especially to the interests of the party leaders, who control the party, including the names that go on their party slate and how high a name falls on the slate. Now who's going to bring you home the bacon and build your local projects? You're no longer at the head of a line, you're just in line. But you can be sure somebody else is at the head of the line. That will be the interests of the biggest parties and their leaders. They will prefer their interests to your local interests, but do you?

No, I want a representative directly responsible to (accountable to) me. I want somebody who will look out for my interests in Congress. Give me "my congressman."

6.12 – Borking

The Senate rejection of Judge Robert Bork's nomination to the Supreme Court gave the language a new word – "borking." Yet this episode gave no more than a hardnosed example of how the Senate uses a familiar and constitutional power. The Constitution says the president "shall nominate, and by and with the Advice and Consent of the Senate, shall appoint … Judges of the supreme Court, and all other Officers of the United States." This clause gives the Senate a power over presidential appointments to the judicial branch as well as within the executive branch.

To stick with Judge Bork for a moment. In 1987, President Ronald Reagan nominated him to the highest bench, an honor long coveted by the judge himself and for which his whole professional life might be regarded as a preparation and seeking. He had already attained to a seat on the D.C. Circuit Court of Appeals, a position that itself required Senate confirmation and for which he had won unanimous confirmation as recently as 1982. His long and impressive resume listed stints as a professor at Yale Law School, as Solicitor General, and as acting Attorney General. But beyond that, Bork's legal career, scholarly writings, and judicial opinions showed him a persuasive advocate for the "conservatives" in the ongoing legal and political battles. Whatever his professional or legal attainments, "liberals" could not but regard this proposal to further elevate him as a threat.

Perhaps the leading liberal light in the Senate, Ted Kennedy (D-MA) wasn't slow off the mark. Within forty-five minutes of the nomination, Kennedy took the Senate floor and in a nationally televised speech made the following statement, "Robert Bork's America is a land in which women would be forced into back-alley abortions, blacks would sit at segregated lunch counters, rogue police could break down citizens' doors in midnight raids, schoolchildren could not be taught about evolution, writers and artists could be censored at the whim of the Government, and the doors of the Federal courts would be shut on the fingers of millions of citizens." Pretty strong stuff, but no stronger than what followed during the Senate hearings. The definition since added to the dictionary for "borking" is to "obstruct someone, especially a candidate for public office, through systematic defamation or vilification."

Not to take sides in that old fight, whatever the right or the wrong, Judge Bork's nomination with his lifelong ambition went down in flames. The Senate rejected him by a fairly solid vote of 50 to 42. But as shown by the later controversy over the nomination of Clarence Thomas by President George H.W. Bush in 1991, "borking" doesn't always work. After a prolonged and heated contest fueled by accusations of sexual harassment with the salacious details served up by his attractive female accuser before a national TV audience, the Senate still confirmed him by a narrow vote of 52 to 48. Justice Thomas presently sits on the Supreme Court, where he has disappointed the expectations of neither his friends nor his foes.

While to assure our impartiality, let's remember both sides can and do play this same hardball game. In 2016, President Barack Obama (a Democrat) nominated Judge Merrick Garland to replace the recently deceased Justice Antonin Scalia. Like Bork, Garland already sat on the D.C. Circuit Court and had a solid resume. But while his supporters tried to paint him as "moderate," Republicans were less than convinced, and they controlled the Senate. Although not subjected to any campaign of vilification, Judge Garland suffered from a tactic perhaps as questionable and surely as hardball. The Republicans simply refused to bring his nomination to the floor for a vote, which lapsed with the end of that Congress in 2016.

As we heard the Constitution say, the Senate's power over presidential appointments extends beyond the judiciary "to all other officers of the United States." Reading on, we find that, "the Congress may by Law vest the Appointment of such inferior Officers, as they think proper, in the President alone … or in the Heads of Departments." Such the press of business, Congress has resigned by statute most appointments to the discretion of the president and workings of the civil service system. But they've kept in their hands the power to confirm the major appointments. Thus, the president's nominees to the highest levels in the executive branch can face the same treatment as meted out to Judges Bork, Thomas, and Garland.

For some outstanding examples, in 1989, President George

H.W. Bush (a Republican) nominated former Senator John Tower as Secretary of Defense. Tower had himself served in the Senate from Texas for twenty-four years (four terms) until retiring in 1986. During most of that time, Tower had been a prominent member on the Armed Services Committee, and after retirement, had been the chief negotiator at the Strategic Arms Reduction Talks (SALT). He looked highly qualified to head the Department of Defense. But as a Republican, Tower was a conservative, and apparently, too, hadn't been the easiest colleague to get along with in the Senate. Amidst allegations of excessive drinking and womanizing, the Democratic controlled Senate rejected him by a vote of 53 to 47. In 2009, another former senator, Tom Daschle, experienced some similar harsh treatment at the hands of his former colleagues, although this time the opposition came from the Republican side of the aisle. Daschle has served three terms in the Senate for South Dakota from 1987 to 2005 and rapidly risen to the leadership. In 2009, incoming president Barak Obama nominated him as Secretary of the Department of Health, Education, and Human Services. Daschle looked a good fit due to his experience with the legislative process and his long-term interest in health care reform about which he had even co-authored a book. It was apparently envisioned Daschle would play a leading role in crafting the legislation that would become the centerpiece of Obama's presidency (Obamacare). But amidst allegations of irregularities over his income taxes, he was forced to withdraw his name.

In sum, the Senate has the power to confirm or not presidential appointees to both the judicial and the executive branches. Now that's a one-shot deal. Once they let the horse out of the gate, they can't stop the horserace. Once confirmed, the man has the office. And no doubt they've occasionally abused the power for mere partisan purposes. Yet it's a power we should want the Senate to have. It forces the president to nominate men with some solid credentials. It forces him to avoid men with questionable pasts or radical views. It serves as a real check upon excessive presidential influence. It's a useful power and serves useful purposes.

6.13 – McCarthyism

Senator Joseph McCarthy (R-WI) is another political figure who gave a word to the language – "McCarthyism." The standard dictionary definition reads, "Making accusations of political disloyalty or subversion upon insufficient evidence, and the use of unfair investigatory techniques in order to suppress opposition." That doesn't sound very nice, and McCarthy wasn't very nice. But rather than starting with an abuse of the process, let's start with how useful the process. Let's start with the Truman Committee from 1941 to 1948.

Way back in 1792, the first congressional committee to investigate anything was over St. Clair's Defeat. In a battle the previous year in the Northwest Territory, an Indian confederacy had nearly annihilated a U.S. force commanded by General Arthur St. Clair. The general, who was among the few survivors, hadn't failed to demonstrate bravery on the battlefield, but the casualty rate was about 88 percent, the near one thousand dead the highest number ever suffered in any single battle during the Indian wars. Congress wanted to know what went wrong and who was responsible.

Ever since, Congress has frequently wanted to know what went wrong and who was responsible, and congressional investigations have gained momentum to where we're familiar with the often noisy routine. An outstanding example of the noise came during the Civil War from the Joint Committee on the Conduct of the War from 1861 to 1865. The first joint committee with members from both the House and Senate, they left behind a not too happy memory. Critics charged them with interfering with Lincoln's successful conduct of the war, pushing the promotion of political generals whose main qualification their affiliation with the party in power (the Republicans), and using their hearings to harass their political foes.

However that may be, when on February 10, 1941, near the start of World War II, then Senator Harry Truman made a speech on the Senate floor calling for a committee to look into defense programs and expenditures, he was careful to avoid the appearance of following this precedent. Concerned with reports from his

Missouri constituents about waste and favoritism in the construction of Ft. Leonard Wood, Truman thought that in the midst of the ongoing massive military mobilization, instances of mismanagement, waste, and outright fraud might not be lacking. Before making his speech, he carefully laid the groundwork with the powers that be in the Senate. To allay President Roosevelt's fear of undue meddling, Truman sent him the message, "I wouldn't conduct the investigation in a way that would hurt defense. You can count on me for that."

Being a man of his word, he kept his word. Formally called the Senate Special Committee to Investigate the National Defense Program, but known popularly as the Truman Committee, since Truman the chairman, the Senate granted the committee wide powers to investigate. But Truman saw they stuck to "the domestic side of the war effort – to industrial mobilization." Interfering not at all with the president's direction of the war or military strategy, Truman conducted the hearings not as an inquisition for partisan and political purposes, but an investigation guided by consultation and consensus.

And the consensus has since favorably regarded the Truman Committee's work as having contributed to rather than obstructed the war effort. They helped resolve conflicts over the allocation of men and material, such as directing resources to assure the adequate production of high octane aviation fuel. They promoted the creation of centralized agencies to better unify the war effort on the home front. They took on numerous cases of waste or fraud. For an outstanding example, "The Committee reported incredible waste and inefficiency [with the camp and cantonment construction program]. A comparison of costs showed that the average cost per man of seventeen camps constructed on a lump-sum basis was $380, while the cost per man of twenty-nine camps constructed on a cost-plus-fixed-fee basis was $684. ... [The] recommendations [made by the Committee] were adopted, effecting a monetary saving estimated ... to be $250 million."

So much for an example of how useful the process. But to come to an abuse of the process, let's come back to Senator Joseph McCarthy. Hollywood has relentlessly portrayed his misdeeds in revenge for having been one of his targets. To recall the history rather than the popular portrayals, McCarthy used the process of congressional investigations to lead the Second Red Scare, lasting from 1947 to 1956, there having been an earlier one back in 1919-1920. Just as Truman started with some real concerns caused by the mobilization to fight World War II, McCarthy started with some real concerns caused by the Cold War. The Soviet Union did mean world domination just as Hitler had. They did engage in espionage and infiltration, tactics at which they were very good and scored some notable successes. The Rosenbergs did steal the secrets for the atomic bomb. The American Communist Party did take orders from Moscow. But whereas the Truman Committee stuck to facts, McCarthy didn't, making ever wilder and less responsible allegations.

No to cover all his mis-deeds in detail, let's take an outstanding example. On July 14, 1951 in long speech on the Senate floor, McCarthy attacked among others General George C. Marshall, who was then serving as the Secretary of Defense in the cabinet of now President Truman. Anyone who knows anything about General Marshall knows him as one of the greatest Americans of the twentieth century. As the Chief of Staff of the Army before and during World War II, Marshall was "the architect of victory." He oversaw the creation in only a few short years of a gigantic military machine. In his famous "little black book" he had written down the names of the officers who had impressed him as the ones to promote when war came (Eisenhower, Patton, Bradley, and a host of others). After the war, he served as the Secretary of State (1948 to 1949), overseeing the "Marshall Plan" that sent billions of dollars to Europe to rebuild their shattered economies, vitally assisting them to resist both internal and external communist pressure. He then served as Secretary of Defense (1950 to 1951).

In his speech, McCarthy gave a long list of American foreign policy failures, nor did this list lack legitimate examples, such as the loss of China to Mao Zedong's Communists. He then went on, "How can we account for our present situation unless we believe that men high in this Government are concerting to deliver us to disaster? This must be the product of a great conspiracy, a conspiracy on a scale so immense as to dwarf any previous such venture in the history of man." As for Marshall, "What can be made of this unbroken series of decisions and acts contributing to the strategy of defeat? They cannot be attributed to incompetence.

If Marshall were merely stupid, the laws of probability would dictate that part of his decisions would serve this country's interest." Finally, "What is the objective of the great conspiracy? I think it is clear from what has occurred and is now occurring: to diminish the United States in world affairs, to weaken us militarily, to confuse our spirit with talk of surrender in the Far East and to impair our will to resist evil. To what end? To the end that we shall be contained, frustrated and finally: fall victim to Soviet intrigue from within and Russian military might from without."

So he went too far. To merely accuse Marshall and Truman's administration of incompetence or even stupidity would have stayed in the realm of opinion and opinions differ. But he accused them of "conspiracy," and in effect, of treason, of betraying the country to the communists. As has been said, everyone is entitled to their own opinions, but not to their own facts. Conspiracy and treason are facts, and McCarthy was basing his facts on no more than his opinions for the reason behind what arguably foreign policy failures. More than that, any rational man knew for a fact that General Marshall a patriot to his core. McCarthy was going farther than the facts could possibly take him.

He constantly went too far, beyond any reasonable conclusion from the facts, constantly abused the investigative process to attack people's reputations and livelihoods. He finally went too far even for the U.S. Senate, an institution proverbially tolerant of its members. In 1954, his fellow senators did what has almost never been done. They passed a resolution of censure against McCarthy. After that stinging rebuke. he rapidly descended into irrelevance and died in 1957

In a radio broadcast on March 9, 1954, the famed commentator Edward R. Murrow, mounted a blistering attack on McCarthy, saying, "No one familiar with the history of this country can deny that congressional committees are useful. It is necessary to investigate before legislating, but the line between investigating and persecuting is a very fine one, and the junior Senator from Wisconsin has stepped over it repeatedly." That well sums up McCarthy and the larger point. Congressional investigations are "useful," but McCarthy stepped over the line into "persecuting." Nor unfortunately, has he been the only one.

President Woodrow Wilson once wrote about congressional

investigations, "There is some scandal and discomfort, but infinite advantage, in having every affair of administration subjected to the test of constant examination on the part of the assembly that represents the nation. The chief use of such inquisition is, not the direction of those affairs in a way with which the country will be satisfied … but the enlightenment of the people, which is always its sure consequence."

Yet for our story about the Constitution, we might wonder whence comes the power for Congress to conduct such investigations. We won't find it mentioned in the text. Let's turn to that question in the next article.

6.14 – Contempt of Congress

At the time of this writing, the headlines say Congress is busy investigating the Russian meddling in the 2016 presidential election. But it wouldn't matter when the writing, Congress is constantly in the news for investigating something or other and often something highly controversial such as the Russian meddling, Watergate, or the Iran Contra Affair. On the morning of this same writing, the headlines also say Congress is contemplating contempt charges against former presidential advisor Steve Bannon, who apparently refused to answer questions before a congressional committee. Such charges for contempt or perjury are also staples of the news.

But whence comes this congressional power to investigate and charge with contempt or perjury? Welcome to another constitutional implication that has acquired wings, taken off, and now constantly in flight. And especially in today's atmosphere, it's hard to imagine how Congress could fly without this power. Members can't arrive on Capitol Hill already equipped with all the required information and expertise, especially when the legislative agenda includes highly technical topics, such as regulating the financial markets or the safety of nuclear reactors. In such an atmosphere, they need to gather the facts and consult the experts. They need the power to investigate.

The Constitution says, "All legislative Power herein granted shall be vested in a Congress of the United States." Logically, that implies the power to investigate, since Congress can't legislate without gathering the required information. Logically, too, the power to investigate implies the further power to compel testimony and truthful testimony. Often people, apparently like Mr. Bannon, have reasons for not wanting to appear and testify, and even when they do appear, sometimes reasons for not testifying truthfully. Logically, then, Congress has to have the power to subpoena (compel) witnesses to appear, hold them in contempt for refusing to testify, and punish them for perjury for false testimony.

But where does this logic run out or does it? Can Congress investigate anything? In 1880, that question came up in the case of Kilbourn v Thompson. Congress had launched an investigation into the collapse and bankruptcy of Jay Cooke & Co. A pioneering figure in modern, big-time finance, Jay Cooke's initial claim to fame came from facilitating the Union to raise the vast sums required to fight the Civil War and making a fortune in the process. But his later fame came from being a financial pioneer in another way. In 1873, his firm went abruptly bankrupt, the size of his collapse setting off a chain reaction in the financial sector. Banks went down like dominoes, their failures causing a temporary shutdown of the stock market. Called the Panic of 1873, the resulting depression lingered around until 1879. Not only did the U.S. economy lose, the U.S. government lost "public moneys" as a result of "improvident deposits made by the Secretary of the Navy of the United States with … Jay Cooke & Co."

No wonder Congress wanted to know what had happened and why. To investigate, the House set up a special committee. As part of their investigation, they served a subpoena on a guy named Hallet Kilbourn. Whatever they wanted to question him about not important to our story, but whatever it was, he refused to testify. Thereupon, Congress found him in contempt and ordered the Sergeant-at-Arms of the House (John G. Thompson) to arrest and throw him in jail, there to rot until he changed his mind and agreed to divulge. Sergeant-at-Arms Thompson promptly did his duty and lodged Kilbourn in the D.C. County Jail. Things being what they are, Kilbourn as promptly sued Sergeant-at-Arms Thompson, alleging Congress lacked the constitutional authority to conduct such an investigation and so his arrest and confinement violated his constitutional rights.

Sound familiar? It should. Just think about all the congressional investigations of the Financial Crisis of 2007, all the witnesses called. But in 1880, such was not yet the settled routine. Before the Supreme Court, Kilbourn's lawyers argued that, "the House of Representatives has no power whatever to punish for a contempt of its authority." The Court didn't go that far, yet found some limits on the congressional power to investigate. Writing the opinion, Justice Samuel F. Miller, created what called "the Kilbourne test," which basically had two prongs, 1) Congressional investigations shouldn't "invade areas constitutionally reserved to the courts or the executive," and 2) Investigations should deal "with subjects on which Congress could validly legislate" and Congress has an actual "interest in legislating on that subject."

Applying this test, Justice Miller held Congress had violated both prongs. He found the investigation invaded an area reserved to the courts, since the bankruptcy case of Jay Cook & Co. was already pending before the courts. And he found that Congress wasn't actually interested in legislating on the subject, just investigating it. He concluded Congress couldn't just go looking into "the private affairs of individuals" and ruled for Kilbourn, who won the case and didn't have to testify.

Granted some limits should exist on the congressional power to investigate, yet this decision doesn't make much good sense. The U.S. government had lost money through the bankruptcy of Jay Cooke & Co. That seems a good reason to investigate. However that may be, the same facts wouldn't result in the same ruling today. Since then, the "Kilbourn test" has been widened into a much broader test. In 1957 in Watkins v U.S., Chief Justice Earl Warren ruled that, "The power of the Congress to conduct investigations is inherent in the legislative process. That power is broad. It encompasses inquiries concerning the administration of existing laws, as well as proposed or possibly needed statutes. It includes surveys of defects in our social, economic or political system for the purpose of enabling the Congress to remedy them. It comprehends probes into departments of the Federal Government to expose corruption, inefficiency or waste. But, broad as is this power of inquiry, it is not unlimited. There is no general authority to expose the private affairs of individuals without justification in terms of the functions of the Congress. ... No inquiry is an end in itself; it must be related to, and in furtherance of, a legitimate task of the Congress."

Under this broader rule, Congress can look "into the departments ... to expose corruption, inefficiency, or waste." Under this rule, Kilbourn would have had to testify or languish in jail. While Congress can also investigate the "administration of existing laws" and "defects in our social, economic, or political system for the purpose ... to remedy them." Putting all that together, it's hard to say what might not fit under such broad powers. Yet Warren does say, "No inquiry is an end in itself; it must be related to, and in furtherance of, a legitimate task of the Congress." Then depending on the facts, some limits may still exist, although it may be hard to find them.

Such describes the present vast extent of the power of Congress to investigate. What about their powers to subpoena witnesses, compel testimony, and charge with perjury? Those are just as extensive. In 1927 in McGrain v Daugherty, a case concerning a congressional investigation into the Teapot Dome Scandals, the syllabus to the case summed those up, "Each house of Congress has power, through its own process, to compel a private individual to appear before it or one of its committees and give testimony needed to enable it efficiently to exercise a legislative function belonging to it under the Constitution." In other words, Congress has the power to issue subpoenas and punish someone who refuses to testify for contempt. In other cases, the Court has held someone can be punished for perjury before Congress as well.

For a lot of folks, a summons to appear and testify before Congress is the chance of a lifetime. Many a professor and many a policy wonk relishes such an opportunity as their fifteen minutes of fame. But whether or not someone wants to bask in the glare of this publicity, the power to compel them to face the cameras is another great power for Congress. It's another power that has grown from small beginnings into much greater things.

6.15 – The Boring Routine

Rather than something exciting and controversial, if you tuned into C-SPAN at 10.00 AM (ET) on February 17, 2018 you saw the boring routine. The House Agricultural Committee was interviewing the newly confirmed Secretary of Agriculture, Sonny Perdue, a veterinarian by trade and former two-term Georgia governor. Such non-exciting, non-controversial hearings describe the grist (most all) of the work done in congressional committees. But the proceedings weren't boring to the participants or folks with a vested interest in U.S. farm policy. Needless to say, the House Agricultural Committee and the Secretary of Agriculture are key players when it comes to U.S. farm policy, which vitally affects the interests, the lives and pocketbooks, of all the other players in agriculture. If you've a mind or an interest, nowadays you don't have to wait and read the *Congressional Record* when it comes out, you can watch them grind it out in real time on TV.

If you do, you're watching "congressional oversight," Congress acting as the overseer to the bureaucracy. You won't find this role explicitly written for them in the Constitution. As one distinguished political scientist says, 'The Founding Fathers had little to say about the nature or function of the executive branch of the new government [the bureaucracy]. The Constitution is virtually silent on the subject." Another gives the reason, "Not much thought was given to the problems of administrative responsibility and accountability in a complex bureaucratic state because a large administrative apparatus was not envisaged at the time." But ready or not, here we come. The rise of "a complex bureaucratic state" has proceeded apace. From 1816 to 1861, the bureaucrats multiplied eight-fold from 4,837 to 36,672. Between 1861 and 1901, the number reached over 200,000. In the 1920s, the figure climbed to 550,000. By 2000, it was well over a million.

The bureaucrats serve in the executive branch, which might lead us to think that under the separation of power the president would oversee this new and "large administrative apparatus." But Congress has to pass the laws to create the agencies and fund their budgets from year to year. Here was an obligation offering an opportunity. On the one hand, if they were going to create and fund the agencies, didn't they have an obligation to see the bureaucrats properly carried out their tasks and spent their funds? On the other hand, here was an opportunity for more power. By exerting a continuous "oversight," they could exert some significant control over the agencies. Congress didn't find that prospect in the least boring. To fill it in, as they set up each new agency, they had only to set up a congressional committee with the power of "oversight" over that agency. In the resulting view, the committees in Congress mirror the bureaucracy.

"In the 100th Congress (1987-88), for example, there were 140 subcommittees of standing committees of the House and 85 in the Senate. Most had narrow jurisdictions matched to the organizational structure of the federal bureaucracy." As codified in the Legislative Reorganization Act of 1946, each was to "exercise continuous watchfulness of the executive agencies concerned of any law, the subject matter of which is within the jurisdiction of such committee." We need only add, "the key members of congressional committees with jurisdiction in their areas are likely to hold office ... longer even than the president, and to have a better idea of what they want. Wise career administrators, therefore, are responsive to congressional committees."

With this formula Congress has both discharged their obligation and seized their opportunity. Their "oversight" lets them compete with and often supplant the president or the cabinet in control over the bureaucracy. If you look at one of those charts showing the organization of an executive agency, you'll see the president or some cabinet officer in the top box. A more accurate chart would add a box right next to him for some congressional committee. An executive officer in the executive branch may head the agency, but some congressional committee is right there looking over his shoulder (charged with oversight). By this technique, Congress has made itself an integral part of the bureaucratic structure

We should also mention Congress has become something of a bureaucracy itself with its own large staff and sub-agencies. Originally back in 1789, a congressman just had a desk. The Senate and House each had no more staff than a Sergeant-at-Arms to maintain decorum and order and an official to record the minutes and keep the records, the Secretary in the Senate and the Clerk in the House. But as the executive bureaucracy has grown, the legislative staff has kept pace. In the first step, congressional committees began to acquire staffs, such as lawyers to advise them on the law or investigators to track down information and witnesses. In the next step, in 1885, a law authorized clerks for individual senators, and in 1893, for the representatives. By 1946, senators were authorized six staff and representatives five. By now, over 7,000 staff work directly for the Senate and 11,000 directly for the House. As a well-known fact, many congressmen lean heavily for guidance on their personal staff, giving the staffers sometimes considerable influence within the Congress. Congressmen also all have staffed offices in their home districts as well.

Several fairly recent bureaucracies work directly for Congress. The Congressional Research Service (the CRS), which dates back to 1914, has around 600 lawyers, economists, and scientists and a budget over $100 million per year. If a congressman has some question about a public policy matter, wants some facts and figures, these guys will dig them out and write him a memo. The General Accounting Office (the GAO) created in 1921 with around 5,000 employees evaluates programs and policies. The Congressional Budget Office (the CBO), not created until 1974, has around 250 economists and accountants with a budget around $50 million. It provides analysis of the cost of budgetary and tax issues. Given the size and complexity of modern government, it's hard to see how Congress could get through all its business in any sort of informed way without some such expert assistance.

To come back to the executive branch of the bureaucracy, the reality is that the president has to share power over them with Congress. As usual with such power sharing arrangements, often a simmering hostility brews and sometimes an open quarrel blows up. Who's on top? Who's running things? It's a tug-of-war. The separation of powers has led to another unexpected result, a divided structure of command and control over the bureaucracy and not an entirely orderly one.

Yet given the separation of powers, what better arrangement might one suggest? We might even argue for a silver lining. Tidiness always looks good in theory. A clear chain-of-command looks more logical and efficient. But experience may teach another lesson. When talking about a bureaucracy as huge as our modern American one, successful top-down management turns out a daunting feat. If not too big to manage, their size, complexity, and density come close. It may be better to have two governors on this engine, even if they sometimes compete for control. Perhaps nothing is quite as effective with the bureaucracy as the transparency forced on them by the boring routine of congressional oversight.

Perhaps President Woodrow Wilson summed it up as well any anyone. "It is the proper duty of a representative body to look diligently into every affair of government and to talk much about what it sees. It is meant to be the eyes and the voice, and to embody the wisdom and will of its constituents. Unless Congress have and use every means of acquainting itself with the acts and the disposition of the administrative agents of the government, the country must be helpless to learn how it is being served; and unless Congress both scrutinize these things and sift them by every form of discussion, the country must remain in embarrassing, crippling ignorance of the very affairs which it is most important that it should understand and direct. The informing function of Congress should be preferred even to its legislative function."

6.16 – Keynesianism

The Constitution grants "the taxing and spending power" to Congress. But the Founders were thinking in the terms traditional to their day. They were thinking about taxing and spending as a way for the government to carry out traditional functions, for example, as the Constitution says, to "raise and support Armies." Back in their day, "fiscal policy" (taxing and spending) wasn't yet conceived as a way for the government to manage the economy to bring about prosperity and avoid recession or depression. But by this day, "fiscal policy" has become an accepted way for Congress to try and manage the economy. Once again, an original and more limited power has become another newer and greater power.

Typically, intellectuals claim credit whenever they can, and since they typically write the histories, they typically claim a lot of the credit. This time around, the intellectual receiving the most credit is John Maynard Keynes, an English economist, lived 1883 to 1946. Under Keynes' theory ("Keynesianism") the government should use "fiscal policy" (the power to tax and spend) to drive the economy toward prosperity and steer away from recession or depression. When the economy losing speed, the government should press on the accelerator, stimulating the engine. It should tax less (leave in more money as fuel) and/or spend more (put in more money as fuel). When the economy too pumped up (inflating a bubble ready to burst), it should take the air out. It should tax more and/or spend less (taking money out). In the years after the Great Depression (1929-1933), Keynesianism became a gospel to many economists. In the years since, the theory has lost some popularity, but continues as part of the spoken language. Anymore, no one discusses the federal budget without mentioning the impact of the taxing and spending on the economy.

Using taxing and spending in such a way gives Congress a newer and greater power than envisioned for them by the Founders. But while power has its pleasures, this one comes with some heavy burdens. Since the Founders' day, we may have learned a great deal about economics, but the science still far from perfected. The best economic minds constantly disagree and as constantly get taken by surprise. Not only did very few predict the Great Depression in 1929, very few predicted the more recent Great Recession in 2007. That leaves it one thing to say Congress has the power to manage the economy through fiscal policy, but still another for them to figure out the right policy. The economists' failures only embarrass them, but with Congress such failures embarrass them with the electorate, the last place they want to be embarrassed.

As much as that, Congress isn't a gathering of professional economists and doesn't operate in the rarefied atmosphere of an academic conference. All sorts of influences pull on the members' economic decision-making. Taxing and spending pick winners and losers, and as an obvious general rule, higher taxes lead to more losers and higher spending to more winners. That leads to another general rule. Congress, being a body that reflects the opinion of the majority of the winners and losers, doesn't like either to raise taxes or lower spending. Reinforcing this rule, fewer and fewer items in the federal budget remain discretionary. The ever-growing entitlements of the welfare state demand the same level or higher of funding year after year. Social Security is famously "the third rail." No politician dares to touch the flow of the benefits for fear of an instant and painful electoral death. These fixed expenses make the federal budget less flexible, leaving Congress less room to maneuver.

Whatever the virtues of Keynesianism, Congress doesn't seem an institution well designed to practice those virtues. As one observer said, "It was one thing to ask Congress to cut taxes and increase spending, not exactly a sacrificial act for elected politicians. But would they be willing to do the reverse when the economy required it? The answer was, they could not. In American politics, the Keynesian ideas seemed to work fine on the upside, but it couldn't work at all on the downside. The political flaw was fundamental." The statistics seem to back him up. The federal budget, the federal deficit, and the federal debt just keep going up and up. Congress seems able to spend, but not able to practice fiscal restraint.

Further limiting Congress as the economic manager, fiscal policy only serves as one of the great tools of macro-economic management, the other being the "monetary supply," the amount of money circulating in the economy. And Congress only has authority over fiscal policy, not over the monetary supply. They've relinquished that other power to the FED (the Federal Reserve Board). As will be discussed in later articles, Congress created the FED as an independent agency with a governing board appointed for a set term of years and not removable except for cause. This institutional design put the FED beyond congressional, or for that matter, presidential control.

As a result of this divided authority, when it comes to managing the economy to try and produce prosperity and prevent recessions or depressions, we have something like two riders on the same horse, one with one rein and spur, the other with the other rein and spur. If you've ever been on a horse, you know he's way more powerful than you, and you may or may not be able to control him. But presuming the economy was a docile horse, which has proved far from the case, these two riders have sometimes reined and spurred him in opposite directions. Congress and the FED haven't always smoothly cooperated. That can make for a rough economic ride.

We'll pick up this topic again when we come to discuss the FED in future articles. But for our tale of the Constitution, let's understand that Congress has once again gained more power. Fiscal policy to manage the economy has become a recognized part of Congress's power to tax and spend. But while eager enough at spending, even sometimes eager enough at cutting taxes, they're seldom eager to lower spending or raise taxes. That makes them not very good at putting this power to good use. Moreover, the FED controls the monetary supply, rather than the Congress. When it comes to the government managing the economy, the present conclusion of the tale seems a somewhat ineffective and confused system of command and control.

6.17 – The Boland Amendment

You may not have heard of the Boland Amendment, but probably heard something about the fall out. With this law, the version passed in 1984, Congress prohibited President Reagan from spending funds to aid the contras in Nicaragua. The fall out was the Iran-Contra Scandal. For our larger story about the Constitution, this episode well illustrates why confusion so often reigns in American foreign policy.

The Constitution confers on the president the power to conduct foreign policy rather than Congress. Not only does the Constitution make him the national leader on foreign policy, he looks better suited to lead. He can settle on a single foreign policy and present a united front to the outside world, whereas Congress is divided against itself between the political parties. Being the chief diplomat and commander-in-chief, he has ready to hand the tools to carry out foreign policy, rather than Congress. He's got immediate access to all the diplomatic and military channels, giving him the widest sources and the latest intelligence, which the Congress does not. Being on call around the clock and every day, he can respond with speed to sudden international crises, while Congress is frequently in recess. The president has even been known to keep diplomatic and military secrets, which Congress has been known to leak like a sieve.

Yet over foreign policy, Congress has some significant ways to check, not to mention obstruct, the president. The Senate has to ratify treaties by a two-thirds majority. But more significant is their power of the purse. Seldom can the president carry out a foreign policy without them funding it, at least not for long. Also significantly, Congress can pass laws directing some foreign policy or even making one illegal. Finally, Congress serves as the center for the "loyal opposition," where congressmen from the party-out-of-power can make speeches and offer resolutions, trying to arouse and lead public opinion against the president. Except when the national existence threatened like during World War II, the other party has seldom failed to oppose the president on some flashpoint foreign policy issues.

As an example of their power of the purse, in 1963, President John Kennedy tried to offer some aid to the Soviet Union with their serious food shortages. In a gambit to ease Cold War tensions, his plan would have let them buy American grain with American financing. But hardline anti-Communists in Congress attached an amendment to the foreign aid bill that blocked the financing and so blocked the deal. As an example of Congress passing a law to block a president's foreign policy, in the lead up to World War II, President Franklin Roosevelt sought to discourage German aggression by offering our support to Britain and France. But the isolationists in Congress passed the Neutrality Acts of 1935 and 1936, making illegal the shipment of arms and munitions to warring countries or any loans or credits for such purchases. These laws cut the ground out from under Roosevelt's feet, since Germany knew once war broke out, no such assistance could go to Britain or France.

As a distinguished commentator has remarked, "All of which amounts to saying that the Constitution … is an invitation to a struggle for the privilege of directing American foreign policy." All of which bring us back to the Boland Amendment, which gives a perfect example of just such a struggle between the president and Congress.

In 1979, the longstanding Somoza regime in Nicaragua collapsed, overthrown by the Sandinista National Liberation Front (the Sandinistas). President Jimmy Carter welcomed this overthrow of a dictator and extended aid to the new government, and Congress went along, approving the funding. He was a Democrat, the Congress was Democratic, and they found themselves in agreement on trying to encourage the emergence of a real democracy in Nicaragua. But events failed to cooperate with their hopes. The leftist among the Sandinistas quickly drove out the moderates, and the leftist leader, Daniel Ortega, looked bent on making himself a "Nicaraguan Castro." Nicaragua signed a treaty with the Soviet Union, Cuban advisors began to arrive, and the Sandinistas began to export their revolution to neighboring countries, especially El Salvador. But they had bitten off more than they could chew, since they proved unable even to quell their opponents within Nicaragua itself. A bloody counter-revolution erupted. Called the "contras" (those *contra* the Sandinistas), these forces were a loose and varied coalition, including moderates as well as right wing supporters of the prior Somoza dictatorship.

Meanwhile back in the U.S.A., the election of 1980 swept Ronald Reagan into the White House. A thoroughly committed anti-communist, the new president viewed communist infiltration into Central America as an existential threat, as menacing America's strategic underbelly ("just two day's driving time from Harlingen, Texas"), and as a crucial component in the worldwide struggle between the United States and the Soviet Union (the "evil empire"). Not surprisingly, then, Reagan supported the contras with the goal to overthrow the Sandinistas. Being themselves disappointed in the Sandinistas, Congress went along and initially voted the funds. But Reagan was a Republican and the Congress was Democratic, a reliable formula to predict a falling out. Sure enough, before too long the Democrats started to profess concerns the president was leading the country into the quagmire of another Vietnam while turning a blind eye to human rights violations perpetuated by the contras. After working themselves up with these arguments for a couple years, the Democrats in Congress were sufficiently convinced to pass the Boland Amendment in 1984.

Actually, there were several versions. Named after Edward Boland (D-MA), the Chairman of the House Intelligence Committee and a widely respected member, this 1984 version read, "No appropriations or funds made available … to the Central Intelligence Agency, the Department of Defense, or any other agency or entity of the United States involved in intelligence activities may be obligated or expended for the purpose or which may have the effect of, supporting, directly or indirectly, military or paramilitary operations in Nicaragua by any nation, group, organization or individual." In other words, this law cut off all aid to the contras. Representative Dick Cheney (R-WY), later more famous as a Secretary of Defense and vice-president, called it "a killer amendment" that would force the contras "to lay down their arms." In a later debate, Newt Gingrich, later more famous as leading the Republican "contract with America" campaign which led to him becoming Speaker in 1995, called a vote restricting military aid for the contras a "vote for the unilateral disarmament of the side that favors freedom in Central America."

Then who was running our foreign policy on Nicaragua? President Reagan had pledged all out support to the contras, but Congress was cutting off their funding. One branch of the government (the chief executive) wanted one policy and another branch (the legislature) was pursuing the opposite policy. America was not presenting a united front. And frankly, our word looked worthless. Congress was repudiating the promises of support made by the president. Nor was this the first time nor the last when such confusion has reigned over our foreign policy, and where Congress has repudiated promises made by a president. For a well-remembered example, as part of ending the Vietnam War, President Richard Nixon had signed an executive agreement to come to the aid of South Vietnam in the event the North invaded. But when the North did invade in 1975, Congress had refused to appropriate the funds for a response.

But notice something about it. Congress has largely a negative rather than a positive power in foreign policy. As has been said, "It is impossible to force a man to wield power if he does not choose to do so." Congress can stop funding or make certain activities illegal, thus frustrating a policy. But they would have a much harder time ever forcing a president to carry out some proactive policy. Say that rather than just cutting off aid for the contras, Congress had voted aid for the Sandinistas. As a legal matter, the president is supposed to spend appropriated money where Congress explicitly expresses the purpose. But as a practical matter, a determined president has lot of ways to delay and frustrate the spending, especially when the money goes to a foreign country. While as a legal matter, if Congress tried to do much more, they would run into serious legal problems themselves. Say they passed a law saying the president had to extend diplomatic recognition or negotiate a treaty with a foreign regime. Not only is it hard to imagine how they could force the president to perform such tasks, but the Constitution reserves both diplomatic recognition and the negotiation of treaties to the president.

At any rate, to such a confused pass has our vaunted separation of powers sometimes brought our foreign policy. Americans like to think we're the sole remaining superpower and we are. But while we may have superpowers, like a lot of superheroes from Achilles all the way to Superman, we have a weakness (an Achilles heel, a kryptonite). We only come together when challenged with an existential threat like with Pearl Harbor or 9/11. Otherwise, we often seem to bumble around like a clumsy giant, easily fooled and easily distracted. Let's follow this bumbling in the next article.

6.18 – The Speaker's Diplomacy

An incident in the career of Jim Wright (D-TX) gives an interesting example of a congressional leader taking an activist role in foreign diplomacy. After entering Congress with the freshman class of 1955, Wright stayed for the next thirty-four straight years until 1989. Representing Ft. Worth in the House, he was one of the large and influential Texas delegation. Starting out a Lyndon Johnson protégé, he eventually advanced into the top ranks of the leadership. In 1977, he became the Majority Leader, the second highest leadership post in the House. In 1987, with the retirement of Tip O'Neal (D-MA), he ascended the final rung, becoming the forty-eighth Speaker of the House, serving until 1989.

Right at this same moment, the Reagan administration was finding itself between the proverbial rock and hard place. The rock was Reagan's pledge to keep the Nicaraguan contras together "body and soul," which reflected his larger commitment to throw back communism in the hemisphere. The hard place was that Congress had cut off all funding for the contras in 1984 with the Boland Amendment. All the twists and turns his administration took, trying to extricate themselves from this cleft, makes for fascinating reading and does makes life seem almost stranger than fiction. Spearheaded by Lieutenant Colonel Oliver North on the National Security Staff, the administration came up with a series of evasions. Rather than sending federal money to the contras, they raised private donations in the U.S. and abroad, particularly from Saudi Arabia. Next, they diverted funds from the sale of arms to

Iran, sales illegal under another law. Thus, they stumbled into the Iran-Contra Scandal, which nearly brought down Reagan's presidency and did result in a number of indictments against members of his administration, including North, several being convicted of crimes, including North. But following this story would lead away from our topic.

Instead, we want to keep our focus on the constitutional aspects. In this connection, in 1987, the Reagan administration tried another tack. They approached Wright, who by then the Speaker, to try and co-opt him onto their team. Turned out Wright was eager enough to suit up for the game. But to the dismay of the Reagan team, he took the ball and ran with it not exactly toward the same goal they had in mind.

Wright had a long-standing interest in Central America and even some fluency in Spanish. In 1980, while still the Majority Leader, he had led a congressional delegation to Nicaragua to meet with the leading elements there. He made another trip in 1982.

Such junkets, billed as fact finding tours, aren't that unusual for congressmen since the days of rapid and easy travel. Seems like a reasonable enough trend. There's nothing like some firsthand knowledge. But such forays can easily insert the congressmen in the front lines of the diplomatic wars. In large part, that's because they've often shown eager to lead the charge and then shown eager to claim the glory and the credit. But particularly when the congressmen not from the president's party, they often don't charge in the same direction as the administration. They meet with foreign leaders, getting some feel for their personalities, interests, and politics. From there, it's a short step to come to favor one of the factions in the country. But it's something of a two-way street. The foreign leaders get some feel for the congressmen's personalities, interests, and politics. It's another short step for the foreign leaders to try and influence the congressmen.

At any rate, that brings the story to 1987, when Wright becomes Speaker and Reagan's administration approaches him with their proposition. Why shouldn't the president and the Speaker join together and offer a peace plan for Nicaragua? No doubt the administration hoped by enlisting the Speaker up front, that would assure congressional support down the line. Nothing loath, Wright promptly agreed to join in offering what called the Reagan-Wright peace plan. These proposals amounted to setting some pre-conditions on the Sandinistas and a deadline for negotiations.

Quite quickly, this joint initiative paid off, leading to a meeting of Central American leaders in Esquipulas, Guatemala in 1986-1987. Brokered by Costa Rican president Oscar Arias, who received the Nobel Peace Prize for his efforts, the resulting Esquipulas Accords created a process for reconciliation and amnesty in Nicaragua. Under the direction of a reconciliation commission, democratization would take place with specific guarantees for individual rights. Neighboring countries agreed to prevent the use of their territory by any rebel group.

But at this point the teamwork between the Reagan administration and the Speaker started to break down. Wright took upon himself to announce and endorse these accords in advance of the White House. Think about that as a designed play in the political game. Wright was claiming the role as the hero of the game by standing up at the podium all by himself and being the first to announce the victory. Not only that, he was prematurely claiming victory, making it very difficult for the Reagan administration to claim the game wasn't quite over, since they had some serious hesitations and reservations. They had tried to co-opt the Speaker onto their team. He was co-opting them onto his.

But the Speaker's lack of team spirit didn't stop there, carrying over into the next phase of the game, the negotiations to finalize the peace. Suspecting strong elements on the Reagan team wanted these negotiations to fail, giving them an excuse to continue their efforts to drive out the Sandinistas entirely, Wright pulled off an end run. He started negotiating directly with the Sandinistas, leaving the administration watching from the sidelines.

For their part, the Sandinistas, sensing a friend in Wright, asked him to personally serve as the intermediary between themselves and the contras in the further negotiations. But rather than run all the interference himself, Wright came up with another name, that of Nicaraguan Cardinal Miguel Obando y Bravo. Wright then met with the cardinal and the Sandinista leader, Daniel Ortega, without notifying the administration, and after looking over the contras' peace proposals, suggested some changes more palatable to the Sandinistas. Although Secretary of State George Schultz objected vehemently against the administration being left out of the process,

Wright plunged ahead anyway, holding further meetings the Reagan administration only found out about through the press. In these meetings, Wright informed the contras that Congress would no longer support them, which left them not much choice except to take what was offered.

Perhaps all this had a happy ending, if only momentarily, since an election in Nicaragua in 1990 raised Violetta Chamorro, a moderate, to the presidency. But important for our tale about the Constitution, let's notice how the Speaker of the House interjected himself into our foreign policy and conducted the diplomacy himself.

A very long time ago in 1799, John Marshall before he became Chief Justice, while serving in Congress, said, "The president is the sole organ of the nation in its external relations, and its sole representative with foreign nations." Whatever their enmity on other matters, Thomas Jefferson seconded him on that, saying "As the president is the only channel of communication between the United States and foreign nations, it is from him alone that foreign nations or their agents are to learn what is or has been the will of the nation, and whatever he communicates as such they have a right and are bound to consider as the expression of the nation, and no foreign agent can be allowed to question it."

But what did we just see happen over Nicaragua? We saw the Speaker of the House acting as "an organ of the nation in its external relations." We saw the president "was not the only channel of communications between the United States and foreign nations," and the Sandinistas were not "bound to accept whatever he communicated to them as the expression of the nation." If they didn't like what President Reagan said, instead they could deal with Speaker Wright.

"Divide and conquer" is an old proverb in foreign affairs. The divisions within our government often offer foreign nations a real chance to do just that. Don't think they don't know it. We imagine we bestride the world like a colossus as the only superpower. But they study us with the keen eyes of intelligent adversaries, and they understand our weaknesses in ways to which we seem blind. They don't even have to start this game. Almost invariably, the other party in Congress starts the game by coming out against whatever foreign policy the president may pursue. All a foreign nation has to do is play off one side against the other in such a way as to win an advantage. If you read the papers, you'll read about them constantly playing this game and to their advantage.

6.19 – A Clumsy Power

Not too long after President Barak Obama took office, you already saw a few bumper stickers – IMPEACH OBAMA. Not a hundred days into President Donald Trump's term, one well-known academic was already calling for his impeachment (Professor Laurence Tribe of the Harvard Law School). During George W. Bush's presidency, some academics and commentators, who apparently took themselves seriously, called for his impeachment. His immediate predecessor, President Bill Clinton, actually suffered through an impeachment, which failed by a wide margin in the Senate. President Andrew Johnson back in 1868 was the only other president impeached, avoiding conviction by just a single vote in the Senate. However, in 1974, Richard Nixon was driven from office through the threat of impeachment.

But has any constitution ever encumbered itself with a more clumsy device for removing the chief executive? Back when the Constitution was written, it mightn't have been so clumsy. Events moved slower and with less urgency. But with the speed and impact things happen now, it's highly inconvenient for Congress and the president to spend a year or more consumed over impeachment.

Back in 1973 and 1974, the hearings over President Nixon's impeachment (the Watergate Hearings) went on for months. However hostile your opinion toward Richard Nixon, it would be hard to exaggerate the toll in time and stress on him. How could he think about or deal with anything else? Yet in the same timeframe, our national security urgently demanded our president's attention elsewhere. Nixon was right in the middle of complex negotiations with the Soviet Union concerning detente and an arms limitation treaty. In October, 1973, Egypt and Syria launched a surprise attack on Israel (the Yom Kippur War), forcing on him a crucial balancing act in foreign policy. He had to make and carry out decisions about how far to support Israel while not overly antagonizing the Arabs, and he had to deal with the real concern the Soviets might intervene on the Arab side, precipitating a superpower confrontation. He had to walk across this tightrope while Congress was pulling their support out from under him, threatening to remove his credibility either to deliver on promises to friends or menaces to enemies.

However clumsy the device, Article II of the Constitution says, "The President, Vice-President and all other civil Officers … shall be removed from Office on Impeachment for, and Conviction of, Treason, Bribery, or other High Crimes and Misdemeanors." The procedure requires a majority in the House to vote for impeachment. The actual trial takes place before the Senate, where conviction and removal from office requires a two-third majority (a very high bar). But while the procedure clear and while "treason" and "bribery" well-defined crimes, what exactly qualifies as the "other High Crimes and Misdemeanors?" Perhaps surprisingly, the meaning remains far from settled.

Like with so much of the U.S. Constitution, the Founders took impeachment from the British Constitution. Over there, the House of Commons voted the charges and the House of Lords tried the case. But they, too, lacked a clear definition of what amounted to "high crimes and misdemeanors." A very famous British case, the Trial of Warren Hastings, illustrates the point. Hastings had served as the British Governor General for India from 1772 to 1785, and after his recall, the House of Common impeached him for his conduct there. His trial before the House of Lords went on sporadically for an incredible nine years from 1788 to 1795. He ultimately won acquittal on all counts, although going through the agony of such a long trial might be punishment enough for most crimes. But although he stood accused of a long list of wrongful acts, it wasn't clear he was charged with any crime.

The great Edmund Burke, who led the prosecution, said in his opening statement that Hastings' acts "were crimes, not against forms, but against those eternal laws of justice, which are our rule and our birthright: his offences are not in formal, technical language, but in reality, in subject and effect High Crimes and Misdemeanors." In plain English, then, Burke was admitting Hastings hadn't violated any criminal law at all. He had violated "not against the forms," and "his offences are not in formal, technical language." In other words, his alleged offences couldn't be stated in "the forms" or "in the formal, technical language" with which defendants are charged with crimes in the ordinary law courts, since he hadn't violated any of the ordinary criminal laws. As one commentator has said, "The high crimes and misdemeanors with which Hastings was charged in 1786 were not offences against the criminal law, as Burke conceded." Nevertheless, Burke claimed he had "violated the eternal laws of justice" which are in "effect High Crimes and Misdemeanors."

Any American, or for that matter, any British lawyer who has ever defended a criminal case would feel his hackles begin to rise at such an opening statement from the public prosecutor. Nothing is more fundamental than "due process of law," and a fundamental principle of "due process" is that crimes must be defined with sufficient specificity to know exactly what conduct is outlawed. As a corollary, a criminal charge must be stated with sufficient specificity to know exactly what crime is charged. Otherwise, no one could know either how to stay within the law or defend himself against an alleged violation. In the ordinary courts, a prosecutor who charged a man with violating "the eternal laws of justice" would be laughed out of court. Hopefully, we all agree the "eternal laws of justice" exist, but when it comes to charging, convicting, and punishing someone for a crime, hopefully we also all agree the prosecutor needs something more specific. Yet the great Edmund Burke himself has just said that for impeachment we don't need something more specific, that to violate the "eternal laws of nature" amounts to "a high crime and misdemeanor."

Impeachment under our U.S. Constitution carried forward this same lack of specificity. Hamilton wrote in *Federalist No. 65*, "The subjects [of impeachment] are those offenses which proceed from the misconduct of public men, or in other words for the abuse or violation of some public trust. They are of a nature which may with peculiar propriety be denominated POLITICAL, as they relate chiefly to injuries done immediately to society itself." Then not for the first or last time, another great authority comes up short of our rational hopes. Because what in the world is that supposed to mean? If the "eternal laws of justice" an imprecise term, surely the same applies to "injuries done immediately to society itself." While if impeachment "may with peculiar propriety be denominated POLITCAL," does that mean no more than a political process like an election? If one party has enough votes in Congress, can they just un-elect the president by impeaching him, claiming he's done some "injury to society?"

Impeachment has been rarely used, which hasn't helped much to clarify the extent of the power. An early case settled that impeachment doesn't apply to Congress, only to the executive and judicial branches. However, Congress can achieve much the same effect by simply expelling a member. Another early case, the impeachment of Supreme Court Justice Samuel Chase in 1804, 1805, seems to have settled that judges couldn't be impeached over the rulings in their opinions, but only for violations of the criminal code. A few judges were subsequently impeached for crimes such as bribery. But for near two hundred years, no member of the executive branch was ever impeached with one exception, President Andrew Johnson in 1868. He, as said, escaped conviction before the Senate by one vote. His lawyers argued that he could only be convicted for "known crimes," that is, acts specifically defined as crimes by the criminal code. But in acquitting him, the Senate rendered no verdict on this narrower, more specific definition for "high crimes and misdemeanors."

When after the lapse of a century, Congress sought to impeach President Richard Nixon in 1973-1974, what amounted to "high crimes and misdemeanors" remained still not clearly defined. The Watergate Committee (who were investigating the president and contemplating the charges) asked their legal staff to furnish them with a definition. Those lawyers came up with this, "Constitutional Grounds for Presidential Impeachment ... (1) exceeding the constitutional bounds of the office in derogation of the powers of another branch of government; (2) behaving in a manner grossly incompatible with the proper purpose and function of the office; and (3) employing the office for an improper purpose or for personal gain."

What does this legalize translate to mean? It didn't say the president had to commit any crime, did it? What it said was broad enough to cover just about anything, wasn't it? What's "derogation of the powers of another branch of government?" What's "grossly incompatible with the proper purpose and function of the office?" What's "an improper purpose?" Who knows?

If that's the definition, maybe we're right back to what Hamilton said about impeachment as a "political process." As a practical matter, if the party-in-power in Congress has enough votes, maybe they can impeach the president. They and their legal staff will never lack the legal agility to make some legal sounding arguments to justify the deed. Their partisans outside Congress will never fail to buy into the justification and support the ouster.

The later 1998, 1999, impeachment of President Bill Clinton (a Democrat) pretty much proves the proposition. The Republicans had enough votes in the House to bring the charges, but the Democrats had enough votes in the Senate to prevent conviction. The members in either chamber pretty much voted along party lines. In other words, it was pretty much "a political process."

While what one party can do this time, the other party can do next time. And impeachment seems picking up speed. Since the Democrats managed to drive President Nixon from office, both the parties seem to regard impeachment as a viable weapon against a president from the other party. Both increasingly seek to wield it.

We may need some way to remove a president from office, but impeachment a very clumsy way. It threatens to virtually shut down the government during the course of the process. While since what amounts to "high crimes and misdemeanors" lacks any specific definition, impeachment threatens to turn into a very dangerous political weapon, repeatedly interrupting orderly government as each party in turn tries to impeach the presidents of the other party.

6.20 – Compared to Them

No point is more crucial to these articles than that the institutional design crucially affects the function. Noting better illustrates than to compare the U.S. Congress with the British Parliament. Both are democratic institutions, yet their different designs cause them to function very differently.

The U.S. Constitution designs Congress as a separate institution (separate from our executive branch), but the British Parliament and executive are linked together. Congress is elected separately from the chief executive, each congressman from his district, the congressional leaders, most prominently the Speaker of the House and Majority Leader in the Senate, by a party caucus in each chamber. This design leaves Congress resting on its own (independent) power base. The executive branch rests on a separate power base, the president being elected by a national constituency and appointing his cabinet. By contrast, the British legislature and executive rest on the same power base (their seats in the House of Commons). All the members stand in the same election. The member who leads the winning party serves as the prime minister and selects his cabinet from other sitting members. The prime minister and his cabinet both lead the House of Commons and head the executive branch. The American design separates, but the British links the legislative and the executive branches.

This difference in their institutional designs crucially affects their function. Congress displays a stubborn, sometimes a downright ornery, streak toward the chief executive. Sam Rayburn (D-TX), who served as Speaker of the House a total of seventeen years, advised members, "If you want to get along, go along." But if they don't choose to get along with the president, they don't have to go along. Their power doesn't depend on his power, leaving them the power to resist. They're rather notorious for wanting to get something out of the process (some of the famous pork) and refusing to go along until they get that something. They're rather notorious, too, for wanting to micro-manage the executive agencies, refusing to pass the budgets until the agency heads kowtow before the appropriate congressional committees. While when Congress under the sway of the opposite political party (divided government), they have every incentive neither to get along nor to go along. Being at political cross-purposes with the president, they're rather notorious for trying to trip up and embarrass his administration at every step.

Rather starkly in contrast, the House of Commons behaves much more British and correct, displaying much better manners toward the prime minister. His nod raises to cabinet rank, and a minister who wants to hang onto his coveted portfolio better say politely things in return. As for the backbenchers (the rank and file), if they want to move up to the front bench themselves eventually, they better show themselves well-behaved. Even more than that, if they're so discourteous as to vote against the prime minister, causing him to lose a key vote (what called a vote of confidence), that forces an immediate dissolution of Parliament and a new election. "To get along, go along." If the backbenchers don't get along, they go along all right, having voted themselves out of office. Their rudeness returns on themselves, forcing them to face all the hardships and perils of standing for re-election. No wonder the British have such a reputation for decorum.

Notice another difference. The Congress has dozens of committees. These committees constantly conduct "oversight," as constantly interfering with the president and cabinet's management of the executive agencies. They also constantly conduct investigations, raking the president and his administration over the coals. By contrast, Parliament never has had many committees and never much interferes with running the executive agencies. Why this difference? It's obvious, isn't it? What prime minister or cabinet want a bunch of pesky committees peering over their shoulders, prying into every nook and cranny, and putting in their two cents worth? And since they control the Commons, they've prevented the growth of a "committee system" with permanent committees to oversee every executive function. But with Congress the incentives reverse. Congress wants all the power it can get, and not being under executive control, has set up innumerable committees to try and run everything it can.

When it comes to foreign policy, you see something similar. The prime minister and Foreign Secretary (their equivalent to our Secretary of State) run British foreign policy. The loyal opposition (the other party, the party-out-of-power) may raise a ruckus in the parliamentary debates, but being in the minority, can't pass laws to limit the foreign policy options or cut off the funding. If a prime minister pursues a foreign policy so unpopular as turns the majority in the House against him, he loses a vote of confidence, and there's a new election. If his foreign policy loses the support of his party, they can replace him as leader and put in a new prime minister. When Neville Chamberlin lost the support of both his party and Parliament in 1940 at the start of World War II, he was simply replaced with Winston Churchill, who then led a coalition government of all the parties. But in any event, the majority in the House ends up behind the prime minister, not opposing him. By comparison, the American president stays in office for four years short of impeachment. Since he doesn't control the Congress, they can take such drastic steps as to cut off the funding for his foreign policy, as we saw them do with the Borland Amendment in 1984, which prohibited funding President Reagan's support for the Nicaraguan contras. We even saw the congressional leadership in the person of Speaker Jim Wright try to negotiate our foreign policy for Nicaragua and then force the outcome on the president.

When compared to them, the U.S. Congress looks a much less efficient design. Their design motivates all hands to man the oars and pull together, rowing in unison and all going the same direction. Our design often causes Congress to row out of sync or even against the president. No wonder our ship-of-state so often has a hard time making headway, occasionally stalls dead in the water.

But before we get too carried away with admiration for our British cousins, let's notice Congress may have some compensating advantages. Efficiency is great when going in the right direction, but when off course, just carries you faster and farther the wrong way. After World War II, several Labor prime ministers steered Britain fast and furious toward a socialist economy. In the 1970s, Conservative Prime Minister Margaret Thatcher reversed course, steering fast and furious back toward capitalism. It may be a question which was the right direction, but they were steering pretty fast and furious off course one time or the other. By comparison, the U.S. economy has more or less muddled along with no strong hand at the tiller. Command-and-control are divided between the Congress, the president, and the FED (an independent agency). These three pilots have sometimes disagreed on which course to set, occasionally sailed on opposite courses. Yet since World War II, the U.S. economy has more profitably voyaged than the British.

At the same time, the British style is more closed (more top-down), the American style more open (bottom-up). The backbenchers in the Commons are submerged in the ranks of the party, marching to the tune played and the cadence called by the prime minister. The members of Congress are all leading their own little parade with their constituents as their audience, all playing a part in some committee or other. In such an open formation, a man who can't find a platform to stand and shout out a speech not really trying. Neither is a man who can't find a way to exert at least some influence. For example, one wonders how a British backbencher can do much of a job at bringing home the bacon, but even obscure congressmen have managed to get something out of the pork barrel.

We used to hear quite a bit about the characters of various nationalities. The British were highly class conscious, stayed in their place, and followed the rules. Americans thought of themselves as a good as everyone else, refused to regard rank, and generally boisterous and undisciplined. Various explanations were offered. The historian Frederick Jackson Turner famously attributed the American character to the frontier, where the law didn't run, every man had to look out for himself, and the devil take the hindmost. There's probably some truth in the explanation. But there might also be some truth in the explanation that the political environment had something to do with it. British politics is top-down and keeps people in line. American politics is bottom-up and people compete for their place in line. It remains a question whether British efficiency costs more than it's worth or whether American inefficiency worth the cost.

6.21 – How Would You Draw

If you had a clean sheet of paper and could draw any constitution you wanted, how would you design your legislative? List all the elements you would want. Compared to your design, how well is Congress drawn?

Heading the list, wouldn't you want a democratic design (representatives elected by and responsible to the people)? Next on the list, wouldn't you want a functional design (to do and get through the people's business)? The first wouldn't do much good without the second.

To accomplish these twin purposes, wouldn't your design want to include the following elements? 1 - periodic elections to hold the representatives accountable to the people, 2 - representation of all the people not just some, 3 – the size not as small as a cabal, where insider and corrupt dealings easy to pull off and hide, yet not as many as a mob, making it hard to function, 4 – legislative procedures that passed the democratic process through from the outside to the inside, rather than procedures that let a few insiders dominate, turning the chamber into an oligarchy, 5 – procedures that let them get through the business and do the business well, and 6 – some mechanisms to let them interface (work effectively) with the executive branch.

If these the specifications, how well does Congress meet the design? Not perfectly, but awfully well. Their two and six-year terms of office with periodic elections every two years keep their noses to the electoral grindstone. Congress represents all the people not just some. The electoral map covers the country, everyone represented. Yet Congress doesn't perfectly represent the people. The Senate is grossly malapportioned, and the gerrymander effect in the House, even when unintended, shorts some people, some groups, and some interests. Some senators have come to represent huge constituencies, for example, a mere two senators from California representing some 39 million people. The size of House districts has grown ever larger, too. In the first House, 65 members represented a population about 4 million (a ratio about 1 to 61,500), while today 435 members represent over 300 million (about 1 to 689,500). With the senators from the larger states, it's hard to see how the head can still be in touch with the tail, while across the board, the representation is much more diluted, often perhaps drowning out the voices of smaller groups or interests. But on the plus side of that ledger, we still elect our senators from their states and our representatives from their districts. They're still tied to and responsible to distinct if large constituencies.

Turning from the outside to the inside, Congress looks neither too large nor too small, but about the right size. The members elect the leadership, most prominently, the Majority Leader in the Senate and Speaker of the House. These leaders, more or less with the acquiescence of the members, appoint the chairmen and other committee members. No doubt the leaders and committee chairs have a great deal more influence than the average member. Yet just about any member has some influence and some significant influence through being on some committee or other. We don't have the sense an inner oligarchy dominates.

As for getting through the business and doing the business well, the committee system gives Congress the benefit of a division of labor and specialization, and the two political parties organize the labor throughout. By dividing the tasks, the committees can get through a great deal of business and all at the same time, and the committee members can specialize and develop the expertise to do the business well. The parties provide the management and the organization. The majority party elects the leaders, holds all the committee chairs, and has a majority on every committee. At the same time, the numerous committees can interface with and oversee the vast federal bureaucracy. The party leadership in Congress gives the chief executive someone to work with.

As for that great bugaboo of excessive government power, what powers does Congress have we would rather erase from the present design? Or might we think some useful powers left out? But such questions don't really amount to very much. As a practical matter, nothing effectively prevents Congress from doing whatever we want, or for that matter, doing what we don't want. They've got the power all right. That leaves the only real restraint the democratic process. But historically, that has proved an effective and the only effective restraint on government anyways. What's so bad about that?

As for that other great bugaboo, the tyranny of the majority, historically, the majority party in Congress has rather frequently clung to control by only a narrow margin, which further narrowed by some dissent within their own ranks. Congress hasn't managed to pass much controversial legislation except after "wave" elections, where a large majority unites behind one party. In those circumstances, something approaching a consensus emerges. Yet this may be changing. More recently, the parties seem to have purged their ranks at the same time as the level of partisan hostility has reached a fever pitch. The parties may now possess sufficient unity, discipline, and antagonism to move against each other with no inner constraints. The passage of Obamacare in 2010 on a fairly narrow and straight party line vote may presage such a development. Only time will tell.

If you can suggest some better design for a legislature, by all means suggest it. Meantime, let's go with the existing congressional design. It looks pretty much like what you would want.

7.00 – THE PRESIDENT

7.01 – The Imperial Presidency

Arthur Schlesinger, Jr., son of a Harvard history professor, himself a Harvard history professor, advisor and speech writer to two-time presidential candidate Adlai Stevenson, advisor and unofficial court historian to President John F. Kennedy, one of the most famous academics of the twentieth century, in 1973, not coincidentally during the presidency of Richard Nixon. came out with a book titled, *The Imperial Presidency*. Among the talents that kept the professor in the limelight, he knew how to pick a title. This one has stuck and come to stand for the notion that American presidents have become too powerful (imperial). But imperial implies an emperor, and American presidents aren't emperors. They're elected, they're term limited to two terms, and they're limited in their powers in numerous other ways. The real question may be not whether they're too powerful, but whether they have enough power to get the job done that we want done.

Political scientists call our American presidency "a strong presidential form," where the chief executive is separate from (doesn't sit in) the legislature. That contrasts with "cabinet government," where the chief executive also occupies a seat in the legislature, for example, like the British prime ministers. Under the theory, the president being independent from Congress makes him a "stronger" chief executive, since his independence keeps Congress from controlling him. But in practice, more often that gets it backwards. More often congressional independence from the president makes him weaker, since he can't control them. By contrast, the British prime minister can control the House of Commons, making him in fact a stronger chief executive.

Consider how British "cabinet government" works. As the first step on his ascent to prime minister, a man must win election to the House of Commons just like the other members. As the next step, he must win election from his party as its leader, Conservative and Labor being the major parties. As the final step, if his party wins to dominance in the House of Commons, the Queen appoints him the prime minister. He then "forms a government" by choosing a cabinet from the other members of his party in the Commons. Thus, the prime minister and his cabinet sit in the House of Commons, and at the same time, serve as the chief executive and heads of the executive departments.

As a practical result, the prime minister occupies a very strong position, effectively able to control both the executive and legislative branches (the cabinet and the Parliament). Cabinet members follow his lead or risk expulsion from the cabinet, and their fondest wish to serve in the cabinet. The rank and file in the Commons (the backbenchers) follow his lead or risk committing another sort of political suicide. If the prime minister loses a key vote (a vote of confidence) in the House, that forces a dissolution and a new election. In other words, by voting against him, they vote themselves out of office. Suffice to say, such an event rarely occurs. In net effect, the prime minister turns out a very strong chief executive. The office has been called as near to an elected dictator as you can get, yet that's an exaggeration, since they remain restrained. If his party grows sufficiently disenchanted, they can vote him out as party leader and vote in someone else, changing prime ministers without forcing a dissolution and a new election. If sufficiently disenchanted, they can bring about a dissolution by voting against him on a vote of confidence, accepting the consequences of a new election. The prime ministers have to watch their step.

By contrast, the American president has much less control over Congress. The leaders of his party in Congress don't owe their leadership to him, rather being elected by the party caucus. His party members can vote against him in Congress without losing their seats. Even more than that, his party may not even have a majority in Congress (divided government). Finding himself in that unpleasant situation, not only does the president lose all hope of much control over Congress, but they routinely become the hostile center for "the loyal opposition." All in all, then, the president's independence from Congress doesn't necessarily make him stronger, rather, their independence from him often makes him weaker.

Nevertheless, American presidents have a lot of ways to influence Congress and have a lot of power independent from Congress. While over the course of our history, they've constantly acquired still more power. In the next articles, we need to turn to examine the whole array of the president's power as it has become. Only then will we be in a position to decide whether he has too much, too little, or enough power.

7.02 – Terms of Office

The last Founding Father to do so, James Monroe served two terms as the fifth president, from 1817 to 1825. Earlier in his career, Monroe had served three terms as governor of Virginia from 1799 to 1802. Pause a moment to do the mental math. His two terms as president added up to eight years, since the presidents serve four-year terms. But his three terms as governor totaled only three years. His terms of office as governor must have been only for one-year each. This calculation reveals a thing of significance about the power of the presidency.

The term of office calculates into the power of office. As Hamilton wrote in *Federalist No. 71,* "Duration in office has been mentioned as requisite to the energy of executive authority." That is, a longer term ("duration") equates to greater power ("energy"). For that very reason, back in Monroe's day, Virginia limited her governor's term of office to a mere one-year. Fearing too much power in her chief executive, the Virginia Constitution weakened the office by shortening the term. In that earlier era, a number of states followed this same formula, limiting their governors and other officials to very short terms of office. A commonly repeated proverb summed up this attitude, "Where annual elections end, tyranny begins." But time and experience disproved the proverb. States found they required more energy in their executive to get things done, and longer terms didn't lead to tyranny. Today, all the states follow the familiar federal formula of two, four, or six-year terms for their officers.

If our presidents had to run for their office every year or two, their power would diminish in proportion. Here today and gone tomorrow leaves little time either to plan or carry out policy. If no one could count on the president's favor for long nor need fear his disfavor for long, he would as quickly lose influence. Constantly running for office would consume him, leaving not much energy left over to do the actual job. On the other hand, lengthen the term of office to say six-years, and presidential power would lengthen in proportion. Stretch the term to say twelve, fifteen, or twenty years, and we would come closer and closer to turning the presidents into virtual monarchs. The Psalmist says, "fear of the Lord is the beginning of wisdom," and we used to hear, "the voice of the people is the voice of God." Let the presidents fear the voice of the people at the next election, that the wisdom of doing something for the people may begin to dawn in their minds, but let not the turmoil of too constant elections deprive them of the power of doing that something.

If the president's four-year term of office fits this prescription, more questionable comes the term limit to only two terms. Washington retired to Mt. Vernon after his second term, setting a precedent. Some of his successors, such as Ulysses S. Grant, longed to break this unwritten rule, but none could overcome the inertia. That was until Franklin D. Roosevelt, who was elected to four terms, serving from 1933 to 1945. Roosevelt regarded himself as the indispensable man, and he may have been right. Name another man who could have done a better job at leading the nation into and through World War II. None perceived the danger sooner, conceived the task more clearly, had more experience and savvy, more courage and confidence. If the crisis might have called forth such another man, in Roosevelt the nation already had the man. The people chose to keep him. How would a two-term limit have served them better?

But of course, his critics would not be stilled. In the 1944 campaign, Republican challenger Thomas E. Dewey said, "Four terms, or sixteen years, is the most dangerous threat to our freedom ever proposed." But Franklin Roosevelt never posed a "dangerous threat to our freedom." His example fails to prove a need to term-limit the president to two terms. If we want further proof, we might look again to Great Britain. Her prime ministers aren't term-limited. Margaret Thatcher served three terms (1979 to 1990), as did Tony Blair (1997 to 2007). Their longevity did no more harm to their freedoms than Roosevelt to ours. As Hamilton wrote in *Federalist No. 72*, "There is an excess of refinement in the idea of disabling the people to continue in office men who had entitled themselves, in their opinion, to approbation and confidence."

But needed or not, in 1951, we ratified the 22nd Amendment. "No person shall be elected to the office of President more than twice." This rigid term-limit clearly impacts the president's power. During the latter part of a second term, his authority wanes, since he becomes less and less a factor in future calculations. Not facing another election, his sense of accountability wanes, too. At the end of his second term and virtually on his way out the door in 2001, President Bill Clinton signed some controversial pardons, not least one for financier Marc Rich, a fugitive from justice hiding out comfortably in Switzerland, evading indictments for tax evasion and illegally dealing oil with Iran during the Iran Hostage Crisis. Would Clinton have granted such a pardon with another election looming? Perhaps, but the choice would not have been made any easier. No longer having to carry the burden of the next election, a term-limited president feels a weight lifted from his shoulders, making unpopular choices easier to carry.

The president's set term of office to four years also carries another consequence. Come hell or high water, we're stuck with him for his term. Again, to compare the British, their prime ministers serve an indeterminate term. Parliamentary elections come around at least every five years, and so the prime minister comes up for election at least every five years. But usually, a new election comes sooner in one of two ways. First, the prime minister can dissolve Parliament, leading to a new election. Picking a moment when his party riding high in the polls, he can sail into the election with a favorable wind at his back. Second and much less to his liking, if his party loses a key vote (a vote of confidence) in the House of Commons, he has to call a new election, whichever way the wind blows. And there's still a third way even less to his liking. His party can vote him out as leader at any time, choosing a new leader to replace him as prime minister. In 1990, Margaret Thatcher suffered this indignity, when the Conservative Party replaced her with John Major. In 1940 at the start of World War II, a coalition replaced Neville Chamberlin, who had lost the confidence of both Parliament and the nation, with Winston Churchill. Such flexibility has been conceived a great advantage of the British system over the American. They can jettison a chief executive, letting them "at the sudden appearance of a grave tempest, to change the helmsman – to replace the pilot of the calm by the pilot of the storm."

Our president serves a four-year term, and he's limited to two terms. Those are his terms of office, do with them what he may. We're stuck with him for his term, do what he may.

7.03 – Presidential Energy

In *Federalist No. 70* Alexander Hamilton wrote, "Energy in the Executive is a leading character in the definition of good government." Why so? The executive (the president) enforces the laws and carries out the policies of the government. Then no matter how good the laws or the policies, we can't have "good government" unless the executive has the necessary "energy" (read power) to enforce and carry them out. A good constitution must give the executive enough energy (enough power).

But while we want to give the executive enough power, we don't want to give him too much power. We don't want him with so much power as able make himself into a dictator. In fear of such excessive power, constitutions ancient and modern have tried a variety of devices to restrain and weaken the executive. One common expedient has been a "collegial system," that is, sharing the office among several men, which weakens the office by dividing the power against itself. The ancient Athenian Constitution carried this remedy to an extreme. Ten Generals commanded their military and ten-member boards managed the other executive functions. No wonder they lost the Peloponnesian War. Such an executive branch brings to mind the remark about a camel being a horse designed by a committee. Riding to war on such a contraption of committees, how could they hope to ride to victory?

Closer to modern times, the French Directory made another valiant effort along the same lines. After their Revolution in 1789, the French went through a swift series of new constitutions. In the 1795 version, "The theorists ... produced [a] surprise. They were afraid a presidential form of government might be the first step toward dictatorship, or to the restoration of the monarchy. Executive power was therefore to be shared between five men, chosen by the legislature, and known as the Directory." These five directors could seldom agree on much beyond their mutual desire to cut each other's throats. Their weakness brought about exactly the result the theorists had wanted to prevent. In 1799, Napoleon staged a *coup d'etat* and wrote still another constitution, eventually making himself a dictator.

In *Federalist No. 70*, Hamilton noted another problem with "a plurality in the executive ... is that it tends to conceal faults, and destroy responsibility." If you have a plural executive, each member will try to hide his faults by blaming the others, making it hard for the public to know who to hold responsible. It's like if you had a baseball team with a committee of managers. When the team has a losing season, who should you fire?

The Founding Fathers did better with the Constitution. Hamilton also wrote in *Federalist No. 70* that, "Decision, activity, secrecy, and dispatch will generally characterize the proceedings of one man, in a much more eminent degree, than the proceedings of any greater number." Wanting these virtues, they vested the presidency in "one man." The president can speak with a single, unifying voice. He can set and push on a definite course. He need not delay, but can act as soon as his mind made up or his options ripen. He can mature his plans in his own mind until ready to act. All these qualities serve especially useful purposes in the conduct of foreign affairs or warfare. He can put in practice the maxim, "Hit the other fellow as quick as you can as hard as you can, where it hurts him most, when he ain't looking!"

In the British Constitution, the monarch still wields the scepter as "the chief of state," serving as the highest embodiment of the "dignity and majesty" of the nation, although the prime minister wields the real executive power, doing the real executive work of government. But by doing away with monarchy, the U.S. Constitution did away with this division of labor. Our president serves both as chief of state, as the symbolic head of the government, and as the real chief executive. In the first role, he

271

performs a number of ritualistic and ceremonial functions. Americans like to think of themselves as not standing on ceremony, yet we have by no means abandoned all ceremony, which still used to signalize significant occasions such as high school graduation or even marriage. Our presidents perform such ceremonies as placing a wreath on the Tomb of the Unknown Soldier on Memorial Day. But they draw more than symbolic power from this role. By using these ceremonial platforms, they can often draw to themselves affection and support.

As for their real executive powers, Article II specifically says, "All legislative Powers herein granted shall be vested in a Congress," yet over the years the president has become the Chief Legislator with more influence over legislation than anyone else. From the beginning, he served as the Chief Executive Officer (the CEO) over the federal bureaucracy. (Article II says, "He shall take Care that the Laws be faithfully executed, and shall Commission all the Officers of the United States"). He's the Chief Diplomat ("He shall have the Power, by and with the Advice and Consent of the Senate, to make Treaties, … and he shall nominate, and by and with the Advice and Consent of the Senate, shall appoint Ambassadors"). He's the Commander-in-Chief ("The President shall be Commander in Chief of the Army and Navy of the United States"). But no enumeration of the president's powers can ever be quite complete, since another, imprecise power always remains (the residual power). That's the power to do whatever needs to be done in a crisis.

Such in general are the energies (the powers) of the president. Such amounts to a lot of energy (a lot of power). But so far, they haven't had enough to usurp the state and make themselves dictators. But do they have enough to get things done? That's a harder question. While the Constitution doesn't divide the executive power against itself like a collegial system, yet the separation of powers between the president, Congress, and the Supreme Court leaves the president with far from all the power. Does he have enough or maybe too much? In the next articles, we need to explore the president's energy (his power) to try to answer that question.

7.04 – Life in the White House

"The life of the White House is the life of a court. It is a structure designed for one purpose and one purpose only – to serve the material needs and desires of a single man." So wrote a guy who should know, George Reedy, who spent a couple years as press secretary to President Lyndon Johnson. He went on, "the most important, and least examined, problem of the presidency is that of maintaining contact with reality." Both points combined lead to a disturbing trend. Over the years, the White House has come to resemble a Versailles, a royal palace where the presidents, surrounded by luxury and the Secret Service, live isolated within an inner circle of loyalists, yes-men, and sycophants. Such a lifestyle can't be a good way "of maintaining contact with reality."

What caused this disturbing trend? We might start with the heightened need for security. During the Civil War, Lincoln and his family lived in the White House with no more than an honor guard and a couple secretaries, John Hay and John Nicolay, who later wrote the great biography of their chief. Just about any citizen could get in, either to ask a favor or just to shake the president's hand. Even Lincoln's assassination and later those of Garfield and McKinley did little to alter this ease of access. But in our times, the threat of assassination has become a constant, as shown by Kennedy's assassination, the attempts on Ford and Reagan, and the attempt on 9/11 to crash a plane into the White House. Angry men and terrorists routinely open fire and set off bombs, and whether we like it or not, they've forced the rest of us to alter our lifestyle, as anyone who has passed through an airport security checkpoint knows. Every major building and public facility requires at least a security guard. While the presidents, as a highest value target, are forced to dwell behind very high security barriers. The outer serenity of the White House conceals an invisible wall manned by heavily armed guards on hair trigger alert. But while a necessity, this barrier cuts off the prior public access. The presidents themselves probably don't mind too much. Being carefully guarded probably only adds to their sense of self-importance, a feeling never in short supply with presidents anyway. At the same time, they avoid a lot of time-consuming and not necessarily pleasant interaction with the electorate. But that's precisely the point. Rather than forced to rub elbows like their predecessors, the presidents have become more remote, more like Louis XIV at Versailles.

Life inside the White House has altered in another significant way. Thomas Jefferson did away with what he regarded as the excessive formality of his predecessors (Washington and Adams). During the Civil War, Lincoln suffered acute embarrassment over the lavish sums Mrs. Lincoln managed to spend on redecorating the White House. But today, the presidents don't seem to regard as excessive or suffer any embarrassment over what has become a lifestyle of the rich and famous. Again, good reasons exist. Since the burdens of the presidency so heavy, why not make his life otherwise as easy as possible? Today, no five-star hotel or luxury spa offers more amenities than the White House. For a change of scene, there's Camp David. For travel, there's Air Force One. As the head of state of the most powerful country on earth, they entertain in a befitting style, too. All in all, presidents and their families have come to enjoy a royal lifestyle. Once again, probably the presidents and their families don't mind too much. Who doesn't enjoy the royal treatment? But once again, that's precisely the point. When the browsing and sluicing are so good at the top, a tendency exists to ignore how bad the reality may be at the bottom.

The White House has changed in another way, too. The place has been converted from the president's private residence and office into an office complex stretching through underground corridors to the office buildings round about. This reflects another change. Thomas Jefferson had no more than a secretary and a messenger. Even by 1900, during the presidency of William McKinley, the president has no more than a chief aide and twelve other onsite staff. But by 1939, during the presidency of Franklin Roosevelt, Congress created the Executive Office of the President, which today has a staff of over 2,000 and a budget of over $300 million. Perhaps most significantly, the EOP includes the White House Office headed by the White House Chief of Staff and the National Security Council headed by the National Security Advisor. Most of the offices in the EOP don't require the Senate's approval like the cabinet offices do, but are solely within the president's gift and serve solely at his pleasure. Naturally, he tends to appoint his own true believers, who got on board early and stayed on board, proving their loyalty through the good times and the bad, long known and trusted. These key players tend to have their offices in close physical proximity to him ("access"). Naturally, too, this inner circle tends to become the president's closest advisors and confidantes. Once again, good reasons existed. The federal bureaucracy had grown so huge that the president required a smaller, more central bureaucracy to help him manage the larger bureaucracy. But notice the tendency to shut out all except loyalists from easy access to the president. If staying connected to reality requires hearing inconvenient truths, this set up is not well-qualified to fulfill that role. It more resembles a royal court with a monarch surrounded by his courtiers.

So is it just me, or don't presidents seem more and more to hunker down behind the security barriers, live the royal lifestyle, enjoy the incense their inner circle burns at their shrine, and play the part of a great leader in their own minds? That's especially true as their term of office winds down. As long as the prospect of the next election looms, that's a powerful incentive to connect with reality. They're highly stimulated to do something to at least look good. But when that prospect fades, what me worry? Might as well enjoy myself. Since by definition the presidents have big egos, one of the main ways they enjoy themselves is by stroking their own egos. They don't just play golf or go on vacation. They work on their "legacy."

And here's another thing about it. A president doesn't really have to do too much if he doesn't want to. Again, to compare him to the British prime minister, the president can exist in splendid isolation. The prime minister doesn't have that luxury. The prime minister is expected to attend in Parliament and even has to answer questions in the "question hour." The prime minister is expected to regularly meet with and consult his cabinet. But the president doesn't attend Congress. He doesn't have to send legislation over to them or even interact with them if he doesn't want to. Nor does he have to hold a cabinet meeting if he doesn't want to. So would it be any wonder if presidents neglected their business? Like everybody else, they go down the slippery slope of the course with least resistance. They let things slide. The mechanism of accountability fails to force them to it, so they neglect it. By contrast, the British system seems to keep the prime minister's shoulder against the wheel.

7.05 – The Disappearing Cabinet

Over the years, the cabinet has pulled off an unusual sort of disappearing act. They've gotten bigger only to fade from the picture. Their fading has left the presidents looking less backed and surrounded with strong advisors. Today, the presidents look more isolated within an inner circle of their own true believers. That can't be better picture.

A painting of Washington's cabinet in 1789 shows just three members, including Secretary of State Thomas Jefferson and Secretary of the Treasury Alexander Hamilton. The well-known painting of Lincoln's cabinet in 1862, conferring over the Emancipation Proclamation, still shows just seven members. But the formal photograph of George W. Bush's cabinet in 2001, the first cabinet of the twenty-first century, shows twenty members, too many to fit comfortably around the conference table or into the picture.

Up until fairly recently, the cabinet held regular meetings and served as the president's closest advisors. Generally, they made up a formidable array. The members had to win confirmation from the Senate, a not insignificant vetting process. The candidates had to present some fairly impressive credentials, some prior track record of political or worldly success, something beyond a mere resume showing loyalty to the president. Many cabinet members had political constituencies and ambitions of their own. Such men weren't reluctant to express strong views or fight hard for them with each other and sometimes the president. Think of Washington's cabinet with Jefferson and Hamilton, both with not so hidden presidential ambitions of their own and whose clashing ambitions caused one, Jefferson, eventually to resign and begin organizing a party in opposition. While not as well remembered, two members in Lincoln's cabinet, the Secretary of State, William H. Seward, and the Secretary of the Treasury, Salmon P. Chase, cherished similar highflying ambitions. The cabinet, then, was a formidable institution hard for a president entirely to ignore.

Whether or not he wanted to hear their advice, whether or not he took it, the cabinet forced on him some experienced, independent, strongminded counsel. What's that old saw about inconvenient truths? The cabinet looked well designed to force such truths on the president.

Gradually, the picture changed. As the federal government got bigger, the cabinet got bigger for the same reasons. To head all the growing executive departments, the cabinet had to grow, too. From a handful, they became more than you could count on all your fingers and toes. At some point, the cabinet got too big for its own good, growing to unwieldy size. The president could no longer consult so big a cabinet with any convenience. Naturally, then, the presidents consulted with them less and less. Rather, the presidents came to rely more on a newer institution.

In 1939, Congress passed a law to set up the Executive Office of the President (the EOP). Good reasons existed. The federal bureaucracy had grown so large that the president needed a smaller, more central bureaucracy to help him manage the larger bureaucracy. The EOP itself has now grown to have a staff of over 2,000 and a budget over $300 million. Central to the EOP are the White House Office, headed by the president's Chief of Staff, and the National Security Council, headed by the National Security Advisor. Their own offices located physically close to the president in the White House complex, both these officials have the coveted "access" to the president. Both are appointed solely by the president, don't require Senator confirmation, and serve solely at his pleasure. Since the EOP's functions overlap with the cabinet's function, the result has been some epic turf wars between it and the cabinet, but increasingly the cabinet seems to lose out to this tighter inner circle of advisors.

Thus, a more modern picture emerges. The cabinet has more and more disappeared, replaced as the president's closest advisors by this tight inner circle. Since this inner circle appointed solely by the president, he tends to appoint long-time supporters and true believers in himself. The president looks much less backed and surrounded by strong advisors and much more isolated within a tight circle of his own true believers. This institutional design looks much less likely to force on him those inconvenient truths.

It has been said, "The net result is the establishment of a

centralizing executive secretariat. This, in turn, frustrates any type of a formalized executive branch with the president and cabinet in close cooperation and collaboration. An even greater reliance is the overreliance of the president on his aides and assistants. … this situation, both quantitatively and qualitatively, effects the amount of information a president receives."

Again, it's instructive to compare the British cabinet system. The prime minister appoints his cabinet from the leading members of his party in the House of Commons. And he can't dispense with them. He has to have their support to keep control over the party in the Commons. If he loses their support, the party can vote him out as leader and replace him as prime minister with another party leader. While his selection of members of his cabinet can include close and long-time political associates, yet can't include only these. He has to select men already elected to Parliament by the voters and those recognized within the party as leaders. The British cabinet continues to meet regularly and exercise considerable influence. The prime minister may dominate them. He may remove them. But he cannot dispense with them or with cabinet meetings. He cannot avoid listening to them. American presidents labor under no such compulsion.

One observer went so far as to conclude, "The cabinet is one of those institutions in which the whole is less than the sum of the parts. As individual officers, the members bear heavy responsibilities in administering the affairs of the government. As a collective body, they are about as useful as the vermiform appendix." But that's not the way it was intended to be. The cabinet was intended as the president's primary advisors. That's the way it started out. For a long time, the cabinet remained the president's primary advisors. So this is change and doubtfully a change for the better. Presidents need to hear inconvenient truths, but seem less likely to hear them.

7.06 – The Federal CEO

The president is the CEO (Chief Executive Officer) of the biggest business in America (the federal government). But a lot of his shareholders (the public) never seem satisfied with his management. The other political party (like a corporate raider) constantly plots to replace him at the next shareholders meeting (the next election). The Congress (like a dissident board of directors) often interferes and tries to oust him from control. The heads of his corporate departments (the cabinet and other agency heads) often either fail to carry out or modify his business plan, as often without telling him, convinced they have a better plan, invariably one more convenient or otherwise more profitable to themselves. Like a highly-unionized workforce, which they are, his millions of employees (the civil service bureaucrats) quietly, but persistently pursue their own business plan, often at the cost of his bottom line. Usually, a strong president can force through a policy he cares enough about to devote the time and energy, yet the size and inertia of this biggest business can easily elude effective management. All in all, the presidents have a hard time running the national business either according to their business plan, efficiently, or to the public profit.

We've heard about too big to fail, but what about too big to manage? From the founding to the present, the size of the bureaucracy has grown relentlessly. Washington's cabinet contained only three departments (State, War, and Treasury), while in 2001, President George W. Bush started out with twenty. By a recent count the bureaucracy had over a million civilian employees divided among fourteen executive departments and sixty independent agencies. That doesn't count a bewildering array of private contractors hired through the bureaucracy. How can anyone manage anything so big?

A president has said, "What I know concerns me. What I don't know concerns me even more. What people aren't telling me worries me the most." But presidents can have no idea what going on in much of the bureaucracy. It's just too big. The bureaucrats are just too opaque. Much of the bureaucracy follows a simple business plan. As long as there's no special inconvenience to them during the business day, what me worry? The management does their best to put a smiley face on their departments, ignoring or hiding the failures, publishing only the side of the facts that make them look good. They seldom fail to persuade themselves that what's good for them is good for the country.

What compounds the problem is the civil service system. The

idea behind civil service was to hire the government employees on merit, promote them on performance, and only discharge them for good cause. Who's going to argue with that? It even works to a large extent. But anyone familiar with the system knows that the merit often not carefully tested, the promotion often not based on performance, and discharge has become a near impossibility. Civil servants have come to occupy virtual sinecures. In the outcome, their productivity and efficiency aren't that good.

What further compounds the problem are the "independent agencies." Congress has deliberately set up a lot of agencies outside presidential control. A board with members appointed for a set term of years manages the agency. The president appoints the members of the board with Senate approval, but can't fire them. Since he can't fire them, he can't control them. The rationale is for the agency to perform some merely regulatory or technical task and/or a desire to remove the agency from the arena of partisan politics. Prominent examples are the Environmental Protection Agency (EPA) that regulates pollution, the Federal Aviation Administration (FAA) that regulates air transportation, or the Securities and Exchange Commission (SEC) that regulates the securities market. This sort of business model makes it hard, if not impossible, for the president to run the business.

The most famous and important independent agency is the Federal Reserve (the FED), which regulates the monetary supply. One of the most famous incidents showing their independence from presidential control came during the run up to the 1992 election between the incumbent, President George H.W. Bush, and the challenger, Bill Clinton. Since the economy not doing too good, President Bush wanted to inject some monetary stimulus. But Alan Greenspan, who headed the FED, refused, fearing inflation. That refusal quite likely cost Bush the election, since the slow economy seems to have been crucial to the outcome.

As much as all this, Congress constantly competes with the president for control over the bureaucracy. The laws that govern the agencies and their funding depend on Congress. That gives Congress a set of leashes to jerk around the bureaucrats. They can change the laws or cut the funding. To keep these leashes tight, Congress has set up a host of congressional committees to oversee every aspect of the bureaucracy. It's a regular sight to see the bureaucrats called before a committee to genuflect and get their marching orders, if not to suffer a painful grilling.

The president is the CEO of the federal business. That gives him a lot of power. But the business is so big and complex, it's hard for him to effectively manage the business. Moreover, the lines of authority often take crucial matters out of his hands. Yet the public holds him responsible for the slightest failure in how this business model performs.

In the days of monarchy, the royal mistresses were said to have power without responsibility. Our presidents often have responsibility without power.

7.07 – The President in Congress

The president doesn't sit in Congress, but has more influence there than anyone who does. We may rightly call him our "chief legislator," with more influence over legislation than anyone else. Yet his troubles in Congress bring to mind that old saying, "too many chiefs and not enough Indians." The competing chiefs in Congress often frustrate his leadership there.

At least once each year, the president does make a personal appearance in Congress for the annual State of the Union Address. This rite originates with words in Article II, "He shall from time to time give to the Congress Information of the State of the Union, and recommend to their Consideration such Measures as he shall judge necessary and expedient." To fulfill this commandant, George Washington, as the first president, started the tradition. Each year during his presidency, he stood up before Congress in formal dress, in that time knee breeches, a wig, a sash, and a sword, and gave an equally formal speech. John Adams, as the second president, followed his lead. However, Thomas Jefferson, as the third president, regarded such ceremony as smacking too much of monarchy, too much like the Speech from the Throne still given by the British monarch at the opening of each Parliament. Besides, Jefferson was an indifferent orator, in his day not a necessary talent for presidential candidates, since they didn't go around making speeches, stumping for office still being regarding as beneath their dignity. Instead, Jefferson sent a written message over to Congress. The presidents after him followed his lead. That was until 1913, when Woodrow Wilson reverted to earlier form, going to Congress in person to deliver a speech. Since then, the live speech has become the expected norm, although in 1981, President Jimmy Carter submitted a written report.

No doubt the advent of radio made such an opportunity too good to pass up and later television only added to the attraction. Cloaked with all the dignity of the highest office, surrounded by symbols of the national government, himself the central image in the spectacle, the president gets to make a long oration to a captive audience, a joint session of Congress. The networks carry the broadcast live without commercial interruption to prove their public spirit. How could the president find a better platform from which to pitch himself, even if the pitch may require some spin? Every year the public tunes in, watching and listening as the president's party loud in applause, while the loyal opposition, if they can restrain their outbursts, sit on their hands or put them together without making any noise.

Presidents have personally appeared in Congress on other memorable occasions. Woodrow Wilson took the rostrum there to call for a declaration of war against Germany on April 2, 1917 (his "make the world safe for democracy speech"). Franklin Roosevelt did the same for a declaration of war against Japan on December 8, 1941 (his "day of infamy speech"). Lyndon Johnson offers another memorable instance, when just days after the assassination of President Kennedy, he sought to reassure and rally the nation on November 27, 1963 (his "let us continue speech").

Although the Constitution says the president shall "recommend to their [Congress's] Consideration such Measures as he shall judge necessary and expedient," for a long time, Congress regarded with a jealous eye any presidential attempt to initiate and steer legislation as improper executive meddling with the legislative branch. James Madison disapproved of President Washington's draft of his first inaugural speech as "its lengthy legislative proposals would be interpreted as executive meddling with the legislature." Before the Civil War, "Although the issues which occupied the attention of Congress were important to the President, Congress was usually regarded as the policy making organ of government." Nevertheless, from the very beginning, the presidents have sought to influence legislation and often successfully. The temptation was just too much for them to resist. The presidents' power was just too much for Congress to resist. And so, once again over time, the original concept of power under the Constitution changed, this time in the presidents' favor.

Today, the executive branch rather than the legislative branch drafts most major congressional bills, which are then handed off to a friendly member of Congress to actually file. Few are more important than the annual Budget of the United States, which runs to thousands of pages and prepared each year under presidential direction by the Office of Management and Budget (OMB). When we recall the Constitution says, "All bills for raising Revenue shall originate in the House of Representatives," we see that while the form somewhat preserved, the substance somewhat altered and greatly in favor of the president's power, since giving him the initiative gives him the chance to mold the budget.

Far beyond specific legislation, modern presidents are expected to come up with a whole program of legislation. Teddy Roosevelt started this modern trend with his Square Deal. Woodrow Wilson followed with his New Freedom Program, Franklin Roosevelt with his New Deal, Harry Truman with his Fair Deal, and Lyndon Johnson with his Great Society. Overall, while the form preserved (Congress as the source of legislation), the substance has greatly altered (the executive branch often taking the lead in formulating legislation and policy).

Yet drafting a bill or writing a program remains a far different matter from passing the legislation. Despite his influence in Congress, the many other leaders in Congress have their own influence, and their agenda may not coincide with the president's grand vision. A good example would be Woodrow Wilson's failure to win ratification for the Treaty of Versailles after World War I. Wilson was an internationalist, and the treaty firmly linked this country to the international community through our membership in Wilson's proposed League of Nations. But a lot of the leaders in the Senate were isolationists and opposed any such link with other countries. To put pressure on the Senate, Wilson in 1919 embarked on an exhaustive speaking tour across the nation, an effort culminating in his debilitating stroke, but not in the ratification of the treaty.

Today's presidents may rightly be called our chief legislators with more influence over legislation than anyone else. But they find it hard to persuade where they cannot command, and they cannot command Congress. Yet they have a lot of tools of persuasion such as logrolling (putting together a coalition to pass legislation by including something to persuade enough wavering members to go along) or the veto (stopping legislation unless concessions made to the president). So a lot of a president's influence in Congress depends on his personal powers of persuasion. Some presidents have proved much better at getting the legislation they wanted than others. Let's consider an example of an outstanding persuader in the next article.

7.08 – Master of the Game

Robert A. Caro has written four thick volumes on a monumental biography of President Lyndon Johnson. Eighty years old and working on the next and purportedly last volume, let's hope Mr. Caro survives to cross the finish line. He tells a fascinating tale, and nothing fascinates him more than the way Johnson acquired and used power. He writes, "to see Lyndon Johnson take hold of presidential power, and so quickly begin to use it … is to see, with unusual clarity, the immensity of the potential an American president possesses to effect transformative change in the nation he leads. … it is possible to glimpse the full possibilities of presidential power."

President John F. Kennedy's tragic assassination in Dallas, November 22, 1963, unexpectedly elevated Johnson to the power of the presidency. But he had already spent a lifetime and had already shown considerable ingenuity in the pursuit of political power and pleasure in the possession. After a decade in the House, he won a very close race for the Senate in 1948 and quickly climbed to become the youngest majority leader in history in 1955. From that vantage point and to a degree never before achieved, he showed a rare capacity to master that stubborn body and bend the members to his will. No wonder Caro titles his book about these years *Master of the Senate.* So when Johnson finally stepped into the presidency, he was already a past master of the legislative arts.

Here was a man uniquely qualified to give a graphic demonstration about how a president could use his power to master Congress and to influence legislation. Nothing showed off his skill better than his role in the passage of the Civil Rights Act of 1964, a true legislative landmark.

In his book about these years (*The Passage of Power*), Caro traces all the twist and turns of this story in graphic detail. At the time of his death, President Kennedy's legislative program was badly stalled in Congress. Besides the civil rights bill, two other key pieces of legislation were pending, the annual federal budget and a tax cut bill. For all his many virtues, Kennedy seemed unable to grasp the right legislative levers to pry these bills lose. It was a logjam with the bills interlocked and blocking each other. Johnson proved a skilled lumberjack. As Caro says, "He not only broke the congressional logjam, he broke it up fast."

The biggest log was the diehard segregationists led by Senator Richard Russell (D-GA). Not so well-remembered today, Russell was a titan of the Senate, who commanded huge respect from his fellow senators. Far from a race baiter, he never failed to express his opposition against civil rights in the highest constitutional terms as rights. And he was himself a past master at working the Senate. In fact, Johnson had been a Russell protégé, their relationship so close Johnson's daughters called Russell "Uncle Dick." Russell's tried-and-true tactic to block civil rights was to clog the Senate with other legislation, delay the other legislation in committee, delay civil rights behind that other legislation, and prevent any civil rights bill from ever reaching the floor until the bill expired with the session.

As a young senator, Johnson had himself helped Russell carry out such tactics. But as the new president he was on the other end of the logjam. He badly wanted to pass the civil rights bill. Not only did he apparently believe in it, but civil rights was part of another logjam, a political one. If Johnson wanted to run for president in his own right in 1964, he badly needed to unjam the hostility felt toward himself by the liberal wing of the Democratic Party, who inherently disliked any man whose accent betrayed him as coming from a wrong culture in their viewpoint, that is, as coming from the South. If Johnson could pass a civil rights bill, he might win over the liberals, at least long enough to win the election.

The other big log in the Senate jam was another senator very familiar to Johnson, Henry Byrd (D-VA). Byrd was seventy-six years old, had served in the Senate for three decades, and was another master at getting what he wanted from that body. He was the Chairman of the Finance Committee where he had blocked those other two key bills, the tax reform bill and budget bill, for an interconnected reason. By "tax reform" was meant lowering taxes to leave more money in the economy as an economic stimulus, and Byrd wasn't set against such a scheme. But lowering taxes meant less money coming in, which would raise the federal deficit, and Byrd was dead set against higher deficits. "He hated public debt with a holy passion." He was holding the tax cut bill as a hostage. Until the budget bill held federal spending down to under $100 billion, neither bill was coming out of his committee. He was stalling both with interminable hearings, and he had enough allies on his committee to keep this up indefinitely.

Turning to the House of Representatives, the jammed log was Judge Howard Smith (D-VA), who chaired the Rules Committee. Generally, every House bill has to pass through this committee to reach the floor. An adamant opponent of civil rights, Smith had killed an earlier civil rights bill simply by staging an early and personal congressional adjournment, leaving town to return to his Virginia farm. With the chairman gone, his committee couldn't hold hearings, effectively ending any hope the bill would come out and go to the floor. Asked for an explanation, Smith blandly explained his barn had burned down, requiring him to go home early to check on things. This stunt led Speaker Sam Rayburn to remark, "I knew Howard Smith would do anything to stop a civil rights bill, but I didn't know he would commit arson."

In the face of such obstruction, Johnson went to work on the logs. First, he unjammed Henry Byrd. Calling him to the White House, Johnson rolled out the red carpet and gave the senator what he wanted and gift rapped. Johnson promised to deliver a federal budget under $100 billion, and in writing, so Byrd could personally go over it and make sure there was no accounting slight of hand. In return, Johnson got Byrd's agreement to let both the tax reform bill and the budget bill out of his committee.

While handling Byrd with one hand, Johnson was busy

neutralizing Judge Smith with the other. Congressional committees can override their chairmen, but such an event a rare occurrence, and Johnson quickly figured out it wasn't going to occur this time either. He couldn't get enough votes in the Rules Committee itself to override the chairman (Smith). So Johnson engineered an even rarer occurrence - a discharge petition. Under this seldom used procedure, if a majority of the House's 435 members sign a petition, they can discharge a bill from the Rules Committee, sending it directly to the floor. Johnson got the petition rolling. When it looked like it was going to gain enough signatures, Judge Smith finally gave in, rather than suffer the public indignity of such a defeat, and the Rules Committee sent the civil rights bill on to the House floor.

By dislodging these first two logs (Smith and Byrd), Johnson had also dislodged a third (Russell's carefully planned obstruction). But now there was a final log, the filibuster in the Senate. Using every lever at his command, Johnson once again proved the master of the game. He rallied grassroots support, particularly among church leaders, black leaders, and union leaders. He politicked the state governors to politic their senators. Nor did he fail to use the power of the presidency to dispense favors. For example, he helped out Charles Halleck (R-IN), the House Minority Leader, by assuring NASA funding for some research at Purdue University, which in Halleck's district. There were numerous other examples. He worked behind the scenes to hammer out last minutes compromises with Senator Everett Dirksen (R-IL), the minority leader in the Senate.

In a historic scene on June 10, 1964, cloture, ending the filibuster, was finally voted (71 to 19). The filibuster had lasted 57 days, the longest in Senate history. One June 19, the civil rights bill itself passed (73 to 27). Johnson had shown himself the master of the game. He had shown how to use all the powers of the presidency to pass legislation.

What did the country get out if it? An annual budget that showed fiscal restraint, a rather unusual creature at any time. A tax cut that spurred economic growth. "The reductions [in taxes] instituted by the bill, and the increased spending they inspired [by the private sector], were a key element in what would become one of the longest economic expansions in American history." Most lasting, the Civil Rights Act of 1964, which finally put an end to the evils of segregation.

What did Johnson himself get? Maybe the gratification of doing what he believed was right. Maybe the gratification of winning a fight. But no doubt the gratification of winning election as president in his own right in that same year, 1964, in a landslide. He had shown strong leadership. Apparently, most of the country agreed with his policies. He even won over the liberal Democrats for a brief moment, although they would soon find other reasons to fall out with him.

For our story of the Constitution, the president has a lot of power to influence legislation. What he can influence depends a lot on his own ability to wield the influence. Not many presidents have mastered the game as thoroughly as Lyndon Johnson.

7.09 - Government by Veto

A recent headline read, "Obama Vetoes Defense Bill in High-Stakes Showdown Over Spending." The story went on to say, "President Obama made good on his threat to veto a $612 billion defense policy bill Thursday, bringing the fight over domestic spending into the realm of national security." As for his reasons, "Speaking to reporters for four minutes in a rare public veto message, … Obama's main objection is that the bill … increase[s] the defense budget without increasing domestic spending." If we only take the trouble to unpack this story, we find a classic instance of how the presidents try, often successfully, to govern through the power of the veto.

Don't forget, the Anglo-American constitutional tradition regards the power of the purse (the power to tax and spend) as the most essential legislative power. Using that power, the English Parliament slowly restrained and finally broke the power of the monarchy. Over that power, the American colonies broke with Great Britain ("no taxation without representation"). Among the powers enumerated for Congress in the Constitution, that power comes very first on the list, "The Congress shall have the power to lay and collect taxes." Then why would President Obama think that as the chief executive he should have the power to interfere with Congress, the legislature, over the budget (over taxing and spending)?

But the Constitution also reserves the president a veto over legislation, including bills to tax and spend. "Every bill ... shall, before it become a law, be presented to the President ... if he approve he shall sign it; but if not he shall return it with his objections." Congress can "override" a veto by re-passing the bill with a two-thirds majority in both houses. But generally, such a solid majority is more than hard to come by. An esteemed commentator on the Constitution has observed, "As to the actual effectiveness of the President's veto ... the testimony of the statistics is conclusive. Between the first inauguration of George Washington and the second inauguration of Franklin D. Roosevelt 750 measures were vetoed. ... Of these 750 vetoes only 49 were overridden, ... Later statistics conform substantially to this pattern. Altogether, it seems just to say that the President's veto is normally effective in nine cases out of ten."

The veto or the mere threat gives the president a lot of power relative to Congress, including over the budget. For a specific example of how this power can work, back in 1959, President Dwight Eisenhower gave a graphic demonstration. Eisenhower (a Republican) faced a Congress solidly controlled by the Democrats (65 to 35 or 65 percent in the Senate and 283 to 152 or 58 percent in the House). As a general, Eisenhower wasn't known for fighting when outnumbered, but as commander-in-chief, he showed willing to take on these odds. He sent the message loud and clear to hold down the spending levels well below the Democrats' desires. To test and break his resolve, the Democrats deliberately picked a highly popular program, the Rural Electrification Administration. Bringing electricity to rural America had been a New Deal initiative, and few failed to see the results as "progress as promised." Relying on this high public approval rating, the Democrats boldly passed a funding bill for the REA that broke through Eisenhower's budget ceiling. But the former general stuck to his guns and resolutely vetoed the bill. When the smoke of the ensuing battle cleared, the congressional attempt at an override had lost by a mere four votes in the House. That set the pattern for the conflict. Never mind their big majority. The Democrats couldn't out vote the president's veto. Congress was forced to come to the table and bargain with the president. Eisenhower managed to cut spending. He had managed to govern through the veto.

What does the more recent headline and story show except President Obama trying to employ the same tactic? But while Eisenhower wanted to hold down spending, Obama wants more domestic spending. But just like Eisenhower managed to govern through the veto, Obama may manage to govern through the veto. Whether it works this time around remains to be seen. Yet what can be seen is the veto not just a negative power, but a positive power. It gives the president not just a negative power over legislation, but a positive power over legislation. It gives him a lever to force Congress to do what he wants. And of course, it's not just over the budget, but over each and every item on the legislative agenda.

Then if the veto serves as part of the separation of powers, as a way for the president to check Congress, it also goes further and lets the president insert himself in the legislative process and exert some control over Congress. Not only does it let him block one law, but he can hold one law hostage against another. Similar to what President Obama did, he can refuse to sign one law he may not like until Congress passes another law he does like. In effect, he can try to force legislation on Congress. The veto is not just a negative power, but a positive power.

7.10 – The Judicial President

Here's a famous veto message, handed down by President Andrew Jackson on July 10, 1832. He was vetoing a law to re-charter the Second Bank of the United States, whose original charter was shortly set to expire. Back in the day, it would be hard to exaggerate the sound and fury of this political controversy (the Bank War). But for our purposes, we can stick with the dry legal narrative. Jackson vetoed the bill based on his view the bank was unconstitutional. He persisted in this view despite the fact the Supreme Court had already ruled such a bank was constitutional back in 1819 in the McColloch Case, which discussed several times in these articles.

Here's what Jackson wrote in his veto message, "The Congress, the Executive, and the Court must each for itself be guided by its own opinion of the Constitution. … It is as much the duty of the House of Representatives, of the Senate, and of the President to decide upon the constitutionality of any bill or resolution which may be presented to them for passage or approval as it is of the supreme judges when it may be brought before them for judicial decision. The opinion of the judges has no more authority over Congress than the opinion of Congress has over the judges, and on that point the President is independent of both. The authority of the Supreme Court must not, therefore, be permitted to control the Congress or Executive when acting in the legislative capacities, but to have only such influence as the force of their reasoning may deserve."

In other words, he was saying that "the opinion of the judges" (the Supreme Court) has "no more authority over Congress than the opinion of Congress over the judges." That is, Congress has as much authority to interpret the Constitution (the highest law) as the Supreme Court. And "the President is independent of both." That is, he has as much authority to interpret the Constitution as either the Congress or the Supreme Court. It didn't matter if Congress thought the bank was constitutional as shown by passing the bank bill. It didn't matter that the Supreme Court had previously held the bank was constitutional. The president had the right to disagree with both of them and interpret the Constitution for himself. That's exactly the power Jackson claimed to be exercising by vetoing the bank bill as unconstitutional.

Since then, Jackson's legal argument has suffered an utter rejection. Not that he lacked the legal power to veto the bank bill. Presidents can still legally veto a bill for any reason they want. But in the years since, the Supreme Court has managed to assert final authority over interpreting the Constitution and the other laws (under the doctrine of judicial supremacy, which we'll come to discuss later in these articles). Presidents no longer make the claim of having a final ("independent") power to interpret the Constitution and the other laws. Today, the Supreme Court is recognized as the final authority.

Yet as a practical matter, the presidents still retain considerable authority to interpret the Constitution and the other laws. That's because the Supreme Court has never ruled on a lot of the

Constitution and a lot of the other laws. That leaves a lot still up for grabs. And that leaves the president some considerable space to assume what amounts to a judicial role. As part of his duty to see "the laws be faithfully executed," he can interpret the laws as part of the process of executing them. That's obviously and especially true with respect to newly passed laws, which never yet interpreted by the Supreme Court. In choosing how to enforce them, the president must first choose between often competing interpretations. Seeing how this initial process works is an easy way for us to see how the authority to interpret the laws, which we think of as a judicial function, actually falls, at least in the first instance, to the president.

In this connection, during President George W. Bush's time in office (2001 to 2009), do you remember the controversy over some of his "signing statements?" Article I, Sec. 7 says that, "Every Bill which shall have passed [Congress], shall, before it become a Law, be presented to the President of the United States; If he approve he shall sign it, but if not he shall return it, with his Objections." Then if a president vetoes a law, he must state his objections, as we just heard Andy Jackson do. But when he goes ahead and signs the bill into law, he may want to state his reasons as well. That's a "signing statement." He may just want to say it's a great law and isn't he wonderful for signing it. But he may want to take the opportunity to do something more. He may engage in what amounts to a judicial function. He may say how he interprets the law and so how he intends to apply it. He may even go so far as to say he objects to some parts of it and doesn't intend to enforce those parts at all.

From the time of the presidency of James Monroe (1817 to 1825) presidents have issued such "signing statements." Monroe signed into law a bill reducing the size of the army and directing him how to select military officers, but issued a statement saying that under the Constitution, the selection of officers was up to him and he didn't intend to follow that part of the law. In 1830, Andrew Jackson signed a bill appropriating money for a road from Detroit to Chicago, but stated he wouldn't extend the road beyond Michigan, since he regarded as unconstitutional the federal government building roads between states. Yet this practice saw not much use until more modern times, when the speed picked up.

In 1971, President Richard Nixon signed a military appropriates bill, but stated that a part of the bill, setting a deadline for the withdrawal of U.S. troops from Vietnam, was "without binding force or effect" (as interfering with a power constitutionally reserved to the president). President Jimmy Carter used signing statements to similar effect, as did Presidents Ronald Reagan, George H.W. Bush, and Bill Clinton.

In 1993, an Assistant Attorney General provided an oft-cited memorandum to President Bill Clinton on the significant of signing statements. He wrote, "such statements may on appropriate occasions perform useful and legally significant functions. These functions include: 1) explaining to the public, and particularly to the constituencies interested in the bill, what the President believes to be the likely effects of its adoption; 2) directing subordinate officers within the executive branch how to interpret or administer the enactment; and 3) informing Congress and the public that the Executive believes that a particular provision would be unconstitutional in certain of its applications, or that it is unconstitutional on its face, and that the provision will not be given effect by the executive branch."

You see, the president is performing judicial like functions. By "directing subordinate officers how to administer the enactment," he's interpreting the law. By determining some part of the law unconstitutional, once again, he's interpreting the law. And it's hard to see how he can avoid either activity. If there's some confusion or leeway in a law, and there often is, how can the executive branch apply it without interpreting it? If the president thinks some part of the law unconstitutional, is he supposed to carry out what he thinks an unconstitutional law? That wouldn't square with the oath he takes that, "I do solemnly swear (or affirm) that I will … preserve, protect and defend the Constitution of the United States."

To come back to the controversy over President George W. Bush's signing statements, where did he go wrong any more than any of his predecessors? A 2006 article in the *Boston Globe* kicked off this dispute, saying, "President Bush has quietly claimed the authority to disobey more than 750 laws enacted since he took office." The paper pretty quickly published a clarification, saying there weren't really 750 separate bills, but that he "has claimed the authority to bypass more than 750 statutes, which were provisions contained in about 125 bills." A blue-ribbon panel of the American Bar Association (the ABA) then jumped in condemning Bush. But the outrage couldn't have been over the mere number of his signing statements, since he didn't issue any more than previous presidents, and in fact, fewer than his immediate predecessor, Bill Clinton. It must have been what he said in some of his messages. And when we remember that President Bush was a Republican, the *Boston Globe* a reliable organ of the Democratic Party, and the ABA something of a satellite of the Democratic Party, perhaps we begin to understand why they were upset with him while they hadn't been with President Clinton (a Democrat). They just didn't like his interpretation.

Let's not get caught up in the partisan squabbling. In the first place, there seems no way for the president to avoid assuming some such judicial role. Since even today so much of the Constitution remains a gray area, and since the same applies to the other laws and especially to new laws, he can't avoid interpreting them in the process of applying them. But in the second place, a danger does exist that he can go too far, that he can try to replace the congressional purpose for a law with his own purpose. Yet there also seems a remedy. An offended party can go to court and asks the courts to overturn the president's interpretation. In addition, the president must still answer to the electorate for his interpretations.

For our purpose of understanding the Constitution, what we want to take away is that the president does have a power that closely resembles the judicial power. He does have a power to interpret the Constitution and the other laws. Once again, the separation of powers proves far from air tight. The activities of the one branch (the executive) bleed over into the activities of another branch (the judiciary). There seems no way to avoid this result in practice.

7.11 – The President's Discretion

Ever been stopped by a cop who cut you some slack and didn't write you a ticket? That's in his discretion. His exercise of that discretion can depend on any number of factors, such as his personality or mood, your speed or your driving record, and how you interact with him. If you come across as a bad actor, your chances of getting a ticket go way up. Prosecutors have a similar discretion. Rather than charging a student at the local university with felony drug possession, they may just file a misdemeanor and later give him a deferred sentence, while a high school dropout may receive less tender treatment. Nor is there anything wrong with such discretion in and of itself. People and their legal indiscretions vary widely. "Let the punishment fit the crime." The maximum penalty doesn't always fit the crime. But we can't help notice such discretion confers a certain power on cops and prosecutors, which they may not always exercise for the best reasons. Their power comes not just from their authority to enforce the law, but from their discretion about whether or how to enforce it.

On a grander scale, the presidents have a similar power that comes from their discretion. The Constitution says that, "he shall take Care that the Laws be faithfully executed." Those words give the president the authority to execute all the federal laws, including the Constitution. But just like the cop or the prosecutor, he can exercise discretion based on any number of factors, political or otherwise. A lot of presidential power comes not just from their authority to execute the laws, but from their discretion about whether or how to execute them.

However, we need to make a distinction. Cops and prosecutors don't have unlimited discretion. A cop working as a driver's license examiner can't refuse to issue a license to someone who passes the test. A prosecutor can't charge someone with a crime without probable cause. Neither does the president have unlimited discretion. If you pay your social security taxes and reach retirement age, he can't order your retirement checks to stop.

What draws the line? In legal terminology, the distinction is between what called a "mere ministerial duty" and a "discretionary act." In the early and famous case of Marbury v Madison in 1803, discussed in several of these articles, Chief Justice John Marshall said, "The President is invested with certain important political powers, in the exercise of which he is to use his own discretion, and is accountable only to his country in his political character, and to his own conscience. ... But when the legislature proceeds to impose on [an executive] officer other duties; when he is directed peremptorily to perform certain acts; when the rights of individuals are dependent on the performance of those acts; he is so far the officer of the law; is amenable to the laws for his conduct; and he cannot at his discretion sport away the vested rights of others." In a later case, the Supreme Court said, "A ministerial duty the performance of which may, in proper cases, be required of the head of a department by judicial process is one in respect to which nothing is left to discretion."

To unpack the legalize, first, what's a "mere ministerial duty?" That's 1) when "the legislature imposes on an executive officer a duty he is directed peremptorily to perform," and 2) "when the rights of individuals are dependent on his performance." You can go to court (invoke "judicial process") to compel an officer to perform such a duty. We could think of almost endless examples. If you qualify, you're entitled to your social security benefits, Medicare or Medicaid, disability benefits, and so on and so forth.

Second, what's a "discretionary act?" Everything else. The Constitution says, "he shall take Care that the Laws be faithfully executed." With respect to everything else, as Justice Marshall said, "he is to use his own discretion, and is accountable only to his country in his political character, and to his own conscience." Not surprisingly, this discretion with respect to everything else gives the president a whole lot of power.

A classic example of such discretionary power was "impoundment." Rather than spending the funds appropriated by Congress for a particular purpose, the president would simply "impound" (not spend) them. In this way, rather than taking care that a congressional law "be faithfully executed," he could totally frustrate the purpose of a law.

Way back in 1803, President Thomas Jefferson refused to spend the $50,000 appropriated by Congress to build gunboats to defend the Mississippi River. He took the view the boats weren't needed. In 1950, President Harry Truman did something similar. He refused to spend $75 million Congress had designated for the support of the Chinese Nationalists on Formosa, remaking in his pithy way, "I've still got [the money] locked up in the drawer of my desk, and it is going to stay there." But President Richard

Nixon got in trouble over the practice, as he got into so much other trouble. Nixon (a Republican) refused to spend the funds appropriated by the Democratic controlled Congress in a number of instances. Enough was enough, and in 1974 Congress passed the Budget and Impoundment Control Act over Nixon's veto. Under this law the president may request Congress to rescind an appropriation, but if they don't grant the request within forty-five days, he's supposed to go ahead and spend the funds for the announced purpose.

In addition, in a 1975 case (Train v City of New York), the Supreme Court ruled a president didn't have discretion to impound funds appropriated for a specific purpose. This case involved the 1972 Water Pollution Control Act Amendments. Under this act, Congress had made available federal financial assistance in the amount of 75 percent for the cost of municipal sewers and sewage treatment works. It further provided that "the [s]ums authorized [including $6 billion for fiscal year 1974] shall be allotted by the Administrator [of the Environmental Protection Agency] not later than the January 1st immediately preceding the beginning of the fiscal year for which authorized." President Nixon had earlier vetoed this act, which Congress repassed over his veto. "Thereupon, the President, by letter dated November 22, 1972, directed the Administrator 'not [to] allot among the States the maximum amounts provided … and no more than $3 billion of the amount authorized for the fiscal year 1974.'"

Several cities, including the City of New York, then sued the Administrator of the EPA (Russell E. Train) on the grounds they were entitled to the funds. The Supreme Court agreed with them, saying, "As conceived and passed in both Houses, the legislation was intended to provide a firm commitment of substantial sums within a relatively limited period of time in an effort to achieve an early solution of what was deemed an urgent problem." The Act left no "discretion" with the president to refuse to spend the funds. The performance was a "ministerial duty." The courts could require the Administrator to spend the funds, and they did.

Thus, the Congress and the Supreme Court cut down president's power of impoundment, although let's recognize a lot of situations still exist where he can exercise discretion in the amount or the way funds spent, since the laws making the appropriates often far

297

from specific and clear. But at any rate, maybe here we have an example of the separation of powers working in action. The legislative and judicial branches checked the executive branch. If you're going to have a separation of powers, surely presidential impoundment threatens the scheme. Not only could the president veto congressional laws, but impoundment let him frustrate the purpose of laws, even ones re-passed over his veto, as this one was.

What we need to take away for our understanding of the Constitution and how it works is that the president's power to execute the laws gives him a lot of power. His discretion about whether or how to execute them gives him a lot of power, too.

7.12 – The President's Laws

People used to say Abraham Lincoln freed the slaves with the Emancipation Proclamation in 1863. Lately, the popular portrayals, such as Steven Spielberg's 2012 film, "Lincoln," more carefully say he just freed some of the slaves, specifically, those in the Confederate States still in rebellion. The rest had to wait until the 13th Amendment in 1865. But if we want to be still more careful, notice something else about the Emancipation Proclamation. It amounts to a law, but Congress didn't pass it, rather the president just proclaimed it. But doesn't Congress pass the laws? How could Lincoln just proclaim something a law?

The Constitution grandly states, "All legislative Powers herein granted shall be vested in a Congress of the United States." Legislative power is the power to make the laws. Yet as a matter of fact, as well as the congressional power to make laws, there has always been an "executive power" to make laws "vested in" the presidents. The Constitution makes them the head of the executive branch and the commander-in-chief. That gives them the authority to issue orders to the bureaucracy and the military. In practical effect, those "executive orders" amount to laws, what we might call "the president's laws."

The Emancipation Proclamation is a perfect example. To quote the actual words, "By the President of the United States of America: A Proclamation. That on [January 1, 1863], all persons held as slaves within any State ... in rebellion ... shall be ... forever free; and the Executive Government of the United States, including the military and naval authority thereof, will recognize and maintain the freedom of such persons."

In other words, the president issued an order. ("By the President: A Proclamation"). He issued the order to the executive branch and the military. ("The Executive Government, including the military and naval authorities, will recognize and maintain the freedom of such persons"). In practical effect, this "executive order" amounted to a law. ("All slaves held within any state in rebellion shall be free.") But the president made it, not Congress.

As a matter of mere necessity, the president has to have such a power to issue "executive orders." As an essential part of his job description, he has to have the authority to give the bureaucracy its directions and the military their marching orders. But modern presidents have used this power more and more to wider and wider effect. And frankly, no one seems to know for sure the outer limits.

This modern trend took off with an activist president, Teddy Roosevelt, who signed twice as many executive orders as his predecessor. The second Roosevelt, his cousin Franklin, another highly activist president, was the most prolific with 1,752 executive orders. Since Franklin Roosevelt served three full terms and part of a fourth, that might be expected, but he also totaled by far the highest number per year. While to give some idea of the overall total, from 1936 to 2001, the presidents issued some 5,392 executive orders.

A lot of these executive orders are mundane. Kennedy's Executive Order 11022 (in 1962) did no more than set up the President's Council on Aging to advise him on the problems surrounding aging. Clinton's 12835 (in 1993) simply set up the National Economic Council to advise him on the economy. But the most famous have made dramatic and significant laws. Roosevelt's 9066 (in 1942) allowed internment of Japanese-Americans during World War II, and some 120,000 were interned for two years. Truman's 9981 (in 1948) desegregated the armed forces. Johnson's 11246 (in 1965) forced private firms with government contracts to institute affirmative action programs. In 1970, Nixon set up the EPA (Environmental Protection Agency) and the DEA (Drug

Enforcement Agency) by executive orders (in 1970 and 1973 respectively), although both were later recognized by congressional laws.

Do clear boundaries limit this power? Not really. In late 1951 during the height of the Korean War, a labor dispute arose between the steel companies and unions and a nationwide strike was set for April 2, 1952. Seeing such a strike as a threat to national security, President Harry Truman issued executive order 10340 directing the Secretary of Commerce to seize the steel companies and keep them running. In the Youngstown Steel & Tube Case (1952) the Supreme Court ruled this order an unconstitutional invasion of the legislative power delegated to Congress. But they really didn't offer much guidance in the way of specific limits on the power.

But while the theoretical limits not quite clear, some practical limits appear. An executive order has to take the form of an order issued either to the bureaucracy or the military. But since the bureaucracy has such wide-ranging powers, that leaves the power of executive orders as wide-ranging. However, since Congress has the final power over the purse, Congress can use that power to rein in an executive order. Nixon expanded the activities of the Subversive Activities Control Board, but a year later Congress defunded the program. While in the last resort, there's always public opinion. If the public doesn't like an executive order, the pressure may result in repealing the order or electing another president who does.

Executive orders are the president's laws. He makes them, not Congress. The limits on this power are far from clear.

7.13 – The President's Treaties

Recently, a sample headline read, "Democrats filibuster vote on legislation opposing Iran deal in Senate." We all know about the filibuster in the Senate, how unless three-fifths (60 percent) vote for cloture, breaking the filibuster, no law can pass the chamber. We've all heard about the Iran nuclear deal. Then we might think the story under this headline was about a filibuster and/or the Iranian deal, and it was about both. But still another story lurked under this story, and one at least as significant. This underlying story is about how the presidents have acquired a power to make treaties all on their own, without Senate ratification.

To dig this story from beneath the headline, recall the sequence of events. First, President Obama through Secretary of State John Kerry was negotiating an agreement with Iran about limiting their nuclear program. Second, back in May, as the negotiations were going on, Congress had passed a law (the Iran Nuclear Agreement Review Act of 2015), saying they should have a vote on whether to accept the final agreement. But notice something here. If Congress later voted against the agreement, that would have amounted to no more than an act of Congress. President Obama can veto an act of Congress, and to override his veto would require a two-thirds majority (66 percent) in both houses. Then as a practical matter, unless two-thirds (66 percent) of Congress were willing to vote against the agreement, their vote would have no effect. Third, when the agreement did finally come before Congress, the House voted against it 269 to 162 (58 percent). But fourth and finally, the Democratic filibuster prevented any vote in the Senate, although the majority voted for cloture 58 to 42 or 58 percent. As a result, the agreement will go into effect.

Stop a minute, back up, and remember that the Constitution says the president, "shall have Power, by and with the Advice and Consent of the Senate, to make Treaties, provided two thirds of the Senators present concur." Two-thirds is 66 percent. But what just happened? The president made what amounted to a treaty. Not only did two-thirds (66 percent) of the senators not concur, but disapproval would have required a vote of two-thirds (66 percent) in both the Senate and the House. The process written into the Constitution for ratifying a treaty was turned totally upside down and reversed.

What's going on? Maybe the name's the thing. Rather than a "treaty," the presidents want to call such things "executive agreements." But that's verbal nonsense. The Iran nuclear "deal" just serves as the latest example. A treaty by any other name is still a treaty (a treaty is a treaty is a treaty). The Vienna Convention on the Law of Treaties defines a treaty "as an agreement concluded between States in written form and governed by international law." In other words, a written agreement between two or more nations amounts to a treaty, whatever the title or label written at the top of the document. By definition an "executive agreement" amounts to a treaty, whatever else you want to call it.

No, once again necessity was the mother of invention and ignored the logical flaws in her offspring. Over time, the constitutional requirement for the Senate ratification of treaties by a two-thirds majority (66 percent) simply turned out too cumbersome to do the work. There was too much work to be done and too seldom could two-thirds (66 percent) of the senators agree on how to do the work. Instead, the presidents came up with a work around. They started working out "executive agreements" and not submitting their work to the Senate for ratification.

For an early example, in 1817, President James Monroe signed an agreement with Great Britain to limit naval forces on the Great Lakes. Much more recently and more well-known, in 1940, President Franklin Roosevelt made an agreement with the British to trade them American destroyers for some island naval bases. In 1941, he made agreements with Denmark to station U.S. soldier in Greenland and with Iceland to defend that country.Over the years, the pace has picked up. "During the first half of the century after independence, of 87 international compacts, 60, and most of the significant ones, were handled through the treaty process. In the next half century there were 215 treaties and 238 executive agreements, but treaties were still used for major matters." However, "In the years 1889 to 1939, of 1441 international compacts 917 were executive agreements and only 524 treaties."

Today, executive agreement come in three recognized types. First, a treaty formally ratified by the Senate may authorize the president to make executive agreements to carrying out the provisions. For example, a number of treaties on tariffs give the president authority to negotiate the actual rates and change them from time to time. Second, Congress may pass a statute authorizing an executive agreement. For example, in 1993, Congress passed a law authorizing the North American Free Trade Area (NAFTA), which approving presidential negotiations to lower trade barriers with Canada and Mexico. Third, still other executive agreements rest on no more than the president's authority to conduct foreign affairs. Prominent examples were Roosevelt and Truman's agreements reached at the Yalta and Potsdam Conferences, both in 1945, for the division of Germany at the conclusion of World War

II. As a footnote, in 1972, Congress passed the Case Act, directing the president to inform Congress of all executive agreements within 60 days. At least if Congress disapproves, perhaps they can take some action.

Yet if "the president's treaties" are a necessity, they remain a somewhat troubling necessity. Let's not get into the argument over the Iran nuclear deal, since no consensus likely to emerge any time soon. Yet as a constitutional matter, one thing stands out. The president did the deal on his own. Two-thirds (66 percent) of the Senate did not concur. In fact, a majority in both the Senate and the House appears not to have concurred. In net effect, the deal shows the presidents have acquired a power to make treaties all on their own unless maybe two-thirds of Congress disapproves. That reverses the original process in the Constitution and gives the presidents a lot more power.

Some other checks and balances do remain. One is that these executive agreements often require some kind of congressional action to implement, and a mere majority can block implementation. Another is the mere pressure of public opinion on the president. Hopefully, that's enough.

7.14 – The President's Wars

Here's another familiar quote from the Constitution, "The Congress shall have the Power ... To declare War." Here's another familiar fact. Congress hasn't declared a war since World War II in 1941, but our presidents have led the country into a number such as the Korea War, the Vietnam War, or the Iraq War. How can we reconcile this quote with these facts, or can we?

Maybe we can just treat the words like a lawyer. When it serves their ends, the lawyers seem capable of finding an ambiguity in virtually any legal document and the Constitution a legal document. Then first of all, what precisely defines a "war?" Such a definition turns out far from easy. World War II obviously amounted to a war, but when in 1986, President Reagan ordered air strikes again the Libyan regime of Muammar Gaddafi in retaliation for his support of terrorism, did such a limited military action amount to a "war?" Second of all, to say "Congress shall have the power to declare war" doesn't say Congress must declare a war before the president takes any military action whatsoever. Third of all, the Constitution says a lot of other things, too, and some of those other things give the president the power to conduct foreign policy and act as commander-in-chief. In either role, "The president has the capacity to order troops into any area of the world, ... And once Americans are placed in a position of difficulty or peril by such orders, Congress has no alternative other than to bail them out."

But these ambiguities over the war-making power are more than lawyerly technicalities or evasions, rather, reflecting a real-world complexity. Clausewitz laid down the dictum, "War is merely the continuation of foreign policy by other means." To conduct a successful foreign policy demands some considerable practical flexibility before coming to the "other means." If you can only press an "on-off" button (peace or war), your options are way too limited. To give peace a chance, you have to give diplomacy a chance. For diplomacy to have a chance, you have to be able to dial up or dial down the pressure on the other side, depending on the circumstances. An alert diplomacy looks to relax international tensions, leading away from war, and diffuse crisis, heading off war. To do so, a successful diplomacy often needs to assume a posture of military strength or even flex some military muscle to deter or convince the other side with a threat.

Remember the lead up to World War II? We tend to regard America's entry into the war as inevitable. Let's trace the trajectory of the events more accurately. President Franklin Roosevelt gave peace a lot of chances. He dialed up the pressure on Germany only gradually throughout 1941. On March 30, he ordered the seizure of Axis ships in our ports. On May 27, he proclaimed an "unlimited emergency" and ordered the U.S. Navy to "sink on sight" any foreign submarine in our "defensive waters" in the North Atlantic. On June 15, he froze Axis assets in this country. On July 7, he ordered the U.S. military to take over the defense of Iceland. In August, he and Churchill met aboard ship in Placentia Bay, Newfoundland, and on August 14, announced they had "discussed lend-lease and other problems of common defense" and agreed upon a postwar "peace program" (the Atlantic Charter). The U.S Navy started convoy duty for all ships as far as Iceland.

On September 11th, he announced that "henceforth American patrols would defend the freedom of the seas by striking first at all Axis raiders ('rattlesnakes of the Atlantic') operating within American defensive areas." On October 8, he issued shooting orders to the Navy to destroy any Axis sea or air forces. While with respect to Japan, in 1940, he had stopped all shipments to them of airplane parts, machine tools, and aviation gas. In early 1941, he shifted the base of the Pacific Fleet forward from San Diego to Hawaii. In July, he stopped all oil exports. On August 24, he warned the U.S would take further steps if Japan attacked neighboring countries. War was inevitable only because Hitler was resolved to conquer Europe and the Japanese imperialists were similarly resolved to conquer Greater East Asia. Roosevelt's diplomacy gave both numerous chances to back off, but both miscalculated their chances.

Throughout our history and all history, a similar story repeats, showing the need for a flexible combination of diplomacy with military force. The presidents require the power to do warlike things without first asking for a formal declaration of war from Congress. There's not space to list just the more recent examples where the presidents used this power. But at some point, they starting crossing the line, and by now they've trampled over so often as nearly to obliterate it. A formal declaration of war no longer seems much of a constitutional requirement.

By any definition, beginning in the latter half of the twentieth century, the presidents repeatedly led the nation into "war" without bothering to ask for a formal declaration of war. In 1950, North Korean invaded South Korea, and President Harry Truman ordered the U.S. military into a war that claimed some 50,000 American lives. Not only did Truman not ask for a formal declaration of war, he acted without even asking for prior congressional approval. Rather, he relied upon the rationale that the Senate had ratified the treaty creating the United Nations, which had voted to intervene militarily, and the Senate's prior ratification of the U.N. treaty authorized him to act. The fact Congress subsequently funded the war was also urged as tacit approval. Beginning in the early 1960s and running through 1973, several American presidents, starting with John F. Kennedy, engaged the military in what became the Viet Nam War, taking another 50,000 U.S. lives. More recently, in

2003, President George W. Bush ordered some quarter of a million U.S. troops to invade Iraq to overthrow Saddam Hussein in what became the Iraq War.

Today, what limits the presidential power to take the country into a war? Right at the close of the Viet Nam War, Congress tried to bring some clarity to the situation by passing the War Powers Resolution over President Nixon's veto in 1973. It says that, "The constitutional powers of the President as Commander-in-Chief to introduce United States Armed Forces into hostilities, or into situations where imminent involvement in hostilities is clearly indicated by the circumstances, are exercised only pursuant to (1) a declaration of war, (2) specific statutory authorization, or (3) a national emergency created by attack upon the United States, its territories or possessions, or its armed forces." It goes on to provide that the president must notify Congress within 48 hours of any such action and that the action must cease unless Congress within 60 days authorizes it or declares war [with a further 30 days for actual withdrawal]."

Since then, presidents have largely observed its provisions, notifying Congress over a hundred times of such action. However, it was complained that President Clinton exceeded the precise limits by continuing the bombing campaign he had ordered in Kosovo in 1999 for more than two weeks after the 90 day deadline had passed. In response Clinton argued Congress has appropriated the funds for the campaign, which implied authorization. In 2011, President Obama committed the military in Libya beyond the deadline, but argued no congressional authorization needed, as we were acting under the leadership of NATO, an alliance created by a treaty affirmed by the Senate.

As a practical matter, presidents require no formal declaration of war to lead the nation into war. "Presidential war power has expanded dramatically in the past half-century, ... We now have presidential wars, set in motion unilaterally by our chief executives."

Today, the only real limits on the presidential power to do war like things appear what he feels the country will support, but that's a very real limit. To start and fight an armed conflict of any size, the president requires strong support in Congress and among the public, and absent some immediate and obvious threat to national security, such support has proved hard to come by. When the going gets tough or goes on for any length of time, keeping such support has proved still harder. The other political party is always more than eager to point out the even imaginary flaws in any president's foreign policy. Congressional and public approval are something presidents aren't likely to start a war without.

7.15 – Domestic Tranquility

The Preamble says, "We the People … in Order to … insure domestic Tranquility … do ordain and establish this Constitution." How did we mean to insure that? By carrying out the laws. Who has the power to carry out the laws? The Constitution says the president "shall take Care that the Laws be faithfully executed."

What power does that give the president? In an 1868 case, the Supreme Court said, "We hold it to be an incontrovertible principle that the government of the United States may, by means of physical force, exercised through its official agents, execute on every foot of American soil the powers and functions that belong to it. This necessarily involves the power to command obedience to its laws, and hence the power to keep the peace." Later, in an 1895 case, they said, "the entire strength of the nation may be used to enforce in any part of the land … all national powers and the security of all rights entrusted by the Constitution to its care."

In other words, the presidents have the power to use force, including military force, to "insure domestic tranquility" (to put down riots, rebellions, or civil unrest). Although they've sparingly used the power, it reminds of what Teddy Roosevelt said, "Walk softly, but carry a big stick." The presidents may walk softly, but they carry the biggest stick.

We've mentioned several times Shays' Rebellion back in 1786 and 1787 in rural Massachusetts. It's perhaps surprising this so long ago local event casts such a long shadow down our history. All that happened was a couple thousand Massachusetts' farmers led by one Daniel Shays, who had served as a captain during the Revolutionary War, shut down the local courts to stop pending foreclosures on their farms. Their underlying demand was for the legislature to pass some fiscal laws more favorable to farmers and debtors. When they went on and tried to seize the Springfield Armory, the state militia easily put them down. Yet though there had been little loss of life or destruction of property, this outbreak threw a scare into the Founding Fathers. It seemed to threaten the rule of law and a descent into anarchy. It reminded them about the fragility, not to mention the importance of civil order. After all, the American Revolution was still fresh in their minds, which had witnessed quite a bit of bloodshed and civil dislocation. Many of their ancestors had fled to these shores from the even greater trauma of the English Civil War (1642 to 1651), and those memories remained with them, too. But beyond their own recent history, they had only to read the history books, which were filled with riots, rebellions, and civil wars.

We should begin to see why the Founders were so concerned "to insure domestic tranquility." To share their concern, we have only to recall our own fairly recent history or read the history books. The Civil War was by far the bloodiest and most costly event in our history. The history books are filled with still bloodier and more costly such events in other lands. Our overall domestic tranquility under the Constitution should rank as a high achievement.

And in the last analysis, this achievement rests only on the fact that the federal government has the power to deploy overwhelming force. Since the use of force an executive function, that means the president has the power to deploy overwhelming force. Although, as said, they've sparingly brought out this big stick, sometimes they've not walked so softly.

Let's recall the Pullman Strike back in 1894. This strike started against the Pullman Company that manufactured the famous Pullman cars, but quickly spread into a boycott against all trains running Pullman cars. Eventually joined by some 250,000 railroad workers across 24 states, the strikers lead by Eugene V. Debs shut down the railroads across much of the country, which meant they shut down the economy across much of the country. At which point, President Grover Cleveland reached for the big stick. He obtained a court injunction ordering the strikers back to work, and when they defied the order, turned to force. He called out thousands of U.S. marshals and some 12,000 troops. In the clashes that followed, about 30 strikers were killed, 4 soldiers died in a train wreck caused when the strikers dynamited a bridge, and property damage was estimated at $80 million. But the president restored "domestic tranquility."

Although this Pullman Strike among the best remembered, presidents have deployed force in some 25 other major industrial disputes over the years. Most occurred in the late nineteenth and early twentieth centuries. But as the industrial unrest died down, the racial unrest came alive. In 1957, President Dwight Eisenhower sent federal troops to Little Rock, Arkansas, to enforce the desegregation of the schools, Arkansas Governor Orval Faubus having defied federal courts orders on desegregation. In 1962, President John Kennedy sent federal marshals to enforce the admission of a black man, James Meredith, to the University of Mississippi, and in 1963, sent the National Guard to enforce desegregating the Birmingham campus. In 1967, President Lyndon Johnson sent federal troops to Detroit to restore order after racial rioting.

Yet it remains fair to say the presidents have sparingly used the power. Why? No doubt mainly because they fear the electoral response. The American public has never liked having the troops called out against them, as who has. The presidents know, too, that any use of domestic force will almost never fail to excite criticism no matter how justified the circumstances.

In this connection, we might remember the Waco Siege in 1993 of the Branch Davidian Compound. The Branch Davidians, an extreme religious sect led by David Koresh, were clearly engaged in illegal activity. When the DEA sought to serve a search warrant on their compound, the Davidians responded with gun fire. Four agents and several members of the sect were killed. The FBI then initiated a siege of the compound, and after fifty-one days, launched a tear gas attack. A fire broke out, whose origin remains controversial, and some 76 Branch Davidians, including women and children died. In the aftermath, which involved several government investigations and dozens of lawsuits, every item of the law enforcement officers' conduct was taken apart and criticized.

But all in all, only the foolhardy or the fanatics go for their guns. They know the federal government has overwhelming force, and the president has the power to use that force. As the man said,

"I don't like them odds."

7.16 – The Residual Power

No enumeration of the president's powers can ever be quite complete since another (imprecise) power still remains. That's "the residual power" to do whatever required by a big enough crisis, forgetting constitutional limits. And surely, that sounds like a rather dangerous power. After all, who decides a crisis big enough? The president? Can he just claim a crisis to justify himself in starting to act like a dictator, and once he starts acting like one, decide when, if ever, to stop?

Abraham Lincoln, during the crisis of the Civil War, gave the most dramatic demonstration of this power. Without any express constitutional authority, Lincoln raised the size of the army and navy, paid out money from unappropriated funds, imposed a naval blockade on the South, suspended the writ of habeas corpus, declared martial law, disregarded orders of the Supreme Court, proclaimed the emancipation of the slaves in the rebel states, and decreed a plan for reconstruction.

In a letter in 1864, Lincoln justified his actions this way, "My oath to preserve the Constitution imposed on me the duty of preserving by every indispensable means that government, that nation, of which the Constitution was the organic law. Was it possible to lose the nation and yet preserve the Constitution? By general law life and limb must be protected, yet often a limb must by amputated to save a life, but a life is never wisely given to save a limb. I felt that measures, otherwise unconstitutional, might become lawful by becoming indispensable to the preservation of the Constitution through the preservation of the nation. Right or wrong, I assumed this ground and now I avow it. I could not feel that, to the best of my ability, I had ever tried to preserve the Constitution, if to save slavery or any minor matter, I should permit the wreck of the government, country, and Constitution together."

Lincoln's reasoning echoes what Thomas Jefferson once wrote in a letter, "A strict observance of the written laws is doubt-less *one* of the high duties of a good citizen, but it is not *the highest*.

The laws of necessity, of self-preservation, of saving our country when in danger, are of higher obligation. To lose our country by a scrupulous adherence to written law, would be to lose the law itself, with life, liberty, property and all those who are enjoying them with us; thus absurdly sacrificing the end to the means."

Such justifications for such power have a long pedigree. The English philosopher John Locke, who lived 1632 to 1704, and as we know, was highly influential with the Founding Fathers, wrote, "it is fit that the laws themselves should in some cases give way to the executive power ... that as much as may be of all the members of society are to be preserved. ... since the end of government being the preservation of all as may be ... . This power to act according to discretion and for the public good, without the prescription of law and sometimes even against it, is called prerogative."

Nor did the assertion of such power stop with Lincoln's presidency. In 1942 during World War II, President Franklin D. Roosevelt peremptorily demanded Congress repeal a certain provision of the Emergency Price Control Act, phrasing the demand in these words, "I ask Congress to take action by the first of October. Inaction on your part by that date will leave me with an inescapable responsibility to the people of this country to see to it that the war effort is no longer imperiled by threat of economic chaos. In the event that Congress should fail to act, and act adequately, I shall accept the responsibility, and I will act. The President has the powers, under the Constitution and under Congressional acts, to take measures necessary to avert a disaster which would interfere with winning the war. I have given the most thoughtful consideration to meeting this issue without further reference to Congress. I have determined, however, on this vital matter to consult with Congress. ... When the war is won, the powers under which I act automatically revert to the people – to whom they belong." In other words, if Congress didn't repeal the law, he would repeal it by executive decree. But the Constitution gives the president no express power to repeal congressional laws.

It all comes down to what James Madison wrote in the *Federalist No. 41*, "It is in vain to oppose constitutional barriers to the impulse of self-preservation." When it comes to national survival, the president has the power to do whatever required. But

311

what amounts to such a crisis or what may be required? No one knows for sure. Nor can it be any other way, since no one knows what crises the future may hold or what may be required. As for any limits on the power, the only effective limits appear what the president reckons he can get away with, that is, what the electorate will support him in doing. Whatever that may be, that's "the residual power."

7.17 – How Come

How come the Electoral College? Why not just elect the president by a direct popular vote of the people? Back in 1787 at the Constitutional Convention, the Founding Fathers had good reasons to come up with this other way. However, as so often with political innovations, the institution never worked as they hoped. As we have good reasons to know, it continues to work less well than we might hope. Then do good reasons still exist for the Electoral College?

The Founding Fathers were nothing if not pragmatic. They stuck as close as they could to political institutions proven in practice, familiar, understood, and reliable. As *Federalist No. 52* says, "Let us consult experience, the guide that ought always to be followed whenever it can be found." In writing the Constitution, they copied as close as they could the English Constitution, leaving out the monarchy and the aristocracy. That gave them a tested model. But when they came to the chief executive (the president), they couldn't follow the model, forcing on them an untried innovation in government.

At the time of the Constitutional Convention in 1787, the English Constitution was itself not fully evolved. Already the prime minister, not the monarch, served as their chief executive, yet the monarch still appointed the prime minister, although he couldn't just elevate some favorite courtier. The royal nod had to go to a recognized leader in Parliament, a man with sufficient support to manage the body, not an easy task. This requirement left the king constrained, yet left him with a range of choices and so left considerable influence with the king. Before too long, this system would further evolve into "cabinet government." Now the monarch had to appoint as prime minister the leader of the dominant party in the House of Commons, leaving the king virtually no discretion and virtually no real power. But back in 1787, when it came to our chief executive (the president), the Founding Fathers weren't able to follow the English model. America no longer had, America no longer wanted a king. Nor did "cabinet government" yet exist to copy.

The Founders wanted a republic, where the people elected the government officials. But in 1787, a national chief executive, elected by the people, had no real precedent. The state governors offered the closest analogy. After the Revolution had swept away royal authority, the states had replaced their royal governors with elected governors with good results. But this state analogy didn't quite fit a national size. All politics being local (as per Tip O'Neil), in the days of the Founder's generation, politics was even more local. They didn't have railroads, steamships, or the telegraph let alone radio, television, or the internet. What roads they had were bad, muddy and near impassable much of the year. Commodities, including those political commodities, the politicians and the news, had to travel by slow conveyances, sail power, oar power, or animal power. Nor were the political parties, which later helped to organize politics nationally, yet invented or even imagined. All of which left political leaders confined in their states or at most to their regions. Except for Washington, who had made himself a national hero during the Revolution and was regarded as a foregone conclusion for the first president, there were no national political leaders.

When the Convention came to debate electing the president by a direct popular vote, they quickly found themselves confronted with some practical difficulties. Leaving aside Washington, who must soon pass from the scene, no candidate would likely win a majority in such an election. Rather, a number of "favorite sons," known and popular in their states or regions, would divide the vote with no clear winner. Say you held a runoff between the two front runners. Look what just happened. Say one candidate haled from Virginia and the other from Massachusetts. The voters across most of the country wouldn't know very much about either one. How could such public ignorance work as a good way to elect the president? Moreover, such an election might elevate a merely local champion, who would govern more in the interest of his state or region than the national interest.

Another idea occurred to some and maybe not such a bad idea. Have Congress elect the president. As experienced politicians, the members of Congress had the sophistication and the information to make an informed choice. Since all the states represented in Congress, such a choice would also reflect the national interest, and the president would govern in the interest of a national body in the hope for re-election. But many saw this method as threatening the cherished notion of a separation of powers between the legislative and the executive. A president who owed his election to Congress and hoped for re-election from Congress might prove subservient to Congress. In addition, since Congress then so small a body, the First Congress had only 26 Senators and 64 Representatives, might corruption find access easy? A wealthy candidate or a candidate supplied with funds by a rich foreign power, say Great Britain or France, would have to corrupt only a few men to buy the election. If not Congress, some suggested the state legislatures elect the president. But many saw this method as threatening the hope for a strong national government. If the president owed his election and hope of re-election to the states, might he not prove subservient to them?

Still another concern worried many Founders. They feared "the ignorance of the masses" as the Achilles heel of democracy. All knew the tale of Julius Caesar and the fall of the Roman Republic. In the classic version, Caesar had won over the mob with bread and circuses, then used them to overthrow the Republic and make himself a dictator. Many Founders feared a direct popular election of the president might open the way for a similar performance in America.

In the end, the Convention came up with what seemed an ingenious solution to all these problems. They came up with the Electoral College. Each state would elect as many Electors as they had members in Congress, senators and representatives combined. None of these Electors could be either members of Congress or federal employees. This restriction sought to maintain the separation between the legislative and executive branches within the federal government. These Electors would meet in their home states to vote for the president. Not bringing them together in a central location sought to make intrigue or corruption near impossible. Each Elector had not just one, but two votes for president, but had to cast their votes for different candidates (couldn't cumulate their votes on one candidate), and one vote had to go to a candidate not from their own state. This rule sought to break up the anticipated "favorite son" effect, forcing the Electors to cast at least one vote for a candidate with national stature. Being men of sufficient stature themselves to be chosen, the Electors would have more sophistication and information than the average voter. They would make an informed choice. Through them the president would owe his election to and might hope for re-election from a national constituency and would serve in the national interest. Finally, since the Electors would be more politically sophisticated, they would not succumb to the appeals of a demagogue.

The Electors' votes were to be transmitted to the President of the Senate, who opened and counted them before both houses of Congress. The candidate with the greatest number became president, provided he received a majority. If more than one had an equal number of votes and a majority, then the House of Representatives chose one of them as president. If no candidate had a majority, then the House choose from the five highest vote getters. As for the vice-president, the candidate with second highest vote total became the vice-president, or if two or more tied, the Senate chose him.

That's how come the Electoral College. That's how it was supposed to work. But like with any political experiment, the good intentions weren't enough to guarantee the results of the experiment, and the theory failed to work as predicted in practice. Let's turn to that story in the next article.

7.18 – As Soon As 1800

As if to prove the Founding Fathers weren't perfect, as soon as 1800, their design for the Electoral College broke down and required a redesign. That was quickly done with the 12th Amendment, ratified in 1804, and counting the votes in the Electoral College is still how we score the game. But this way of counting doesn't exactly reflect the popular votes and slightly tilts the playing field. Not only have a number of presidents won the game without scoring a majority of the popular votes (only a plurality), but worse, a few have actually won with fewer popular votes than their opponent and twice recently. No wonder that we constantly hear calls for a further redesign, coming from the theorists, who long for a more logical system, and the losers aggrieved over a particular election.

To see what went wrong as soon as 1800, recall the rather complicated way the College was supposed to work. Every state selected a number of Electors equal to their representation in Congress, their senators and representative combined. Each of these Electors had two votes for president, which they couldn't cumulate, but had to cast for different candidates. The candidate with the most Electoral votes won the presidency, provided he had a majority. If two or more tied and had a majority, the House of Representatives chose one of them as president. If no candidate had a majority, the House chose the president from among the five with the highest vote totals. The candidate for president with the second highest vote total became the vice-president, but if two or more tied, the Senate chose one as vice-president.

But when after the election of 1800, they came to count the Electoral votes, up popped the dreaded law of unexpected and unintended consequences. Thomas Jefferson, the Republican challenger, had soundly drubbed the sitting president, John Adams, the Federalist incumbent. But remember, each Elector cast two votes for president. The Republican Electors had duly marked one of their ballots for their party's candidate for president (Jefferson). But they as duly marked their other ballot for their party's candidate for vice-president (Aaron Burr of New York). The Electors meant to elect Jefferson as president and Burr as vice-president. But no way existed to differentiate when they marked their ballots. All they could do was check one box for Jefferson (for president) and one box for Burr (for president, too). The unexpected consequence was that Jefferson and Burr tied for president.

Such a tie threw the election into the House of Representative to choose between Jefferson and Burr. And another flaw in the original design of the Constitution was that a new Congress didn't take office until March 3rd the year after their election in November. Although the Republicans had won a solid majority in the new, incoming Congress, the old, outgoing Congress, which still dominated by the defeated Federalist, would decide the election. As an aside, not until 1933 did the ratification of the 20th Amendment finally change the date a new Congress takes office to January 3rd, doing away with such long lame duck sessions.

Politics being politics, during the presidential campaign of 1800, the Federalists had demonized Jefferson as next of kin to the devil, but hadn't demonized Burr near as much, since he was less of a threat. Being in that frame of mind, a strong contingent of the Federalists hatched a plot to keep Jefferson out by voting Burr in, even though they knew the Republican Electors, not to mention the people, had meant to elect Jefferson as president. As for Aaron Burr, who this episode as well as his later career showed really did have a fairly close relationship with the devil, while publicly supporting Jefferson, he intrigued behind the scenes to supplant him.

When it came to the voting in the House of Representatives, the chamber deadlocked through an interminable thirty-five ballots over seven days. This impasse threatened to bring down the still new federal government. Some of Jefferson's supporters made serious noises about marching on the Capitol to install him as president by force. Finally on the thirty-sixth ballot, better sense prevailed with a little help from some behind the scenes maneuvering and compromise by Jefferson himself. In the end, as we all know, Thomas Jefferson took office as the third president of the United States. America had witnessed the first hostile takeover of the presidency. The new federal government and the U.S. Constitution had survived the crisis by the narrowest of margins.

This defect in the Electoral College design led to the 12th Amendment ratified in 1804, which changed the way the Electors vote. Now each Elector has one vote for president and one for vice-president, one of whom still has to come from another state than the Elector. If no candidate for president wins a majority, the House of Representatives chooses the president from the top three. If no one wins a majority for vice-president, the Senate chooses the vice-president from the top two.

Since then, only one election has been thrown into the House. In

1824, Andrew Jackson drew both the most popular votes (153,544 out of 356,038 or 43 percent) and the most Electoral votes (99 out of 261 or 39 percent). Since that wasn't a majority, the House choose from among the top three (Jackson, John Quincy Adams, and William H. Crawford). Rather than the front-runner (Jackson), they chose his nearest rival (Adams with 31 percent of the popular vote and 32 percent of the Electoral votes). But Andy Jackson got his revenge in the next election (1828), when he romped home a clear winner.

More significantly, in forty-eight presidential elections since 1824, eighteen presidents have received less than 50 percent of the popular vote while winning in the Electoral College. Abraham Lincoln in 1860 offers a prominent example, winning only 39.9 percent of the popular vote. However, most of these presidents won by a plurality (more votes than their nearest competitor). For examples, Woodrow Wilson in 1912 won just 41.8 percent of the popular vote, but a solid 81.9 percent of the Electoral vote, and Bill Clinton in 1992 won 43 percent and 67.8 percent respectively. But of more concern, some presidents have won fewer popular votes than their opponent, and two of these examples are quite recent. George Bush in 2000 got only 47.9 percent of the popular vote, while Al Gore got 48 percent, but Bush squeaked by in the Electoral College with 271 to 266. Donald Trump in 2016 got only 46 percent of the popular vote, while Hillary Clinton got 48 percent, but Trump won fairly handily in the Electoral College by 304 to 227. The only losing presidential candidate to ever actually win a majority (51 percent) was Samuel J. Tilden back in 1876, who still lost by one vote in the Electoral College to Rutherford B. Hayes (184 to 185).

A run of seriously out-of-step results between the popular vote and the Electoral vote might begin to call in question the democratic legitimacy of the system. What might be a workable redesign? Let's turn to that in the next article.

7.19 – A Little-Known Provision

We're all pretty familiar with how the Electoral College works. You cast your vote for a candidate for president, but you're really voting for a slate of Electors in your state pledged to your candidate. The slate of Electors with the most votes (a plurality) wins the election in your state. These Electors later meet and cast their votes for your candidate. Their votes are what really elect the president.

And we're all pretty familiar with the great grievance against the College. Since the slate with the most votes wins in each state, a presidential candidate can lose the popular vote nationally, but still win election as president. That can happen when a candidate wins by a narrow margin in some states, but loses badly in others, causing him to win a majority of Electors while winning fewer popular votes overall. When such an outcome occurs, the election doesn't accurately reflect the will of the majority. Majority rule being a fundamental democratic principle, such an outcome violates the principle.

But we're less familiar with why the College works that way. That's caused by a little-known provision in the Constitution, which reads, "Each State shall appoint, in such Manner as the Legislature thereof may direct, a Number of Electors, equal to the whole Number of Senators and Representatives to which the State may be entitled in the Congress." In other words, each state legislature "may direct" how their states "appoint" their Electors. It's the state legislatures who have set up the Electoral College to work the way it does, not the Constitution itself or Congress. Once again, when we look into it, we find another example of interests operating on institutional structure to decisively influence how things work.

Early on, the states experimented with a variety of ways to appoint their Electors, some extremely odd. For example, in 1792, the North Carolina legislature divided the state into four districts, and the members of the legislature residing in each district appointed three Electors. The people didn't even get to directly vote for the Electors. Sometimes, too, the legislatures altered the method from election to election. For example, Massachusetts altered her method in every election up until 1828. While if we look carefully inside all these methods and alterations, we find the dominant party in the legislature trying to game the system to their own advantage, often with success.

Despite these early variations, "Three modes were usual:

election by the legislature; election by the people in districts; election by the people on a general ticket." Today, the last (a "general ticket") has won out. Let's consider all these modes and why the last won out.

As for selection by the legislature, that mode always seemed insufficiently democratic to a lot of folks, and several instances proved the potential for obvious abuse. For an extreme example, in 1812, New Jersey law provided for the people to vote for the Electors on a general ticket. But just eight days before the election, the legislature passed a new law for election by themselves, cancelling the popular election and returning to themselves the selection of the Electors. Needless to say, the legislature took this remarkable step under the strong impression most of the people differed with the legislative majority over the better candidate. The legislative majority gamed the system to their advantage. This instance and others helped bring this mode into such disrepute as to disappear.

As for selection by the people in districts, this mode appears likely to reflect the votes of the national majority, although still without mathematical certainty. Rather than standing as a slate (on a general ticket), the Electors stand in districts. "The people in each district would have cast their vote for President according to a sense of their own interest; and a majority of districts, in a nation-wide constituency, would have chosen the President." Usually, this mode will divide a state's Electoral votes among the candidates. and the winner of the popular vote will likely win the vote in the Electoral College.

Why did this mode, too, lose out? Remember how the "general ticket," which is what we have, works. As said, the Electors stand as a slate and the slate with the most votes (a plurality) wins, and all the states' Electoral votes go to just one candidate. Next consider the point made in a Senate Committee Report in 1826 at a time when Congress was considering constitutional reform of the Electoral College, "If uniformity by districts is not established by the free consent of the states, uniformity by general ticket or legislative ballot, must be imposed by necessity. For, when the large states consolidate their votes to overwhelm the small ones, those, in their turn, must concentrated their own strength to resist them."

Senator Thomas Hart Benton (D-MO), who served in the Senate from 1821 to 1851, authored this report and understood his politics. If a state uses the district system, it will divide its votes among the candidates. If a state uses the general ticket system, it will cumulate all its votes for one candidate. Thus, under the district system, a state loses influence on the outcome as compared to a state with a general ticket. If some states used a general ticket, and out of a desire to maximize their influence on the election, some states would, the states that did would "overwhelm" the others who didn't with the "consolidation" of their Electoral votes.

Exactly as Benton predicted, the general ticket was "imposed by necessity," the necessity felt by all the states to maximize their influence in the election. The general ticket became standard in all the states. By now, it's so long-accepted as to be taken for granted. But it's not set in constitutional concrete. Any state legislature could still alter its mode at any time.

But this little-known provision is carved in constitutional stone. The states have a right to "direct" how to "appoint" their Electors. And the words on this boulder seem to block the often-suggested reform of a national plebiscite, where the voters would elect the president directly by popular vote. Such a change would require a constitutional amendment, and it's unlikely enough states would ratify. As a political scientist of some profundity said, "The national plebiscite system has one great handicap that cannot be overcome. It could be established only by constitutional amendment, and no amendment establishing it stands any chance whatever of passing the Senate or being adopted by the states. The difficulty can be briefly stated. The national plebiscite system would completely alter the relative weight of the states in the election of the president."

To illustrate, he analyzed the 1952 presidential election with this result, "It will be seen that of the twenty-four small states only two, Oklahoma and Connecticut, would gain by a change from the Electoral voting to the popular voting system. Oregon would maintain its weight. All the rest could lose." Since nearly half the states would lose influence, such an amendment wouldn't likely gain the consent of the necessary three-fourths of the states for ratification. The states' interests operating on the institutional structure block the change.

321

The main purpose of these articles being to describe the Constitution as it is, rather than suggest reforms, let's leave the Electoral College. But numerous proposals for reform are constantly advocated. All have complicated consequences and very likely unintended consequences, making any reform problematic. Even if a reform were doable, the remedy may prove worse than the disease. Just recall how another reform in the mode of electing the presidents that sounded so good in theory worked in practice, which neither as intended nor foreseen. For that, on to the next article.

7.20 – A School for Demagogues

At this writing, Donald Trump is the president-elect to the amazement of virtually all, surely even himself. Mr. Trump ran as a Republican, but didn't start out and never became the preferred choice of that party's establishment. Nothing succeeds in politics like success, and right now the establishment looks busy reconciling with his success and scrambling for the offices in his power to dispense. But during the primaries, the "National Review," a recognized voice of a branch of the Republican establishment, had this to say, "Trump is a philosophically unmoored political opportunist who would trash the broad ideological consensus within the GOP in favor of a free-floating populism with strong-man overtones." In other words, they were calling him what the Founding Fathers called a demagogue. They were calling him an "unmoored political opportunist," rather than a man of principle, who was appealing to whatever popular with the masses ("a free-floating populism") and out to gain power for himself ("with strong-man overtones").

Too bad for the Republican establishment that the Electoral College didn't work out the way the Founding Fathers hoped. Rather than a direct, popular election of the president, they planned a two-tiered, indirect election. First, the people elected the Electors, then the Electors elected the president. An important motive was to screen out the demagogues by filtering the ignorance of the masses through the better-informed Electors. As Alexander Hamilton envisioned in *Federalist No. 68*, "A small number of persons, selected by their fellow citizens from the general mass, will be most likely to possess the information and discernment requisite to so complicated an investigation." As John Jay added in *No 64*, "As [the Electoral College] ... will in general be composed of the most enlightened and respectable citizens, there is reason to believe that their attention and their votes will be directed to those men only who have become the most distinguished by their abilities and virtue, and in whom the people perceive just grounds for confidence. The constitution manifests very particular attention to this object."

In other words, the Electoral College was designed to keep the demagogues from seizing center stage by placing a more discerning set of critics between them and the ignorant rabble in the pit. The public might prefer rock and roll, but the Electors would prefer classical music. Rock stars weren't going to play the White House. Classically trained conductors were going to bring their more disciplined and elevated art to the venue.

But the unforeseen rise of the political parties very soon upset the staging of this event. Being unforeseen guests, the political parties exercised an unforeseen influence on the behavior of the invited guests. They quickly reduced the Electors to no more than the staff at the event, who took the tickets and checked the hats and coats. Rather than running the show, using their independent judgment, the Electors quickly came to simply punch their party ticket, rubber stamping their ballots as previously pledged to their parties. So much for the best laid plans.

Yet the rise of the parties had another and saving unintended consequence. Under the parties' control, presidential elections continued a two-tiered process, and this process still worked to screen out the demagogues. At the first tier, the parties nominated their candidates; at the second tier, the people elected one party's candidate as president. And the first tier only nominated candidates acceptable to the party establishment, since the party leaders could control the party. And the party leaders were professional pols, hard-headed, long-serving, and battle hardened in democratic elections. To win their support a man had to pay his dues and establish some serious bona fides with them. They weren't going to let some rank outsider like Mr. Trump seize the baton out of their hands and take over their orchestra. The demagogues weren't going to make it to the second tier (the popular election).

Back at the start, the parties selected their nominees through a party caucus of the party leaders in Congress. Jefferson, Madison, and Monroe, all got their nominations that way. But as popular participation spread with the lowering of property qualifications, which admitted more people to the franchise, and as the country spread across the continent with the opening of the west, which admitted new states, complaints began to sound against the caucus. State and local leaders, not to mention the party members at large, felt and were excluded from the process. They began to raise a hue and cry against the caucus as not sufficiently open and democratic, as an insider deal, concentrating power in the party leaders at the capitol.

And so, just as American political genius created the political parties, now American political genius created the party convention as a way of opening the process. Under this new system, state conventions elected the party's delegates to a national convention, and the national convention elected the party's candidate for president. The Democratic Party Convention of 1832 was the first national convention by a national party, although the sitting president, Andrew Jackson, was already their nominee for president, and they did no more than nominate Martin van Buren for vice-president.

But just as complaints were raised against the caucus as not sufficiently democratic, eventually similar complaints began to be raised against the convention. Within the conventions, the party leaders could control the proceedings and their state delegations. Within the conventions, too, one party faction invariably lost the interparty fights. Frustrated and angry, the losers tended to turn on the process. They began to allege that the party bosses, who gathered in the "smoke-filled rooms" off the convention floor, were cutting deals that cut the people out. They began to demand a more open and democratic process and came up with a reform they touted to fill the bill. They wanted "primary elections," where the party members in each state would directly select the party candidates by voting for delegates to the national convention pledged to support that candidate. The idea was to sideline the party leaders, the bosses, and put the process directly in people's hands. And lo and behold, not only did they win their reform, they accomplished their purpose.

But up jumped the unintended consequences. At this point, the party establishments began to lose control over selecting their party candidates. That was the intended consequence. But as the unintended consequence, the process no longer filtered out the demagogues. Candidates for president no longer had to pay their dues to the party establishment by showing some serious bona fides to the professional insiders. Instead, they could appeal over the leadership's heads directly to the party members. Instead of being "party centered," the elections began to become "candidate centered."

In 1959, John F. Kennedy had far from proven his chops during his time in the Senate, where he was far from a leader. But he had the charisma, the organization, and the funding (his father's millions) to take his candidacy directly to the people in the primaries. And he took the nomination away from a proven party leader, Lyndon Johnson, who had proved himself in the Senate. In 1999, Barak Obama had proved even less during his even shorter tenure in the Senate. But by appealing directly to a coalition of African-Americans and the more liberal wing of his party, he won the nomination in the primaries, knocking off the seasoned insider, Hilary Clinton. All of which brings the story back to Mr. Trump in 2013, who no more than carries this trend to the extreme.

Then we might want to ask, have presidential elections become more "open and democratic" or a school for demagogues? Does the process set up a healthy competition or teach the lowest political arts, the appeal to ignorance, inexperience, and prejudice? Only time will tell. But the trail having been so clearly blazed, it's hard to imagine more candidates won't try to follow the same trail to the hallelujah land of the presidency. Get ready for more candidates with little proven political experience and more billionaires, who can finance their own campaigns. Get ready for more candidates from the radical wings of the parties, who while out of step with the electorate as a whole, can yet hope to carry their party and then hope to carry the electorate as a whole, perhaps as the lesser of two evils.

So get ready for more presidents with little or no experience of how the machinery of government works, and who even if they bring an aptitude to the job, will have to learn on the job. So get ready for more presidents with few ties or maybe even at odds with their parties' establishments. So get ready for more presidents who may have a hard time governing, since they lack a working relationship with the members of their party in the Congress.

Not entirely as an aside, it's instructive to compare the British system for selecting their prime ministers. Over there, the two major parties each have their own method. In the Conservative Party, "the Party-in-Parliament" (members of the party elected to the House of Commons) select two of their party leaders as their candidates for prime minister. The party as a whole ("the Party-out-of-Parliament") elects the party leader from these two choices. Since the members of Parliament highly knowledgeable and experienced, they have selected a series of highly capable leaders. By contrast, in the Labor Party "the-Party-out-of-Parliament" (not their members in Parliament) elects their leader (the party's candidate for prime minister). Lacking the same knowledge and experience, they recently elected Jeremy Corby as Labor leader. Not only was he not the choice of "the-Party-in-Parliament" (the sitting members of the Labor Party in the House of Commons), but by any measure appears the worst leader ever to lead a major political party in the long history of Great Britain.

There may be something to be said for the Founders' foresight and good intentions with the Electoral College. There may be something to be said for a two-tiered process that screens out the demagogues. Unfortunately, the College didn't work out as they planned, and the reform of going to direct primaries hasn't worked out quite as planned either. Any future plans for further reforms might want to take into account this something to be said for a two-tiered process. We might want to find a way to consult the wisdom acquired through experience, say through holding elected office, in electing our presidents.

7.21 – President Cheney

Did you know that Dick Cheney was President of the United States not once, but twice? But it's a trick question. He was only the "acting president," once in 2002 and once in 2007, both times only for a few hours. While incapacitated by a medical procedure (both times a colonoscopy), President George W. Bush transferred temporary power to Cheney, the Vice President, under the 25th Amendment ratified in 1967. Nor was he the only "acting president." When Vice-President back in 1985, George H.W. Bush also served as president a few hours when President Ronald Reagan was incapacitated by a medical procedure (again a colonoscopy that led to further surgery).

Originally, the Constitution said no more than the following about the presidential succession in Article II, Sec. 1, "In Case of the Removal of the President from Office, or of his Death, Resignation, or Inability to discharge the Powers and Duties of the said Office, the Same shall devolve on the Vice President." That seems clear enough in cases of death or resignation, but what about cases of presidential "inability to discharge the powers and duties of the said office." Who exactly had the authority to make that decision?

President William Henry Harrison suffered the misfortune of being the first president to die in office in 1841. Some suggested the Vice President, John Tyler, would then only serve as an "acting president," but Tyler promptly had himself sworn in and moved into the White House. Since then, we've followed this "Tyler precedent" on the deaths of the presidents. "The king is dead. Long live the king."

No problem appears, except the vice president's elevation left that office vacant, and who would succeed in the case of another sudden presidential vacancy? However, Article II, Sec. 1 went on to plug this gap, saying, "the Congress may by Law provide for the Case of Removal, Death, Resignation or Inability, both of the President and Vice President, declaring what Officer shall then act as President, and such Officer shall act accordingly, until the Disability be removed, or a President shall be elected." Under this authority, Congress passed a law designating which officials next in the line of succession, although none were ever called upon to serve.

Then the Constitution provided for the succession on the death, resignation, or removal of the president, but what about presidential "inability to discharge the powers and duties of the said office?" No mechanism was provided to make such a determination. Several events showed how easily this neglect might cause serious problems. In 1881, after being shot by an assassin, President James A. Garfield lingered in an incapacitated state for over two months before death. In 1919, President Woodrow Wilson suffered a stroke, leaving him incapacitated for several months. His wife (Edith Wilson) and his doctor (Dr. Cary Grayson) concealed how serious his condition and no one assumed the president's powers. In 1955, President Dwight Eisenhower suffered a heart attack, putting him in the hospital for six weeks, and in 1956, underwent emergency surgery for a bowel obstruction. On both occasions, Vice President Richard Nixon assumed the duties on a limited basis, but made no claim to be the acting president.

President Kennedy's assassination in 1963 seems to have served as the catalyst to put something more specific in the Constitution. The 25th Amendment, as said, ratified in 1967, was the result. Sec. 1 simply says, "In case of the removal of the President from office or of his death or resignation, the Vice President shall become President." That changed nothing. However, Sec. 2 provides that when "there is a vacancy in the office of the Vice President," the President nominates a new one "subject to confirmation by a majority vote of both House of Congress."

So far, we've seen two such appointments. When Vice President Spiro Agnew resigned in 1973, President Nixon nominated Michigan Congressman Gerald Ford and Congress confirmed him. When Ford became president on Nixon's own resignation in 1974, he in turn nominated New York Governor Nelson Rockefeller as vice president and Congress confirmed him. It's possible, then, to become President of the United States without ever being elected by the people, as Gerald Ford did, although he's still the only instance. The requirement of confirmation by Congress probably assures only someone well qualified will ever travel this route.

Going on to Sec. 3 of the Amendment, we find an attempt to deal with the issue of presidential incapacity. The president can inform Congress "that he is unable to discharge the powers and duties of his office, and until he transmits to them a written declaration to the contrary, such powers and duties shall be discharged by the Vice President as Acting President." That's the provision under which Vice Presidents Cheney and George H.W. Bush both served as "acting presidents." No hitch appears with this process so far, which looks to have filled a hole and what could be a dangerous hole in the Constitution. With the fast pace of modern events, not to mention the possible need to respond immediately to a nuclear attack, we don't want a vacuum at the top.

But that leaves a dangerous problem. What if the president doesn't recognize or disagrees about his incapacity? The next section (Sec. 4) tried to come up with a solution, saying, "Whenever the Vice President and a majority of either the principal officers of the executive departments or of such other body as Congress may by law provide, transmit to [Congress] their written declaration that the President is unable to discharge the powers and duties of his office, the Vice President shall immediately assume the powers and duties of the office as Acting President." That will probably work smoothly enough when the president in a coma, but what about when he's wide awake and disagrees?

Let's just hope we never have to cross that bridge. At that point, Sec. 4 becomes a rickety constitutional structure. If the president sends a written denial of his incapacity to Congress, he takes back up the job. Except, "the Vice President and a majority of either the principal officers of the executive department or of such other body as Congress may by law provide" can persist in their view about his incapacity. If they so inform Congress within four days, Congress must then decide the issue by a two-thirds majority against the president. They must decide within twenty-one days. If not in session, they must re-assemble within forty-eight hours and decide within twenty-one days of when they reassemble.

Talk about your constitutional crisis. Let's hope this one never happens. "The king is dead. Long live the king." But what happens when the king goes mad? Throughout history, that's never been an easy situation to handle. At least the 25th Amendment makes an attempt at a practical solution. Who knows? It might work, if it ever comes to that.

Once again it makes one long for the British system of cabinet government. If his party becomes convinced the prime minister incapable of doing the job for any reason, they can just vote him out as party leader. They simple vote in a new party leader, who takes over as prime minister. It seems a lot easier way to handle the situation, but our system with our beloved separation of powers denies us such an easy out.

7.22 – January 20

"Those who either attack or defend a minister in such a government as ours, where the utmost liberty is allowed, always carry matters to an extreme, and exaggerate his merit or demerit … . His enemies are sure to charge him with the greatest enormities, both in domestic and foreign management; and there is no meanness or crime, of which, in their account, he is not capable. … To aggravate the charge, his pernicious conduct, it is said, will extend its baleful influence to posterity, by undermining the best constitution in the world. … On the other hand, the partisans of the minister make his panegyric run as high as the accusations against him, and celebrate his wise, steady, and moderate conduct in every part of his administration."

The Scotch philosopher David Hume made those observations as far back as 1741, speaking about Great Britain. Yet his long-ago words half remind of the now American president, Donald Trump. Only half remind, since while his enemies charge Mr. Trump with the greatest enormities, few even of his partisans celebrate his wise, steady, and moderate conduct. But the words apply fully to his two immediate predecessors, George W. Bush and Barack Obama. Their enemies charged them with the greatest enormities, including undermining the Constitution, but their partisans made the panegyrics run as high. Such generally applies to any occupant of the presidency.

But what happens on January 20 every fourth year? The 20th Amendment, ratified in 1933, says, "The terms of the President … shall end at noon on the 20th day of January." Before that, the date was March 4. But while the date has changed, the ceremony has not. On that date, every president for over two hundred years has handed over the power of office to his elected successor exactly as prescribed by the Constitution.

In and of itself, such a peaceful transfer of office and of power confirms the Founders attained one of their chief goals with the Constitution. Our chief executive hasn't turned into a dictator, as has so often happened elsewhere. Whatever their "baleful influences," none of the presidents has "undermined" the fundamental nature of the office. They're elected by and so responsible to the people, and they've stepped aside for their elected successors at the end of their terms. "And that has made all the difference."

When so many chief executives who started out democratically elected have managed to turn themselves into dictators, why not here? Can't be entirely due to the law which sets the limits on their term. Virtually every usurping dictator broke a similar law along the way. Rather, a great deal must relate to the Founders' forethought in setting up the institution. By limiting the term of office and the powers and by the separation of powers, they didn't leave the presidents enough power to break through the laws as so many chief executives have done elsewhere. Over the years, the presidents have acquired much greater powers, but apparently still not sufficient to bring off such a feat. But a great deal does relate to the law and the habitual observance of that law. To quote Hume again, "Habit soon accomplishes what other principles of human nature had imperfectly founded; and men, once accustomed to obedience, never think of departing from that path, in which they and their ancestors have constantly trod, and to which they are confined by so many urgent and visible motives."

But to come back to a question earlier asked, Do the presidents have too much power? If they don't have enough to usurp the government and turn into dictators, maybe we can say they don't have too much. But that leaves this perhaps more difficult question. Do they have enough power to get the job done the way we want it done?

And it's like the course of true love, which never did run smooth. The course of our government never has run smooth. Yet it's hard to see how giving the president more power would have caused us to run a better course. If he could have done some good more smoothly, he might as easily have done some bad more smoothly. While surely, it's better to trust him not too far. There's always the danger that a man with too much power will turn the relationship from one of consent into compulsion. Romantic love, at least, isn't a matter of command, but constant courtship. The lady doesn't do well who surrenders herself totally into her lover's power. Better to keep him constantly yearning and ardent after her favor. She doesn't want to end up the inmate of an oriental seraglio (the slave of a sultan). We, the public, would do well to be as jealous of a president's power.

Indeed, that's where his enemies' raging jealousy serves a better purpose. If his own partisans might convince themselves to surrender more power to the "wise, steady, and moderate conduct of his administration," his enemies are never so enamored. American history conclusively shows they will never fail to charge him with "the greatest enormities," never fail "to carry matters to an extreme," never fail to charge him with "undermining" the Constitution. Their hypervigilance makes it hard for him to conceal any philandering, hard to deviate from the constitutionally straight and narrow.

Nevertheless, over the course of our history, the presidents have acquired more power, as seen in these articles. Yet this has always been done only through a consensus, when the force of changing circumstances convinced most people about the need. In addition, when Congress has ceded more power to the presidents, they have either tried to limit such cessations or call them back when circumstances changed. For example, the crisis of the Great Depression forced Congress to concede a great deal more economic intervention, management, and regulation to the executive branch. Yet Congress hedged the concessions, either by keeping oversight of the new executive agencies in their hands or sometimes by setting up independent agencies outside presidential control, such as the FED. During the Civil War, Lincoln exercised greater powers than any prior president, yet in the succeeding era, Congress reclaimed a new found primacy, and for a while, ran roughshod over the presidents. In the World Wars, vast powers were given to Presidents Wilson and Roosevelt to control the economy, but after the wars, these powers were largely called back. During the Cold War, presidents carried their discretion in foreign policy to the point of fighting undeclared wars. But as the Cold War subsided, Congress re-asserted itself, for example, with the passage of the War Powers Act in 1973, which attempted to limit the president's power to carry out military action without congressional approval.

Look to January 20 every fourth year. It's a litmus test. If the president surrenders power to his successor, he's not yet a dictator. In all history, only two other significant examples exist of such a consistent and peaceful transfer of the office of the chief executive for such a long period of time – the Roman consuls and the British prime ministers. That's pretty good company. That's quite an accomplishment.

8.00 – THE SUPREME COURT

8.01 – If You Can Keep It

At the close of the Constitutional Convention, as he emerged from the hall, a lady asked Benjamin Franklin, "Well, Doctor, what have we got – a republic or a monarchy?" To which Franklin replied, "A republic, if you can keep it." But to tell another truth about the Constitution, we never entirely had a republic. To tell still another truth about it as it has become, we haven't kept as much as we had.

We call America "the Great Democracy," and it is. But merely as a matter of definition, our government was never entirely a democracy or a republic (a representative democracy), but rather a mixed form. The Constitution set up two democratic institutions (Congress and the presidency), but also an aristocratic one (the Supreme Court).

That's no more than a matter of definition. Political scientists define a democracy or a republic (a representative democracy) as a political institution where the people possess the sovereignty (the ultimate power). They define an aristocratic institution as where some select few possess the ultimate power outside the people's control. The first definition precisely fits Congress and the presidency, where the people retain ultimate control through elections. But the second precisely fits the Supreme Court, where a select few (the nine justices) hold the power outside democratic controls.

Article III says, "The Judges, both of the supreme and inferior Courts, shall hold their Offices during good Behavior." In practical effect, the justices on the Supreme Court have lifetime tenure. While the president nominates and the Senate confirms them, they never again have to stand for any sort of election. The nine justices completely control the power of their institution (the Supreme Court) outside all democratic controls. That precisely fits the definition for an "aristocracy."

Now they're not a "hereditary aristocracy" like European feudal nobility, where title passed down from father to son. But history offers numerous examples of non-hereditary aristocracies. The Roman Senate was one of the most famous and powerful aristocracies ever, but the senators weren't born in tunics with a purple fringe (their badge of office). To attain the Senate, a man had to win a series of elections to ever higher executive offices in balloting before the Roman Assemblies. To successfully run this arduous course took years and many fell by the wayside. But once promoted to the Senate, a man sat for life. The question isn't how you make it into the aristocracy, rather it's one of power. With an aristocratic institution, those on the inside control the power (outside other control).

Since the Founding Fathers were committed republicans (believed in representative democracy), why did they set up the Supreme Court as an aristocratic institution? Once again, they copied the British Constitution for what seemed good reasons.

Many centuries before, British judges had started out serving at the will of the monarch. He appointed and removed them as he saw fit. Much later, during the events before the Glorious Revolution of 1688, some hotly contested political disputes between king and Parliament found their way into the courts, for example, over the king's power to tax without parliamentary consent. Lo and behold, what happened? The judges either ruled for the king or suffered a defrocking, the king stripping them of their robes. Not surprising, the king's lawyers generally won their cases in front of such judges. But when Parliament finally got the upper hand, they crafted a careful remedy. They cut the judges' leading strings, giving them "judicial independence." While the king still appointed them, now the judges served during good behavior (effectively for life). Under the formal justification that went with the reform, judges required "judicial independence" (freedom from outside control) to render impartial justice. In the succeeding years, British judges did serve as models of impartiality, well upholding the rule of law.

But British judges never escaped all parliamentary control.

Having just fought free from a royal autocracy, the British Parliament had no purpose to thrust themselves beneath the rule of a judicial oligarchy instead. In Britain, "judicial independence" never came to mean the judges were supreme (sovereign) over Parliament itself. A way remained for Parliament to remove a judge. Moreover, the British Constitution remained and still remains unwritten, and Parliament could and still can change it by just passing a new law. That pre-eminent authority, Sir William Blackstone, in his *Commentaries on the Law of England* (published between 1764 and 1769) stated the still settled rule, "[Parliament] hath sovereign and uncontrolable authority in making, confirming, enlarging, restraining, abrogating, repealing, reviving, and expounding of laws." This fundamental legal principle left the British Parliament in ultimate (supreme) control over their constitution, not their judges. The British Constitution was and is a system of "parliamentary sovereignty" (or parliamentary supremacy), where the elected legislature has the ultimate control, not the unelected judges.

Coming to 1787, when our Founding Fathers came to write the U.S. Constitution, the British judicial system looked good to them. They wanted impartial judges who would uphold the rule of law. In addition, under the theory of the separation of powers, they wanted a judicial branch independent from the other branches. Once again, they copied an admired part of the British Constitution, writing "judicial independence" into the U.S. Constitution. They gave the federal judges lifetime tenure. From there the law of unintended consequences gradually took over due to other differences between the two constitutional systems.

Under the U.S. Constitution, it turned out Congress lacked an effective way to remove a judge. That omission wasn't entirely clear back at the start since impeachment looked a way. The *Federalist No. 81* says, "The power of instituting impeachments … is a complete security. There never can be danger that the judges by a series of deliberate usurpations on the authority of the legislature, would hazard the united resentment of the body entrusted with it, while this body was possessed of the means of punishing their presumption by degrading them from their stations."

But when in 1804, the Jeffersonian Republicans in Congress

tried to impeach a Federalist justice (Samuel Chase), not only did the Senate fail to convict, but the case gave rise to a rule limiting future impeachments to where a judge commits a crime. The justices lost all fear of being removed when Congress merely disagreed with their rulings, even if these rulings "usurped the authority of the legislature." Moreover, the U.S. Constitution wasn't only written, but Congress received no power to change it. Yet American judges didn't lose their power to interpret the law, including the constitutional law. Thus, if Congress disagreed with the Supreme Court's rulings, either their interpretation of the law or the Constitution, Congress had no effective remedy.

These differences between the two constitutional systems gave the Supreme Court huge and unforeseen advantages not shared by their British brethren. Over time, the Supreme Court leveraged these advantages to an unforeseen extent. They gradually reinterpreted the Constitution to acquire more power for themselves. Slowly but surely by this process of reinterpretation, the Court left behind the British system of "parliamentary sovereignty," where the legislature possesses the supreme power in the government. Instead, they reinterpreted the Constitution into a system of "judicial supremacy," where the Supreme Court possesses the sovereign power over the laws and the Constitution.

In the end, they have managed not only to change the original relationship between the branches of the government, but between the people and the government. Rather than the democratic institutions (Congress and the presidency) predominating, the aristocratic institution (the Supreme Court) has come to dominate over much of the national agenda. Rather than "popular sovereignty" where the people retain the ultimate power, under "judicial supremacy" the Supreme Court has acquired ultimate power over the people.

"Well, doctor, what have we got – a republic or a monarchy?" As merely a matter of definition, we got a republic mixed with an aristocratic element (a democratic Congress and presidency mixed with an aristocratic judiciary). Back at the start, the powers of the Supreme Court were so narrowly confined as left the overall structure properly described as republican. "A republic, if you can keep it." But over the years, the justices have managed to re-define their powers much more widely. We haven't managed to kept as much as we had.

To understand the Constitution as it has become, we have to understand how the Supreme Court has acquired a great deal more power. Like always with the lawyers, and the justices are nothing if not lawyers, they did it with words. Like always, they were clever with the words. To understand how they did it, we have to read and see through a lot of clever words. On to the next article.

8.02 – Judges in their Own Cause

As a young lawyer, one quickly learned that judges don't look with favor on challenges to their jurisdiction (their authority, their power). When they can find a way to rule in their own favor (for their jurisdiction, their authority, their power), generally, they rule that way. Just as generally, where there's a will, there's a way, since the law only words, and a clever lawyer or a clever judge can generally make the words say whatever he wants to hear. A renowned case from our very own county shows how this general, but unspoken rule works. Mention Creek County around any group of lawyers in America and one of them will likely say, "Oh, the Volkswagen Case." They've all studied the case in law school.

Here are the facts of the case. Back in 1976, the Robinsons, who lived in New York, bought an Audi car made by Volkswagen, both foreign corporations. The next year, 1977, driving cross-country on vacation, they got rear-ended, where else but right here in Creek County. The wife and two of the children suffer grievous burns. The guy who rear-ends them turns out judgment proof (with no insurance and no assets). But Audi and Volkswagen are what the trial lawyers call "target defendants" with deep pockets to pay big damages. The lawyers for the Robinsons sued both corporations, alleging faulty design, causing the gas tank to explode and the doors to jam.

Now "jurisdiction" is the authority (read power) in a particular court and its judge to hear a particular case. Under these facts, which court had jurisdiction over this case? If they wanted to, and they did, the Robinsons' lawyers could file this lawsuit in the county where the accident happened, in the state court, the district court in and for Creek County. Usually, the court where something happens has jurisdiction. But if they wanted to, and they did, the lawyers for Audi and Volkswagen could then "remove" the case to the federal court for the Northern District of Oklahoma, which sits over in next door Tulsa County.

In America, we have a rather unique two-tier legal system due to the federal nature of the union. The state and the federal courts often have "concurrent jurisdiction," where the jurisdiction of the two court systems overlaps. Where what called "diversity jurisdiction" exists (where all parties on the opposite sides of the case come from different states), any party can elect to "remove" the case to federal court, choosing the federal over the state courts. The reason relates to an old and not unjustified fear that the state courts will favor their own citizens, while hopefully the federal (national) courts lack such a bias. As *Federalist No. 80* put it, "that tribunal [the federal court], which, having no local attachments, will be likely to be impartial between the different states and their citizens."

An even more urgent reason existed why Audi and Volkswagen wanted out of Creek County, wanted to move the case to the federal court over in Tulsa County. In those not too distant days, Creek County still possessed a certain fame, if not notoriety, across the entire nation. We were known as a premier "plaintiff's jurisdiction." Our juries routinely soaked "target defendants" for multi-million-dollar verdicts.

Why was that? Back then, the Creek County Bar still fielded some great trial lawyers, who knew how to play on a jury as well as any lawyers who ever lived. These lawyers played off and on the county demographics. Back in the oil boom days, the oil companies drilled and pumped their wells in this county, making it home to oil field workers, blue-collar types with a strong populist streak, hostile to corporations and big business. As jurors, they showed willing to break into the corporate coffers and spread the wealth around. Next-door Tulsa County had housed the oil company headquarters and was populated with white-collar types. They were much more conservative about giving away other people's money.

To try and keep the case in Creek County, the Robinsons' lawyers came up with a rather clever legal tactic. As well as suing Audi and Volkswagen, remember both foreign corporations, they also sued two New York corporations, the regional distributor and local dealer who sold the car to the Robinsons. Remember, to make a case "removable" from the state court in Creek County to the federal court in Tulsa County, all the parties on the opposite sides had to come from different states. Since the Robinsons, the plaintiffs, came from New York and these other two corporations came from New York, joining these latter as defendants would have "broken up the diversity."

Unfortunately for them, this attempt ran into another rule about jurisdiction. To sue someone or some company in a state requires they have some "minimal contacts" with that state. Otherwise, anyone could sue anyone anywhere. Think of the potential abuse. Turn it around and say you live in Oklahoma and have absolutely no contact with New York. If someone can sue you in New York just because they want to, they can jerk you around much to your inconvenience and expense. Under this rule, Audi and Volkswagen, although foreign corporation, couldn't complain about being sued in Oklahoma. They had significant contacts with this state, doing business here by selling their cars here. But the local New York dealer and regional distributor didn't sell any cars here. And they objected to being sued in Oklahoma.

This case went all the way up to the U.S. Supreme Court. And how would you predict the judges at the different levels would rule? Simply apply the unspoken rule that judges don't favor challenges to their jurisdiction (their authority, their power), and generally, they can find a way to rule in their own favor. That gives you the answers. The state judge in Creek County ruled against the challenge to his jurisdiction. The Oklahoma Supreme Court affirmed him, ruling against the challenge to their state courts' jurisdiction. Up at the U.S. Supreme Court, the justices reversed, ruling against the challenge to the federal courts' jurisdiction.

In other words, the state courts ruled in their own favor (for their authority, their power), and the federal courts ruled in their own favor (for their authority, their power). Being the higher courts, the federal courts won the argument as a matter of power politics. In the end, the case was removed to the federal court in Tulsa County and ultimately went to trial there. As a footnote, the Robinsons lost. Apparently, the jury concluded their injuries resulted from the negligence of the guy who rear-ended them, not a faulty design of the car.

Why don't judges favor challenges to their jurisdiction? Why do they generally find ways to rule in their own favor? It's nothing more than Hobbes' first principle of political psychology in action. "So that in the first place, I put for a general inclination of all mankind, a perpetuall and restless desire of Power after power." Judges rule for their own jurisdiction, since their jurisdiction is their power. They share with "all mankind" a "desire of Power after power."

Yet a legal maxim so ancient as to descend from the Roman is *nemo iudex in causa sua* ("no man should judge in his own cause"). In the *Federalist No. 10,* Madison gave the reason, "No man is allowed to be a judge in his own cause, because his interest would certainly bias his judgment, and, not improbably, corrupt his integrity." Yet in the Volkswagen Case, what happened? The judges sat as judges in their own cause (the challenge to their jurisdiction, to their authority, to their power). Not only that, up at the Supreme Court, they sat as the final judges in their own cause without further appeal. So over and over, the same thing has happened as in the Volkswagen Case. When their jurisdiction has been challenged (their authority, their power), the judges have over and over sat as judges in their own cause. Not only that, but the Supreme Court has sat as the final judges in their own cause without further appeal.

No wonder that over the course of American history, the Supreme Court has constantly acquired more power (more jurisdiction). As the final judges of their own jurisdiction without further appeal, they have constantly found ways to rule in their own favor. If you don't believe it, read on to the next articles.

8.03 – Judge Made Law

You often hear said, "Judges should interpret, not make the law." But in the Anglo-American legal tradition, our judges have always made law in the process of interpreting it. Just a brief consideration will show such judge made laws not only a necessity, but good and useful. So instead, we should say, "Judges shouldn't become a law unto themselves." Unless we grasp this admittedly rather complicated distinction, we can't grasp the proper powers for judges in a democracy.

In the first place, judges have to make law in the process of interpreting it. The laws have to be written in more or less general (abstract) terms, but every case involves a concrete and more or less unique set of real-world facts. To "interpret the law" requires the judges to apply the general laws to the particular facts of each case, as the lawyers say, to determine the "law that governs the facts" or to determine "the controlling law." Much of the time, this process allows a straightforward, merely mechanical application of the law, and the judge can, as we say, "follow the law." Yet frequently, the unique facts of a particular case come to a fork in the legal path, forcing the judge to choose which path to follow. Frequently, too, some unexpected facts will plunge beyond the previously cleared legal right-of-way, forcing the judge to break a new path. In choosing and breaking these paths, the judges cannot avoid, in effect, making new laws. Unless the judges could make such new laws, justice herself would come to a halt, come to the end of the road.

Take an interesting old English case, Bushell's Case from way back in 1670. Even after all these years, that case still possesses vitality (made a law still in effect on both sides of the Atlantic). Way back then, the young William Penn, whose later fame was as the founder of Pennsylvania, but who we also recall as an ardent Quaker convert, one day felt compelled to preach a sermon on a London street corner together with a fellow enthusiast, one William Mead. Such public preaching deliberately defied the Conventicle Act, a law closing churches other than the official Church of England. The spectacle quickly attracted a crowd of some 400 to 500, and the authorities about as quickly arrived on the scene to take both men into custody. But their later trial before a London jury resulted in an unexpected outcome. Most Londoners being themselves religious non-conformists, the jury turned out packed in the defendants' favor. Although the trial judge (Sir Samuel Starling) instructed them to convict, the jurors refused. Enraged, the judge held them in contempt of court for failing to follow his instructions and jailed them. One member of the jury (Edward Bushell) appealed.

However, the law was far from clear. The law said that jurors should follow the judge's instructions on the law. Not being learned in the law, they must rely on him to instruct them in it, and if they can ignore his instructions, they wouldn't be following the law. But the law also said jurors should exercise their independent judgment in reaching their verdict. If the judge not only instructs them on the law, but could instruct them how to rule, why have a jury at all?

To interpret and apply the general law to the specific facts of the case, the judge who heard the appeal (Sir John Vaughan) could not just "follow the law." He had to choose one pathway over the other. In his opinion, he ruled that jurors couldn't be held in contempt for their verdict, establishing a still important principle of jury independence, and incidentally, freeing Bushell. In effect, he had made a new law (a judge made law). From that day to this, jurors can freely render their verdict without fear of being held in contempt for not following the judge's instructions, even though they're supposed to follow them.

Then do we begin to see why such judge made law not only a necessity, but good and useful? Since the law often comes to such a fork or even the end of the road, unless the judges could make new law in this way, justice herself would come to a standstill. But where does judicial lawmaking come to the end of its road, or does it?

Take a famous American case, McPherson v Buick Motor Company from back in 1916. Later Supreme Court Justice Benjamin Cardozo crafted this opinion while on the New York Court of Appeals. The plaintiff (McPherson) bought a Buick car, but the wooden wheel (this was a long time ago) crumbled, causing him injury. He sued Buick. But under a long-settled legal doctrine called "privity of contract" you could only sue a manufacturer when you bought the product directly from them, that is, were in "privity" or directly contracted with them. McPherson hadn't bought the car directly from Buick, but through a dealer.

Except with his opinion, Justice Cardozo changed the law. He wrote, "If the nature of the thing is such that it is reasonably certain to place life and limb in peril when negligently made, it is then a thing of danger. … If to the element of danger there is added knowledge that the thing will be used by persons other than the purchaser, … then, … the manufacture of this thing of danger is under a duty to make it carefully." Thus, Judge Cardozo created a whole new law and a judge made law of "products liability." In the future, manufacturers could be held liable for faulty products, regardless from whom the ultimate consumer bought them.

His new judge made law was widely praised. As the industrial revolution had begun to flood the marketplace with factory made products, the old rule had become more and more obsolete. Since almost all these products were sold through middlemen, manufacturers could escape liability for turning out defective and dangerous products. This new "products liability" law was more realistically adapted to industrial conditions. Yet we can't but see that Cardozo, the judge, made a new law in a highly dynamic way. The law was already settled and clear. He didn't just come to a fork in the path or the end of the road. Rather, he decided to move the road (to reverse prior law and make an entirely new law).

Then we might begin to wonder what limits the power of judges to make law? Or is there a limit? Moreover, so far, we've just talked about the ordinary law, not the constitutional law (the highest law from which all other laws flow). Can or should the judges make constitutional law as well? If so, what limits their power to make constitutional law? Or is there a limit? Are they simply a law unto themselves? Let's turn to these interesting and momentous questions in the next article.

8.04 – A Law Unto Themselves

In the last article, we saw that judges have to make law in the process of interpreting it, which not only necessary, but good and useful. The lawgiver can never state the law so clearly or so completely as not to leave a lot of gray areas. If judges couldn't fill in these gray areas with their interpretations, that would leave too much in the shadows outside any clear interpretation. In coloring in these areas, often the judges can't avoid making, in effect, new law (judge made law). In this article, we'll see the same applies not just to ordinary laws, but also applies to constitutional law and for the same reasons.

The Constitution leaves a lot open for interpretation. If the judges couldn't fill in with their interpretations, that would leave too much not filled in. The judges have to make constitutional law exactly the same way they make ordinary laws, which again, not only necessary, but good and useful. All of which brings on the ultimate question. Are there or should there be any limits on judicial lawmaking, or are the judges a law unto themselves?

To take an early and classic example of judge made constitutional law, let's go back to 1819 and the still famous case of McCulloch v Maryland, which was discussed in an earlier article. To recall the facts, back in 1816, Congress had passed a law to charter a national bank. But the Constitution says nothing about a national bank, which many strongly opposed, such as state banks, who feared a national bank would siphon away a lucrative share of their business. These opponents arranged a lawsuit to challenge the bank as unconstitutional, as beyond the powers of Congress. Thus, they forced on the Supreme Court a question of constitutional magnitude, forced the justices to interpret a gray area in the Constitution.

The Constitution delegated to Congress certain "enumerated powers" such as to regulate commerce, tax and spend, fund the military. It went on to say Congress should have all "necessary and proper powers" to carry out these enumerated powers. Then was a national bank implied as a "necessary and proper" way to carry out these "enumerated powers?" For example, the argument went, a national bank would serve as a needed and convenient way for the government to securely deposit and disperse the receipts from taxation, say to fund the army and the navy. But the counter-argument went a national bank not needed, however convenient, since the government could just use the existing state banks. Here was a classic gray area in the Constitution, one of many.

In his opinion, Chief Justice John Marshall came down for the bank, writing, "After the most deliberate consideration, it is the unanimous and decided opinion of this Court that the act to incorporate the Bank of the United States is a law made in pursuance of the Constitution." He could have ruled exactly the opposite way with exactly as much logic. But it was necessary for him to answer the question one way or the other. He was forced to interpret the Constitution one way or the other. While today, who argues a national, central bank not good and useful? Without the

Federal Reserve, a much more complicated and powerful successor to this earlier bank, our economy couldn't operate with much success.

But what limits this power of the judges when making constitutional law or are there any limits? Take a more recent and still controversial case, Roe v Wade from 1973, the abortion case. In his opinion, Justice Harry A. Blackmon, writing for the majority, went beyond filling in a gray area and blotted out prior laws. The states had long ago passed laws against abortion, which at the time, no one thought beyond their constitutional powers. But Blackmon suddenly reinterprets the Constitution, finding implied a new right to abortion, overturning the existing laws. To reach this ruling, he engages in a very loose process of interpretation. To begin, he finds a "right to privacy" implied in the Constitution, and to conclude, he further finds, "This right to privacy … is broad enough to encompass a woman's decisions whether or not to terminate the pregnancy."

Once again, we see a judge making a new constitutional law, this time the new right to abortion. The "pro-choice" camp views this particular new judge-made law as good and useful, which the "right to life" camp does not. But either camp has to admit that Roe v Wade shows a judge making constitutional law at the fringes of any reasonable interpretation of the Constitution. It would be absurd to pretend the Founding Fathers contemplated the Constitution would ever guarantee a right to abortion. It would be about as absurd to pretend they contemplated some guarantee of a "right to privacy." So it's hard to pretend the judges filled in some gray area in the Constitution. So it's hard to pretend the judges just didn't make law all on their own at the constitutional height. So you've come a long way baby, not just winging the implications, but flying all on your own.

All of which brings on the ultimate question. What if anything limits the judicial power to make new law, even new constitutional law? The rule inherited from England hadn't drawn a bright line, but instead relied on an effective restraint. The English judges could and still can make new law, even new constitutional law. But Parliament remained and remains supreme over their judiciary. When Parliament makes a law, and Parliament can make even constitutional law, their judges are bound by the law (must follow and can't overturn it). A way remains for Parliament to remove a judge, and if Parliament disagrees with a judicial interpretation, Parliament can pass a new law to reverse the interpretation. While not only is the judiciary restrained by Parliament, but Parliament is restrained by the people, since Parliament elected. Thus, the English judges never became a law unto themselves.

But under the U.S. Constitution something different happened. Our judges turned out virtually un-removable by Congress except for crimes, and Congress has no power to change the Constitution. But our judges didn't lose their power to interpret the laws, including the Constitution. So in effect, our judges could still make laws, even constitutional laws, and Congress had no effective check against them. So over time, our judges would manage to make themselves supreme over Congress ("judicial supremacy"). So our American judges became a law unto themselves. The only restraint is their self-restrain, notoriously weak in the face of temptation, as well as their sense of what they can get away with. So in effect, the judges became restrained neither by Congress nor the people. Let's turn to unfold this story in the next articles.

8.05 – The Fine Print

If you don't take the time to read the fine print, the lawyers who draw the contract will rob you blind. But why take the time, when you have to sign whatever they put in front of you anyway? Doesn't that pretty much describe our situation nowadays? Whether taking out a mortgage, making an auto loan, or applying for a credit card, you have to sign the contract they put in front of you drawn by their lawyers. You don't get the chance to negotiate, but have to put your name to the bottom line on their printed form right where the lady across the desk obligingly marks an X. Over the internet, you can click the "read" button and pull up the "terms and conditions," but to proceed you have to click "accept." So since it doesn't seem to matter, we've fallen into a bad habit of not taking the time to read the fine print drawn by the lawyers, but taking their terms as a given.

That brings to mind the famous legal doctrine called "judicial review." The terms of this doctrine give the Supreme Court the power to declare unconstitutional and hence void laws passed by Congress. Back in 1803 in the famous case of Marbury v Madison, the lawyers on the Supreme Court slipped this doctrine, a term much to their own advantage, into our social contract (our Constitution). Ever since with later cases, they've been slipping in further terms further to their own advantage. But why take the time to read their terms? The doctrine works like an irrevocable power of attorney, where we, the people have signed away to them, the lawyers on the Supreme Court, the power to sign for us, putting our names to whatever terms they want, and there's nothing we can do about it. So we've fallen into a bad habit of taking their terms as a given.

But let's break a bad habit. Let's take the time to read the fine print in Marbury v Madison and the other later cases that slipped in their other terms. Otherwise, we can't understand how the Supreme Court has changed our social contract (our Constitution) over the years much to their own advantage. We can't understand the present awesome powers the lawyers on the Supreme Court have acquired over us, which much greater than originally. We can't understand the Constitution as it has become.

Then welcome to Constitutional Law 101, but not as taught in the law schools. In those seminaries, they burn their incense at the professional shrines and no site more holy than the Marble Temple at One First Street in Washington, D.C., inside which the nine high priests on the Supreme Court preside over the professional mysteries. Besides inspiring their eager acolytes to keep the faith of the professional religion, the law professors don't teach much more than a dry orthodoxy of legal doctrines and legal procedures. The legal doctrines amount to no more than definitions like the definitions of the degrees of homicide, all the way from negligent homicide to murder in the first degree. The legal procedures amount to no more than when, where, and what papers (pleadings) to file like to sue someone or probate a will and all the stages a case passes through in the courts (through all the hearings and trial to final judgment).

Learning this side of the law takes no more than memorization, which why by the third and last year, law students are bored out of their minds. They're worn out with no more than cramming to pass the exams and can't wait to get out into the real world and do some real things like making some real money. They're more than ready to turn to the other side of the law. They're ready to put the law to doing its real work to serve their clients' interests, but above all to serve their own interests. They're ready to start doing things like slipping onerous terms into the fine print of a contact or the Constitution for the matter.

Then finally we've come to the side of the constitutional law we want to study. We've come to side they don't teach in the law schools. We've come to what we might call the money side (or power side) of the law. That's the side where the lawyers and others as well try to use and do use the law to make money and acquire power. Not only don't they teach this stuff in law school, but you have to read the fine print in the law cases and put together the implications to find it. That's because like when they slip the fine print into a contract, the lawyers and judges don't quite want you to notice what's going on with this other side of the law. On the surface of the cases, they constantly talk about high ideals like "justice," "equality," and "rights," but beneath this surface another logic is as constantly at work. That's the logic of the money and the power. On this side of the cases, the logic always seems to work out so that the lawyers and judges acquire more money and more power.

Any college course needs a syllabus. Here's the one for our version of Constitutional Law 101. First, we need to study the origins of the doctrine of judicial review. Where did the idea come from for the Supreme Court to have a power to declare acts of Congress unconstitutional and hence void? Second, we need to study how the Supreme Court actually acquired that power. You can read the Constitution (the contract) with a microscope and you won't discover any such power for the Court, even in the fine print. Rather, in that famous case in 1803 (Marbury v Madison), Chief Justice John Marshall will claim to find that great power for his Court implied in the Constitution. In other words, he wrote it into the fine print himself. Third, we need to study the original, highly limited nature of the doctrine. Originally, the judges pledged never to declare an act of Congress unconstitutional except in a clear-cut case where all reasonable men would agree. Since seldom even all the justices agree an act unconstitutional, you can see that amounted to a highly limited power. Fourth, we need to study how the Court in the 1857 Dred Scott Case later slipped some more into the fine print by erasing the original limits on the power. That case created a new paradigm for "unrestrained judicial review," where the justices can simply declare laws unconstitutional with no real limits, thus greatly enlarging their power. Fifth, we need to study some of the cases in more modern times, where the Court has continually slipped into the fine print still more power for themselves. Today, the courts can run nationwide social programs such as massive busing to integrate the public schools. They can take over and run huge bureaucratic agencies such as a state prison system. They have even occasionally levied taxes. Finally, we need to study the overall implications for the Constitution as it has become.

Not only is this a course without grades, you can drop out at any time, but not without signing your name to the bottom line and taking their terms as a given. Unless you take the time to read their fine print, you're signed onto a social contract you don't understand.

8.06 – Professor Thayer

Back in the day, James Bradley Thayer, who lived 1831 to 1902, was a guru at Harvard Law School, which still has a lot of gurus, although none seem following the path blazed by Professor Thayer. Teaching there from 1873 until his death, Thayer was a major influence on such as Oliver Wendell Holmes, Jr., a near contemporary, and later Felix Frankfurter, both impressive legal scholars in their own right, both who made it onto the Supreme Court. Thayer advocated "judicial restraint," a path along which Holmes and Frankfurter followed him in theory, though not always in practice as justices. But their later brethren on the highest bench have pretty much obliterated this path, which few law school professors nowadays at Harvard and elsewhere travel much either. By "judicial restraint" Thayer meant that the Supreme Court should defer to the legislative judgment (defer to Congress) by not holding laws unconstitutional except in "clear-cut" cases where all reasonable men would agree. No wonder, then, so few Supreme Court justices or law school professors travel this path anymore, since who prefers "restraint?"

Thayer wrote a famous essay, "The Origin and Scope of the American Doctrine of Constitutional Law," published in 1893. The "American doctrine" was his scholarly way of saying the "doctrine of judicial review." That doctrine is peculiarly "American" and gives the Supreme Court the power to declare acts of Congress unconstitutional and hence void. Even though America took over her legal system virtually whole cloth from Great Britain, the mother country, yet British judges didn't possess this power. Few other countries have ever given their judges such authority either, although their judges have sometimes sought to make such a claim. This lack of precedent led Professor Thayer to ask about "the origin" of the doctrine. He wrote, "How did our American doctrine come about, which allows to the judiciary, the power to declare legislative Acts unconstitutional, and to treat them as null? ... How came we then to adopt this remarkable practice?"

Professor Thayer's research found no direct precedent, but revealed the doctrine originated from a similar practice. Each of the thirteen American colonies began with a royal grant. The king would issue a charter, say to the Virginia Company or the Massachusetts Bay Company. Each charter not only authorized the formation of a colony, but provided a government for the colony along the same familiar lines as the mother country's government. These charters served like mini-constitutions. A royal governor was the chief executive and a colonial legislature with an appointed chamber like the House of Lords and an elected one like the House of Commons passed the local laws. But the British colonial authorities had no purpose to let these colonial legislatures slip the leash.

To prevent that, they carefully wrote some restraints into the charters. One such provision prohibited the colonial legislatures from passing any law that either contravened their charters or British law. To make this restraint effective, they tied it back to a royal override. They reserved a right to appeal to the monarch against any law passed by the colonial legislature. When we see how this procedure worked, we see why Professor Thayer found the origin of the doctrine of judicial review in this royal prerogative.

An old case from colonial days, Winthrop v Lechmere from

1728, illustrates. This lawsuit involved the estate of a man with the grand old Puritan name of Wait Still Winthrop, who died in 1717, leaving two children, John Winthrop and Anne Lechmere, and some land in Connecticut. Under English law, all land passed to the eldest son (the rule of primogeniture), and with the usual generosity of heirs, John claimed all his father's land. But Anne objected under a law passed by the Connecticut colonial legislature. This law had modified primogeniture in the colony, giving the eldest male no more than a double share. Beneath these facts, we sense a degree of colonial hostility for the British aristocracy, since inheritance of all land by the eldest male greatly assisted the concentration of wealth in a few privileged families.

Not surprisingly, Connecticut's colonial courts preferred their own colonial laws and ruled Anne entitled to her share of the land. But John took that appeal reserved against colonial laws, appealing across the water to the British royal authorities. His lawyer argued that Connecticut existed by virtue of her charter from the crown and that when the colonial legislature altered the rule of primogeniture, their act violated that charter. "For," the argument as recorded in the reports reads, "by the Charter [the General Assembly's] power of making laws is restrained and limited in a very special manner (namely), such laws must be wholesome, and [not] contrary to the laws of the realm of England." Primogeniture being a venerable law of the realm of England, they argued the Connecticut legislature could not change the rule. When John "threaten[ed] an appeal to the King in Council, [h]e was taken into custody for contempt; but escaped ... and went to England, where he brought his appeal."

Again not surprisingly, the British royal authorities favored British over colonial law, ruling as follows, "Their Lordships, upon due consideration of the whole matter, do agree humbly to report as their opinion to your Majesty, that the said Act [abolishing primogeniture in Connecticut] should be declared null and void, being contrary to the laws of England, ... and is not warranted by the Charter of that colony." In other words, John got all the land and Anne was excluded.

But do you see how this practice resembles the later doctrine of judicial review? Under the British practice, someone could appeal against an act of a colonial legislature to a higher authority, the

British colonial authorities across the water. But after the American Revolution, the newly independent states assumed full sovereignty, took all the power of government unto themselves. But what happened to this royal prerogative to void laws? Had it been merely an onerous restraint on the power of the people to govern themselves through their elected representatives? Did it now just disappear and a good thing too? But it had been a very valuable power, as power usually is to those who possess it. And some judges in the newly independent states reached out to claim the power for themselves in slightly altered form. They came up with the idea that someone could now appeal to them as the higher power against the legislature. If someone alleged a legislative act violated the state constitution, the judges could declare the statute unconstitutional and hence void.

As Professor Thayer notes, this assumption of a not inconsiderable new power by the judiciary went down by no means without dissent. At least some saw anti-democratic tendencies. As an example, Thayer cites a commentator on the laws of Vermont, writing back in 1777, a guy named Swift, who served as chief justice of that state, who said, "No idea was entertained that the judiciary had any power to inquire into the constitutionality of Acts of the legislature, or pronounce them void for any cause. Long after [that] period ... the doctrine ... that the judiciary have authority to set aside ... Acts [of the legislature] ... was considered anti-republican." In 1784, when a New York court overturned a law passed by their legislature, the indignation brought forth a public meeting, which declared in an Address to the People of the State, "That there should be a power vested in the Court of the Judicature, whereby they might control the Supreme Legislative power, we think absurd in itself. Such powers in courts would be destructive of liberty."

However that may be, Professor Thayer has shown "the origin of the American doctrine of constitutional law," that is, of the doctrine of judicial review. And isn't it interesting that this judicial power should descend from a royal prerogative? Indeed, it will turn out a royal power for the Supreme Court, as we shall see in future articles. But before turning to that, let's look in the next article at what the Constitution says about judicial review, if it says anything.

8.07 – The Silence of the Document

We're talking about that great power of judicial review, the power for the Supreme Court to declare acts of Congress unconstitutional and hence void. In the last article, we saw how the idea originated with a royal prerogative, the power of the British royal authorities to void laws passed by the colonial legislatures, either as violating the colonial charters or British law. We saw how after the American Revolution, the judges in some of the newly independent states claimed a similar power for themselves, claiming a power to void laws passed by the new state legislatures that violated the new state constitutions. But we saw their claim went down by no means without dissent, being seen as anti-democratic.

Coming to the Constitutional Convention in 1787, what did the Founding Fathers write into the Constitution about judicial review? The document is persistently silent. Nowhere do we read an express delegation of this power to the Supreme Court. Nevertheless, we've already seen a great many powers not expressly delegated, yet later found implied. Did the Founders imply this power (was such their original intent)? As usual over such questions, one side will later answer emphatically "yes," and the other side as categorically "no."

But without knowing more, which way would we expect the Supreme Court to answer the question? We have only to remember the unspoken rule about judges not favoring challenges to their jurisdiction (their authority, their power), and that generally, since the law and the Constitution only words, they can generally find a way to rule in their own favor. Before long, such exactly describes the answer the Court will give. In the famous 1803 case of Marbury v Madison, the Court will successfully lay claim to this great power of judicial review, that is, the justices will find a way to rule in favor of their own power.

But before coming to that case, first let's visit the Constitutional Convention to determine the Founders' original intent, if we can determine it. Although the Convention deliberated in secret and kept no official records, yet some delegates preserved fairly detailed accounts. Most notably, James Madison, the Father of the

Constitution himself, made copious notes, published many years later, his *Notes on the Debates in the Federal Convention of 1787*. Reading through these, we discover judicial review mentioned no more than a few times and never directly. All the references come in the debates over the proposal for a "council of revision." Under this proposal, the president and some of the judges would have formed a council of revision to review laws passed by Congress. If they rejected a law, it wouldn't have become effective unless repassed by Congress. Obviously, this idea didn't survive to the final draft, but a similar idea lingers in the presidential veto.

In the debates on this proposal, Elbridge Gerry of Massachusetts, one of the most brilliant speakers at the Convention, was recorded as saying, "Mr. Gerry doubts whether the Judiciary ought to form a part of [the council of revision,] as they will have a sufficient check against encroachments on their own department by their exposition of the laws, which involved a power of deciding their Constitutionality. In some States the Judges had actually set aside laws as being against the Constitution. This was done too with general approbation." In other words, he thought the Supreme Court would have a power of judicial review.

But as soon as he sat down, Gunning Bedford, Jr., a delegate from Delaware, obtained the floor to oppose such a power. "Mr. Bedford was opposed to every check on the Legislative, even the Council of Revision first proposed. He thought it would be sufficient to mark out in the Constitution the boundaries of the Legislative Authority, which would give all the requisite security to the rights of the other departments. The Representatives of the people were the best Judges of what was for their interest, and ought to be under no external controul whatever." Thus, he thought the Supreme Court should not have a power of judicial review.

Taking the same side, John Francis Mercer of Maryland observed that, "He disapproved of the Doctrine that the Judges as expositors of the Constitution should have authority to declare a law void. He thought the laws ought to be well and cautiously made, and then to be uncontroulable." John Dickinson of Delaware supported him. "Mr. Dickinson was strongly impressed with the remark of Mr. Mercer as to the power of the Judges to set aside the law. He thought no such power ought to exist. He was at the same time at a loss what expedient to substitute. The Justiciary of Aragon he observed became by degrees, the lawgiver."

And so, looking through the record, it goes. No one thoroughly discusses the pros and cons of judicial review. Other topics absorbed the delegates main attention like congressional apportionment. Then where does that leave the Founders' original intent about judicial review? In all fairness, the record leaves either side a plausible, but neither a conclusive argument. Delegates who might favor judicial review could depart the Convention fairly satisfied. They could argue the power implied in the Constitution. Delegates opposed could depart as fairly satisfied. Judicial review not being expressly mentioned in the document, they could argue this silence expressed a purposeful omission. While whichever side they stood on, judicial review must have remained a somewhat vague idea in all their minds. It wasn't a tried and true (tested) mechanism of government. So far it had seen very little application in practice. The limited debates at the Convention had done nothing to develop the complete contours of this new theory of judicial power. Like so much else about the Constitution, a great deal was left to future events and later interpretation.

Nor did events standstill, and during the controversy over ratification of the Constitution, judicial review picked up a ringing endorsement. Alexander Hamilton, writing in the *Federalist No. 78* came out for it. Since James Madison, the Father of the Constitution himself, together with the lesser known but still influential John Jay, later the first chief justice of the Supreme Court, collaborated with Hamilton, and due to the high level of their tone and reasoning, the *Federalist* has always occupied a special niche on the shelf of those who cherish the Founders' "original intent." Hamilton's *No. 78* is, then, a proof that carries considerable weight. Yet all agree Hamilton wrote this number, and Madison would later publicly repudiate judicial review. And as already seen, there was no consensus among the Founders about judicial review. Once again, the argument appears inconclusive.

Yet Hamilton provided a persuasive rationale picked up and sounded to the echo by Chief Justice John Marshall in Marbury v Madison in 1803, the case which successfully claimed that power for the Supreme Court. Let us turn to that great case in the next article.

8.08 – Marshall v Jefferson

Maybe we should rename the great case of Marbury v Madison in 1803 as the great case of Marshall v Jefferson. The actual lead plaintiff was one William Marbury, an individual otherwise unknown to history. Three other actual plaintiffs joined with him in bringing the lawsuit, names still unknown to history, although you can look them up. By contrast the actual defendant was James Madison, a name otherwise illustrious in our history as Father of the Constitution and with title to several other major accomplishments. But actually, as so often with constitutional cases, the named parties were the catspaws in a larger game of power politics. The real protagonists were John Marshall, the new Chief Justice of the Supreme Court, versus Thomas Jefferson, the new president, and the larger game was a rivalry for power between themselves and their respective political parties.

John Marshall and Thomas Jefferson would have denied hating each other, preferring to rest their motives on higher ground. Their actual motives rested on highly familiar ground. We need only look back at the contentious election of 1800, only the fourth national election on our history, to understand their mutual hostility. If you think elections nasty nowadays, we didn't have nothing on our illustrious ancestors. Jefferson and his Republican Party accused John Adams, the incumbent president, and the Federalist Party, who controlled Congress, with plotting a coup to overthrown the new republic and set up a monarchy and aristocracy. The Federalists labeled Jefferson a dangerous radical and accused him of sexual misconduct with a slave mistress. Probably this mudslinging failed to much affect the outcome, which resulted more because the Republicans were better led and better organized. They routed the Federalists in the battle at the ballot box.

But in the interval between their defeat in late 1800 and their forced march away from the Capitol on March 3, 1801, when the Jeffersonians took office, the Federalist hatched a scheme to beat a retreat into the bastion of the judiciary. On February 13, 1801, they rammed through a law to create sixteen new federal judgeships (life-time posts). President Adams promptly nominated faithful

Federalists, and the Senate as promptly confirmed. Then on February 27, Congress passed a law to create justices-of-the-peace for the District of Columbia, not lifetime posts, but just five-year terms. Again, Adams quickly named faithful Federalists, one of his choices falling on our William Marbury, who shortly ended up serving as the lead plaintiff in Marbury v Madison. The Senate confirmed on March 3, 1801, Adams' last day in office.

Perhaps justifiably outraged, Jefferson and the Republicans had no intention to let the Federalists snatch such a victory from the jaws of defeat. Labeling these last-minute appointees "the midnight judges," as soon as they occupied their seats in Congress, they repealed the law creating the new federal judgeships (the life-time posts). And here was a thorny legal thicket. The Constitution says the Congress can create federal judgeships and federal judges hold office for life. Then once Congress creates the judgeship and the judge takes the office, can Congress thrust him out by abolishing the judgeship? In the event, none of the ousted judges mounted a serious challenge in court. Probably discretion appeared the better part of valor. In their hour of triumph, the Jeffersonians dominated the stricken field in too much strength, making a frontal assault on Congress too risky. Swallowing their disappointment with their courage, these judges silently folded their tents and disappeared into the outer darkness.

But something else happened with those justice-of-the-peace (the five-year posts). Their commissions had been signed and sealed by the Secretary of State, but in the last-minute rush, not actually delivered to them. When the new Secretary of State, James Madison, arrived in the office, he found these documents laying on the desk and quietly filed them away in the archives. President Jefferson's administration took the position that the offices were simply vacant, that not actually having been delivered, the commissions never went into effect.

It was at this point that Marbury and the other sued James Madison, as said, the new Secretary of State. This particular type of lawsuit goes under the name of "a petition for a writ of mandamus." It amounts to this. When an officer in the executive branch fails to perform a mere "ministerial duty," that is, a duty the law requires him to perform, an aggrieved citizen can file a petition for a writ of mandamus, an order from a court compelling the officer to perform the duty. To take a modern and trivial example, say you pass a driver's license test, but not liking your looks for some reason, the examiner decides not to issue you a license. That's a mere ministerial duty. The examiner has no discretion. If you pass the test, the law requires him to issue the license. You can file a petition for a writ of mandamus and the court will order him to issue your license. In exactly the same way, Marbury and the others argued that the delivering the commissions was a mere ministerial duty that the law required Madison to perform. They asked for an order of the court compelling him to deliver their commissions, effectively, to put them in their offices.

Marbury and the others filed this lawsuit in the Supreme Court itself, where it fell into the hands of the new Chief Justice, John Marshall. Like Jefferson a Virginian, yet Marshall was no follower or admirer of the new president, but rather a staunch Federalist. And actually, the new Chief Justice was himself one of the "midnight judges," having being appointed in January and taking the oath as Chief Justice only on February 4th. Also actually, before his last-minute elevation to the highest bench, Marshall had been himself the Secretary of State in President Adams' cabinet, where he continued to serve until the end of Adams' term. Actually, he had been the very man charged with signing, sealing, and delivering the commissions to Marbury and the others. Then actually, not only was Marshall a Federalist and a foe to Jefferson and the Republicans, but intimately connected to the very facts the case. Modern rules on conflict of interest would have prevented him presiding, yet we're told under the standards of the day, Marshall did nothing improper in hearing the case. But we've out of space and need to pick up the story in the next article.

8.09 – Jefferson by a Decision

To pick up where we left off, the new Chief Justice, John Marshall, a Federalist, looked like he had just been handed a golden goose on a silver platter. The case of Marbury v Madison looked like a perfect chance for him to sharpen his judicial knife and start carving up the opposition by ruling against Jefferson and the Republicans. But back then, things didn't yet have their present look.

Back then, Americans weren't yet habituated to the present practice where the Court habitually overrules the Congress. The Court had never yet ruled a single act of Congress unconstitutional and hence void, and it wasn't yet even clear the judges possessed such a power. Americans still regarded their elected Congress as the predominant branch. Madison no more than reflected the attitude when he had written in Fede*ralist No. 51*, "In republican government the legislative authority, necessarily, predominates." For the life-time judges to start overruling the elected Congress risked raising the cry of "anti-democratic" against the Court.

The Republicans in Congress, who were nothing if not hostile to anything they perceived as "non-democratic," had already shown willing to take on the judiciary with the repeal of the law creating the life-time judgeships. Above all, Thomas Jefferson wasn't a man to trifle with. If Marshall started carving him up, Jefferson was perfectly capable of sharpening his own knife and finding a way to start carving up Marshall and his Court instead.

Having all this in mind, Marshall came up with a clever opinion generally regarded as a judicial masterwork, as showing off a genius level legal dexterity. With one hand, he tossed a scrap to the rabid Federalist (mollified his base) by saying some nasty things about Thomas Jefferson, while careful never to mention him by name. With the other hand, he came up with a way to let Jefferson actually win the case (mollifying him). Sticks and stones may break my bones, but words will never hurt me. Then get off my back, Mr. President. And oh, incidentally, the really clever thing was that Marshall came up with a way to rule in his own favor by claiming that great power of judicial review for himself and his Court. To understand how he brought off all these legal feats and simultaneously, we have once again to read some more fine print.

Remember, Madison, as Jefferson's Secretary of State refused to deliver their commissions as justices-of-the-peace to Marbury and his friends. Chief Justice Marshall starts off by getting in his licks against Madison and through him, Jefferson, over that. The Chief Justice writes, "It is … decidedly the opinion of the Court that, when a commission has been signed by the President, the appointment is made, and that the commission is complete when the seal of the United States has been affixed to it by the Secretary of State. ... To withhold the commission, therefore, is an act deemed by the Court not warranted by law, but violative of a vested legal right."

To translate from the legalize, Madison and through him Jefferson have deliberately broken the law and violated the rights of Marbury and his friends. To translate into the more common tongue, they weren't honorable and high-minded men at all, but power-hungry politicians ignoring the law to advance a partisan agenda. Yet let's not fail to see that however "decided," Marshall's ruling was no more than his "opinion." His opinion was no better than the opinion of Madison or Jefferson, who had some pretty strong legal arguments on their side.

Not to go into all that, in the formal language in which legal duelists issue their challenges to mortal combat in the courts, the Chief Justice looked to have just slapped Madison and Jefferson across the face and thrown down the gauntlet. Looked like he was going to wield his judicial carving knife to rule against them despite the danger of inciting a killing counterstroke. But then, Marshall did what generally regarded as so clever. He found a way to withdraw the challenge without losing face by wrapping himself in the mantle of the Constitution.

To understand how he managed this feat, first we have to understand the legal distinction between a court of "original jurisdiction" and a court of "appellate jurisdiction." A court of original jurisdiction is where a case is originally filed, usually a lower court. A court of appellate jurisdiction hears appeals from the lower courts, and so, the higher court. Of course, the Supreme Court is the highest court of all. Yet Marbury's lawyers had filed their case "originally" with the Supreme Court. In doing so, they relied on a congressional law that gave the Court "original jurisdiction" to hear petitions for writ of mandamus.

If we look at what the Constitution says about the jurisdiction of the Supreme Court, Article III reads, "In all cases affecting Ambassadors, other public Ministers and Consuls, and those in which a State shall be a Party, the supreme Court shall have original Jurisdiction. In all other Cases ... the supreme Court shall have appellate Jurisdiction, ... with such Exceptions, and under such Regulations as the Congress shall make." In other words, in the specifically listed cases the Supreme Court has "original jurisdiction," and you can file the case there. "In all other cases," the Court has "appellate jurisdiction," and you cannot file the case there, but can appeal there. Yet "with such exceptions as Congress shall make."

Thus, we come to another gray area in the Constitution. In a few cases, the Supreme Court has "original" jurisdiction, in "all other cases" has "appellate" jurisdiction," yet "with such exceptions" as Congress "shall make." What exactly does that mean? It would seem to mean Congress can do whatever it wants about the Court's jurisdiction, that is, make any "exceptions" Congress wants.

But the Chief Justice willfully ignores the "exceptions." Instead, he rules the Court can only have "original" jurisdiction in the cases specifically listed. Then do you see the next step he has forced on the logic? If the "original" jurisdiction covers only those specific cases, Congress cannot extend the jurisdiction to writs of mandamus to cover such cases as Marbury. In other words, Congress has violated the Constitution by passing such a law. Taking this next step in the logic, Marshall rules, "The authority, therefore, given to the Supreme Court, by the act establishing the judicial courts of the United States to issue writs of mandamus ... appears not to be warranted by the constitution." Then do you see what the Marshall has so cleverly done? He has cleverly reasoned the law into a contradiction. First, he ruled Marbury and his friends have an absolute right to their commissions, although he could have ruled the other way with just as much reason. But if he had ruled the other way, the case would have been over. Not being entitled to their commissions, they would have lost and Jefferson won. Next, he ruled Congress cannot give the Court original jurisdiction over writs of mandamus, although he could have ruled the other way with as just much reason. But if he had ruled this other way, the case would have been over. Since the Court had jurisdiction, it would have ordered the commissions delivered and Jefferson would have lost. By this clever reasoning, the Chief Justice has contrived a legal contradiction between the absolute right to the commissions and the Court's lack of a right (lack of jurisdiction) to hear the case.

Then do you see the clever result? He has maneuvered into this contradiction to claim the power of judicial review for himself and his Court. Read his famous words for yourself, "It is emphatically the province and the duty of the judicial department to say what the law is. ... If two laws conflict with each other, the courts must decide on the operation of each. So if a law be in opposition to the constitution; if both the law and the constitution apply to a particular case, so that the court must decide that case conformably to the law, disregarding the constitution; or conformably to the constitution, disregarding the law; the court must determine which of these conflicting rules governs the case. ... If then the courts are to regard the constitution; and the constitution is superior to any ordinary act of the legislature, the constitution, and not such ordinary act, must govern the case to which they both apply."

Then do you see? With these words, he claimed the power of judicial review for the Supreme Court. It's a classic syllogism like if all men are mortal and Socrates is a man, then Socrates must be mortal. If "the constitution is superior to any ordinary act of the legislature" and "it is emphatically the province and the duty of the judicial department to say what the law is," then the Court must have the power to "decide the case conformably to the Constitution, disregarding the ordinary law." In other words, the Court must have the power of judicial review to void congressional laws ("the ordinary act of the legislature") that violate the Constitution ("in opposition to the constitution").

And so, he both rules the Court has the power of judicial review and exercises the power for the first time. He declares the congressional law giving the Court original jurisdiction unconstitutional and hence void. The Court not having jurisdiction to hear the case, he dismisses it.

Who won this heavyweight fight between these two political giants? Thomas Jefferson won by a decision. Marbury and the others didn't get their commissions and weren't made justices-of-the-peace. Yet John Marshall could walk away with his head held high. He had stayed in the ring with the champ and not been knocked out. He could even claim a moral victory by claiming to have won the power of judicial review for the Supreme Court.

Yet what did this claim amount to? Back then, it was far from clear. The Chief Justice had voided a minor congressional law as unconstitutional. Big deal. Nor, back then, did the power of judicial review look like much of a big deal. That's because as originally claimed, it wasn't much of a power, rather very limited.

Let's turn to those original limits in the next article.

8.10 – The Limits of the Rationale

Lawyers break a case down into the facts, the issues, the ruling, and the rationale. With the famous case of Marbury v Madison from 1803 we looked at the facts, including the clash between Chief Justice John Marshall and President Thomas Jefferson. We saw the issue, whether the Supreme Court had the power of judicial review. We heard the ruling. Yes, the Chief Justice ruled, he and his Court had the power. But what about the rationale, the reasons to support and justify this ruling?

Marshall put forward a simple and seemingly compelling rationale. He wrote, "The original and supreme will [of the people] organizes the government and assigns to the different departments their respective powers. … The powers of the Legislature [Congress] are defined and limited; and that those limits may not be mistaken or forgotten, the constitution is written. To what purpose is that limitation committed to writing, if these limits may at any time be passed by those intended to be restrained? … It is a proposition to plain to be contested that the Constitution controls any legislative act repugnant to it."

To unpack that, the Constitution expresses the "original and supreme will" of the people. They have "defined and limited" the "powers of the Legislature" (Congress). To keep "those limits" from being "mistaken or forgotten, the constitution is written." To keep those limits from being "passed," Congress must "be restrained." Therefore, the Supreme Court must have the power of judicial review to "restrain" Congress by ruling unconstitutional any law "repugnant" to the Constitution. Otherwise "to what purpose" have a written constitution at all?

Many at the time and since have found this rationale completely convincing. Over the years, countless historians, political scientists, and law professors have taught this theory and as completely convincing. Yet not everyone convinced then or now. Take the most prominent example from back in the day, Thomas Jefferson. He went on record as follows, "You seem ... to consider the judges as the ultimate arbiters of all constitutional questions; a very dangerous doctrine indeed, and one which would place us under the despotism of an oligarchy. ... When the legislative or executive functionaries act unconstitutionally, they are responsible to the people in their elective capacity. The exemption of the judges from that is dangerous enough."

To unpack that in turn, have we not repeatedly seen that the Constitution leaves a lot open to interpretation, a lot of gray areas? Some "limits" may be written, but not many are clearly written. Then the writing may express the "original and supreme will" of the people, but only when clearly expressed. Otherwise, we come to another gray area where the people's "original and supreme will" far from clear. Then when we arrive at such a gray area, which rather frequent, how decide the "limits" on Congress, or for that matter, on the president or the Supreme Court? Put another way, as a practical matter, who fills in the gray areas?

As Jefferson says, when the elected Congress does the job, fills in the gray areas, not only do they represent the people, but "they are responsible to the people in their elective capacity." But when the unelected judges do it, not only do they not represent the people, but they're not responsible to the people. And so, we should begin to see why Jefferson called judicial review "a very dangerous doctrine indeed." Since so much of the Constitution and the limits are open to interpretation, whoever has the final power over the interpretation ("as the ultimate arbiters") has near an open-ended power with no clear limits. For the Court to possess this power, rather than Congress, threatens to replace rule through a democratic institution ("responsible to the people") with rule by an aristocratic institution ("place us under the despotism of an oligarchy").

Then if Marshall gave a pretty good rationale for Marbury v Madison, Jefferson and his followers gave a pretty good refutation. That left Chief Justice Marshall and his supporters needing some further rationale. Nor was such an effort beyond their ingenuity. To cut the base from under this counter-attack, they shortly came up with a formula of words. They pledged never to declare a law unconstitutional except in a "clear-cut case, beyond a reasonable doubt, where all reasonable men would agree" Over the years, they kept repeating this formula in various forms like a protective incantation against the attacks on judicial review.

For example, Chief Justice Marshall himself in 1810 in Fletcher v Peck said, "The question, whether a law be void for its repugnancy to the constitution, is at all times of much delicacy, which ought seldom, if ever, to be decided in the affirmative, in a doubtful case. ... it is not on slight implication and vague conjecture that the legislature is to be pronounced to have transcended its powers, and its acts to be considered as void. The opposition between the law and the constitution should be such that the judge feels a clear and strong conviction of their incompatibility with each other."

For a much later example in an 1878 case, Chief Justice Remick Waite, "This declaration [that an act of Congress is unconstitutional] should never be made except in a clear case. Every possible presumption is in favor of the validity of a statute, and this continues until the contrary is shown beyond a rational doubt. One branch of the government cannot encroach on the domain of another without danger. The safety of our institutions depends in no small measure on a strict observance of this salutary rule."

Thus, they limited the rationale. By limiting judicial review to "clear-cut" cases, the Court could claim to be doing no more than defending the will of the people as "clear-cut" expressed in the Constitution. Since they would be doing no more than that, no one could accuse them of replacing the will of the people or the people's representatives in Congress with their own judicial will, replacing democracy with "the despotism of an oligarchy."

Nor would judicial review so limited to "clear-cut" cases have amounted to very much of a power. Almost always, Congress can make a strong argument to act constitutionally, so almost always the case not "clear-cut." Seldom even all the judges agree that a particular law is unconstitutional, so seldom even all the judges agree the case "clear-cut." Then under the limits of the rationale, the elected Congress would have filled in the gray, rather than the unelected Court.

Such describes the "original doctrine of judicial review" or the "limited" or "restrained" doctrine. And for over fifty years the Supreme Court regarded the limits of the rationale. For over fifty years, they never declared another congressional law unconstitutional.

But these "limits" might be written in the cases like the Constitution written, yet what "restrained" the judges from "mistaking or forgetting" them, as Chief Justice Marshall had been so concerned in Marbury to restrain Congress from "mistaking or forgetting" them? His rationale was that the Court would restrain Congress within the "limits" written into the Constitution. But in turn, what restrained his Court within the "limits" written into the doctrine of judicial review? Nothing really. Those pledges to "judicial restraint" were no more than words on the printed page. No effective mechanism enforced the limits. Even the laws against murder are no more than words on the page without a mechanism of enforcement. How much less any pledges to self-restraint made by government officials, including the judges.

So finally, the time would ripen. In the Dred Scott Case in 1857 the Court would for only the second time declare a congressional law unconstitutional. In the process, the Court would abandon the original limits on the rationale. Reneging on their pledges to limit themselves to "clear-cut" cases, the Court would shift the paradigm for judicial review. In the future, judicial review would have no clear-cut limits. Let's follow this story in the next article.

8.11 – The Dreadful Case

Has any case ever had a more appropriate name than Dred Scott in 1857? Dred is in the very name of the case. Indeed, it was a dreadful case. Not just for the reason usually given, but for an underlying reason as well. On the surface, Dred Scott was all about slavery. In his opinion and notoriously, Chief Justice Roger Taney somehow discovered a "right to slavery" implied in the Constitution. But under this surface and almost silently the case was all about the Court's power. On this side of the case (the power side), the Chief Justice shifted the paradigm on judicial review, leaving behind the limit to "clear-cut" cases, leaving the power with no clear limits. Let's turn over this dreaded case and look at both sides.

First, for the surface issue – slavery. What exactly does the Constitution say about slavery, if anything? Absolutely nothing openly, but we find what Abraham Lincoln later called in the

Lincoln-Douglas debates three "covert" references. In Article I, "Representatives ... shall be determined by adding to the whole Number of free Persons ... three fifth of all other Persons." In other words, slaves were counted in determining the number of representatives (the "three-fifths compromise"). Also, in Article I, "Migration or Importation of such Persons as any of the States now existing shall think proper to admit, shall not be prohibited ... prior to [1808]." In other words, Congress couldn't prohibit the African slave trade before January 1, 1808, and incidentally, Congress did prohibit it on that day. Lastly, in Article IV, "No Person held to Service or Labour in one State ... escaping into another, shall, in Consequence ... be discharged from such Service or Labour, but shall be delivered up on the claim of the Party to whom such Service or Labour may be due." In other words, slaves escaping to another state would be returned to their masters, later leading to the highly controversial "fugitive slave laws."

Did these covert references imply a "right to slavery" (prohibit Congress form abolishing slavery)? Congress didn't think so. The very First Congress in 1789 passed the famous Northwest Ordinance, prohibiting slavery in what later would become Ohio, Indiana, Illinois, Michigan, and Wisconsin. The Ordinance reads, "There shall be neither Slavery nor involuntary servitude in the said territory." Nineteen members in that First Congress had attended the Constitutional Convention, and George Washington, who as president signed into law the new Northwest Ordinance, had presided at the Convention. Apparently, all these gentlemen thought Congress possessed such authority. In 1820, Congress passed the Missouri Compromise, extending westward the old Mason Dixon line between Maryland and Pennsylvania and prohibiting slavery north of the line. In 1850 with the Compromise of 1850, Congress prohibited slavery in still other territories.

Congress thought the majority had a right to prohibit slavery, but a minority, the slaveholders, didn't like that thought. They preferred to think the Constitution guaranteed them a "right to slavery" against the majority. Nowadays, a "right to slavery" may sound rather odd to our ears, although perhaps no more odd than some present rights may sound to future ears. That just shows that minority rights can mean about anything you want, depending on what minority you want to prefer.

As a matter of fact, one of the earliest minorities in our history successfully to claim their rights against the majority was that old slaveholding minority. While they've fallen out of fashion, their method remains very much in fashion, and in fact, they largely invented the method. First, they claimed to find their minority rights implied in the Constitution just like so many other minority rights have since been found implied there. Next, they turned to the courts to defend their rights just as so many other minorities have since turned to the courts to defend their rights against the majority.

The political calculations before the Civil War explain their preference for this method. In those antebellum years, the slaveholding minority faced a bleak political future when calculated by the democratic method. The slaveholders controlled only the South. The free states were way ahead statistically, demographically and economically, and pulling farther away each year. The slaveholding states were already outnumbered in Congress, and as the free states multiplied across the continent ("go west, young man"), the free majority would reach overwhelming proportions both outside and inside Congress. Slavery was doomed by the math of majority rule (by the democratic method). If Congress and the majority had the power, eventually, Congress and the majority was going to prohibit slavery across the whole nation, not just in the territories.

Well, change a losing game. If you don't like the way the math adds up, invent some new math. Long-cherished American notions about our "inviolable rights" stood ready to hand. All the lawyers for the slaveholders had to do was reach for and wield their version just like today the civil rights lawyers reach for and wield their version. All they had to do was discover an "inviolable right to slavery" implied in the Constitution just like the civil rights lawyers have since discovered so many other inviolable rights implied. That way, they could remove the controversy to another venue, from the democratic arena in Congress to the judicial forum before the Supreme Court. That way, they could change the method, change from playing a losing democratic game to playing a judicial game, where the math would likely add up the opposite way.

Much later a Supreme Court justice well summed up the

argument always made to support such motions for a change of venue. In a 1943 case, Justice Robert H. Jackson wrote, "The very purpose of the Bill of Rights was to withdraw certain subjects from the vicissitudes of political controversy, to place them beyond the reach of majorities and officials and establish them as legal principles to be applied by the courts. One's ... fundamental rights may not be submitted to vote; they depend on the outcome of no elections."

Under this reasoning, all the slaveholding minority had to do was convince the Supreme Court about a "right to slavery" being implied in the Constitution just as the civil rights lawyers have since convinced the Court about so many other rights. If they could only succeed, that would "place it beyond the reach of majorities" as a "fundamental right," which "may not be submitted to vote ... depend on the outcome of no elections." The right would be "established as a legal principle to be applied by the courts."

But before the Civil War, although Justice Jackson's argument already popular, this method still faced what looked an insurmountable obstacle. Everyone liked and likes the notion their "fundamental rights may not be submitted to vote." But the Constitution leaves a lot about "our fundamental rights" open to interpretation, not clearly expressed. And remember, the Supreme Court had pledged under the original doctrine of judicial review never to declare a law unconstitutional except in a "clear-cut" case, where the Constitution clearly expressed the right. No "right to slavery" was clearly expressed. Then the Supreme Court itself had no "right" to declare the laws prohibiting slavery unconstitutional. However much the slaveholding minority might want to remove "the subject from the vicissitudes of political controversy," they had no "right" to do so. Looked like they were stuck with the democratic method.

But not to despair. After all, that pledge to limit judicial review to clear-cut cases was only words, and lawyers never despair when it's only words. That just made the task more challenging. Not only would the slaveholders' lawyers have to convince the Court a "right to slavery" was implied in the Constitution. They would also have to convince the Court to break that pledge about "clear-cut" cases. They would have to convince the Court to take an increase in its power, since clear-cut cases limited the Court's power.

Fortunately for them, arguments for more judicial power have never been too hard to sell the Court. In the next article, we'll see how the justices managed to convince themselves to buy the argument and take the increase.

8.12 – Channeling Justice Taney

During oral argument in a recent case, the Obergefell Case in 2015, the same-sex marriage case, Associate Justice Elana Kagan went on record with this remark, "We don't live in a pure democracy, we live in a constitutional democracy. And the Constitution imposes limits on what people can do and this is one of those cases ... where we have to decide ... whether the Constitution... prevents the democratic processes from operating purely independently." Justice Kagan may not have realized that she was channeling Chief Justice Roger Taney from the Dred Scott Case in 1857, the right to slavery case. And she's not the only one. Modern justices may not like his cause, but they love his method. They channel him all the time.

With the Dred Scott Case (1857), Chief Justice Taney shifted the paradigm on judicial review. Before the Court could only declare a law unconstitutional in a "clear-cut" case "where all reasonable men would agree." Taney abandoned that original restraint without ever admitting to the deed. In its place, he substituted "unrestrained judicial review" with no clear-cut limits.

Thus today, when Justice Kagan and other justices like her say things such as, "we have to decide … whether the Constitution … imposes limits," they don't mean decide "whether the Constitution" imposes clear-cut limits. Instead, they're channeling Justice Taney. By his method, the Constitution "imposes limits on what people can do," but there are no clear limits on what the justices can do. Instead of "the democratic processes operating purely independently," only the Court operates independently. No wonder the justices love this method (this power).

Turning to the facts of this dreadful case, who was Dred Scott anyway? Born in 1796, Dred was a slave in Missouri, a slave state, who belonged to a Dr. John Emerson, an army surgeon. As the army transferred the doctor around to various military posts, he took Dred with him, and their travels carried them into free territory where Congress had prohibited slavery by the Compromise of 1820. Under existing law, an owner who took a slave into free territory freed the slave by the owner's own act. In the increasingly heated conflict over slavery, this law assumed a fundamental significance. If a slaveholder could take a slave into free territory and the slave remained a slave, there would no longer be any free territory and slavery would exist across the whole nation.

Although we know he was illiterate, signing with an X on legal documents, Dred Scott knew about this law. When Dr. Emerson died in 1843, Dred filed a lawsuit seeking his freedom on precisely those grounds. We might be surprised a slave could sue his master, but a number of slaves had previously taken this same path to the courthouse and won their freedom.

Not to follow all the twists and turns, which were several, the case eventually reached the pinnacle up at the U.S. Supreme Court. There Dred's fate fell into the hands of Chief Justice Roger Brook Taney. Born way back in 1777, Taney was eighty years old, but still possessed the mental vigor of one of the finest lawyers of his day. Earlier in his career, he had practiced law with Francis Scott Key, the composer of the "Star Spangled Banner," whose sister Taney married. He served as Attorney General and Secretary of the Treasury in the cabinet of President Andrew Jackson and became a close confidant of Old Hickory. In 1836, Jackson appointed him as Chief Justice, succeeding the legendary John Marshall. Taney did good work on the Court in adapting the laws to the emerging commercial and corporate environment. You couldn't have found a more distinguished lawyer and jurist.

As for slavery, Taney came from Maryland, a slave state, and in 1857, the same year as he authored Dred Scott, wrote a letter to a Massachusetts' clergyman much quoted against him. "Every intelligent person whose life has been passed in a slaveholding state, and who has carefully observed the character and capacity of the African race, will see that a sudden and general emancipation would be absolute ruin to the negroes, as well as to the white population." Nevertheless, thirty years gone by, he had freed his own slaves and supported eventual emancipation.

But the times they were a changing, and despite his advanced age, Taney was still pliable enough to change with them. As a Jackson man, he shared his chief's passionate commitment to the national union, a true patriot in that sense. As the conflict over slavery grew ever more violent, he saw that union threatened with imminent and violent dismemberment. The Chief Justice put this two and two together in his mind and took two other crucial mental leaps. In the first leap, he came to believe the slaveholders' legal theory about a "right to slavery" being implied in the Constitution. In the second leap, he came to believe the free states, the majority, had provoked the crisis by their wrongful aggression against this legal right belonging to the minority in the slave states. Around these beliefs, he had formed a fiercely held set of convictions.

Here were all the ingredients that call upon a man to do the right thing. If he could save the union, he must do so; if he could defend the minority's rights, he must do so; if he must bend a legal nicety to do so, even to the breaking point, he would do so. This psychology should be all too familiar to anyone who studies the history of the Court. While the causes change over time, the psychology within the judicial mind stays the same. Becoming convinced of the righteousness of their cause, the justices follow the dictates of their moral imperative. They do the right thing. Such is frequently lauded as the very highest source of judicial conduct. To this way of thinking, we may condemn Taney's cause, but not his method. Indeed, it was he who invented the method right here in Dred Scott.

Remember two things. First, no "right to slavery" was clearly expressed in the Constitution. Second, under the original, then existing doctrine of judicial review, the Court could only declare a law unconstitutional in a clear-cut case where all rational men would agree. Yet first, Taney, writing for a seven to two majority, rules, "The right of property in a slave is distinctly and expressly affirmed in the Constitution." Second, he uses judicial review to declare a congressional law unconstitutional for only the second time.

He declares the Missouri Compromise of 1820, the congressional law prohibiting slavery in the territories, unconstitutional and hence void. Under his ruling, the slaveholding minority had won and the free state majority had lost just as so many other minorities have since won and so many other majorities have since lost before the Supreme Court. Congress lacked the power to prohibit slavery, which now existed permanently across the whole country.

For our tale of the Constitution as it has become notice two things. First, Taney had followed his conscience. He meant to save the union by handing down an unalterable decree of the Supreme Court, laying to rest for all time the conflict over slavery. With the same decree, he meant to defend the rights of the minority against the majority. But second, he did not follow the law, did not follow the original limits written into the law on judicial review. A right to slavery simply was not clear-cut, not clearly expressed in the Constitution. All reasonable men did not agree, even two justices on the Court dissenting. To do the first, follow his conscience, he had had to abandon the second, not follow the law.

Not that the Chief Justice admitted to his deed. Assuming a pose still constantly assumed by the justices, he publicly denied what he privately did. He wrote, "The duty of the court is to interpret the [Constitution], with the best lights we can obtain on the subject, and to administer it as we find it, according to its true intent and meaning when it was adopted." What else was Justice Kagan still pretending in 2015 when she said, "we have to decide ... whether the Constitution... prevents the democratic processes from operating purely independently." But who fooled by this then or now?

For one, Abraham Lincoln wasn't fooled. Referring to the Dred Scott Case in his first inaugural address on March 5, 1861, he said, "The candid citizen must confess, that if the policy of the government upon vital questions affecting the whole people is to be irrevocably fixed by decisions of the Supreme Court, the instant they are made in ordinary litigation between parties in personal actions the people will have ceased to be their own rulers, having to that extent practically resigned their government into the hands of that eminent tribunal."

Let's not get fooled either. Chief Justice Taney shifted the paradigm on judicial review. A judicial review not limited to clear-cut cases is a much more powerful judicial review, no longer with any clear limits. From that day to this, judicial review has had no clear limits. Present justices may not like his cause, but they love his method. They love the power. They channel Justice Taney all the time.

8.13 – Interpreting Away

If the Constitution was a gold mine of power, the Supreme Court kept expanding their claim. Initially, we saw them just stake a narrow claim, just to judicial review as the power to void laws in "clear-cut" cases. Next, we saw them move their stakes, widening their claim to judicial review as a power with no clear limits. Now, we'll see them jump a claim already staked out by Congress and the people. By so doing, they will claim a power to interpret away the clear-cut meaning of the Constitution itself. If this had been a gold rush, somebody would have got shot.

The Court filed their papers on this latest claim over the Reconstruction Amendments, which so important as sometimes called the "Second American Constitution." Back at the founding, America had a problem. How bring the thirteen states together into a national union? The Founders brought them together with the Constitution, which notice, a democratic solution. After the Civil War, during Reconstruction, running from about 1865 to 1876, America had a similar problem. How bring the rebel states back into the union and bring the new freedmen with them? The statesmen of this later era tried with the three great Reconstruction Amendments, which notice, another democratic solution.

The 13th Amendment, ratified in 1865, abolished slavery. "Neither slavery nor involuntary servitude … shall exist within the United States." The 14th Amendment, ratified in 1868, guaranteed all citizens their equal rights. "No State shall … deny to any person … the equal protection of the laws." The 15th Amendment, ratified in 1870, specifically guaranteed the vote (the fundamental democratic right). "The right of citizens of the United States to vote shall not be denied or abridged … on account of race, color, or previous condition of servitude."

Notice that these amendments put democracy to work on both ends of the problem. Going in, democracy worked out the solution for Reconstruction. The Congress, the people's elected representatives, passed the amendments, and the state legislatures, again the people's elected representatives, ratified them. To come back into the union, the rebel states had to accept these additional amendments as a precondition. The people had spoken. Coming out, democracy would work out the remaining solutions. With slavery gone and their other rights in hand, most importantly the ballot in hand, all citizens, including the new freedmen, would have the wherewithal to look out for their own interests in the reunited nation. The people would speak again, everyone finding their own place in the democratic scheme of things.

Sounds like a great solution, doesn't it? But it wasn't to be. In no more than a few short decades, the Supreme Court would interpret away the clear-cut meaning of these great Reconstruction Amendments. By a narrow reading, the justices would interpret away the promise of votes and equality for the freedmen. Yet by this same narrow reading, they would more widely read the doctrine of judicial review. They would expand that claim into a power to interpret away the clear-cut meaning of the Constitution itself.

Since the vote the fundamental democratic right, what happened with it offers the best example of what happened overall. As already quoted, the 15th Amendment reads, "The right of citizens of the United States to vote shall not be denied or abridged … on account of race, color, or previous condition of servitude." Surely, these words spoke clear-cut enough that any reasonable man would understand. The 15th Amendment meant to guarantee the freedmen their votes. The people had spoken by ratifying the amendment.

But beginning with the Reese Case in 1876, the Supreme Court spoke in turn, and once we carefully sort through their words, clearly enough for any reasonable man to understand. They interpreted away the guarantee (and so interpreted away the clear-cut meaning of the 15th Amendment). Chief Justice Morrison Remick Waite writes the opinion. Read carefully to catch his subtle legal quibble. He writes, "The Fifteenth Amendment does not confer the right of suffrage upon anyone. It prevents the States, or the United States, however, from giving preference in this particular, to one citizen over another, on account of race, color or previous condition of servitude."

Did you catch it? He made a crucial distinction. He said the 15th Amendment didn't guarantee the freedmen's right to vote ("does not confer the right of suffrage upon anyone"). Rather, he said the words merely prevented discrimination against them on certain specific grounds ("prevents giving preference on account of race, color or previous condition of servitude"). Then do you see the momentous consequence? If the 15th Amendment doesn't guarantee the freedmen's right to vote, but only protects them against discrimination on certain specific grounds ("race, color or previous condition of servitude"), this interpretation leaves them open to discrimination on some other grounds, if someone clever enough to think up some.

They were clever enough all right. Voting laws shortly began to appear on the statute books in some states like the following, "He [the elector] shall be able to read and write, ... If he is not able to read and write ... then he shall be entitled to register and vote if he shall ... be the bona fide own of property assessed ... at the valuation of not less than three hundred dollars. ... No male person who was on January 1, 1867 ... entitled to vote ... and no son or grandson of any such person ... shall be denied the right to register and vote in this State by reason of his failure to possess the educational or property qualifications prescribed." Do you see? Since few freedmen were literate, few owned much property, and neither they, their fathers, nor grandfathers voted before 1867, such "grandfather" laws effectively disenfranchised them.

Thus, clearly enough for any reasonable man to understand, the Supreme Court interpreted away the clear-cut meaning of the 15th Amendment, interpreted away the guarantee of the vote to the freedmen. In the same era in other cases, the justices also interpreted away the clear-cut meaning of the 14th Amendment, interpreted away the guarantee of "equal protection of the laws" to the freedmen. All of which clearly destroyed the democratic program for Reconstruction as enacted by the people through Congress and their state legislatures. Having lost the vote and their other rights, the freedmen could no longer participate in the democratic process and lost the power to defend their interests. The Court had rejected democracy both coming in and going out. They had rejected both the democratically arrived at program and democracy as the way to move forward with the program.

For our tale of the Constitution as it has become, the people through the elected Congress and state legislatures had filed their claim to Reconstruction. They had claimed to guarantee the freedmen their votes and equal rights. But the unelected justices on the Supreme Court found a way to invalidate this claim.

Instead, the Court expanded its own claim to power over the Constitution. Back in 1803 in Marbury v Madison, they had claimed the power of judicial review. But at the time, the doctrine was no more than a narrow power to declare congressional laws unconstitutional in clear-cut cases. But then, in 1857 with the Dred Scott Case, they had widened their claim, claiming they were no longer limited to clear-cut cases, leaving their claim with no clear limits. Now, they had further expanded their claim. Now, they had acquired the power to interpret away the clear-cut meaning of the Constitution itself.

With this line of cases, the Supreme Court rendered the noble purposes of the Reconstruction Amendment a dead letter. Yet the words lingered on the face of the Constitution like unfulfilled promises or broken pledges. In the last half of the twentieth century, these promises would finally be fulfilled and these pledges redeemed. Through a long process for which the Supreme Court can rightly claim much credit, the Reconstruction Amendments were revitalized, the vote and equal rights were restored.

Yet the justices have never restored the power they claimed for themselves with these cases. We might say that by interpreting away the Reconstruction Amendments, they reconstructed the Constitution. Today they still have and use the power to interpret away the clear-cut meaning of the Constitution itself. It has been a gold mine of power to them. And they will shortly further expand their claim, as will be seen in the next articles.

8.14 – Interpreting In

If you can subtract, why can't you add? If the Supreme Court could interpret away (subtract), why couldn't they interpret in (add)? The one operation attracted them as much as the other and for the same reason. Interpreting away the clear-cut meaning of the Constitution was one power, but interpreting in a whole other meaning was still another power. And so, having just watched as the justices interpreted away the clear-cut meaning of the Reconstruction Amendments, the promise of equality to the freedmen, now we will watch them shortly go on to interpret in a meaning clearly never meant (legal segregation). Not only could the Court both add and subtract, their math totaled up to an opposite solution, opposite to the democratic solution for Reconstruction arrived at by the people and Congress. The only constant was the power side of the equation, where the Court constantly raised itself to a higher power.

In the last article, we watched the Court subtract. In such cases as Reece in 1876, they interpreted away the Reconstruction Amendments, interpreted away their promise of the vote and equal rights for the freedmen. On the surface, these cases subtracted out the clear-cut meaning of those amendments. On the other side (the power side), these cases raised the Court's power to become a power to interpret away the clear-cut meaning of the Constitution itself.

In this article, we'll watch the Court add. In the famous or infamous case of Plessy v Ferguson from 1896, they will interpret in the Constitution the doctrine of "separate but equal" (legal segregation). On the surface, this case added a meaning to the Constitution clearly never meant. On the other side (the power side), the case raised the Court's power still again to become a power to interpret in meanings clearly never meant.

It surprises many to learn that as far back as 1875, Congress passed a law against segregation, the Civil Rights Act of 1875. This law read, "That all persons within the jurisdiction of the United States shall be entitled to the full and equal enjoyment of the accommodations, advantages, facilities and privileges of inns, public conveyances on land or water, theaters and other places of public amusement; subject only to the conditions ... applicable alike to citizens of every race and color, regardless of any previous condition of servitude." Violations carried a fine of up to $500.00, a pretty stiff penalty in those days, and people could also sue for damages. Since Congress presumably represents the majority, this law presumably represented the majority view against segregation.

How did America get from a national law against segregation to state laws mandating segregation, as we know later happened in some states? In the first part of the answer, the Supreme Court interpreted away the Civil Rights Act of 1875 just as earlier we saw the justices interpret away the Reconstruction Amendments.

That subtraction happened with the Civil Rights Cases in 1886. But we've already seen the Court subtract (interpret away), and now we're ready to see them add (interpret in). That brings us to the second part of the answer. In the case of Plessy v Ferguson in 1896, the Court interprets in the Constitution the doctrine of "separate but equal." Their judicial addition let states pass laws to segregate.

Plessy v Ferguson, as said in 1896, concerned a challenge to a "separate car law" passed by the state of Louisiana in 1890. This law read, "All railway companies carrying passengers in their coaches in this State shall provide equal but separate accommodations for the white and colored races, by providing two or more coaches for each passenger train, or by dividing the passenger coaches by a partition so as to secure separate accommodations." Not only "shall" the companies provide "separate accommodations," but the "white and colored races" shall occupy the "separate accommodations." The law mandated (ordered) the segregation, didn't let people sit where they wanted.

But if we will only remember another law and a constitutional law at that, the 14th Amendment ratified in 1868, had clearly stated, "No State shall make or enforce any law which shall … deny to any person … the equal protection of the laws." Remembering that, we immediately perceive that the Louisiana "separate car law" was an attempt to evade the 14th Amendment. The Louisiana state legislature was trying to pass off a difference as without a distinction, pass off "equal but separate" as still "equal protection of the laws."

Would they get away with it? Justice John Marshall Harlan, the lone dissenter in Plessy v Ferguson, would memorably, but vainly protest, "The thin disguise of 'equal' accommodations for passengers in railroad coaches will not mislead anyone." Nor did it. All knew what was meant. Yet Justice Henry Billings Brown, writing for the majority, had the last word, "The object of the [14th] amendment was undoubtedly to enforce the absolute equality of the two races before the law, but in the nature of things it could not have been intended to abolish distinctions based upon color, or to enforce social, as distinguished for political, equality, or a commingling of the two races upon terms unsatisfactory to either. Laws permitting, or even requiring their separation in places where they are likely to be brought into contact do not necessarily imply the inferiority of either race to the other."

In other words, they got away with it. The Court had interpreted in the Constitution a meaning clearly never meant. They had reversed the clear-cut meaning of the 14th Amendment. Going in, Justice Brown says, "the object of the [14th] amendment was undoubtedly to enforce the absolute equality of the two races." Coming out, he says that state "laws permitting, or even requiring their separation" didn't violate "equal protection of the laws."

The Court had interpreted in the Constitution the doctrine of "separate but equal." Wearing this "thin disguise," America got from the national laws against segregation, the Civil Rights Act of 1875 and the 14th Amendment, to state laws mandating segregation such as the Louisiana Separate Car Law of 1890.

The justices had proven they could not only subtract, they could add. They had interpreted in the Constitution a meaning never meant. By so doing, they further added to their own power. Now, they had both the power to subtract and add (interpret out and interpret in). But the Court wasn't through adding to its power, as we shall see in the next articles.

While as a footnote, notice something else. We always hear the Supreme Court protects minority rights against the majority. But "minority rights" isn't a self-defining term. Depending on how you want to define the minority, their rights can lead not only to different, but to opposite outcomes. The freedmen were a minority. But the majority in the Louisiana legislature was also a minority across the nation as a whole. The majority across the nation lined up on the side of the freedmen's minority rights. How else explain the Civil Rights Act of 1875 and the 14th Amendment, which the national majority passed. But the majority on the Supreme Court chose to line up with the segregationist minority. Presuming the Court protects minority rights, how do they choose which minority, and how does this instance show them better at choosing the more worthy minority than Congress or the people themselves?

8.15 – Interpreting Again

The present moral authority of the Supreme Court flows directly from Brown v Board of Education in 1954. That was the greatest case ever handed down by the Court, greatest in principle, greatest in effect. The applause has not yet died. Yet for our tale of the Constitution as it has become, the Court acquires still more power with the case.

Chief Justice Earl Warren wrote for a unanimous Court, "Does segregation of children in public schools solely on the basis of race ... deprive the children of the minority group of equal educational opportunities? We believe it does. ... Separate educational facilities are inherently unequal. Therefore, we hold that the [minority group] ... are, by reason of the segregation complained of, deprived of the equal protection of the laws guaranteed by the Fourteenth Amendment."

With this ruling, the Court finally returned to the original, clear-cut meaning of the 14th Amendment that, "No State shall make or enforce any law which shall ... deny to any person ... the equal protection of the laws." Since "separate educational facilities are inherently unequal," the laws that segregated violated "equal protection of the laws." Therefore, such laws were unconstitutional.

Great stuff. That's clear-cut. What reasonable man disagrees? Yet to turn to the power side of the case, the Court acquires still more power. Remember, it was the Court itself that back after Reconstruction had interpreted away the original, clear-cut meaning of the 14th Amendment, interpreted away "equal protection." It was the Court itself with Plessy v Ferguson in 1896 that had interpreted in "separate but equal," a meaning clearly never meant and that opened the way for legal segregation. Now, the Court itself is interpreting again, reversing their prior interpretations. So now, they have the power to interpret out of the Constitution, interpret into the Constitution, and interpret again the Constitution.

When we remember the original rationale for judicial review, we see how far their power has come. When the Court first seized this power back in 1803 in Marbury v Madison, Chief Justice John Marshall had said the "purpose" for judicial review was to defend the "original and supreme will" of the people as "written" in the Constitution. But since what "written" was often far from clear, this original doctrine came with a limitation. Only when the "original and supreme will" of the people was clearly expressed ("clear-cut") would the Court void a law as unconstitutional. Otherwise, the justices ran the risk of writing their own will into the Constitution with their interpretations. But by the time of Brown in 1954, what has happened? The Court has gradually seized the power to make, unmake, and remake the Constitution, however they want. The "original and supreme will" of the people matters for nothing. Today, "the Constitution is what the justices say it is."

As much as a power to interpret again the Constitution, Brown began to interpret again the Court's power in still another way. Brown v Board of Education actually consists of several opinions. In the first, called Brown I, in 1954, we just heard Chief Justice Warren declare legal segregation unconstitutional. But beyond the declaration, what was the remedy? In the next year in 1955, in what called Brown II, the Court came back to try and answer that question. Once again, Chief Justice Warren wrote for a unanimous Court, "In fashioning and effectuating the [remedies], the courts will be guided by equitable principles. Traditionally, equity has been characterized by a practical flexibility in shaping its remedies ... . These cases call for the exercise of these traditional attributes of equity power." Further, [T]he cases are remanded ... to take such proceedings and enter such orders and decrees consistent with this opinion as are necessary and proper to admit to public schools on a racially nondiscriminatory basis with all deliberate speed the parties to these cases."

To someone not versed in the legal terminology, these words must sound opaque. He says, "These cases call for the exercise ... of equity power." What exactly is "equity power?" And the law makes a distinction between a "legal remedy" and an "equitable remedy." A legal remedy is money damages. An equitable remedy is an order from a court to do or not to do something.

This distinction is rooted in the fact that money damages are sometimes not "adequate." Take a textbook example. A man goes on your land and cuts down some trees. You can sue him for money damages, which are adequate, since the money makes you whole, or at least, as whole as the law can make you, the trees being gone. But say a man moves on your land, cuts down some trees, builds a log cabin, and starts farming. Money damages are no longer adequate. Land is unique, and you have an exclusive right to occupy your own land. You can sue and get an order from the court, evicting him and putting you back in peaceable possession. Obviously, there are numerous other situations where money damages are "inadequate." These are the cases that call for the "exercise of equity power."

As obviously, desegregation calls for the exercise of such a power to order things done. Money damages are inadequate. In the first place, the money damages would be impossible to calculate. In the second place, what wanted was an equal education, which may require spending some money, but will require something beyond money. The federal courts across the country will have to order something done to desegregate. Nor was such an easy or one-off task. Desegregation would require not just one order, but orders reaching across the whole country, directed to thousands of schools, affecting millions of children, impacting as many communities. It would also require ongoing orders for years to come. No wonder Warren says, "These cases call for the exercise of these traditional attributes of equity power."

Yet his words began to interpret again this "equity power" in a highly non-traditional way. Back in 1896, when Plessy v Ferguson interpreted "separate but equal" into the Constitution, the Court could act merely through a negative. They could just open the constitutional gate, get the hell out of the way, and let the states stampede out of the corral, letting them enact state laws to segregate. The Court didn't have to lead. But to carry out Brown and desegregate, they would have to boss the cattle drive, prodding the states all the way up the trail to the railhead, all the way to desegregation. The Court would have to lead. It was the difference between writing elegant opinions in the cloistered quiet of your chambers and coming down out of the ivory tower to ramrod your opinion through the wilderness of the real world. Rather than the "traditional" role of judges, handing down rulings, they would have to take on something more like traditional executive functions to carry out their orders to desegregate.

When the Chief Justice used the word "traditional" with respect to "equity power," it was somewhat misleading. By this time, if it was not quite yet "traditional" for the Court to interpret again the Constitution (interpreting out segregation and interpreting in desegregation), it was still less "traditional" for judges to take on the role and the powers he was suggesting for them. However wonderful Brown, with the case the Supreme Court acquired still more power. On to the next article to learn more about this latest innovation in the Court's power.

8.16 - The New Model

In the last article, we covered Brown v Board of Education in 1954. We heard Chief Justice Warren, writing for the Court, declare legal segregation unconstitutional. Next, we covered Brown II in 1955. We heard Warren say the courts should use their "traditional equity powers" to order desegregation ("with all deliberate speed"). But our larger topic concerns the Constitution as it has become, and right now, especially the power of the Supreme Court as it has become. On that side of the case (the power side), Brown creates a new model judicial supremacy. With this latest model, the Supreme Court would acquire the power not just to make national policy through their interpretations of the Constitution, but directly themselves carry out vast social policies across the whole nation.

To see how far the power has moved toward the Court, let's begin by recalling what Abraham Lincoln heard to say back in his first inaugural address, on March 5, 1861, "The candid citizen must confess, that if the policy of the government upon vital questions affecting the whole people is to be irrevocably fixed by decisions of the Supreme Court, the instant they are made in ordinary litigation between parties in personal actions, the people will have ceased to be their own rulers, having to that extent practically resigned their government into the hands of that eminent tribunal."

Lincoln was talking about the Dred Scott Case in 1857, which covered in an earlier article. If we will remember, that case was "ordinary litigation between parties in personal actions." There were only two "parties," the slave Dred Scott and his owner John Stanford. It was a "personal action," a case between just the two of them. It was "ordinary litigation," the Court handing down a ruling just between the two of them. To this point, all the other cases covered in these articles have been the same, just between individual plaintiffs and defendants. In 1803 in Marbury v Madison, Marbury and three others sued James Madison, the Secretary of State. In 1896 in Plessy v Ferguson, the parties were just two, Homer Plessy, the man who got arrested for refusing to sit in the colored section of a New Orleans streetcar, and Judge John Howard Ferguson, the state judge who had upheld the Separate Car Law.

But by the time we reach Brown in 1954, to talk about "ordinary litigation between parties in personal actions" no longer fits the reality on the ground. For convenience, we cite the case as Brown v Board of Education, but in reality, the plaintiffs were thirteen parents "on behalf of" their twenty children. It was a "class action." Soon much larger classes became the norm, such as in a later case, "all school children in the City of Detroit." In a "class action" one or several plaintiffs can sue "on behalf of all those similarly situated." Such a legal device has a long history. But after Brown, the use and size exploded and not just along racial lines. Public interest lawyers filed class actions all over the place, say on behalf of all the mentally ill in a state's mental institutions, all the prisoners in the penitentiary, all the disabled, and so forth. We're no longer talking about "litigation between parties in personal actions." We talking about mass litigation between mass political constituencies.

But that's not all. In the last article, we heard Chief Justice Warren say in Brown II, "In fashioning and effectuating the [remedies for desegregation], the courts will be guided by equitable principles. … These cases call for the exercise of these traditional attributes of equity power." Now "equity power" is a court's power to order someone to do (or not to do) something. But what more precisely are the "guiding principles of equity," the "attributes of equity power?"

To put flesh on those bare bones, let's turn to *Corpus Juris Secundum*, a standard set of law books that across 164 volumes summarize all American law. Here with the usual density of legal prose is what the editors say, "Equity … adapts its relief and molds its decrees to satisfy the requirements of the case … its purpose is the accomplishment of justice amid all the vicissitudes and intricacies of life. … equity has always preserved the elements of flexibility and expansiveness so that new remedies may be invented or old ones modified to meet the requirements of every case ... In other words, the plastic remedies of equity are molded to the needs of justice ... and the flexibility of equitable jurisdiction permits innovation in remedies to meet all varieties of circumstances which may arise in any case. Moreover, the fact there is no precedent for the precise relief sought is no consequence."

Obviously, this fellow "Equity" packs a lot of muscle on his bones (has near super powers). He has "flexibility and expansiveness." He "may invent new remedies or modify old ones." His "remedies are plastic." He can "innovate remedies." His "purpose is the accomplishment of justice." With this superhero on their side, once the judges set out to "accomplish justice" (become convinced they're right), what can't this dynamic duo accomplish together? Together their powers appear almost limitless.

Then you've just heard described the "new model judicial supremacy," if you put the earlier cases from the prior articles together with these powers. Putting together all their powers, "the Constitution is what the judges say it is." As Lincoln said of the Dred Scott Case, "vital questions affecting the whole people [can be] irrevocably fixed by decisions of the Supreme Court, the instant they are made" by their re-interpretations of the Constitution. But their decisions are no longer "made in ordinary litigation between parties in personal actions." Rather, with class actions, the Court has acquired a power over mass political constituencies. With equitable remedies, the Court has acquired a power to order just about anything.

If as a result of the Dred Scott Case, Lincoln said, "the people will have ceased to be their own rulers, having to that extent practically resigned their government into the hands of that eminent tribunal," what would he say now? Now, to what "practical extent have the people ceased to be their own rulers?" To answer that question, on to the next article to see the new model judicial supremacy in action.

8.17 – In Action

A recent headline from May 26, 2016 reads, "62 years after Brown v. BOE [Board of Education], court orders schools to desegregate." Reading on, we learn a federal judge has just handed down this order to the folks in Cleveland, Mississippi. Perhaps more surprising, we learn this wasn't the first order to desegregate handed down to them by a federal judge. The case was originally filed way back in 1965, and over the years, several federal judges handed down desegregation orders. More than that, the school board had complied with all the prior orders. Perhaps as much, the schools seemed fairly good and the public, white or black, hadn't expressed much dissatisfaction. But the U.S. Department of Justice didn't share the satisfaction. The prior federal judges just ordered the children to attend the closest schools with an option to transfer to any school of their choice. Since whites lived on one side of "the tracks," and blacks on the other, that left the races still attending mostly separate schools. And the latest federal judge assigned to the case agreed with the DOJ. This new judge has now ordered all the schools consolidated so that whites and blacks will now attend the same schools. If you thought "desegregation in education" had run its course (no longer in action), you may need to think again.

Going back and tracing the history of this case is a good way to see the "new model judicial supremacy" in action, a good way to understand the Supreme Court's power as it has become. Under this new model, "the Constitution is what the judges say it is." No limits exist on the Court's power to interpret or reinterpret the Constitution. The justices can use a few words in the text such as "equal protection" to make and re-make national policy. Using class actions and equitable remedies, they can directly carry out their policies and run vast social programs across the whole nation. No limits exist either on the size of the classes, which can run into the millions or even assume a national size. Nor do any limits exist on the equitable remedies, which lets them order whatever they become convinced in the interests of justice and for however long. After all, over sixty years of court orders and still counting is a lot of court orders and a long time.

Brown v Board of Education back in 1954, sixty-two years before this recent case, created this new model. Brown held legal segregation unconstitutional as violating the "equal protection clause" of the 14th Amendment. That reversed the Court's prior decision in Plessy v Ferguson from 1896, the case that had written "separate but equal" into the Constitution, that is, authorized legal segregation. Thus, with Brown we see the first part of the new model judicial supremacy in action. The Court reinterprets a few words in the Constitution ("equal protection") to make new national policy, in fact, reversing their own prior policy. Next, it was time to see the second part of the new model in action, for the Court to use class actions and equitable remedies to carry out their new policy across the nation. In Brown II in 1955, we saw the Court order the lower federal courts to carry out desegregation ("to admit to public schools on a racially nondiscriminatory basis with all deliberate speed").

But wait. There was a crucial omission. What is "desegregation in education" anyway? That turns out a complex, not to mention contentious, question. With Brown, the Court had neglected to give an answer. And their later answers would fall between two stools. "De jure segregation" is legal segregation (ordered by law). "Desegregation in education" was able to take a firm seat against such laws. "De facto segregation" is any racial separation caused by the facts on the ground, particularly by the fact cultures tend to congregate separately, forming their own neighborhoods and communities. "Desegregation in education" has never been able to take as firm a seat against this cultural separation, although it's still trying and may ultimately succeed.

You can easily read Brown as no more than striking down legal (de jure) segregation (racial separation order by law). That's all the face of the case seems to say. In 1955, a federal appeals court handed down an opinion which was highly influential at the time, interpreting Brown exactly that way, "The Supreme Court ... has not decided that the states must mix persons of different races in the schools ... What it has decided, and all that it has decided, is that a state may not deny to any person on account of race the right to attend any school that it maintains. ... The Constitution, in other words, does not require integration. It merely forbids discrimination. It does not forbid such segregation as occurs as the result of voluntary action. It merely forbids the use of governmental power to enforce segregation."

On this reading, Brown canceled the laws that ordered segregation, but "did not require integration," that is, "racial mixing in the schools," doing away with racial separation however caused. Under this interpretation, children should attend schools where they lived, the neighborhood schools. Such a reading certainly grasped the easier handle. If a law ordered segregation, simply strike the offending language from the statute books. Brown drew a heavy stroke of the judicial pen across those very pages, which now stood mute and fading, testament to a bygone era.

Yet for whatever reasons, which not important for our story about the power of Supreme Court as it has become, a lot of civil rights activists and their public interest lawyers preferred another interpretation. They wanted to read Brown as "requiring integration," as requiring "racial mixing in the schools." They wanted not just to forbid de jure segregation (ordered by law), but to forbid de facto segregation, any racial separation in the schools, even when "the result of voluntary action." As a necessary corollary, they wanted not "merely to forbid the use of governmental power to enforce segregation," they wanted to use "governmental power" to force "integration," to "racially mix." As practical matter, they advocated such remedies as realigning school districts, and more controversially, massive busing. They didn't want just hands off, but hands on.

When we remember that Brown v Board of Education was based on "the equal protection clause" of the 14th Amendment, perhaps we begin to see how their demands called for a radical increase in governmental power and especially the power of the courts. The 14th Amendment merely reads, "No State shall make or enforce any law which shall … deny to any person … the equal protection of the laws." If you do away with the laws that order racial separation, how do you any longer have "state laws" to "deny to any person the equal protection?" Under their demands, that must not be enough. Rather than laws that didn't order racial separation, they wanted laws that ordered "racial mixing." They didn't want just to "forbid the use of governmental power to enforce segregation," they wanted to "use governmental power" to force "integration." There was no place in their scheme of things for any racial separation in the schools as a result of "voluntary action."

And so, we begin to see why their version of "desegregation in education" never rallied the same support as Brown's renunciation of legal segregation. Cultural groups naturally live together as a result of "voluntary action," as witness the renowned ethnic neighborhoods in American cities. At some past time, living together gave rise to culture in the first place, bonds running deep and lasting long, reacting strongly against dilution. Traditionally and naturally enough, children went to school near their homes, and uprooting that relationship touched more than one nerve. People wanted their children physically close, in schools just down the street, part of the community, where parents knew the local actors and had a voice, usually through elected school boards. That tradition tied into another American tradition, people being accustomed to conduct their affairs locally, quick to resent interference from higher ups, as quick to reflect their resentment at the ballot box. But we've run out of space and need to pick up the story in the next article.

8.18 – Still in Action

There's a little considered aspect of the present judicial supremacy. Since the Supreme Court has seized authority to finally interpret the Constitution, when the justices speak their final word, they render Congress mute. The law can never change until the Court decides, if ever, to change it. Back in 1896 with Plessy v Ferguson, we heard the Court speak such a final word, interpreting into the Constitution "separate but equal" (legal segregation). After that doleful word, Congress could no longer say anything (pass any laws) against segregation. But when in 1954 with Brown v Board of Education, the Court finally interpreted again, reversing itself and holding legal segregation unconstitutional, that finally took the muzzle off Congress. And Congress promptly responded by passing the Civil Rights Act of 1964, a landmark piece of legislation.

Thus, as one significant inconvenience, judicial supremacy forces change to wait on the delays of the law. When Congress makes a law, they can change it the next session or in the same session for that matter. When the Supreme Court makes a law, they can only make a change when and if another case comes up. Such a case may not arise for a long time or never.

For example, back in the 1976 case of Elrod v Burns, we saw the Supreme Court outlaw patronage, the hiring and firing of government employees on a partisan affiliation. Instead, the Court mandated a thoroughgoing civil service system, touted as hiring and promotion based on merit, termination only for cause. Recently, some commentators have advocated a change back to some patronage as a way to reinvigorate the political parties, which drew some of their lost vitality from the practice. But how could we ever change back, presuming we should? The legislative branch would have to pass a law in deliberate violation of the Court's prior ruling, the executive branch would have to hire some employees in deliberate violation on a partisan basis, and both would have to hope they won the ensuing case before the judicial branch. That's an awfully cumbersome way to change the laws, not to mention an awful risky way, opening the officials to the threat of monetary damages.

To come back to the main point, we need to come back to the Civil Rights Act of 1964. As previously seen, Brown v Board of Education had ordered "desegregation in education," but failed to define the term "desegregation." But the Court having spoken a new word, Congress could dare to speak its own new word, and they so dared with Civil Rights Act of 1964.

With this law they set up a program for desegregation in the public schools. The Act read, "'Desegregation' means the assignment of students to public schools and within such schools without regard to their race, color, religion, or national origin, but 'desegregation' shall not mean the assignment of students to public schools in order to overcome racial imbalance." Of major significance, it went on to say, "Nothing herein shall empower any official or court of the United States to issue any order seeking to achieve a racial balance in any school by requiring the transportation of pupils or students from one school to another or one school district to another in order to achieve such racial balance." As for the program to carry it out, Congress provided for lawsuits and funding cutoffs to school districts that failed to comply.

Reading carefully, we see Congress as carefully defined "desegregation in education." They condemned the "assignment of students to public schools" based on "race, color, religion, or national origin." But they also condemned "the assignment of students to overcome racial imbalance" and specifically condemned "the transportation of students to achieve such racial balance," that is, condemned busing. Congress had opted for "neighborhood schools." Children should go to school where they lived with the freedom to transfer around as wanted.

But under judicial supremacy, the Court still had the final word. And no need to follow this story in detail, since we already know the turn the plot now took. In a series of cases, the Supreme Court would hold constitutionally insufficient the Civil Rights Act of 1964. Rather, the justices would impose a more radical definition of "desegregation in education." They would rule that "equal protection of the laws" in the 14th Amendment required the "assignment of students to achieve racial balance" and the "transportation of students to achieve racial balance" (massive busing). In the coming years, thousands of school districts would be realigned and millions of students ride the bus to "integrate" ("racially mix").

All of which brings us back to the 2016 headline with which the last article began, "62 years after Brown v. BOE, court orders schools to desegregate." The whites and blacks in Cleveland, Mississippi, lived in largely separate neighborhoods. The children attended school in their neighborhoods and could transfer to the school of their choice. This looks entirely in line with the Civil Rights Act of 1964. Nor were the black schools inferior to the white, and no one really complaining, except the Department of Justice. Nevertheless, the federal judge ruled this situation not "desegregation in education" and ordered the schools consolidated to eliminate the racial separation.

Let's not go into the pros and cons of these competing definitions of "desegregation in education," the congressional versus the judicial version. What we want to understand is the Constitution as it has become and the powers of the Supreme Court as those have become. And what we see is the "new model judicial supremacy" is still very much in action. Under this new model, the Court interprets or reinterprets a few words in the Constitution, here "equal protection." Not only do they have the power to interpret those words anyway they want, they have the power to order massive social programs across the whole nation to conform to their interpretation.

Do you remember how this journey started? It started back in 1803 in Marbury v Madison with the Supreme Court pledging to protect the "original and supreme will" of the people as clearly expressed in the Constitution. The justices were going to defend the rights of the people as clearly expressed in the Constitution against the majority in Congress.

Do you see where we've arrived? Under the new model judicial supremacy, who is going to protect and defend the rights of the democratic majority of the people or the Congress either one against the majority on the Supreme Court? It all goes to prove a very old observation, "Whoever hath an absolute authority to interpret any spoken or written laws, it is he who is truly the lawgiver, to all intents and purposes, and not the person who first wrote or spoke them."

8.19 – The Bureaucratic Synergy

Neither the judges nor the bureaucrats are overly fond of the elected officials. The judges feel a need to keep the elected officials in their place, firmly under the judicial thumb. The bureaucrats resent being under the thumb of these same elected officials. While "the enemy of my enemy is my friend," and political alliances being what they are, recently the judges and the bureaucrats have often found it convenient to form alliances against the elected officials.

We've already watched how the judiciary constantly claims precedence over the elected officials. Conceiving themselves as the superior under "judicial supremacy," they don't mean to let their inferiors get above themselves, so constantly swat them down. The bureaucrats conceive of themselves just as highly, and being relegated as inferiors to the elected officials, constantly look for ways to avoid or escape their servitude.

Increasingly, in this connection, they, the bureaucrats, have come to realize being sued may not be such a bad thing. Let the public interest lawyers sue their agency. Let the judge rule their agency has failed to perform some constitutional duty, say to provide adequate care to the mentally ill or adequate housing to the inmates in the penitentiary. Let the judge take over and run their agency, supplanting the elected officials and running it up to the judge's constitutional standards. Their agency may have lost the lawsuit, but far from being handed a lemon, the bureaucrats often discover they've just been served lemonade, and the party has just begun.

During the twentieth century, they, the bureaucrats have vastly proliferated. After civil service reform in the late nineteenth century, they came to occupy virtual sinecures. Gathering in their growing enclaves, they did a great deal of useful work, but at the same time breeding the familiar "bureaucratic cultures." These cultures seldom failed to rationalize a need for bigger staffs and greater funding for their agencies. They as seldom failed to rationalize their motives as the very best. If they couldn't save the world, they longed to save more of it.

Who stood in the way of their doing these good things? Who but the elected officials, the legislature and the chief executive? Mindful of the unpopularity of bureaucratic schemes, the elected officials reined in the schemes. Mindful of the unpopularity of taxes, they rein in the costs of bureaucratic budgets.

But only let a federal judge take over their agency as a result of a lawsuit. It might look like the bureaucrats had done no more than exchange one master for another. But frequently, they found they had escaped servitude to a narrow-minded and miserly master and entered the service of a more open-minded and generous man, one after their own heart. Being unelected, the judge needed not concern himself with either the unpopularity or the costs. Frequently, their bureaucratic schemes for human progress appealed to him as much as to them, and as their pleasure grew in doing good, his pleasure grew to the same extent. Here was a master with the where-with-all to gratify the desires of his servants as well as himself, a man with a bottomless purse, and the more money his servants spent, the richer it made him, since all the expenses come out of someone else's pocket. Never mind the credit largely went to him. They were willing to take the cash and let the credit go.

Why did the judge's pleasures so frequently coincide with the bureaucrats' pleasures? The judge had confirmed his superiority by putting down those inferior elected officials again by taking their agency away from them. And the judge no longer just decided cases in the isolation of his chambers. He had made himself the center of the action. He ran things. He had surrounded himself with a little court of obsequious bureaucratic minions, eager to gratify his every whim and run his every errand. Nor should we forget the court's lawyerly retainers, who assist by filing the lawsuit and joining with the judge to supervise the agency, their reward a steady flow of rich fees paid from the public coffers. What can these three not accomplish together? Jilting the legislative and executive, the judiciary, the bureaucracy, and the lawyers form a more perfect union, replacing a clash of interests with a harmonious *ménage a trois*.

Nothing better illustrates how this bureaucratic synergy works than the Adams Case, filed in 1970 and going on for twenty years until 1990. This litigation generated from the discontent over the election of Richard Nixon to the presidency in 1968. During the campaign, Nixon had pursued a so-called "southern strategy," among other things promising to "cool off" the pace of desegregation in the public schools. If we will recall, the Civil Rights Act of 1964 had provided that the federal government could cut off funding to school districts that failed to comply. The federal agency assigned this task (HEW) was nothing loath to boss around the states and had shown a laudable zeal in cutting off the funds. But once installed as chief executive, Nixon used his authority over the agency to tighten their reins and slow their speed. In fairness to Nixon, we should add he denied opposing desegregation, insisting he was only opposed to the heavy handedness of the bureaucrats, which he argued was damaging to educational quality.

His policies excited considerable opposition within the bureaucracy, who of course, regarded themselves as warriors in an utterly just cause (racial desegregation). At HEW, the director, Leon Panetta, resigned in protest. On the day his successor was announced, 125 members of the staff, more than one-third the total, expressed their "bitter disappointment" in a letter to the president. Over at Department of Justice, 65 of the 100 lawyers in the Civil Rights Division signed a petition declaring the administration's action "inconsistent with clearly defined legal mandates." It was a classic instance of the bureaucrats chaffing at the authority of an elected official, here the president, over them.

The bureaucrats weren't the only ones upset. Enter the civil rights lawyers to file a lawsuit, alleging the president was violating the Constitution. A reliable source advises these lawyers were working "covertly with disaffected HEW bureaucrats." Next enter the local federal judge to find against the president and take over and run the program. This was the Adams Case, which as said, was filed in 1970 and went on for twenty years until 1990.

Before it was over, this case would reach national size. Rather than the president running the national program for desegregation outlined in the Civil Rights Act, the federal judge would run it. Rather than the president running his version, the federal judge would run his version. Rather than the president ordering funding cutoffs, the federal judge would order them. Rather than the executive branch running the bureaucratic agencies involved, the judicial branch ran them.

Nixon's alleged violation of the Constitution was perhaps more than a dubious claim. About cutting off federal funding, the Civil Rights Act of 1964 said, "Compliance ... *may be* effected ... by the termination of ... assistance." And "may" isn't "shall." That is, Congress has said the president "may" cut off funding to force compliance with school desegregation, not "shall." That clearly says the president can do it or not, or as much or little as he wants. It was up to his discretion. How can the president's acting within his discretion somehow violate the Constitution?

But never mind. For our purposes that's really almost beside the point. What we want to understand is the Constitution as it has become and the power of the judiciary as it has become. What we see in action is the fully developed new model judicial supremacy. Based upon a few words in the Constitution, a federal judge takes power over the national program for school desegregation. Using a class action, his orders run nationwide; using equitable remedies, he directly carries out his judicial program. In the final refinement, he takes over and runs a huge bureaucratic program, supplanting congressional or presidential management, the management of the elected officials, with his judicial management. All the pieces in place, the new model displays in a plentitude of judicial power.

Not only have the bureaucracy discovered that a federal lawsuit may come on them like a blessing in disguise, freeing them from their subservience to the elected officials. The federal judges have discovered such lawsuits allow the judiciary to develop a bureaucratic synergy, where the judges can use bureaucratic power to help along their judicial power. The Adams Case exemplifies such a bureaucratic and judicial embrace.

But while both parties come willingly to this union, the terms hardly amount to a modern marriage of gender equality, rather the old-fashioned patriarchal type, the bureaucratic bride pledging to honor and obey the judicial groom, so eager to escape the household of her legislative and executive parents, she eagerly pays the price of legal tutelage to a judicial husband.

8.20 – Inside the Temple

The U.S. Supreme Court didn't have its own building until 1935, instead being crowded into the Capitol with Congress. But in 1929, then Chief Justice William Howard Taft, incidentally the only chief justice also to serve as president, from 1909 to 1913, finally persuaded Congress to appropriate the funds for a separate building to separate the two branches physically as well as functionally.

Back in that day, America still preferred her public buildings in an impressive, neo-classical style, and whoever visits the Supreme Court Building will admit the architect rather let himself go along those lines. According to the Court's own website, "The building was designed on a scale in keeping with the importance and dignity of the Court and the Judiciary." Apparently, that "importance and dignity" called for something on the order of a Greek temple. Everywhere the visitor looks, one sees soaring marble columns and over the top iconography. Over the west front façade appear in huge letters the words, "Equal Justice Under the Law." Over the east pediment, "Justice, the Guardian of Liberty." Who cannot but be overwhelmed with the dignity and the majesty of what quickly came to be called the Marble Temple?

But we don't want to fail to go inside the temple. We've seen that the Supreme Court's great and famous cases all have two sides, the surface, where they talk about high ideals, and the other side (the power side), where the power moves and always toward the Court. The outside of their temple resembles the surface of their cases, all about the high ideals. But if you look around inside, you'll find the other side (the power side). Engraved in marble you'll find these words which come, as they say, from the famous case of Marbury v Madison, a case visited in some detail in the prior articles.

"IT IS EMPHATICALLY THE
PROVINCE AND DUTY OF
THE JUDICIAL DEPARTMENT
TO SAY WHAT THE LAW IS."
MARBURY v. MADISON
1803

But notice the words quoted thus in isolation somewhat distort the meaning of the case. Marbury v Madison stood for the proposition the Supreme Court had the power of judicial review to declare congressional laws unconstitutional and hence void. But the doctrine came with a severe limitation. The Court could only do so in "clear-cut" cases. Since not much about the Constitution clear-cut, this original limitation left this judicial power highly restrained. But when you take the quoted words out of context, it makes it sound like the Court has the power "to say what the law is" with neither limits nor restraints.

Indeed, that describes what the Court has pulled off, starting with that very case of Marbury v Madison in 1803. The justices have always claimed to act on the noble slogans outside their building. "Equal Justice Under the Law. Justice, the Guardian of Liberty." They write such words on the surface of their cases. But in the name of these noble slogans, on the other side of their cases (the power side) they have constantly exalted the motto engraved inside their building. By so doing, they have gradually seized the power "to say what the law is" with no limits or restraints any longer attached.

Such describes the present awesome powers the Supreme Court has gradually acquired. Today, as we have seen, "the Constitution is what the justices say it is." As we have also seen, "Whoever hath an absolute authority to interpret any spoken or written laws, it is he who is truly the lawgiver, to all intents and purposes, and not the person who first wrote or spoke them."

To summarize those present powers: 1) The Court may void congressional laws at will; 2) The Court may ignore or change the clear meaning of the Constitution itself; 3) The judiciary may order and directly carry out vast social programs across the whole nation; 4) The judiciary may directly control bureaucratic agencies and programs; and 5) The judiciary may even order taxation.

What's most sacred to the Supreme Court? "By their deeds you shall know them." Their deeds worship not so much the noble slogans on the outside of their building as the motto on the inside. Inside the Marble Temple, they worship nothing so much as their own judicial power. In these articles, we have seen how they have constantly distorted the noble slogans to serve their power.

This record recounts a remarkable ascent to power. Let us frankly admit our situation and come to understand the Constitution as it has become. Let us no longer accept the lawyerly evasions and misrepresentations. Let us understand that the Court has succeeded in transforming the very nature of the Constitution. The Constitution was all about power to the people (democracy). Today, the judicial aristocracy rules over much of the national agenda.

8.21 – When They Did Better

Hamilton says in *Federalist No. 72*, "The best security for the fidelity of mankind is to make their interest coincide with their duty." When it comes to the Supreme Court, we've seen their interest didn't coincide with their duty, and so their fidelity wasn't secured. Their duty was to defend the Constitution, which meant above all defend democracy, the people's right to self-government. But the Court's interest was to acquire more power for itself. Human all too human, the justices stayed faithful to their interests and betrayed their duty, while all the time denying what they did, claiming to defend the Constitution. Gradually, they interpreted the Constitution to acquire more and more power for themselves, taking away more and more power from the people. By today, rather than the American people governing themselves in their own interests, they are much ruled over by the Court (by the judicial aristocracy in their own interests).

But in one specialized way, the Court's interest did coincide with their duty. When it came to defending "the due process of the law," the one marched with the other. Since due process consists mainly in the rights to careful legal procedures, and since the legal profession, including the judges, make much of their living by running such procedures and so protecting such rights, here their interest called a cadence that kept them in step with their duty. As a result, the Supreme Court and the judiciary as a whole did better when it came to protecting the due process of the law. Nor has this conferred an inconsiderable benefit on the people.

The 5th Amendment ratified in 1791 and the 14th Amendment ratified in 1868 both guarantee against the taking "of life, liberty, or property without due process of law." As correctly understood, this guarantee relates mainly to the procedural (the processes of the) law rather than the substantive law. In legal parlance, the "substantive laws" are the substance of the law, say the law that makes murder a crime or the law of intestate succession as to who inherits in the absence of a will. The "procedural laws" are the procedures to carry out the substantive laws, say a jury trial to determine guilt or innocence or the probate of an estate to determine the heirs. Having in mind that "due process of law" refers to procedure in the courts, we can begin to see what the "due process clause" in the 5th and 14th Amendments meant to guarantee.

Over the long history of Anglo-American law, a number of careful legal procedures were developed to protect the people's rights. The Constitution specifically guarantees several of the best known and most important. Article I, Sec. 9 says, "The privilege of the Writ of Habeas Corpus shall not be suspended." This ancient protection of the English common law lets anyone held in custody force the authorities to bring him into court and show a lawful cause for their detention. That may not sound like a big deal, but effectively prevents arbitrary arrest followed by indefinite detention, a practice near and dear to the hearts of autocratic regimes. Even when the arrest lawful, the 8th Amendment says, "Excessive bail may not be required," preventing the authorities from using minor charges as an excuse to lock up people for extended periods while awaiting trial. Some other specific guarantees are "the right to a speedy and public trial, by an impartial jury," the right "to be informed of the nature and cause of the accusation," the right "to be confronted with the witnesses against him," the right "to have compulsory process for obtaining witnesses in his favor," and the right "to have Assistance of Counsel," all in the 6th Amendment. Nor should we neglect to mention the right "against unreasonable searches and seizures" in the 4th Amendment and the right against self-incrimination ("to take the fifth" as in the 5th Amendment).

But there's no complete list written down in the Constitution or anywhere else. In general terms, the Supreme Court has said in a 1985 case, "The Due Process Clause provides that certain substantive rights – life, liberty, and property – cannot be deprived except pursuant to constitutionally adequate procedures." In another, earlier case in 1970, they said, "The fundamental requisite of due process of law is the opportunity to be heard," which requires timely and adequate notice of the government's action and an effective opportunity to defend, confront adverse witnesses, and present one's own evidence and arguments.

Whatever touches "life, liberty, or property," which arguably just about anything the government does, requires "due process" (a notice and a hearing). All of which should make it easy to see why "due process" a favorite refrain with the judges and the lawyers. Due process confers on the judges a vast, supervisory power over all the other government officials; at the same time, it raises up a vast and profitable business for the lawyers. No wonder they love it. Indeed, some might say almost too well. Under their influence, due process has grown like all their other powers, until we're almost overgrown with due process. Today, so much notice and so many hearings are required as almost to delay and cripple the courts and the government from getting through their business with any expedition.

Yet if in medieval times the saying was that "town air makes free men" due to the legal rights people enjoyed in the towns, today, we might say a similar thing about due process. If we still breath free air in this country, the due process of the law guarded by an "independent judiciary" deserves much of the credit. If we can have too much of a good thing, yet we should hesitate to conclude we breath too much of the free air of due process.

Notice, too, that the "due process of law" guarantees two of the requirements for "the rule of law." We earlier saw the rule of law requires three things – clearly stated laws, clearly established and fair legal procedures, and equal protection of the laws. Due process guarantees the first two requirements– clearly stated laws and clearly established and fair legal procedures. The 14th Amendment "equal protection clause" guarantees the third requirement.

Anyone caught up in the toils of American courts may have cause to rue the day. They should have a sign outside every courthouse. LAWYER ZONE – ENTER WITH CAUTION. Few except the lawyers exit without paying a price, not just in money, but in agony of mind. Uneasy lays the head with a lawsuit hanging over it. Yet you would be hard put to find another legal system that so carefully protects your life, your liberty, and your property.

What they did best was take power, but when they did better, they protected the due process of the law.

9.00 – THE BUREAUCRACY

9.01 – A Modern Marvel

Remember Hurricane Katrina back in late August, 2005? Remember the natural disaster, followed by the human disaster, followed by the disaster of the disaster relief? As one journalist put it, "Hurricane Katrina crashed into Mississippi and Louisiana with unbridled fury, and by nearly every account, the federal response was an abject failure. It's hard to imagine how the Department of Homeland Security, the sprawling colossus that was supposed to have made the country safer, could have failed so spectacularly."

But no, it's not "hard to imagine." The Department of Homeland Security ranks as a bureaucracy, and the ranks of the bureaucracy have many a time "failed so spectacularly," but usually they fail more quietly, since they prefer the quiet. Bureaucrats don't aspire to costar as the foils with those star reporters on *60 Minutes* or *Dateline*. To their way of thinking, out of sight is out of mind. They prefer to pull down their sufficient salaries, never miss a day of their ample vacation time, not work too hard in the meantime, and not draw too much attention to themselves. If the Marine Corps motto is *semper fi* (always faithful), the bureaucratic motto might be "always faithful to our quiet comforts." Quietly pursuing these comforts, the ranks of the bureaucracy have often as quietly failed to do their duty.

But while that's true enough, in fairness we should start with bureaucracy at the other end. We should start by recalling that modern bureaucracy a modern marvel. What's that you say? Absolutely. Bureaucracy may sometimes fail, but more routinely succeeds. But just like bad news outsells good news, no one tends to notice their successes. But let's notice.

The way America cooks today, the bureaucrats have a finger in every pie. People disparage this cook, but can't get enough of his cooking. How many millions of checks does the SSA mail out every month to the right address and on time? That bread feeds a lot of budgets. How about the money itself (the monetary supply)? Who mixes those ingredients if not the FED? Their dough spends pretty good. While if you want gourmet fare, what about NASA? Sending a man to the moon or the Hubble Telescope is the icing on the cake. The alphabet soup goes on and on, as does the sustenance served up. Think DOD (defense), DOJ (justice), DOT (highways), FDA (food quality), EPA (water quality).

A modern American standard of living is unimaginable without the successes of a modern bureaucracy. Bureaucrats might complain as victims of their own success. They've done so much for so many for so long, they're expected to do everything for everyone and right now. Yet over Katrina, FEMA failed spectacularly and noisily, and the quiet failures may turn out just as spectacular, only since they don't make much noise, we don't hear about them or not until too late. "What I know concerns me. What I don't know concerns me even more. What people aren't telling me worries me the most." A hurricane makes a big noise, but no one hears a drip in a cavern unless they go down there. But a steady drip can wear away solid rock. What might the bureaucrats' quiet failures be wearing away beneath our feet? We better descend beneath the quiet and check them out. Except down there are caverns measureless to man.

One count had the bureaucracy occupying 2.6 billion square feet of office space, four times as large as all the office space in the ten largest cities. Beneath such a vast structure, how locate a small leak before the leak turns into a flood? Then, too, vast reaches of the structure have been made deliberately hard of access, since the bureaucratic occupants don't want to be disturbed. How get back into their hidden recesses to search for leaks? Then how measure what leaking away? How measure laziness, putting it off, passing it down the line, not making a decision, or evading responsibility? They signed the sign-in sheet, didn't they? They put in their eight hours a day, forty hours a week. They moved the paperwork from the in-basket to the out-basket. But how measure the actual quality or efficiency of their work?

Take a prominent example that has to make one wonder about

the quiet leaks. In 2009, the headlines announced that Bernard L. Madoff had been sentenced to 150 years in prison for running the biggest Ponzi scheme ever, the size of the fraud running perhaps as high as $65 billion. In the story behind the headlines, we learned Madoff had operated his scheme for over twenty years in one of the most highly regulated sectors of the economy, the securities markets. Why did the regulators, the bureaucrats over at the Securities and Exchange Commission, take so long to catch him? Madoff himself confessed in an interview that he found it "inconceivable" that the SEC ignored tips on him and that he "was astonished" their investigators didn't find him out sooner. The SEC's internal investigation found that "the SEC received more than ample information in the form of detailed and substantive complaints over the years to warrant a thorough and comprehensive examination and/or investigation of Bernard Madoff ... for operating a Ponzi scheme, and despite three examinations and two investigations being conducted, a thorough and competent investigation or examination was never performed." The SEC is one of the most important bureaucracies regulating the financial sector. If they didn't detect a leak as flagrant as Madoff for twenty years, what other leaks might they not detect until way too late?

The Founders gave not much thought to bureaucracy, which in their day counted for not much. In 1789, the First Congress saw a need for only three executive departments (State, Treasury, and War). George Washington supervised only some 3,000 officials. Two centuries later, President George W. Bush looked out over agencies in the hundreds with well over two million civilian employees. In sheer size this huge "fourth branch" has come to totally overtop the others. Thus, today we face a problem the Founding Fathers never had to face. How assure the accountability and efficiency of this huge bureaucracy (the fourth branch)? Modern bureaucracy a modern marvel, but it's also a modern problem. We want the routine successes, but not the spectacular (Katrina like) failures or the drip, drip, drip (like over Madoff). The question is how we can have the one without the other (the feast without the famine).

9.02 – Never Believe

One of those things we're told never to believe is, "I'm from the government and I'm here to help you." But the government seems determined to help us more and more. While frankly, our grumbling seems not so much over their help, but rather that it came not soon enough or sufficient enough, not up to our exacting standards and soaring expectations. So what we should really believe is the government will just keep getting bigger, since to help more and more, it will have to keep getting bigger. Both sides (the government and we, the public) are really pushing in the same direction.

Accepting that belief would go a long way to explain the relentless rise of the bureaucracy, since to say government gets bigger is really to say the bureaucracy gets bigger. The House of Representatives hasn't gotten bigger since 1911, when a law set the size at 435 members. The Senate hasn't gotten bigger since 1959, when the admission of Hawaii as our fiftieth state set the size at 100 senators. There's never been more than one president. Nine justices have sat on the Supreme Court since 1869, when a law set the size. What has grown is the bureaucracy. A recent, but probably by now out-of-date count, tallied some 2,600,000 bureaucrats, up from about 3,000 in 1789.

What drove this growth? The bureaucrats drove their own growth. As already said, they're determined to help more, and political scientists even have a term for their determination – "budget maximization." To help more, they need more of everything, more staffing, more facilities, more programs, and more of everything requires ever more money in their budgets (budget maximization). But at the same time, we, the public, drove their growth. We want more of everything from the government, instant gratification of our every need and desire.

Modernity drove the growth as well. Modern technology drove the growth. Invent the radio and you need an agency to allocate the bandwidths. Invent the airplane and you need an agency to man the control towers and coordinate the flight plans. Modern size and complexity drove the growth. As the modern economy became nationwide and interconnected with the Industrial Revolution, we needed a bunch of agencies to manage the economy, say to prevent monopolies or regulate the stock exchange. We needed a central bank to manage the monetary supply (the FED). Modern demographics drove the growth. When people moved from down on the farm to the cities, they became much less self-sufficient, needing all sorts of government services, such as highways and parks, water and sewers, gas and electricity. Great modern events drove the growth. To fight World War I and II and the Cold War, we needed huge agencies to coordinate the economic and military effort. The rise of the modern welfare state drove the growth, adding still more bureaucrats to deal with poverty, medical care, retirement, and disability. Modern demands for social and racial justice drove the growth, leading to still more bureaucracies, such as the EEOC (the Equal Employment Opportunity Commission).

Bureaucrats grew not just by the numbers, but in authority and discretion. Just their greater numbers were one reason. Washington could fairly directly supervise some 3,000 bureaucrats, but a modern president has to manage in the millions. This growing size forced the delegation of authority downward to the bureaucrats to manage themselves. In Washington's day, a bureaucrat described basically a clerk, who did such routine tasks as keep ledgers or issue vouchers. In more modern times, bureaucrats came to carry out numerous complex and ongoing tasks. Think of the DOD (Department of Defense). Think of the weapons systems the DOD bureaucrats must acquire (everything from rifles to nuclear missiles), the logistics they must manage (everything from soldiers' rations to the fuel for nuclear submarines), the facilities they must maintain (everything from the Pentagon to hundreds of overseas bases). Such tasks have forced the delegation of a great deal of authority down the line, empowering the bureaucrats.

We're beginning to come to what folks really mean when they say, "never believe I'm from the government and I'm here to help you." To help us more and more, we've asked the government to do more and more. In the process, we've had to give the bureaucrats more and more authority and discretion to do it. But all too often, they've used their greater authority and discretion neither too wisely nor too well. Rather than helping more, they've often neglected their tasks. Coming to interfere more often, they've more often badly interfered, messed things up, and gotten in the way.

Why would that be? Whenever we look carefully into it, we find the same old thing. We find a neglect of that golden word in government – accountability. We find we've neglected to properly design our bureaucratic institutions so as to hold them accountable to us. What happens next is what always happens whenever there's such a neglect. The government officials, this time the bureaucrats, start leading comfortable lives and doing little or shoddy work. They start gaming the system to help themselves rather than helping us.

Never believe that the government is not going to keep getting bigger. So never believe that the bureaucracy is not going to keep getting bigger. Their interests drive the growth. They want more of everything. Our interests drive the growth. We want more of everything. Everything about modernity drives the growth. The bureaucracy is not only here to stay, but is going to steadily grow. That leaves just one real question. Can we design our bureaucratic institutions to stay accountable to us? If not, we're won't stay in control of them, rather they're going to get in control of us. When that happens, we'll be right never to believe, "I'm from the government and I'm here to help you."

9.03 – All Other Officers

The tale of our American bureaucracy begins with some words in the Constitution, and once again, a tale about our constitutional law begins with some vague wording. In the very First Congress in 1789, these particular words caused a dispute about the president's power over the bureaucrats. Settled at the time in what seemed a commonsense and satisfactory way, the same dispute would surface again during Reconstruction right after the Civil War. Finally, in a 1926 case, the Myers Case, the Supreme Court stepped in and seemingly settled the meaning once and for all. But not really, since our bureaucratic tale would later take some other surprising turns.

Article II contains the particular words underlying the institutional structure of our bureaucracy, our presently huge fourth branch. Among the list of the president's powers, we read, "He shall … nominate, and by and with the Advice and Consent of the Senate, shall appoint … all other Officers of the United States whose Appointments are not herein otherwise provided for, and which shall be established by Law: but the Congress may by Law vest the Appointment of such inferior Officers, as they think proper, in the President alone."

The Constitution says virtually nothing else about "the other officers" or "the inferior officers," in other words, the bureaucracy. Nor when we read carefully do these few words say much except for two things. First, the president has the power to appoint them with the consent of the Senate ("He shall … nominate, and by and with the Advice and Consent of the Senate, shall appoint … all other Officers … whose Appointments are not herein otherwise provided for, and which shall be established by Law"). Second, "Congress may be Law vest the Appointment of such inferior Officers, as they think proper, in the President alone" with no need for Senate approval.

These words might seem clear enough, seeming to put the president over the bureaucrats. He has the power to appoint them. But turn it around and ask, all right, the president can appoint them, but can he unappoint (remove them from office)? In the First Congress in 1789, that question caused some serious controversy. At least when the consent of the Senate was required for their appointment, some senators thought such consent should be required for their removal as well.

Their argument rested on the doctrine of the separation of powers and system of checks and balances. If the Senate could deny their consent for the removal of an official, that would amount to another legislative check upon presidential power. But James Madison, who sat in the House and was urged on by President Washington, successfully turned this argument against itself. He argued that the separation of powers should prevent such congressional meddling with the chief executive. In the debate, he said, "If there is a principle in our Constitution … more sacred than another, it is that which separates the Legislative, Executive and Judicial powers. If there is any point in which the separation of the Legislative and Executive powers ought to be maintained with great caution, it is that which relates to officers and offices." In other words, if the chief executive couldn't remove the officers in the executive branch without the consent from the Senate, that would mix together the executive and legislative branches, violating the separation of powers. And at the time, Madison's counter-argument fairly easily carried the day. The record shows that, "The question was now taken and carried, by a considerable majority, in favor of declaring the power of removal to be in the President."

Madison's argument just made common sense. As Chief Justice Taft would later say in that case previously mentioned, the Myers Case in 1926, "The reason for the principle is that those in charge of and responsible for administering functions of government who select their executive subordinates need, in meeting their responsibility, to have the power to remove those whom they appoint." He went on, "The vesting of the executive power in the President was essentially a grant of the power to execute the laws. But the President, alone and unaided, could not execute the laws. He must execute them by the assistance of subordinates." The opposite rule, "by fastening upon him, as subordinate executive officers, men who, by their inefficient service under him, by their lack of loyalty to the service, or by their different views of policy, might make his taking care that the laws be faithfully executed most difficult or impossible." Taft was our only chief justice who also served as president, before becoming chief justice. No doubt he knew whereof he spoke.

Accepting Madison's argument, the First Congress in setting up the bureaucracy in 1789 gave the president the power to remove any officer and without Senate approval. The question seemed settled. But right after the Civil War, the Congress, which was controlled by the Radical Republicans, had a serious falling out with President Andrew Johnson over how to run Reconstruction. Famously, Congress went so far as to impeach the president for the first time in our history, although unsuccessfully. But as a less famous part of this episode, Congress also passed the Tenure of Office Act in 1867, which took away the president's power to remove officers appointed with the advice and consent of the Senate. The purpose was to prevent Johnson from removing cabinet officers, and especially the Secretary of War, Edwin Stanton, who had sided with the Radical Republicans against the president over Reconstruction. Johnson vetoed the law, but

Congress re-passed it over his veto.

What a strange law, which effectively left the president not able to control his cabinet even though he stayed responsible for their performance. No need to follow this story any farther, but only to fast forward to 1926 and the Myers Case again. In that case, the Supreme Court finally got around to declaring this law unconstitutional. Chief Justice Taft wrote, "the Tenure of Office Act of 1867, insofar as it attempted to prevent the President from removing executive officer who had been appointed by him by and with the advice and consent of the Senate, was invalid, and that subsequent legislation of the same effect was equally so." In other words, the president possessed the power to remove them, and Congress could not constitutionally take away his power.

Then we might start to think that case concluded our bureaucratic tale. We might start to think that presidents have the power to remove the bureaucrats. We might think they can hire and fire them at-will, whoever they want, whenever they want. We might think that leaves the presidents owning and running the bureaucratic shop. But turns out such thoughts would carry the tale only as far 1926 when the Meyers Case handed down.

Because right in this same timeframe, our bureaucratic tale began to take some unforeseen and surprising turns. Facing modern circumstances, Congress began to re-design the bureaucracy in more modern ways. And as so often with our constitutional tale, rather than the plot becoming clearer, the plot thickened. As this tale unfolds, the president not only loses a great deal of his earlier power over the bureaucracy, but the bureaucracy will acquire a great more power all their own outside presidential control.

To understand the bureaucracy as it has become, we need to turn to these re-designs of the bureaucratic structure. Once again, the Constitution as it has become will turn out near unrecognizable from the original words.

9.04 – Humphrey's Executor

Few have heard of William E. Humphrey, who served as a member of the Federal Trade Commission from 1925 to 1933. But a famous case memorializes him, and students of constitutional law all know the case. Humphrey himself died before the Supreme Court finally handed down the opinion (you've heard of the laws delays), and the executor of his estate being substituted as a party gave the case the formal caption - Humphrey's Executor v United States (1935). The decision conceals a story of some significance about our bureaucracy as it has become and our Constitution as it has become.

Justice George Sutherland, on the Court from 1922 to 1938, wrote the opinion and begins with the facts. "William E. Humphrey, the decedent, on December 10, 1931, was nominated by President Hoover [a Republican] ... as a member of the Federal Trade Commission, and was confirmed by the United States Senate. He was duly commissioned for a term of seven years expiring September 25, 1938." However, on October 7, 1933, some five years before his term expired, the new president, Franklin Roosevelt [a Democrat], wrote him a letter that read, "Effective as of this date, you are hereby removed from the office of Commissioner of the Federal Trade Commission." But "Humphrey ... continued thereafter to insist that he was still a member of the commission, entitled to perform its duties and receive the compensation provided by law at the rate of $10,000 per annum." Eventually before his decease, he sued for his salary, thus making up the case.

What's going on here? In the last article, we visited the Myers Case in 1926, where the Court affirmed in ringing tones the president's power to remove "any officer" confirmed by the Senate. Humphrey "was confirmed by the United States Senate." Why didn't he think President Roosevelt could hand him his walking papers?

That question leads back to Federal Trade Commission Act of 1917, which brought into being the FTC. This law said, "That unfair methods of competition in commerce are hereby declared unlawful." And, "The commission is hereby empowered and directed to prevent ... unfair methods of competition in commerce." Not to go into the specifics of what defined as "unfair methods of competition," which rather complex, Congress gave the FTC extensive powers to issue cease and desist orders, levy fines, and bring cases in the courts.

413

As for makeup of the Commission, the Act "creates a commission of five members to be appointed by the President by and with the advice and consent of the Senate," who "shall be appointed for terms of seven years" with staggered terms so not all the members came up for re-appointment at the same time. So far nothing should sound new or unusual.

But the Act went on to say, "any commissioner may be removed by the President for inefficiency, neglect of duty, or malfeasance in office." In others words, in the Act, the Congress had limited the president's usual powers of removal, since he could only remove "for inefficiency, neglect of duty, or malfeasance in office" (couldn't remove them at-will, but only for cause). But in his letter terminating Humphrey, the president had given no such "for cause" reason, rather merely informing him, "I do not feel that your mind and my mind go along together on either the policies or the administering of the Federal Trade Commission."

Why did Congress want to limit the president's power to remove the commissioners? The debates in Congress show they wanted to create an "independent agency." With a traditional "executive agency," the president had the power to hire and fire the agency staff, giving him effective control over the agency. But with this newer type (the "independent agency"), a board or commission runs the agency. The president appoints them, but the members then serve for set terms, and they're only removable for cause. This limitation leaves the president effectively not able to control the agency, leaving the agency "independent."

Why would Congress want to create such a new type of the bureaucratic creature? The underlying aspiration seeks to take the partisanship out and leave the experts in. To hopefully accomplish this transformation, Congress writes the law and turns the enforcement over to a board or commission of experts, who supposedly do nothing except enforce the law. To quote from the congressional debates, "The commission is to be nonpartisan, and it must, from the very nature of its duties, act with entire impartiality. It is charged with the enforcement of no policy except the policy of the law." And, "the Congressional intent [was] to create a body of experts who shall gain experience by length of service -- a body which shall be independent of executive authority except in its selection, and free to exercise its judgment without the leave or hindrance of any other official or any department of the government."

Then you get the idea. But to pretend that this new type of bureaucratic offspring (an "independent agency") a gleam in the eye of the Founding Fathers imagines way too much. They never conceived of such a creature as an "independent" bureaucrat outside the president's control. They provided for no such bureaucrat with the Constitution. Moreover, in the earlier 1926 Meyers Case, we heard the Supreme Court declare in no uncertain terms that Congress could not take away the president's power to remove executive officers. Then how can this new type of bureaucracy pass the test as constitutional?

But as so often happens, when a legal rule turns out inconvenient, the Court crafts a convenient legal exception. Justice Sutherland creates the exception right before our eyes with his opinion, saying, "The authority of Congress, in creating [bureaucratic] agencies, to require them to act in discharge of their duties independently of executive control cannot well be doubted, and that authority includes, as an appropriate incident, power to fix the period during which they shall continue in office, and to forbid their removal except for cause in the meantime. For it is quite evident that one who holds his office only during the pleasure of another cannot be depended upon to maintain an attitude of independence against the latter's will."

If the case of Humphrey's Executor didn't give birth to a new sort of bureaucracy (Congress did that by passing the law), yet the Court just baptized the infant. Thus was brought to constitutional life the "independent agency" (independent of the chief executive, the president). And over the years, Congress has brought into being a great many more such progeny. To name a few in this now illustrious line, the Federal Reserve (the FED), the Environmental Protection Agency (EPA), the Federal Communications Commission (FCC), the Federal Election Commission (FEC), the National Labor Relations Board (NLRB), the Securities and Exchange Commission (SEC), the Social Security Administration (SSA), the Securities and Exchange Commission (SEC), and the Nuclear Regulatory Commission (NRC).

So now you've heard of William E. Humphrey if you hadn't before. He made history if only posthumously. His case established the constitutional status of independent agencies outside the president's control.

But was such a creature a good thing or a bad thing? Like so many other constitutional innovations, it was probably a mixed blessing. On the one hand, sometimes it may make good sense to remove an item from the partisan agenda and turn it over to some experts to run according to the laws laid down by Congress. On the other hand, you want to be careful what you remove and how you do it. You want to be careful how much power you give away and not to give away all accountability. Let's consider these further issues in the further articles.

9.05 – The Dirty Word

In an early instance of political correctness back around 1900, the progressive reformers of that era made "patronage" a dirty word. Instead, you had to say "civil service." But if patronage developed a seamy side, it started out with some real virtues and never lost all virtue. Nor did civil service turn out a paragon of all the virtues either. As so often happens, the reformers' zeal and their idealism carried them and their reform too far.

Boiling away the bad taste left by the progressives' propaganda, a patronage system was nothing more than bureaucrats who served "at-will." The chief executive could hire and fire them, whom he wanted, when he wanted. And this lack of job security conferred on them a basic virtue. They stayed accountable to the people, if by one step removed. Whom one can hire and fire, one can control. Since the president was accountable through elections, the bureaucrats were accountable through him. As James Madison would sum up this issue in a debate in the First Congress in 1789, "If the President should possess alone the power of removal from office, those who are employed in the execution of the law will be in their proper situation, and the chain of dependence be preserved, the lowest officers, the middle grade, and the highest, will depend, as they ought, on the President, and the President on the community."

The virtue of this logic made good sense to the Founding Fathers. They wrote patronage into the Constitution while not using the actual word. Article II says, "He [the President] shall ... nominate, and by and with the Advice and Consent of the Senate, shall appoint ... all other Officers of the United States whose Appointments are not herein otherwise provided for, and which shall be established by Law: but the Congress may by Law vest the Appointment of such inferior Officers, as they think proper, in the President alone." In other words, as we saw in an earlier article, although the Senate might have a say on who was appointed, they president could remove whoever he wanted. While "with such inferior officers as they think proper," Congress could vest both the appointment and removal "in the president alone." And they very soon did that with almost all except the top jobs, not having the time themselves to supervise the hiring and firing of all the lower level bureaucrats.

However, their logic failed to account for the rise of political parties, which not mentioned in the Constitution since not foreseen. But patronage fit with party politics like hand in glove, and the party politicians quite soon figured out the fit. When filling the some 3,000 places available under the new government, Washington stressed ability over faction, helped by the fact real political parties didn't yet exist. Yet even Washington favored men who shared his views, men who were gravitating toward the emerging Federalist Party. But already by 1801, when Thomas Jefferson (Democrat-Republican) carried out the first hostile takeover of the presidency by defeating the sitting Federalist president, John Adams, the election was as much between the parties as the candidates and as bitter between both. In an obvious coincidence, the occasion also witnessed the first large scale use of patronage as a party device. Finding the bureaucracy filled with Adams' Federalist friends, Jefferson replaced many with his Democratic-Republican friends.

In the election of 1828, Democrat Andrew Jackson soundly beat another Adams (John Quincy). Although careful studies reveal that during his two terms and eight years in office, Ole Hickory replaced no more than one-fifth the bureaucrats and perhaps nearer a tenth, yet patronage began to pick up a negative connotation. His foes hammered relentlessly away at "King Andrew," one of their accusations being he was feeding his Democratic mobocracy with public jobs. Look, they cried out in indignation, see virtuous and unoffending merit departing the halls of government, cast out in the cold to reward these political hacks. Senator William L. Marcy (D, NY) didn't help matters when in a speech defending his chief, he made the frank remark, "to the victor go the spoils." The other side turned the phrase against him, and the label "spoils system" stuck to patronage ever after.

But Abraham Lincoln, a still beloved president, wielded the bloodiest patronage ax. Arriving in Washington in early 1861, he found the bureaucracy a nest of Copperhead Democrats, many actively Confederate in sympathy, some suspected of actual spying and sabotage. Lincoln promptly decapitated the snakes, separating from their offices a whopping 89 percent of direct presidential appointees (1,457 out of the 1,639). Nothing daunted by this decimation, the Republican Party faithful stepped forward with eager courage, ready to fill the gaps in the ranks and turning the bureaucracy into a solid Republican phalanx. Lincoln's use of patronage remains the most profound of any president and graphically illustrates that basic virtue of presidential control. How fight and win the Civil War working through a lukewarm and obstructive bureaucracy?

Patronage showed other virtues, too. Patronage excited popular participation and bound together the parties. People hoped for a government job like postman, or better yet postmaster, and once on the payroll, feared to lose the paycheck. With this incentive, they joined the party, gave their time and money, went to precinct meetings and conventions, crowded the marches and rallies, and voted for the party. Today, the editorial writers never cease to bemoan voter apathy and low turnout. Such complaints were much less heard when patronage still motivated the rank and file. And patronage gave party leaders sticks and carrots, ways to manage the party, not always a bad thing, if leadership sometimes a good thing.

But whether or not Americans have any genius for politics, "the business of America is business." Somewhere along the line, some keen-eyed entrepreneurs conceived a merger. They came up with a scheme to turn politics into a business run at the public expense. This hybrid turned local party organizations into "machines" under "bosses," who used patronage as their lubricant. The bosses oiled the party workers (ward heelers and so forth) with patronage jobs.

In turn, the workers oiled the machine by donating back a share of their salaries and cranking out the vote by manning the levers of the organization.

In some cities, this not so subtle contraption performed only too well, virtually taking over the municipal governments. At which point the bosses, having replaced a true democratic process with a business they controlled, found themselves ruling virtually unchecked. And giving into the temptation, they started adulterating the product to further milk the profits. Rather than sticking to the legitimate side of the business, they expanded into an illicit side. They handed out public projects to their cronies for bribes and kickbacks. They rigged elections. They evaded justice by corrupting prosecutors and courts. Boss Tweed in New York, Tom Pendergast in Kansas City, their exploits make up a colorful, but inglorious chapter in the history books.

The time had come for reform, and the reformers, called the progressives in this era, already had a reform ready to hand. They wanted to replace patronage with a civil service system. Rather than the politicians handing out government jobs on a partisan basis, they wanted government employees hired on merit through testing and only terminated for good cause. They pointed to European countries like Great Britain, for an early and prominent example, where such a "merit system" had proved a great success. Here was a good idea whose time had come.

But if the ancient Greek motto "nothing in excess," the modern American motto seems "everything in excess." Rather than remembering the virtues of patronage, the reformers remembered only the vices. They made patronage into a dirty word and civil service sound like a paragon of all the virtues. Rather than finding the happy medium, their reforms went too far. They eliminated the virtues of patronage right along with the vices. But that's the rest of the story.

9.06 – Irish Eyes Were Smiling

For those who find in cultural affiliation some explanation for political affiliation, Justice William Brennan's long career on the Supreme Court from 1956 to 1990 might serve as a good illustration. As his name suggests, Brennan was an Irish-American, both his parents being first-generation Irish immigrants. And he seems to have regarded Anglo-Americans much the way the Irish regard the English in the old country, and we know how that is. In his eyes, the Anglo-Americans could do nothing right, which to say, the democratic majority could do nothing right, since the Anglo-Americans were the majority. Once elevated to the highest bench, he found himself perfectly situated to correct the many errors of this majority through replacing their democratically arrived at laws with his judicially arrived at laws. He was able to operate much like a great bishop of the Irish Catholic Church could have operated, if the bishop had found himself in an Ireland suddenly converted into a theocracy. Justice Brennan infallibly and constantly re-interpreted the sacred text (the Constitution) to confound the Sassenach. No wonder in those solemn, posed, group photos of the Court, Justice Brennan's eyes seem to possess an irrepressible Irish twinkle of pleasure.

His attitude toward patronage serves as a good example of his overall cultural hostility toward Anglo-American political culture. In 1976, he wrote the decision in Elrod v Burns, a case that utterly demolished the prior bureaucratic structure as designed by the majority in Congress and the states. On the ruins, he raised a monolithic meritocracy, a thoroughgoing civil service system. But while his new structure turned out monolithic all right, the meritocracy turned out rather too often a mediocracy. At the same time, he inflicted considerable collateral damage on the political parties. Being riveted on doing down his cultural foes, Justice Brennan failed to perceive the unexpected consequences.

By the time the Court and Justice Brennan got around to Elrod v Burns, as said in 1976, the bureaucracy had already been largely reformed, the old spoils system a thing of the past. With the Pendleton Act way back in 1883, Congress had already made the federal bureaucracy into a civil service system, and in the years following, the states had done the same with their bureaucracies. But as usual with democratic solutions, it was a gradual process with some compromises. By no means did all patronage disappear nor all government employees become civil servants. In pursuit of purposes good, bad, or indifferent, Congress and the states had left a lot of jobs still patronage (at-will). In these enclaves, an elected official could still decimate his staff, either to enforce policy or reward retainers. As much as that, the civil service laws weren't written in constitutional stone. Congress and the states retained the legislative authority to alter and tinker with the system at any time.

Now patronage was a practice "as old as the republic." And the Supreme Court has frequently laid down the rule that, "A legislative practice such as we have here, evidenced not by only occasional instances, but marked by the movement of a steady stream for a century and a half of time, goes a long way in the direction of proving the presence of unassailable ground for the constitutionality of the practice, to be found in the origin and history of the power involved, or in its nature, or in both combined." Or stated another way, "Long settled and established practice is a consideration of great weight in a proper interpretation of constitutional provisions of this character."

In the face of this legal rule, how did Justice Brennan manage to find that patronage had suddenly come to violate the Constitution? Well, a clever lawyer never has much trouble making the words say what he wants to hear. An admirer of Justice Brennan would later write of him, "Once Brennan determined what the desired end should be, he never had any difficulty in fashioning the legal means to achieve that end." In this instance, Justice Brennan "fashioned the legal means" out of the 1st Amendment guarantee of freedom of speech. Not do go into the details, needing only for our purposes to know the result, he held that discharging government employees on a patronage basis violated their right to free speech. So suddenly, we, or least the bureaucrats, had a new constitutional right. All the bureaucrats except the very tip-top ones now had a constitutional right to civil service status. They could not be hired, fired, promoted, or disciplined except on merit. Moreover, that system was now written in constitutional stone. Congress and the states could no longer change it.

If you're one of those to whom patronage a dirty word, probably you agree with Justice Brennan's opinion. But for me, patronage had some real virtues, and his wholesale slaughter extinguished the virtues right along with the vices. But at any rate, Justice Brennan once again did down his foes, the Anglo-Americans and their political culture. Today, the federal and state bureaucracies must be monolithic meritocracies, thoroughgoing civil service systems. Unfortunately, the system developed some problems not foreseen by Justice Brennan. In addition, by eliminating patronage root and branch, the decision tore up a tap root of the political parties, who had drawn much of their nourishment from patronage. Nowadays, you hear quite a few lamenting the parties' present weakness, and you need look no farther than this case for a main cause.

Yet as a footnote, civil servants don't have quite all the rights Justice Brennan wanted. While the good justice won most of his fights on the Court, he didn't win 'em all. In particular, he didn't win the fight over the Hatch Act, officially, "An Act to Prohibit Pernicious Political Activities." Passed by Congress back in 1939 and since amended several times, this law restricts the right of civil servants to engage in political activity. For example, one provision prohibits them from taking "an active part in political management or in political campaigns." In a 1973 case, the Letter Carriers Case, this law was attacked as an unconstitutional interference with free speech as protected by the 1st Amendment. But the majority on the Court turned back the challenge.

Writing the opinion, Justice White reasoned that, "A major thesis of the Hatch Act is that to serve this great end of Government – the impartial execution of the laws – it is essential that federal employees … not take formal positions in political parties, not undertake to play substantial roles in partisan political campaigns, and not run for office on partisan political tickets." And, "Another major concern of the restriction against partisan activities by federal employees was perhaps the immediate occasion for enactment of the Hatch Act in 1939. That was the conviction that the rapidly expanding Government workforce should not be employed to build a powerful, invincible, and perhaps corrupt political machine." With these concerns in mind, the Court upheld the Hatch Act and it limits on civil servants' participation in the political arena.

That left Justice Brennan to join the dissent written by Justice Hugo Black, who said, "We deal here with a First Amendment right to speak, to propose, to publish, … . Time and place are obvious limitations. Thus, no one could object if employees were barred from using office time to engage in outside activities, whether political or otherwise. But it is of no concern of

Government what an employee does in his spare time, whether religion, recreation, social work, or politics is his hobby -- unless what he does impairs efficiency or other facets of the merits of his job." They would have allowed only some very narrow limitations on the participation of civil servants in politics, but as said, they, including Justice Brennan, lost.

There you have it. The Supreme Court has ordered a civil service system for all government bureaucracies, federal, state, or otherwise. Only a few jobs at the very tip-top are exempt from the requirement. Moreover, that's a constitutional right and can never be changed short of constitutional amendment or another re-interpretation by the Court, either an unlikely event. But at the same time, civil servants are prohibited from engaging in a wide range of political activities. Perhaps somewhat oddly, then, although government employees have a constitution right against being hired or fired for their political activity, they don't have a constitutional right to engage in political activity. But maybe that's not a contradiction. Maybe that just a sensible solution that takes the bureaucracy largely out of politics. At any rate, such describes the present situation of our bureaucracy.

9.07 – Their Bottom Line

A lawyer friend repeated a story a local postman told him. The postman was laughing about it. The Post Office kept trying to fire him, which might not seem a laughing matter. But the same thing kept happening. After losing the termination hearing at the local level, he kept winning on appeal to the higher level in Kansas City. These occurrences had become so regular he could just laugh at them anymore. Knowing this postman, one was glad for him not losing his job, but wondered whether some pretty good reasons didn't exist from him to have lost it. An affable enough fellow, he didn't strike one as probably a very reliable employee, probably being somewhat over fond of the bottle. Anyone who knew the local postmaster would doubt him firing someone without good cause even to provocation. However that may be, anyone who's ever worked in the bowels of the federal bureaucracy has probably seen not a few instances that remind of this postman's story.

Notoriously, it's near impossible to discipline, demote, or fire a federal bureaucrat. That's a main thing that went wrong with civil service reform. It wasn't supposed to work that way, but it came to work that way. Bureaucrats have come to occupy virtual sinecures and so lost much of their accountability. "Neither snow nor rain nor heat nor gloom of night stays these couriers from the swift completion of their appointed rounds." Oh, yeah? Any business that can't hold its employees accountable won't deliver the mail, and the same goes for the business of government. But another main cause relates to the very nature of the bureaucrats' business. With them, it's hard to measure what they do or how well they do it, making it hard to find their bottom line.

Max Weber, the great German sociologist, who lived 1864 to 1920, formally identified six elements as making up a modern civil service system, 1) hired and promoted on merit and only disciplined, demoted, or discharged for cause, 2) paid fixed salaries, rather than a rake off from the collected fees, 3) a clear chain of command from top to bottom, 4) a clear division of labor, 5) the public treated objectively upon the merit of the cases, rather than based on their status or influence, and 6) governed by express, written rules.

Weber regarded this modern model as a great advance over late medieval bureaucracies, which ramshackle affairs permeated by influence. Those bureaucrats had gained their offices through influence, and shamelessly used their own influence to benefit their patrons and themselves. By the nineteenth century, leading European nations had moved toward this newer model. Especially in Great Britain and Germany, this reform proved strikingly successful, the bureaucracy becoming much more rational and efficient. Following in the footsteps of this trend, American reformers began to call for a similar makeover on this side of the Atlantic, and slowly but surely, they carried the day. In 1883, Congress passed the Pendleton Act, changing most federal bureaucrats into civil servants. In 1939, Congress forced the states to follow suit, requiring them to administer any state programs receiving federal funds through a civil service. While as we saw in an earlier article, with the 1978 Elrod v Burns Case, the Supreme Court ordered a thoroughgoing civil service system for all except the very tip-top jobs.

Yet a civil service system didn't turn out entirely progress as promised. Over the years and one way or another, the civil servants managed to game the system. Tested, hired, and promoted on merit? If exceptions prove the rule, exceptions have amply proved these rules. Through one exception or another, the unqualified and incompetent have been often hired and often promoted. Disciplined, demoted, and discharged for cause? The hurdles have been raised so high as to make such leaps a Herculean task. The postman's story has repeated again and again.

Finding their bottom line has proved at least as hard. With private enterprise, you can find their bottom line. Just examine their books. The competition to make money forces some efficiency. Otherwise, they lose money, and sooner or later, enough red ink on their bottom line equates to bankruptcy. "Commerce is like war; its result is patent. Do you make money or do you not make it? There is as little appeal from figures as from battle."

But government bureaucracies don't compete to make money. No balance sheet measures their profit and loss. Without that, how do you calculate their efficiency? They may have built huge projects, piped clean water to a city, built a superhighway, or sent a man to the moon. But they may have wasted huge amounts of time and money doing it. However horribly inefficient, they don't go bankrupt. Rather, the more they spend, the more they come back and request in next year's budget. How measure their bottom line?

What can their lack of efficiency cost? Take a recent report about the Social Security disability system. The authors concluded that, "Our particular estimate is that failings by the administrative law judge system have led, on net, to more than $72 billion being paid out to disability claimants over their lifetimes through unwarranted benefit awards over the period from 2005 through 2014." In other words, this particular bureaucratic inefficiency had cost $72 billion. That's how much these particular bureaucrats, the administrative law judges, had wrongly paid out in excess of what they should have paid. Apparently, you could have figured out their bottom line, but nobody was doing it. These bureaucrats weren't being held accountable, letting them slip into inefficiency.

Let's take away a couple lessons. Modern bureaucracy was a great advance. It's much more rational and efficient than the earlier, feudal model. But when we pass a law for a bureaucracy, let's never fail to write in strict accountability. Let's really hire and promote our civil servants on merit. Let's not make them immune from discipline, demotion, or discharge. Since we can't measure their efficiency by their profitability, let's write in other standards to calculate their bottom line. Let's make them work, and work for us.

9.08 – All on Their Own

The recent Obamacare Case (King v Burwell, in 2015) seems a good place to start on the problem with the bureaucrats making laws. The Constitution clearly states, "All legislative Powers herein granted shall be vested in a Congress." Legislative power is the power to make laws. So we might wonder how can the bureaucrats make laws at all. But once again, we come to some more words in the Constitution that turned out not to mean quite what they seemed to say. Today, our bureaucrats make a lot of our laws, although technically called just "regulations." That's not the problem. Rather, the problem comes when the bureaucrats start making laws all on their own. The Obamacare Case shows how it can easily happen.

Bureaucratic laws (regulations) turned out not just a convenience, but a necessity, especially with modern circumstances of size and complexity. Congress wants a job done and passes a law to do the job. Often the business in hand is so large and/or so technical, they don't have the time with so much other pressing business to write all the details into the law. Instead, Congress not only passes the job onto the bureaucracy, but also passes on the details for the bureaucrats to fill in. Congress long ago passed a law to regulate nuclear power plants. The law passed both the job and the details onto an agency, today the Department of Energy. In essence, Congress simply said, "Assure the safety of nuclear reactors." The bureaucrats at the DOE, their expert engineers, wrote the detailed regulations to assure hopefully the safety of nuclear reactors. Such bureaucratic regulations amount, in effect, to laws, since people have to obey them or face a sanction, a punishment.

Under the formal theory, Congress still makes the laws (legislates), not the bureaucrats. The bureaucrats merely do the job assigned them by Congress. But in practice, a problem can quickly occur. What if the Congress passes a law, but includes so few specific guidelines as to pass the real lawmaking down the line to the bureaucrats?

Back in 1933, Congress passed the NIRA (National Industrial Recovery Act). In a huge rush to deal with the crisis of the Great Depression in the "hundred days" after Franklin Roosevelt took office as president, Congress passed a record number of laws, some not fully thought out. Among these, the NIRA stood out for size and vagueness. The Act merely stated a policy to promote "industrial recovery," whatever that might mean. Next, it authorized the president to create a bureaucratic agency, "To effectuate the policy of this [act], the President is hereby authorized to establish such agencies ... as he may find necessary." Next, it authorized the making of bureaucratic regulations, "The President may approve a code or codes of fair competition for [each] trade or industry." That was about it. Roosevelt promptly signed an executive order bringing into being a huge agency, the National Industrial Recovery Agency (the NIRA). The agency as promptly promulgated thousands of regulations, covering every industry from the 3,500,000 workers in retail to the 45 workers in the animal soft hair trade, altogether some 23,000,000 workers. That was a lot of regulations. That amounted to a lot of laws passed not by Congress, but by the bureaucracy.

In a case in that day rivaling the fame of the Obamacare Case in this day, the Supreme Court rightly called down Congress. In the Schechter Poultry Case (1935). Chief Justice Charles Evans Hughes wrote, "The discretion of the President in approving or prescribing codes, and thus enacting laws for the government of trade and industry throughout the country, is virtually unfettered. We think that the code-making authority thus conferred is an unconstitutional delegation of legislative power." In other words, Congress had, in effect, delegated the real lawmaking to the president and hence to the bureaucracy. Such a total abdication was "an unconstitutional delegation of legislative power" as violating the separation of powers.

Thus, a fundamental principle of administrative law (the laws governing administrative agencies, the bureaucracy) is that Congress must specifically with sufficient clarity and detail assign the bureaucracy their mandate. If this were a military operation, we would say the civil authority (the Congress) must clearly define the mission and spell out the rules of engagement. Otherwise, nothing keeps the military (the bureaucrats) from going off on a rogue mission and making up their own rules of engagement, which would violate the principle of civilian control. It's the same principle in either context, and in either context, it makes both common sense and constitutional sense. You need to keep the military under civilian control, and you need to keep legislation under the control of Congress.

But that just brings on the hard part. It's all very well to say Congress must pass laws with sufficient clarity and detail, but what if they don't? What if Congress flubs or fudges? Even more, what's sufficient clarity and detail? Many a man has walked smiling into a courtroom with what seemed an ironclad contract in hand, only to depart frowning with nothing in hand. The lawyers on the other side seem able to twist and confuse the clearest seeming words. The same happens with any law. People constantly twist and confuse the clearest seeming laws into shapes more useful to themselves. So it turns out hard, really near impossible, for Congress to pass the laws with sufficient specificity.

This legal background sets the stage for our present-day case, the Obamacare Case in 2015. But we also have to understand the background for the Obamacare law. Officially, the Patient Protection and Affordable Care Act of 2010, that law meant to extend insurance coverage to most Americans. For obvious reasons, the insurance companies wouldn't sell or only at a prohibitive price health care policies to people with a "pre-existing condition" (at high risk of becoming or already sick). Thinking that looked easy enough to fix, some states passed laws forcing the companies to sell a policy to anyone who applied and the same policy at the same price. But as Chief Justice Roberts wrote in the Obamacare Case, these laws "had an unintended consequence. They encouraged people to wait until they were sick to buy insurance. Why buy insurance coverage when you are healthy, if you can buy the same coverage at the same price when you become ill? This consequence ... led to a second: Insurers were forced to increase premiums to account for the fact that, more and more, it was the sick rather than the healthy who were buying insurance. And that consequence fed back into the first: As the cost of insurance rose, even more people waited until they became ill to buy insurance." For one example, Washington state passed such a law in 1993, and over the next three years, premiums sky rocked by 78 percent and coverage plunged by 25 percent. Within a few more years, all insurance company either fled that state or were planning their flight.

All right, hopefully that's clear so far. The state fix having failed, it was time for the federal fix, time for Obamacare. But we've run out of space and need to come back in the next article for part two of this story.

9.09 – Part Two

To pick up where we left off, the Obamacare law runs to 906 pages in the statute book, and the provisions are long on complexity, too. No wonder not many people have read it. As an easier way to understand it, let's quote Chief Justice John Roberts from his opinion in the Obamacare Case (King v Burwell) from 2015. But that's neither short nor easy itself. Justice Roberts wrote, "The Patient Protection and Affordable Care Act adopts a series of interlocking reforms designed to expand coverage in the individual health insurance market. First, the Act bars insurers from taking a person's health into account [a pre-existing condition] when deciding whether to sell health insurance or how much to charge. Second, the Act generally requires each person to maintain insurance coverage or make a payment to the Internal Revenue Service [pay a penalty]. And third, the Act gives tax credits to certain people to make insurance more affordable."

Got that? The law was "designed to expand coverage" so virtually everyone would have health insurance. To do that, "First, the Act bars insurers from taking a person's health into account." The law forced insurance companies to sell a policy to anyone despite any "pre-existing condition" and at the same price. "Second, the Act ... requires each person to maintain insurance coverage [or pay a penalty to the IRS]." The law forced everyone to buy insurance. "And third, the Act gives tax credits to certain people to make insurance more affordable." The law took money from some taxpayers to give to others to pay for their insurance. In net effect, the law meant to force everyone into the insurance pool, raising the water level with the funds flowing in so that the premiums from the healthy people, whose health care costs were lower, would raise the level to cover the costs for the unhealthy people. To help lower income folks afford the insurance, the law redistributed to them some liquid assets from higher level income folks.

Got it so far? Hopefully, because next the real confusion sets in. Under the Act, the states could set up their own insurance exchanges where people could buy insurance after comparing prices and coverages. But when a state failed to set up one, the federal government would set up one. But in drafting this part, the Congress made a crucial "mistake." On its face, the law reads that the tax credits to low income folks were available for "an Exchange established by a state," but neglected to mention the ones established by the federal government when a state failed to establish one. Either Congress thought all the states would set up their own exchanges, or more likely, just didn't think it through. Either way, the "mistake" turned out crucial. Only 16 states established their own exchanges, while 34 states did not, forcing the feds to establish most of them.

Now the way the law reads, the tax credits to help low income folks afford the insurance were only available when a state established an exchange, and so were only available in the 16 states with their own exchanges, not in the 34 where the feds had to set up one. That was crucial, since under another part of the law, people who didn't get the tax credits were exempted from having to buy the insurance. In practical effect, Obamacare would have gone down the drain. Millions would have escaped the requirement to buy insurance. Of course, the unhealthy would still have bought it, since they needed the health care. But the healthy wouldn't have bought, since they could have waited until they needed it. The anticipated premiums paid by the healthy needed to pay the health care costs for the unhealthy would have drained away, leaving Obamacare either massively underfunded or bankrupt.

But the bureaucracy, which recall under the control of the

president the law named after, saddled up and rode to the rescue of his law. The IRS promulgated a bureaucratic regulation, saying people would still get the tax credits anyway, not only in states with their own exchanges, but in states with federal exchanges, too. But hold on. How can a bureaucratic regulation change a congressional law? Supposedly, the Congress passes the laws, and supposedly, the bureaucracy does no more than fill in the details with their regulations. Didn't this IRS regulation go way beyond that, changing the congressional law, not just filling in the details?

But we should already be well aware no legal rule exists a clever lawyer, or for that matter, a clever bureaucrat, can't reason his way around. Here's another example. The IRS bureaucrats simply claimed the congressional law wasn't clear enough and claimed to be merely clarifying the law. They argued the bureaucracy wasn't really changing the law, but merely filling in the details.

Thus, we finally come to the crux of the Obamacare Case. The plaintiffs in the case challenged this IRS regulation. They argued what the congressional law said on its face was the law; that the IRS bureaucratic regulation changed the law; and that the bureaucracy couldn't do that. Of course, just as the bureaucrats had an agenda, these plaintiffs had a not so hidden agenda. They wanted to bring down the whole Obamacare law.

Whatever the motives on either side, the extent of the bureaucracy's power to make regulations, which in effect laws, is an important issue in and of itself. What are the limits on this power? And as said, Congress is supposed to pass the laws and the bureaucrats only supposed to fill in the details with their regulations. But often an argument can be made a law is somewhat confusing. That's particularly true, as it was true here, when someone has a motive to claim confusion. And an express legal rule already existed to deal with such claims laid down in the Chevron Case in 1984. In his opinion, Chief Justice Roberts cites to this case, "When analyzing an agency's interpretation of a statute, we often apply the two-step framework announced in Chevron. Under the framework, we ask whether the statute is ambiguous, and if so, whether the agency's interpretation is reasonable. This approach is premised on the theory that a statute's ambiguity constitutes an implicit delegation from Congress to the agency to fill in the statutory gaps."

Using this rule, here's what Chief Justice Roberts does. He applies this "two-step framework." First, he finds the congressional law "ambiguous." Second, he finds the IRS interpretation in their regulation "reasonable." He finds the IRS didn't change the law, only filled in the details. In the outcome, he upholds the regulation. Obamacare was snatched from the jaws of an early death.

Whether they supported or didn't support Obamacare seems to have a lot to do with whether the legal commentators either agreed or disagreed with this reasoning and outcome. That's beside the point for our purposes. What we want to understand is the Constitution and the bureaucracy's powers under the Constitution. Let's look at the case from that angle.

First, the bureaucracy clearly has the power to fill in the details of congressional laws with their regulations. Second, if a law "ambiguous," they have the power to fill in the details with their "reasonable" interpretation. And since what amounts to an ambiguity often itself open to interpretation, this rule greatly increases their power. But third and somewhat disturbing, in instances such as this one, Congress can lose all effective power over bureaucratic regulation (bureaucratic lawmaking). We discover this last point when we consider the larger political context.

The Congress that passed Obamacare was controlled by the Democrats and it passed strictly on party lines. The Republicans had since taken over control of Congress. If the law had any ambiguity, Congress could have passed another law to clarify it. But the Republicans were hostile to Obamacare. They weren't going to pass a clarification to save the law. But say they wanted to clarify it the other way. Say they wanted to pass a law that disapproved the IRS regulation. Well, effectively Congress lacked the power. Any such law would have been vetoed by President Obama and to override the veto would have required a two-thirds majority. But there was no such super-majority in Congress. In such a situation, Congress is no longer in control of making the laws. The bureaucracy when backed by the president can in effect make the laws with their regulations and Congress becomes helpless to intervene. This sort of thing may happen all the time, only we're not aware of it because it's usually a smaller deal and never makes the headlines.

All in all, as a matter of convenience and necessity, the bureaucrats, in effect, make a lot of laws (with their regulations). They're supposed to just fill in the details. But that leaves them a lot of room to maneuver. Congress often has a hard or impossible time reining them in. The bureaucrats have a lot of power to make laws all on their own.

9.10 – The Proxy Bureaucracy

At least somebody seems to have some affection for the bureaucrats. Political scientist John J. Dilulio, Jr. wrote a book called *Bring Back the Bureaucrats*. A professor at the prestigious University of Pennsylvania, the cover of the book describes him as "one of America's most respected political scientists." Academics need to publish or perish, and to make the big splash they long for, need to come up with new and startling insights. These needs combined with this longing help to explain why they're constantly re-writing and revising our history in newer and ever more startling ways. And the call made by the title of this book surely qualifies as new and startling. The bureaucrats don't seem to have gone away in the first place, and who would want them back if they had? In trying to convince us, the good professor draws our attention to a recent innovation in our government – the rise of the "proxy bureaucracy."

Being a thoroughly up-to-date political scientist, Professor Dilulio is heavy into statistical analysis. His first set of statistics doesn't start out surprising, but turns surprising. He writes, "America's federal government has grown bigger and bigger over the last half century. In 2013, Washington spent more than $3.5 trillion. Adjusted for inflation, that was five times more than it spent in 1960." Well, that's not surprising. We all know the budget just keeps going up and up. But he goes on, "And yet, during the same half century that federal government spending increased fivefold, the number of federal bureaucrats increased hardly at all. … In fact, … when Ronald Reagan won reelection in 1984, there were slightly *more* federal bureaucrats (about 2.2 million) than when Barack Obama won reelection in 2012 (about 2 million)."

Well, that's surprising. The federal government got "bigger and bigger," the budget got "fivefold" bigger, but the number of bureaucrats in the government (the civil service) stayed about the same? How can that be?

Turns out this first set of statistics masks another set. This other set shows the federal government has been doing a lot of "outsourcing." Rather than the federal bureaucracy getting bigger, the federal government has been getting bigger through the "proxy bureaucracy." The feds have been hiring out their work to the state bureaucracies and to independent (private) contractors and so masking the actual growth in the size.

The professor's next set of statistics makes the point. "More than two dozen federal departments and agencies spend a combined total of more than $600 billion a year on more than 200 intergovernmental grant programs for state and local governments. ... In 2011, there were 14.8 million full-time and 4.8 million part-time workers employed by state and local governments." Further, "The federal government spends more than $500 billion a year on contacts with for-profit firms. ... All, told, in 2012, businesses that received federal contracts employed an estimated 22 percent of the U.S. workforce, or about 26 million workers." And finally, "In 2012, governments entered into about 350,000 contracts and grants with about 56,000 nonprofit organizations ... and paid $137 billion to nonprofit organizations for services. ... In 2010, the nonprofit sector employed about 10.7 percent of the U.S workforce, or nearly 11 million people."

The federal government has become like the proverbial iceberg, most of the mass concealed beneath the surface. The federal bureaucrats are the visible part above the water. But beware, a much larger mass lurks hidden below, made up of state and municipal bureaucrats and private contractors, these last both for-profit and not-for-profit.

Within this newer bureaucratic structure, the "federal civil servants function mainly as grant monitors or contact compliance officers. ... 'Big government' in America is a Washington-led big *inter*government *by proxy*. ... Big government's proxies are state and local governments, for-profit businesses, and non-profit organizations." And "big government" it is. For a final statistic, "It has been estimated that total government spending in the United

States as a percentage of GDP (46.8 percent) is just a couple points below the average for the seventeen so-called Euro Area democracies (49.3 percent). ... Thus, America's big government does not spend or borrow significantly less than the supposedly more 'statist' European democracies do."

Why the rise of the proxy bureaucracy? Professor Dilulio sees the answer in the strong American aversion for "big government" together with the strong American attraction for the benefits paid out by big government. With the proxy bureaucracy, Congress has saved appearances and had it both ways. The federal government doesn't appear to get any bigger, the number of federal employees staying near the same. But the benefits can keep getting bigger, since the proxy bureaucracy can distribute them.

Overall, Professor Dilulio sees quite a few things wrong with the way our American bureaucracy has come to operate. He goes so far as to say it "reflects a derangement of our constitutional system." It's worth the time to go over his list of concerns, since it pretty well sums up complaints more widely heard. First, Congress and the federal courts have often managed to take control of the bureaucracy away from the president. ("Subverting the separation of powers, Congress and the federal courts, not the executive branch and the president, lead in deciding how to 'faithfully execute' federal laws"). Second, the states have lost much of their independence to the federal government. ("State and local governments function ever less like sovereign civic authorities and ever more like Washington's administrative appendages"). Third, Congress has used the proxy bureaucracy to "shroud government's size and attenuate their accountability for its performance." Fourth, the money flowing through the proxy bureaucracy creates strong interest groups who feed on the money. These third-party actors in turn form powerful lobbies to protect their food supply, setting up power loops that gorge on the government. Congressmen vote the money for the lobbies' programs; in return, the lobbies support the congressmen, voting for them, working for their re-election, and donating back some money to their campaign. By thus working together in their own interests, they cut out the public interest. And fifth, the system has become so complex as almost impossible to manage.

All of which explains the title of his book, *Bring Back the*

Bureaucrats. Crucial to his solution, he says we need to "hire 1 million more full-time civil servants by 2035." He argues that a normal (civil service) bureaucracy will function more transparently and straightforward than the proxy bureaucracy. He makes a good argument. The media likes nothing better than to expose bureaucratic incompetence and waste, which never in short supply. But the multi-levels of the proxy bureaucracy make ferreting out such stories a near impossible task. Whatever its other faults, a well-constructed civil service bureaucracy has an easy to read organizational chart and clear guidelines. The chain of command runs from top to bottom, from the chief executive down. The bureaucrats operate according to laws passed by the legislature and their regulations.

Compared to what we have, it makes one think of what a Victorian lady once said, "Thank goodness for the quiet of the marriage bed after the hurly burly of the chaise lounge." A more regular relationship might not be such a bad thing.

9.11 – A Fistful of Dollars

Economists like to ask, "Who's the most powerful person in the world?" Then surprise you with their answer, "No, not the president, the Chairmen of the Federal Reserve." But they're exaggerating for effect. The Commander-in-Chief is more powerful than a guy who just commands the monetary supply. Money may be the sinews of war, but a man with a gun is more powerful than one with a fistful of dollars. Not to mention, the president has a lot of other powers in his hands. But they're not exaggerating too much. The Chairman of the FED does rank second, at least inside our borders. That means an unelected bureaucrat is more powerful than any of the elected leaders in Congress, the members of the cabinet, or even the life-time, also unelected justices on the Supreme Court.

Yet we won't find either its Chairman or the FED mentioned in the Constitution as originally written. How and when did he and his institution get written into the script and with such starring roles? It turns out a tale of the good, the bad, and the ugly. Congress had good intentions when they wrote the FED into law, originally in 1913, but with a significant re-write in 1935. But the critics have accused the FED of bad acting, or at least acting more in its own and its constituents' interests than the public interest. And the ugly episodes (the recessions and depressions) have a way of stealing whole scenes. In the end, whether the FED comes across as a hero or not seems to depend a lot on the target audience. Wall Street and the bankers, the FED's constituency, have generally applauded its exploits, but the wider public mostly sits silent, apparently having inexplicably lost interest in the show.

Once upon a time in America, the public took a lively interest in the "monetary supply." They understood the significance. The debt-ridden Massachusetts' farmers who joined Shay's Rebellion in 1786 and 1787, discussed in an earlier article, understood. The dirt-poor farmers and sharecroppers who made up the backbone of the Populist Movement from around the 1870s to just after the turn of the century understood. In 1896, a young dark horse candidate, William Jennings Bryan, electrified the Democratic National Convention with his "cross-of-gold speech," saying, "We shall answer their demands for a gold standard by saying to them, you shall not press down upon the brow of labor this crown of thorns. You shall not crucify mankind upon a cross of gold." The delegates erupted, carried him around the arena on their shoulders, and made him the youngest nominee for president ever for a major political party (at thirty-six). They understood.

And it's easy enough to understand. But the terminology is a bit confusing, since to say "inflation" means the value of money goes down, and to say "deflation" means the value goes up. An annual inflation rate of say 10 percent means a bushel of wheat that say costs $10 one year will cost $11 the next. The value of your money (what your money will buy) went down. An annual deflation rate of 10 percent means the bushel cost $10 one year and only $9 the next. The value of your money went up. And the "monetary supple" can move the value of money either way. More money in circulation can cause inflation and less can cause deflation. It's no more than another exemplification of the law of supply and demand, since more of a commodity causes the market price to fall, while less causes the price to rise. It works the same way with money as with any other commodity.

Since the monetary supply can cause inflation or deflation, it's not a neutral factor in the economy or our lives. Generally, inflation benefits the debtor class (the ones who owe the money, as generally the ones without wealth) and deflation the creditor class (the ones owed the money, as generally the ones with wealth). As a well-known economist observed, "The average middle-income homeowner is the big winner in inflation. His labor income keeps up with prices, his home appreciates in real terms, and his home mortgage payment does not increase at all." The same holds true for those lower on the economic scale. But for the wealthy this outcome reverses. They live off the returns (the profits) from their stash of money (their wealth), and inflation lowers the value of their pile, while deflation raises it.

Take what happened to the farmers and sharecroppers who backed the Populist Movement. They got caught in the Great Deflation, running from around 1870 to 1890. Year after year the prices paid for their crops went down. In 1866, a bushel of wheat sold for $2.06, but ten years later brought only a lone one-dollar bill. By the 1880s, it was down to 80 cents, by the 1890s down to only 60 cents. In 1866, corn sold for 66 cents a bushel, but three decades later for 30 cents. Their incomes dropped drastically. But their mortgage and loan payments to their bankers and landlords (the wealthy) stayed the same. Those sums were written in the contracts and didn't go down. The farmers and sharecroppers were caught in a squeeze that benefited the bankers and landlords.

Caught in this squeeze, even the most diligent and hardworking often went from broke to utter destitution. To them, that looked an ugly outcome. But beauty being in the eye of the beholder, few rich folks viewed it the same way. They got richer, since the value of their investments (those mortgages and the loans owed to them) didn't go down, but up. They got repaid in money with a greater value that bought them more.

Who controls the monetary supply (controls inflation or deflation)? The government, of course. In the old days, they could just print more or less money. Today, it's more complicated, but still amounts to the same thing. Not surprisingly, in American history, the country has always been of two minds about the monetary supply. The debtors (the borrowers) have always wanted "easy money" (an ample monetary supply, at least some inflation). The creditors, who owed the money, have always wanted "hard money" (a tight monetary supply, or even better, some deflation).

To come back to the Populists again, after briefly going off the "gold standard" (money backed with gold) during the Civil War, America had quickly gotten back on. Since the supply of gold was limited, this monetary policy restricted the supply of money, helping cause the Great Deflation. That's what Bryan was talking about when he said, "We shall answer their demands for a gold standard by saying to them, you shall not press down upon the brow of labor this crown of thorns. You shall not crucify mankind upon a cross of gold." He wanted to abandon the gold standard and free up the monetary supply. But he lost that election to McKinley, and America stayed on the gold standard. The political outcome led to economic outcomes, and the political winners also turned out the economic winners.

As said, in 1913, Congress created the Federal Reserve. It was past time for America to have a central bank. Modern economic conditions demanded it. The British central bank (the Bank of England) goes all the way back to 1694, which shows how late we were getting in the game, and every industrialized nation has a central bank. And a crucial role for any central bank is controlling the monetary supply. But in America we did something unique. We made our central bank "independent." Once again, the idea was to turn over a complex problem to the experts and let them run it free of political influence. As Representative Carter Glass (D-VA) and one of the most important architects of the legislation said in the debates, the FED was to be an "altruistic institution … a distinctly nonpartisan organization whose functions are to be wholly divorced from politics."

So it was a tale of the good, the bad, and the ugly. Congress had good intentions. They put the monetary supply in the FED's hand and told them to do the right ("altruistic") thing. In the past, both sides had bad or at least interested motives. But now, being "wholly divorced from politics," the FED could act in a "distinctly non-partisan" way. And the FED always claims to do just that. They claim to play the role of the hero who rides off at the end of the movie, the gold safely stowed in his saddlebags. They claim to have killed off the bad guy (the bad motives). But he's not yet safely buried. While as for those sometime ugly outcomes, such as the Great Depression in 1929 or the Great Recession in 2007, they keep stubbornly stealing scenes. But we've run out of space and need to pick up in the next article.

9.12 – A Few Dollars More

To pick up where we left off, the Federal Reserve (the FED) is the most powerful "independent bureaucracy." An institution deliberately set up outside control by either Congress or the president, these guys can control our monetary supply. Since not much more important than the economy, and since not much more important to the economy than the monetary supply, we should begin to conceive why the FED and its chairman so important and so powerful. But while independent from Congress and the president, and we should add, from democratic control by the people either, they're not entirely independent from politics. The FED just serves a narrower constituency.

In the terms used by classic political science, the Federal Reserve was cast in an aristocratic mold. A seven-person Board of Governors runs the institution. Appointed by the president and confirmed by the Senate, the members serve fourteen-year terms, staggered so not all come up at the same time. The president also appoints the chairman for a five-year term from among the sitting members, which also requires Senate confirmation. Neither the governors nor the chairmen are removable except for cause. Thus, the FED possesses that essential characteristic of an aristocratic institution. The in-group (the Board) controls the institution outside other control.

Emblematic of such high status, since 1937, they've occupied their very own impressive marble clad building on Constitution Avenue in Washington, D.C., named the Marriner S. Eccles Federal Reserve Board Building after a former chairman. It's a site to visit comparable to the better-known Capitol, White House, or Supreme Court Building. The power and influence exercised inside easily compare with the others.

As said, they can control the monetary supply. For our purposes, it's not important to understand how (the mechanisms), only to understand they can. In addition, the FED performs other extremely important functions. It regulates the nation's banks and watches over the financial system. When things get really bad, it's the lender of last resort, where banks have to go hat in hand to beg for enough funds to stay afloat.

All of which makes the FED an "independent bureaucracy" with huge powers. Yet looking carefully, we'll see they're not entirely independent from politics. To start with, their Board must live with a constant potential threat to their independent power. The FED's preferred policies have sometimes run into serious conflicts with the preferences of Congress or the president. Since the FED's independence depends on a congressional law, creating the agency, if Congress and the president ever got upset enough, together they could amend the law to take away the independence. This forces the FED to play politics in two ways. First, they constantly have to politic Congress and the president, explaining, cajoling, and even compromising. But second, they play politics by recruiting outside support from their own narrow, but influential constituency.

Because remember, the FED regulates all the privately-owned banks. These are the Main Street banks located on the main streets across every town and city in America, and these banks have tremendous influence. Is the banker in your town or city not among its most influential people? As long as the FED keeps the private bankers happy, they can rely on support from this tremendously influential interest group, the Main Street banks. As much as that, what the FED does crucially impacts the Wall Street bankers, the biggest actors in the financial sector located mainly in New York. If they keep the investment banks, investment firms, and investors happy, they can count on Wall Street's tremendous influence as well.

What keeps the Main Street and Wall Street bankers both happy? They're the ones with the money, and so they're the ones who don't like inflation. Then no one should express surprise when the FED consistently manages the monetary supply to minimize inflation and keep their constituents happy. And that may be a good thing, since too much inflation surely a bad thing. Just ask them in Venezuela, where inflation presently running about 3,000 percent a year. Yet remember, too, some inflation benefits the middle and lower economic classes. As much as that, too tight a monetary policy also retards real economic growth (the creation of production, opportunity, and jobs). Tighter money equates to higher interest rates, taking away the easier credit needed to fund real economic growth. Under such a tight monetary regime, what makes money is money (the high interest returned on investments). So its critics complain that the FED has consistently pursued policies more beneficial to those with money (the rich) than the average man on the street.

As one commentator put it, "The policy makers [the FED] were voting, after all [by keeping money tight with a high interest rate], to avoid one kind of economic risk that mattered most to their institution – the risk to money [inflation] – and to authorize other kinds of economic loses – lost jobs and income, lost production and opportunity, lost equity in society. Even though … the real economy suffered grievously as a result, this was the posture of caution that the Federal Reserve would always find most comfortable. It was the choice its own constituencies in finance and banking would always applaud. In their own minds, central bankers could never be wrong in principle as long as they came down on the side of money."

For all the FED an "independent" bureaucracy, it's not entirely independent of politics. To maintain its own independent power, it plays politics. The way it plays the game tends to benefit the interests of its own narrow constituency. It strongly tends to protect the value of money to keep inflation down. That's a good thing, but you can have too much of a good thing. The FED will always tend to be out for a few dollars more for its constituents (the Main Street banks and Wall Street). That will always tend to leave the rest of us with a few dollars less.

9.13 – A Dual-Control Car

A congressman named Wright Patman (D-TX), who served in the House nearly fifty years from 1929 to 1978, a populist and an early and persistent critic of the FED, said this, "As things stand now, economic policy making is run like a dual-control car driven by two drivers, each one of whom insists on his independent right to use the brakes and accelerator as he and he alone sees fit. It is pure luck if the motor is not constantly stalling. To say the least, that is a most inefficient way to get anywhere." To understand what he was talking about, let's look at what happened during the presidency of Ronald Reagan from 1981 to 1989.

Reagan came in office pledged to balance the budget while at the same time cutting taxes and raising defense spending. His persuasive rhetoric claimed we could have it all (a balanced budget, lower taxes, and more defense spending). In this "rosy scenario," the lower taxes would stimulate the economy, which would bring in more revenue, while slashing wasteful spending would save money, overall leading to a balanced budget, despite more defense spending.

But as the president, Reagan didn't control taxing and spending. That's "fiscal policy" and controlled by Congress. And Congress showed willing enough to cut taxes and spend more on defense (popular policies), but proved unwilling to cut back other spending (other popular policies). We should easily see where this car was headed. We arrived at lower taxes with more spending, and rather than a balanced budget, we arrived at a soaring federal deficit of over $200 billion a year, doubling the national debt in five years.

In terms of "fiscal policy," Congress was stimulating the economy, leaving more money in with lower taxes and putting more in with higher spending. But in the same timeframe, the nation was suffering from a high inflation rate. By adding money to the economy, Congress wasn't dampening down the fires of inflation, but pouring more gas on the flames. Meanwhile over at the FED, the Chairman, Paul Volcker, was determined to fight and drive down inflation using the FED's control over monetary policy. To do it, Volker raised interest rates ever higher, having the effect of taking money out of the economy. In the net effect, the government was simultaneously pursuing contradictory policies. At the very same time Congress was using fiscal policy in a way that fueled inflation, the FED was using monetary policy to take away the accelerant. Moreover, since Congress's fiscal policy was inflationary, the FED's monetary policy had to be all that more stringent. The not too happy outcome was a recession in 1981 and 1982.

Now we should see what Congressman Patman was talking about. The car was the economy. The dual controls (the brakes and the accelerator) were fiscal and monetary policy. The two drivers were Congress and the FED. Each claimed an independent right to use their controls as they saw fit. One was accelerating while the other was braking. The motor was stalling.

Yet the economy isn't a car, and even if it doesn't look very efficient to have dual controls, some good reasons may still exist. To see why, let's recall a number of presidents have regretted the independence of the FED. With their re-election looming on the horizon, no president likes the prospect of running into the headwinds of an economic downturn, the blame for which will take the wind out of his sails. But since the FED is independent, it's not sailing in the same boat with the president. Headwinds for him may be tailwinds to them. Just when the president may want a monetary policy to stimulate the economy, adding wind to his sails, the FED may want a deflationary policy to take the inflationary air out of the economy. In fact, for the president and the FED to tack on opposite courses has happened more than once. Richard Nixon blamed his loss to John F. Kennedy in the presidential election of 1960 on the FED for just such a reason. The loses of Jimmy Carter to Ronald Reagan in 1980 and George H.W. Bush to Bill Clinton in 1992 are widely attributed in large part to the same cause.

Without an independent FED, what would happen? What if the president controlled them like a traditional, non-independent bureaucracy? We know what would happen, don't we? The president would tip the FED the word to stimulate the economy right around election time. He would use monetary policy as a tactic in his campaign for re-election. Such a single-driver car might go more efficiently in one direction than our dual-control car, but would it be a better direction? Following the road signs of a president's political ambitions won't likely coincide with the underlying fundamentals for a stable and prosperous economy.

While however the critics may rail against the FED for working in the interests of its constituents (the Main Street banks and Wall Street), the monetary policy that best benefits them is sound money (a low inflation rate). And there's a lot to be said for sound money. It may not be very logical or very efficient to have a dual-control car. But given the alternatives, maybe it's not such a bad car after all.

For our story of the Constitution as it has become, we're

reading a chapter never written by the Founders. It's a chapter they couldn't have written, since they could never have anticipated the need. But that was the whole idea. As practical men with lots of experience, they knew they could only vaguely anticipate future events and circumstances, and the farther in the future, the vaguer their predictions. "No plan of battle survives beyond the first serious contact with the enemy's main force." On the battlefield, the commanding general has to delegate discretion downward, letting the commanders on the ground adapt to a situation in flux. On the political battlefield, the Founders pursued a similar strategy. They created the institutions and delegated to them the discretion to deal with the future. That's exactly what Congress did when they created the FED in 1913. A modern economy requires a central bank to manage the monetary supply. They chose to make our central bank (the FED) an "independent bureaucracy." Understanding the temptations to play politics with the monetary supply, maybe they didn't do so badly to deny such temptations to the presidents.

9.14 – A Government Mule

During the Financial Crisis of 2007 to 2008, an article in "Time" magazine began this way, "Fannie Mae and Freddie Mac are in trouble. … But who are they, exactly, and what have they done to prompt the federal government to announce it was standing by with a possible multibillion-dollar bailout?" Good questions both and both important to understanding the Constitution as it has become.

Political scientists call Fannie Mae and Freddie Mac "government-sponsored enterprises" (GSEs). As the term suggests, they're hybrid institutions (a cross-breed, mixing the government with private enterprise). You won't find them mentioned in the original Constitution, but they've been around a while. Like that other cross-breed, the mule, they've proved a superior adaptation in some ways, better at some sorts of work than either parent, but like the mule, with some not so desirable traits as well.

Congress bred the first of this line with the Federal Farm Loan Act back in 1916, over a century ago. Entitled, "An act to provide capital for agricultural development," that law intended to "provide capital" (money for loans) to farmers. It set up twelve regional Federal Land Banks. Just like ordinary banking corporations, these Land Banks sold stock to raise the capital (the money) to operate (to make the loans to farmers). But not only could private investors buy this stock, the federal government could own it. Each bank was initially capitalized at $750,000. If enough private investors didn't buy in, the feds would take up the rest, assuring full capitalization. These Land Banks were supervised by the Federal Farm Loan Bureau, a federal agency under the Secretary of the Treasury. But to run the day-to-day operations each Land Bank had its own board of directors, three appointed by the government and six by a borrowers' association.

So we see this institution was a hybrid, mating the government with private enterprise. The government "sponsored" the enterprise and kept some supervision. But the enterprise engaged in a business (loans to farmers), had investors like a business, seeking a return on their investment, and managed its own business. The hope was this institutional cross-breed would have the strengths, but avoid the weaknesses of both parents.

Private lenders are risk-adverse by nature, and loans to farmers carried a high risk of defaults. So private lenders shied away from this sort of work, causing a scarcity of credit, stunting the output and growth of the agricultural sector. The government was reluctant to make the loans itself for a couple reasons. The American public have never shown much fondness for socialism, the government running businesses such as banking. The fact private businesses, including banks, don't want to have to compete with government probably partly explains the source of this attitude. But it's also partly explained by the fact the government has seldom run any business as efficiently as private enterprise. Nor did the government (read Congress) want to foot the bill, that is, appropriate all the money for the operating capital.

With the Land Banks, Congress tried its hand at a creative solution. They hoped that under their local board of directors, the banks would operate as efficiently as private enterprises. They hoped as "government sponsored," the banks would attract plenty of private investment, leaving Congress to come up with very little or none. When a private bank fails to collect on loans, they go belly up, and their investors lose their money. But since the federal treasury backed the Land Banks, private investors could buy the stock without fear of losing their money. Even if the farmers failed to repay, the feds could be expected to swallow the loses and protect the investors. As a result, the Land Banks should attract enough private capital to operate.

Lo and behold, this government mule turned out well-adapted to do the work. Private capital flowed into the Land Banks, giving them the money to loan out to farmers. So well did they work, that today the Federal Land Banks have grown into an enormous enterprise with over $300 billion in loans on their books. Over the years, this readily available credit has greatly contributed to outstanding success in the agricultural sector. Dare we ask for a round of applause for that so much maligned institution, the Congress?

But where does the Constitution enumerate a power for Congress to pass such a law? That question came up in the Smith Case in 1921. And that question should remind us of the earlier McCulloch Case from back in 1819 so often mentioned in these articles. In that earlier case, Chief Justice John Marshall had found the power to charter a national bank implied in the Constitution. In this later Smith case, the Court simply relied on the same logic, but pushed to somewhat greater lengths.

Writing the opinion, Justice William Rufus Day said, "Since the decision [in the McCulloch Case] it is no longer an open question that Congress may establish banks for national purposes, ... That the formation of the bank [the earlier Second Bank of the United States] was required in the judgment of the Congress for the fiscal operations of the government was a principal consideration upon which Chief Justice Marshall rested the authority to create the bank, ... We therefore conclude that the creation of these banks [the later Land Banks], and the grant of authority to them to act for the government as depositaries of public moneys and purchasers of government bonds, brings them within the creative power of Congress although they may be intended ... to facilitate the making of loans upon farm security at low rates of interest."

Thus, the prior power to create a national bank "to act for the government as depositaries of public monies and purchasers of government bonds" now expanded to the power to create banks "to facilitate the making of loans." The logic was pushed to somewhat greater lengths.

With this Smith Case, the Supreme Court passed through its constitutional portal such "government-sponsored enterprises." Which brings the story back to Fannie Mae and Freddie Mac. Those institutions are no more than later and larger elaborations on the same scheme, and they carry the logic still somewhat farther. Fannie (officially the Federal National Mortgage Association) was created in 1938 and Freddie (the Federal Home Loan Mortgage Association) much later in 1975. As their names suggest, they meant to infuse liquidity (more money to make loans) into the home mortgage market just as the Land Banks had infused liquidity in the farm loan market. By so doing, they meant to make the American dream of owning your own home come true for many more people.

We think of a typical home mortgage as a thirty-year loan with a fixed-rate of interest. But private investors don't regard such loans as very attractive. For one thing, the risk exists the homeowner may default, and for another, the risk exists over such a long period, inflation will eat away at the investor's profits. So to attract private investors and infuse liquidity, Congress came up with another creative solution similar to the Land Banks. Fannie and Freddie didn't directly make loans to homeowners. Instead, they bought loans already made. By so doing, they again took away the risk for private investors. Lenders could make loans with a guaranteed place to sell the paper. They could cash out up front for a sure profit. That gave them every incentive to make the loans. Moreover, once they sold one loan, they could turn around and use that same money to make another. Their capital wasn't tied up for thirty years. And once again, since Fannie and Freddie were government-sponsored enterprises, investors were willing to put their money into them, since the government implicitly guaranteed they wouldn't lose it. Fannie and Freddie were able to raise the capital to buy up all those loans.

And once again, this government mule turned out well adapted to do the work. As one observer wrote, "Fannie and Freddie, with the help of the U.S. government, accomplished something that Rumpelstiltskin would envy. They took the worse possible investment – a 30-year fixed-rate fully repayable mortgage – and turned it into the second most liquid instrument in the world, just behind Treasuries. … Fannie Mae and Freddie Mac were long viewed by many as shining examples of public-private partnership – that is, the harnessing of private capital to advance a social goal: in this case, homeownership." As a result, "Since the Great Depression of the 1930s, homeownership had steadily expanded from 44 percent to 66 percent of all families."

So we see these GSEs are like a government mule. Private enterprise was too cautious by nature to do the job. The government by nature recoiled from the taint of socialism and having to foot the bill. The cross-breed seemed to combine the strength of the government's backing with the efficiency of private enterprise. It seemed to do a better job than could either of the parents.

Once again, we might want to pause for some applause for Congress. But during the Financial Crisis of 2007 to 2008, that turned into a chorus to boos. Fannie and Freddie had gotten way over extended. They held $5.3 trillion in outstanding debt. And the government may have taken away the risk for private lenders, but the risk hadn't gone way. All Fannie and Freddie had done was transfer the risk to the government. And in the eagerness to spread homeownership as wide as possible, a lot of loans had been made to people who weren't very good credit risks (the subprime mortgages). When the housing bubble burst (when home values unexpectedly stopped going up and instead went down), a lot of people could no longer make their mortgage payments. As a result, "Fannie Mae and Freddie Mac were in trouble," and the government (read the taxpayers) had to come up with a "multibillion-dollar bailout" for them.

For our tale of the Constitution as it has become, let's notice two things. First, these "government-sponsored enterprises" are an innovation on the original Constitution and one that has been greatly extended. Second, on the plus side, they obviously brought about some good, but just as obviously, they have a negative side. Let's turn to that negative side in the next article.

9.15 – The Kick of the Mule

In the last article, we talked about how Congress started setting up "government sponsored enterprises" (GSEs) such as Fannie Mae and Freddie Mac. These institutions cross-bred the bureaucracy with private enterprise. The resulting government mule proved well-bred to do some hard and useful work. Fannie and Freddie injected massive liquidity into the mortgage market. By so doing, they made a thirty-year fixed rate mortgage the American standard. That made owning your own home the America standard, and that made the American standard of homeownership the envy of the world. "Broad ownership of family homes was one of the federal government's fundamental social policies and one of its most effective programs. ... Since the Great Depression of the 1930s, homeownership had steadily expanded from 44 percent to 66 percent of all families." Such an accomplishment ranks as quite an achievement and quite a unique one, shared by no country other than tiny Denmark.

But while mules are well-adapted to do some hard and useful work, proverbially, they have minds of their own ("stubborn as a mule") and "the kick of a mule" is just as proverbial. Fannie and Freddie would soon exhibit such unpleasant traits. With the Great Recession of 2007, Americans would find out these government mules had minds of their own and just how hard they could kick.

In the years leading to 2008, Fannie and Freddie grew into giant enterprises. "By the end of the decade [the 1990s], Fannie Mae had become America's third largest corporation, ranked by assets. Freddie was close behind. The companies were ranked one and two respectively on *Fortune's* list of the most profitable companies per employee. ... By the end of the 1990s, Fannie and Freddie's combined assets exceeded the GDP of any nation except the United States, Japan, and Germany." Their top executives made fortunes. "In 1991 David Maxwell retired as chief executive of Fannie Mae. He was sixty-one years old and had held the post one day short of ten years. He walked away with a lump sum of $27.5 million, most of it accrued retirement benefits ... . [It was] reported that Raines [his successor] had been paid $90 million between 1998 and 2003." The investors who bought their stock did very well, too.

Fannie and Freddie grew as powerful and influential as they were big and rich. By injecting massive liquidity into the mortgage market, they made a booming market, which made big profits for all the banks and financial firms in the market, making Fannie and Freddie a lot of very influential friends. Fannie and Freddie also contributed big bucks to political campaigns and ran one of the most influential lobbies in DC. For those who go through the revolving door, back and forth working for the government and private enterprise, Fannie and Freddie were often lucrative stops along the way, making a lot more influential friends.

But for all their accomplishments in making mortgages available and affordable, they didn't escape criticism. As "government sponsored" but business "enterprises," their hybrid nature served as essential to their success, but violated free-market principles. Fannie and Freddie existed only because the feds sponsored them, and this sponsorship gave them a big competitive advantage. Being implicitly backed by the federal treasury, they could raise capital more readily and on better terms than anyone else, since investors weren't worried about losing their money. As Claude Pope, Jr., the chairman of GE's huge mortgage insurance business, testified before Congress, "No truly private company can compete effectively with Fannie Mae or Freddie Mac." In effect, the critics said, Fannie and Freddie and all those making money out of them were profiting with the government's assistance. If not quite a form of welfare for the wealthy, yet was that fair to anyone else?

Less noticed was the "moral hazard." By that term economists describe a situation where one man can take a risk, but shift the cost to someone else. In the familiar but imaginary scenario, say a casino let a man pocket his winnings, but the house covered his loses. With such a guarantee of good luck, a man could gamble without fear, and since riskier gambles pay off bigger (having higher odds), such a man would throw caution to the winds and gamble wildly. Gimme them dice, man. I'm on a roll. I can't lose.

That pretty much describes Fannie and Freddie. Backed by the bottomless reservoir of the federal treasury, they gave into moral hazard. Didn't look like they could lose, and they started making riskier and riskier bets. They neglected the due diligence required for making loans, failing to check out borrowers' credit worthiness or the soundness of the collateral, lending out tons of money to people with poor credit ratings and on insufficient collateral. The investors lending money to Fannie and Freddie gave into the same hazard. They failed to watch and evaluate Fannie and Freddie's mortgage portfolio the way they would have done with a private mortgage lender. Nor it should be added, did the government regulators catch what was going on.

So Fannie and Freddie had minds of their own, and they were soon to show just how hard they could kick. By 2008, they between them owned or guaranteed $5.3 trillion in debt. That wasn't money they had on hand, but money they were owed (had loaned out or guaranteed). That's not a big number, that's a huge number. By comparison, they between them only had $84 billion in capital (money on hand). That seems a huge number, but by comparison, only a big number. They were leveraged about 63 to 1 (had loaned out about 63 times their assets). If something started to go wrong with just a fraction of their loans (about one in sixty-three), they would burn through their available capital. In 2008 with the financial crisis, they began to do just that and with astonishing speed.

On August 6, Freddie reported a loss of $821 million, and just two day later, later Fannie topped that figure with a $2.3 billion loss. By September 7, 2008 the feds had to step in and take over both under a recently passed law. But that didn't stop the bleeding. "By November 2009, Fannie and Freddie would eat through all their capital, and the government would be forced to inject more than $110 billion." They had become "too big to fail." If they had gone bankrupt, their fall would have pulled down the whole financial system and the economy. To keep them from going down, the feds (read the taxpayers) had to pump in all those billions. As for Fannie and Freddie's investors who had bought their stock, their faith in the government's implicit pledge to stand behind the GSEs proved only partially right. The feds saved Fannie and Freddie, but wiped out the investors, although they're still hoping and fighting for some recompense at this writing. While it should also be mentioned the taxpayers didn't lose all their money, as Fannie and Freddie later paid some back and may pay back some more.

Nevertheless, that was a pretty vicious kick. What can we learn from this episode? Government sponsored enterprises (GSEs) have their uses, but you better be careful how you set them up and carefully regulate them. They have minds of their own and can kick you pretty hard.

9.16 – Military Bureaucracy

You can't count all the coups the military has carried out in history. If "political power grows out of the barrel of a gun," the military has the guns and has frequently used that firepower to seize political power. Yet so far the U.S. military hasn't staged any coups against the Constitution. Given Americans "can do" attitude, what's holding our generals back? Don't say the legal doctrine of "civilian control." Every military coup violates some law. Something more solid than a legal doctrine must stand in their way.

To start with, we inherited a British tradition based on some similar geographic good luck. "Fog In Channel – Continent Cut Off." Just that narrow sleeve of the sea, just about twenty miles at the Dover Strait, spared the British Isles the constant threat from overland invasions. That spared the British monarchy the expense of a large standing army in a constant state of preparedness. While later on when Parliament began to fall out with the kings, Parliament didn't fail to perceive another advantage. A king with no more than a few regiments at his back like their Stuart monarchs wasn't nearly as formidable as a king with a continental style professional army like Louis XIV over in France. After the Glorious Revolution of 1688, which permanently established Parliament's supremacy, settled British policy became a small army in times of peace, which they expanded only in times of war and only for the duration. The small size of their army not only saved them the expense, but by limiting the size of the army, limited the size of the threat to the civil government.

If the Brits had the Channel, the Americans had the Atlantic and Pacific Oceans. If Parliament didn't like the expense or the threat of a large standing army, neither did Congress. Taking another page from the British playbook, America maintained only a small professional army, expanding it during wars. We even went them one better. Article II said, "A well regulated Militia, being necessary to the security of a free state, the right of the people to keep and bear Arms, shall not be infringed." Thus was the "right to bear arms" enshrined in the Constitution. Why was it "necessary to the security of a free state?" Not only as security against foreign threats, but as security against a military coup. In the days of the musket, an armed militia could match up pretty well against disciplined regulars with cannons, as shown during the American Revolution.

All the way through the first half of the twentieth century, this British style military policy served us fairly well. It got the country through the Mexican-American War (1846-1848), Civil War (1861-1865), Spanish-American War (1898), World War I (1917-1918), and even World War II (1941–1945). But with the Cold War, much of the protection offered by the oceans suddenly evaporated. Technology had shrunk the globe. ICBMs and long-range bombers could deliver their payloads to these shores within a matter of hours. Unless we stood ready to defend our interests with military force on a moment's notice, we risked losing before we could even get ready. The era of small armies was over.

"If you want peace, prepare for war." During the Cold War, beginning really in 1945, Congress heeded this advice. Today we have one of the largest armies in the world and the most expensive one. The officers and men aren't short-term conscripts, but professionals. The days of the muzzle loader being long gone, their firepower widely outclasses anything in civilian hands. Not only that, but as President Dwight Eisenhower warned in his Farewell Speech (January 17, 1961), "We have been compelled to create a permanent armaments industry of vast proportions." The resulting "military-industrial complex" has brought into being a set of institutions (military and industrial) whose interconnected interests exert a strong influence in our national life. Not entirely unnoticed, as witness several Hollywood portrayals of imaginary military coups, these alterations somewhat increased the potential for the mis-use of military power.

What today restrains our military? First does come that doctrine of civilian control, which subordinates the military to the civil authority. Being so long taught and practiced, this doctrine has come to exercise a strong influence over men's minds. The military appear to have thoroughly internalized it as among their highest duties. Despite such flights of fancy as "Dr. Strangelove," a real-life military coup is a national taboo (unthinkable). Strongly seconding that, the laws place the military chain-of-command firmly under a civilian bureaucracy (the Department of Defense). The DOD is as firmly under the president. By law, only the president has the legal authority to order military action. Not to be left out, congressional committees constantly supervise and snoop into the military. Overall, the habits of obedience and existing institutional arrangements appear deeply ingrained.

Also of significance is the "up or out" system of promotion for military officers. The officers either gain promotion to the next rank within a set time (up), or they're cut lose or retired (out). The ones who make it all the way to the top (the four star generals) still must face a similar fate. Not being able to advance (up) to any higher rank, after a set time, they're retired (out). General Winfield Scott ("Old Fuss and Feathers") served as the Commanding General, the highest general, for twenty years from 1841 to 1861. Such a long tenure can no longer happen. Just as a short term of office restrains a civil politician, being a short-timer restrains the power of a general and for the same reason. He doesn't have as much time to build influence, and since no one can count on his influence lasting for as long, he can't build as much in the time he has.

You won't find many movies made before 1950 that failed to celebrate the American military in a heroic light. Since the 1960s, a strong trend has set in to portray the military as proto or crypto fascists. In this newer genre, the generals are seldom up to any good and not seldom bent on a military takeover. Perhaps the behavior of generals in other times and other places, as well as human nature itself, justifies such fears. Yet in point of fact, our American generals have continued to scrupulously regard the Constitution and the doctrine of civil control. It's rather striking to contrast them in this respect against the men who claim to be specifically designated as the defenders the Constitution (the justices on the Supreme Court). While the justices have constantly usurped power, as discussed in the articles on the Supreme Court, the generals have so far usurped none. However, it's unlikely the generals have any less will-to-power than the justices. Rather, the institution structure hasn't given the generals the same opportunities as the justices.

Let's remember the Preamble says, "We the People of the United States, in Order to … provide for the common defense … do ordain and establish this Constitution." Providing for the national defense was one of the Founders most important purposes, since subjection to a foreign conqueror would defeat all their other purposes. As absolutely essential to the "national defense," the Constitution authorized Congress "to raise and support Armies." But the Constitution also embodied the doctrine of civilian control by making the president the "Commander in Chief of the Army." The Founders purpose was to guard against a military coup, since they regarded a military dictatorship as among the worst forms of government. So far, the Constitution has achieved both these purposes and at the same time. We have a powerful army, yet we've had no military coups. Let's keep having it both ways.

9.17 – Off the Books

Ian Fleming wrote the first Bond novel (*Casino Royale*) in 1952. He found it easy enough to translate a secret agent into entertainment. At about the same time in 1949, the U.S. Congress wrote the law that created the CIA. But a secret agency didn't translate so easily into constitutional language. For one obstacle, Article I says, "a regular Statement and Account of the Receipts and Expenditures of all public Money shall be published from time to time." How could Congress write a law for an agency with a secret (off the books) budget? For another obstacle, Article I also says, "The Congress shall have the Power … to declare War." How could Congress give this secret agency a license to kill, not just to carry out assassinations, but raise and fight proxy armies in undeclared wars?

Necessity proved the mother of another constitutional invention. "The course of the Second World War was determined in part by intelligence failures … beginning with a series of unanticipated and devastating attacks – by Germany on France in May 1940, by Germany on Russia in June 1941, and by Japan at Pearl Harbor that December." Better intelligence might have prevented the 9/11 terrorist attacks. Being so disastrously taken by surprise proves the necessity for good intelligence, while the CIA is a prime example of the birth of the invention.

Entering World War II, America was the only great nation without a "central" intelligence agency. Scattered around within various civilian agencies and the military, intelligence was something of a step-child. After World War I, we had a highly successful code breaking unit (the Black Chamber). These guys broke a bunch of codes, including those of China, France, Britain, Germany, Japan, and the Soviet Union, and decoded thousands of top-secret messages. But when the new Secretary of State, Henry L. Stimson, learned about the project in 1929, he shut them down, remarking, "Gentlemen do not read each other's mail." After Pearl Harbor in 1941, Stimson, now the Secretary of Defense in President Roosevelt's wartime cabinet, left behind such Marquis of Queensberry Rules, as did the country. Under the leadership of Major General "Wild Bill" Donovan, a highly decorated World War I veteran, but whose postwar career not as a soldier, but a lawyer, the Office of Strategic Services (OSS) was quickly created. But this immediate predecessor to the CIA was demobilized at the end of the war with the same speed as the American armed forces, going out of existence in 1945.

Rather quickly, the Cold War changed the attitude back again. In 1949, Congress passed the law creating the CIA. But although called the "central" intelligence agency, all intelligence is far from centralized in this agency. Another huge intelligence agency is the National Security Agency (NSA), which specializes in "signal intelligence" (SIGINT), intercepting communications however sent and cryptoanalysis, breaking encrypted messages. They're the ones listening in on your cell phone. In all, we have a number of intelligence agencies with tens of thousands of employees and billions in budgets.

Accepting their necessity, these intelligence agencies are no more than a bureaucracy with a special, two-sided mission. On the "intelligence side" they collect and interpret intelligence, and on the "operational side" they carry out often covert operations. All the big nations and some of the smaller are in this game.

On the "intelligence side" it's somewhat like stud poker. Some of the cards are showing, but potentially, the most potent cards are concealed. A good poker player can infer a lot from the face up cards. A good intelligence agency can learn a lot just by careful analysis of the publicly available information. But if you could read the other players' hidden cards without them knowing, you would gain a winning edge like playing with a marked deck. Gentlemen may not read each other's mail or cheat at cards, but the essence of this side of the game is somehow to purloin and read the other fellow's letters without him knowing. On the "operational side" it's the old cloak and dagger. The players are out to stab each other in the back, and to get away with it, conceal their daggers under their cloaks.

To all sides in the intelligence game, secrecy is a crucial rule. But while secrecy crucial, quite a few U.S. intelligence operations have eventually made the headlines, giving us a pretty good idea of the sort of things they do. Beginning in 1956, the U2 overflights of the Soviet Union photographed every visible object, purportedly with enough detail to make out a golf ball. U.S. agents masterminded successful coups against unfriendly governments in Iran (1953), Guatemala (1954), and Chili (1973). In between, a similar attempt in Cuba resulted in the Bay of Pigs debacle (1961). During the Vietnam War, agents ran Operation Phoenix, assassinating dozens of suspected Viet Cong officials and sympathizers. That just gives some of the highlights or lowlights.

Rather than the details, we want to consider the basic problems such a bureaucracy poses for our democratic government. In a democracy, the golden word in government is accountability. But since intelligence agencies necessarily operate secretly, how can we know what they're doing? If we don't know what they're doing, how can we hold them accountable?

"Secret agent man. They've taken away your name and given you a number." But while we know the names of our secret agencies (the CIA, the NSA, etc.) we don't know their numbers. Their budget is off the books, a secret, as is their size. Making this opaque surface even darker, these agencies keep secrets from themselves. Internally, their organization is highly compartmentalized. It's "need to know." Each department keeps its secrets from the other. These many chambers are designed to minimize the damage done by a compromise (leak) in any chamber like the watertight compartments on a ship. But with so many chambers made so hard of access, can the top (the agency heads) know for sure what's going on at the bottom in the private recesses of all the chambers? Notice, too, that these agencies are somewhat desensitized to breaking the law, since their activities are routinely illegal under the laws of the target country. Notice, too, that while directed outside at other countries, their activities bleed back inside this country. Since just like we're trying to penetrate them, they're trying to penetrate us, we forced to meet them on our own ground inside our own country.

All of which creates a somewhat disturbing situation and one ripe for abuses. If ordinary bureaucrats seek to hide their ineptitudes and failures, these secret agents have some big advantages for such a pursuit. If ordinary bureaucrats might often prefer their own agenda rather than the policy handed down by Congress or the president, these secret agents have some big advantages for such a pursuit. With so much black off-the-books money floating around, does the right hand know what the left doing? Might not some light fingers within the agency stick to some of this easy cash, diverting the funds from the agency's wallet to their own wallets? With so many black ops (covert operations) going on, might not some over-zealous ideologues within the agency go off on a rogue mission, say to assassinate a foreign leader or overthrow a foreign government? While the agency supposed to pursue foreign enemies, might not the ideologues within the agency prefer to pursue the enemy within (their ideological enemies within this country).

Indeed, American intelligence agencies have been accused at times of all these faults. But we're not so much interested in the lurid details as the question of how we try to hold these secret agencies accountable and prevent such faults. In *Federalist No. 64*, John Jay, in connection with discussing the treaty making power, says that the president "will be able to manage to business of intelligence in such manner as prudence shall suggest." That's still the first line of defense. The president controls the agencies and we rely on his prudence. But there's a second line. All these agencies report to committees in Congress, who control their budgets.

"Oh, where hath our intelligence been drunk? Where hath it slept?" We don't want ever have to make such an exclamation again like we had to after Pearl Harbor or 9/11. Of necessity, we need these intelligence agencies to prevent being taken by surprise.

But we don't want to sleep on them either. We need to hold them accountable and stay wide awake on this job.

9.18 – Special Persecutors

Recently, the custom has become to assign a special prosecutor to investigate every president. In this connection, we might want to remember what a justice of the Supreme Court once said, "Therein is the most dangerous power of the prosecutor: that he will pick people that he thinks he should get. With the law books filled with a great assortment of crimes, a prosecutor stands a fair chance of finding at least a technical violation of some act on the part of almost anyone. In such a case, it is not a question of discovering the commission of a crime and then looking for the man who has committed it, it is a question of picking the man and then searching the law books, or putting investigators to work, to pin some offense on him." We need only add, the president's many political enemies never fail "of picking him as the man" they "should get." And we should begin to understand both the motives for this recent custom and the peril to the presidents

The Constitution says, "The President ... shall take Care that the laws be faithfully executed." Those words gave the executive branch the authority to investigate and prosecute federal crimes, and traditionally, the Attorney General, appointed by and under the president's direction, handled this duty. But when criminal allegations were made against the president himself or his administration, an increasingly frequent occurrence in the modern era, a conflict of interest immediately appeared. Since the Attorney General under him, that left the president with ultimate control over any investigation and prosecution of himself or his administration. Just as we don't let a man sit as the judge in his own cause, we don't let a man serve as the prosecutor in his own case and for the same reasons.

Not that the Constitution lacked a remedy in such cases, which was impeachment. Article II, Sec. 4 provides, "The president, Vice President, and all Civil Officers of the United States, shall be removable from Office on Impeachment for, and Conviction of, Treason, Bribery, or other High Crimes and Misdemeanors." After removal, any officer, including the president, can be charged with and tried for the crime in the ordinary way. Removing the man from office also removed any conflict of interest.

But as noted in an earlier article, impeachment turned out a clumsy device hard to use. So beginning in the later nineteenth century, another procedure started to assume a considerable constitutional significance. When criminal allegations were made against their administrations, the presidents began to appoint "independent counsel" to handle the investigation and prosecution. Under the idea, the president would turn the matter completely over to that official. Yet since the president appointed him, the president still retained the constitutional power to fire him. In 1875, President Ulysses S. Grant appointed a special prosecutor over the Whiskey Ring Scandal, which involved allegations against the president's private secretary and close personal friend, General Orville E. Babcock. When the first prosecutor turned out over zealous, Grant fired him and designated a new one.

The modern use of special prosecutors took off with the Watergate Scandal stemming from the break in at the Democratic Party headquarters in the Watergate Complex, June 17, 1972. The Democrats controlled Congress and their suspicions naturally focused on the Republicans, and particularly on the just re-elected Republican President, Ricard Nixon. In his confirmation hearings in 1973, they extracted a pledge from Nixon's nominee for Attorney General, Elliot Richardson, to appoint a special prosecutor. Richardson appointed Archibald Cox, whose resume included stints as a professor at Harvard Law School and as Solicitor General under President John F. Kennedy. No wonder he proved such an enthusiastic prosecutor of Richard M. Nixon. But when Cox proved so enthusiastic as to subpoena the tape recordings of Nixon's private conversations (the White House tapes), Nixon ordered Richardson to fire him. Richardson refused and resigned, as did Deputy Attorney General William Ruckelshaus. That left the Solicitor General, Robert Bork, the third in line at the Justice Department, to finally carry out the president's order (in what became known as the Saturday Night Massacre, October 20, 1973). Nevertheless, Cox and his successor as special prosecutor (Leon Jaworski) played a key role in uncovering evidence that drove Nixon from the presidency. No wonder from that day to this, every president's political foes have sought the appointment of a special prosecutor in the hope of equal success.

Nixon's firing of Cox led the Congress to pass a law fundamentally altering the nature of special prosecutors for a while. Called the Ethics in Government Act (1978), this law put special prosecutors beyond presidential authority. Either Congress or the Attorney General could request a special prosecutor. A special court of federal judges decided whether to grant the application and appointed the special prosecutor. He wasn't removable except for cause, and Congress retained oversight of his investigation and prosecution.

But as we just read above, Article II says, "The President ... shall take Care that the Laws be faithfully executed." Recall also the "separation of powers." Then ask yourself, How can such a law be constitutional? The investigation and prosecution of federal crimes belongs to the president as part of his executive powers. How can Congress take away his power to appoint prosecutors and turn that over to the courts, the judicial branch? How can Congress exclude the president from supervising the prosecutor and confer a power of oversight on themselves?

Well, per usual, if you want the Supreme Court to go along with a constitutional innovation, just make sure they, the judiciary, acquire more power in the process. This law conforms to that maxim by taking the power to appoint prosecutors away from the president and giving it the federal judges. In the case of Morrison v Olson in 1988, the Supreme Court in turn conformed to the maxim by finding this law constitutional.

Every single president in office under this law suffered through an investigation by a special prosecutor, Presidents Jimmy Carter, Ronald Reagan, George H.W. Bush, and Bill Clinton. Over the Iran-Contra Affair (during Ronald Reagan's administration), the special prosecutor, Lawrence Walsh, appointed in 1986, indicted fourteen administration officials, including then Secretary of Defense, Casper Weinberger. Some were acquitted, some convicted, and the next president, George H.W. Bush, who had served as vice-president under Reagan, ultimately pardoned all those convicted or still awaiting trial. In 1994, a special prosecutor, Kenneth Starr, was appointed for the Whitewater Investigation into President Bill Clinton and First Lady Hillary Clinton's real estate dealings back in the 70s and 80s. His investigation kept expanding until finally exposing the president's sexual liaison with a White House intern (Monica Lewinsky). At which point the special prosecutor having finally dug up an arguably criminal offense, the investigation turned into the failed impeachment attempt against President Clinton in 1998.

Perhaps this run of constant investigations and prosecutions wearied the participants as well as the country. In 1999, Congress let the special prosecutor law lapse, and it looked like we might be in for a pause. But the Attorney General can still appoint a special prosecutor under rules promulgated by the Department of Justice. These rules say such a special prosecutor only removable for cause. But since only bureaucratic regulations promulgated by the Justice Department, not a law passed by Congress, it would seem the president retains the constitutional authority to dismiss them.

However that may be, the office of special prosecutor has seldom remained vacant for long. In 1999, during the presidency of Bill Clinton, Senator John Danforth was appointed to investigate the FBI handling of the Waco Siege. In 2003, during the presidency of George W. Bush, Patrick Fitzgerald was appointed to investigate the Plame Affair. In 2017, during the presidency of Donald Trump and at the time of this writing, Robert Mueller has been appointed to investigate Russian involvement in the 2016 election.

All I can tell you for sure is this. All of us believe in the rule of law. None of us believe someone should be above the law, even the president. But don't be so naïve. I've seen a lot of high-powered lawyers at work in the courts. It helps them if someone has actually done something wrong, but they don't need for someone to have done something wrong. That's why they're high-powered, highly paid lawyers. They can turn very little or even nothing into a verdict. And anyone who has ever done anything in the big time, either politics or business, has arguably done something wrong. As much as that, by the time they've finished the investigation, you don't have to have done anything wrong to start with. You will have arguably done something wrong during the investigation, either obstructed justice or committed perjury (lied to the FBI). Like I said, they don't need much. They're great lawyers. They'll get you.

All in all, it's become an odd way to run a government. Neither the presidents nor those closest to them can concentrate on doing the job. Rather, they have to expend enormous amounts of time and energy trying to fend off the special prosecutors. The presidents live under a legal siege, constantly surrounded and beset by subpoenas, grand juries, and legal charges (not to mention the leaks to the press about the supposed wrongdoing), their resources consumed by the constant legal warfare against them. You'd think it hard enough to carry out the onerous duties of that high office without being the target of a relentless criminal investigation.

Only the lawyers could love such a setup, as indeed they do, since they find lucrative employment in both camps. They don't call America "the litigious society" for nothing. To the president's other duties, we've added the unofficial duty to serve as the chief target of the highest-profile litigation.

9.19 – Outside Either House

A provision of the Constitution seldom given much thought has some big consequences for our bureaucratic design. Article I, Sec. 6 says, "no Person holding any Office under the United States shall be a Member of either House during his Continuance in Office." In other words, no one "holding any office" in the bureaucracy can simultaneously serve in Congress ("be a member of either House"). Why did the Founders write such a restriction in the Constitution, and what are the big consequences?

We might think their main reason the sacred theory about the "separation of powers." And that would be correct. As Madison stated their reasoning in *Federalist No. 47*, "The accumulation of all powers legislative, executive, and judiciary in the same hands, … may justly be pronounced the very definition of tyranny." Faithfully following their theory, they wrote this prohibition against "dual office holding" into the Constitution against holding an office in the executive and legislative branches at the same time.

Their reasoning drew additional strength from a perceived flaw in the English Constitution. Members of Parliament not only could hold executive offices, but such was the customary practice, and by the way, still is the customary practice. This custom gave critics an easy opening and those not gifted with such an office were usually the first to go through it. They charged the king and his inner circle of ministers, who handed out the offices, were using this power to corrupt the Parliament. By distributing the offices and the sometimes lucrative incomes that went with them, they alleged this inner circle was able to pull Parliament's strings, in essence, through bribery. There was some truth to the allegation, although probably not as much as claimed. However that might be, this perception reinforced the Founders' determination to totally separate Congress from the bureaucracy.

What are the consequences? Once again, the consequences weren't quite as intended. In the first place, the separation between the Congress and the bureaucracy hasn't turned out near as total as the Founders imagined. Congress creates the agencies and funds their budgets. Since responsible for both, they rather reasonably wanted to exercise some ongoing supervision over both to see the bureaucrats doing their jobs and spending the money as intended. This led to the now familiar process of congressional oversight and investigation. The spectacle of some unfortunate bureaucrat being raked over the coals by a congressional committee has become a staple of the national life. More quietly and routinely, every agency has to constantly cultivate a relationship with some and sometimes several congressional committees. To get what they want and need from Congress, the bureaucrats have to constantly give Congress what it wants and needs. As a practical matter, Congress has enormous power and influence over the bureaucracy. Many observers go so far as to charge that Congress has, in effect, supplanted the president in his intended role as the chief executive (the CEO) over the bureaucracy.

In the second place, note Congress doesn't have much direct authority over the agencies. The president still has the direct authority. As another practical matter, then, the bureaucrats often find themselves trying to serve two masters at the same time, Congress and the president. Two heads may be better than one, but the bureaucrats must sometimes feel like a body with two heads that give conflicting and even contradictory commands. No wonder they're sometimes clumsy and ill-coordinated. And when things go wrong, it's sometimes hard to know who to blame, obscuring responsibility. Congress blames the president, the president blames Congress, and both blame the bureaucrats. To top it all off, as we saw when discussing the Supreme Court, the judiciary sometimes takes a hand in running the bureaucracy, taking control away from both Congress and the president and further confusing the situation.

By contrast, let's go back and look again at the British bureaucracy which the Founders were so eager to leave behind. Today, they still practice the custom of dual office holding. The prime minister appoints members of Parliament from his own party as the heads of their agencies, some of whom sit as prominent members in the cabinet such as the Chancellor of the Exchequer or the Secretary of State for Defense. The bureaucrats themselves (the civil service) are the permanent staff, who remain whichever party in power. There's not a separation, but a fusion. There's much less confusion about who's in charge. The prime minister (the chief executive) is in charge. The cabinet and the bureaucracy all follow his lead, and since as earlier explained, the House of Commons follows his lead as well, the chain of command works in a much more orderly fashion.

Which system is better, the American or the British? We heard Madison say, "The accumulation of all powers legislative, executive, and judiciary in the same hands, … may justly be pronounced the very definition of tyranny." The opposite of tyranny is presumably liberty. But the British don't have less liberty than ourselves. And the British system looks more efficient, since the lines of authority and responsibility more clearly drawn. Yet maybe less efficiency not necessarily such a bad thing. Maybe two heads are better than one. Despite the occasional confusion, maybe a more diffuse management style works better. Rather than the commands just coming down from the top from the chief executive, maybe the American system more open to complaints and requests that come up from the bottom from the people, through their congressman.

It's hard to say for sure who has the best of it, the Americans or the British. But let's understand how the different systems work. If our American bureaucracy sometimes seems near dysfunctional, it's not just the size. It results from the design of the system. If the British, well, more British (more well-mannered and orderly), it results from their design. But if their system looks more functional, ours may actually be more accountable and responsible to the people, since the bureaucrats report not just to the executive heads, but to the legislative body, which also more independent from the chief executive.

9.20 - All Under One Roof

Don't tell me bureaucracy can't make or break a modern nation state. There's a biography of Stalin with the subtitle, *Breaker of Nations*. But Stalin didn't break nations. He just issued the directives to his bureaucrats (the *apparatchiks*). They did the breaking. For an outstanding example, in 1930, they deported some 15 million kulaks (somewhat better off Russian peasants) to labor camps and the Arctic. Millions died and more millions lived out a miserable existence on arrival. That's pretty terrible, but by so doing, the bureaucracy broke and re-made the Soviet nation state.

What makes bureaucracy such a powerful tool of the modern state? Above all, the multiplier effect. They multiply the government. Our main set of government institutions are Congress, the presidency, and the Supreme Court. They're the queen bees who lay the eggs (lay down the laws and policies). The bureaucracy (a much larger set) multiplies their effect many times over. They're the drones who do all the drudge work around the hive and forage far afield to gather the honey. They're the ones who will sting you if you disobey the laws of the hive, disturb it, or get in the way of its business.

A bureaucracy resembles a mini-government within the larger government. In its fullest institutional form, it carries out legislative, executive, and judicial functions all under one roof. Being assigned its task (its mandate) by a queen bee (Congress, the president, or the Supreme Court), the agency drones will then promulgate their own, more detailed regulations (their legislative function). They then enforce their regulations (their executive function). Individuals or entities charged with violations have a chance for a hearing before the agency (their judicial function).

To take a routine example, Congress created by law the Environmental Protection Agency (EPA). As their name says, they were assigned the task of protecting the environment. As part of that, they were assigned to regulate the pollution put out by power plants. The EPA then promulgated detailed regulations on power plant emissions (its legislative function). EPA inspectors then enforced the regulations by inspecting power plants and citing them for violations, which could result in a fine or even closure (its executive function). Any company charged had a right to a hearing before the EPA (its judicial function).

For another routine example, take the Social Security Administration (the SSA). Congress created a program for retirement benefits. SSA then promulgated more detailed regulations on how to apply for the benefits, calculate the retirement age, and the amount of the benefits (its legislative function). It then paid out the benefits (its executive function). Those who feel aggrieved that either their age or benefits wrongly calculated could have a hearing (its judicial function).

We should easily see the multiplier effect. To see how far the bureaucracy multiplies the state, let's remember what we earlier heard a respected political scientist say, "Just try to identify any activity in which you engage; any space you traverse; any building that you enter (including your own private home); any product or service that you produce, buy, or sell (including private health insurance); or, for that matter, any air that you breath on which there is no government policy, program, or regulation."

While despite their reputation for the reverse, bureaucracies can also raise the efficiency quotient. By carrying out all their functions (legislative, executive, and judicial) under one roof, they can gain the big efficiencies that come from a division of labor and specialization. It works just the same way as the factory system, another harbinger of modernity. One man would take forever to fabricate a car. By breaking the production down into the component parts, a factory of men can crank out hundreds or more a day. Each man can become quick and good at his particular task. The same goes for the bureaucracy.

Why do they have a reputation for the reverse (for a low efficiency quotient)? A couple of factors figure in. In a private business, a man's income will closely relate to his productivity, giving him a strong incentive to hard and efficient work. But civil servants' salaries aren't tied to their productivity, taking away that incentive. Private business also has a motive to stay lean and mean (keep costs down and profits up). But bureaucracies tend to bloat. The bigger they grow, the bigger their domain. Rather than cutting costs, they tend toward "budget maximization" by constantly seeking more funding to expand their domain.

Bureaucrats also tend to cozy up with their clientele ("bureaucratic capture"). Say you put an agency to regulating the railroads. Before you know it, rather than regulating the railroads, they're in bed with them. Rather than looking out for the public's interest, they start working for the railroads' interests. Why? For one thing, people are social creatures, and who wants to be a bad guy all the time? The agency guys are constantly interacting with the railroad guys, and "why can't we be friends?" Rather than a frown, let me put a smile on your face. Let's go to lunch and work out a deal. For another thing, the agency guys and railroad guys are the only ones in the room. To make all their lives easier, they find a way to work in harmony. Since the public not in the room, they become the "forgotten man," left out of the harmony. For still another thing, both agency guys and the railroad guys quickly perceive how they can operate to their mutual benefit. The agency guys wouldn't mind working on the railroad themselves at a cushy job with a sufficient salary. The railroad guys wouldn't mind working for the agency at least for a while, taking an inside stand, making some contacts, and influencing some policy. So they set up a "revolving door." Guys work a while for the agency and a while for the railroad, going back and forth, moving up the ladder in rank with each rotation. It turns into a cozy relationship, where the same guys milk the agency to profit the railroads (at one station), then milk the railroads for their share of the profits at the next station.

Unlike bees, the bureaucrats aren't instinctively programmed to work for the good of the hive. Rather, they've programmed to fly off and gather honey for themselves (to work in their own interests). To counter this natural tendency, you have to re-program them somehow or other. And unfortunately, it's mainly negative incentives, which never work as well as the positive incentives in private business. The one positive incentive is that people like to think well of themselves. Bureaucrats are no different. They want to take pride in their work and feel they're doing a good job. That's not an insignificant incentive. But beyond that, it's negative incentives. You have to force them to do the work through holding them accountable somehow or other. You have to institute some quality control and some quotas and try to hold them to the standards. But good luck. They're past masters in the art of the alibi.

Alexander Hamilton wrote in *Federalist No. 13*, "Civil power, properly organized and exerted, is capable of diffusing its force to a very great extent; and can, in a manner, reproduce itself in every part of a great empire by a judicious arrangement of subordinate institutions." Nothing better exemplifies this truth than modern bureaucracy. They can do amazing things. Just look at what they did for Stalin. But this example should serve as a cautionary tale. Lest we forget, lest we forget, like all government institutions, the bureaucracy won't work in the public interest unless held accountable to the people through effective mechanisms. Nor will they work efficiently unless held accountable through effective mechanisms. It's a difficult problem we can never expect to perfectly solve.

10.00 – THE STATES

10.01 – Indestructible States

Back in an 1869 case (U.S. v Texas), the Supreme Court said, "The Constitution … looks to an indestructible Union composed of indestructible States." But "an indestructible Union" wasn't finally established by any words out of the justices' mouths, but at the canon's mouth as an outcome of the Civil War. However, some words in the Constitution did establish the "indestructible States."

The Constitution guarantees the states their indestructability by guaranteeing their territory. Whatever other aspects of sovereignty they surrendered to the federal government, they kept that crucial one ("a defined territory"). Article IV says, "No new state shall be formed or erected within the jurisdiction of any other State; nor any State be formed by the Junction of two or more States, or Parts of States, without the Consent of the Legislatures of the States concerned as well as of the Congress." Thus, the territory within a state's "jurisdiction" cannot be lost without its own consent ("the consent of the legislature concerned"). Since the power that goes with "jurisdiction" a very valuable possession, whoever possesses some not likely to have any interest in surrendering the possession. So such consent is an unlikely eventuality.

Since every legal rule seems proved by the exceptions, our history offers more than one. In the case of Kentucky, which admitted as the fifteenth state in 1791, Virginia, of which Kentucky has been a part, consented to creating a new state from her former territory. In the case of Maine, admitted as a state in 1820, Massachusetts, of which Maine had been a part, consented to creating a new state from her former territory. In the more colorful case of West Virginia, when Virginia in 1861 at the outbreak of the Civil War seceded from the union, her western counties in turn seceded from Virginia. Populated by farmers with few slaves and no love for the tidewater aristocracy, they had no interest in fighting for the one or the other. In 1863, Congress admitted these counties as the new state of West Virginia. If so doing technically violated the Constitution, in an 1870 case (Virginia v West Virginia), the Supreme Court found a highly technical excuse for the violation and confirmed the existence of West Virginia. In addition, a number of border disputes have inevitably sprung up between states, and the Supreme Court has assumed the authority to settle such disputes. How else decide such cases when neither state willing to cede the territory? But these have never involved more than slivers of land.

Nevertheless and despite these exceptions, the states remain "indestructible." Why did the Founders do it that way? Simple. The thirteen existing states would not have come into the union without some guarantees for their continued sovereignty, and this was one of the guarantees. Each state already had a government, another crucial aspect of sovereignty, which both reflected and protected the interests of their citizens. The general view prevailed among the people about needing a stronger national government, yet the people were enamored with and jealous of losing their states. This double-faced attitude put the Founders to the task of serving two masters at the same time by somehow accommodating the need for a stronger central government with the continued existence of the states. They rather creatively came up with a fairly unique solution by designing a "federation."

All the large European nations had and have "unitary governments." All the sovereignty (all the power) was "unified" in the national, central government. Their form resulted from their origins. All of them had grown around the centralizing power of a king, who had gradually managed to concentrate all authority in himself. As part of this process, the lesser political subdivisions such as provinces, counties, or municipalities came to depend for their very legal existence upon the will of the central government. For example, after the French Revolution in 1789, their central government reorganized their hodgepodge of feudal provinces into more orderly departments by abolishing and consolidating a number of older ones. That's exactly what the American states weren't willing to let happen. They weren't willing to surrender all their independence to the central government.

History offered examples of another government form at the other end of the political spectrum – the "confederation." In such nations, the political subdivisions had predominated over (had more power than) the central government. Such exactly describes our government under the Articles of Confederation from 1781 until 1789. Both other historical examples and our own confederation had proved the weakness of the form. Without sufficient power to govern effectively, the central government failed to accomplish much in the way of national defense, foreign policy, internal order, or economic prosperity. Without sufficient power at the center, over time, these governments had all tended to disintegrate into their constituent parts. As *Federalist No 1* said, this form had already proved it "inefficacy."

The Founders needed another alternative, and they turned to a "federation." In this form, the central government and the political subdivisions (the states) share power, but the central government predominates (has more power). And the way this power sharing arrangement started out, the states retained a lot of their former sovereignty, a lot of their former powers.

Yet today, although the states remain "indestructible" with their territory intact, their "jurisdiction" (their power) has gradually and greatly eroded away. The federal torrent has washed away the substance beneath their feet until they stand on not much more than a foothold of their former powers. In these articles, we've watched the constant workings of this process. Despite some efforts to dam the flood or reverse the flow, that old man river (federal power) has just kept rolling along, eating away all the obstacles in its path. The power has accumulated more and more, making up a greater and greater federal jurisdiction.

With our "federal union," the Founders meant for the federal and state government to share power with the feds predominant. It's still that way. But the feds have become a lot more predominant. Nevertheless, however much the states have lost power, they're still "indestructible." If anything about the Constitution looks hard to change, that looks hard. A state can't go out of existence without its consent, which no state likely to give. The only way to get rid of them would be a major re-write of the Constitution. But we don't want to get rid of them. Let's consider why in the next articles.

10.02 – The Republican States

The Constitution in Article IV says, "The United States shall guarantee to every State in this Union a Republican Form of Government." Of course, the original thirteen states all had republican constitutions. Article IV went on to say, "New States may be admitted by the Congress into this Union." As new states applied for admission, they submitted their proposed constitutions to the Congress. All were republican in form, and Congress admitted them in such a form. So far, no local demagogue has managed to usurp a state government and make himself a little dictator. Not that complaints haven't sounded over details, such as the old complaints about malapportioned or gerrymandered legislative districts. Yet while no one seriously complains their state doesn't have "a Republican Form of Government," let's not take this guarantee entirely for granted or lose sight of the significance.

An old Supreme Court case, Luther v Borden, decided back in 1848, shows how a serious complaint can come up about the details. The background was a bit complex and concerned Rhode Island. Unlike most others states, Rhode Island didn't write a new state constitution after American independence. Instead, the powers-that-be preferred to keep the government granted under a charter issued by King Charles II way back in 1663. The legislature passed a few laws to account for the absence of the monarch, but that was about it. Called the "charter government," this constitution severely limited the franchise, setting such a high property qualification as to disenfranchise the majority of citizens.

Gradually more and more frustrated with their exclusion, the majority were as gradually more and more angered with the legislature's refusal to remedy the situation. Finally, in 1841, they took matters into their own hands. Under the leadership of one William Dorr, they called a constitutional convention, wrote a new constitution with a wider franchise, and elected a new state government with Dorr as governor. But the old state government refused to cease existence, and instead, declared martial law. In response, Dorr's followers flew to arms (the Dorr Rebellion). But while the two sides faced off a few times with rifles in hand, neither side managed to work themselves up sufficient to fire on the other. No blood was shed, but Dorr was eventually arrested, convicted of treason, and sentenced to life at hard labor, although released after a couple years. But while the rebels may have lost the war, they won the peace. The state legislature fairly quickly passed a law extending the franchise much more widely.

Today, this same complaint should never come up. Today, the U.S. Constitution and other federal laws guarantee all citizens the franchise. And while other complaints may occasionally sound, all the states have "a Republic Form of Government." Along the familiar American lines, all have bicameral legislatures except Nebraska, which has a single chamber, together with elected governors and independent judiciaries. For our purposes, the details aren't important, but the overall scheme is fundamentally important.

Look at a map of the United States. The nation covers half a continent, half North America. The distance from New York to Los Angeles is almost 2,500 miles. The distance from Minneapolis to Houston is well over 1,000 miles. The total land surface calculates to more than 3,000,000 square miles, leaving out Alaska and Hawaii. Across this vast space live more than 300,000,000 people. No longer can we say, as John Jay did in *Federalist No. 2,* "that Providence has been pleased to give this one connected country, to one united people, a people descended from the same ancestors, speaking the same language, professing the same religion ... very similar in their manners and customs." Nor even in that prior day did all these regions and peoples get along perfectly, as the Civil War later dramatically showed. While today, the political map with deep red states and deep blue states reflects not just some stark political contrasts, but some deep divisions along cultural and economic lines.

How govern such a mass of land and so many people? You can do it top-down like continental European countries. You can give the national, central government all the power. But the "republican form" of our states leads to a much more bottom-up sort of country. The political subdivisions beneath our federal government (the states) retain a considerable significance and influence in the federal government through their congressmen, and remember, even the small states have two senators. The lowest political subdivisions (the counties and municipalities) retain a considerable significance and influence within their state governments through their state legislators. The people themselves retain a considerable significance and influence through all levels through the elections at all levels. Thus, that guarantee of "a republican form of government" to the states prevents a total concentration of power at the top in the national government. Rather, significant power continues to reside at the bottom.

Thus, the "guarantee to every State in this Union a Republican Form of Government" has a large significance, particularly when put together with the guarantee of the "indestructible states" as discussed in the last article. Together, these two provisions in the Constitution guarantee a diffusion of power away from the top toward the bottom, toward the people.

No matter how big the crowd, in America you're never just a face in the crowd. You're able to make your voice heard at the local, state, and even national level. It may take some effort, but you see it happen all the time. From the point of view of the average citizen, more bottom-up is a lot better than more top-down. Since we're all just average citizens, let's value these guarantees and our states as we should.

10.03 – The Two Congress Solution

Some political scientists talk about "the two Congress problem." They say we have, in effect, two congresses. They say the congressmen are elected to represent the national interest. That's one Congress. But since elected from their states, they also represent their states' interests. That's a second Congress. These political scientists see a "problem." They see the congressmen as frequently putting their states' interests above the national interest, since their own interests in getting elected depend on a state rather than a national constituency.

But how would you ever separate one from another? How can the nation do well unless the states do well? Aren't the states' interests in the national interest? How can the states do well unless the nation does well? Isn't the national interest in the states' interests? It's "one nation, indivisible." What we want are congressmen who multi-task, looking out for all our interests (national and state) and all at the same time. And isn't Congress well designed to pull off such a double feat?

The Constitution never meant to leave the states behind, saying, "The House of Representatives shall be composed of Members chosen every second Year by the People of the several States." Further, "each State shall have at Least one Representative." And, "The Senate of the United States shall be composed of two Senators from each State, elected by the people thereof." The states were guaranteed their representation in Congress, and by the same motion, the congressmen were bound to their states through "being elected by the people thereof."

Now when the French make what we call French fries (*frites* to them) they slice the potato vertically from top to bottom, making round shaped fries. When Americans make French fries, they slice horizontally, making fries in strips. You can slice and dice the electorate several ways, too, depending on what you want to cook. While the way America has always cooked politically, we've divided the electorate along geographic lines, electing our representatives from geographic districts.

In a famous case, Chief Justice Earl Warren wrote, "Legislators represent people, not trees or acres. Legislators are elected by voters, not farms or cities or economic interests." He was speaking in the context of "apportionment" (the population size of legislative districts). He was making the point that each district should have an equal number of "voters" ("one-man, one-vote"). True enough, but that doesn't change the fact we elect our "legislators" from geographic districts ("trees and acres"). As an inescapable result, although "elected by voters," they also represent the "farms or cities or economic interests" in their districts as well as "the voters."

Why has America always followed this recipe? To start with, it was simply home cooking. Our palate was simply familiar with the taste. We brought over the mother country's political cookbook in our cultural baggage, and the British elected and still elect their House of Commons from geographic districts. By the time the Founders wrote the Constitution, carving up the political turkey along such lines suited American tastes for still another reason. Electing our congressmen from districts in their states was another way to guarantee the states their continued existence and influence and persuade them to join the union. It was also seen as a way to prevent an excessive concentration of power in the federal government, which many greatly feared. While by today, it's not only a settled taste, but the states are addicted to the power and influence their representatives give them in Congress.

But you can cook your politics other ways. Over in Europe, they much prefer a *haute cuisine* called "proportional representation." This recipe adds the ingredient of parties to their legislative cake in proportion to their votes in the national election. In the purest form, this cooking leaves out the ingredient of geographic districts altogether. To imagine a simplified illustration, say a country has 10 million voters and 100 seats in the legislature. Say Labor wins 4 million votes (40 percent), the Conservatives 3 million (30 percent), the Liberals 1.5 million (15 percent), the Socialists 1 million (10 percent), and some other minor parties get the rest (5 percent). The legislature will have 40 Labor members, 30 Conservatives, 15 Liberals, 10 Socialists, and 5 members from some minor parties. None of these legislators represent any specific geographic district. Rather, they represent tranches of voters spread across the whole country.

Such a political oven bakes representatives with very different tastes from our American variety. Our congressmen represent geographic districts. That may sound like representing "trees or acres," but amounts to representing "communities" (the ones located in their districts). This recipe gives our congressmen a taste for representing the folks back home who elected them and the communities in their districts. Under proportional representation, the legislators aren't elected by the folks back home or from any particular community. They have different tastes. They prefer the taste of representing the political parties which elected them.

The elites have always run Europe, and their elites love proportional representative. It's easy to see why. They claim their recipe better represents the variety of opinions across a society and especially minority opinions. They claim their political cooking leaves behind the baneful influence of vested local interests, instead appealing to the higher ideals which each party claims embodied in their party's platform. But what they really love is the power this cooking gives them (the elites) as the leaders of their parties.

A long time ago in 1816 a Frenchman who goes by an English name, Benjamin Constant, said, "A party is a group of men professing the same political doctrine." That's what the political elites all say and what they want you to believe. They want you to believe they're pursuing the high ideals "professed by their political doctrines." But even before that, the Scotch philosopher David Hume in 1760 had "made the shrewd observation that the programme [the doctrines, the ideals] plays an essential part in the initial phase, when it serves to bring together scattered individuals, but later on organization comes to the fore, the 'platform' becoming subordinate." That describes what parties end up doing. Their "platform becomes subordinate" and their "organization comes to the fore."

And their "organization" is out for one thing above all else – to win political power. Proportional representative lets the political elites win power as the leaders of their parties, but leave behind what American politicians call "case work," that is, leave behind the onerous task of looking out for the needs of the people and communities in their districts. Proportional representation lets them play on the stage of grand ideas without ever having to play the provinces. No wonder they love it. They can ignore the yokels in the pit and shot right to stardom over their heads.

We should much prefer "the two Congress problem," which not so much a problem as a solution. The Constitution forces the election of congressmen in their states. That mechanism binds them to their states and to the people and communities in their states. That's only "a problem" to political leaders who want to slip the leash and run free from the burden of responsibility (accountability) to the people. It's "a solution" for the people, who should want to keep the reins in their hands and never let the team run away.

What about the second half of the problem? Do their ties to their states cause the congressmen to neglect the national interest? No doubt they look out for their states. But the business before Congress is the national interest. That business stares them constantly in the face. While they may have a care for their states, they're also forced to have a care for the nation. Then aren't they as nearly in the right frame of mind as we can put them? The constitutional design neglects neither the state or the national interest. The "two Congresses" aren't a problem, but a solution.

10.04 – The Tenth

If ever history illustrated that institutions matter, the history of our state and federal governments illustrates it. The words (the laws) in the Constitution limiting the feds haven't proved much of a barrier. Since they (the feds) have the final say on the meaning, they've constantly re-interpreted the words (the laws) to take more power over the states. But institutions matter. The institutional design has imposed some limits.

The institutions of the states were guaranteed both their permanent institutional existence and their representation in the institution of Congress. So far, these features of the design have proved an obstacle against "all power to the feds." It makes the Congress of two minds. With half their minds, the congressmen have often led the assault on the states, since when the feds acquire more power, they as federal congressmen acquire more power. With the other half their minds, the congressmen have sometimes defended the states and will undoubtedly defend them against any threat of total extinction. Since their own power based there, they want to protect their base. The institutional design has let the states survive and retain some powers.

But exactly what powers do the states retain? The 10th Amendment, ratified in 1791, the last one in the Bill of Rights, says, "The powers not delegated to the United States by the Constitution, nor prohibited by it to the States, are reserved to the States respectively, or to the people." There you have the formal legal theory.

To unpack the theory, first, let's remember that federal law is supreme over state law. The "supremacy clause" in Article VI says, "This Constitution, and the Laws of the United States which shall be made in Pursuance thereof… shall be the supreme Law of the Land." Their supremacy gives the feds the last word on the law. Having that last word has let them constantly re-interpret the law to acquire more power for themselves.

Second, the feds have the powers "delegated to the United States by the Constitution." It takes those powers specifically away from the states. We've mentioned most such powers in these articles. For example, we saw that the "commerce clause" in Article I, Sec. 8 says, "The Congress shall have Power ... to regulate Commerce with foreign Nations and among the several States." That took the power to regulate international and interstate commerce away from the states, but not intrastate commerce solely inside a state.

Third, some powers are "prohibited ... to the states" (specifically taken away from them). We've covered most of those, too. For example, the 14th Amendment says, "No State shall ... deny to any person within its jurisdiction the equal protection of the laws."

Fourth and finally, all other powers are "reserved to the States respectively, or to the people." But what's left over? In a recent 2012 case the Supreme Court answered the question this way, "The Federal Government can exercise only the powers granted to it. The same does not apply to the States, because the Constitution is not the source of their power. The Constitution may restrict state governments — as it does, for example, by forbidding them to deny any person the equal protection of the laws. But where such prohibitions do not apply, state governments do not need constitutional authorization to act. ... In our federal system, the National Government possesses only limited powers; the States and the people retain the remainder. ... Our cases refer to this general power of governing, possessed by the States but not by the Federal Government, as the 'police power'."

So the states possess a "general power of governing" called the "the police power." But what does that amount to? In the formal language of the law, this term the "police power" doesn't refer just to the "police" (as in the cops). *Black's Law Dictionary* defines "police power" as, "The power vested in the legislature to make, ordain, and establish all manner of wholesome and reasonable laws, statutes, and ordinances ... as they shall judge to be for the good and welfare of the commonwealth, and of the subjects of the same." Well, when you start throwing around such vague words as "wholesome and reasonable laws" or "for the good and welfare of the commonwealth," it can mean just about anything you want it to mean. We might just as well say that the "police power" amounts to an almost limitless power.

Then the states might seem to possess almost limitless power. But not at all. Not only does the Constitution specifically delegate some powers to the feds and specifically prohibit some to the states, but the states own constitutions limit the powers of the state governments just like the federal one limits the feds. For example, all the states have their own bill of rights, limiting what their governments can do. While finally, since all the states guaranteed a republican form of government, the power of the people at the ballot box acts as the most fundamental restraint on the state governments.

In general, we might say the Constitution meant to give the feds the power over national matters, leaving the states with the power over state and local matters. But that turns out nowhere near a bright line, rather leading to complex and ongoing questions. Let's try to sort some of it out in the next article.

10.05 – Travel About the Country

Remember the old Southwest Airline ad, "You are now free to travel about the country?" They meant their low airfares made travel about the country affordable if not quite free. A more fundamental reason is the Constitution guarantees you a right to travel about the country and really for free. We take that for granted, but it's a significant right. And it's only one in a set of complicated rights that try to draw the boundary between national and state powers in our "federal system."

The Constitution took away from the states their prior power over their external affairs. Article I, Sec. 10 says, "No State shall enter into any Treaty, … No State shall, without the consent of Congress, lay any Imposts or Duties on Imports or Exports … keep Troops, or Ships of War." The states could no longer conduct their own foreign policy, regulate their own foreign commerce, or maintain their own military, although Congress can let them, for example, maintain a militia, which the 2nd Amendment will later say "necessary to the security of a free State." By signing onto the

Constitution, the states surrendered these powers to the feds.

But under the Constitution, while the feds acquired power within the national borders, the states retained powers within their own borders. Since the national borders now overlapped the state borders, the feds' powers now overlapped the states' powers. What rule drew the boundary between them?

In the last article, we saw the states had the "police powers," that is, "to make, ordain, and establish all manner of wholesome and reasonable laws, statutes, and ordinances ... for the good and welfare of the commonwealth." But some powers were specifically "delegated to the United States" and so taken away from the states. For example, the "commerce clause" delegates to Congress the power to "regulate Commerce ... among the several States." The feds had the power to regulate commerce between the states (interstate commerce), but the states still had the power to regulate commerce within their borders (intrastate commerce). But sometimes it turned out hard to tell the one from the other, and so this general rule required some more specific guidelines.

Take a well-known case out of Oklahoma from 1911, West v Kansas Natural Gas. Back in 1907, the Oklahoma legislature had passed a law permitting the construction of natural gas pipelines in the state, but prohibiting any pipeline from crossing the state line. Apparently, the Oklahoma legislature wasn't in a sharing mood, but wanted to keep the state's abundant natural gas for domestic consumption only. However, the neighboring states, particularly Kansas and Missouri, lacked such an abundance and very much wanted and needed a share.

Obviously, piping natural gas between the states amounts to "commerce," being no different than freighting any commodity around the country, say Pennsylvania coal, Oregon timber, or Idaho potatoes. And as seen, the "commerce clause" gave the feds the power "to regulate commerce among the several states," although back at the time, Congress hadn't passed a law regulating the commerce in natural gas. So a couple pipeline companies brought a suit against Oklahoma. They alleged the state was unconstitutionally interfering with the feds' power over interstate commerce.

To defend the suit, Oklahoma's lawyers argued the law related only to intrastate, not interstate commerce. After all, the Oklahoma law applied only within the state's borders. They argued Oklahoma was only exercising its "police powers" to pass "all manner of wholesome and reasonable laws … for the good and welfare of the commonwealth." They argued this law was "for the good and welfare" of Oklahoma's commonwealth, as a conservation measure preventing the depletion of the state's natural gas reserves.

Who has the better of this argument? Well, Oklahoma lost. Justice McKenna, writing for the Supreme Court, said, "If the states have such power, a singular situation might result. Pennsylvania might keep its coal, the Northwest its timber, the mining states their minerals. And why may not the products of the field be brought within the principle? … To what consequences does such power tend? If one state has it, all states have it; embargo may be retaliated by embargo, and commerce will be halted at state lines. And yet we have said that, 'in matters of foreign and interstate commerce, there are no state lines.'" The good justice found the Oklahoma law unconstitutional as violating the "commerce clause."

In reaching this decision, he cited two general rules, "No state, … may prevent or unreasonably burden interstate commerce … nor may any "state … substantially discriminate against or directly regulate interstate commerce or the right to carry it on." And when it comes to the "commerce clause," there's also an older, more general rule, called "the Cooley Doctrine." It comes from the Cooley v Board of Wardens Case (1852) and says, "Whatever subjects of this power [the federal power under the commerce clause] are in their nature national, or admit of only one uniform system, or plan of regulation, may justly be said to be of such a nature as to require exclusive legislation by Congress."

Together, these legal rules draw the boundary between "interstate" and "intrastate" commerce. Where commerce is in its "nature national" or requires "one uniform system," the states don't have the power to interfere. Nor can they "unreasonably burden" or "substantially discriminate against" interstate commerce. Not that these rules aren't complicated and sometimes hard to apply themselves. But in general, they've worked pretty well to accomplish one of the Constitution's overriding purposes.

As Hamilton wrote in *Federalist No. 11*, "An unrestrained

intercourse between the States themselves will advance the trade of each by an interchange of their respective productions, not only for the supply of reciprocal wants at home, but for exportation to foreign markets. The veins of commerce in every part will be replenished, and will acquire additional motion and vigor from a free circulation of the commodities of every part." The Constitution meant to set up a great national marketplace where commerce could flourish free of restraint.

It's still relevant to recall that in feudal Europe travel about the country wasn't free. Every petty feudal lord and every town had barriers across their roads, rivers, and bridges. They mulched a fee at the tollbooths. By so doing, they laid a heavy burden on travel and trade. These tolls gradually disappeared with feudalism, neither much regretted, but even in the Founding Fathers' day, hadn't entirely disappeared. As Hamilton noted in *Federalist No. 22*, "The commerce of the German empire is in continual trammels from the multiplicity of the duties which the several princes and states exact upon the merchandises passing through their territories, by means of which the fine streams and navigable rivers with which Germany is so happily watered are rendered almost useless." And as feudalism receded, the modern nation states replaced these feudal barriers with their customs sheds and tariffs at the national borders. Only very recently has the European Union made travel and trade free across much of that continent.

In America prior to the Constitution, our commerce had fallen into the same trammels. After winning their independence, the states had quickly begun to levy duties and raise tariffs against each other. One of the Founders' biggest purposes with the Constitution was to tear down these barriers and create a great national marketplace. Who will say they didn't succeed in that purpose and succeed big time? Not only are we free to travel about the country, our huge national marketplace has given us a huge economic advantage. It goes far to explain American prosperity over the years. We were two hundred years ahead of Europe, and we've reaped a rich reward.

To return to the larger point. The boundary between federal and state powers is a complicated topic. When it comes to the "commerce power," the above rules try to sort out the situation. They've worked pretty well, but new questions constantly come up.

10.06 – Something There Is

"Good fences make good neighbors." Originally, a stout fence kept the feds from trespassing on the states' domain. But "something there is that doesn't love a wall." Over time, this wall has fallen into a radical state of disrepair. Today, as we have seen, the feds graze their cattle and raise their crops all over the landscape. More than that, state and local governments and also the private-sector have often found themselves reduced to the status of tenant farmers, forced to work on the fed's acres for a share, or worse, sometimes pay for the privilege.

Starting post-World War II and gaining speed over the next decades, the feds started making "grants" (of money) to state and local governments, but with "mandates" (orders) attached. To reach into the feds' pot and take their gold, the state and local governments had to perform the attached mandates (had to work for the feds by carrying out some program or other). Major areas for such programs were civil rights, education, and the environment. By the 1970s, the money from such grants spread over some 500 programs made up about 25 percent of state and local budgets. One authority concluded, "When the entire spectrum … is examined, it is difficult to identify a major state or local service that has not been touched by one or more federal mandates."

But at least these were "voluntary grant-in-aid programs." State and local governments could "opt-out." If they were willing to forego the money, they didn't have to carry out the federal programs. If they opted to sign on, at least they received a share of the federal money for doing the work.

However, in the 1970s, Congress started passing "mandatory" programs with no opt outs. Whether the state and local governments wanted to or not, they had to carry out the federal programs. While before too long, the feds came up with a further refinement of the technique. Congress started passing "unfunded mandates." They not only ordered state and local governments as well as the private-sector to work for them, but to pay for the privilege. Congress mandated (ordered) the programs, but didn't fund them. Instead, they passed the costs on down the line by ordering the state and local governments and the private sector to come up with the money.

To take a couple routine examples and there are hundreds, take a closer look at something as mundane as your monthly water bill. You're liable to see a special charge for something like "storm water runoff." Under the Clean Water Act, most recently revised in 1987, the feds ordered every city in America to construct an up-to-date storm water runoff system to prevent pollution. The cities have to pick up the costs, which they pass on to you. For another example, have you noticed those kiosks by the roadside that advertise free cell phones? But those phones aren't free. Rather, the feds passed a law (the Telecommunications Act of 1996) that ordered the phone companies to give phones to lower income folks and pass on the costs to other folks. Look at your monthly phone bill. If you don't have a free phone, you're one of the folks picking up the tab. You'll see the fee on your bill (the universal service fee).

How far have these unfunded mandates gone? It's hard to find complete statistics. For an example, it has been estimated an EPA mandate that required the schools to pay for asbestos removal cost some $2.5 billion for a program whose usefulness later seriously questioned. For another example, it was estimated it cost the private-sector some $1.5 billion over ten years to comply with Department of Labor's enforcement of the Fair Labor Standards Act. In 1993, America's counties spent $4.8 billion on unfunded federal mandates (12 percent of their locally raised revenue).

What's wrong with these unfunded mandates? Quite a bit. As one authority remarked, "Experiencing the joy of creating new benefits while passing down the pain of paying for them, federal officials had seemingly little discipline in foisting new responsibilities on the state and local sector." He went on, "mandates can serve to undermine accountability in our intergovernmental system. At the federal level, the link between the joy of enacting benefits and the pain of paying for them is broken, removing an important discipline on the creation of public programs."

The feds may not have felt the pain, but increasingly, the state and local governments together with the private-sector did. Banding together, they raised enough of a ruckus for Congress to pass the Unfunded Mandate Reform Act of 1995. More an early warning system than a firewall, this law doesn't prevent the practice. Under the provisions, the Congressional Budget Office (CBO) provides an estimate for the cost of any unfunded mandate. Mandates imposing more than $50 million a year on state or local government or more than $100 million on the private-sector are subject to a point of order. That is, a member of Congress can raise a point of order and the whole chamber then votes on the mandate. Only a very few have ever been disapproved. From 1996 through 2018, Congress passed some 114 intergovernmental bills and 421 private sector bills exceeding those dollar limits.

"Something there is that doesn't love a wall." What would that be? "Mandates are the product of deeply rooted political forces in our society." The feds lusted after the power, the states lusted after the fed's gold, and the wall stood in the way. These forces eroded and toppled the wall. On the other hand, "before I built a wall I'd ask to know what I was walling in or walling out." The wall stood in the way of filling a lot of needs that would have otherwise gone largely unfulfilled, either because the states lacked the resources or the will, such as environmental pollution, aid to the handicapped, Medicaid, and many more. It also blocked a national uniformity on such programs.

Such is the state of the wall today. The original federal system has been greatly eroded and toppled. It's still another example of how the Constitution has become very different from the original. Once again, there's a downside and an upside.

10.07 – State rights

Sometimes you still hear that old cry raised – "state rights." But the potency of the slogan faded with rebel yell. When Lee surrendered at Appomattox, the feds just didn't defeat the rebs, the feds defeated the states. Today, the doctrine of "state rights" looks no more likely to revive than the South to rise again. Having lost that final appeal to arms, the states lacked the weapons to offer much further resistance. They lost the war, and they've been losing the battles ever since. The feds have continually invaded and overrun whole provinces originally occupied by state power. Yet the states still possess some stubborn rights.

In the extreme form, state rights never made much sense anyway. Not to re-tell that old story entirely, the doctrine of nullification argued a state had a right to "nullify" (void) federal laws. If a state didn't like a particular law, their legislature could just vote to void it, and the state could ignore it. The doctrine of secession argued a state had a right to secede from the union. If they didn't like where the country headed, they could just leave. The first doctrine threatened to render the federal government a nullity and the second to dissolve it altogether. Both disappeared as an outcome of the Civil War, and good riddance.

Yet leaving aside such extreme views, the states were not only the foundation on which the Founders erected their constitutional structure, but meant to serve as crucial to the design. The rights "reserved to the states" meant to leave local government in state hands, while the powers "delegated to" the feds meant to transfer national government into national hands. But as seen, the power in the feds' hands has constantly trumped the rights in the states' hands until the feds hold most of the cards.

As Woodrow Wilson wrote in his *Congressional Government*, published in 1884, long before he became president, "Manifestly the powers reserved to the States were expected to serve as a very real and potent check upon the federal government." State rights were meant to serve as part of the separation of powers and system of checks and balances. But as he goes on, "yet we can plainly enough see now that the balance of state against national authorities has proved, of all constitutional checks, the least effectual." So once again, the Founders' design failed to perform in practice as hoped for by their theory.

Nevertheless, the states still possess some stubborn rights designed into the constitutional structure. Being "indestructible" and having a right to their representatives in Congress, they've blocked a complete consolidation of power in the national government. Being elected in their states, the representatives and senators still look out for the interests of their constituents, the folks and communities back home. Having a right to a "Republican Form of Government," all the states have their own governments.

These officials will always defend the continued existence of their states and their rights, since their power and influence depend on that existence and those rights. And the states have a right to their "police powers" ("to make, ordain, and establish all manner of wholesome and reasonable laws, statutes, and ordinances"). They still pass and/or administer much of the local laws. Despite the feds' constantly winning more of the deck, the states still hold quite a few cards. The game didn't play out as the Founders' planned, but quite a few state rights are still left over that still serve as crucial to the constitutional structure.

The states still serve to devolve the government downward to the people. The 50 states are subdivided into over 3,000 counties and around 30,000 cities and 85,000 towns, not to mention thousands of school boards, rural water districts, and so forth. All the states pass their own law codes, not to mention the ordinances passed by the counties, cities, and towns. These laws govern whatever the feds haven't gotten their hands on yet such as most crime and punishment, property rights, inheritance, marriage and the family, education, public health, insurance, corporations, and much more. These laws often impact people's day-to-day lives more than the federal code. The states and their political subdivisions administer these laws, and as we have seen, even many of the federal laws, as well as carry out all the myriad tasks of local government such as trash hauling, water and sewer, police and fire protection. Since all this mass of state and local government is democratic in nature (accountable to the local electorate), that leaves a lot of local power in the people's hands.

All these thousands of mini-democracies serve as America's "schools of democracy." By running for office, holding office, and participating in the process, the people learn practical lessons in self-government you can't learn any other way. It's the difference between reading the rules for a complex card game like bridge and actually learning to play the game. No amount of book learning can replace the practical experience. While just as the American education system is accessible to virtually everyone, this multiplicity of political subdivisions makes this education in democracy widely accessible and taught. In America, there's not just one educational path. We don't administer a test to divide people, separating them into those who can go onto the university and relegating the rest to learn a trade. You may not get into an elite university unless you score high on an aptitude test, but there's still a multiplicity of trade schools, community colleges, and universities you can get in. Nobody is shut out from about as much education as they want. All the multiplicity of political offices serves the same purpose. If you want to put your foot on the political ladder, they are plenty of rungs on which to start.

The states also serve as "laboratories of democracy," a phrase popularized by Justice Louis Brandeis in the case of New State Ice Co. v Liebmann in 1932. Brandeis wrote, a "state may, if its citizens choose, serve as a laboratory; and try novel social and economic experiments without risk to the rest of the country." Nor have the states failed to grasp this opportunity for "novel social and economic experiments." Nevada, somewhat a leader in the field, early legalized gambling and made marriage and divorce as easy as changing your clothes. Whether good or bad, these experiments obviously caught on. Recently, a number of states legalized marijuana, another experiment that seems catching on. Such programs as unemployment insurance, wage and hour laws, bank deposit insurance, food stamps, and Social Security also all started out on the state level.

Hamilton wrote in *Federalist No. 17*, "It will always be far more easy for the State governments to encroach upon the national authorities, than for the national government to encroach upon the State authorities." It may have looked that way back in 1788. But that's not how it turned out. The national government has constantly encroached upon state rights.

State rights ain't what they used to be many long years ago. But we don't want to send them to the glue factory. They still do a lot of good and useful work around the farm.

11.00 – CLOSING ARGUMENT

11.01 – The Day of Battle

Ladies and gentlemen of the jury, remember, this is the case of the critics versus the U.S. Constitution. I not so modestly self-appointed myself as the lawyer for the defense to appear for the Constitution. All the evidence being in, the time has now come for closing arguments. That gives the lawyers a chance to sum up the case and make an argument to the jury.

Then to begin, if you've been patient enough to read these articles, I hope you feel your efforts have had some reward. I hope you feel you've learned a thing or two about the Constitution as it has become. But I wouldn't blame you for feeling we've fought a long campaign without a decisive battle. Some of the loudest criticisms of the Constitution have yet to receive a reply. So my conscience would trouble me toward you, if I couldn't say, "I have not yet begun to fight." So far, I've just been clearing the decks and making the ship ready for action. Now I mean to pour in my broadsides until the foes of our Constitution strike their colors or sink beneath the waves of public disapprobation.

As usual, the campaign takes longer than the slaughter on the day of battle. In this conflict, we can't count the victory by the ships sunk, prizes seized, and corpses bobbing in the water, yet we have a quick and reliable way to judge who wins and has the right to erect the trophy on this stricken field. Hopefully, we already agreed, up front, back at the start on how to judge success in government and so how to judge the Constitution or any constitution. Hopefully, we agreed to measure by the Index of Freedom, the Per Capita Gross National Product, and the progress in both. If the critics refuse to weigh with these impartial scales, they do no more than reveal their own bias.

Then the battle is over. By these standards, the Constitution sinks its critics. The Index of Freedom combines the measure of "political rights" (self-government) with the measure of "civil rights" (individual rights) to arrive at the overall rank on the scale of "freedom." On this front, the Constitution led the world in 1789 and has led ever since. The per capita GDP ranks the standard of living. On this front, America has also constantly led. Not stood still on either front, but advanced on both. For example, the Constitution gradually extended the vote to all citizens over eighteen. A higher standard of living extends much farther as well with a wide safety net of welfare programs extending still farther. Both flanks of this battle line (freedom and the GDP) have constantly made progress. By these objective standards, the Constitution sends its critics to the bottom.

But rather than statistics, let's go with the voice of the people. And the word is out. If you think there's a more welcoming constitutional shore somewhere else, set sail. But the tide sets toward these shores. The flood of immigration throngs toward the safe harbor of the U.S. Constitution. They come for American freedom, the American standard of living, and American progress. And they've been crowding the boats for a long time. "Send me your poor, your tired, Your huddled masses longing to be free." If life on arrival turned out not quite as rosy as their hopes, apparently, life turned out pretty good by comparison. Apparently, the word of mouth confirmed the advertising. The masses have kept boarding for the destination. How can the critics refute this living testimony to the good life under the U.S. Constitution?

But the Constitution didn't just "lift the lamp beside the golden door." It shined a light on the world. Imitation being the sincerest form of flattery, the peoples of the world have constantly longed to flatter the Constitution. The sincerer their imitations, the nearer their constitutions came to their longings. But few have managed more than a pale imitation. Doesn't that show the original a masterwork? People admire the sound of a Stradivari, but it's not so easy to make a violin sounding as good. People admire the U.S. Constitution, but it's not so easy to make one as good. But modern violin makers have succeeded in making violins that sound as good as a Stradivari. There's every reason to believe modern constitution makers can succeed as well. They just need to make sincerer imitations.

Do the critics have a better model to imitate? No, they're left with no more than *ex post facto* (after the fact) arguments or a longing for still greater perfections. As for the first, an English historian wrote, "It is one of the penalties which great men must pay for their greatness, that they have to be judged by posterity according to a standard which they themselves could not have recognized, because it was by their greatness that the standard itself was created." The same goes for the Constitution. If some of our constitutional past not up to modern standards, what else created the modern standards except our Constitution? Can the critics show some other constitution that would have faster created still better standards? If not, their criticisms of the earlier shortcomings miss the mark.

As a youth, Abraham Lincoln walked beside an ox drawn wagon all the way from Kentucky to Indiana. We wouldn't blame his family for not traveling faster and more comfortably in a car. Let's not make the error of anachronism (an error in chronology) with the Constitution either. The present builds on the past. Thank your lucky stars when your national present better than your national past (progress rather than regression).

As for the second, who doesn't want more perfection? But we're never going to reach ideal perfection. If the Constitution made progress and it has, by all means, suggest the ways to make more progress. But if they want to criticize the Constitution as delaying progress, they need to show how some other constitution would have brought about faster or better progress.

Then the battle is over. The critics are sunk. But let's not fail to understand why the battle was won. Throughout history, peace has served as no more than a prelude to the next war. If you won a war, you might celebrate a triumph, but you better start getting ready to fight the next war. And unless you understood how the last victory was won, you weren't likely to understand how to win the next one. Notoriously, generals get ready to fight the last war, but the next one turns out not exactly like the last one. You better not just understand how you won the last war, but how the next will differ and how to win it.

Why did the Constitution do better than other constitutions? How well is the Constitution likely to fare in the future? We better try to figure it out.

11.02 - Why Nations Fail

We know why nations fail. It's not even hard. A book with that same title (*Why Nations Fail*) will tell you, if you don't already know. After reading these articles, you might want to read that book. The authors, two professors named Daron Acemoglu and James A. Robinson, say, "poor countries are poor because those who have power make choices that create poverty. They get it wrong not by mistake or ignorance but on purpose." If we unpack that together with some more they have to say, we'll understand why our Constitution didn't fail, but succeeded.

First, "poor countries" are failures. If you don't believe it, you can read the statistics about their lack of a decent standard of living, which consistently goes along with a sorry record on human rights. Better yet, visit some underdeveloped country and take in the sights and smells. You may be charmed by the people, but their standard of living isn't so charming. Incomes are low, poverty rampant, housing substandard, infrastructure lacking, education scarce, medical care primitive. Civil rights and the rule of law are virtually non-existent. You can't help but wish them a better, richer, and freer life.

Second, nations "fail because those who have power make choices that create poverty." That is, their governments ("those who have the power") cause the failure. And third, "they don't get it wrong by mistake or ignorance but on purpose." That is, "those who have the power" intentionally get it wrong for their own purposes. As Acemoglu and Robinson go on to say, poor countries are invariably "ruled by a narrow elite that have organized society for their own benefit at the expense of the vast mass of the people, … Political power has been narrowly concentrated."

This narrow concentration leads to what they call "extractive" institutions. They say, "There is a strong synergy between economic and political institutions. Extractive political institutions concentrate power in the hands of a narrow elite and place few constraints on the exercise of this power. Economic institutions are then structured by this elite to extract resources from the rest of society. Extractive economic institutions thus naturally accompany extractive political institutions. In fact, they must inherently depend on extractive political institutions for their survival." These extractive institutions create "great wealth for those who possess it" (the narrow elite), but strangle the free-market with taxes and expropriations, leading overall to a failed, poor nation.

By contrast, "inclusive" institutions foster the free-market and lead to successful, rich nations. They say, "Inclusive economic institutions foster economic activity, productivity growth, and economic prosperity. Secure private property rights are essential. A businessman who expects his output to be stolen, expropriated, or entirely taxed away will have little incentive to work, let alone any incentive to undertake investments and innovations. But such rights must exist for the majority of people in society. ... Allowing people to make their own decisions via markets is the best way for society to efficiently use its resources. When the state or a narrow elite controls all the resources instead, neither the right incentives will be created nor will there be efficient allocation of the skills and talents of the people."

In other words, nations fail through failing to write constitutions like our Founding Fathers wrote. To translate into the terms of classic political science, "extractive" political institutions amount to autocracies (monarchies or aristocracies), where one man or a very few are "those who have the power." By contrast, our Constitution creates "inclusive" political institutions (a democracy), where "those who have the power" are held effectively accountable to the people as a whole. It's as simple and easy as that. Our inclusive political institutions lead to our free-market institutions. Our success as a nation depends on both.

Autocracy and democracy operate on the same basic principle of human psychology – self-interest. "So that in the first place, I put for a general inclination of all mankind, a perpetuall and restless desire of Power after power." This psychology operates like the force of gravity in the physical universe. But the institutional architecture in the differing forms of government bends the force. Autocratic "political institutions concentrate power in the hands of a narrow elite and place few constraints on the exercise of this power." They're top-down. Those at the top can assert their force downward with "few constraints," forcing everyone else to get and keep in line, crushing freedom to crush political opposition and the free-market to own it all themselves. By contrast, democracy is bottom-up. The people have the power. To win political power the officials have to win periodic election from the people. This mechanism flips the officials' self-interest. To win power they have to serve the people's interests not just their own. Since the people want their freedoms, they get their freedoms. Since they want their property, they get the free-market, the right to their property and to the freedom to buy and sell it.

That's why this nation didn't fail. The Founding Fathers wrote a constitution that created "inclusive institutions" (democratic and free-market institutions). That's the bedrock. In the next articles, let's consider the details.

11.03 – Why Them

Why did the Founding Fathers succeed with the Constitution? Why them, when so many others failed? Used to be, their names were heaped with accolades. George Washington was "the father of his country," James Madison "the father of the Constitution." The Convention was "the miracle at Philadelphia." Why them?

The short answer is they like everyone else were products of their culture. As John Jay wrote in *Federalist No. 2*, "With equal pleasure I have as often taken notice that Providence has been pleased to give this one connected country to one united people – a people descended from the same ancestors, speaking the same language, professing the same religion, attached to the same principles of government, very similar in their manners and customs." In other words, they were Anglo-Americans, heirs to that culture, including its "principles of government."

In the face of all the Founders' expressed hostility toward King George III during the American Revolution, it's easy to forget that British culture was republican rather than monarchical in its "principles of government." Britain may have had a king, but the elected House of Commons was the real power. As immigrants from Great Britain, the American colonists had brought over those same "principles of government" in their cultural baggage. And over here in the colonies, they had lived in so many mini-republics.

The British Parliament may have had the final say over colonial affairs, but the elected colonial assemblies held much of the real power. The Founders knew their way around republican institutions and enjoyed the protections offered to their property, their liberty, and their lives. If every culture has its own briar patch, they was raised in that briar patch.

Nowadays, when somebody says "the culture needs to change," what they mean is the culture needs to change so the speaker has more power. That's what the Founding Fathers meant with the Revolution, too. They wanted to change the existing political culture to have more power for themselves. But cultures die hard, being habitual ways of thinking and behaving, and beyond that, they had good and rational reasons not to leave behind their culture's "principles of government."

They well knew that British political institutions were the best in the world, had produced the freest and most prosperous culture in the world. At the Constitutional Convention, Alexander Hamilton went on record as saying, "he had no scruple in declaring, supported as he was by the opinion of so many of the wise & good, that the British Gov^t was the best in the world." Another delegate said, "Much has been said of the Constitution of G. Britain. I will confess that I believe it to be the best Constitution in existence." Others expressed similar views.

But as another delegate, Elbridge Gerry from Massachusetts remarked, "The maxims taken from the British Constitution were often fallacious when applied to our situation which was extremely different." Others made similar observations. We didn't have and didn't want a king. Then who would fill the monarch's role in our Constitution? Nor did we have or want an aristocracy. Then who would fill the seats in the upper house of our legislature, presuming it had two chambers? As much as that, Britain had a single sovereign government with England, Scotland, Wales, and Ireland amalgamated in the whole. But America had thirteen independent states, none willing to surrender all their sovereignty to a national government.

In the debates at the Convention, the delegates showed themselves severely pragmatic. They didn't want some high-sounding theory. They wanted to go with political institutions proven in practice. John Dickinson, a delegate from Delaware, well expressed this attitude, when he said, "Experience must be our only guide. Reason may mislead us. It was not Reason that discovered the singular & admirable mechanism of the English Constitution. It was not Reason that discovered or ever could have discovered the odd & in the eye of those who are governed by reason, the absurd mode of trial by Jury. Accidents probably produced these discoveries, and experience has given a sanction to them. This is then our guide."

Where they couldn't copy British institutions, they looked for examples of republican institutions from elsewhere. First, they looked at the governments of the newly independent states. When they couldn't find what they wanted there, they searched through the governments of other nations ancient and modern. The record is full of references to ancient Greece and Rome, the Republic of Venice, the Netherlands, Germany, and so forth.

Were the Founding Fathers more selfless and patriotic than other men? Perhaps. Of all the men who made the American Revolution, George Washington was the one best situated to have turned the Revolution to serve his personal ambitions, as so many other revolutionary heroes have done. There were even murmurs about making him our monarch. But Washington slept with a copy of Joseph Addison's "Cato," a play that was a paean to the virtues of republicanism, on his bedstand. He was a committed republican. Whatever their shades of political opinion, it was a shared commitment among all the Founding Fathers. And committed republicans are more selfless and patriotic than other men because that commitment forces them and trains them to think in the public interest, not just their own self-interest.

But they were also lucky. As John Jay wrote in *Federalist No. 5*, "The history of Great Britain is the one with which we are in general the best acquainted, and it gives us many useful lessons. We may profit by their experience without paying the price which it cost them." The Founders were lucky to have this experience as their cultural heritage. They could use the "discoveries" produced by "accident" and "sanctioned by experience" as their "guide." They didn't have to "pay the price" these had cost their cultural ancestors (the British) in the past.

Why them? The Founding Fathers were Anglo-Americans. Republican institutions were their cultural heritage. That's why.

11.04 – A Thriller

About the most thrilling thing you could ever read is James Madison's *Notes of Debates in the Federal Convention of 1787,* first published in 1840. There's another book to read after you read these articles, and one readily available over the internet for free. But to get the drama, you'll have to keep in mind the stakes, the whole future life and happiness of the country, and grasp the complications of the plot.

The Constitutional Convention deliberated in secret. But Madison "chose a seat in front of the presiding member [George Washington], with the other members on my right & left hands. In this favorable position for hearing all that passed, I noted in terms legible & in abbreviations & marks intelligible to myself what was read from the Chair or spoken by the members; and losing not a moment unnecessarily between the adjournment & reassembling of the Convention I was enabled to write out my daily notes." By so doing, he bequeathed us a faithful record of the proceedings.

In 1787, America looked sliding down the slippery slope to national failure. As we earlier heard Alexander Hamilton say in *Federalist No. 15,* "We may indeed with propriety be said to have reached almost the last stage of national humiliation. There is scarcely anything that can wound the pride or degrade the character of an independent nation which we do not experience." How right he was.

But while most nations have slipped down that slope because "political power has been narrowly concentrated" and they're "ruled by a narrow elite that have organized society for their own benefit at the expense of the vast mass of the people," we were slipping down the opposite way. We were sliding toward anarchy. As James Wilson, a delegate from Pennsylvania, said in the debates, "Bad Govern^{ts} are of two sorts. 1. that which does too little. 2. that which does too much: that which fails thro' weakness; and that which destroys thro' oppression. Under which of these evils do the U. States at present groan? Under the weakness and inefficiency of its Govern^t. To remedy this weakness we have been sent to this Convention."

Try to imagine the nation as he spoke. The national government existed in not much more than name, leaving a power void at the center like a planetary system with no sun. The sun also rises, but the federal sun had not yet risen. The president, the Supreme Court, the bureaucracy, the federal law code, all were still over the horizon.

The "subsisting government" under the Articles of Confederation was a single, weak institution, a one chamber Congress. Supposedly, they had the authority to conduct foreign affairs and provide for the national defense, but lacking the authority to collect taxes, had no money to do the one or the other. In this void the thirteen states blundered around on their own independent orbits, each state almost a little nation, each little nation going its own willful way. This absence of a central power left the nation as a whole weak and divided, vulnerable to foreign intervention and invasion, vulnerable to internal dissension and civil strife. Over time, the states would doubtless have found ways to collide and come to blows with each other. Nor in such a chaotic situation could the national economy gravitate along a steady and prosperous course.

But if we needed a stronger national government, how much stronger? As Madison's journal reveals, the delegates to the Convention weren't even agreed among themselves. A number would ultimately refuse to put their name to the completed document and depart to oppose ratification.

In the first place, was the Convention to settle for some revisions to the Articles or write an entirely new constitution? William Paterson, a delegate from New Jersey, argued strenuously "that the amendment of the Confederacy was the object." A few others backed this half-way course. But the overwhelming majority of the delegates were resolute for more radical reform. They were determined to abandon a weak confederacy and unite behind a strong federal government.

But if a new constitution was the train coming down the tracks, the debates reveal a lot of obstacles threatened to derail the train or derange the tracks so the train could never have run on them. Were we to have a national legislature, national chief executive, and national judiciary all three? If so, was the legislature to have one or two chambers? In either case, how elect the members, say by the people or the state legislatures? To what term of office, say three years, seven years, or maybe for life? Were we to have a single chief executive or maybe two or three at once (a collegial system)? How elected, say by the people, the Congress, the state legislatures, the state governors, or maybe some other way? To what term of office, say four years, seven years, or maybe for life? Who would appoint the judges, say the chief executive, the Congress, or maybe the states?

What's thrilling about the debates is how the train keeps threatening to get side-tracked or jump the tracks altogether. All sorts of unworkable notions were floated. Rufus King, an otherwise sensible member from Massachusetts, proposed that Congress have three chambers, not just two. Our legislative train runs slow and bumpy enough with just two rails. Imagine the ride with three. Hugh Williamson from North Carolina "wished the Executive power to be lodged in three men taken from three districts into which the States should be divided." Imagine three conductors on the train, each with a different schedule and destination. Another suggestion was never to admit any more states than already existed. That sure would have shortened the line. George Mason from Virginia "moved to enable Congress "to enact sumptuary laws" (laws against extravagant personal expenditure on luxuries in dress, furniture, or food). Imagine if the federal government had the authority to regulate extravagant ladies' fashions and men's apparel. So much for the red carpet.

The biggest blockade turned out apportioning the states' representation in the new Congress. Under the Articles, each state had one vote in that Congress, a rule that greatly favored the small states. Not surprising, the big states insisted the new constitution apportion the new Congress by population. They had a very strong argument on their side, an early version of "one man, one vote." After all, the most fundamental democratic principles are for the people to elect the representatives and majority rule. As Madison himself from the big state of Virginia said, he "considered an election of one branch at least of the Legislature by the people immediately, as a clear principle of free Government."

However strong their argument, Mr. Paterson, as seen, from the small state of New Jersey, countered with the blank statement that "the small States would never agree to it." David Brearly, also from New Jersey, said, "There will be 3 large states, and 10 small ones. The large States by which he meant Mass^{ts} Pen^a & Virg^a will carry every thing before them." Luther Martin from Maryland said, "that the propositions on the table were a system of slavery for 10 States: that as V^a Mass^{ts} & P^a have 42/90 of the votes they can do as they please without a miraculous Union of the other ten: that they will have nothing to do, but to gain over one of the ten to make them compleat masters of the rest."

It was all about the power as usual. The two sides debated back and forth for weeks, coming close to losing their tempers with each other, almost causing the delegates to throw up their tools and go home in despair. But as we know, they finally constructed a work around, the Great Compromise. They apportioned the House by population, giving the big states an advantage there, but each state had two votes in the Senate, giving the small states an advantage there. So have these built in advantages and disadvantages stayed to this day.

As we also know, they managed to work through or around all the other obstacles as well, even if the tracks not perfectly laid and the train has not always run smoothly or on time. The delegates managed to reach the destination for which they set out. The new Constitution replaced weakness with strength. Congress, the presidency, and the judiciary all received strong powers. Federal law became "the Supreme Law of the Land." America left behind the Confederacy's fatal weakness.

It's a great read. The heroine was tied to the tracks while the train came inexorably on. Would she be snatched from destruction? Yes! Barely in the nick of time and by the skin of our teeth. Let's not forget that one of the Constitution's first and lasting accomplishments was to rescue the nation from the weakness of disunity.

11.05 – A Saga

Except for the ancient Roman Republic, no republic in history has lasted as long as our American Republic, except again, the British. Most past attempts disintegrated into some sort of disaster, only sorted out by descent into some sort of despotism. But the Founders managed to write not merely a republican short story, but start a saga. How did they manage that?

The word "institution" in the sense of "organization" doesn't appear in the Convention's debates. The word in that sense wasn't much in vogue in their day. Yet increasingly, political scientists have come to describe their success in those terms. The Founders managed to create a lasting republican institution that went on living. This living institution has been writing the saga ever since.

Earlier it was said the Constitution or any constitution more like a jury trial than a verdict. It sets up the processes that arrive at the verdicts (the laws and policies). But looked at another way, it was a final verdict. The Constitution rendered a final verdict for republican institutions. From that verdict all other verdicts flow. Those institutions have handed down all the other verdicts ever since by passing the laws and deciding the government's policies.

It's not like the lawyers try to tell you. It's not like your rights are indelibly written in the Constitution, and "being entrenched in parchment to the teeth," keep the government from violating your rights. Rather, your right to self-government is written in the institutions, and so those institutions keep the government from violating your rights, as well as keep it working in your interests. It's easy to see how the architecture of republican institutions structures these results. Since the officials are elected, to get elected they have to do what the people want, and the people want their rights protected and their interests served.

When the architects designed the U.S. Capitol Building, they didn't want just an impressive and elegant structure. They wanted the damn thing to stand up, rather than collapse in ruin. That required taking into account all the gravitational forces pulling on the building. They had to design enough strength into the structure, sometimes by balancing one force against another, say with an arch. In designing our constitutional architecture, the Founders were obsessed with the same concerns. They wanted an impressive and elegant institution that protected the people's rights and served the public interest. But they wanted the damn thing to stand up and last. That required them to account for all the forces pulling on the structure. They needed to design in enough strength, and one way they tried to do so was by balancing one force against another with the separation of powers.

The gravitational force in the political universe is still that same old self-interest (that "perpetuall and restless desire of Power after power"). The Founders carefully designed this force into their structure. In the debates at the convention, John Francis Mercer from Maryland said, "It is a great mistake to suppose that the paper we are to propose will govern the U. States. It is the men whom it will bring into the Govern[t] and [their] interest in maintaining it that is to govern them. The paper will only mark out the mode & the form. Men are the substance and must do the business." In other words, "the paper" (the Constitution) "only marks out the mode and the form" (the republican institutions). This mode and form "brings the men into the government," into office through elections. It then becomes their "interest to maintain" the government under which they hold office.

The Founders meant to use this force (the officials' self-interest) as the central pillar, but they also meant to use this same force to raise other buttresses. They perceived a well-designed republic could attract a vast array of other interests as further support. Remember the questions we earlier heard asked in a critical way, "Did the men who formulated the fundamental law of the land possess the kinds of property which was immediately and directly increased in value or made more secure by the result of the labors at Philadelphia? Did they have money at interest? Did they own public securities? Did they hold western lands for appreciation? Were they interested in shipping and manufacturing?" Whether or not the delegates had such interests, they knew lots of other people who did. Rather than turning away those interests, they meant to attract them to support their new edifice of government.

Nor did their design fail in this ambition. "Have money at interest?" The new government put in place a sounder monetary system, assuring lenders (those with "money at interest") would get repaid in sounder, not inflated currency. As a result, banking, lending, and capital formation proceeded apace, attaching these interests, since they depended on the monetary system. "Own public securities?" The new government could effectively tax and so pay its debts. As a result, people bought government bonds, attaching their interests, since they wanted to get paid back. "Hold western lands for appreciation?" The new government could raise an army to defend the frontiers. As a result, thousands of settlers surged into the territories, attaching the interests of both the speculators, who held "western lands for appreciation," and the settlers, since they both depended on the protection. "Interested in shipping and manufacturing?" Such interests prospered as well, attaching them.

These interests were only the start. Through one interest or another, directly or indirectly, the new government fairly quickly attached the people as a whole. Today, you couldn't count all the interests attached to and depending on the federal government and so supporting it. That's why, for example, Social Security is the "third rail." Politicians don't dare touch the benefits for fear of instantaneous electoral death. The people are attached to the benefits and no one better short-circuit the flow.

Not the least force attached was the people's patriotic allegiance. People tend to support their national government. Even evil governments can usually count on this force when attacked by foreign foes. The Russians fought with fury in World War II, but as Stalin was astute enough to see, fought for Mother Russia, not for communism or him. In 1787, Americans already had a strong sense of national identity, and the new government quickly firmed up and reinforced this sense, giving it still another support. When the Japanese bombed Pearl Harbor, men flocked to the recruiting offices and the Republican Party even buried momentarily its difference with the Democratic President, Franklin Roosevelt. The terrorist attack on 9/11 excited a similar, if less intense and shorter lived response.

Yet throughout history, what except this same force of interests has repeatedly toppled republics? Acting in their own self-interest, someone or other has managed to seize all power for themselves, altering the government into a tyranny or oligarchy. Well knowing that long story, the Founders sought to design still another reinforcement for their structure. They wrote in the "separation of powers." By separating the branches (the Congress, the president, and the judiciary), they meant to balance the competing forces. Under the theory, this balance would keep one branch from toppling the structure and rising to total dominance on the ruins.

And so, in the familiar architecture of our republic, our Congress has two chambers. The force of the one does often check the force of the other. Often a bill passed in one house suffers amendment in the other and the two houses have to reach some compromise, and sometimes one house simply blocks the other. The president's force often checks the Congress and vice versa. He can and does veto their bills, and they have to reach a compromise with him or muster the two-thirds majority needed to override his veto. Since they can sometimes do neither, he sometimes totally blocks them. While for their part, Congress often refuses to pass bills in the form he prefers, forcing him to compromise with them or totally blocking him.

Yet of late this element in the design has come under increasing criticism. The critics argue the separation of powers causes too much inefficiency, obstructing the timely and efficient conduct of business, sometimes blocking crucial business altogether. For the proof to their argument, they point to the British Constitution, which is republican, but has no separation of powers. Look, they say, the British are as free and their government works as well in the public interest, and as a matter of fact, their government is more efficient. Then what's the good of the separation of powers?

Let's take up their argument in the next article. But before going on to that, let's not forget to give credit where credit due. The Constitution created a living republican institution that has gone on living for a long time now. Since staying alive is the first law of the political or any other jungle, that fact alone must say our Constitution uniquely well designed. That living institution has gone on to write quite a saga.

11.06 – Greener Grass

Proverbially, the grass looks greener on the other side of the fence. It's been a long time now since, as discussed in an earlier article, that guy Montesquieu looked across the English Channel and thought to see greener constitutional grass. Nor was he wrong. The English Constitution (their representative democracy) was highly preferable to the French (absolutist) monarchy. But he didn't quite understand what grew the greener grass. He thought the "separation of powers" between the legislative and executive was the fertilizer and the rain. But the English Constitution didn't and doesn't have such a separation. Rather, exactly the opposite is true. "The efficient secret of the English Constitution may be described as the close union, the nearly complete fusion, of the executive and legislative powers." What grew the greener grass was just rooting their constitution in democratic soil. But the Founding Fathers bought into the Frenchman's theory on constitutional agronomy. In the U.S. Constitution, nothing is more prominent than the separation of powers.

Coming down to the present day, a lot of American political scientists have gone through an experience similar to Montesquieu. Looking across the Atlantic Ocean, the British constitutional grass looks greener to them than our American variety, but for a reverse reason. They see "the close union, the nearly complete fusion, of the executive and legislative powers" in the British Constitution as much more efficient, as growing a much more verdant and well-mannered lawn. They see the separation of powers as causing constitutional dysfunction, as a grass killer combined with weed seed, causing large brown patches and a proliferation of noxious weeds.

We've touched on this topic a number of times. The British Constitution unites and fuses the legislative and executive branches. The legislative power to pass laws resides in the House of Commons, the vestigial branch of the House of Lords retaining almost no power. The executive power to carry out the laws lodges with the prime minister assisted by his cabinet. But they share a single residence. Under the terms of their lease, everyone first has to win election to the Commons. The member who leads the dominant party gets the royal nod as prime minister. The prime minister invites into the cabinet other leading members of his party from the Commons. The prime minister and his cabinet sit in the legislative branch at the very same time they occupy their seats in the executive branch.

Their political ambitions (incentives) further unite them. MPs seldom cherish a fonder wish than cabinet rank, and once they reach the front bench, fear losing their portfolio. Since the prime minister can either bestow or take away this gift, they strongly tend to court his favor and follow his lead. As for the backbenchers, hope lingers eternal in the human breast that the prime minister may yet summon them to serve in the cabinet. Nor do they want to lose the seats they occupy. If they fail to follow their party's prime minister, causing him to lose a crucial vote in the Commons (a vote of confidence), his government falls, and they fall right along with him. Such an event triggers an immediate election, and everybody has to fight for their seats all over again.

No wonder the British system is more efficient. The Commons follow rather than obstruct the prime minister. And their system has other virtues. If the prime minister flagging at the course, they don't have to wait for the next race (wait for the next election), they can run in a substitute at any time. His party can simply scratch him (vote him out as party leader) and vote in a new leader. In any event, a new election comes around every five years, but they don't necessarily have to wait that long either. If a government drifts far enough off track to lose its majority in the Commons, it loses a vote of confidence and a new election immediately held.

With such perils hanging over his head, a prime minister can never retreat into the comforts of 10 Downing Street and bid the Commons defiance. He may have the whip hand, but has to manage his reins with some dexterity. Intrigue, insurgency and insurrection tend to fill the heads of the cabinet and even the backbenchers, not to mention the other party. Nor can he afford to dispense with the advice and consent of his cabinet, rather must constantly meet with and consult them, forging some sort of consensus to keep their backing. If their support erodes, his support in the Commons will likely erode in proportion, since they lead factions and wings within the party themselves. Finally, he has to personally attend the Commons and directly answers questions during "the question hour."

When you compare them with our American system, you see why so many political scientists view the British grass as greener. Our Congress is separated into the Senate and the House, and the Congress is separated from the president. When the same party controls all three institutions, there's some incentive to cooperate, but not even then a very compelling one. During the presidency of John F. Kennedy (a Democrat), the Democratic Party enjoyed a comfortable majority in the Congress, but his big tax cut and civil rights bill looked permanently stalled at the time of his death. While if the other party can seize on any of the institutions (divided government), it can become hard to get even essential business done. Witness all the recent government shutdowns, where a divided government couldn't even keep the government funded (up and running). Such dysfunction could never occur under the British Constitution.

Moreover, we're stuck with all of them (the Senate, the House, and the president) to the end of their terms. There's no way to change the helmsman (the president) at the appearance of the storm. Impeachment is hardly a viable course. Come hell or high water, we're stuck with him. No matter how incompetent or unpopular he becomes, there he is for four years. There's not even a reliable way to replace a physically or mentally incapacitated president. Nor does he even have to do much of anything if not so inclined. He can simply throw up his hands and retreat behind the comfortable, not to mention luxurious walls of the White House. Nothing compels him to meet with his cabinet. Traditionally, he gives the State of the Union Address in person to Congress each year, but if he prefers, he can just send over a written message. Certainly, he never has to appear before them and answer questions nor even hold a press conference.

The separation of powers has caused still another distinction to develop between the two systems. The British Parliament has never had a lot of committees, but the American Congress quickly developed a bunch. Nor is the reason for this variation far to seek. Congress quickly evidenced a natural desire to oversee the executive branch to make sure things were running right. Particularly when one of the chambers controlled by the other party, they as quickly evidenced a similar desire to constantly investigate the president, his cabinet, and associates. Since nothing prevented them, Congress quickly developed a lot of committees to realize these desires. Thus, America has come to enjoy the constant spectacle of congressional oversight and interference with the running of the executive departments, as well as the constantly sensationalized congressional investigations. But over in Great British, the prime minister and the cabinet heads sit in and control the House of Commons. They've never evidenced much desire to have a bunch of committees constantly looking over their shoulders and investigating them, and being in a position to do so, have generally nipped such spectacles in the bud.

Well, for my part, the grass looks about as green on either side of the fence, but my taste prefers the grazing on this side, maybe for just the same reason you prefer mom's cooking since you grew up eating it. But the proof is in the pudding, and looks to me like we cook as good a pudding. Britain may cook more efficient and orderly, but to me, America cooks more free and open. Over there, it's a place for everyone and everyone in their place and everyone bows to the Queen. Over here, you can make your own place, and we don't bow to no one. Our economy cooks more dynamic and innovative and has cooked the best and newest recipes such as computers or the internet. They may have served up a more thoroughly baked version of the welfare state for those whose tastes run that way, but we've served up a pretty thorough version ourselves.

Moreover, their system has recently developed a bad flaw. This relates to the way they select their party leaders, who then serve as the prime minister when their party wins power. In the Conservative Party, the Party-in-Parliament (the members of the party who sit in Parliament) select two potential candidates for leader, and the Party-out-of-Parliament (the other party members) then selects one of these two. Since the members of Parliament a pretty canny and experienced lot, this method picks good leaders. But the Labor Party lets the Party-out-of-Parliament (a list of members not in Parliament) select their leaders. Since the Party-out-of-Parliament tends to be dominated by the most vociferous and radical members of the party, this method tends to select as the leader someone from the radical fringe, which reliably the more intractable and less practical. As a result, the Labor Party now has surely the worst leader (Jeremy Corbyn) of any major party in the long history of Great Britain. If Labor wins power, he'll be the next prime minister.

For the dangers this poses, let those who abhor our present president (Donald Trump) contemplate how much more they would abhor him cloaked with all the powers of a British Prime Minister. Let those who support him contemplate how much they would abhor one of his radical foes cloaked with similar powers. Perhaps the grazing on this side of the fence isn't so bad after all.

11.07 – Get the Money

Have you heard about the first three rules for law practice as taught by older lawyers to younger? "Get the money, get the money, get the money." The first three rules for practicing politicians amount to the same thing. "Get the power, get the power, get the power." Being thoroughly familiar with these rules, the Founders' sought to write into the Constitution some limits on just how much power the politicians could get. But they wrote most of them deliberately vague, and we've been arguing ever since over what they meant. But whatever their "original intent," by today the feds have gotten the power all right, far more with far fewer limits. That leaves the only live questions whether their gains to the good or the bad and what effective limits might remain.

The formal doctrine of enumerated (or delegated) powers still says the government can "exercise only the powers granted to it" by the Constitution. Since only some powers granted, that sounds like a limit. But the Constitution spoke in broad generalities, not specifics ("the power to regulate commerce" or "provide for the general welfare"). Moreover, it goes on broadly to say the government shall have all the "necessary and proper" powers to carry out the granted powers, and again, we hear no specifics. We can argue over the original intent as long as we want, but the original intent was broad generalities with few specifics. Who can doubt that legal draftsmen as capable and experienced as the Founders deliberately wrote in that vagueness?

Why? Alexander Hamilton tells why in *Federalist No. 34*, "Constitutions of civil government are not to be framed upon a calculation of existing exigencies, but upon a combination of these with the probable exigencies of ages, according to the natural and tried course of human affairs. Nothing, therefore, can be more fallacious than to infer the extent of any power, proper to be lodged in the national government, from an estimate of its immediate necessities. There ought to be a CAPACITY to provide for future contingencies as they may happen; and as these are illimitable in their nature, it is impossible safely to limit that capacity."

Since the Founders couldn't know all the "probable exigencies," they meant to leave the government with "a capacity to provide for future contingencies as they might happen." They deliberately meant to leave some room for the system to evolve. Some room. The feds have evolved their power to fill the room and burst the seams, no doubt way beyond any anticipation or expectation in the Founders' minds.

Under the commerce clause, "The Congress shall have Power ... to regulate Commerce ... among the several States." Originally, we saw they didn't even have the power to regulate or outlaw a monopoly. Later, we saw that power so far evolve that they could order a farmer not to grow wheat for personal consumption by his family. Under the taxing clause, "Congress shall have the Power To lay and collect Taxes." Later, we saw that power so far evolve they could order everyone to buy something (insurance). If the government can order you what to produce and what to consume, we might wonder what limits remain on their powers under the commerce and taxing clauses.

Nor is the government limited to the enumerated (specifically granted) powers. We heard the Supreme Court rule that, "when Congress acts under the Spending Clause [the power to spend the taxes], ... Congress can use that power to implement federal policy it could not impose directly under its enumerated powers." So for example, we saw that although the Constitution grants no specific power to pay people's medical bills, yet the Spending Clause gave them the power to set up Medicaid. We might wonder what limits remain on their power under "the Spending Clause."

Nor let's forget the foreign policy and war powers. The Constitution says the president, "shall have Power, by and with the Advice and Consent of the Senate, to make Treaties, provided two thirds of the Senators present concur." We saw that power so far evolve President Obama could sign a nuclear treaty with Iran without Senate approval and even in the face of a majority opposed. The Constitution goes on to say, "The Congress shall have the Power ... To declare War." We saw the president's power so far evolve as to lead us into a number of undeclared wars like Vietnam. While under their war powers, we've seen Congress can order a command-and-control economy, virtually taking over the economy.

If that not enough power, remember we heard President Franklin Roosevelt call for a Second Bill of Rights way back in 1944. These new rights included, "the right to earn enough to provide adequate food and clothing and recreation; ... The right of every family to a decent home; The right to adequate medical care and the opportunity to achieve and enjoy good health; The right to adequate protection from the economic fears of old age, sickness, accident, and unemployment; The right to a good education." In other words, he called for the welfare state, a work well along if still a work in progress. But the power to do many of these things was nowhere granted in the Constitution. To start doing them, the government had to take still more power and will have to take still more to finish the job.

That still ain't all. The 14th Amendment says, "No state shall make or enforce any law which shall deny ... to any person ... the equal protection of the laws." Originally, that meant "the laws" could make no invidious distinctions, that is, no distinctions not based upon some rational reason. For example, we saw the laws could treat juveniles different than adults, but not blacks different than whites. Later, we saw that power evolve so far as to reverse its meaning. It was no longer enough for "the laws" to make no invidious distinctions. Rather, now, "the laws" had to outlaw all conduct deemed invidious. For example, we saw that even though the laws no longer ordered segregation (racial separation), the laws now ordered integration (racial mixing). Businesses couldn't refuse to serve blacks, and the public schools had to contain a proper racial mix.

Today, this power has evolved so far it's like the old Mormon case over polygamy (Reynolds v U.S. in 1878). In that case, the Supreme Court ruled the Mormons could believe in polygamy, but couldn't practice it. Today, maybe you still can believe whatever you want in the privacy of your mind, but you can't practice any belief the government deems invidious. As a famous example, take the "dear colleague letter on transgender students," which was an order issued to the schools by the Department of Justice and Department of Education. The letter ordered as follows, "Gender identity refers to an individual's internal sense of gender. ... Restrooms and Locker Rooms. A school may provide separate facilities on the basis of sex, but must allow transgender students access to such facilities consistent with their gender identity." If you want, you can still read Supreme Court cases that say, "the National Government possesses only limited powers." But if the National Government can tell people what restrooms and locker rooms to use, we might wonder where to find any remaining limits.

Get the money. Get the power. The feds have gotten both. Today, they have power over the people to almost any extent. That leaves the only live questions whether their gains to the good or the bad and what effective limits might remain. But we've run out of space again and need to pick up the discussion in the next article.

11.08 – The New Colossus

You're not allowed to question the theory of evolution. That would commit a heresy against a prime tenet of the secular religion, which you better believe or else. The modern, secular version of the Spanish Inquisition would promptly hold an *auto da fe* and roast you alive in the public square. Then not to risk such a fate, it certainly seems true that unless you can adapt, you'll go extinct. That applies not just to species, but to societies, institutions, and governments.

The Founding Fathers may not have known the theory, which became a truth beyond question after their day. But they got it. They created a living institution of government, and they understood it would have to evolve. In *Federalist No. 82*, Hamilton wrote, "Tis time only that can mature and perfect so compound a system, can liquidate the meaning of all the parts, and can adjust them to each other in a harmonious and consistent WHOLE." That looks toward an evolution.

As we heard him say in *Federalist No. 34*, "Constitutions of civil government are not to be framed upon a calculation of existing exigencies, but upon a combination of these with the probable exigencies of ages, … . Nothing, therefore, can be more fallacious than to infer the extent of any power, proper to be lodged in the national government, from an estimate of its immediate necessities. There ought to be a CAPACITY to provide for future contingencies as they may happen; and as these are illimitable in their nature, it is impossible safely to limit that capacity." That looks toward an evolution in the powers of the government "to provide for future contingencies as they may happen."

Knowing the government's power would have to evolve, they wrote its powers into the Constitution somewhat vaguely, leaving some space for the evolution. But they believed in "limited government," too, and so at the same time, they tried to write in some limits. But as seen throughout these articles, those limits have failed to restrain very much. The forces pushing on the evolution have long since generated a "New Colossus," a government with powers far beyond the anticipation of the Founders and far beyond any reasonable interpretation of their "original intent."

At every step along the way, some critic or other was constantly heard to complain the government was exceeding the limits on some constitutional power or other. This set of critics is still very much with us. But what would you have? Would you rather the limits had failed or the government had failed? If the limits hadn't failed, the government couldn't have evolved, and if the government couldn't have evolved, the government would have failed.

It's been the old two-edged sword. By this time, either edge has cut pretty deep. We've felt the pain as one edge has cut ever deeper into our lives, constantly intruding upon and interfering with us. But would we want a government that couldn't, say, have cut out the pain that monopoly was causing us? That for some other examples, couldn't regulate our modern economy, hopefully to bring us the pleasures of prosperity and prevent the pain of recessions and depressions? That couldn't provide for healthcare? That couldn't enter into informal treaties, since the formal treaty making process so cumbersome as largely unworkable? That short of a declaration of war couldn't deploy the military to protect our national interests and ward off the outbreak of actual war? That couldn't manage the economy in war time so we could win the war? That couldn't provide the benefits of the welfare state to give us a safety net against "the economic fears of old age, sickness, accident, and unemployment." That couldn't remedy the wrongs of racial segregation?

In the past at least, Americans have been accused of being

overly pragmatic, not idealistic enough. Some might offer this evolution as ample proof. We repeatedly reasoned our way around theoretical limits to reach practical goals. We took the cash and let the credit go. We largely acquiesced in the government taking more power over us as a pragmatic necessity.

But that doesn't mean this criticism lacks force. Who doesn't believe in "limited government?" Who doesn't believe the government has gotten too much power in some respect or other? But there our New Colossus stands astride our national life. What effective limits continue to restrain his powers over us, if any?

Well, let's remember something else Hamilton said in *Federalist No. 31*, "A government ought to contain in itself every power requisite to the full accomplishment of the objects committed to its care, and to the complete execution of the trusts for which it is responsible, free from every other control but a regard to the public good and to the sense of the people. ... all observations founded upon the danger of usurpation ought to be referred to the composition and structure of the government, not to the nature or extent of its powers."

Right. We want a government with "every power requisite to the full accomplishment of the objects committed to its care, and to the complete execution of the trusts for which it is responsible." But that doesn't leave the government "free from every control." No, rather he says, "free from every control but a regard to the public good and to the sense of the people. ... all observations founded upon the danger of usurpation ought to be referred to the composition and structure of the government, not to the nature or extent of its powers."

Right again. The "composition and structure of the government" is the only real defense against "the danger of usurpation." No words on a printed page ever effectively limited the powers of any government. The only real defense has always come from "the composition and the structure" (the institutional nature of the government). Democratic institutions set the limits through their reference to "the sense of the people" through elections.

Then today, what limits the power of our New Colossus? Well, notice. His powers have grown huge, but he still retains the same shape. He's still a democratic institution. And his shape still limits his powers. The effective restraint is nothing except his democratic nature. And how well has that restraint worked? Pretty well. We're still pretty free. Moreover, we have the means in our hands to further restrain him through the democratic process. It's just a matter of having the understanding and the will to do it.

While the Founders' attempt to write in limits may have largely failed, their attempt to write in a strong enough institution largely succeeded. As long as our democratic institutions continue to succeed, we can hope to continue to succeed. That sets the effective limits on the powers of the New Colossus.

11.09 – We the People

The Preamble reads, "We the People … do ordain and establish this Constitution for the United States of America." But reading the debates in the Convention, the delegates expressed quite a few doubts about "the people." They wanted democracy, but not too much democracy. Rather than a direct democracy, where the people rule more or less directly, they wanted a republic, a representative democracy, where the people elect their representatives to rule for them. Today, no one dare say anything against "democracy," yet perhaps the Founders weren't wrong in fearing too much democracy.

As for the delegates doubts about "the people," Elbridge Gerry from Massachusetts said, "The evils we experience flow from the excess of democracy." Edmund Randolph from Virginia seconded that, "in tracing these evils to their origin every man had found it in the turbulance and follies of democracy." Speaking of the proposal to popularly elect the president, he said, "The people are uninformed, and would be misled by a few designing men." Others expressed similar sentiments.

These reservations about an "excess of democracy" help explain the Electoral College and why senators started out elected by the state legislatures, rather than directly by the people. The Founders wanted to filter and refine the people's voice to speak through more informed mouths. The same reservations go to explain why they limited the franchise with property qualifications. They wanted to keep the ballots in the hands of a more informed electorate.

But since their day, the call for more democracy has repeatedly triumphed. The Electoral College still functions, but the election of the president has become a much more directly democratic event with the people directly selecting the candidates through primaries. Senators are now directly elected by the people due to the 17th Amendment ratified in 1913. Not only have property qualifications been rejected, any qualifications for voters, such as say, having a high school diploma or not having a felony conviction have been rejected. Today, the call is to "count every vote," even if someone has to carry the ballots to the people, show them where to place their marks, and haul them back for counting.

But more democracy hasn't necessarily translated into better democracy. For example, around the 1900s, the progressives of that era campaigned for more democracy by advocating the "referendum." Under this proposal, a law or constitutional amendment would be referred directly to the people for them to vote on. A number of states adopted the idea, most notably California. But the results have disappointed. As the example often given, in 1978, about two-thirds of Californians voted to pass Proposition 13, an amendment to the California Constitution to cap property taxes at 1 percent of assessed value. Who wouldn't want to cap their taxes? But this rigid ceiling later received much of the blame when the quality of California's public education declined. The schools' funding depended on this source of taxation, which was now constricted.

Whether or not this particular criticism valid, the general criticism looks valid. A referendum turns out a highly cumbersome way to makes laws. It can only present laws to the voters one at a time (in "a silo"). But the laws exist in context, the cost and effect of one impacting others. When the question is solely whether or not to cap or lower our taxes, who wouldn't vote yes? But that badly narrows the question, leaving out connected questions, obscuring the effect on essential government services such as education. It's also all or nothing, up or down, take it or leave it, with no chance for further compromise or tinkering with the provisions. And it makes very rigid laws, hard to change no matter how the law works in practice. When phrased as constitutional amendments, the legislature can't later reverse the outcome. Even when phrased as just an ordinary law, the legislators are reluctant to make changes and face the accusation of reversing the will of the people. A referendum also has to appear on the stump. A speaker on the stump has to boil down the issues and swing a wide lasso to catch the widest possible audience. That badly tends to crowd out the nuances and replace a reasoned approach with an emotional appeal. Finally, but not least, the average voter simply lacks as much experience and information as the average member of the legislature.

By contrast, passing laws in the legislative chamber forces the legislators to "bundle" them, consider how the costs of one impact another, consider the overall effects. They can compromise and tinker right up to the last moment. In the very next session, they can respond to the effect the law has in the real world, altering provisions or even repealing the whole thing. The same speaker who made simplistic arguments on the stump can make more nuanced arguments to his colleagues, who possess considerably more knowledge and experience than the average voter. Thus, the referendum doesn't appear as good a way to make laws as the legislative process and a more direct democracy didn't necessarily translate into a better democracy.

Maybe the Founders weren't so wrong not to want too much democracy. We might want to keep that in mind and exercise some caution with proposals for still "more democracy." What may sound like a good reform, may not always turn out such a good one. Good reasons exist for passing your laws through an elected legislature.

Then, right on. "We the people." But what we "ordained and established" was a republic, a representative rather than a direct democracy. As Madison said in *Federalist No.* 10, "it may well happen that the public voice pronounced by the representatives of the people, will be more consonant to the public good, than if pronounced by the people themselves." Not only may it happen, generally, it will happen.

11.10 – Mr. Jefferson Goes to Washington

Thomas Jefferson famously said, "If I could not go to heaven but with a party, I would not go there at all." As famously, he later invented the first American political party (the Democrat-Republicans), and traveling at the head of this party, passed through the pearly gates to the White House, as close as it gets to political heaven. After all, "A foolish consistency is the hobgoblin of little minds."

Jefferson wasn't alone among the Founding Fathers in condemning political parties. In his Farewell Address, Washington fulminated at length against them. "Let me ... warn you in the most solemn manner against the baneful effects of the spirit of party generally. ... the common and continual mischiefs of the spirit of party are sufficient to make it the interest and duty of a wise people to discourage and restrain it. It serves always to distract the public councils and enfeeble the public administration. It agitates the community with ill-founded jealousies and false alarms, kindles the animosity of one part against another, foments occasionally riot and insurrection. It opens the door to foreign influence and corruption, which finds a facilitated access to the government itself through the channels of party passions."

But time taught another lesson, as Jefferson learned another lesson. Not that Washington was wrong about parties "agitating the community" and "kindling animosity." If Americans fiercely divided against themselves, what more causes the divisions than the "mischiefs of the spirit of party?" Yet political parties turned out essential to democracy. If you want to go there at all, you have to go with a party. Otherwise, welcome to chaos. Without the political party, democracy lacks an institution to organize and express public opinion in an effective way and to organize the legislature in an effective way.

To see that, imagine a national election without political parties. Hundreds or probably thousands of candidates would run for the 435 House and 100 Senate seats, all unaffiliated, all standing on their own platforms. "I'm for capitalism. Well, I'm for socialism. Well, I'm for the best of both. I'm a free-trader. Well, I'm a protectionist. Well, I'm for the best of both. I'm an internationalist. Well, I'm an isolationist. Well, I'm for the best of both." How could the voters sort out such a cacophony of voices? How could they choose among the voices to send any sort of clear message to Washington? How could the lucky winners sort themselves out on arrival to decide whose platform to carry out?

We've learned another lesson about political parties. How you structure your electoral system decisively structures your party system. In turn, your party system decisively structures how your government functions.

Political scientists refer to "the Westminster system," also called the single-member district system (SMD). The name comes from the British Parliament, which sits in Westminster. It's also called "the single-member district system," since a single-member is elected from each district. Such a system differs from an array of other alternatives, all based on some form of proportional representations (PR). In the purest form of PR, candidates don't stand in districts, rather, each party runs a nationwide slate of candidates. Each party wins legislative seats in proportion to their percentage of the total national vote with some minimum, say 3 percent, to win any seats.

The results under the different systems lead to radically different outcomes. The Westminster system (SMD) leads to a two-party system. Proportional representation leads to a multi-party system. In single-member districts, two dominate parties will emerge. Smaller parties may win a seat or two on occasion, but usually, voting against one major party only gives the election to the other major party. Smaller parties or defectors from a major party soon grow discouraged and merge or return to a major party. But with PR, smaller parties can flourish on a narrow margin. Usually, a couple or three main parties will emerge, but even fringe parties can hope to win some seats. For an example of the variation in results, in the 2015 British election, the UK Independence Party (UKIP) won only one seat in Parliament. But across the whole country, it won about 3.9 of the 30.4 million votes (about 12.8 percent). Under PR it would have received around 83 of the 650 seats in the House of Commons.

The resulting party system decisively influences how the government functions. The Westminster (two-party system) pushes the government toward the middle ground and the majority rules. Look at the polling on most major issues. Despite all the present talk about polarization, the actual statistics form a bell curve. Fewer people occupy the extremes, more the center. Whichever the ruling party, they're forced toward the rise on the bell curve, toward the center. To win power, they have to appeal to a majority view. To keep power, they have to govern in line with the same view. The radical fringe can seldom call the shots, leaving them in a constant state of frustration. But with PR, a single party seldom wins a majority of the legislative seats. To govern requires the forming of some sort of coalition among the parties. Since such coalitions are formed after the election, the bargains struck will likely change the outcome of the election. Some bigger party will likely have to surrender some part of their program to coalesce with some smaller party. This coalition government may only poorly reflect the majority view. Even fringe parties can sometimes call the shots as the price for joining a coalition. No wonder the radical fringe love PR.

If democracy should govern in line with majority rule, the Westminster system will govern much better than a PR system. On the other hand, if what you want is a government that caters to minorities and the fringes, you might say PR better.

At the same time, a two-party legislature will function more efficiently that a multi-party one. In a two-party system, one party will have a majority in the chamber. Since they control the chamber, they can get through the business. But in a multi-party system, the parties in the governing coalition have differing agendas. Getting them all to agree and sign off makes it much harder to get through the business. There is often not much reason for smaller parties to compromise, since their issue their reason for existing.

When Thomas Jefferson created the first American political party (the Democrat-Republicans), he had none of this in mind. But since America inherited the single-member district (SMD) system from Britain, electing our congressmen that way, the result quickly led to a two-party system, today, the Democrats and Republicans. This result decisively influences how our government functions. The parties have to move toward the middle ground to win elections. The majority rules rather than the extremes. At the same time, the result provides a crucial element around which Congress organizes, helping them to get through their business.

The Constitution nowhere contemplates political parties. Parties quickly emerged, spontaneously generating out of the other institutions. Today, the parties have become an essential feature of the institutional design. Once again, we got lucky. We inherited "the Westminster system," which leads to a two-party system. That looks highly preferable as a design.

11.11 – The Forge of Democracy

Congress has been called "the forge of democracy." That brings to mind the old Greek legend about an age of gold, an age of silver, and an age of iron. In the golden age, men possessed all the virtues. But the race declined, first to silver and then to iron, harder men with harder weapons, but fewer virtues. Our congressional forge has turned out a few golden laws, some silver, and some iron, but more often some sort of alloy often mixed with some baser metals. We can't look back on a golden age of legislation. But so far, Congress has turned out laws good enough to pass as coin of the realm with sufficient gold and silver content. From time to time, some debased laws may have found their way into circulation. But just like the dollar accepted around the world, overall, our congressional laws have served as sound money and circulated to good effect.

Why? First and foremost, Congress is a democratic institution. Elections are frequent and fair; everyone can vote and stand for the office; there's a free press and freedom of association. Accountability is the golden word in government. Congress is accountable. But it's not enough just to hold your legislators accountable through elections. A lot depends on how you elect them, the electoral system, and a lot on the internal structure of the institution.

To start from the inside, Congress is a "linked, dual channel" legislature. The two political parties and the committees serve as the "dual channels." The parties give Congress an organizing principle otherwise lacking. The majority party elects the leaders such as the Speaker of the House and Majority Leader in the Senate, while the minority party forms "the loyal opposition" under their own leaders. The majority leaders preside over and run the proceedings, but their majority seldom solid enough to run roughshod. Not infrequently, some of their members desert them over one thing or another, forcing them to reach across the aisle for sufficient support to pass a particular measure and forcing some compromise between the parties. At the least, the minority constantly scrutinizes for defects and flaws, real or imagined, in legislation, keeping the majority on their toes and more or less to the straight and narrow. While the committees gain for Congress the advantages that come with a division of labor and specialization. The numerous committees can simultaneously work on numerous laws while simultaneously overseeing the numerous bureaucracies. The committee members, some who serve for years, can develop an expertise in their areas. And since the majority party appoints all the chairmen and has a majority on all the committees, these dual channels are "linked." Congress can move as a whole and in a coherent way, which it otherwise could not. In addition, the party leaders give Congress a way to interface with the chief executive which otherwise lacking.

As for the electoral system, Congress is modeled on the Westminster (single-member district) system. We elect our congressmen from single-member (geographic) districts. You get "your congressman," who looks out for the folks and communities in your district. Other electoral systems by electing legislators at large across the whole country break such an intimate tie, leaving local voices shouting in the wilderness with no legislative ear attuned to hear their cry, leaving local interests small chance of raising enough sound to be heard all the way to the corridors of power. While at least as much, the Westminster system results in a two-party system with just two major parties, and as seen, having just two parties coherently organizes Congress. Electoral systems that result in multi-party legislatures lack such an organizing principle, but must govern through forming coalitions. Not only are such coalitions often unstable, frustrating the transaction of business, their formation requires cutting backroom deals made between the party leaders after the election, a process not only lacking transparency, but lacking any approval by the voters. Since most voters occupy the middle ground, the Westminster system also forces both parties toward the same middle ground. The will of the national majority generally prevails in Congress. In the multi-party systems, the will of the majority is never clearly expressed, but chopped up into fragments. The radical fringe can often call some key shots as the price for their often crucial cooperation in forming a coalition.

Nor let us forget that rather than a direct democracy, Congress is a representative institution. To win a seat requires the candidates to run against the competition and keeping a seat requires constant competition. "You can fool all the people some of the time, some of the people all the time, but not all the people all the time." If there's any truth in the adage, the people will sort out the better competitors, and the better competitors will figure out it's in their interest not to try to fool the people, but to govern in the people's interest. The institution doesn't just select on average like a lottery, but selects for better than average. It picks those better at the business, and like any business, once in the business they gain the advantage of experience, becoming even better. To repeat again what Madison said in *Federalist No. 10*, "it may well happen that the public voice pronounced by the representatives of the people, will be more consonant to the public good, than if pronounced by the people themselves."

Observe the overall good results. Congress is a democratic institution. Accountability is the golden word in government. Congress is accountable. It's not just accountable to the people as a whole across the country, but to local folks and communities. It can move as a coherent whole. The party-out-of-power never ceases to scrutinize and call to account the party-in-power. It can interface with the executive branch. It can get through a lot of business and can get good at the business. It's forced toward the middle ground to govern in line with the will of the majority.

In the terms political scientists like to use nowadays, it's an open institution (transparent). Not only can anybody run for a seat, but virtually every viewpoint has a chance to be heard in the halls. The institution is bottom-up rather than top-down. Rather than dictating to the bottom, the top has to respond to the bottom. It has an effective feedback mechanism, which rapidly and effectively feeds back information from the bottom to the top, and the top can't ignore the bottom. Far from being dysfunctional as so often claimed, it's functional.

The institutional design for a democratic legislature turns out not so easy, as witness all the failures throughout history and around the world. Most legislatures have turned out laws so tight as to strangle the nation or as loose as runaway inflation. They govern too much in the interests of a narrow elite or too little, leading to a situation close to national anarchy. But Congress has minted laws with enough gold and silver content to circulate to good effect. It's the forge of democracy.

11.12 – The Run of Presidents

Ranking the presidents ranks a national pastime. Washington and Lincoln come in close for first. Franklin Roosevelt comes in third. The stock of some has fluctuated over the years. Thomas Jefferson and Andrew Jackson used to rank high, but being slaveholders recently devalued their stock. James K. Polk holds pretty steady near the top. He may have lacked charisma, but "what Polk went for he fetched." He fetched the remaining half of the American subcontinent for the nation, mainly by taking us into the Mexican-American War from 1846 to 1848. Millard Fillmore and James Buchanan appear mired at the bottom. But if there's always room at the top per Daniel Webster, there's always room at the bottom. Some recent presidents appear consigned there, at least by their critics.

Yet it's not entirely the man, it's his chances. A president can't be great without a great chance. Not all the presidents got the chance to found the nation (Washington), enlarge the nation (Polk), or preserve the nation (Lincoln). Some had lesser chances and lesser chances to score clear-cut wins. When the Japanese attacked Pearl Harbor, it was pretty clear what Roosevelt needed to do and unconditional surrender a clear win. When the terrorists attacked on 9/11, it wasn't as clear what President George W. Bush needed to do or what would count as a clear win. Likely enough, his critics would have derided whatever he did, and they certainly have.

But it's not entirely the man or his chances. The office makes the man. "Power reveals." The annals of kingship reveal that "absolute power corrupts absolutely." That office will corrupt the ordinary run of men. From the glories of David and Solomon, the biblical kings quickly descended into a run of regicides, only interrupted by the occasional "good king." The Roman emperors descended in a brief two generations from the wisdom of an Augustus to the madness of a Caligula. If later some "good emperors" such as Marcus Aurelius momentarily rescued the line, the corruption finally set in irreversible. The European kings, Chinese emperors, and Turkish sultans only lengthen the list. A reigning queen like Elizabeth I of England is the rare exception. The general rule is a run of rulers who bankrupt and ruin the nation, succeeded by another dynasty who repeat the process.

By contrast, the run of American presidents has never fallen below a certain level. As their oath of office says, "I do solemnly swear (or affirm) that I will faithfully execute the Office of President of the United States, and will to the best of my Ability, preserve, protect and defend the Constitution of the United States." None of them have failed to keep their oath. None have usurped the Constitution and turned themselves into a tyrant. They've preserved the "Union," assured "domestic tranquility," provided for the "common defense," and promoted the "general welfare" (the purposes for the Constitution proclaimed by the Preamble).

Why the difference? Why have we had such a long run of at least comparatively successful presidents, good enough for government work? Such a run can't be the roll of the dice (chance). We can't have been lucky enough to have the right men randomly turn up at the right time and place for over two hundred years. Rather, it must be something about the office that makes the man. The office must somehow choose them, form them, and let them succeed, or at least not fail too drastically.

Of course, in the first place, American presidents don't have absolute power, and so they're not absolutely corrupt. If that sounds like damning with faint praise, it's about the highest accolade we can ever bestow on any run of political leaders. "Let us now praise famous men." You'll not find many to praise whose absolute power revealed their inner man. You'll find less to condemn with American presidents for the simple reason they don't have absolute power.

More than just restraining their vices within tolerable limits, the office inspires them to virtue of a certain sort. "All the world's a stage, and one man in his time plays many parts." To play the president's part, a man can't inherit, buy, or seize the office. He has to audition before a critical audience. "America's Got Talent." He has to win an open competition by showing enough talent to beat his rivals for the role. The lucky winner gets to actually play the role on stage for four years. And he better give a compelling performance. Unless he can sell tickets at the box office, he'll soon find himself playing to an empty theater. His production will close, and he'll be ushered off the stage.

What sort of virtue does playing this part inspire? Hollywood has turned out far more mediocre or worse than great movies. But you can't accuse them of not trying to sell tickets at the box office. The same goes for American presidents. Only a few have been great. But you can't accuse them of not trying to sell tickets at the box office. They try to play to the public taste.

But is that a virtue? Old Socrates didn't think so. Hollywood and the presidents share the criticism uttered so long ago by that oracle against democracy. Their audience is the common (average) man. He accused them of playing to the lowest common denominator, rather than appealing to a more elevated taste. What about that?

Leaving out Hollywood, about which the complaint appears to possess a lot of validity, what's the taste in the public theater, the political theater in which the presidents act? It is pretty average, isn't it? The average audience will applaud a performance that meets their individual needs. That is, they want a family, a decent education, a good job, adequate health care, a nice house, and the opportunity to flourish and lead a meaningful life. Since they can't get these needs except in society, they also applaud a performance that attains their society goals. That is, they want security against foreign invasion, a good economy, law and order, and freedom. In short, their tastes strongly run toward a high standard of living and high index of freedom. And these preferences coincide with the purposes proclaimed in the Preamble for the Constitution (to preserve the "Union," assure "domestic tranquility," provide for the "common defense," and promote the "general welfare").

If you want to call such tastes the lowest common denominator, what's so wrong with hitting such an average? What's so wrong with the virtues inspired by playing to the tastes of such an audience? The president plays his part so as to try to win their applause. This virtue explains why their performances haven't fallen below a certain level. The office makes the man.

Except for the consuls of the Roman Republic and British prime ministers, no other run of chief executives in all history can compare with the run of success of our presidents. The Roman consuls' run lasted around four centuries, but finally ran out. The British prime ministers' run has lasted near three centuries and still running. Whether our presidents' run of success has run out may be a matter for debate. But even those who make the claim hope to see that run resumed after the next election, when their candidate sworn in as president.

However you rank the presidents, none of them has fallen below a certain rank into the ranks of tyrants. None of them has failed to try to play to the public taste. By so doing, none of them has failed too badly. That's about as good as it gets in politics. We better hope it never gets any worse.

11.13 – A Shibboleth

What's a shibboleth? The dictionary says, "a custom, principle, or belief distinguishing a particular class or group of people, especially a long-standing one regarded as outmoded or no longer important." Then what's the rationale for judicial review? It's a shibboleth. But what's hypocrisy? The dictionary says, "feigning to be what one is not or to believe what one does not." Then when the Supreme Court still feigns to believe this shibboleth, what's that? It's hypocrisy.

If that seems a bit complex and opaque, let's sort it out. Remember? Judicial review is the Supreme Court's power to declare congressional laws unconstitutional and hence void. Remember, too? The rationale as propounded by Chief Justice John Marshall way back in the case of Marbury v Madison in 1803 was that, "The original and supreme will [of the people] organizes the government and assigns to the different departments their respective powers. ... The powers of the Legislature [Congress] are defined and limited; and that those limits may not be mistaken or forgotten, the constitution is written. To what purpose is that limitation committed to writing, if these limits may at any time be passed by those intended to be restrained?"

In other words, the people expressed their "original and supreme will" with the Constitution. They "defined and limited" the "powers of the Legislature" (Congress). To keep "those limits" from being "passed," Congress must "be restrained." To do that, the Supreme Court must have a power of judicial review to declare laws unconstitutional and hence void. Chief Justice Marshall's rationale for judicial review was that the Supreme Court would defend the "original and supreme will" of the people as expressed in the Constitution.

And so, with this rationale and with this very same case of Marbury v Madison in 1803, the Court successfully claimed the power for judicial review for itself, a power nowhere specifically granted it. But remember, too? Originally, this rationale came with a major limitation. Some "limits" may be "written" into the Constitution, but not many clearly written. Then the Constitution may express the "original and supreme will" of the people, but only where clearly expressed. As a logical result, the Supreme Court could only declare laws unconstitutional in "clear-cut" cases where all rational men would agree. Otherwise, the power of judicial review threatened, as Thomas Jefferson warned at the time, to "place us under the despotism of an oligarchy," replacing rule by the democratic Congress with rule by the life-time judges. Unless the judges were limited to clear-cut cases, they wouldn't be defending the "original and supreme will" of the people, but merely imposing their own version of the Constitution. If they could do that, they could impose their will on Congress and the people themselves.

To defuse this criticism at the time, the Court came up with a formula of words. They repeatedly pledged never to declare an act of Congress unconstitutional except in a "clear-cut" case. As Chief Justice Marshall himself put the rule in 1810 in the case of Fletcher v Peck, "The question, whether a law be void for its repugnancy to the constitution, is at all times of much delicacy, which ought seldom, if ever, to be decided in the affirmative, in a doubtful case." As Chief Justice Morrison Remick Waite said in a later case in 1878, "This declaration [that an act of Congress is unconstitutional] should never be made except in a clear case. Every possible presumption is in favor of the validity of a statute, and this continues until the contrary is shown beyond a rationale doubt."

That was the "original" or limited doctrine of judicial

review. But just as the limits on so many of the government's other powers have evolved largely away, this limit on the Supreme Court's power has evolved entirely away. Beginning with the Dred Scott Case in 1857, the Court began to forget all about clear-cut cases. Not to tell that story over again, who doesn't know that today their power has become virtually unrestrained. By now, it's a commonplace for the Court simply to void congressional laws at will. Going way beyond even that, the Court can at will simply change a previously accepted (clear) meaning of the Constitution itself.

Then what's the shibboleth? What's the "custom, principle, or belief distinguishing a particular class or group of people, especially a long-standing one regarded as outmoded or no longer important"? That's the rationale for judicial review, that the Court defends the "original and supreme will" of the people as expressed in the Constitution. That's a "belief distinguishing a particular class or group of people," most of the legal profession and a host of fellow travelers. But it's also "regarded as outmoded or no longer important" by them. Rather, today, they regard the Constitution as "whatever the judges say it is" with no regard whatsoever for the "original and supreme will" of the people.

What's the hypocrisy, the "feigning to be what one is not or to believe what one does not?" That's the Court's still "feigning to be what one is not," feigning to be the defender of the "original and supreme will" of the people as expressed in the Constitution. That's the Court still feigning "to believe what one does not," to believe in the rationale for judicial review. Rather, today, they do just whatever they want to do, and they believe in their power to just that.

This hypocrisy is not the least cost of judicial review. We, the people, established the Constitution. We were supposed to make the laws through Congress. But the Court has usurped the power to remake the constitutional law at will. In so doing, they constantly feign to defend the will of the people as expressed in the Constitution. But who cannot see the hypocrisy? They don't defend our will, but constantly impose their will on us. How can this open hypocrisy not bring our highest law into contempt? But there are other costs as well. The country goes down a course steered by the self-interest of the lawyers and judges, rather than the course set by the people. Their self-interest does not necessarily coincide with the public interest. Even if it did, this "judicial supremacy" violates fundamental democratic principles.

If there's a valid criticism of the Constitution, this is a valid criticism. We're told we live in a democracy. In reality, the Court has usurped out democracy. When the Congress or the president take more power, they're still responsible to the people. The democratic nature of our government doesn't change. But by taking more power, the Court has changed the very nature of our government. The Court isn't responsible to the people. Rather, it has usurped power over the people and rules above and beyond responsibility to them. If anything about the Constitution as it has become ought to change, that would be a good place to start.

Yet let's not neglect to give the them credit for when they did better. The Supreme Court hasn't guarded democracy, but they have served as good guardians over the rule of law, the "due process of the law" and "equal protection of the law." In America, the government can't take your life, liberty, or property without adequate notice and an adequate hearing. In guarding these rights, the justices have rendered a not inconsiderable service to the people.

11.14 – The Birth Defect

A good lawyer looks up the law. When the other lawyer starts arguing the law says thus and such, quoting back at him the actual law often reveals him as blurring and twisting the words to win the argument. But lawyers aren't the only ones guilty of blurring and twisting the words to win an argument. When it comes to attacking the Constitution, such tactics might qualify as a national pastime and go way back.

For a classic example, a persistent set of critics say the Constitution was "born with a birth defect" – slavery. Like good lawyers, let's look up the law. What does the Constitution actually say? The word "slavery" nowhere appears in the original Constitution. When the word finally did make its appearance, it was only to abolish slavery. The 13th Amendment ratified in 1865 says, "Neither slavery nor involuntary servitude … shall exist within the United States." Since the original words didn't mention slavery and the later words abolished slavery, whence the defect?

Oddly enough, these present-day critics have taken over an argument earlier made by the other side. In the agitation over abolition prior to the Civil War, the slave states were losing the argument in the democratic arena. They were losing the demographic and economic battles, and eventually, they were going to lose the political war. The free states were wealthier and more populous. Their growing population was heading west, filling the territories with free homesteaders, which must invariably lead to still more anti-slavery states. Sooner or later the non-slave states were going to have the votes in Congress to abolish slavery. Trying to find another way to win the argument, the advocates for slavery began to blur and twist the words. They began to claim the Constitution guaranteed them a "right to slavery," a guarantee beyond the reach of majority rule.

Again, like good lawyers, let's look up some more law. And we've already read this law back in the articles on the Supreme Court, but to recap more briefly. While the Constitution as originally written didn't mention the word "slavery," yet there were "three covert references." First, "the three-fifths compromise" let the slave states count their slaves for purposes of apportioning the House of Representatives. Next, a second provision prevented Congress from outlawing the African slave trade until 1808, which incidentally, they did outlaw on January 1, 1808. Finally, a third provision provided for the extradition of escaped slaves back to their masters, later leading to the highly controversial "fugitive slave laws."

But nowhere do we find any words that say Congress lacked the power to abolish slavery. In fact, Congress passed several laws against slavery. The famous Northwest Ordinance in 1789 had prohibited slavery in the Northwest Territory, an area that later went to make up Ohio, Indiana, Illinois, Michigan, Wisconsin, and Minnesota. The Missouri Compromise in 1820 had prohibited slavery north of the Mason Dixon line between Pennsylvania and

Maryland, and the Compromise of 1850 extended the prohibition to still other territories. Of course, all the northern states had prohibited slavery within their borders.

Not only did the words of the Constitution fail to guarantee "a right to slavery," the actual practice refutes such a reading of the words. Slavery existed in 1787 in some states, but no words prevented Congress from outlawing it at a later time in all the states. Rather, the Constitution left to the people the right to decide this great question through the democratic process.

But while two wrongs don't make a right, the people would shortly witness two wrongs successfully claimed as a right. To start with, the slave states would wrongly claim a "right to slavery" by twisting and blurring the words in the Constitution. Next, the Supreme Court would wrongly take away from the people their right to decide the question by twisting and blurring the words in the Constitution to claim such a right for their Court. Both wrongful claims would succeed. But those weren't the sins of the Constitution, rather those were sins against the Constitution and against the people and democracy.

Again, like good lawyers, let's look up the law, and again, we already read this law back in the articles on the Supreme Court. In the 1857 Dred Scott Case, the Supreme Court found a "right to slavery" guaranteed in the Constitution. Chief Justice Taney ruled that, "The right of property in a slave is distinctly and expressly affirmed in the Constitution." But since the actual words weren't in the constitutional law, he had to blur and twist other words to win his argument with a wrongful implication. But not only was his ruling wrong, the Supreme Court had no right to make that ruling. Even assuming the Court had the right of judicial review, a doubtful implication itself, they had pledged never to declare an act of Congress unconstitutional except in a "clear-cut" case. Otherwise, the people retained the right to decide, acting democratically through Congress. Not only was a right to slavery not "clear-cut," it wasn't even there.

Thus was the Constitution doubly sinned against. First, the justices wrongfully took away the people's constitutional right to decide on slavery for themselves, and next, they wrongfully ruled slavery a constitutional right. If they so insist, let the critics who claim the Constitution was born with this "birth defect" side with the slaveholders and the Supreme Court. Let us side with a truer view of the Constitution.

Let us side with what Abraham Lincoln said in the Lincoln-Douglas debates in 1858, "Again; the institution of slavery is only mentioned in the Constitution of the United States ... three times, and in [none] of these cases does the word 'slavery' or 'negro race' occur; but covert language is used each time, and for a purpose full of significance. ... and that purpose was that in our Constitution, which it was hoped and is still hoped will endure forever – when it should be read by intelligent and patriotic men, after the institution of slavery shall have passed from among us – there should be nothing on the face of the great charter of liberty suggesting that such a thing as negro slavery had ever existed among us. This is part of the evidence that the fathers of the government expected and intended the institution of slavery to come to an end. They expected and intended that it should be in the course of ultimate extinction."

No, the criticism that the Constitution was born with the birth defect of slavery rests on blurring and twisting the words. The Constitution guaranteed no right to slavery. More than that, the Constitution provided a democratic mechanism through which slavery could later be abolished. And the Constitution did later abolish slavery with the 13th Amendment ratified in 1865.

As much as all that, this criticism is *ex post facto* (after the fact). And it's only the most outstanding example of a lot of "after the fact" criticisms, such as, for example, women didn't get the vote until the 19th Amendment in 1920. All these criticisms suffer from several defects themselves. First, how validly criticize the Constitution for not being farther ahead of its time that it was? In 1787, it was the cutting edge, extending equality to more people than ever before. That would seem to cry out for congratulation, rather than condemnation. Second, if the Constitution later extended equality still further, that would seem a matter for compliment, rather than a ground for insult. Third, if the Constitution hasn't moved fast enough for them, can the critics point to some other constitution that did or would have moved faster? If not, what are they complaining about?

11.15 – The Moral of Segregation

The present moral authority of the Supreme Court flows directly from Brown v Board of Education in 1954. That case finally declared legal segregation unconstitutional. Good for the Court. Legal segregation violated the "equal protection of the laws" written in the Constitution by the 14th Amendment as well as the fundamental democratic principle "all men are created equal" proclaimed in the Declaration of Independence. But let's not mistake the moral of the story.

The lawyers want to hang a false narrative on this hook. First, they want to claim the Court saved the nation from segregation, from the oppressive majority and the errors of democracy. Next, they want to claim the moral of the story teaches "guardian democracy." That is, since the majority will oppress the minority as shown by segregation, we need the justices to serve as "guardians." Rather than Congress or the people, the Court should be the highest power in the land (judicial supremacy). Being above and beyond the reach of majority rule with their life-time offices, they will serve as the "guardians" for the Constitution and correct the errors of democracy. As Brown shows, they will interpret the Constitution so as to defend our rights. And what's more sacred than our rights?

But that's a false narrative constructed in their own interest. Instead, let's remember the facts, which tell another story. We've already covered those facts, but briefly to recap. It wasn't democracy or the people who enacted legal segregation. After abolishing slavery with the 13th Amendment in 1865, the majority went ahead to pass a series of laws against segregation. In 1868, the 14th Amendment guaranteed the "equal protection of the laws." In 1870, the 15th Amendment guaranteed the freedmen their votes. The Civil Rights Act of 1875 even prohibited segregation on public transportation and in places of public accommodation. Since democracy and the people passed these laws against segregation, how blame them for its later enactment?

Rather, put the blame where it belongs. It was the Supreme Court that later interpreted away the people's will (the will of the majority) and interpreted in legal segregation (in the name of minority rights). As we earlier read, with the Reese Case in 1876, they interpreted away the 15th Amendment right to vote. By so doing, they gave a body blow both to democracy and the freedmen's rights, and "kill the body, and the head will die." The Court seized from the people's (the majority's) hands the right to democratically decide about segregation, seizing the power to decide for themselves, the life-time justices. With the ballot seized out of their hands, the freedmen could no longer defend their other rights through the democratic process.

As a further and final blow, the Court interpreted the doctrine of "separate but equal" into the Constitution with Plessy v Ferguson in 1896. That is, they interpreted in a "minority right" to legal segregation. Today, when minority rights interpreted to reach far other outcomes, their reasoning is roundly condemned. But their logic was no worse than a lot of more recent outcome-driven legal logic. It rested on the rights to freedom of contract and association to do business and associate with whom you want. Nor are those insignificant rights. Yes, people should have such freedoms. But to interpret them into a right to legal segregation distorts the logic to reach a false conclusion. Legal segregation doesn't protect freedom of contact and association, but denies both. A law that makes a man ride in the back of the bus denies his right to freely contract and associate. It denies "equal protection of the laws." And of course, once the Count interpreted away the will of the majority, that's exactly what happened. A minority of the people, who with the freedmen now disenfranchised were a majority in some states, used their new "minority right" to pass laws for legal segregation.

What's the true story? The Supreme Court, not democracy or the people interpreted away "equal protection of the laws." They did so in the name of "minority rights." The Court, not democracy or the people, enacted "separate but equal." One minority wanted to oppress another minority. The majority tried to prevent it, but the Court prevented the majority. Then good for Brown. The justices finally changed their minds. But they didn't save the nation from an oppressive majority and the errors of democracy. They finally rescued us from their own earlier errors about "minority rights,"

What's the true moral of the story? Not the one the lawyers and judges want to teach. They want "guardian democracy." They want the Supreme Court to have ultimate power over the Constitution. Why? Because the more power the Court has, the more power the lawyers have and the more money they will make. They're self-interested. But if the Court got it so wrong in the past, acting in their own interest, why should we have faith they'll get it right in the future? As shown by segregation, their interest doesn't necessarily coincide with the public interest.

No, the true moral of the story is "keep the faith." Don't lose faith in democracy and the people. If they got it right in the past, why shouldn't we have faith they'll get it right in the future? Their interest is more likely to coincide with the public interest, since they're the public.

11.16 – A Natural Heavyweight

Back in the 1930s, my father worked in the oil fields outside Kiefer, Oklahoma. It was a rough time and place. One day out on the rig, a hard customer wanted to pick a fight with him. At seventeen, my father stood about six-four or a little more and weighed two-forty, none of it fat. In his senior year he captained his high school football team to an undefeated season. But like a lot of naturally large men, he was more of a placid disposition. He pointed out the size differential, but the other guy responded with that old line, "The bigger they are the harder they fall." "Yeah," my father said, "but it's hell when they don't fall." The guy took another look and thought better of it.

A boxer can't punch much above his natural weight. Roberto Duran and Sugar Ray Leonard were great welterweights (140 to 147 pounds), but for them to venture into the ring against a Joe Frazier, a very good heavyweight, over 200 pounds, would have been an act of reckless bravado. But it's not all size. Skill, agility, and stamina count, too. Duran or Leonard would have whipped up on some couch potato no matter how big and the fatter the better. The rule in boxing is a heavier man will beat a lighter one, and the farther apart their weights, the more the outcome will favor the heavier man. But a well-trained boxer with beat an unskilled and/or out-of-shape man of any size.

The same goes for nation states. They fight in weight classes. A bigger nation will beat a smaller nation, and the bigger the size differential, the more certain the outcome. In 1914 and 1940, little Belgium stood no chance against big, bad Germany. Unless a nation wants to get sand kicked in its face, it better be a natural heavyweight. But it's not all size. Back in the 330s BC, lean and mean little Macedonia under Alexander the Great demolished the hulking Persian Empire in the ring. A nation better not be a couch potato. It better have some skill, agility, and stamina. It better keep in some sort of fighting trim.

All of which brings up a side of the Constitution often taken for granted. It let America grow to an impressive (super-heavyweight) size. In 1787, America consisted of only the thirteen states along the Atlantic seaboard, and the first decennial census in 1790 counted a population of only 3,929,326. Today, the nation stretches from "sea to shining sea" across half a continent, and the most recent census in 2010 was 308,745,538. This feat proved something about which a lot of doubt existed back in 1787. It showed that a democracy could expand to cover a very large landmass and include a very large population without losing its democratic character.

And while obesity may be an epidemic and a lot of the population couch potatoes, the other guy better take another look and think twice before picking a fight with the U.S. We're not just a very large nation. We're a naturally healthy body politic and pack a lot of muscle on our frame. The hard customers who went ahead and threw the first punch had reason to regret it. Ask the Japanese Imperialists or the German Nazis.

Traditional empires were top-down. Some young contender in fighting trim managed to knock out the other challengers and grow into a heavyweight, the Persians, the Romans, the Turks. And "down with the defeated." These champions didn't share their crowns. Theirs was the power and the glory of being the "undisputed heavyweight champion of the world." These were "empires" not just in size, but in government. The brain at Persepolis, Rome, Istanbul ruled despotically over the rest of the body politic. The nervous system carried commands with ease from top to bottom, from the capital to the provinces, but messages traveled only slow the other way and weren't regarded as very urgent on arrival. The digestive system carried back nourishment (the taxes), and as long as plenty of this food flowed up, any symptoms of distress in the lower limbs weren't regarded as very urgent either.

But such empires weren't a healthy mind in a healthy body. Invariably over time, the bottom, the vast bulk of the body, began to suffer from neglect. Sores festered in the provinces. A creeping paralysis overcame some of the organs. Some of the muscles atrophied. Invariably, too, the champ gave into the easy living at the top and gradually got fat and out-of-shape. Until eventually, these empires were bloated, weak, and unhealthy bodies. At which point, they routinely succumbed to one of two fates. Some fresh contender in fighting trim knocked them out and took away their title like Alexander the Great did to the Persian Empire. Or the scavengers tore off chunks from their not quite dead carcass as they slowly expired from the inner rot like the decline and fall of the Roman Empire.

But America is a different sort of empire, if empire the right word at all. As a democracy, it's much more bottom-up. The brain doesn't entirely rule the body, but is often ruled by the body. The nervous system carries the messages back from the bottom, and the top hears the messages. Rather than neglecting the lower limbs, the brain cares about every ache and pain. It constantly tries to apply cures and remedies, even sometime practicing some preventative medicine. We're not only a very large guy, we're a very healthy large guy.

But are we in fighting trim? What about our skill, agility, and stamina? "The sinews of war are infinite money." Our sinews are in great shape. The economic organs of our body politic are immensely strong. Since World War II, we're able to say the same for our military muscle. Since then, we've kept our military in fighting trim. But staying in shape is a constant challenge. There's always a tendency to slack off the training and indulge in the pleasures of the flesh, and you hear people all the time urging exactly such a course on us.

Then let's not entirely forget December 7, 1941. Back then, our military was weak and unready. The Japanese Imperial Navy sucker punched us pretty good that day at Pearl Harbor. And to be frank about it, we had some luck in the early rounds, particularly at the Battle of Midway in 1942. If they'd landed that punch, which we dodged as much by luck as skill, no doubt we would have had the strength to get up off the canvas and win the fight. But the bout might have gone into the later rounds, and who knows about our will-power, our staying power? As we'll discuss in the next article, our natural will-power is much less than our natural muscle power.

A lot of hard customers around the would still want to pick a fight with the U.S. But they've taken another look and thought better of it. They've noticed we're naturally a very large guy. And they've gone to school on the mistakes made by those guys who went ahead and threw the first punch. But they've also noticed that like my father was a very large man with a placid disposition, the U.S. is a very large nation with a placid disposition. We'd rather avoid the fight, and we're quick to stop the fight, even before the other guy knocked out. Once incited sufficient to take the field, we're mobile, agile, and hostile, but we're slow to suit up for the game and quick to pick up our ball and go home. Putting two and two together, the tough guys have come up with another game plan. They cuss us out from a safe distance, pick fights with smaller nations, and avoid a direct confrontation with the U.S. The present foreign policy of Russia or Iran shows how to do it.

Why don't we have much natural willpower (staying power)? Why would we rather avoid the fight? On to the next article.

11.17 – Hardly Roman

Remember the line from "The Hustler," "You're a Roman, Bert. You have to win them all." That script made Bert the bad guy all right, but why did that trait make him a bad guy? Why shouldn't we want to win them all like the Romans? But we're hardly Roman, not having won all our wars. As a recent editorial in a national newspaper noted, "There have now been three big U.S. strategic defeats over the past several decades: Vietnam, Iraq and now Iran."

As for the last (Iran), this editorial writer was referring not to a war, but to a "strategic defeat" in foreign policy, the Iran Nuclear Deal. He counted that as a defeat, since he concluded the U.S. failed to achieve its goals as stated going into the negotiations. He went on, "The big question is, Why did we lose?" On that "big question" he concluded, "The first big answer is that the Iranians just wanted victory more than we did."

Roger that. But to say "the Iranians" mis-personifies the answer. It wasn't "the Iranians" who "wanted victory more than we did." No doubt individual Iranians and Americans want their countries to win just about as much, whether in foreign affairs or an international soccer match, nor do the Iranians, as individuals, have more will-power than Americans. Rather, the Iranian Constitution, whatever its other failings, has more will-power in foreign policy than our Constitution. The same fundamental lack of will-power underlies our defeats in Vietnam, where we did lose the war, and Iraq, where we won the war, but seem to have lost the peace.

To come back to the Romans, unlike us, the Roman Republic did win them all. But once again, not because the ancient Romans, as individuals, had more will-power than modern Americans, but because their constitution had more will-power. Under their constitution, their Senate controlled their foreign policy, and that institution had a lot of will-power. Roman senators held their seats for life. Before winning that final promotion, a man had to win election to a series of ever more responsible offices, ending by winning the consulship, the highest executive office. It was like running a gauntlet. To keep running, they had to keep winning the elections, which took place before the Roman assemblies. To keep winning, they had to keep proving their competence for the next promotion. It was a training in a harsh and competitive school of practical experience, where ability and stamina thoroughly tested.

It's a remarkable fact that for some two hundred years the Roman Senate plotted a consistent course in foreign policy, steered upon four guiding principles. First, Rome never fought any except just wars, which they interpreted in such a way as to mean the elimination of all potential rivals. Second, Rome never quit on a war, relentlessly doubling down on loses regardless of the costs, which forced opponents into a zero-sum game, facing catastrophe as the price to stay in. Third, despite some well-known exceptions when forced to teach an object lesson, say to Carthage or the constantly rebellious Jews, Rome treated the vanquished with unusual generosity. Rather than enslaving conquered peoples, they promoted them to allies and left them largely autonomous. Fourth,

Rome scrupulously honored her treaties, allowing reliance upon her word.

In combination, Rome meant to conquer, and she put other nations to a stark either-or choice. Either negotiate an early out, taking easy terms reliably kept, or face ceaseless war to annihilation. This formula applied naked power and self-interest to both ends of the equation, and most made the necessary calculation. Many surrendered without a real contest; Rome built a network of loyal alliances, which further increased her strength; the recalcitrant suffered obliteration like Carthage. With this foreign policy Rome conquered the known world.

Nor could they have won them all without the institutional nature of the Roman Senate. The Senators had extensive and practical experience, forming them into exactly the sort of hard-headed men to come up with such a long-sighted foreign policy. Since they held their offices for life, their elevation above day-to-day politics took much of the factional strife out of the process, facilitating a consensus. Their life-time offices, fresh senators gradually added as others died off, also gave the policy a long-term stability. The institutional structure decisively influenced the institutional function, charting a course otherwise unimaginable.

The Iranian Constitution has a lot of will-power in foreign policy, too. Their Supreme Leader is a religious scholar who holds office for life. He makes all the big calls, including the ones on foreign policy. In other words, he's a virtual dictator, and for all its faults, dictatorship is an institution with a lot of will-power to carry out the dictator's will.

By contrast, American foreign policy depends on institutions with much less will-power than either the Roman Senate or the Iranian Supreme Leader. Our president and Congress constantly sail into the headwinds of party politics, and so generally, our foreign policy makes way against a fierce gale of criticism from the party-out-of-power. During President John Adams' undeclared Quasi War against the French, running from 1798 to 1800, the Jeffersonians tirelessly assailed him. The same thing has gone on ever since. When Democratic President Bill Clinton took military action on Kosovo in 1999, the Republicans relentlessly assailed him. When Republican President George W. Bush took military action in Iraq in 2003, the Democrats relentlessly assailed him. Our institutions don't unite us against the foe, but divide us against each other, sapping our will-power in foreign policy.

It's hard to fight a foreign war while fighting an endless political civil war. In fact, it's hard even to steer a straight course. America may be militarily strong, but her will-power is comparatively weak and inconsistent. We've seldom set a steady course in foreign policy, let alone a course for world domination. When right after World War II, the atom bomb gave us a brief superiority, we imposed no *Pax Americana*. Instead, we swiftly demobilized and returned to the pleasures of civilian life, preferring to ignore the threatening shoals that loomed all around. We haven't doubled down on our wars, but routinely retreated in the face of adversity.

Historically, we've managed to move into vacuums and take advantage of still weaker nations. We occupied the empty interior of the North American continent, brushing aside the weak resistance of the American Indians and the Mexicans with the Indian Wars and the Mexican-American War of 1846 to 1848. We did somewhat the same with various adventures in the Caribbean and Central America. But Gary Cooper in "High Noon" we were not. When the going gets rough, the rough get going. That wasn't us. We got out of town, leaving the townsfolk to fend for themselves such as in Vietnam or Iraq. We haven't even reliably kept our word, as for example, President Nixon signed an executive agreement to aid the South Vietnamese if the North invaded, but Congress refused to honor his word.

But there's an exception. We're capable of responding to existential threats, that is, threats to the national existence. If you draw your sword and try to run us through the vitals, you scare the whole body enough to unite against the foreign foe. As Admiral Yamato is supposed to have remarked after the Japanese surprise attack on Pearl Harbor, "I am afraid we have awakened a sleeping tiger." Indeed, they had. When after that war, the Soviet Union posed another clear existential threat, we got ourselves together sufficient to fight the Cold War, too. But our national front dissolves as such threats fade, and we quickly return to the usual partisan civil war over foreign policy.

As we heard the recent editorial say at the top, "There have now been three big U.S. strategic defeats over the past several decades:

Vietnam, Iraq and now Iran." Right. Let's admit we lost. Why? Not because we lacked the military power to win. We lacked the will-power to win. Unless faced with a clear existential threat, we're not much of a threat to get it together or stay the course.

Does our weakness in foreign policy amount to a valid criticism of the Constitution? Some say no. They see the result as a peace-loving nation. No doubt a nation too weak to unite except against existential threats will have a peace-loving nature. Who dares not love peace? But others see a glaring and dangerous defect. We inhabit the same world as nations with more hostile natures. They despise our weakness as an invitation to aggression. You want to build a nuclear capacity, the bombs and the missiles? Do it! The U.S. is too weak to stop you, as witness North Korea. You want to prop up the dictator next door, helping him murder thousands of his people to stay in power, thus making him your dependent and indebted ally? Do it! The U.S. won't stop you, as witness Russia and Iran in Syria. We're hardly Roman. We don't eliminate all threats with our strength. We grow them with our weakness.

Lacking the will-power to act proactively, we've fallen back on the old adage, "If you want peace, prepare for war." We spend more of our vast GNP on our military than any other nation, and we're generally conceded to have the best military out there. But as the Cold War has faded, the consensus behind even this defensive posture appears fading. Only time will tell. If the next existential threat catches us as flat-footed as Pearl Harbor, we may not manage to snatch our brand from the burning this time around.

You hear a lot of talk about the "American Empire." But we're hardly Roman. Our past wins give us a false confidence. Indeed, World War II and the Cold War were wins for the history books. But we haven't won them all, and lately we've been pretty steadily losing them. Rome only won them all as long as her constitution gave her the will-power to do it. When her constitution changed, she started to lose them, too. Our Constitution never has had much will-power in foreign policy. Lacking any existential threats, we just look to be tending back to our baseline.

Federalist No. 62 says, "Every nation consequently whose affairs betray a want of wisdom or stability, may calculate on every loss which can be sustained from the more systematic policy of its wiser neighbors." We haven't shown much "wisdom or stability" lately. So we can probably count "on every loss which can be sustained from the more systematic policy of our foes." They don't have "wiser" constitutions, but they have ones with more will-power in foreign policy.

11.18 – Ben's Advice

Ladies and gentlemen of the jury, lawyers have been known to use closing argument as a chance to gloss over their client's faults, obfuscate the facts, misquote the law, and try to throw dust in the jury's eyes. Rather than following their example, let me follow Ben Franklin's advice offered at the close of the Constitutional Convention in his Final Speech, "I confess that there are several parts of this Constitution which I do not at present approve, … In these sentiments, Sir, I agree to this Constitution will all its faults, if they are such. … I doubt too whether any other Convention we can obtain, may be able to make a better Constitution. For when you assemble a number of men to have the advantage of their joint wisdom, you inevitably assemble with those men, all their prejudices, their passions, their errors of opinion, their local interests, and their selfish views. From such an assembly can a perfect production be expected? It therefore astonishes me, Sir, to find this system approaching so near to perfection as it does; … Thus I consent, Sir, to this Constitution because I expect no better, and because I am not sure, that it is not the best."

Let me say, ladies and gentlemen of the jury, "It astonishes me to find this system approaching so near to perfection as it does." Does it not astonish you? Yet, "I confess there are several parts of the Constitution which I do not present approve." Some you may not approve either. But, "I doubt too whether any other Convention we can obtain, may be able to make a better Constitution." Do you not doubt that with me? Thus, "I consent to this Constitution because I am not sure that it is not the best and because I expect no better." Should you not consent for the same reasons?

Ladies and gentlemen, Franklin said, "when you assemble a number of men to have the advantage of their joint wisdom you inevitably assemble with those men, all their prejudices, their passions, their errors of opinion, their local interests, and their selfish views." No doubt this remark applied to the delegates at the Constitutional Convention. For an instance, we saw their "selfish views" of their "local interests" prominently on display in the controversy over how to apportion Congress, causing the Senate today to be the most malapportioned legislative body in the world. But their "joint wisdom" recognized these very faults in themselves. "We're no angels." They accepted human nature as they found it in themselves. And so, they followed the recommendation found in *Federalist No. 51*, "what is government itself, but the greatest of all reflections on human nature? If men were angels, no government would be necessary. ... In framing a government which is to be administered by men over men, the great difficulty lies in this: you must first enable the government to control the governed; and in the next place oblige it to control itself. A dependence on the people is, no doubt, the primary control on the government."

And so, in "their joint wisdom" the Founding Fathers brought forth a republic with "dependence on the people the primary control on the government." Lately, a great many people have taken issue with American "exceptionalism." But no one can deny America started out and remains exceptional in that way. In 1789, a republican constitution was highly exceptional, and today, it's still exceptional. That's the exception "from whom all blessings flow." Republican institutions re-align the forces in the political universe much more favorably for "We, the people."

This exception alone should astonish us, but when we come to the details, does it not "astonish you to find this system approaching so near to perfection as it does?" In these articles, we've looked in detail at Congress, the presidency, the judiciary, the bureaucracy, and the states. Not to say we found "perfection," but "approaching so near" as not finding clearly better alternatives. Indeed, we found each institution about as well designed as human ingenuity could devise.

Yet, ladies and gentlemen, "I confess there are several parts of this Constitution which I do not at present approve." As a convinced republican, as the Founding Fathers were, the "judicial usurpation" fills me with dismay. As Jefferson warned back at the time, the doctrine of judicial review was "a very dangerous doctrine indeed, and one which would place us under the despotism of an oligarchy." Since his time, his prophecy has proved only too true. The Supreme Court has usurped a power never intended for them. Until by this time, we find ourselves ruled over to a very great extent by the un-elected judges, rather than ruling ourselves democratically. But while that unfortunately, if accurately, describes the Constitution "as it has become," it's more sinned against the sinning. We should direct our ire against the true offenders, the judges, who in their power lust, have cleverly corrupted the republican virtue of our original Constitution.

Other parts of the "system" we might not "presently approve" either or should at least concern us. The separation of powers seems becoming more and more a problem, constantly stalling even urgent business, such as keeping the government funded and up and running. Since Congress succeeded in driving President Nixon from office, they seem to have reconstituted themselves as a permanent tribunal to investigate and harass the presidents. Not content to wait for news of a misdeed, they go searching in the hope of finding a misdeed or arguably one, and hoping if no crime already committed, the president or his associates will commit some crime under the pressure of the investigation, either perjury or obstruction of justice. Anymore, Congress often seems consumed with playing a game of "gotcha," rather than playing their role in running the government. Along the same lines, a bad habit has developed of setting on a special persecutor to dog every president. Anymore, rather than playing his role in running the government, the presidents and their associates are often consumed with warding off a pack of legal pit bulls. Nor should we approve the way the Electoral College unreliably reflects the popular will. Nor with the way primary elections have degraded the process for selecting presidential candidates. Nor perhaps, should even long habit entirely accustom us to the Senate's gross malapportionment. Nor should our national weakness in foreign policy fail to concern us.

But ladies and gentlemen, despite these reservations or others we may have, "I doubt too whether any other Convention we can obtain, may be able to make a better Constitution." Do you not doubt that with me? Franklin said, "when you assemble a number of men to have the advantage of their joint wisdom you inevitably assemble with those men, all their prejudices, their passions, their errors of opinion, their local interests, and their selfish views." Any present assembly of men would bring with them the same defects, yet where would we find any "joint wisdom" in a present assembly?

Not that the race of men has declined. We could find delegates as capable and informed about human nature and political theory. Indeed, the intervening centuries have added a great deal to our experience and knowledge. But the Founding Fathers possessed some advantages we no longer possess. Their common culture unified them, all being Anglo-Americans, and the political parties hadn't yet divided them into two hostile camps. But today, "diversity" is the watchword and, "To your tents, O Israel." Our diverse cultures have retreated to their tents to fight the relentless "culture wars." The political parties have recruited and excited this cultural hostility to serve in their partisan warfare. Today, our present breed of political leaders are utterly ruthless partisan and cultural warriors. The Constitution barely holds them together. How could we expect them to write a better one?

Then wasn't Ben's advice good? Ladies and gentlemen, are you not "astonished to find this system approaching so near to perfection as it does?" Do you "except a better?" Are you "sure that it is not the best?" Finally, "Thus I consent, Sir, to this Constitution because I expect no better, and because I am not sure, that it is not the best." Should you not consent for the same reasons?

Ladies and gentlemen, in a criminal case, the state has to prove the case against the defendant "beyond a reasonable doubt." In a civil (non-criminal) case, the plaintiff need only prove the case "by a preponderance of the evidence." In closing argument, you often hear a lawyer pleading with the jury to give his client the benefit of the doubt under either burden of proof. Forget that. Let me submit to you, my client doesn't need the benefit of the doubt. Let me submit to you, the plaintiffs, the critics, have failed to prove their case against the defendant, our Constitution, by any reasonable burden of proof. Not only have they failed to prove their case, let me submit to you, our Constitution stands vindicated.

Ladies and gentlemen, in your deliberations, take the advice Ben Franklin offered to the delegates themselves back at the Constitutional Convention. It's still sound advice. Cast your votes for, not against our Constitution. But before submitting the case for your final verdict, permit one last word in the last article.

11.19 – The Question Left Over

Ladies and gentlemen of the jury, the time has come to submit the case for your judgment. Permit one final word. Ladies and gentlemen, the question isn't whether you have a great constitution. You have a great one. But there's a question left over. Are you good enough for your constitution? That's a tougher question. At times, I've had my doubts about you, but I have my better hopes, too.

The Declaration of Independence proclaims, "We hold these truths to be self-evident: that all men are created equal, that they are endowed by their Creator with certain unalienable rights, that among these are life, liberty, and the pursuit of happiness. That, to secure these rights, governments are instituted among men, deriving their just powers from the consent of the governed."

Ladies and gentlemen, the Constitution has never failed to live up to the spirit of those words. Whatever your "rights" mean to you, the Constitution has never denied your rights. Not as long as you agree "all men are created equal" and have the same rights as you. And so, not as long as you agree "governments derive their just powers from the consent of the governed," on democracy as the way to decide on your rights. While if you don't agree, let me suggest you're failing to live up to the spirit yourself.

Whatever the failures in the past or present, those belong to you, the people, not the Constitution. The Founders opened the door for you to democracy. If you pushed through only to take a wrong turn, blame yourselves, not the Constitution. A constitution can chain you down like a slave or make you free, but a constitution can't both make you free and still chain you down to do the right thing. With your freedom comes your responsibility. Now you have to make your own choices for good or ill. Own up to your responsibility. Make haste back through the same door and take a better turn this time. Whatever the failures in the future, those are going to belong to you, too.

Then what are you complaining about except yourselves and the choices you've made? And frankly, some of your choices, past and present, raise some serious doubts about you, and some people seem to think you've never done anything right. But "America, love it or leave it." Even those who don't love it, don't seem to want to leave it. According to the nightly news, people are climbing the walls to get in. They're voting with their feet, and how interpret their votes? How except that you, the people, have made far more better choices, rather than worse ones? Otherwise, America wouldn't be such a great place to live, and people wouldn't want to stay in or get in.

The fact is, "You never had it so good," and other people want to have it as good as you. If you deserve the blame for some wrong turns, I don't see why you don't deserve the praise for the far more better turns. Someone told me "rational optimism" was an oxymoron, but I'm rationally optimistic about you. I think you've made far more right than wrong choices and made steady progress. You've come so far, why can't you keep on going still farther? So I have my better (rational) hopes about you.

Ladies and gentlemen, in a 2017 survey, the Pew Research Center (that oracle) reported, "Fully 86 percent describe the country as more politically divided today than in the past." What about these deep divisions about which we hear so much? All I can say is, that if the polls often reveal a shocking public ignorance on political issues, they as often reveal a shockingly bad memory about the past. To remember better, only glance through some old newspaper archives, which now readily available online. In their day, the Jeffersonian newspapers denounced Presidents Washington and Adams as closet monarchists, who longed to come out of the closet, and later, the Whig editors railed against President Jackson as "King Andrew." Routinely, we've been more or less and bitterly divided against ourselves. If now and then the political divide has spit open like a dangerous chasm, we've only gone off the edge once, with the Civil War.

As much as that, this one poll in isolation makes it sound like, "Things fall apart; the centre cannot hold." But not only has the center held in the past, again, with the exception of the Civil War, but look at the wider polling across all the current controversial issues. This wider sample assumes the shape of the familiar bell curve. On the issues, most people still cluster near the center. We may be politically divided between Democrat and Republican, but we still agree on much more than we disagree. So once again, I have my better hopes about you, that the greater numbers in agreement will outvote the lesser numbers on the fringes and you won't go off the edge again.

Ladies and gentlemen, your situation brings to mind still another old lawyer adage. In a town with only one lawyer, the lawyer will starve. Let another lawyer move into town, and both will begin to thrive. A single lawyer can make just the sound of one hand clapping. You require at least a pair to raise the sound of litigation and the fees made from the business. It's not just that the lawyers stir up the litigation, although they do, but every town contains quite a bit of potential litigation beneath the quiet. The townsfolk are more or less divided against themselves by their interests, economically, socially, and culturally. They've suffered some wrongs at each other's hands, real and imaginary. They're cherishing some grudges and grievances against each other. A legal monopoly stifles this underlying dissonance, but some legal competition will release the noise. Given the chance, the freedom, the people will start to litigate against each other.

The Constitution gave you your chance, your freedom, and you have your two lawyers, the two political parties. The volume of your political litigation soon reached a crescendo. "Sue the bastards!" became your battle cry, and you turned loose the dogs of partisan political warfare against each other "and damned be he that first cries, hold, enough." But what would you rather have? You could have the quiet of a town with just one lawyer, a political monopoly, a one-party state. That would silence the political litigation. But wouldn't you rather have your freedom to litigate despite all the partisan sound and fury?

Ladies and gentlemen, for once learn a lesson from the lawyers. I've seen lawyers get real upset with particular judges and particular verdicts. Even saw a lawyer cuss out a judge in the corridor one time. But you want to be careful and not go too far. You can find yourself held in contempt of court, and carried far enough, disbarred. Never met a lawyer who wanted disbarred and kicked out of the courts. That's where they make their living. Without the courts, they would starve. The lawyers practice some enlightened self-interest. They don't go too far, and except for a few outliers, avoid the fate.

The Constitution is your court. Litigate all you want. Raise all the sound and fury you want. But practice some enlightened self-interest. Don't go so far as to disbar yourselves. Don't kick yourselves out of the Constitution. That's where you make your living and a good living. Without the Constitution, you'd starve.

Ladies and gentlemen, once heard a big-time criminal lawyer use an old story in closing argument. Didn't think he told it in a very good cause, but it's a good story. Let me tell my version in a better cause. It goes this way. There was a wise old man, and there was a young man, who as the young so often want to do, longed to show up his elders. One day the young man caught a bird in the forest, small enough to hold between the palms of his hands. He went to visit the wise old man. "Old man," he said, holding up his cupped hands with the trapped bird, "you're reputed to be wise. Tell me, is the bird in my hands alive or dead?" If the old man said "dead," he meant to open his hands and release the bird alive. If the old man said "alive," he meant to crush it between his palms and show the bird dead. The old man looked the young man in the eyes and said, "It's in your hands." The young man paused a moment, opened his hands, and the tiny bird flew away.

Ladies and gentlemen of the jury, our Constitution is in your hands.

END